MW01047945

Things Seen
and Unseen

Things Seen and Unseen

Discourse and Ideology in Tokugawa Nativism

H. D. Harootunian

The University of Chicago Press
Chicago and London

H.D. Harootunian is the Max Palevsky Professor of
History and Civilizations and professor of Far Eastern
languages and civilizations at the University of
Chicago.

The University of Chicago Press, Chicago 60637
The University of Chicago Press, Ltd., London
© 1988 by The University of Chicago
All rights reserved. Published 1988
Printed in the United States of America
97 96 95 94 93 92 91 90 89 88   54321

Library of Congress Cataloging-in-Publication Data

Harootunian, Harry D., 1929–
  Things seen and unseen.

  Bibliography: p.
  Includes index.
    1. Japan—Intellectual life—1600–1868.   2. Kokugaku.
I. Title.
DS822.2.H313   1988   001.1′0952   87-19069
ISBN 0-226-31706-4
ISBN 0-226-31707-2 (pbk.)

For Polly

Contents

Acknowledgments

When it takes as long to write a book as it has this one, an author is bound to incur some heavy debts along the way. In my case, I have been fortunate to have good friends and colleagues who have taught me more than I can say; in the words of nativists, they represent a *mimegumi*, a blessing, that can only be paid in the last instance. My first expression of thanks must go to my friends and colleagues at Chicago and elsewhere: to Tetsuo Najita, who has been a constant intellectual companion, who has discussed this book with me at every stage and who may very well have suggested the topic to me; to Bernard Silberman, who read an earlier draft and offered a detailed and rigorous critique; Irwin Scheiner, of the University of California, Berkeley, whose close readings of an earlier draft and the penultimate version have contributed substantially to refining the content; Masao Miyoshi of the University of California, San Diego, for his vast knowledge of Japanese life and culture; William LaFleur of the University of California, Los Angeles, for an informatively critical reading for the press; Naoki Sakai, from whom I have learned much; and Hayden White, of the University of California, Santa Cruz, whose writings on historical criticism and text production have provided continual guidance in fashioning my own project. I would like also to thank Norma Field and William Sibley for their support and generous encouragement.

It would have been very difficult to write this book without the assistance of "strong readings" by Japanese scholars. Although the secondary literature on *kokugaku* is staggeringly large, I would like to single out the following whose works I have relied on: Professor Matsumoto

Sannosuke, formerly of Tokyo University, whose classic monograph on the politics of late Tokugawa *kokugaku* paved the way for all subsequent studies; to Professor Haga Noboru, of Tsukuba University, whose countless books and articles on late Tokugawa nativism constitute an oeuvre which no student can or should ignore and have been crucial to my study; to Professor Watanabe Hiroshi, of Tokyo University, for his essays on the poetics of late nativism that form the core of my own understanding; to Professor Koyasu Nobukuni, of Osaka National University, whose book on *Norinaga to Atsutane* first alerted me to the idea of seeing nativism as a narrative; and Professor Tahara Tsuguo, of Hokkaido University, whose books on major figures like Motoori and Hirata, and articles on Ōkuni I have found indispensable.

I would also like to record my thanks to Maggie Zansitis for producing a penultimate draft on disk, editing, and proofreading the manuscript along the way; and Betsey Scheiner for her sensitive and skillful copyediting. I want to thank Anne Walthall, of the University of Utah, for suggesting the book cover, and the staff of the Seminary Cooperative Book Store of Hyde Park for what can only be described as the best book store in the United States.

Finally, I would like to record my gratitude to both the Japan Foundation and the Suntory Foundation for generous gifts enabling the publication of this book. I am also grateful to the Historiographical Institute of Tokyo University and its director for permission to reproduce a detail from *Tawara kasane kōsaku emaki*.

Abbreviations

Gs   *Kokugogaku taikei: Gohō sōki.* Tokyo: Kōsei Kaku, 1938.

HA   *Nihon shisō taikei,* vol. 50, *Hirata Atsutane, Ban Tomo-yuki, Ōkuni Takamasa.* Tahara Tsuguo, Saeki Arikiyo, Haga Noboru, eds. Tokyo: Iwanami Shoten, 1973.

HAz (old)   *Hirata Atsutane zenshū.* Muramatsu Iwao et al., eds. Tokyo: Isseidō, 1912.

HAz (rev)   *Shinshū Hirata Atsutane zenshū.* Tokyo: Meicho Shuppan, 1978.

IYz   *Ikuta Yorozu zenshū.* Gakuzōkai, ed. Tokyo: Seikatsu-sha, 1944.

Kcks   Ono Takeo. *Kinsei chihō keizai shiryō.* Tokyo: Yoshi-kawa Kyōbunkan, 1958.

Kjk   Mutobe Yoshika. *Kenyūjun kōron.* In *Shintō sōsho,* Tokyo: Kyōbundo, 1896.

Koku   Kamo Mabuchi. *Koku-i kō.* In *Iwanami shisō taikei,* vol. 39, *Kinsei shintōron zenki kokugaku.* Tokyo: Iwanami Shoten, 1972.

Kotoba   Kamo Mabuchi. *Kotoba-i kō.* In *Iwanami shisō taikei,* vol. 39, *Kinsei shintōron zenki kokugaku.* Tokyo: Iwanami Shoten, 1972.

Ksi   *Kinnō shishi ibunshū.* Inoue Tetsujirō, Ueda Mannen, Inobe Shigeo, eds. Tokyo: Shunyodō, 1937.

Kus   *Nihon shisō taikei,* vol. 51, *Kokugaku undō no shisō.* Haga Noboru and Matsumoto Sannosuke, eds. Tokyo: Iwanami Shoten, 1971.

xii   Abbreviations

MIki   *Maki Izumi no kami ibun.* Tokyo: Kenshōka, 1913.
MNz (new)   *Motoori Norinaga zenshū.* Ono Susumu, ed. Tokyo:
              Chikuma Shobō, 1970.
MNz (old)   *Motoori Norinaga zenshū.* Motoori Toyoei, ed. Tokyo:
              Yoshikawa, 1904.
Nk   Suzuki Shigetane. *Norito kōgi*, vols. 1 and 2 (Vols. 13
              and 14 of *Kokubun chūsaku zensho.*) Tokyo: Kokuga-
              kuin Daigaku, 1909.
Nmc   Sagara Akira, ed., *Nihon no meicho, Hirata Atsutane,*
              24. Tokyo: Chuo Koronsha, 1972.
Nsd   Suzuki Shigetane. *Nihonshokiden.* Tokyo: Kokugakuin
              Daigaku, 1910.
OSs   *Kindai Nihon shisō taikei*, vol. 22, *Origuchi Shinobu
              shū.* Hirosue Tamotsu, ed. Tokyo: Chikuma Shobō,
              1975.
OSz   *Origuchi Shinobu zenshū.* Origuchi Hakushi Kinenkai,
              ed. Tokyo: Chūō Kōronsha, 1956.
OTz   *Ōkuni Takamasa zenshū.* Nomura Senshirō, ed. Tokyo:
              Yūkōsha, 1939.
SMk   Itō Shirō. *Suzuki Masayuki kenkyū.* Tokyo: Aoki Sho-
              ten, 1972.
Tck   *Tenchūki.* In *Kokugaku taikei: Satō Shin'en shū,* Anzu
              Motohiko, ed. Tokyo: Jiheisha, 1943.
TMz   *Tomobayashi Mitsuhira zenshū.* Sasaki Nobutsuna, ed.
              Osaka: Yūkawa Kōbunsha, 1944.
Yi   *Yōzōka ikuron.* In *Kokugaku taikei: Satō Shin'en shū,*
              Anzu Motohiko, ed. Tokyo: Jiheisha, 1943.
Yk   *Gendai Nihon shisō taikei*, vol. 29, *Yanagita Kunio.*
              Masuda Katsumi, ed. Tokyo: Chikuma Shobō, 1965.
Yt   Katsura Takashige. *Yotsugigusa tsumiwake.* Niigata,
              1883.

Things Seen
and Unseen

Then, the creation deity Takami musubi no kami sent back the two gods (Futsu-nushi and Take-mika-zuchi) with a commandment to Ōnamuji no kami, saying: " . . . Our imperial grandchild will now administer the visible affairs that you have directed. You must now administer the affairs of the gods (*kami no koto*)." . . . To this, Ōnamuji replied, "Since the imperial instructions of the heavenly deity are courteous, how can I disobey the command? I have hitherto ruled over visible things, which hereafter will be administered by the imperial grand-child. I will withdraw to govern things concealed and mysterious (*kakuretarukoto*)."

    Nihonshoki, book 2, part 2

What is a Wife and what is a Harlot? What is a Church and what
Is a Theatre? Are they Two, and not One? Can they exist separate?
Are not Religion and Politics the same thing? Brotherhood is Religion,
O demonstrations of Reason, dividing families in cruelty and pride!

    William Blake

For man, then, origin is by no means the beginning—a sort of dawn of history from which his ulterior acquisitions would have accumulated. Origin, for man, is much more the way in which man in general, any man, articulates himself upon the already-begun of labor, life, and lan-guage; it must be sought for in that fold where man in all simplicity applies his labor to a world that has been worked for thousands of years, lives in the freshness of his unique, recent, and precarious exist-ence a life that has its roots in the first organic formations, and com-poses into sentences that have never before been spoken (even though generation after generation has repeated them) words that are older than all memory.

    Michel Foucault

Prologue: Historians' Discourse and the Problem of Nativism

Several years ago, I published an essay called "The Consciousness of Archaic Form in the New Realism of *Kokugaku*," which represented my first effort to map the contours of nativism in the early modern period.[1] The initial purpose of that essay was to explore the possibility of finding a theoretical perspective on this intellectual episode in the Tokugawa period that might avoid relying excessively on the vast secondary literature Japanese have produced on this subject, in order to find a detour around the strong (mis)readings that have come to dominate our understanding of its historical place. It was my hope to say something Japanese scholars had not yet said, and to find a form in which to say it. What I then tried to envisage, as a preliminary and totteringly tentative move, was the outline of a program (one critic described it as a manifesto) that might enable me to grasp nativism—as I decided to call *kokugaku* (instead of the more established translation, "national learning," which bordered on unintelligibility while risking associations with "nativist" movements elsewhere)—as a form of textual productivity that resulted in an ideological contestation of official representations of order and, therefore, a hitherto unsuspected struggle over the signifying process itself and the mechanisms for determining meaning during the Tokugawa period.

Before taking on this task, I believed it was necessary to embark on a study of theory that might simultaneously offer escape from the more commonsensical strategies currently in fashion in the social sciences—such as modernization theory, which invariably trivialized considerations of culture and thought—and disclose a new vista capable of releasing the study of ideology from the distortions of reflection theory. It was my conviction then, as it remains, that theory might be employed as a powerful instrument for an understanding of textuality and ideological production in general (even though there can never be a general ideology). This strategy required examining the utility of conceptual schemes as a form of play, to see what they might yield, in an effort to grasp the nativist moment without relying on standard Japanese interpretations or recuperating a metaphysics of the text that simply recounted the text's content as if it knew itself. The article I published elicited widespread commentary that denounced the informing impulse and, by extension, all such exercises as theoretically top-heavy, materially insubstantial, jargonistic, and generally insensitive to the conventions of "lucid" historical writing. Critics seized upon its theoretical load, rather than the resulting interpretive yield; in their dismissal of my first effort to situate one of the possible meanings of nativist texts within another level of activity, they ignored the "interpretation" altogether. Confronting the spectacle of theory, historical "criticism" assumed that the interpretation of nativism I had developed had no logical relationship to the methodological meditation rehearsed in the first part of the article. When critics turned to my conclusions regarding the nativist program, they appealed to received canons of historical narrativity and charged my interpretation with a lack of clarity and insufficient evidence, without demonstrating the necessary privilege accorded to certain styles and establishing quantitative criteria for evidential authority. Most remained unconvinced that historical practice should be implicated in theory at all and closed ranks to defend the "consensual" conviction that history as a reconstructive act was the cure to the illness symptomatized by theory. Yet "reconstructing" in narrative form is an act that seeks to displace a loss of immediacy and inevitably falls into representation, which is no more exempt from theoretical assumptions than language is from the powers of figuration.

At bottom, all historical practice is an act of criticism. At the same time that theory enables us to imagine the framing operation involved in the formulation of any analytic program, it must teach us that our own perspectives possess no privilege over others, since its power lies precisely in the capacity to make visible the frames from which our categories for representation derive. In this way, historical criticism can never be far from political purpose.

This book is an attempt to put into practice the program that I tentatively envisaged for the first time in "Archaic Form" and to pursue its methodological agenda. Although the passage of time, changing perspectives, and a much closer look at the materiality of the nativist intervention (its texts) have forced me to abandon some of the earlier proposals as naive, I see this book as an effort to fulfill the spirit of the earlier essay. It is not my purpose to write either a historical narrative of the development of nativism, explaining how and why it originated at a determined point in time, or to describe its subsequent unfolding. Nor will it be my intention to satisfy conventional claims to coverage and account for its content comprehensively. Work of this sort has been done exhaustively and extensively by Japanese scholars, virtually from the moment nativism appeared in history. It would be difficult, if not impossible, to replicate this tradition in any case, and any effort to do so would, at the very best, result in the reinvention of an imperfect wheel. My interests, which draw freely on this tradition of scholarship[2] as a necessary means for "reading" the texts produced by nativists, seek, first of all, to define the space that *kokugaku* occupied as a discourse in the historical field of late-Tokugawa Japan. Discourse belongs to the order of language usage, the possible forms of utterances, and the particular way nativists were able to talk, write, and think. This form of enablement was directly related to specific objects and their modality of relating, which produced for nativists a knowledge of things that they sought to represent in discourse. One of the central objects nativists talked and wrote about was language itself. To concentrate on the content of nativist discourse, however, is to de-emphasize nativists as authors and personalities. Instead of attending to biography and seeking motives and intentions, which are rarely, if ever, available to analysis, I will focus on the texts themselves as they were disposed by the discourse. There are other very good reasons to shift attention from author to discourse, which I will note along the way. But it is important, at the outset, to announce the scope of my own inquiry.

The objective of this study will also be to examine how the nativist discourse functioned ideologically. My use of the much-maligned term *ideology* may be quite unfamiliar to the conventional historical understanding, which has associated it with doctrine or a coherent system of beliefs, deliberate distortions or false consciousness (as against a putative real consciousness) corresponding to a social reality reflected in it. The view of ideology I propose in this study favors production (and signification) rather than reflection. Such a choice is prefigured by a rejection of "expressive causality" and the more traditional Marxian commitment to base/superstructure in favor of what Louis

Althusser has called "structural causality," with its emphasis on the semi-autonomous levels of the social formation. This conception of social formation consists of a number of semi-autonomous but inter-related levels, such as the economic, the political, and the ideological, each with its own practice. These levels enabled Althusser to call attention to the importance of ideology both as a material practice and as a function in the reproduction of social relations of production. (By practice he meant the transformation of "raw materials" into a "determinate product," made possible by labor employing a specific mode of production.) While there are problems with this view, it avoids seeing ideology as a distorted reflection of society's material base or as a form of be-witchment but, rather, as a material practice that plays an autonomous role in the constitutive process. When textual and intellectual production is seen as a process, the text, because it has been produced, must be apprehended as a component of the general system of production and the "real" must be understood not as its object to reflect but as its institutional conditions of existence. Because textuality is a productive activity, its own components—texts—must be seen as distinct practices of signification, which are related not to extra- or non-discursive truths but to other practices of signification. Since ideological practice is semi-autonomous and constitutive, it may also affect other levels of the social formation. The result of a productive process itself, it also functions to produce a consciousness of the lived experience of groups or individuals in an imaginary (imaged) way: it diverts people from what is contradictory in their experience and directs them toward renewed "recognition" (and thus misrecognition) of what they already believe or know about themselves. But accepting this conception of ideology (which I will specify below) means acknowledging the subsequent task of investigating the texts for traces of this ideological effect by submitting them to political calculation.

Ideology, in the sense I have provisionally indicated, is *inscribed* in specific discourses insofar as it is written or spoken in them; it inheres in words because they themselves represent significations capable of mobilizing people to act or perceive their world in specific modalities, either to conform to forms of domination or to contest them.

In this view, ideology loses its function as a master referent employed for evaluative purposes and ceases, therefore, to be a specific set of representations; it becomes an analytic, and thus a nonrepresentational, category that must be grasped semiotically within the operation of discourses. The "signifieds," or contents of discourses, are not motivated by extradiscursive forces, an "externality" that the theories of expressive causality—whether of the Marxian or the Hegelian variety—demand as if it were a court of last appeal. They are prompted instead within "specific processes and practices of signification." As a result, the principal criterion of analysis can no longer insist on a symmetrical relationship between discourses and a "reality" that is external to them, because discourse can only be grasped as instances of an interdiscursive construction, as mosaics of utterances crisscrossing one another and establishing their own categories of adequacy. In this book, I have taken the line of argument, proposed by Michel Foucault and others, that discourses must always be seen as moments of power as well, since power is invariably implicated in any effort to represent knowledge. Such a view also rejects the received distinction between a "symbolic" order and the "real" as ontologically given in favor of a view of these claims as effects of historical and social forces. Discourses disclose in social practice how "reality" and the "symbolic" are constituted and related to each other; at the same time, they themselves are products of "real structures." According to John Frow, discourse "covers a spectrum of semiotic systems from both realms ['real' and 'symbolic']." Just as specific material structures secure representations in a semiotic process, so semiosis itself "involve[s] varying degrees of motivation, explicitness, and systematization."[3]

Such a view clearly departs from what we might call historical common sense. Historical common sense, perhaps best articulated by W. G. Gallie and most rigorously criticized by Hayden White, approaches history not as a self-conscious and deliberate practice, a method based on a reasoned theoretical position (thus inviting talented amateurs to write more readable histories than professionals), but as the "obvious" mode or natural way of doing history. Any effort to introduce critical theory into historical practice (most vociferously refused by the talented amateurs but resisted uniformly by professionals as well) incurs the risk of either violent denunciation—as if in fear of the death of history itself—trivialization and marginalization, or outright indifference, leading to what Japanese have called *mura hachibu* (ostracism). If recent outbursts are testimony, the defenders of historical common sense charge that theory is misleading, interfering with the natural way historians write history. It perplexes and deliberately confuses the minds of readers and students with unnecessary and obfuscating philosophical speculation and leads to "overingenuity," "jargon," the sin of opaqueness, and the loss of direct contact with the unmediated "reality" of the historical field. This particular charge recalls Paul DeMan's perceptive juxtaposition of "common sense" to theory. "What we call theory," DeMan wrote in *Resistance to Theory*, "is precisely the confusion of linguistic with natural reality, of reference with phenomenalism. . . . Those who reproach literary theory for being oblivious to social and historical (that is to say, ideological) reality are merely stating their fear at having their own ideological mystifications exposed by the tool they are trying to discredit. They are, in short, very poor readers of Marx's *German Ideology*." DeMan rightly observes that theory works like Marx's conception of the scandal of the dialectic itself to undermine deeply entrenched significations by revealing their mechanics and up-setting established practices. And it "blurs the borderlines between literary and non-literary discourse."[4] The governing assumption behind historical common sense is the belief that the documents transparently reflect an invariant reality, which is always there and is secured only if the historian sticks to the facts and tells the story the way it is.

Although historical common sense has shown a sensitivity to questions of theory on occasion, especially when directed toward the question of historical knowledge, it has concentrated principally on the status of content and the methodological approaches that assist the telling of the story line. In consequence, the problem of form has remained unnoticed and its meaning uncontested. The form of history, narrative, is invariably reduced to questions of technique, style, and writing (the "tyranny of lucidity") largely because of the unexamined conviction that a knowledge of the past unravels as a continuous story. Thus, narrative appears as common sense and common sense as narrative.

When a philosopher such as W. G. Gallie turned to an examination of the historical narrative as a mode of understanding, it was less to explore the form of representation than it was to identify the "concept of the story" as a principal vehicle of "all historical thought and knowledge."[5] Gallie saw in narrative the starting point of historical inquiry, its basic form; his identification of the status of the story constituted a supplement to philosophic efforts (begun by the Windelband-Collingwood school) to authenticate the claims of historical understanding against the charge that "purposive thought and action" could never be apprehended as natural phenomena, obeying scientific laws or theories. Hence, Gallie's attention was directed toward constituting the historical by demonstrating that a proposed explanation "contributed a description and substantiation of something that is worth narrating"—something worth following through to a conclusion.[6] The story, for historical writing, was the analogue to theory for science. The common element was the articulation of "critical dissatisfaction" with received theories and the subsequent acknowledgment of the need to construct a method for testing and evaluating them. Even though historians were denied the specificity or certainty of method allowed scientists, they did, nonetheless, proceed critically in order to test the often-vague truth content claimed by the story. To validate this analogy, Gallie focused on the story itself, almost as if narrative constituted a cognitive mode, and on the means the historian must, therefore, *necessarily* devise to determine the story-worthiness of an action.[7] By establishing an "adventure," "notable elements of surprise," accident, and the unforeseeable as the criteria for worthiness, Gallie was able to effectively privilege content over representational form—narrative—as the problem for historical knowledge. Ultimately, he confused content for form itself by making the latter a condition for the former. Only content possessed meaning, while form appeared as a natural and obvious vehicle claiming no autonomous status in the determination of meaning.

But valorizing content, determining how worthy an action is for subsequent "emplotment," betrays a fundamental belief that events and actions are mediated by the very form that confers upon them the status of the historical. To argue for the worthiness of content, the plausibility of the story, as it conforms to the criterion of the "non-routine ventures" and functions as a test for established moral and intellectual habits, is to ignore the power of representation, the crucial determination by which such adventures ultimately reaffirm received conventions. In this view, the form of history in narrative is simply given. It requires no consideration of its constitution and its possible functions for meaning. Nor is the historian obliged to consider how the materials that are used to tell a worthy story have themselves been constituted or reconstituted. In fact, in telling a story, the materials do not demand that they be represented in narrative; it is the narrative form that arranges the materials in order to establish the sequential order of a "story-worthy" event. Many premodern cultures and societies other than our own have developed encoding procedures that are unconstrained by a mode constructed, as Hayden White argues, on the model of the realistic novel.[8]

Gallie specifically enumerated the properties of the story. He was quick to announce that its conclusion could never be deduced from its beginnings, but he was equally certain that later events unconditionally required earlier ones.[9] Such fixed relationships satisfied a general criterion for "intelligibility" or "acceptability" and, thus, sanctioned the claims of context, which historians invariably made a principal condition for telling their stories. Yet this appeal to "intelligibility" and "accountability" is merely another way of talking about common sense and the evident. It suggests how the sequential code governs the transmutation of an event into a story-worthy representation. The appeal to the authority of common sense implies strongly that the form of representation will function to make familiar the particular event, action, or incident, because the "ground of intelligibility, of stories matches exactly with that of everyday life."[10] But such an assertion surely fails to account for the vast disparity in experiences over time and place and the very real possibility that no credible correspondence can be made between the thought and actions of a Japanese in the eighteenth century and the representations of everyday life as we know it. Moreover, it overlooks the very crucial distinction made by Émile Benveniste between discourse and history, between dialogic texts, which are organized between speaker and listener, and narrative, in which events are made to speak for themselves.[11]

If Gallie is to be taken at his word, then we must assume that the appeal to common sense and the necessity to match experience with everyday life as we know it invests narrative with an ideological function scarcely evident to him. For narrative, in this sense, would operate to deproblematize the life it is seeking to retrieve, in order to make the Other look like us. But this correspondence between representation and "life" is possible only if we are willing to accept the form of narrative as unproblematic, synonymous with cognition itself, a natural and commonsensical dictation that reflects the world innocently rather than constituting it according to an unstated plot line. Indeed, it is the "followability" offered by the story line that gives to history its explanatory force, and followability requires precisely the kind of ordered succession one might find in any story endowed with structure and meaning, continuity and fullness. Yet the problem is even more complex than it is made to appear, because the very form that authorizes and secures fullness and continuity, succession and closure, which historians have confidently identified with history itself, neither arises naturally from nor corresponds directly to life and the quotidian experience.

If historians have been slow to recognize the problematic nature of representational form, literary critics, cultural theorists, and semioticians have, in recent years, registered continuing complaints concerning the privileged status of narrative and contested the very codes that lie in suppressed silence under its construction. Hayden White has proposed, in his decomposition of nineteenth-century historical consciousness, the possibility of fusing all historical writing to the philosophy of history by identifying the prelinguistic strategies (tropes) that have disposed narratives to order "facts" in a particular sequence so that they may tell a story of a certain kind.[12] White's argument discloses how tropic strategies prefigure and, thus, determine the actual emplotment and structure of meaning, which the historical narrative is pledged to illuminate. Yet his own tactic uncovers the moral-aesthetic positions enabled by such strategies, which historical explanation seeks to suppress in validating its own claims to truth. And Fredric Jameson, in *The Political Unconscious*, has shifted the terms of understanding itself by foregrounding the status of narrative as the problem of analysis.[13] The central purpose of Jameson's analysis is to identify, beneath layers of displacement, the ideological functions performed by narrative form, yet to reveal how such symbolic acts reveal a positive, utopian vision.

Common sense, then, functions as the identifying emblem of history when it is nothing more than the historian's discourse. Yet it "betrays" its discursive allegiance by its own "incoherencies," "contradictions," and "silences." Its weakness appears most clearly when it eschews theory altogether and presents its own claims as nontheoretical and "obvious," its story the most plausible one accessible to the historian. But it is precisely in this claim to the "obvious," and "naturally given" that common sense declares its exemption from demonstrating its "internal consistency." The discourse on historical common sense merely effaces the question that its own account of the world is incoherent or inconsistent or simply at variance with elemental experience and enjoins its practitioners to get on with a simple reading of the documents (not texts) in order to extract the story that is already there. This practice discloses a deeper conceit, which equates the absence of theory with the attainment or "guarantee of objectivity." Here, historical common sense avoids any "confrontation with its own problematic presuppositions," valorizes "whatever procedures and methods are currently dominant" without questioning their agendas, and secures the reverse of objectivity by perpetuating "unquestioned assumptions."

In brief, there can never be any practice without theory, even though historical common sense seeks to conceal its own "theory" in the doing of history. The most amateurish practitioners of history, who are no less naive than its most professional purveyors, function as an army of accomplices supporting the claims of common sense. Yet they all "presuppose," by the very act of reading "documents," "a whole theoretical discourse about language and meaning," about the relationships between words and things, signs and significations, and surely about themselves and their place in the world and in history. It is ironic that nativists, the subject of this book, early recognized the mediating role of language and the effect of usage on intent and feeling and meaning itself. But this recognition was quickly effaced in the practice of writing history in Japan, just as it was elsewhere. The irony doubles back since history is, as nativists acknowledged, the most idiographic discipline among the human sciences and becomes possible only because what we call the traces of the past appear in language. Hence, "common sense appears obvious because it is inscribed in the language we speak" and others have spoken. The importance of the post-Saussurian "revolution"—structuralism, post-structuralism, neo-Marxism, etc.—lies in its willingness to interrogate language, to assume that it is not a neutral, transparent means with which "individuals transmit messages" as innocent exchanges "to each other about an independently constituted world of things." Rather, it is language that constitutes the world of things. An exchange of signs is always an exchange of differing values. There is simply no innocent usage of language, just as there is no innocent reading, in which an invariant reality is transparently reflected in words; words are, as nativists observed, opaque, layered, filled with differing and contrary valences, ideologically charged; lucidity is illusory, as is its claim that an utterance must necessarily be *true* because it is "obvious," "familiar," and "clear." [14]

Despite considerable differences among them, the new theoretical strategies all contest the authority of received positions as socially constituted practices and challenge claims to validity founded in common sense and the presumed neutrality of language. This assault has often been expressed in difficult and even syntactically obscure formulations, not out of pedantry or perversity but from the belief that resistance to familiar values and presuppositions in discourse must not reproduce these assumptions and values by being easily readable and understandable. To do so risks losing the critical point the newer strategic practices wish to make and threatens to bend us to a complicitous relationship with the very assumptions we seek to contest. New and unfamiliar concepts and theories invariably require unfamiliar and difficult discourses to enforce the distance from the object of critical practice. My initial reworking of the concept of ideology is a case in point, as will be my decision to employ concepts such as production, reproduction, and social formation (for society). Although I am aware of the dangers in a commitment to exploring the promises of a new and unfamiliar discourse and in the seeming inaccessibility of new theories and perspectives, the undertaking is worth these and other risks. But it is also evident that complaints demanding the dismissal of theory as "unnecessary" and "jargonistic" are merely the reflex of common-sense discourse when it encounters challenges to its own claims. They lead to an avoidance of conceptual confrontation altogether and, perhaps unintentionally, to a repudiation of the liberal-humanist appeal to "open-mindedness" and "pluralism" that authorize common sense. This is not to say that jargon does not exist. Yet if we can agree that no language act is immune to ideology, then it is not enough to imply ideological complicity by calling attention to jargon and theory or by discounting terms because they appear new or different. It is my conviction in this book, a lesson learned first from nativists but recently reinforced by a reading of new critical strategies, that when we "resist linguistic innovation, we assert that we know all we need to know." The act of rejecting such a conceit establishes the relationship between this prefatory explanation and the subject of nativism itself. The task requires making the newer strategies accessible without, as Catherine Belsey has so aptly put it, "recuperating them for common sense by transcribing them back into the discourse of everyday life."[15]

It is for this reason that I have tried to retain, wherever possible, the terminology of the new critical strategies and their unfamiliar formulations as a way of "reading" *kokugaku* texts. I have also tried to avoid the conventional narrative form of a "followable story." One of the ironies of historical practice is that much of the material it draws on to tell a story comes from discourse, which is distinguished from historical narrative insofar as it invariably assumes a dialogue between a speaker and a listener; whereas history effaces the speaker altogether in order to give the impression that the "events seem to narrate themselves."[16] Discursive texts, which are idiographic notations of speech, are positioned by a privileged historical narrative to tell a coherent story. By securing coherence, this device establishes closure, when the texts are, in effect, open. Moreover, this tactic reduces the intelligibility of texts to a single, fixed position as the means to foreclose plural meanings. The language itself that is found in the texts of history (called documents) confers the official status of a single meaning and reduces the range of possible meanings found in the plural text to a solitary, authoritative voice—interpretation. This is why narrative so often appears in a third-person voice, omniscient, even Olympian, and why historians strive for comprehensiveness and the illusion of the "definitive study." But to write history that insists on narrative closure and the fixed position of the text's intelligibility, eliminating voices in dialogue for the sake of an automatic unfolding—"the events narrating themselves"—is to accept a view of life that is both given and completed. By "the presentation of an intelligible history" or, better yet, a followable story, "which effaces its own status as discourse," historical common sense performs as ideology to suppress "the relationship between language and subjectivity." Its practitioners become "accomplices of ideology," inasmuch as they seek to oppose a view that would result in producing historical practice.[17] Narrative signals ideological complicity principally because of its "propaedeutic value" to the contemporary social order and its capacity to constitute an image of the notion of continuity-in-change that is the presupposition of the kind of society we value.[18] But what we value as innocent description is indistinguishable from what we prescribe as necessity. Hayden White has concluded, in this connection, that "narrativity, the kind of narrativity that we associate with modern Western culture, full, coherent, finished or closed, summons up an image of the Real which will possess a coherence, order, fullness and continuity-in-change that social practice never displays. Or one should say: never displays to those privileged groups of a society for whom what should be is indistinguishable from what is."[19] The narrative of Japan's modernization fails to conceal this compulsion for both coherence and closure when the story line betrays its ideological complicity with prescription masked as description.

"Producing historical practice" usually refers to the process of production by which the texts used to construct a history are "deconstructed," that is, an analysis directed toward disclosing the conditions of textual production out of the available discourses. This view stands in rather stark contrast to historical common sense, which seeks to read documents as transparencies for truths that are always there, fixed and accessible to skilled historical extraction. For our purpose, in "reading" nativist texts, this means interrogating as far as possible their process of production, not simply as private experiences of authors or as the "authority" of authorial intention but as the mode by which works come to be produced, the materials used and how they are arranged. If we proceed in this manner, we are led to "point(s) of contradiction(s)" in the texts, which are usually suppressed: how and at which point nativist texts exceeded the limits they had constructed and how their form was constrained. To propose that nativist texts, like all texts, were riddled by contradictions is to break away from the assumption of a univocal, single interpretation, a, coherent, "authoritative reading" that, for Japanese interpreters, has portrayed *kokugaku* as a smooth, consistent movement, obeying the requirements of a familiar story line. Texts are neither free from contradictions nor constrained by invariant truths authorizing a single, authoritative interpretation. Instead, nativist texts show a remarkable degree of openness and what Paul Ricoeur has called a "surplus of meaning"; they are accessible to different articulations precisely because they were not fixed for a followable story. They must be seen as objects to be worked on by us for the production of *meaning*. My aim, then, has been not so much to seek the principles unifying nativism but to discover its "multiplicity" and "incompleteness, the omissions that it displays but cannot describe," its "contradictions." In the space of these "absences," or "silences" as Pierre Macherey calls them, "texts implicitly criticize their own ideology"; they possess the means available for a "critique of their own values," insofar as they provide for a "new process of production" by the analyst—the reader.[20] As a result of this operation, we are granted a glimpse of the limits of ideological reproduction. It is easy to accept the prevailing Japanese interpretations that *kokugaku* was enlisted as a support for the managerial ideology of the Tokugawa order.[21] We can go further, however, and suggest that nativism made available, from within, a critique of its own discourse and a process of producing meaning, which the received interpretations have failed to uncover. Tentatively, we can say that this meaning was inscribed in the *kokugaku* valorization of an order that was vastly different from the polity it was enjoined to rescue, and of a vision of culture that sought to unite mental and physical work in contrast to an official version that presupposed their division.

This kind of reading differs from more conventionalized Japanese practice, which seeks either (with Maruyama) to reduce *kokugaku* to ideological complicity or (with Muraoka) to establish its unity and coherence, to repair any inconsistencies by referring to the author's philosophy or by inserting the writers of the texts into the contemporary context.[22] By smoothing out these texts, closing them by creating a "canon" and an "acceptable interpretation," suppressing precisely those elements that conflict with dominant ideologies, historical criticism acts as an accomplice in perpetuating an ideology.

An approach that interrogates texts for their conditions of production and their corresponding ideological effects prevents us from reading texts as notations of reality, containing essential truths, as if there were a "metaphysics of the text." It also cautions us against using what Pierre Bourdieu has identified as native categories.[23] In the case of the former, it has been my purpose to "read" nativist texts not for an invariant truth but for operational truths belonging to different modes of authorial production. Reading for "truth" inevitably results in recapitulating the content of the texts and implies a privileged autonomy of its own. Moreover, such an exercise (its worst form is simply translating long portions of the text) replays the content and suggests that knowledge found in the text is given, already constituted, complete; to recount content (the text's "knowledge") is to reify the text as the source of its own value and to establish preemptive closure. To propose that knowledge is given is to say that the text's object is already constituted and fixed, that the text knows itself (just as, we are told, the facts speak for themselves). But the text's content may not know itself, or it may seek to divert the reader from what it cannot or will not speak about. Any reliance on the text's knowledge will secure only a pseudo-knowledge. In advising a distrust of native categories, Bourdieu has called attention to the disjunction between the explanation an informant may give of a practice when asked by an outsider and the "true nature of this practical mastery, 1.q. that is learned ignorance . . . a mode of practical knowledge not comprising knowledge of its own principles." He has warned that native theories are dangerous because they lead to the "superfluous reinforcement" of an "intellectualist tendency" signifying the objectivist approach to practices. Native explanations, whether extracted from an informant or culled from a text, invariably distill principles of practice and thought about actions from responses articulated in emergency or extraordinary moments in everyday life and establish them as governing norms. Such an approach inhibits the "logic of practice" that regulates the quotidian life. Bourdieu's example is the ideological use many societies make of lineage models and the legitimizing function of genealogical tables, which are reclaimed as representations of the real. Although such texts function as effects of the real, they must be examined for what they suppress from themselves—a discourse of familiarity—which leaves unsaid all those things that go without saying. Precisely because these aspects of practices are taken for granted, they are subject to "the censorship inherent in [the agent's] *habitus*, a system of schemes of perceptions and thought which cannot give what it does give to be thought and perceived without ipso facto producing an unthinkable and unnameable." Yet to perform this operation, to name what has hitherto been unnamed or unthinkable, as *kokugaku* illustrates, is to raise questions about a practice on which prevailing discourse has remained silent. Nativist theory and knowledge, produced by the "operation of the second power," "presupposes the structures it analyzes": nativism, produced by the same practices it sought to account for, reinforced prevailing structures by providing them with a form of rationalization. It is nonetheless true, however, that nativism went beyond mere reinforcement, because "whenever the adjustment between structures and dispositions is broken, the transformation is doubtless of the generative scheme, reinforced and accelerated by the dialectic between the schemes imminent and the norms produced by reflection on practices, which impose new meanings on them by reference to akin structures." As I hope to show, nativism not only reproduced the social conditions of existence but reconstituted and even transformed them in the process. What started out as thinking about practice became a practice.

The new strategies consulted for this inquiry define the object of study as the text rather than the past, which can never be known. They also authorize an interrogation of texts for the intervention they embody at the moment they appear in a determinate cultural field, not for invariant truths of time and place that they can never reflect. This approach requires us to ascertain the positions that different intellectual forms and practices occupy in relationship to one another within a given cultural (or historical) field.[24] The position of any form of cultural practice within this field is never fixed; it constantly shifts as the relationships that define the field are rearticulated. Hence, as Tony Bennett observed, there are no forms that are forever "oppositional" or "dominant"; rather, their functioning and effects depend politically on the place they occupy within the changing set of relationships that define their position. A redefinition of the cultural field requires a critical intervention by historians to "structure relations" to *produce* for texts a particular position as "support" for a particular ideological or political program. Historians, I believe, have long practiced this kind of restructuring unwittingly, as we can observe in the narrative of modernization or in Marxism, under the sanction that the field they designate and its distinguishing relationships are natural and commonsensical. Yet the position any text occupies within a field is not natural to it; it is the result of a "historically specific organization of the field of cultural relations," shaped into a particular discourse directed toward achieving specific effects for some group and purpose. Just as it is important to break with an idea of common sense that argues for the naturalness of a text's position, it seems equally imperative to reject the Marxist insistence on the essential politicality of texts, as if they reflected invariant truths. Marxists have devoted themselves to making the text's politics explicit because it is there, just as modernizers have worked to depoliticize or deproblematize texts, or, indeed, to rob them of a politicality. But to suppress or to tease out what is already there is an act of political intervention. Texts do not always necessarily have a politics or even a "political unconscious" that waits to be suppressed or brought to light; they must be made to speak politically by an act of "politicizing, by producing a new position for them within the field of cultural relations and new forms of use in the broader social process."

When Maruyama Masao wrote his great work *Nihon seiji shisōshi kenkyū*, he situated Ogyū Sorai's and Motoori Norinaga's texts within a certain field that was produced by a historically specific organization to give expression to a hegemonic or dominant ideology. We have no reason to suppose that such relationships are either natural or permanent and no reason to assume that we are prevented from producing different positions for *kogaku* and *kokugaku* texts by redefining the set of relationships governing the cultural field of the eighteenth century. We can propose, for example, that the relationships were determined not by the necessity to supplement a failing ideological order (as Maruyama believed) or even to contest it, but by a recognition that that word and meaning had become uncoupled in what Motoori Norinaga referred to as a separation of word, thing, and intent (*kotoba, koto, kokoro*). If we can agree upon this shift in the eighteenth-century problematic, then we are enabled to read the very same texts for different political effects. But such a "reading" does not "reflect" a work of transformation on ideological form that *kogaku* and *kokugaku* have always been able to perform and the historian now discovers. No text "has such an 'effect' independent of the way it has been worked" by historical criticism.

To explain the conditions producing texts, which is what Maruyama sought to do in his "reading," constitutes a critical intervention. Eighteenth-century texts did not signify the ideology they were said to have naturally; Maruyama made them signify it as a means of explaining contemporary (the 1930s) state ideological control and dissolving its claims to naturalness, common sense, eternity. Nothing is ever restored to history, as if it had been lacking or required "natural" supplementation; everything is put there.

But even if, as suggested above, ideology is a misrecognition of the real, it is, nonetheless, a product of the real that can be grasped through effects. Such a view conforms to prevailing Japanese interpretations of *kokugaku* as an ideological handmaiden to the hegemonic Tokugawa ethos. However, it goes further. When *kokugaku* tried to answer the "question of its question," the disjunction between language and experience, it sought to represent a world in words (leading to practice) that hitherto had not been externalized to certain social groups. Specifically, it offered to represent the experience of groups that had formerly remained on the borders of the dominant ideology. By turning to the task of establishing a condition for discourse in the knowledge (and thus interest) of the lived experience—especially in worship and work—of the ordinary folk (*aohitogusa*), *kokugaku* offered a voice to groups that had possessed none before and produced an audience that was conscious of social class. This effect was made possible by centering a lived experience in discourse in an imaginary way, as an authentic and "natural" reality that needed to be separated from the constraints of culture and artificiality in order to return to a whole and integrated life in the supposed natural relationship between deities, land, and people.

If Japanese interpreters of *kokugaku* are correct that nativism offered support to the crumbling Tokugawa order by admonishing people to work hard and to submit voluntarily to authority, it is also important to add that *kokugaku* imagined an order vastly different from the polity it sought to support. The reason for this difference stemmed from the rarely observed fact that *kokugaku* had *reworked* (not "discovered") earlier forms of literature and religious practice, which had remained on the sidelines of official culture and ideology. Late-Tokugawa *kokugaku* brought those forms from a preclass, folk culture (in fact, the "folk" itself, which had existed apart) into a direct relationship with official ideology and culture. In their valorization of work (and worship), *kokugakusha* were able to show, within the context of Tokugawa life, the origin of culture in the separation of mental and physical labor. The withdrawal of culture from the material production—the "existent," as Adorno put it—resulted in defining life in its negativity.[25] This process gives meaning to the nativist denunciation of *karagokoro* (Chinese mind), with its presumption of artifice and contrivance (*sakashira*). It also explains why so much activity appeared to concentrate on considerations of death and the migration of the spirits. And it enabled *kokugaku* to dramatize the juxtaposition of two different conceptions of culture by inserting a world apart into the official world within. Yet to suggest this juxtaposition between two cultures—one based on a separation of mental and physical labor and the other seeking to unify the two realms—is to propose that *kokugaku* went well beyond its assigned role to assist the flagging managerial order. Of course, the *kokugakusha* did not "intend" such an effect; but it can be plausibly argued that the manifest content of *kokugaku* signified an autonomous ideological role that *refracted* a socioeconomic existence entirely its own. Here, *kokugaku* functioned as a mediate point between popular culture and official Tokugawa ideology. In this way, it must be seen as the result of a new, historically produced set of social and cultural relationships that mediated between two distinct realms to establish the condition for conjuncture; these relationships were subsequently appropriated by a rural class seeking to solve the problem of disorder, rebellion, and production in the countryside.

The purpose of this historical illustration has been to show that whenever we encounter texts we are constrained to interrogate them for their effects within the set of relationships of whatever historical field we have articulated. Yet to make this move is to embark on a political intervention in which the past is always a displacement for the current situation and where the principle of historical determinations is rescued from the shadows of the unconscious and relocated in the site of language—the text.

If we aim to produce a knowledge of the texts, rather than extract a knowledge from them, our concern shifts from historical narration to an act of criticism that seeks to transform what has been given to us. Such an operation, it seems, qualifies less as a form of "recognition" than a practice working to produce meaning. Moreover, instead of merely complying with an ideology secured through recognition, the procedure moves to "construct its own object" by producing the work. Although we are always obliged to account for authorship, inasmuch as texts are produced by somebody for somebody else, the author relinquishes control of the text since, as Pierre Macherey put it, "the work that the author wrote is not precisely the work that is explicated by the critic."[26] Motivation is rarely, if ever, accessible to us; intentionality presumes a neutral reading. Neither adequately describes the task for historical discourse, because the practices of an author and a historical critic are generated by discourses that are relatively autonomous. Nativism, for example, can be produced—written, not read—in the twentieth century by using the knowledge of our time, rather than that of eighteenth-century Japan. The point is, however, to escape from the positivist dream of a simple communication model that presumes a symmetry between author and reader, despite the passage of time or distance of space, as if we had privileged access to experiences of epochs long past. To recognize that we are separated from nativist texts by time and cultural space (as are contemporary Japanese who study these texts) is to acknowledge that an ideal intersubjectivity is impossible. Yet to release the texts and us from such an intersubjective program is to prepare the ground for the kind of production of meaning that will account for the fact that texts and readers exist in discourses and ideologies belonging to different modes of cultural production. To see the text as *productivity* is to locate it in relation to the prevailing language codes and to apprehend its status within the intertextuality of utterances taken from other texts. Julia Kristeva, writing about the Russian literary critic M. M. Bakhtin, has observed that when the status of the word or utterance is raised, the text is implicated in history and society, "which are then seen as texts read by the writer and into which he inserts himself by rewriting them." The diachronic dimension is transmuted into the synchronic; in the transformation, linear history appears simply as an "abstraction." The only way *any* writer can participate in history, according to Kristeva's reading of Bakhtin's conception of carnivalesque discourse, is to contest this historical abstraction by the act of "reading-writing," by self-consciously juxtaposing the practice of one signifying structure or discourse to another.[27] Here is a promising way to imagine textual production in any given time or place without trying to account for authorial intention or motivation and appealing to an "unproblematic" *con*text, external to the text, as a ground base for both explanation and meaning. Just as we produce texts that are composites of other utterances and texts in order to maintain the dialogic demands of discourse, we can safely assume that texts have always functioned intertextually as representatives of specific signifying systems.

If we can accept this move, then we can say that nativists, or indeed any thinkers or writers from the past, are always our contemporaries, since we can never participate in the experiences of texts rooted in historical imaginaries no longer available to us. We are not eighteenth-century Japanese—neither are twentieth-century Japanese—and are forever prevented from experiencing texts as they were experienced by contemporaries of Motoori Norinaga and Hirata Atsutane. We are, however, able to work on these texts as *productivities* in order to reconstruct an ideology that we must assume they sought to suppress as a condition for saying to their interlocutors what they said, an ideology that is present in the texts by its apparent absence.

It should be evident from all that has been said that my purpose in writing this book has been to supply merely a "reading" of nativism, not to reconstruct its moment in history. Nevertheless, I have been concerned with questions of historicity. Beyond this reading stands the enabling conviction that every cultural object resembles a text, inasmuch as it reveals a surplus of meanings and interpretations that can never be exhausted, recovered in their entirety, or authoritatively reconstructed from their "context." By reading, I am not referring to the act that, according to Jacques Derrida, is easily reducible to identifying theme and content and thereby reproduces the official value of texts. Nor do I mean a biographical effort to locate a unified intention through the medium of a "transparent" language capable of reflecting accurately what the text's content "reveals." Instead, I have tried to "read" nativist texts for their internal "heterogeneity"—that is to say, for the conditions attending the construction of a content that must necessarily present the appearance of a unified intentionality in order to suppress or smooth over the very heterogeneity that has constituted it as a text—and to make visible the slips, slidings, and obvious silences that betray the claims of unity. When "reading" replaces "reconstruction" as the task for historical understanding, it points to the inherently political purpose marking the practice of historiography, which has been displaced or suppressed as an institutional condition for the teaching and writing of history.

The practice of reading that I have tried to apply in this book contests the institutional limits that have defined the disciplinary boundaries of history, not simply by calling attention to the postulates of historical continuity (already demolished by Michel Foucault) but, more important, by raising questions concerning the aporetic nature of historical understanding itself.[28] Ideally, such an approach should lead to what might nervously be called a "re-exoticization" of the historical past, which emphasizes its difference from, not its identity with, the present and reminds us of how narrative seduces us into believing that the past leads to the present. It would also, however, oblige us to concede our recognition of the genuine otherness of texts we stand in a position to "receive" from times and cultures distant from our own—all texts that come to us as traces or inscriptions of losses, as reminders of absent presences. Yet we would also be compelled to acknowledge what Ernst Bloch once called the "non-synchronicity" of the present and the effort to portray it as homogeneously complete. Far from seeing through such a program, I have managed only to retain, on occasion, the sign of textual difference. Reading nativist texts at the level of trying to follow them, I have been constantly aware of how distant and remote remains the world that gave them expression, even as I recognized that any attempt to capture their foreignness would result in mere unintelligibility. But this loss was lessened by my conviction that the act of reading demands accountability for its own historical situation when seeking to secure historical understanding. Earlier, I proposed that the knowledge produced by texts depends on the purposes to which they are subject, given the boundaries of what is socially permissible. As John Frow has written:

> The historical problems of assessing the ideological intensity of a text, the degree of its break with ideological norms and the level at which this occurs, is finally the problem of the historicity of reading: what we notice in a text is guided by our situation within a field of ideological struggle. A concern with the lines of power which structure this situation precludes the relegation of the text to the apparently closed context of its initial writing. It can be situated neither in an unmediated pastness nor in an unmediated presence. [29]

This recognition amounts to the formulation of reading strategies that will not only "consume" texts for their content but, resisting this commoditized idolization of the artifact, "produce" them as well, working them over and emphasizing their utility. Such a move aligns the reader's productive role with the image of how the text was produced, in spite of intervening distances of time and cultural space, and seeks to establish the terms of a "conversation" between representatives of different modes of cultural production. This strategy breaks with received regimes of reading, invariably presented by historians as reconstructions of the past, and with those institutional guarantees that transmute the historian's discourse into the autonomous discipline of history. "Politicizing" our own context of reception in this manner means that every act, however neutral it claims to be, is charged with a politicality, even as it tries to suppress it. The appeal to autonomy that history, along with other disciplines, has made demands the drawing of hard-and-fast boundaries between the internal concerns of a discipline devoted to producing knowledge and its external concerns, which are usually implicated in the world of politics. By their nature, disciplines like history have made their indifference toward politics an enabling condition for their practice. But it is precisely the claims of this kind of disciplinary privilege—its removal from the world, its insistence on a separation from politics—that make possible its refusal to recognize its own inescapable historical placement as a condition for practice. Just as there is no outside to textuality—an observation made years ago by Derrida—so can there be no outside to the reflection made inside a discipline. By the same measure, we can claim no privileged authority for our reading, since our reception of texts will always be mediated, and even constrained, by how we choose to integrate our own situation into the effort to account for the values stored within the texts that have been transmitted to us.[30] Such a move would entail the reordering of our priorities: the removal of the disciplinary constraints that derive their "authority" from claims of "autonomy" and "separation" and, thus, insist on the necessity of a division between "inside" and "outside" as a condition for serious historiographical practice. Yet, the sanction of newer priorities authorizing different strategies, which themselves appear as the Sign that the older disciplinary divisions were arbitrary and undecidable, would now oblige us to offer our own work, not as still another donation to the continuing consecration of History, but hopefully as a contribution to the current discussion, devoted precisely to questioning those disciplinary boundaries which, for so long, have resisted 'welcoming the Other.' In this way, our own efforts might reveal a historicity which our histories have consistently sought to repress.

1 Discourse/Ideology : Language/Labor

The Language of Ideology

One of the apparent paradoxes of Tokugawa intellectual history is that, while Japanese society was undergoing perceivable economic transformation and newer productive forces were undermining prevailing modes, *kokugaku* remained silent on these momentous changes and issues. Yet nativist texts, by the early nineteenth century, were mobilized to reconstitute agricultural work and valorize its practice as an application of the "ancient Way" (*kodōron*). Such an operation required nativism to exceed its own constraints, imposed by form and content, to speak about politics and the necessity of public order. Seemingly literary, linguistic, and religious texts were made to speak to questions of political practice even though their muted stand had simply signified assent to the way things were. This political vocalization disclosed a conjuncture between the original content of *kokugaku* and what we might call leading elements among the upper peasantry (*meibōka*), who sought to reorder agricultural life and restore productivity in the countryside by centering work and peasantry as the real meaning of nativist texts. As *kokugaku* was being made to resolve the rural problem, the leading elements of village life designated themselves, not the authorities, to be in the best position to reinstate order. Although nativism rarely specified any social group in Tokugawa Japan, since it presumed to speak to all peoples (employing the archaic word *aohitogusa*—ordinary folk—to denote the human community), the ordinary folk was increasingly equated in the early nineteenth century with the peasantry and the ancient Way with agricultural labor. But there was nothing inherent either in nativism, or in the social groups that sought representation from it, to explain the conjuncture and the subsequent appropriation.

A clue to resolving this seeming paradox is offered by Max Weber in his masterful *Protestant Ethic and the Spirit of Capitalism*. Weber tried to explain vast changes in material life and consciousness without reducing one to the other; he wanted to show how capitalism was mediated by new forms of spirituality, where each—Protestantism and capitalism—represented different, independent kinds of activity. He was less concerned with historical representation than with the possibility of reaching a value-oriented interpretation, which, he believed, was not necessarily *in* history but *of* history. This interpretation authorized the means to construct what he called a "historical individual."[1] For Weber, such an approach led to the formation of "ideal types," typifications rather than historical explanations; interpretation was directed toward imputing value to an object, instead of determining what people who created the object felt at the time. The imputation of possible value also permitted him to escape the reductionism demanded by the base/superstructure relationship ("expressive causality") and to propose the relative autonomy of ethos (which I reread as ideology) as a causal force in the constitutive process. Far from proposing that Protestant spirituality caused capitalism, Weber identified the processes by which capitalist activity was able to appropriate new religious impulses without taking on the baggage of its content as well. In all probability, capitalism had no need for such a theory of motivation; there was no inner logic compelling it to seek such authoritative representation. Weber suggested that an ethos (or ideology) need not be—and often was not—produced by the group that became bonded to it.[2] A particular cultural product was given an ideological effect by the act of appropriation and, thus, became the ideology of a group—indeed, defined it as a group, even when there was no "natural" fit authorizing the alliance. Hence, ideology was produced when a group or class sought to supply or supplement its interests with a body of "authoritative" knowledge. Yet, Weber noted of capitalism and its informing ethos: "The capitalistic form of an enterprise and the spirit in which it is run generally stand in some sort of adequate relationship to each other, but not in one of necessary interdependence. . . . This, however, is justified by the historical fact that the attitude of mind has on the one hand found its most suitable expression in capitalistic expression, while on the other the enterprise has derived its most suitable force from the spirit of capitalism."[3] When the interaction of knowledge and interest displaced base/

superstructure, form and content, knowledge, or discourse—a certain way of talking about a specific set of objects—became ideological. The conjuncture and the subsequent bonding between discourse and a social group revealed something about the principle of history enabling the alliance, yet it was precisely the function of ideology to repress history in the interest of representing the merger as natural and self-evident. History, here, referred to the specific forces of production and social relations characterizing the social formation. Weber also noted that linking capitalist organization and Protestant spirituality required suppressing the conditions that produced religious reform or new productive arrangements. He implied, and others explained, that new productive processes offered the raw materials for speculation, even though they were quite independent of the philosophic forms that ultimately supplied representation.[4] A convergence, making possible an appropriation of forms from one level of the social formation to another, signified the possible mode of relating between semi-autonomous domains. In the case of nativism, as I hope to show, its view of nature, which was steeped in an earlier productive process, made possible the incorporation of raw materials—content—of agriculture from the side of social relationships into a generalized view of the world. What may have functioned originally as a form of reproducing the conditions of social existence—leading Japanese interpreters of *kokugaku* to interpretations that call attention to its complicity with the Tokugawa managerial ideology—ultimately had a totally different function. In response to the transformation of the dominant mode of production occurring in the late-Tokugawa period, nativism signified the *nonreproduction* of political and ideological conditions of existence.[5]

Nativist discourse apparently attracted different social groups, whose interests were assimilated to its claims of knowledge. But neither reflection theory nor appeals to historical contingency adequately explains the conjuncture. The conjuncture changed both the social group appropriating it for representation and the content of nativism; in the case of the latter, *kokugaku* was increasingly mobilized as a solution to rural problems and, in the case of the former, the upper peasants changed their role to that of "natural" leaders—agrarian sages—of the newly conceptualized village, by virtue of their possession of authoritative knowledge. Despite the seemingly contingent nature of the coupling, there was good reason prompting leading groups in the countryside to *recognize* in *kokugaku* a representation of their interests.

Such "recognition" (really a misrecognition) was tied to the central concerns of the nativist project and the ways they might offer "meaning" to social groups that became associated with it.

Most Japanese interpreters of nativism separate the discourse into the two "schools" of Motoori Norinaga and Hirata Atsutane. Such a view discerns a significant break between Motoori and his "pupil" Hirata; it also contends that the ruralization of nativism was implicit or inherent in Hirata's religious meditations, even though he was attempting to provide support to the beleaguered ideological order. But Hirata was not a peasant, and his students in the Ibukiya (established in Edo) were not necessarily recruited from rural constituencies. If peasants appeared on the school rolls consistently, so did recruits from other groupings in Tokugawa Japan. It is hard to demonstrate that Hirata's message, which aimed to reformulate native religious practices, directed its appeal primarily to peasants. Moreover, his own formulations of the "ancient Way" and his attempt to define the meaning of *kokugaku* were surely, according to his own declarations, consistent with the received tradition of discourse as it had been established in the eighteenth century by Kamo no Mabuchi and Motoori. It is true that Hirata altered relationships in the body of discourse to introduce elements that, in the writings of earlier nativists, had remained marginal or peripheral. But this activity—reemplotting nativism—merely supplemented what he believed to be already present in a doctrine whose adherents insisted upon plenitude and presence. His intervention constituted a contestation within *kokugaku* over how certain claims should be expressed. This surely explains Hirata's so-called break with the Motoori line as articulated by Ōhira (more will be said on this subject later), and his decision to alter the emphasis from poetry (and linguistics) to practical religiosity. Native religious practices were not alien to the *kokugaku* of Kamo and Motoori. Hirata was seeking to show that the "ancient Way" and its religious claims were *central* to *kokugaku* but had been obscured by an excessive concentration on poetry and aesthetics. His purpose was to demonstrate, on textual authority, that religious practice preceded the representations in language, song, and poetry that practical spirituality produced.

At the same time that this argument distanced Hirata from the established mainline, it permitted him to enlarge the scope of nativism and ring it with an "untranscendable horizon," so that all forms of thought became either local manifestations of nativism or simple distortions. It is for this reason that he launched a broad-based attack on all "rivals" in the 1820s: "vulgar Shintoists," "stinking" Confucianists, misguided students of Dutch Learning, Buddhists, and nativists working in different idioms. But to contest received nativist formulations he had to seek authorization in an already constituted audience recruited from among Edo townsmen (*yūmin*), the same audience his rivals sought to reach, or he had to create one that had not hitherto existed. This impulse prompted him to dramatize the religious problem and demonstrate how the distortion of genuine spirituality had led to aberrant forms of private behavior as a consolation for profound unhappiness. Here, Hirata's rhetorical skills, possibly unmatched among contemporaries, transformed impressive learning into a message of universal urgency: he tried to convince his audiences that despite the pleasure found in the Edo culture of play—*ukiyo*—such behavior grew out of unhappiness inspired by the fear of death and the migration of the spirits to the place of permanent pollution (*yomi*).[6] People had been diverted from a meaningful, productive, and orderly life out of the anxiety that thoughts of death introduced. He offered both an "authoritative" explanation of life after death and a promise of consolation by reasoning that the spirits could not possibly migrate to *yomi*.

I do not mean to suggest that Hirata was interested merely in grandstanding in the hope of recruiting larger numbers of followers, even though some contemporaries like the writer Takizawa Bakin were convinced that he was driven by self-interest. But Hirata was, more than most, able to make rhetoric an integral condition for transmitting discursive content. Because his rhetorical strategies often modified that content, his speeches contributed to making *kokugaku* into a practice. Such an explanation narrows the contextual referents of nativism and escapes reducing *kokugaku* to contemporary social conditions, as if its choice of concerns mirrored a material history external to its texts. It would be difficult to say that people were more agitated by considerations of death in the late eighteenth and early nineteenth centuries than at any other time in Tokugawa Japan or, indeed, in the long duration of Japanese history. Yet such a centering, as it was performed by Hirata, was obviously more than a rhetorical ploy and undoubtedly signified, by distancing and displacement, something about contemporary reality. Insofar as Hirata called attention to the prevailing life-styles of Edo townsmen and argued that the absence of seriousness was a symptom of profound disorientation, we can acknowledge the intervention of history into his discourse. But the entrance of history was only an

indirect effect of the real, which was the meaning of Hirata's considerations on death and his theory of consolation (*Shizumari*).

Hirata's intervention sought to solve the problem of death by
showing how it occupied only one part in a larger conception of existence, one that was whole and in which the parts stood in a relationship
of kinship to one another. He was offering *kokugaku* as a supplement
to prevailing ideological formulations that could no longer contain or
conceal negativity and the contradictions occasioned by the uncoup-
ling of life and experience. Death and the prevalence of unhappiness
were dramatic means to call attention to the willful pursuit of personal
interest and its inevitable result—disorder, the fragmentation of life
into disconnected parts, the dissolution of wholeness, and the intrusion
of differences. The sundering of the relationships that had made for a
whole life was the not-said in his effort to show how life, experience,
and its representation constitute a seamless narrative in which all things
past and present—spirits, ancestors, and the living—were held together
in a web of interconnecting relationships by virtue of their common
descent from the creation deities (*musubi no kami*). To overcome the
fear of death was to restore unity to life and culture when before it had
been absent in society.

The offer of consolation to the ordinary folk involved a comprehensive cognitive strategy, which nativism shared with contemporary
discourses in the eighteenth century.[7] In this scheme, connectedness
showed family resemblances, despite apparent differences to the eye,
and family resemblances revealed the essential relationship of all things
past and present, because of the common creative powers of the *musubi no kami*. Both Hirata and his rural appropriators increasingly saw
that their task was to discriminate among different identities and account for these discriminations and the proliferation of differences
(fragmentation) while demonstrating the inevitable kinship of all parts
and series. This demonstration of connectedness and kinship derived
from a cognitive strategy that sought to dispose of, and thus represent,
the world through reduction to the modality of contiguity. The issue
struck at the root metaphor of Tokugawa Neo-Confucianism itself,
which, in its effort to apprehend the world in a series of resemblances,
could simply no longer account for "differences" as mere anomaly.

The new choice *kokugaku* offered to the failing Neo-Confucian
"hermeneutic" was to explain the world in such a way as to accommodate the apparent differences manifest among phenomena and to
secure the promise of continuity that the Neo-Confucian model of

knowledge had previously made possible. Contiguity called forth the model of the syntagm—in contrast to the spatial-relationship paradigms of Neo-Confucianism—and the categories of order, measurement, calculation, and discrimination. In nativism, the world of appearances was broken down into dualities, oppositions, or contiguous linkages, such as cause and effect, agent and act, visibility and invisibility. Such concerns disclosed the destruction of the earlier guarantee of kinship between the seen and the read, the eye and the ear; hereafter, discourse would be directed at showing that what was stated was distinct from what the utterance really represented. Activity consisted less of drawing things together, inducing emulation or sympathy through the operation of principles in order to secure resemblance and the promise of sameness. It would now account for the relationships between apparently different things in a general effort to establish the identity of objects and to argue that connections and identities were no longer local manifestations of principle (*ri*). The act of discriminating privileged a comparative method capable of recognizing the primacy of differences. Although measurement and discrimination presupposed starting from a whole and dividing it into its constituent elements, it was the parts themselves that observers ultimately equated with the whole. By the same token, the presumption of order required establishing elements—the simplest that could be found—in order to arrange differences in series characterized by a "family resemblance," according to the smallest degrees of the set. This "metonymic" strategy (the term was not used by Japanese) allowed observers to make qualitative distinctions that previously, under the regime of the paradigmatic model of knowledge, had been difficult to make; eighteenth-century discourses increasingly spoke of distinctions between, for example, competence and incompetence, equality and inequality, past performances and present experiences. In time, the concern for comparison itself became a function of the search for orderly series.

By resorting to what I have called a metonymic strategy, nativism, together with other contemporary discourses, was able to create an apprehension of a world in which one thing—the part—was reduced to another or substituted for the whole.[8] In this epistemological scheme, parts of presumed totalities functioned to construct a series of attributes that were adequate to the whole and could reveal the web of relationships that bound entities together. Metonymy promised to make sense of things that appeared to be different and discontinuous by relating them to each other in contiguity or, even, in propinquity. Perhaps the most distinguishing feature of this new strategy was its power to reduce things to essential parts, to search out, as a consequence, their genetic origins. This form of reduction to origins is a necessary condition of metonymy, and the genesis it reveals usually offers powerful warrants for action and practice in the present. The most dramatic instance of this expressive mode was *kokugaku*, not to mention *Mitogaku*, which returned to origins to establish the essential connectedness of apparent differences. The reductive strategy that propelled restorationists' impulses—what nativists called "adhering to the base"—was neither romantic, nostalgic, nor necessarily conservative. Rather, it constituted a conception of the real that was rooted in specific social practices of the eighteenth century, since it sought to retrieve essential and tangible meanings no longer available to contemporaries. This impulse lay at the heart of the nativists' emphasis on words and representations, their search for a primary and natural language that was capable of expressing things tangibly and accurately, and their attempt to rescue the traces of *kotodama* itself—the spirit of language—which had preserved the true vehicle of expressibility. The principal purpose of this reductive strategy was not to invite the present to slavishly imitate the ancient past or even the original language, but to recall meanings and functions in their essential forms to serve as guides for the present and to demonstrate that tangibility and wholeness derived from naturalness, not contrivance. To achieve the promise of interconnectedness, wholeness, and tangibility, Hirata and his rural followers sought to provide a systematic classification that could demonstrate, by representation, the relationship of all things. Like many others in the late-Tokugawa period, Hirata chose the form of cosmological speculation as his mode of relating, because it promised to show in visual diagram how "history" functioned as a crucible that held together all relationships.

Yet the initial purpose of this vast classification system was to show that it was impossible for the spirits of people to migrate after death to the dreaded, foul world of *yomi*. Its purpose was to provide comfort to ordinary people who, Hirata believed, feared death and consequently expressed their anxieties and unhappiness in activities such as peasant rebellions, village out-migrations, and self-indulgence in the privatized pleasures of city life. The argument for consolation was made possible by convincingly elaborating, in diagrammatic form, a fundamental division between "visible things" and "invisible things." But this classification was already presupposed by nativist cognitive strategy, which was capable of relating seemingly unrelated objects to

one another by showing how their shared identity derived from the
divine intervention that had fixed the invisible world as the source of
the phenomenal realm of visible things. By linking the visible to the
invisible in a relationship of cause and effect, agent and act, and
thereby making one's conduct in the phenomenal realm the basis of
judgment in the invisible world, Hirata and his followers were able to
offer representation and meaning to groups that had hitherto remained
marginal to official discourse. Under this arrangement, the evaluation
of behavior and judgment was based on morally informed activity,
which came to mean work and productive labor. Echoing Ogyū Sorai's
defense of the "little virtues," nativists believed that whatever a person
did was important, since everyone was obliged to perform according to
the endowment and disposition bestowed by the heavenly deities. This
theory did more than enjoin the ruled to fall into line and work hard.
Its really significant consequence was to transform the ordinary folk
into knowing subjects capable of occupying a position of autonomy by
ethicizing their quotidian life and the productivity of their daily labor.
It drew attention to the centrality of such activities as work and productivity, which had formerly been consigned to the margins of Confucian
discourse, and shifted the axis of activity from the performance of specific behavior that satisfied norms to the essence of life itself as the
criterion of all performance and knowledge and the indispensable basis
of community. The idea of a hidden world took on specific associations
in the late-Tokugawa period when it became linked to the sanctuary of
the ancestors. We know from Hirata's own studies of tutelary worship
that this sanctuary of the spirits and ancestors was the village. But now,
the original sense of a hidden world changed to overlap increasingly
with the world of village, family, and household. In time, when the
invisible realm was symbolized by the tutelary shrines (which themselves were associated with Ōkuninushi no kami, ruler of the invisible
world), it became identical with the world of the village, concealed,
powerless in the space of visible, public authority, yet vibrant with real
activity. Here, nativist discourse pitted a horizontal reality, close to nature, against the vertical world of the Tokugawa *daikan*, daimyo, shogun, and even emperor, against the artifice of contemporary history
itself. Hence, when Hirata argued that the living inhabited the visible
world and the spirits and deities resided in the invisible realm, he suggested the possibility of an interesting dialectic between creation and
custom. Each realm was separate but, nonetheless, related to the other;
the living were the descendants of the ancestors and the deities. And

each bespoke the whole. Creation was, to be sure, the work of the gods, yet it was also a continuously productive act in which humans participated to literally reproduce the initial act of origins. For nativists, "creativity and productivity" (*musubi*) established the divisions, the classes of events and things, inner and outer, human and sacred, visible and invisible; yet such categories were not limited to the singular moment of creation but applied, rather, to life itself as an ongoing process. Because, as Ōkuni Takamasa observed, *musubi* also denoted linkages, binding together, and union, it served as a leading principle in a theory of human harmony (*wagō*). The fact that the most explicit evidence of the continuing activity of the creation deities was agricultural work explains its primacy in nativist thought and its identification with worship. Moreover, work, in the sense of a fulfillment of the divine intervention, functioned to call attention to the sacred purpose informing human intention and, thus, acted as the bond (much like language) holding together community. It offered an alternative means of securing social solidarity that was easily as important as mere political obedience and loyalty.

At its most fundamental level, the world envisaged by nativists was one of linkages and kin relationships. It was a realm where microcosm, the household and the village (the part), served as a substitute for the macrocosm, the "national soil," where emperor as a living deity met the tutelary deities and ancestors administered by Ōkuninushi no kami and where the verticality of public authority collided with the horizontal claims of village life.

The argument for an autonomous and self-sufficient village, removed from the centers of power, hinged on the idea that people were obliged to return blessings to the creation deities. They were obliged to duplicate the archetypal act of creation by their agricultural work and reproduction. Judgment and the final authority lay in the hidden realm, which was now identified with the village and administered by Ōkuninushi no kami, not the living deity who was the emperor. This duty was described as a form of entrustment (*yosashi*) deriving its power from scriptural authority; the land was a trust bestowed by the gods so that human beings might work and make it habitable. Work now was seen as a reenactment of the archetypal event of creation. Late-Tokugawa nativists (invariably recruited from village leaders or priests) employed this idea of trust to emphasize the importance of agricultural life and the role of the village as the most appropriate means of organizing people for work. The notion of an autonomous village merged, however, with the idea of an administration pledged to take care of the people. The result was the increasing presentation of *kokugaku* as a method for solving current problems in the countryside. Such a method was dramatized as caring, assistance, and mutual aid, which also could be justified as aspects of entrustment. Because entrustment became the grounds for rural self-sufficiency, the nativist intervention in the late-Tokugawa period ultimately elevated the village as a space responsible for its own administration and economic well-being. The proposed arrangement, and the new religions such as Kurozumi, Tenri and Konkō as well, conjured up an enchanted realm that reunited politics and religion in the new shape of community and invited its occupants to secede and seek relief from the negative constraints of contemporary history, structures, and mediations.

The Problematic of Discourse

To call attention to the way nativist cognitive strategy permitted the ideological resolution of aporias posed by contemporary history is to raise the fundamental problematic that determined the formation of the discourse and the "question of its question" it sought to answer: the disjunction between language and experience. Nativism was one among several discourses in the eighteenth century that proposed to represent, in words and practice, a world that hitherto had not been "externalized" to social groups. It drew its authority from the groups to which it was directed and over which it was able to exert its power; it literally produced groups by expressing them. This "extraordinary discourse," as Pierre Bourdieu has called it, invariably derives its power from the "capacity to objectify unformulated experiences, to make them public." Yet the impulse to externalize a world inevitably discloses the disjunction between language and experience and summons the historical circumstances that, in some way, have prompted systematic expression—"externalizing" what previously "had up to then been lived nameless."[9] This naming of the unnamed, for nativism and other discourses in the eighteenth century, presumed an identity between language and experience. Specifically, it meant offering authoritative expression to groups and, hence, experiences that had been represented only on the borders of the dominant discourse in Tokugawa Japan. As *kokugaku*, along with other discursive formations, made an "unnamed" experience into public common sense as a means to authorize the constitution of groups that had not hitherto gained access to signifying practices, it provided a powerful justification for practical action.

Underlying this valorization of different and local "experiences" was the more fundamental recognition that the received codes of meaning specified the limits of what could be said or understood at any given moment. Understanding depended on a person's position in a given signifying practice. In Neo-Confucianism, groups were classified along the lines of a fixed division of labor between head and hand that entitled the former to rule over the latter. Since ruling relied on certain forms of moral knowledge, only those who had acquired it and who possessed the proper credentials could become rulers. Most social constituencies belonged to the category of the ruled and were either denied access to the dominant signifying practice or were simply marginalized. The classification between ruler and ruled carried an additional distinction between those who possessed subjectivity and those who did not. Meaning was principally directed toward the subject, the person in a position to know—and therefore speak, in this case, a member of the warrior class. "To be a subject is to have access to a signifying practice" and thereby become identical with either the "I" of an utterance or discourse or with its speaker. The subject becomes fixed to a specific position in a discourse and, hence, to a specific knowledge that constrains the availability of meaning. Signifying always precedes the individual, whose own sense of self must derive from it; it is always learned. In this way, the subject is always "an effect of the meaning it seems to possess."

Although it had been the initial intention of the Tokugawa to control discourse, to determine what could be said and understood as well as what it was possible to be, to make sure that the ruled acted according to the positions they occupied in order to produce and reproduce the specific social formation, this sense of surety began to break down early in the eighteenth century. The opposition of ruler and ruled was beginning to exhaust its productivity; it was losing the capacity to sustain a vision of the political that could successfully accommodate the complexity and plurality of the social urban environment. Physical and demographic expansion stimulated an acceleration of the social and cultural life, which began to present itself as a vast spectacle of social surplus juxtaposed to the "rational" and organized structures of the Tokugawa "order," as imagined by Neo-Confucian ideologues. Social surplus spilled over status lines and destabilized fixed meaning by fostering play and plural identities.

It should be noted that signifying practices are never static and discourses are never fixed for all time, even though they claim the authority of timelessness. By the same measure, meaning can never be single. Instead, it is constantly deferred, owing to its capacity to imply difference, and, therefore, "displaced by the absent trace of alterity" (otherness) within the identity made possible as an "effect of difference." Just as utterance determines a particular identity, what it includes, which constitutes presence, is possible only because of those meanings that have been excluded to represent a difference that is literally absent. As a result of these exclusions, discourses are always threatened by challenges to their "boundaries," that is, to what is admissible, legitimate, and appropriate. They must defend their limits and seek to arrest the play of meaning as it slides toward plural articulations. Failure to stem the "slide toward plurality" risks the establishment of new discourses and alternative forms of knowing capable of producing new subject positions, new determinations, and new definitions of the real. The successful installation of new discourses and alternative forms of knowledge converges with the recognition that meaning itself is no longer fixed and that newer possibilities for what it is to be a subject are already being enacted.[10]

Nativism was one among a number of discourses that called into question the suppositions of a political ideology rooted in the logic of sameness, which had divided the political and cultural spheres neatly between ruler and ruled, mental and manual labor. Yet it went even further; it challenged the very fixity of the social identity of the ruled in a closed hierarchic chain of resembling elements that reflected the "order" found in nature. The material expansion of Edo, the hub of a world not yet imagined, made it possible to reject these fixed identities, because the subject positions that people occupied as a condition of urban life had begun to proliferate. At the same time that the multiplication of needs and the differentiation of services contributed to the city's expansion and blurred the established identities between ruler and ruled, the city secured powerful symbolic representation in the notation of a discordance between language and experience.

As nativism revealed the relationship between the formation of an "extraordinary discourse" and the acknowledged separation of received language usage from experience, it recognized the necessity to reassess the status of both. At its beginnings in the eighteenth century, *kokugaku* concentrated on locating an authentic experience which had been suppressed by contemporary conditions that could be found only

in literary works produced in the native idiom. *Kokugakusha* quickly
recognized, however, that the representation of such experience in
texts had been seriously compromised by the use of Chinese conventions and that it was necessary to resuscitate the native language, which
was buried under alien and unnatural Chinese words, syntax, and
sounds. Their observation was reinforced by a conviction that contemporary language usage had become opaque, laden with foreign elements, and powerless to reflect accurately; it occluded genuine feeling
to such an extent that words failed to convey life accurately. Only a
language free from artificial constraints and distorting elements could
guarantee a successful return of expression to the experience of daily
life. Nativists turned to finding ways of restoring a correspondence between a natural language and authentic feeling and unifying, as they
put it, intent (*kokoro*), word (*kotoba*), and deed (*koto*). They began to
investigate the texts of the native tradition, to locate traces of original
Japanese before the fateful adoption of the Chinese script and its distorting vocalizations. Nativists were convinced that a return to these
texts and this language would enable them to "hear" echoes of the
authentic sounds generated by the inaugural voice of the gods. But proposing a "return" in this manner presupposed an ontological grounding
since language was created. Within the space opened up by language,
the inaugural act of enunciation (*kotodama*) established a type of reference that made the speaking of Japanese and the vocalization of native sounds the ontic dimension of being. In short, for the nativist
intervention, language signified an inaugural act and a specific referent; speaking a language transparently reflected the divine moment of
creation. To speak a language that could adequately *refer to* the founding act of creation and the human habitat was to secure a promise that
the identity of sameness would be reinstalled as the solution to differences caused by the language of the Other (Chinese) and the loss in-
curred from the effacement of the ontological.

It was clearly the problem of difference—the division and fragmentation in life—that commanded the attention of early nativists.
The disclosure of a language prior to Chinese and coterminous with
the creation of the folk who were divinely appointed to speak it dramatized another opposition between the natural and the artificial. This
view, which had immense implications for nativist conceptions of culture, history, and nature, permitted a shift toward the "real" or
"natural" as the object of coherent verbal expression. Discourse first
apprehended culture as Chinese—alien, unnatural, and remote, a

sedimentation smothering genuine existence; a return to the real existence that was tied to production and reproduction meant getting out
of culture (history). Then the discourse could easily transfer its concerns to the details of daily life as further manifestations of authentic
experience. It should be noted, in this connection, that nativists
stressed the primacy of speech over writing, voiced expression over
script, since the spoken word was seen as immediate, present, and always complete in itself. Voice was the living breath (*iki*), the body
acting. Hirata and rural nativists enlarged this emphasis on the immediacy of voice to include work and daily affairs. By the time of the late-
Tokugawa nativists in the early nineteenth century, the problem of
explaining the instance of difference was no longer urgent; it was succeeded by a question that had become more compelling—of working
out a theory of practice to realize the promised sense of identity and to
transpose the terms of fragmentation into wholeness. By turning to the
task of establishing a knowledge that corresponded to the lived experience of the ordinary folk (*aohitogusa*), especially in their daily work
and worship, nativism offered a voice (and identity) to groups where
none had existed before and produced an audience as an effect of that
knowledge. It centered on lived experience, daily life as *kokugakusha*
defined it, as an authentic and natural reality that demanded to be
liberated from the constraints of culture, and its fragmenting consequences; by escaping from culture—second nature, as it were—it was
possible to return to a natural and unmediated relationship between
the deities, land, and people, to secure once more a union with the
tangible real, the quotidian experience of the folk, which had been
realized first in antiquity.

In this process, *kokugaku* reworked earlier forms of literature and
religious practice that had become remote from official ideology and
culture. This activity explains their summoning of the Japanese language and their claim that it referred directly to more genuine forms of
expressibility—the real. But the quest for a prelapsarian language also
provided the sanction to interrogate official forms of writing, especially
where they were suffused with alien syntax and words. This call to a
primary language and its associations with a natural religion—life
itself—represented a world apart, if not exactly an inversion. Late-
Tokugawa nativism succeeded in bringing elements from folk culture—in fact, the folk itself—into a direct relation with official ideology and culture, which, through a set of devices, was transfixed and
revealed from within as the ideology of a changing and failing order.

Nativists repositioned language, and subsequently work and worship, within the context of the established order, bringing new elements from the outside into a relationship of propinquity to change the meaning of the context itself, perhaps even to "discrown" it. Work, as I hope to show later, was merely a code for worship; it had existed safely at a distance from Tokugawa ideology. When it was made into a central subject of the world of official culture, it provided an ideology of daily life that could replace the official version by making the action of the body equivalent to the operation of mental discipline—mind. Here, nativism converged with the culture of popular verbal fiction (*gesaku*) and the floating world of infinite play, which privileged the ceaseless activity of body over mind.

In their valorization of work, nativists were able to show the origin of culture in the separation of mental and physical labor within the boundaries of official Tokugawa life. The withdrawal of culture from material production, the "existent," work and life, resulted in defining life negatively in terms of a fear of death. Authorized by this recognition, nativists were now able to insert a world apart into the context of Tokugawa life. Some historians have argued that the nativist project signalled the installation of local culture, but this view represents the achievements that hindsight assigned to it rather than the effects derived from its immediate program. Since nativists rejected culture itself because it had been generated by the division between physical and mental labor—which produced inequality (desire), social failure, and fragmentation—it is unlikely that they would have been willing to project another conception of culture. The purpose of their discourse was to overcome the artificial divisions in social life by unifying head and hand. By working on forms of writing and material culture where native language and productive labor had always occupied a central position, which, hitherto, had remained remote from official life, *kokugakusha* established the possibility of a direct encounter between them and the official world. Such a view means reading the nativist project, especially its concentration on language and forms of writing, as possessing an autonomous ideological role that refracted a socioeconomic existence entirely its own. In their effort to resuscitate the traces of an authentic linguistic tradition found in the poems of the *Man'yō*, in the accounts of the *Kojiki* and the *Nihonshoki*, and in other "literary" genres, they aimed less at showing these works as "literature" than at installing them as significations of reality and products of particular, socially constrained practices of writing, which simultaneously revealed a specific constellation of class relationships within language. The quest to locate a prior—originary—language, to establish original meanings lost in the superimposition of Chinese, prompted nativists not only to mobilize words by juxtaposition but also to contest the realm of fixed associations upheld in official usage. They also challenged the claim of official culture to define the real and the appropriate. The invocation of a native language offered a different signification of reality as well as different social associations, ones that represented the voice of the deities and the ordinary folk and the activities of their world.

Even more important was their invocation of a folk life preoccupied with natural forms of worship and daily work, indistinguishable from each other, which was long forgotten but clearly present outside official Tokugawa culture. Such a world may well have renewed official ideology from time to time by temporarily subverting fixed hierarchies, especially in religious practice and festivals. But now, nativists transformed this received folk "culture" by bringing it into a direct relationship with official ideology. No longer would folk culture merely invert official ideology for a fleeting moment. This transformation gives meaning to the consistent effort to show in poetic practice the consequences of hardened conventions in contrast to those of fresh, spontaneous, and genuine archaic Japanese; it explains the need to dramatize the indissoluble ties between a natural religion and daily life in contrast to the propensities of alien religious forms, which insisted upon separating worship from spheres of existence, and the importance of physical work in contrast to the privileging of moral contemplation and mental labor. Nativists sought to undermine the very division between high and popular cultures by reintegrating the two as a condition for securing wholeness, a disposition shared by the Edo culture of play, but with different consequences. The act of incorporating forms of life into an integrated whole must be read as an instance of ideological criticism, charged with social and political meaning. Wholeness, the promise of similitude, meant representing contemporary life as a unity of fragmented and disconnected parts. Nativism, along with *gesaku*, must, therefore, be seen as a mediate point between popular culture and official Tokugawa ideology. Yet this function was the product of a new, historically produced set of social and cultural relationships that established the condition for a conjuncture. Nativism's situation at this point of confluence historically determined the contours of its writing but also disclosed specific social, political, and ideological determinants.

The Ideology of Language

Nativism functioned as a critique of ideology by showing, through the agency of juxtaposition and propinquity, how dominant forms of representation failed to contain the contradiction between language and experience; the authority for this claim derived from a powerful criticism of language usage itself. In fact, it was a concern for the status of language, not simply for poetic or literary form, that marked the beginning of the nativist project in the late seventeenth and early eighteenth centuries.

Language as Ideological Production

Embedded in the nativist discussion of language was a differentiation between individual speech and the larger system that authorized performance. Nativists believed that even though utterance ultimately depended on a system of language, the general system, which nativists vaguely called *kotodama*—the spirit of the language—could only be apprehended through performative expressions in poetry and prose. Concentration on the instance of utterance invariably problematized how and why one sentence connected with another into a whole. I noted earlier that discourse is simply the act of making sentences, speaking about certain objects in a specific and recognizable modality. In addition, Émile Benveniste, following Ferdinand de Saussure's insight into the relationship between *langue* and *parole*, has proposed that, with the sentence, one leaves the domain of language as a "system of signs" and enters "another universe . . . whose expression is discourse."[11] Although structuralist linguists have argued that discourse is not synonymous with communication and that only the most arbitrary relationship exists between a signifier and the signified or sound and its referral to a concept, nativist thinkers defined utterance not as an effect of communication but, rather, as its central function. Underlying this move were two principal assumptions that informed much of nativist practice: (1) language must be a transparent medium if it is to communicate, and (2) the subject is a self-sufficient individual, given prior to language and standing outside of it but still able to intend and communicate a message external to its realm.

Even more important to this conception of language was the way nativists related signifier to signified. They proposed that signifiers or phonemes—sound—are naturally adapted to convey the signified because the meaning represented in a word is naturally, not arbitrarily, motivated by an authorizing signifier. *Kokugaku* language theory sought to link two basically different things into a unified and natural series of relationships. Nativist theorists consistently emphasized the primacy of Japanese sound, but they compromised the essential autonomy of the signifier by trying to show how specific sounds found perfect correspondence in lexical representation. Instead of insisting that the phonemes of a language defined one another in a system of mutual differentiations or that signifiers related to one another and not to any signified, nativists sought to show that the articulation of a specific sound system was bonded to the intention (*kokoro*) of the speaker. Hence, they saw the signifier as a necessary but passive conveyer of communication, although they also argued, rather contradictorily, that the sound—the signifier—was active and determining because it was necessary and specific to Japanese. The intention of the speaker seeking to communicate was coterminous with the action of the signifier. Nativist phonology mandated a ground of intentionality shared by the signifier and the speaker who signified meaning. When they subsequently gave priority to speech over writing, they believed they had found the way to show how the voice expressed the mind—that is, *kokoro*—just as later writers argued that work expressed the body's intention without mediation. Although contemporary language theory has demolished the presumption of transparency between signifier and signified by demonstrating the absence of a relation between signified and reality, writers still recognize that a discourse can claim to give knowledge by referring to "reality." In the case of the nativist production of knowledge in discourse, readers or listeners had to be positioned in such a way as to read or hear the discourse as transparent and treat it as referential.

By aiming their critique at the usage of language and the practice of culture it validated, nativists were able to foreground the question of ideology itself and its prevailing and dominant manifestation in Tokugawa Japan. They charged that contemporary forms of representation were not adequately referring to "reality" and that form had been separated from content, language from authentic experience. Arguing that the communication of reality depended on finding the correct means of expressing the correspondence between intention, thing, and word, they proposed that any real correspondence between form and content stemmed from the view that the text was transparent and able to represent something outside itself, which, in this case, was ideology. Thus,

kokugakusha distinguished the signified, which they located in contemporary writing as the site of the ideological, from the signifier,
which they installed as a neutral means of representation. As we shall
see, this distinction in itself constituted an ideological act, because ideology cannot be restricted to the signified. In their valorization of poetry, they made visible as ideological what otherwise was disregarded as
merely a means or instrument of representation.

Hence, the nativist assessment of language usage concentrated on
demonstrating how sense and meaning are conferred on "reality"
through conventionalized forms. It contested the very terms employed
to represent reality and the claim of those who reserved for themselves
the authority to do so. According to V. V. Voloshinov, ideological practice is equated with the production of signs and, conversely, the world
of signs is endowed with social value from ideological production.
Signs are objective, material objects, always socially constituted; language and all ideological forms are invested with an "autonomous reality," "imposing a signification on 'reality'" (not a correspondence to
it) that "reflects" and "refracts" "its own systemic organization." This is
not to say that these forms are reducible to economic and social relationships, even though it is conceivable to suppose that they are ultimately explicable by them; literature—forms of writing as ideology—is
not identical with the economic base, for if it were, it would not be
visible as something separate from it. What makes discourse discourse
is also what makes it ideological. Nativism was produced by a certain
history, yet it also produced history by contesting forms of language
usage and cultural practice.[12] It is ideological precisely because it lived
and died in history. But a specific discourse produced readers and listeners who produced it—nativism—as they read and listened in their
present. As the nativist discourse on language disclosed, the actual
transmutation of words into signs and the entry of signs into the world
of meaning reveal whose words they are and for whom they are meant.
This move requires an accounting for the particular set of relationships
between speaker and listener within which the "dialogue" is conducted
and shaped. These interactions, in turn, are affected by the larger
economic, political, and ideological relationships that constitute the
broader referent. It is for this reason, Voloshinov concluded, that a
word—its usage—is related to a class-based struggle for the terms employed in signifying reality. When nativists set about appraising contemporary language usage, they were challenging the terms that the
dominant Tokugawa ideology employed to establish reality and, by ex-

tension, the very supremacy of its leadership, whose authority consisted of securing assent to these terms.

The nativist linguistic project early revealed a dissatisfaction with the claim that language constitutes fixed and given meanings. Insofar as words and syntax are mobilized and fought for by different constituencies to express their experiences—to endow social meaning by the act of usage—language becomes an "arena of class struggle." "Only that," Voloshinov observed, "which has acquired social value can enter the world of ideology, take shape and establish itself there."[13] The social formation recognizes situations in which an ideological theme (an ideologeme) functions as a social accent. Although only one sign community may prevail, language serves as the site for intersecting social interests, the space where the clash of social values takes place, where "multi-accentuality" seeks to "reflect" and "refract" existence. Class never coincides with the sign community but appears within the space offered by it. As the example of the nativist intervention discloses, diverse social groups will share the same language only to advance their claims to establish meaning by attaching differently oriented accents to every ideological sign.

In eighteenth-century Japan the managerial class sought to establish a "supraclass" and, thus, convey an eternal character to the ideological sign. This aim was represented best by the Neo-Confucian insistence on identifying words with what they were meant to denote in order to extinguish or suppress by driving inward any possibility of conflict between fixed social judgments and any effort to endow one sign with several meanings. Ideological hegemony consisted of making the sign "uniaccentual." Until the eighteenth century, this kind of linguistic hegemony had been able to enforce a certain uniformity in representation—even though "spoken" language was beginning to find its way into texts of popular verbal fictions—by forcing the sign to withdraw from the pressures of struggle over accent and meaning.[14] Nativists had early noticed this operation, when they sought to exhume a lost, originary language that, they believed, had been allowed to degenerate into allegory and historical memory. The retrieval of this language was first made possible by an act of philosophical apprehension that sought to reinvest the lapsed language with a living intelligibility and accent. Once this meditation passed from philosophy into linguistics, from metaphor suppressing difference to metonymy supplying a means to account for it, from dead convention to active intervention, language itself became a powerful instrument in the struggle for meaning and order. When language became life and experience, life itself could no longer remain the same.

Too often, interpreters of *kokugaku* have apprehended the discourse as a textual tradition that established a method of reading. Writers as diverse as Muraoka Tsunetsugu and Hani Gorō proposed that, in its effort to rescue a native literary tradition, *kokugaku* developed a rigorous approach to texts, which was analytically philological (Muraoka) and scientifically critical (Hani).[15] Yet despite its apparent production of texts about texts, nativism was really opposed to textuality. This "paradox" is easily resolved if we recall what textuality meant for its practitioners. For nativists, the text represented the repository of the written word and was identified with China—with history, the mediations of culture, "second nature"—whereas a return to Japanese meant recovery of an originary language in sound and speech, not in script. This impulse to recover a lost presence prompted the linguistic intervention that marked writers from Keichū (1640–1701) through early-nineteenth-century proponents of the spirit of language (*kotodama*); the privileging of a spoken language that sounded natural to the Japanese, rather than the phonemic distortions of Chinese and its script, explains the nativist rejection of both textuality and history. Nativism directed its attention less toward developing a methodology to decode settled inscription than toward demonstrating how writing perverted and suppressed genuine meaning; it was less interested in approaching texts with a theory of reading than in showing conclusively how writing failed to convey the experience of presence and immediacy promised by speech. Speaking defined the ground of being; being authorized the state of doing, practice. Only sound in speech offered a transparent representation of an underlying reality; only Japanese sounds and syntactical organization revealed an authentic reality, as the first songs (*uta*) and fables disclosed, in their natural correspondence between what people said and how they said it. In emphasizing the spoken word and its associations with presence and doing, nativists believed they had found the way to evade the snares of written script altogether. This sense of the immediate opposed the mediate—history or culture; a continuing present opposed a past accessible only in imperfect traces. For the ancients, past and present were indistinguishable; for the nativists, Japan was always present, while China belonged to a dead past.

Nativists were not alone in recognizing the problematic nature of contemporary language usage. Throughout the eighteenth century, there was general agreement among several discourses that what could be said simply did not correspond to how it could be said. Philosophical activity had already shifted attention, through the intervention of ancient learning (*kogaku*), toward the failure of contemporary language to grasp and represent reality.[16] To recover language as an adequate mode of representation, writers interrogated the most ancient pre-Confucian texts and their language, seeking the true relationship between word, deed, and intent. Here, the presumption that the ancients had achieved a perfect correspondence meant that, although language must reflect reality, reality constantly mediated its usage. Such a view introduced a powerful relativism in the shape of historicism, which mandated the changing nature of language to adequately represent a changing reality; it also opened up the way to privilege intent and thing over word. To privilege intent over mere word is to suggest that people knew how to act long before they had found words to express their performance. At this juncture, as we shall see below, nativist linguistic theory turned toward emphasizing the kinship between language and performance by developing a theory of the verb that defined activity and the immediate in order to make language transparent to itself.

The assumption informing this restoration of an authentic language was that routine and public usage no longer served as an adequate vehicle for expressing and communicating experience. What needed to be said could not be said with received conventions. As a result, confusion was manifest everywhere, misunderstanding was leading to the proliferation of difference between meaning and intent, and, at the same time, the real remained occluded, hidden by contemporary usage. Beneath the exchange of everyday spoken words, nativists believed, there existed a language capable of denoting reality, a form of more fundamental human contact, which the early songs and poems had disclosed but time had obliterated. *Kokugakusha* were proposing a juxtaposition between a public and private language—the former, heavily freighted with Chinese expressions brittle with clichés, had been corroded by publicly received ideas, conventionalized, and imprisoned in idiographic script; the latter, whose traces were inscribed in ancient poetry, illuminated the existence of a genuine life continuing beneath the dead surface of social routine. The task *kokugakusha* recognized was to recover this fresh, nonalienated, originary language in which the ancients' preverbal and nonverbal events and deeds were rendered translucently, clearly, and tangibly.

The nativist linguistic intervention secured another effect that is important to our analysis. By emphasizing the role of voice in express-

ing the mind's intention and the primacy of signifier over what is signified in representation, nativists were led to concentrate on poetry and
song as the perfect instances of the correspondence between form and
content. Their attention to a speaking voice called forth the status of
the subject, a speaker speaking to others, not the solitary reader. The
presence of subjectivity in language, as suggested earlier, is revealed in
any effort to distinguish who is speaking or making the utterance, in
the distinction between the act of enunciation (the speech event) and
the enounced (the narrated event).[17] The enounced is what is uttered
or stated, while enunciation refers to the act of utterance in discourse.
Recent theory has elaborated further to distinguish between the "subject of enunciation" (the participant of the speech event) and the "subject of the enounced" (the participant of the narrative event). For the
subject of the enounced, the word is seen as meaning, "the signifier is
lined up with the signified," and discourse appears transparent, since it
is identified with the subject who speaks. Subjectivity is centered in a
fixed position where the ego—self—is present to itself, since it is presumed to be identical with the subject who speaks. For the subject of
the enunciation, the word functions as a thing, the signified slides under the privileged signifier, and discourse is revealed as material process. Subjectivity is decentered, and the fixed position of the ego is
shown to be a temporary point in the process of the Other.[18] Just as the
signified depends on signifiers, the enounced relies on enunciation.
When nativists began to theorize about language, they quickly "recognized" that Japanese privileged the "I" who speaks, whereas Chinese
did not. In both their move to show the importance of Japanese sounds
over Chinese pronunciation and their epochal discovery of an inflected
system capable of distinguishing between "this" and "that" (*ji ta*), the
deictic and demonstrative dimensions of language, nativists clearly indicated the space for designating a subject voice and subjectivity that
had hitherto remained unarticulated. They argued further that the disjunction between speech and narrated event, undoubtedly created by
the superimposition of Chinese on Japanese, had caused the contemporary confusion between the immediate and the mediate and the un-
ceasing decentering of the subject, as evidenced in both the emulation
of the Other (China), which could never be realized, and the drift away
from fixed positions such as work and worship toward the gratification
of desire through pleasure and profligacy.

This distinction prefigures Benveniste's differentiation between
"history" and "discourse." Although subsequent commentators have

refined the categories so that they apply to both narrative and discursive utterance, Benveniste's formulation suitably covers the kind of classifications nativists were trying to establish. History, as the impersonal act of narration practiced by the Chinese, emphasizes the subject of the enunciation, the "I" of the utterance, where the narrator is omniscient and implied; whereas discourse is a personal mode where the narrated is presented explicitly and directly by the "I" who speaks.[19] Whereas history always privileges what is narrated over the narrator, the signified over the signifier, discourse shifts the locus of priority to a represented speaker who appears prior to what is being said, so that the signifier dominates the signified. The importance of discourse for nativists, especially as located in the speech acts of song and poetry or even in the orality of "histories," such as the Kojiki and the *Nihonshoki*, and other ancient narrations, such as compilations of Shinto prayers, was that it invited the reader or listener to identify himself with a represented speaker, to become the subject of the enounced. As we shall see, nativist poetics disavowed the distant impersonal voice of enunciation (the Other) and promoted only a position for a subject of the enounced, so that each reader, reciter, and listener—Hirata directed his remarks to listeners who had no leisure time to read and study books—would see that the speaker of the text was none other than himself. This operation was supported by explicit forms of "hailing" the subject in both Motoori, who constantly referred to the ordinary person (*bonjin*), and Hirata, who elaborated a number of indicators drawing attention to common folk (*aohitogusa*), the "people of the present," the "men of the times." Poetry produced a subject voice while suppressing the conditions—history—that generated the text in the first place.

Very early in the nativist program, Kamo no Mabuchi, an enthusiast of the ancient poems of the *Man'yōshū*, proposed that poetry and song "assist governance" by "moving the heart" (or intention) and "consoling humans." Kamo rejected didactic poetry, which impersonally instructed people how to behave, and praised a tradition where the "songs [*Man'yō*] recite things that touch the intention." Poetry did not correspond to conventional political values, as it did in China, but encouraged the receiver to act naturally and to identify with the way things were (*tenchi no mama naru kokoro; Koku*, 376, 384).[20] As Motoori Norinaga argued in his *Ashiwake obune*, this "poeticizing of politics" aimed to demonstrate the distance between mere political narrative, which directed the lower orders to fall voluntarily into line, and the "poetry of genuine feeling," which moved people to act naturally in their daily encounters with the world of things. Politically, this operation transformed the object of domination into the dominance of the subject. Motoori's central concept of *mono no aware*—the sense of being affected deeply by *things* in everyday experience—dramatized this shift toward the subject of the enounced and the listener's (or reader's) identification with the representative speaker as if he himself produced the poem or song. The strategy was expanded by Hirata Atsutane when he announced to his listeners that the ancient Way (*kodō*) involved nothing more than their daily lives. And in the late-Tokugawa period, as we shall see later, the power of "poetic perception" was transmuted by Tomobayashi Mitsuhira into a knowledge constituted by an interest to restore presence, authorizing forms of radical political action. Each commentator aimed to secure a sense of identity, completion, and centeredness.

This nativist effort to create a subject voice and discount historicity as a distortion installed, by an act of misrecognition, a coherent position for the subject of the enounced in a closed, syntagmatic chain; at the same time, it foreclosed the process of enunciation and, indeed, history itself, by a number of operations that closed the gap between past and present. The *kokugaku* emphasis on sound as signifier and, thus, on the whole dimension of voice and speech conformed to the shift to an emphasis on metonymy and what might be called a syntagmatic hermeneutic rather than the metaphor and regime of paradigm so closely associated with Neo-Confucianism. As Roland Barthes (following Saussure) has argued, the nature of speech is syntagmatic since, quite apart from "phonation," "it can be defined as a [varied] combination of (recurrent) signs; the spoken sentence is the very type of the syntagm; it is . . . certain that the syntagm has very close similarities to speech."[21] For nativists, the coherence of the subject and its capacity now to convey its place as intending meaning, whether in poetry or prose, was produced along this syntagmatic chain, that developed as a single voice to sustain meaning and itself in linearity and contiguity. Linearity fixed the subject in a closed chain of signifiers that, according to Jacques Lacan, "insists" meaning in and for it.[22] The meaning intended in the syntagmatic chain must exclude other signifiers and contexts; it ultimately relies on the systematic nature of language itself and the syntactic and grammatical rules that have produced it. Here, it seems, is the major function of nativist linguistic theory. When it sought to hold back the process of enunciation, it suppressed the historical conditions accounting for the production of poetry, song, and

even forms of narrative prose. Motoori's poetic method opposed any
procedure that derived its meaning from the accumulation of history
and sought to uphold, according to an observation of Barthes, a "language without writing," by which man, in the example of the ancients,
"confronted the world of objects without going through any of the
forms of history or social life."[23] Here, too, is the meaning of *mono no
aware* and its promise to close the distance between past and present in
order to secure an empathic community, unbound by the constraints
of history or social forms, and more important, of Hirata's cosmological
narrative, what Hegel once called "unhistorical history," and its ever-
present interaction between production and reproduction, creation and
custom.

This strategy created a space for a subject that could be mobilized
for ideological contestation against the received authority and its form
of representation. Hirata's discourse, for example, was appropriated (reworked) by rural notables (*meibōka*) fearful of riot, rebellion, and the
diminution of productivity in the countryside in the 1830s and 1840s.
The price they paid for naturalizing work and getting peasants to fall
into line was the establishment of a political order whose subjects became the authors of their own lives and actions. Something of the same
process was undoubtedly experienced by townsmen, whom Motoori
invited "to know *mono no aware*." In both cases, ideology was produced as an effect of discourse, enabling people to constitute themselves as coherent subjects and to "see" themselves as the originators of
certain actions and practices. But such a recognition was really an act
of "misrecognizing" their "imaginary" relationship to the conditions of
existence. Even though nativists, from Motoori through Hirata, insisted that the constituted subject had no history since it had been produced by a history that ideology had effaced, nonetheless this subject
was now in a position to produce history. As Barthes has noted, "In the
text, only the reader speaks." Although nativist language theory, with
its emphasis on the phonetic properties of language, acknowledged the
signifier as an action of the body, it also produced a place for the subject
of the enounced, which depends on the process of enunciation. This
was the intended meaning of Hirata's use of the lapidary phrase *kan-
narae, aohitogusa narau*—"to know about the deities is to know the
folk" insofar as the gods had created the conditions of existence which
humans were appointed to reproduce—and Ōkuni Takamasa's later
articulations, which sought to demonstrate how the folk merely continue by work and mutual assistance what the *kami* had produced at

the time of creation. By centering the folk, the speakers and doers, nativists were able to show that the creation of custom, speaking and doing, was not different from the primal acts of the deities who had made the cosmos. Yet this act of centering did not necessarily remove the desire of the Other. Speaking the native language and working to reproduce creation merely induced people to recognize the real Other in the primal deities and, ultimately, in themselves. Such a move did not lessen desire, which both speaking an unalloyed language and working the "native soil" (*kunitsuchi*) sought to satisfy in an endless process of creation and custom, production and reproduction. When nativists noted that the folk were obliged to repay the "blessings" (*mimegumi*) of the gods by providing for the land and making it habitable, they were simply relocating the object of desire itself. At the same time that the folk were invited to imagine themselves as speakers of the discourse, they were, as subject speakers or actors, confronted with relations outside their control; they had to face the repetition of identity and difference so necessary to the constitution of subjectivity.[24] Divine intervention and human intentionality were linked in a necessary dialectic, but they remained separate terms, just as creation and custom, production and reproduction, constituted discrete events. Human intentionality worked to approximate the conditions of divine intervention, but it was destined to fall short of perfect attainment, fixed subjectivity, and closure, as it participated in an endless process toward the Other. The unbridgeable space between divine intervention and human intentionality constituted the fathomless locus of desire, despite Motoori's effort to humanize the deities or Hirata's attempt to deify humans.

The Sovereignty of Sound

The nativist critique of language was manifest in the attack on Chinese learning (*karagokoro*) and in the celebration of "wonder," silence, and the things that could not be explained. This position was earliest articulated by Kamo no Mabuchi (1697–1769), who sought to understand and, thus, represent the world as it is given, in wonder, in silence if necessary, rather than in abstract principles and written words. Such speculative artifices as the mediations in the task of representation merely introduced disorder by multiplying distinctions and differentiations that, accordingly, could no longer be comprehended in the modality of similitude: "That which says man is different from the birds and beasts is, in human terms, self-praise and contempt for others. This, too, is characteristic of the Chinese. The Chinese despise the realms of the world as barbarian realms, which is an incorrect usage of the word *ebisu*. Are not all things that live within the universe insects? Among them why should man alone be esteemed? Why should man alone be different?" (*Koku*, 379). Kamo attributed the Chinese conception of man to the linguistic confusion wrought by categorization and differentiation. He contended that rational understanding, now equated with ideographic representation, inevitably led to the proliferation of differences, to misunderstanding, and to disorder. Finding evidence for this conviction in an examination of the usefulness of Chinese characters as instruments for representation, he concluded that it was not only too burdensome for the mind to recall so many of them but that they also delayed understanding by obscuring real intent and meaning. They were invariably too opaque.

In order to remove opacity from language usage, Kamo formulated a subject voice capable of giving expression to sincere human feelings. An example was already accessible in the poetry and song of the ancients, which managed to convey the most unadorned and honest sentiments. By contrast, he noted, contemporaries had lost the competence to express genuine sentiment, owing to the distortions of hardened public conventions. Kamo's major linguistic text, *Kotoba-i kō*, published twenty years after his death in 1789, compared the elegance of the native Japanese language with Chinese and Sanskrit and concluded that its autonomy explained its superiority. The ancients were disposed naturally to the simple and the gentle and consequently, required fewer words to denote their deeds. Since it was sufficient to transmit deeds by spoken voice, ideography was unnecessary; instead, the ancients constructed words by a simple vocalization consisting of fifty sounds.

Kamo's argument rested upon a conception of archaic simplicity. The ancients established a correspondence between sound and deed; since deeds and words were few in number, it was a time when nobody was perplexed and forgetful and there was perfect comprehension (*Kotoba*, 395). Heaven saw fit to bestow fifty sounds. Acts preceded sounds, which, in turn, were identified with forms of conduct necessary for the formation of words. Yet, Kamo observed, words depended on the "differentiation of sound that has been transmitted from earliest antiquity." He explained that the correspondence between words and the differentiation of sounds relied on a relationship between the basic phonemes—[a i u e o]—and fundamental action and word formation.

The first phoneme, he wrote, was the sound—[a]—for the beginning and occurrence of deeds; the second—[i]—was the sound for "body words," words that did not indicate (fixed things, such as a fan, or words of time, which referred to an action that would be fixed later); the third—[u]—referred to sounds that indicated moving things (living or action words such as putting on clothes, which were concerned with the deeds of things); the fourth—[e]—was the sound for words of command; and the fifth—[o]—was the sound that assisted things. The last category, he explained, consisted of sounds linked to a variety of words in order to make their meaning possible. This fifth form presumably contained particles like *o, so, to, no, mo, yo, ro,* as well as forms of conjugation guiding the transformation of verbal tenses. "When one understands this [classification]," Kamo insisted, "one will be able to clarify the words for things" (*Kotoba*, 396, 398–405). It was important to understand this classification of sounds, because the words they authorized were not found in foreign countries. "If one assembles these fifty sounds, one will not be divided from the ancient Japanese [*utsu-kushiku aokusa*]." These sounds had been granted, he continued, to show the foundations of the realm of spoken words, which has not changed for fifteen hundred centuries, since the beginning of imperial rule in the age of *kami* learning. It was for this reason that Japan had been called the land of the spirit of language (*kotodama*) since antiquity. Words were composed of basic sound patterns linked together in a contiguous series and generated by natural and simple deeds from the common experience of daily life.

Kamo's conception of language was linked to a privileging of sound over the formation of words. Speech—the spoken—revealed the inscription of sound. He sought by this emphasis on sound to restore to language its materiality, and to words their kinship with the world of things and deeds. "When children are born in our country," he noted, "they elicit the sound of aahh; soon after, they grow up and hear words." But sound and words were not separate entities. Sounds were made according to geographical area; people had to learn the words of the place where they lived. Sounds produced words and constituted the sign (*shurushi*) of the realm's words. "Contemporaries, however, hear and learn and are thus at the mercy of sounds derived from Chinese ideographs. Since they apprehend and interpret sounds with such words, they invariably make mistaken calculations" (ibid., 379). Over time, the Japanese were obliged to borrow Chinese ideographs in order to write down their deeds. The adoption of this writing system resulted in confusion, because Chinese tonal values differed markedly from those of spoken Japanese. As a result, the Japanese were compelled to invent a notational system by which to make the conversion. Kamo observed that this operation was especially noticeable in the ancient classics, when the same ideograph was often enunciated differently. What it sacrificed, he feared, was the sound system of the ancient language and the meaning of archaic words: Chinese sounds were made to accommodate Japanese by Japanizing Chinese words. The observation inspired a rhetorical question: "How can we understand the ancient period, its books, and traces?"

Thus, in ancient Japan sounds came before words and spoken words were formed from a combination of their natural sounds, even though later scholars reversed the order of the relationships. Kamo's researches led him to assert that word formation ultimately depended on the prior sorting out of the sounds that characterized the ancient communicative mode. These sounds were not human inventions but products of the "national soil" (*kunitsuchi*) and revealed their oneness with other things in the land. To propose a relationship between the production of sound and the land was to suggest the possibility of a central dialect, what he called "correct sounds," shared by all who were born in Japan. In his day, he believed, the "correct sounds" could be found in the Kinai region of Kyoto and Nara. People who readily acknowledged the existence of diverse dialects throughout the land could have no real argument against a standardization of sound. The standardization of sound, which apparently the ancients had secured, guaranteed perfect understanding among users and supplied the best defense against a proliferation of confusion. "If the heart of humans in this country is straight," he advised, " . . . deeds and words will be few in number; there will be no dispute over the [meaning of] words, one will hear well, and if one does not forget, it [meaning] will be transmitted far and wide over a long period of time. Indeed, when there is a correct heart [intention] among the folk, the imperial edicts of the emperor will also be few in number" (ibid., 399).

Kamo expanded these thoughts in *Koku-i kō*, published in 1765. He observed in this text that India had formalized its sound system with fifty letters, similar to the Japanese, yet over five thousand writings on Buddhism had been transmitted. Even with a scarce supply of alphabetic letters, the Indians had available to them an "unlimited number of words." But they were not simply letters. Since the fifty sounds represented the voices of heaven and earth, they contained nature itself.

Even though they were different from Japanese sounds, they were, nevertheless, natural to the area in which they "grew" and were used, in contrast to the Chinese tonal system, which the ancient Japanese had adopted. Archaic Japanese, before the importation of Chinese, had developed some sort of notational system to indicate properly the reading of sounds, but it had been destroyed with the introduction of Chinese. This meant that the most ancient texts were inaccessible to later Japanese, who had no sure way of knowing how the earliest sounds were vocalized. Still, the words from antiquity that had been preserved, Kamo believed, revealed something of the concordance between the "principle that everything can be expressed with fifty sounds and that fifty sounds accommodate all things." Hence, "the words referring to flowers—'bloom,' 'decay,' 'sprout,' 'wither,' 'pistil,' 'stamen,' etc.— good as well as evil, are expressed easily without extraneous letters and without difficulty" (*Koku*, 380).

When Chinese was adopted, the ideographs were used simply to denote words. "Words were the main things," Kamo claimed, and the "ideographs were the slaves." In time this order of things was upset; the preeminence of the words (and, thus, the sounds out of which they were formed) was lost and they became servile to the ideographs. The reason for this unhappy circumstance derived from the fact that the "evil custom that enabled slaves to become emperors in China took hold in Japan" (ibid., 381). On the "evidential" authority of this observation, Kamo was able to note that a phonetic notation system corresponded naturally to sound, and a writing or inscriptional system based on it "relates to common life and has nothing to do with refinement." The Chinese system, because of its association with theoretical thinking, had always been considered refined, but, inevitably, it led to confusion. A natural mode of expression was vastly superior, because it was not forced or labored (ibid.).

Later in the *Koku-i kō* he joined his conception of language to a consideration of the problem of difference. In this essay, as in some of his earlier texts on style and poetry, he elevated the earliest songs and poems as exemplars manifesting the correct and straight intention. Intention, he reported, invariably produced deeds that found perfect expression in spoken words: "Songs wholly express the intention of humans. To be sure, they do not appear to be of any use as regards the world. But if one understands them well, one will also know the human intention, and if one knows the human intention, one will automatically understand the cause . . . of confusion" (ibid., 377–78).

The primacy of poetry, revealing true intentionality, related to the problem of language itself. Kamo despaired over the number of ideographs currently in use, which he estimated at thirty-eight thousand, and noted that rather than lead to real understanding, the very multiplicity of words inspired the confusion and disorder that scarred ancient Chinese political history. "With reference to the one word for flower," he reasoned,

> . . . it is necessary to use the ideographs for "bloom," "decay," "petal," "stamen," and "stem," and more than ten other words. In addition to names of countries, place names, the names of grasses and trees, special ideographs are employed that otherwise might not be used in everyday speech. Is even one who takes the trouble supposed to be able to retain so many signs? There will either be confusion, or the characters will change from generation to generation. Consequently, they cause a great deal of confusion and, as they bring no advantage, they become extremely burdensome. (Ibid., 380)

Since Chinese teachings had violated nature by seeing it as culture, "they interfere with its continuity [literally, harden nature]" (ibid., 383). Therefore, the Chinese emphasis on a morality marked by "benevolence," "honesty," and "knowledge" went against the dictates of nature itself—the movement of the seasons, for example—and introduced dangerous discontinuities and rigidities, distinctions and differences that had nothing whatsoever to do with reality. "It is better," Kamo asserted, "to follow the heart [*kokoro*] of heaven and earth without [recourse] to names" (ibid., 384). He proposed that the Chinese practice of naming, which was produced by writing and led to theory and speculation, caused the proliferation of differences that were clouding the minds of contemporary Japanese. Differences, he observed, forced people into divided purpose; but the upright intention, he wrote in the last pages of the *Koku-i kō*, "requires little, since it is founded on simplicity," the surest defense against the entanglements of division. Writing, then, represented invention, trickery, and philosophic illusion; it was manipulated by men seeking power and control in order to show their achievements as natural endowments of heaven and earth. The poems of the *Man'yō*, however, revealed how the "ancient spirit" was in "harmony with the intentions of heaven and earth." In the end, Kamo identified the natural sound system with the common daily life experience of the ordinary folk. The words of the most ancient poems and songs provided a glimpse of this world of ordinary, natural lives and the intentions of people living in a remote time. Yet, like most nativists, he recommended neither the slavish imitation of an antiquity accessible only in fragmented traces nor the impossible task of recuperating it in the present. To remember this time, he said, was to recall how the ancients, who seemed never to forget, were able to avoid making distinctions between the common experience and its adequate mode of representation. Because contemporaries had ignored this lesson, they had relied on an artificial language and writing system that had diverted their intentions and made them slaves to culture. Kamo's renunciation of the Chinese language and its inscriptional system made little effort to conceal its harsh political judgments. His observation that writing was cynically used by men seeking power revealed a deep equation between writing and state formation: writing had made possible a bureaucratic apparatus that could only be eliminated by returning to the speech and the time when "words for things were fewer in number."

The Model of the Syntagm

Motoori Norinaga (1730–1801) refined Kamo's thinking and defined more fully a subject position for the speaker of Japanese. His modest effort to refine the master's theories resulted in a rather significant supplement to the meditation on sound. In a series of linguistic texts written late in his career (*Kotoba no tama no o* and *Kanji no san onkō*, published in 1785), Motoori sharpened the essential features of this authentic voice and supplied an explanation of how it differed from the public language of contemporary speech. The *Kanji no san onkō* continued Kamo's investigations of the naturalness of sound in the original formation of words and their occultation after the importation of Chinese ideographs; the *Kotoba no tama no o* expanded the concern for difference by examining the system of conjugating verbs and the operation of postpositions in Japanese. The move toward verbs and postpositions acknowledged a space for action and performance along the syntagmatic chain, at which Kamo's elevation of sound had only hinted. Motoori's intervention successfully brought together the sovereignty of sound and the relevant grammatical protocols as the preparatory condition for transforming subject voice into acting agent and author of signification. Politically, the privileging of speech over writing sanctioned the primacy of activity over receptivity (naming), to open the way for an encounter with the immediate and effacement of the mediate.

In the *Kanji no san onkō* Motoori announced that ideographs were not the original wording system in Japan. Although Kamo had observed the way that the sound values of Chinese ideographs had destroyed the original Japanese vocalization in the process of accommodation, Motoori wished to demonstrate that the distortions were even greater than Kamo had imagined, because of the complexities of the Chinese sound system. The importation of ideographs to Japan had brought three distinct patterns of sound from the Chinese historical experience: *kan'on*, the Sui-Tang vocalization transmitted to Japan by returning students and Buddhist monks; *goon*, more ancient sounds, akin to southern dialects; and *toon*, sounds brought to Japan from the China of the Song, Yuan, and Ming (*MNz* [new] 5:381, 392–95). Even if one system was probably superior or more pure than the others, all were inappropriate to the Japanese. "In discussing the facts relating to the pronunciation of Chinese sounds," he wrote, "it is necessary to note first the fundamental differences between natural sounds in Japan and in foreign countries" (*MNz* [new] 5:381). Once the various systems were sorted out, the problem of difference would happily disappear. His reason for disentangling the mixture of sound systems sprang from the conviction that Japan, owing to its divine origins, had always been superior to all other countries. Because of this status, it "stands as the head does to the human body" and, thus, directs rather than being directed (ibid.). Since the Japanese language—"translucent and bright" and "strongly fresh"—excelled all others, it demanded to be purified of foreign lexical and tonal corruptions. When one, for example, gazed upon a sky with no trace of clouds, there are "correct and elegant and pure sounds" available to express this sentiment within heaven and earth. In this regard, Motoori proposed that spontaneity and truthfulness always prompted the user of language to elicit the correct word covering a situation, because the sounds forming them were themselves produced naturally. To express spontaneity in the form of a written script rather than natural speech introduced artifice and compromised the sentient nature of the experience.

Motoori was following Kamo's formulations concerning the status of sound as he began to explore the archaic system, which, by his reckoning, consisted of forty-seven distinct sounds—fifty, if [i], [e], and [wa] were included (ibid. 5:382). These additional sounds were, according to his findings, unnecessary in ancient Japan and seldom used. The ancients "used only the purely correct and elegant sounds found in heaven and earth and never mixed them with confusing [literally, murky] and incorrect sounds" (ibid.). Natural sounds appeared to Motoori as a kind of transcendental signified, guaranteeing appropriate utterance. Their usage, recalling Kamo, was exceedingly scarce, whereas action and movement, silent activity emulating the gods, was perfectly understood and never required additional explanation. But, because of the operation of verbal inflection, and its "inexhaustible" capacity to join "this" to "that," Japanese "has accumulated a large supply of words" (ibid. 5:382).

At this point, Motoori introduced his conception of verbal conjugation (*katsuyō*) as a crucial factor in authorizing phonemes and producing a space for the subject voice. The ancient Japanese verbal system had clearly distinguished between the "natural voice" and the ability to inflect verbs in order to designate mood, tense, and forms of activity. Since the inflective system was authorized by the prior privileging of sound and voice, *kokugakusha* sought to establish the natural, rather than arbitrary, relationship between the sound-image and its content, what it signified. By discovering the capacity of the language to transform words into verbs and verbs into different modalities, the generative power to create innumerable words out of one, they could reveal how the subject voice—and the *kotodama*, the signifier beyond—indicated performances, actions, and moods. By recognizing the powers of inflection, they could establish graduated meanings capable of accommodating differing and changing situations. The identification of this verbal system related closely to Motoori's cognitive view, which postulated "knowing" on the basis of feeling profound sensitivity to some thing(s) (*mono no aware*) and the capacity of the knower to respond to each situation as it required. It should be pointed out that earlier linguistic concerns had concentrated chiefly on the status of nouns; it was not until the eighteenth century that interest shifted to the performance of verbs. Epistemologically, this shift may be explained by the displacement of a paradigmatic mode of organizing knowledge by one that was essentially syntagmatic and relational: the former stressed similitude, verticality, nomination, and stasis; the latter accounted for differences by relating them in a specific modality along a horizontal grid, to indicate the occurrence of action. Emphasis on the noun—the name, which "resembled" the thing it denoted—conformed to a system that could only relate things by imitation and emulation, by proposing the essential similitude of all things generated and informed by principle; an act of naming differentiated things in a vertical hierarchy in order to constitute a static cosmic chain of resemblances. The verb or an inflected system stressed what Motoori called a "relationship between trunk and branch" that emphasized linkage and the power of conjugation; it brought forth the possibility of change and action, a performative dimension that responded to different situations, and an infinite capacity to generate words to meet changing states of being and existence (ibid. 5:17, 383).

In the *Kanji no san onkō* Motoori noted that even the simple words "to say" (old spelling: *ifu*) and "to think or feel" (old spelling: *omofu*) could be converted by substituting different sounds, such as [ha], [hi], [fu], or [he]. The result was a series of conjugations that included forms such as *ihamu, ihi, ifu, ihe* or *omohamu, omohi, omofu, omohe* (ibid. 5:383). The term used to describe this action, *hataraki kotoba* (working—or acting—words), carried in it the sense of life and living. This move revealed what we have called a metonymic disposition to order; it reduced words (or things) in a single series to their basic and most tangible property, which, in this case, happened to be voice/sound. Yet such an operation permitted substitution: *yuku* (to go) could become *yukamu, yuki*, or *yuke*; *kaheru* (old spelling; to return) could become *kaheramu, kaheri*, or *kahere*—all, of course, denoting differing verbal states of action and performance. By contrast, Chinese words were all fixed. In addition, Motoori observed, identifying still another class of verbs found in the *Man'yōshū* and *Kogo shūi*, "When joining words to each other to make [other] words, there are the postposition particles such as *wa, mo, zo, koso, te, ni, wo, ya, ka, mu*, etc. In this manner it is truly wondrous that they divide meaning minutely by serving as verbs and particles and auxiliary verbs. They do not extend to foreign [Chinese] words. In heaven and earth it is believed that there are probably no national words as exquisite as these" (ibid.).

Motoori tried to clarify what he meant when he described Chinese sounds as muddy and dim (*mōrō*). As an example, he offered the occasion of gazing on a cloudy evening sky. When looking on such a scape, he wrote, the natural response (at least in Japanese) was immediately "aa"; but "aa," as a result of the Chinese intervention, was heard as "oo" or "wa" (ibid.). There were other, similar cases; they all showed that such sounds were not as clearly discriminated in China as they were in Japan. The almost inexhaustible number of written graphs in China created a great capacity for rich visual differentiation but a poverty of the aural, because there were fewer sounds and a greater chance for homonyms and infinite confusion. This disparity stemmed from the fact that Chinese words could not be inflected, declined, or conjugated to accommodate differing states of experience and meaning. Elaborating upon an insight derived from Kamo, Motoori saw the Chinese language as a great device for naming things as if they occupied fixed positions in a static hierarchy (or even cosmos) of meaning. In Japanese, one could easily denote differing states to action words such as "eat" and "drink," whereas in Chinese there was simply no way to make comparable differentiations; the basis of Japanese was "living words" (*ikita kotoba*), in contrast to foreign languages such as Chinese, which consisted of "dead words" (*shinda kotoba*; ibid. 5:388). The opposition between living and dead languages, already expressed in the opposition between Japan (similitude) and the Other (difference), was prefigured by the *kokugaku* juxtaposition of nature and culture. It made possible the more fundamental oppositions between performing, acting or doing, and passive, inactive states, between manual labor (work) and mental labor (meditative non-action). However, the oppositions that Motoori's linguistic intervention had brought to light could be overcome by the very act of recognizing that certain normative practices required supplementation, which the emphasis on sound and an inflection system promised to provide. Here, Motoori found the necessary sanction to embark upon his major project—to literally rewrite the *Kojiki* (*Kojikiden*) in terms of what he called "correct words," reconstructions of the natural sounds of archaic Japanese before its corruption, by using the traces of ideographs.

Just as privileging Japanese sound over ideographic writing could recreate a lost sense of presence and immediacy, the working word, reflecting life itself, could overcome the fixity, distance, and detachment that writing had imposed. Voice and the capacity to make verbal moves with "working words," whose functions derived from relations of contextual usage rather than fixed positions, permitted *kokugakusha* to see language as an ongoing practice. This discovery was important for two reasons: it provided nativists the means to realize the immediate over the mediate, the subject voice over its removal in writing, presence over absence, proximity over distance, attachment over detachment, and practice over the abstracting propensities of principle (*ri*) or theory; and it disclosed the link between language and labor, in which the working word transposed itself into the working subject—the existent, life itself—by identifying language as action, doing as a guarantor of being, and work as a correlate to speech or its extension. Nativists

believed that speech, which represented an original displacement of
the gesture or cry, had degenerated into disembodied writing, and the
remedy lay in the action of the body and its work, the natural substitution to which speech referred until it was stalled by the importation
of writing.

At the heart of this formulation was Motoori's theory of "living
words," the postpositions mentioned above, whose operation permitted
Japanese to move beyond the static world of naming into a domain of
multiple meanings, active and constantly changing (ibid., first mentioned on p. 383). Although Motoori did not invent the study of these
postpositions but merely continued a practice begun in the middle
ages, his mediation, which consisted of a tabular classification of usage,
resulted in far-reaching consequences for the nativist discourse and Tokugawa Japan.[25] The *Kotoba no tama no o* sought to illuminate the
nature of these particles not as fixed words or even as established auxiliary verbs (although they could play this function in certain contexts)
but as rules of relations and connections, exemplifying the relationship
between "trunk and branch," means and end (*moto sue*) (MNz [new]
5:5, 17). He believed that because these particles were fundamental to
"living" or "working" words, it must be shown how they function rela-
tionally between words in the construction of meaningful speech.[26]
Motoori was convinced that the particles in Japanese were natural endowments from the age of the gods. They had always determined how
the "trunk" and "branch" were to be united. In antiquity, they had
arranged themselves naturally in speech and poetry, with scarcely any
mistakes, but in the poetry and prose of later ages, the order of the
particles had been regularly mistaken. Hence, he declared the intention of *Kotoba no tama no o* to counteract a tradition of abuse—"the
variety of bias"—transmitted down to the present as well as to provide
detailed, correct instruction (MNz [new] 5:5, 17).

Early in this text Motoori rejected the popular identification of
Chinese auxiliary verbs and Japanese particles; he cautioned that,
despite apparent similarities, this kind of misapprehension had led to
misunderstanding. "If one fails to discriminate between the two systems," he wrote, "there will be no ordering among words; poetry and
all things will become useless" (ibid.). He wished to show the primacy
of ordering words according to correct, "natural," determinations and
how the particles were able to relate each word to the one that followed
in a syntagm. Ancient poetry illustrated how this ordering process was
a "natural principle," rather than a personal contrivance, by privileging

the "three great connectives"—*wa*, *mo*, and *tada* (ibid. 5:18). The very title of the text—"the strand that links the stones together"— implied that ordering according to particles merely obeyed the arrangement of things: "Jewels become beautiful necklaces principally because of the power of the string to relate one to another in a chain." "Jewels" served as a metaphor for words, which were strung together by the postpositions to avoid formlessness, while the "string" called forth the model of a syntagm. Motoori placed great emphasis on the proper ordering of language and the avoidance of disorder; if language order fell into disarray, nothing remained but misunderstanding and political disorder (a theme he was later to amplify in his *Naobi no mitama*). In another metaphor, he proposed that, without the ordering provided by the particles, words resembled formless cloth stitched by clumsy hands (*tsutanaki te*); the particles functioned to stitch together a whole cloth out of independent pieces (ibid. 5:253). The "skill" to string things together into proper relationships constituting a whole derived from the "natural intention" found in the position of the particles, which later ages neglected.

Motoori Haruniwa (1763–1828), Norinaga's son, pursued this theme in greater detail. In *Kotoba no yachimata* (1808) Haruniwa concentrated on the rules governing working words, which, he believed, were "miraculous." The ancients never mistook the activity of such words, but in later ages usage degenerated into disorder and the natural endowment was transformed into showy contrivance. To avoid misunderstanding and the threat of disorder, he recommended the study of ancient poetry, which would "naturally" reveal the functioning of such words even if one had not studied the rules systematically (*MNz* [old] 6:2).[27] His plan of work consisted of a vast classification system to identify the categories of rules governing the expression of the fifty sounds. The work called attention to an order of transitive and intransitive verbs, which Norinaga may have suggested in *Tama arare* (1792) by noting the "differences between *ji* and *ta*" (oneself and the other) in several words, but never explicitly articulated (*MNz* [new] 5, 479). Years later Haruniwa turned to detailing the functions of this verbal form in a work called *Kotoba no kayoiji* (1828), a supplement to Norinaga's formulations on the particles and working words.

Haruniwa argued that, since word meanings depended on understanding the determination of the particles and the circumstances of their usage, context must be seen as a principal factor in explaining the varying changes of mood and tense. "In differentiating all things in order to signify the deeds recited in poems and written in books and in knowing their conditions in detail," he wrote, "one should aim principally at the working words concerning oneself and others, this and that" (*MNz* [old] 6:6, 48). The importance of his classification of verbs lay in its effort to define the relationship of subject to other. It made a division between verbs indicating action toward a future result, passivity ("the body receiving" [*ukemi*]), causativity, possibility, self-initiated action, and the actions of another agent. Until recently there has not been complete agreement among linguists concerning the existence of transitive and intransitive verb forms in premodern Japanese, what Roy Miller has called "endoactive" and "exoactive" pairings. Miller has seen the presence of such pairings as unproblematic and as evidence of the historical kinship between Japanese and Korean and "other Altaic languages."[28] However, some Japanese linguists have discounted the distinction between "oneself" and "other," and others have admitted the possible existence in certain usages. The likelihood of some sort of verbal differentiaton along these lines appears justified for many Japanese verbs, because of the presumed distinctions they make between forms of action and the relationship between agents. Even if scholars cannot reach an agreement on the specific terms to designate the operation, it still seems possible to concede a space for such verbal activity, since discourse would be impossible without the presumption of a subject-object relationship. An awareness of "endoactive" and "exoactive" verbs appeared in medieval poetic studies and concentrated on explaining the relationship between demonstratives, such as "this" (I) and "that" (you). A distinction was made in the interpretation of Japanese *waka* poetry between "skillful seeing," reading about a place from the perspective of oneself, and "seeing from the place," locating viewing in the object rather than the outside viewer.[29] This pairing of self (*ji*) and other (*ta*) was also manifest in rules governing the recitation of linked poems (*renga*). The medieval text, *Sōgisho shinsho* made an important division between "the deed that humbles the body" and the "body that speaks in its entirety."[30] Finally, Fujitani Nariakira (1738–79), perhaps the most original linguist of the time, came closest, before Haruniwa, to articulating a clear-cut classification of transitive and intransitive verbs by dividing self and other into surface and subsurface words.[31] If Nariakira had lived to complete his systematization of grammatical usage, he would have provided a detailed classification of the operations of transitives and intransitives and their transformations. Haruniwa sought to provide a body of detailed examples of how such "words" behaved. Inherent in his classification scheme was the important differentiation of things into three subjects: "self," "other," and "thing" (*ji*, *ta*, and *mono*), all implying, without necessarily making explicit, the property of materiality—body. In the *Kotoba no kayoiji* he broke down *ji* into two subsets, oneself or self (*mizukara*) and natural or nonself (*onozukara*); *ta* referred to other self, and *mono* evoked the outside world. By relating to objects in certain modalities, these subjects constituted the occupants of a linguistic community. Yet such distinctions implied changing relationships in space and time as well. An awareness of spatial and temporal relationships summoned into place a community of communication (the empathic community) and the possibility of shared meaning among its practitioners (intersubjectivity). Haruniwa's transitive-intransitive coupling gave sharper distinction to the subject voice by designating a subject that related in space and time to something beyond itself or a subject being acted upon by something outside itself. Failure to discriminate the proper usage in designating verbal relationships—in "not understanding this deed in detail"—risked throwing this and that, self and other, into confusion and disorder.

The Bodily Origins of Language

Haruniwa sought to define the function of the subject actor and its temporal and spatial relationship to the object world; his student Suzuki Akira (1764–1837) identified this relationship with formal conduct. In a text less oriented to specifying tenses than to establishing a practicum—*Hanareya gakkun* (1814)—Suzuki envisaged language as a key element in learning, and practice as a condition for realizing its rules. Although he and Haruniwa showed the same interest in the formal rules of relationships between words, Suzuki went further to speculate about the origins and the production of language itself and the movement of words (*hataraki kotoba*) resulting from their "miraculous spirit" (*tama*). Despite accepting the causal role of "spirit," a proper nativist conceit, he ultimately located the origins of language in sound and the operation of voice, and in the body itself.

Suzuki proposed that language be counted as one among the four disciplines, or deportments; the other three were ethics, political affairs (*matsurigoto*), and literary studies. All must be taught together in order to discriminate between letter (refinement), conduct, loyalty, and truth (*Kus*, 346). "One comes to the skill of literature by teaching letters, to morality by teaching correct conduct, to political affairs according to the doctrine of loyalty, and to truth through language." Since the practicum naturally divided into four distinct disciplines, when one called attention to the others, it showed how the part summoned the whole. Unless the skills belonging to the four disciplines combined, genuine learning was impossible. Like the other disciplines, language was composed of an inside (*hana*), or essence, and an outside (*jitsu*), or reality. The "*hana*," he wrote, was found in both Japanese and Chinese; it constituted "the rules that [govern] all good things, such as elegance and the avoidance of rustic language." The outer aspect of language, its reality, referred to the intent that gave speaking the name of truth; because both speaking and political affairs could inspire disloyalty and untruth, both were linked to loyalty and truth. But because the Way was unified, it was equally important for moral behavior and speaking to cohere. "Ethical behavior occurs when one conducts the body toward the Way, and it is language [speech] that relates this [act] to the mouth" (ibid., 367). Hence, speech and conduct constituted the "two wheels of a cart" and the "two wings of a bird." Speaking was insubstantial, "empty," a receptacle; conduct was full and substantial.

Moral conduct presupposed an inner and outer division—the "substance of moral conduct" and "dignity" (*igi*)—with the former privileged over the latter, just as language (speaking) consisted of a combination of essence and reality. Here, it seems, Suzuki was relying on the nativist differentiations between visible and invisible realms (to be explained later), where essence (*hana*, the invisible) actually determined phenomenal reality. Explaining reason or principle (*dōri*) meant acknowledging its constancy, speaking of real things meant knowing real things; a stated intention sprang from true feelings and never betrayed the truth. Suzuki believed that voice represented the inner side of language and gave adequate expression to words denoting "reality." But his argument was prefigured by nativist linguistic strategy, which had proclaimed the primacy of sound and speech over writing. In Suzuki's thinking, the "force of voice" appeared as an enabling power, an essence that made possible the truthful expression of external reality. Quoting from the Chinese, he asserted that "words come from the spirit of man's voice; in the words of a composition there is force" (ibid., 403). It was this enabling function he delegated to the particles—*te, ni, o, wa*—in his classification of grammar to explain how the power of voice governed conduct and how language determined proper behavior.

In *Gengo shijūron* (1820) Suzuki categorized language into four parts: (1) "the names of all things," "body words," or words that do not move; (2) the particles; (3) "words of form"; (4) words of deeds. He saw the operation of the other three forms in relation to the functioning of the particles (*Gs* 1:152–53). Chinese lacked postpositions, and their function—a form of absent presence—could only be inferred contextually from words themselves (*Gs* 1:155–56). But words in Japan derived their capacity to become "living words" from the power of the particles, the "wondrous spirit of language [*kotodama*] of our great and august country" (ibid. 1:155). Japanese excelled over the words of all other countries in its happy reliance on the particles, which were "polished precision" compared to the "rough" words of China (ibid. 1:156). "The three varieties of words," he wrote,

> are places that indicate an object, the *te, ni, o, wa* is voice, the former are words that express deeds and things, the *te, ni, o, wa* is the voice of intention attached to these words; words are like the jewel, the particles resemble the strand; words appear as tools, the *te, ni, o, wa* function as hands manipulating them. Add the particles to body words, and they become living words. (Ibid.)

Suzuki positioned the origin of words in the "voice of the particles" by generalizing it into a structuring principle: the objective of the particles was to direct the "body words." Then he was able to classify the functions of particles into such categories as interjections (particles separating and isolating words), adverbs and conjunctions (particles preceding words), particles within words, terms and word endings, and auxiliary verbs.

So expansive was the role assigned to the particles and, hence, to voice that it constituted the source of language itself. "The expression in voice of what moves the heart (*kokoro*) of man begins with the particles," Suzuki asserted; as a result, the particles represented the "spirit" and "marrow" of words. They were both the driving force and the substance (ibid. 1:158). Elsewhere in the text, he announced that the particles formed "the great foundation [*taisō*] of language" and that voice differentiated and "signified" (*shirushi*) the names of all things. However different things seemed to appear, they were all, at bottom, informed by this enabling voice and linked naturally to one another, just as things, deeds, and people of the realm were united because of the productivity of the creation deities. The particles permitted the conversion of "body

words" into "living words" and the subsequent naming of all things
(ibid. 1:157, 159). Indeed, the voice of the particles came forth to
pierce (*ugachi*) the circumstances of human intention (ibid. 1:159).
Here, Suzuki came closest to the project of contemporary writers of
verbal fiction (*gesaku*), whose books, filled with the sound and speech
from the streets of the cities, concentrated on the action of the body,
whether in the act of speaking, eating, drinking, making love, or disposing of waste. *Gesaku* writers saw their efforts as "piercing the hole"
(*ana no ugachi*) and penetrating the contradictions in social life that
the masses, who experienced them, might recognize but would never
understand. Just as verbal fiction was made to "pierce" custom in order
to create a condition for changing conventions by revealing what most
failed to see, so Suzuki assigned to voice the power to differentiate and
sort out things and deeds in order to imitate the changing circumstances of custom (ibid.). In *Gago onjōkō* he even categorized four
essentially mimetic sounds that played the role of a phonemic master
code: "those imitating the voice of birds and beasts, sounds imitating
the voice of humans, those replicating things, and the voice copying
forms, circumstances, and deeds."[32] Here, it seems, Suzuki went further than most nativists in seeking to slide signifier under the signified.
His classification produced two immediate conclusions: that sound
plainly imitated things and acquired the force of materiality; and that
the process of imitating real things as they were—what both Kamo and
Motoori saw as the *magokoro*, or true intentionality—led to recognizing real circumstances, rather than a supposed reality on the surface.
But the mimetic force of sound (that is, the particles that were signifiers
and signified) also introduced a powerful conception of change, or its
possibility, by juxtaposing the real to the merely apparent. Although
this strategy had been prefigured in the earlier nativist attempt to pit
Japan, as nature, against China, as culture, once it was applied to a
community of speakers in an environment dogged by aporias, it easily
became a powerful instrument of political criticism. "Language [speak-
ing] derives from sound," Suzuki remarked, and it "has form, shape,
and intention."[33] If sound and speaking corresponded naturally to the
reality of things, then the claims of the written and its users represented
a deception.

Although Hirata Atsutane, whose interests were less linguistic
than "religious," assimilated this move to privilege the materiality of
voice and the bodily association of speaking, Suzuki articulated it first
in the conviction that speech always resembled the "body performing

correct conduct." His favorite metaphors, in which the voice directed words in a manner comparable to hands employing tools, underscored the role accorded to the body in the constitution of language. Suzuki probably derived this impulse from Haruniwa as well as from Fujitani Nariakira, whose grammatical system resorted to articles of clothing in order to differentiate functional categories. In Fujitani's fourfold scheme, *na* covered the operation of naming; *yosoi*, or "bodily dress," designated "determining deeds"; and *kazashi*, a type of hairpin used in the Edo period, and *ayui*, a variety of legging, played the role of "assisting words." Nariakira went on to explain that *kazashi* called attention to the head, *yosoi* to the body, and *ayui* to the "lower extremities" (*shimotsukata*). In more functional terms, *yosoi* stood for the inflectional operation, while *kazashi* and *ayui* signified pre- and postpositional words. But all called attention to the role of the body, including the voice, in conveying true intention. Both Nariakira and Suzuki believed that words clothed speech to make it appear human; speech also formed a model in the body's utilizing and manipulating tools for the performance of work. In their assignment of the ideal of a working word to verbs and inflections, nativist grammarians seemed to have discovered a way to overcome the putative division between the mind meditating quiescently and the body performing manual labor; both mind and voice (mouth) resided in the head, which was attached to the body and its "lower extremities."

It was Hirata, however, who gave the sharpest expression to the materiality of the voice and its relationship to the body. The voices of humans produced the "miraculous fifty sounds" identified first by Kamo.

> In considering the source [of these sounds], it exists for all men in the mother's womb. They are not able to breathe until this breath is received from the umbilical cord. If there is no breath, there is no voice and there would be no sound heard outside. The sound that must be raised first is lodged within the body. It is contained within the throat and mouth. This was bestowed by the creation deities, our primal ancestors, and has continued down to the present day. . . . It is called the force of spiritual origins. (*HAz* [rev] 7:438 [*Koshibon jikei* 1:24])

Hirata's interpretation was no doubt related to his effort to resuscitate the Izumo version of the myths, with its emphasis upon Susanowo, the wind god, and his principal descendent, Ōkuninushi no kami. Susanowo and his progeny represented breath, breathing, life, all encom-

passed by the word *iki*; their divine qualities were housed within the
body to enable it to speak and work (*hataraki*). The act of forming
sound was imitative and, thus, essentially reproductive in intent and
function (*HAz* [rev] 7:438). Language and speaking originated in voice,
and its natural intention was found in the fifty sounds. According to
Hirata, voice had shape (*sugata*) and form (*katachi*).

> It is experienced in the world of humans. Since it consists of deeds [*ko-
> towaza*] and dense things [*shikekimono*], it is related to things seen and
> heard. Intentions move within it [speaking]. Voice occurs variously.
> Since it is a thing, it has shape; since it has shape, it is reflected in the
> eye; since it is reflected in the eye, it touches intention; and, as it touches
> intention, it emits voice. This voice, relying on the shape and form of
> things it sees, is one that acquires its [own] shape and form. We call this
> tone color [timbre]—*neiro*. (Ibid.)

Hirata wished to demonstrate how the body, as represented by the
speaking voice, reproduced shapes and forms in sound that were
equivalent to those things seen and heard. Because he viewed language
as essentially onomatopoetic, his theory, which aimed at restoring language to the world of things and deeds, authorized the nativist quest
to unite words to things and intention. It lay at the base of Motoori's
decision to rewrite the *Kojiki* in terms of real sounds, in order to show
how the ancients gave form and shape to things and deeds inhabiting
their world, as well as Hirata's move to link all things together into a
cosmic narrative. Even more important, it disclosed the terms nativists
subsequently employed to identify the operation of language with the
dynamics of labor.

Perhaps the late-Tokugawa nativist Ōkuni Takamasa conveyed
best this sense of speech conforming to things seen and heard: he proposed that the meaning of sound provided privileged understanding,
because it organized all things and, therefore, functioned like principle
(*kotowari*). "If one understands the forty-seven phonetic sounds [Ōkuni
reduced the fifty sounds by three], one should exhaust principle."
Ōkuni's appropriation of the Neo-Confucian conception of "exhausting principle" provides an example of how nativists inverted the Other
into a "self-same identity"; he gave the term a new meaning, which
excluded, or even suppressed, the original intention associated with
"the extension of things and the penetration of principle" (*kakubutsu
kyūri*). In Ōkuni's "inversion," the sound system served as the basis of

all things and deeds, and an examination of it promised to yield the "secret" spiritual force informing the cosmos. The "Great Way" glimmered through words as well as things and deeds on earth (*OTz* 4:348).[34] "Since the deeds of heaven and earth are all in words," he wrote, "the principle ingrained in the universe must be endowed in words. If one only inquires into the intention of the forty-seven phonetic symbols [*iroha*], it should be possible to exhaust principle within the world" (*OTz* 4:348). In words, he believed, one encountered the sacred principle holding all life together.

Language into Labor

The nativist linguistic project was, above all else, concerned with the production of language. Activity was directed toward an excavation of the conditions attending the primal act of constructing words and sentences and a determination of the relationship between utterance and the world of things and deeds. To discover the inaugural act of language in the late eighteenth century, it called attention to an otherness, which was consistently suppressed in nativist texts but enabled nativists to envisage their project. If nativists in the late eighteenth century sought to talk and write about the production of language, they must have believed that language usage had become problematic. They must have been convinced that a clarification of proper linguistic usage was the key to solving other problems. The intensity of their activity pointed to a kind of linguistic alienation, in which eighteenth-century language had become a commodity and its users consumers with no knowledge of the conditions producing the language they "consumed." Linguistic acts appeared increasingly as given products, extraneous to the real operations of language, its productive modality, and performance. For this reason, nativists like Okuni Takamasa were quick to distinguish the substance (*karada*) of language from its mere use; to use language correctly required a knowledge of its production—how it had been constituted at the moment of inception. Nativists noted that a profound transformation had taken place in the eighteenth century, which changed linguistic producers into linguistic consumers. To counteract it, they valorized archaic song and poetry as traces of the moment of original production. Arguing strongly for conducting poetic studies in order to acquire a knowledge of how the ancients used words and produced language, Motoori Haruniwa, for example, criticized a language that was merely handed down, where mechanical uses had supplanted production, and where users no longer thought about what they were doing (*MNz* [old] 6:98). Discussions of ways to summon the intention of words contained an attack on the prevailing autonomization of language usage; for example, Motoori Ōhira, the successor to Norinaga, defended the recitation of ancient poetry as the surest method for avoiding the thoughtless use of language.

Nativists asserted that contemporary speakers had lost contact with both the natural and the human, especially the sense of connectedness that the ancient poems so powerfully illustrated between humans and the world of things and deeds that presided over the formation of language. They complained that foreign sounds and locutions had added the rubble of sedimentation to bury the authentic language and had displaced, therefore, its productive operations into mere exchange-value. Hence, language had come to suppress the conditions of its production; it was reproduced only for the purpose of thoughtless consumption. As a result, the times appeared opportune to restore to daily life a language that made possible self-expression, communication within a preclass division of labor, and imitation of the world of deeds and things in order to illuminate things and intention in their undifferentiated unity. Nativists believed that identity could be secured by resituating language (speaking) to its locus in the body. But this relocation also implied a recovery of property and a return to direct ownership of the means of communication, since words belonged to the speaker who uttered them.

Nativists believed that pure and unadulterated sound and speech attended the formation of language in antiquity. They unequivocally agreed that voice and action, the work of the body, were one and the same thing. Voice also signified the social, since the whole grammatical project aimed at showing the transaction between speakers who shared correct sound and the things and deeds it sought to imitate. But this attempt to reunite voice and body meant that language itself, as practiced in the eighteenth century, had become external to its users and that body no longer belonged to oneself: surely, this is what nativists were driving at in their insistence on the primacy of voice, sound, and the function of working and acting words. Just as voice signified the social—an "empathic community" making dialogue possible because of the translucent correspondence between words, things, and deed—the operations of language showed how words assisted one another to form a perfect replication of community itself, as Hirata observed and Okuni reformulated in his theory of mutual assistance (*wago*). The return of voice to body insured that language had once more become the property of living subjects; it would guarantee against the fetishization and commodification of language into mere subjectivism and solipsism. Language, like all other things, possessed concreteness, tangibility, and materiality. Thus, the first songs, like the creation fables, identified the physical transformation of sound into voice with its supposed referent to show that the production of language consisted in making it into a working body.

Hence, song and poetry were inscriptions of voice and speech, as Ōkuni Takamasa clearly had in mind when he proposed (*Kotoba no masamichi*, 1836) that humans were limited to what the eye saw and the ear heard. Intention (*kokoro*) was in the body, just as the *kami* were in heaven and earth. But one did not see the shape of this intention; it was linked to the voice and found in words. In the same way, even though the spirits (*kami*) of things came before things and created them, their shapes were hidden from view. Knowledge was restricted to things seen and heard, made manifest by the spirit. When Ōkuni turned to the performance of working words, he established a more explicit relationship between the materiality of speech and the movement of the spirit, a bonding that mirrored the "miraculous principle" bequeathed at the time of the creation of the universe (*OTz* 4:348). The division of a word into its "beginning" (birth), "middle" (existence), and "end" (death) would exhaust the intention found in working words.

> All things, all deeds, all principles in the cosmos are embodied in the ascent and descent, joining and separating of spirit [*tama*], energy [*ki, ke*], and substance [*mi, shitsu*]. Spirit and energy are without shape but they are not identical. Substance depends [*noru*] on energy and spirit and is associated with earth. Energy, or force, depends on spirit and is associated with sky. This is the principle of animality . . . and comes before [all things]. . . . It is called the spirit of good fortune and the founding spirit. (Ibid. 4:348–49)

The linguistic sign, like the human body, housed a spiritual force that could be recognized by the act of speaking or doing. The living body of language was the form manifesting the *kotodama*; its forthcoming, as Husserl might have said, was realized in its coming forth.

Finally, nativists all asserted that speech originated in gesture and developed as a response to the things and deeds humans encountered in remote antiquity. The body, therefore, *reproduced* in sound and speech the things inhabiting the world. But because this reproduction was evidence that a relation between speakers had occurred, it was related to the constitution of an Other. This formulation implied a conviction that the linguistic community could always be retrieved in its subject-speakers. What had been forgotten or presumed dead could be revived and re-presented because it lived in the speaker. Nativists believed that this revival could be realized if contemporaries could be persuaded to abandon idealized words, clichés, and alien meanings and recover the operations that had produced the ancient songs. To "restore" an authentic language, they recommended retracking the traces of primal speech left in the ancient texts and prayers. They proposed attaining a "second origin of language" by a direct immersion in the substance of words and speech that embodied the spiritual process attending the creation. In fact, many writers were convinced that the very opacity of language, its inertia, now offered the occasion for reuniting the present with the intentionality of antiquity, from which the contemporary world had been set adrift. Here, too, there was a connection between language and work. Just as language could be revived by replicating its original operations, by returning words to the body, so could work be restored to the body as its instrument. Voice and work belonged to body. It is hardly surprising that nativists often used the image of hands manipulating tools or compared the operation of speech with working words. Nor was it an aberration for people like Hirata to equate worship, the recitation of prayer (in place of poetry), with the activity of physical labor, as if they constituted a natural coupling. They saw the recovery of tangible linguistic activities and bodily work as the same thing, because both signified imitative gestures denoting things, deeds, and relationships as they existed in a precategorical past. Nativists often cited the way children learned gestures and sounds mimetically, as if the operation functioned as a model for archaic linguistic practice. Their recognition of the imitative function of speech immediately drew attention to the world of things, the model for mimesis in the archaic time when body was bonded to nature itself. They also insisted that workers had imitated the intention of creation to make the land habitable for succeeding generations. To work with matter, workers had to use their bodies as instruments of productivity. Basically, both speakers and workers reproduced the conditions of existence before they had been removed from the body. This characterization of their performance suggests that nativism constituted a nonreproduction of the conditions of social existence in the eighteenth century and the radical production of conditions of social life that were not yet available to immediate experience.

Although it is difficult to ascertain from nativist texts whether speech existed prior to work or vice versa, the authority of the body diminished the importance of this question and established a firm grounding for a relationship between the two activities. Ultimately, as we shall see, late-Tokugawa nativists were less concerned with the niceties of language study and more urgently interested in the status of work as a gestural repayment of the blessings handed down by the creation deities. But often what they said about work had been prefigured in their discourse on language. Both voice and work "imitated" things and called forth the social and the presence of an "empathic community"; both involved knowing the most fundamental conditions of production in order to reunite body to matter (nature) and reappropriate the product—word and work—for the body. This coupling implied mutual assistance and made it possible to reach a second origin, which promised to restore to contemporaries links to a forgotten past. However, this recovery was powered by a mimetic instrumentality aimed less at a literal return to the remote past in every detail, as if propelled by an insurmountable nostalgia, than at a restoration of the relationship between body and nature that had been lost in the society of eighteenth-century Japan.

Since both language and work had been covered by a sedimentation that concealed their true purpose to humans, nativists believed it was possible to remove the rubble in order to initiate a praxis that would recover its lost meaning. The importance of the nativist linguistic intervention was that the renovation of meaning implied not only the recovery of the body proper and the reinstatement of its status in discourse but also the rescue of material nature, labor, and even technology. In turn, this implied the juxtaposition of a precategorical economic structure and a subjective and intersubjective founding economic operation to the fundamental structural modes of late-Tokugawa Japan. This juxtaposition revealed a space between prevailing ideological representations and called forth an effort to supplement what many believed was missing. The object of desire inspiring this "supplement" was to overcome the separation between mental and manual labor (coded by the acknowledged separation of public and private), in which contemporary culture and its "crisis" had originated. The way to reunite mental and manual labor was to return to the identity of speech and work as activities centered in the body.

The nativist linguistic project rejected the normative claims of an official language suffused with alien elements, authoritative, hierarchical, monologic, finished, and fixed; it demanded a return to a living language and an expressibility that would be open to active responses rather than passive "understanding." Nativists believed that the spoken word always preceded finished and fixed ideographic writing; they were also convinced that utterance was invariably social, insofar as it defined the contours of a communicative community. Words stood as the products of socially organized persons in the process of their interaction. But according to the lesson taught by the ancients, the re-presentation of a living sign community could never be far from the specific socioeconomic prerequisites of the group's existence. In order for any item to enter the social concern of the group, however inadvertently, it would have to make contact with the basis of material life, just as the ancients imitated in sound the things and deeds of the world. More important, *kokugakusha* insisted on contextual changeability in language usage and resisted copying the forms of expressibility practiced by the ancients. Time and again, Motoori warned his contemporaries against the strict imitation of ancient words and style; instead, he recommended emulating the freshness and spontaneity of their language practice. Because the language community that the nativists envisaged generated different "accents" depending upon the conditions of interaction—as described by Voloshinov[35]—it permits us to reread the nativist linguistic intervention as a disclosure of ideological production, where existence found its way into words and signs through a process of interaction and refraction. When *kokugakusha* juxtaposed their own accentuality to contemporary convention, they were also promoting their own social interest, which effectively challenged the claim of the Tokugawa ruling class to impart a supraclass, eternal, and uniaccentual character to the ideological sign.

2 Archaism I: The Origin of Discourse

Language and the Question of Form and Content

When Kurozawa Okinamaro (1795–1859), a student of Norinaga's school, the Suzunoya, published his *Kotodama shirube* (Guidance in the spirit of language) in 1852, the nativist linguistic project was already congealing into history, and interest was turning to questions of worship and work. Kurozawa's text constituted an inventory of nativist linguistic intelligence and an effort to systematize the various strands of thinking into a coherent grammatical statement. By the time he wrote his text, it was taken as common sense that access to the ancient songs and books was impossible without a knowledge of working words, the "connections of the particles,"and the "uses of the phonetic syllabary." A person who was deficient in this knowledge of language, he warned, was like a man without legs and a bird without wings.[1] A reading of ancient texts that did not apply this knowledge would only reflect the unrestrained vulgarity found in contemporary speech and writing. In order to avoid the confusion produced by apprehending the "reality" of one age with the words and intent of another, Kurozawa faithfully reproduced Norinaga's message to establish a correspondence between intent, deed, and word. Inherent from the very beginning in this quest for correspondence was the question of how form should be related to content. By privileging intent and thing over word, nativists presupposed that a content (experience), which hitherto had been unnamed, preceded form, the means to express experience adequately. Their criticism of the "Chinese mind" aimed at showing how form had constrained content and made it conform to alien requirements.

In a discussion of the status of the *Nihonshoki* as a "reliable" historical text, Hirata Atsutane claimed that the *Kojiki* constituted a superior source because it did not conform to the style of Chinese dynastic histories. Obviously, this sentiment had been inspired by the thoughts that Motoori had recorded about this text in his *Kojikiden*. Owing to a reliance on Chinese historiographical convention, Hirata wrote, the *Nihonshoki* had assimilated a Chinese intention and, thus, forfeited much of the reality of antiquity. "Intent, deed, and word must correspond. In antiquity there were the conditions of antiquity in intent, word, and deed; in later ages there was the condition of later ages in intent, word, and deed." Moreover, intent, deed, and word in China belonged to the Chinese. Because the *Nihonshoki* had recorded the deeds of Japanese antiquity with the intention of later ages and other places, there was no possibility for the necessary correspondence (*HAz* [old] 1:18–19 [*Kodō taii*]).[2] By contrast, the *Kojiki* had been able to escape all "contrivances," and secure the perfect correspondence by transmitting the words of antiquity as they were. As a result, it successfully avoided the confusion expressed by men of later times. Elsewhere in this text Hirata described Japan as a "country of words" that existed well before the importation of ideographs. His complaint about writing focused on the presumed identification of "principle" and ideographs. Because ideographs had been superimposed upon Japanese words, there were many instances in which principle fell short of an appropriate fit with the native word. Scholars throughout the ages had failed to make this discrimination and had mistakenly referred to principle (ideograph), rather than to its true referent, as the basis of explanation (*HAz* [old] 1:18–19).

Nativists believed they had found a solution to this "practice" of reversing the order of things and a way to reinstate an authentic experience—content (custom, in Hirata's thinking)—to its privileged place of primacy. It was necessary first, however, to show how experience would reveal a form adequate to itself and how to bond practice (content) with the affairs of daily life. Even Motoori's more formal meditations on poetry and song evinced an explicit preference for practice and action. His explorations into the language of ancient song stemmed less from a sterile impulse to return to a golden age than from a desire to use ancient poetry—that is, speaking—as an example of the adequate form to express daily practice and sentiment because of its equivalence with the mundane order. The freshness of language— speaking—that the *Man'yōshū* manifested disclosed the purity of intent

(*magokoro*), practice, and performance unmediated by an inappropriate form. Thus, it would be foolish, he advised his contemporaries, to
merely copy the language and the style (*aya*) of the ancients. The important point was to recognize the primacy of sincerity and honest practice—content—that caused the ancients to resort to song as a natural
correspondence to the content of practice. Consequently, any effort to
imitate this form and its language in the present risked recuperating the
primacy of form over content, a lifeless formalism, and a suppression
of the experiential texture of contemporary life. Motoori believed that
appealing to the example of the ancient poems would illustrate how
form had once adequately reflected the experience of life. Yet he was
also mindful that subsequent changes in content required a reconsideration of the form and language that might best serve it. This conviction was at the heart of his attack on contemporary poetic convention;
it provided one of the functions for his conception of *mono no aware*,
a theory of cognition that described the knowledge and understanding
of objects that arose from a profound feeling for them.

On closer examination, Motoori's theory was an expansion of
nativist belief in that operation that produced words from sound and
the grammatical project that established a mode of relating subject to
object. Since poetry was speaking and speaking was a reproduction of
things and deeds encountered in the world, entering empathically into
an object meant employing the correct word to express it. Like language, the world of things was not fixed and timeless, but fluid and
ever changing, constantly requiring a reassessment of one's relationship
to it. In short, the model for Motoori's larger theory of cognition was
the example of language itself.

This theory of cognition, which defined the fluid relationships
between perceiver and perceived, explains the apparent shift in nativist
problem-consciousness from poetic and linguistic studies in the late
eighteenth century to formulations on religious (Shinto) devotion and
work in the early nineteenth century. Although interpreters of *kokugaku* have seen in this move a break between Motoori's strong emphasis
on poetic and exegetical studies and Hirata's preferences for religion, it
was less of a rupture than a working through of the possibilities authorized by the nativist cognitive program. Evidence abounds throughout
Hirata's writings to suggest that knowing things deeply meant "knowing
things of the times," which increasingly referred to a knowledge of daily
affairs that most *kokugakusha* had ignored. An even more accurate
indicator of the shift was the nativist preoccupation with stabilizing the

relationship between form and content. Whereas Motoori saw in song (*uta*) the form most adequately corresponding to the "true intent," Hirata, who earlier accepted this formulation, turned to narrative to demonstrate how the web of relationships figured work and worship. But the shift was prefigured by a tropical strategy for apprehending the problem of differences (China, the Other), which first prompted nativists to emphasize metaphorical identification (similitude) and only later to explain difference through the agency of metonymical and contiguous association. Kamo and Motoori had privileged poetry, since it taught them how the ancients had reached a metaphorical understanding of reality. Hirata moved from poetry to a cosmic narrative that promised to relate apparently different things to form a complex whole. The most dramatic instance of this problematizing of form was disclosed in the way each thinker viewed the ancient histories.

The Poetry of Things

It is well known that Motoori turned to "historical" studies in midlife, when he concentrated his considerable energies on examining in exhaustive detail the *Kojiki*—Japan's earliest surviving written "history" (compiled in the late seventh century). Until the middle years of the Tokugawa period, the *Kojiki* had not drawn much scholarly attention; it had existed largely within the shadows of the *Nihonshoki*, a later "history." The *Kojiki* had been seen by most as a repository or source for understanding the *Nihonshoki* and the *Man'yōshū*. Motoori's "discovery" of this languishing text was inspired by the recognition that, even though it had been written in Chinese ideographs, it had been meant to be read in Japanese. Hence, far from being an aid to understanding other texts, the *Kojiki* was a major mine of ancient words, which made the ancient intention accessible to contemporaries. This is not to say that the *Kojiki* had not been worked on before Motoori. Kada Azumamaro (1669–1736), an earlier nativist, wrote a "report" on the text (*Kojiki satsuki*) and Kamo no Mabuchi recommended a close reading of it, in order to understand better the language of the *Man'yōshū*. But it was Motoori who saw that other texts, because of their reliance on Chinese, had lost the ancient intention and forfeited any understanding of ancient words. Despite Motoori's apparent reverence for this text, as exemplified in a strategy that sought to clarify the pronunciation and meaning of words contained in it, piety did not prevent him from virtually "rewriting" it for his contemporaries. He saw the *Kojiki* as a kind of master text granted by the ancient deities as a record of their gift to the folk, an account of the creation of the land and its purpose. He saw his task to illuminate and clarify the traces of ancient intention, which was, he believed, the site of all meaning. Time and erosion caused by alien practices and language had altered the meaning of the ancient words contained within the text. Hence, he embarked on an exegetical and linguistic inquiry that was both phonological and etymological. But, it should be added, this effort to provide an authoritative reading of the *Kojiki* was the most problematic part of his project. If reading ideographs for what they might reveal of ancient Japanese sounds was not accompanied by the effort to exhume archaic words then there would be no way to gain access to the "reason" of the *Kojiki*. In order to penetrate the recesses of reason, he recommended a strict examination of the words in the text, which consisted principally of a detailed consideration of the ancient language and the development of a method of reading (*MNz* [new] 9:31). He believed that the text was directly transmitted orally "by the mouths of men" to be "heard by the ear" (ibid. 9:16, 17). Only after the importation of Chinese script was the text written down in ideographs representing the sound values of the oral transmission. Because the *Kojiki* recorded deeds and things that the ancients had *spoken* about, it closely resembled the ancient songs and poems, which also expressed the primacy of speaking over writing (ibid. 9:18). This belief validated Motoori's claim to "rewrite" the *Kojiki* as ancient speech, using phonetic syllabary (*kana*). It also authorized his claim that "word" (*koto*) and "deed" (*koto*), possessing the same sound in Japanese, constituted an identity that revealed true intention (*kokoro*), signifying the unity of experience and expression.

Michel Foucault, writing about the sixteenth-century episteme in Europe, has suggested that the meaning of signs, what they signified, was identified with the signs themselves, since the signs, it was believed, originated from what was similar, just as their constitution depended on discovering similitude. By this act, semiology was superimposed on hermeneutics to demonstrate similitude.[3] This observation comes close to describing Motoori's effort to collapse the distinction between intention—meaning—and word and thing. He defined what was irreducibly Japanese—the voice—as a semiological procedure, and a hermeneutic—his reading of it—would fix its meaning. Throughout Motoori's writings, and explicitly in his preface to the *Kojikiden* and his late methodological essay *Uiyamabumi*, he consis-

tently privileged the status of language—speaking—as the true index
to meaning and thing. His discussion of *mono no aware*, informed by
the ancient songs and poems as well as the later *Genji monogatari*,
continually tried to show how a true response to things inspired genuine feeling toward an identification with the object world. Word became the thing itself, and semiology, the production of signs, was
welded to semantics, the construction of meaning. Archaism for
Motoori meant returning to the tangible; it demanded closing the gap
between word and thing in order to reach the origin of discourse itself.

According to Motoori, the *Kojiki* resembled no other text. Because it had not been worked on by successive generations of writers, it
provided the virgin "traces" of primal acts and deeds in the only language that could have expressed them: "To aim at principle [*kotowari*],
unconnected to things as such, has been expressed in the books of
admonition by Confucians and Buddhists. The ancient books of the
great august country proclaim in writing the teachings of common
men. The discussion of the principle of things [in the *Kojiki*] does not
contain hidden intent and principle apart from the words that have
been recorded in antiquity" (*MNz* [new] 9:32–33). The *Kojiki* had
escaped the disjunction between representation and represented because of its oral transmission. Here, Motoori registered dissatisfaction
with writing itself, especially the ideographic system, because it constituted a "secondary revision" and functioned as a mediation that displaced immediacy, presence, and the act of production. To emphasize
the effects of this displacement, he contrasted the *Kojiki* with the later
Nihonshoki and observed that the latter was a text "directed by the
Chinese style," which the former had assiduously avoided even though
it employed ideographs. Since the *Kojiki* never became mired in the
snares of the Chinese style, it preserved the words and things of the age
of the gods. Hence, the "unification of intent, things, and word correspond completely," because the words used in the text relayed with
unerring accuracy the circumstances of the most remote past (ibid.
9:6). The real record of the *Kojiki* was "public" (*ōyake*)—that is, it
referred directly to the affairs of the emperor and ordinary folk—while
the "histories" of the Chinese style remained representative selections,
informed only by "private opinion" (ibid. 9:5, 6, 8).

Antiquity and the later ages, Motoori believed, each had its own
sense of intent, things, and words. Yet the *Nihonshoki* recorded the
facts of antiquity with alien words that belonged to a later age: "Because
it [*Nihonshoki*] transmits the will of our country in Chinese words,

there are several instances of disagreement [between word, thing, and intent]; the *Kojiki* has not added private [selfish] knowledge [to the deeds] . . . and records things as they were handed down by antiquity; its intent, things, and words all correspond. It [*Kojiki*], thus, conveys the truth of ancient times, as it aimed principally at the words of the ancients" (ibid. 9:6). Precisely because the words recorded these events truthfully, they constituted the subject of the text.

Motoori's resolution of the "disagreement" between word, thing, and intent, and the subsequent separation of sign and meaning, proceeded on two levels: on one level, he criticized the use of Chinese words that referred to principle rather than reality, which inevitably equated words and deeds with "reason"; on the other, he attempted to articulate a conception of truth that, he believed, had been absent in subsequent "histories." In the first case, he directed attention to the ways Chinese texts had dealt with the question of origins. Whatever the circumstances relating to the beginnings of heaven and earth, he wrote, Chinese explanations were invariably fabrications produced by "ordinary minds employing reason (*kotowari*). But the ancient accounts of Japan are not like this. Before there were words to express things, there were things and deeds, which ultimately were transmitted to other and succeeding generations" (ibid. 9:8). When these two methods were compared, he continued, the Chinese approach, founded on the primacy of reason, appeared to be superior, and people were persuaded to believe that such reasoned explanations were true. In comparison, the method of ancient transmission (*koden*) seemed shallow (ibid. 9:8–9). Consequently, "intelligent people throughout the ages, down to the present time, have been perplexed." But as he proposed in the *Naobi no mitama* (an independent book in the first volume of the *Kojikiden*), the deed to "govern" the realm corresponded to the Way of the gods; it inhered in "things," not in "contrivances." The purpose of imperial governance was to pursue the intent of the deities who created the realm. This arrangement was what the *Man'yōshū* called the *kannagara*, the Way of the gods: "In the august time of antiquity, there was no disputing this Way. In ancient words this Way referred to the land of water and ears of rice, the land that does not dispute the Way of the *kami*. This was the Way that preceded things. As for *michi* (Way) it was written *umashimichi*; the prefix for 'august' [*mi*] was attached to road [*chi*] in things such as mountain roads, field roads, and it was a road that proceeded only in things" (ibid. 9:50). In antiquity there was no word for the Way; the word for *chi* and *michi* were the same, meaning only "road" or "path" (ibid.; also 2:148 [*Isonokami sazamegoto*]). Any other meaning simply did not exist. Here was a truth that was present by its absence as a word: the ancient Japanese knew what the Way meant, even though they possessed no means to give it nominal expression. By contrast, the Chinese contrived to make the Way into a prior principle, an abstraction that preceded things but did not inhere in them. "When ideographs were imported to Japan, the [word for] way ceased to refer only to road; it was used to convey a variety of things, and the ideograph acquired accumulated intentions and meanings, such as 'morality' [*dōtoku*], 'ethical principle' [*dōgi*], 'heavenly way' [*tendō*], and 'reason' [*dōri*]. When all of these ideographs are read as road . . . the word for it comes to be used variously [*izura mo*] for the idea of the ideograph *michi*" (ibid. 9:50; also 2:148). Despite a convention that *michi* meant nothing more than a physical path, people continued to believe in the idealizations summoned by the Chinese ideograph.

Just as the imperial descendants made the august intention of the heavenly deities their own, there could never be a separation between the divine age and the present. The Way always existed in the land and among its people as a condition indistinguishable from the divine creation and the subsequent ordering of things, especially the trust of governance invested in the imperial lineage. It was a sign that denoted (*shirushi*) correctness, elevation, and respect, which, Motoori argued, will never be found in any place other than Japan because it has been bestowed according to the august spirit of the first deities (ibid. 9:55, 57, 59). The specific relationship he wished to make, which was later and more fully articulated by Hirata, was that, since all humans acquired life from the creation deities, they knew well the deeds (*waza*) that their bodies were supposed to perform. People knew naturally what they had been intended to do by virtue of their divine creation, just as they knew naturally how to speak correctly. In the imperial age, all people, from high to low, had had no trouble in making the "great intention of the emperor" their own. By contrast, people of the present received instruction in the Way, in the deeds they should perform. This was the reason, he believed, why people must study the *Kojiki* and the *Man'yōshū* carefully in order to know, once more, that the Way is realized in actual conduct and performance, not in instruction or in the acquisition of title and name.

Motoori believed that, before associations had sedimented, there had not been any occasion to establish a conscious "learning of the

Way." In *Naobi no mitama*, he announced that, since there was nothing called a Way in the age of the gods, it must mean that one could easily find it (ibid. 9:50–51).[4] Even before language, before the naming of things, there was something that constituted the reality of the world. It involved grasping and understanding what inheres in things, by "entering into things with the circumstances of speech [*monoii no sama*]. By this method of entering into things [*oshi hakaru mono*], everything will be understood" (*MNz* [new] 9:33).

Both the *Kojiki* and the *Man'yōshū* illuminated the encounter of humans with the world of nature, in which the recitation of poetry and the singing of songs constituted natural responses by people "touched by things," "deeds," and stimuli (ibid.).[5] Motoori believed in the inseparability of the songs and human achievement, because the deeds prompting them gave expression to the proper words, which immediately showed the kinship between meaning and the feeling for things, experience and expression. The things and deeds transmitted by words in the ancient texts were accomplished by gods in the age of high antiquity and involved an encounter with the creation, birth, and formation of men and women, plant life, fields, and mountains. The texts presented a picture of the wholeness of life, which constantly "touched" and "moved" people deeply. Encounters were with things (*mono*), whose forms determined the words used to express them. Meaning always inhered in things; it was transmitted by humans who understood things immediately as a result of the sensation elicited in the encounter with the world but were forced to grasp and convey the experience in words. As a result, the circumstances of speaking (*kotoii*) in antiquity required an identification of the things prompting the formation of words.

Yet Motoori warned against an exclusive reliance on etymology as a method for learning the Way. The explanation of words was important, he wrote in the *Uiyamabumi*, but the quest for original meaning often led to a variety of interpretations. Even though scholars had made the study of words their first order of business, it would have been better if they had not, because there was no profit to be gained from it. Rather, it was necessary to know well how the words had been used. A simple consideration of original meaning led only to lifeless imitation in later ages. But an association between things and their expression revealed the interaction between the world and its meaning. A failure to know how words had been used would, in time, prevent any genuine understanding of how and where they had been constituted (ibid. 1:16

[*Uiyamabumi*]). Motoori complained about interpreters "devoted to the learning of the Way" because he was convinced that writing, by accumulating meaning and abstraction, buried the true intent of the deed. Learning about the Way signaled an opposition to it. The notion of a *kami* Way, a Way of the gods, came into existence only after the introduction of Confucian speculation and Buddhist practice. Studying these texts led only to a knowledge of "foreign customs" and an erroneous differentiation of the great customs of Japan's august antiquity as a separate "Way of the gods." By their juxtaposition to Confucianism and Buddhism, the ancient customs assumed the character of a doctrine and rules that could not be known without study. But, Motoori was convinced, even if one read the ancient texts, the meaning of antiquity was still difficult to grasp. The meaning of the ancients came from knowing their deeds (*waza*), which were difficult to understand. It was not through study and learning that one came to know the gods' Way. Instead, one must have known, from the time of birth, that the Way was nothing more than the true intention of the gods, and this true intention was simply the "customs of the times," whether good or bad. When men of later generations turned to the blandishments of Chinese "meanings," they failed to nourish the true intention. If one sought to study the Way today, he would not succeed in grasping its true meaning. Learning required, first, an abandonment of the conventions of Chinese scholarship for an empathic penetration into the recorded deeds of antiquity. Just as the ancients secured knowledge by entering the things and deeds they encountered, so contemporaries would be able to reach the Way naturally by their own sympathetic understanding. "With the pure, clear intent of our country, study well the ancient texts. If this is done, one will know naturally that no other Way should be received; that is, to know this is to conduct the Way of the gods" (*MNz* [new] 9:62).

The model for this kind of knowing remained the production of song and poetry, whose operation continually confirmed the cognitive mode humans first employed in their encounter with the world. This was, of course, the purpose of Motoori's intense engagement with *mono no aware*. Ironically, the valorization of an empathic cognitive mode securing entry into objects presupposed the very division between subject and object that it promised to dissolve. Nativist grammar had already called attention to this division and provided it with a systematic classification. But the exercise of a deep feeling for certain things or deeds and "knowing" how to express such sentiment required a return to the kind of metaphorical identification Motoori had observed in the archaic language. Poetic language summoned power, energy, a kind of materiality of physical objects; there was little or no emphasis on a clear separation between subject and object, word and thing. The recognition that subject and object in ancient poetry were linked by a common power implied a belief that words offered control over certain things and deeds. Motoori believed that as speech utterances recording encounters, the ancient poems and songs were intensely material or physical, anchored in images connected with bodily deeds and specific objects. It was the fact that the language of ancient song was clearly metaphorical—something could always be said for something else— that secured a kinship between subject and object. By contrast, Motoori's own language (and cognitive strategy) was remote from this innocent and naive metaphoricalness; it was metonymical by nature, separating subject from object, differentiating between outward expressions and inner thoughts, feeling, and sentiments (the familiar distinction between surface and subsurface, visible and invisible), with the part calling attention to the whole. He sought a metaphorical merger of human and natural life and power through the modality of metonymical reduction, and this involved, as we shall see, trying to think his way back to a conception of language in which words conveyed power and bodily associations, rather than their suggestion. The project inspired criticism, largely on the grounds that Motoori had ignored the meanings of words that lay beneath the surface. This basically metonymical response was inaugurated by Fujitani Mitsue (1768–1823), son of Nariakira, who complained that Norinaga's Kojikiden, especially its etymological preoccupation, failed completely to delve below the surface of words to the spirit of language beneath. But this very operation happened to be the point of Motoori's poetics, to close the gap between presumed outward expression and "inner reality." By the same measure, Tachibana no Moribe (1781–1849) condemned Motoori's method for failing to distinguish between "fundamental words" and "narrative words" (katari kotoba), literal and figural meanings in transmission of ancient tales.[6]

The poetry of things represented Motoori's effort to rethink a return to the concrete language of the ancients, to restore a "second historical origin" in the present. He favored the poetic form, principally because it—like speech—expressed naturally the world of things and deeds and promised to close the distance between content and form, subject and object, public and private. Early, he recognized the importance of things (*koto, mono*). He accounted for their apparent differences by the action of human sentiment (*ninjō*), which was possessed universally—a fact that Japanese Confucianists had not recognized until the early eighteenth century. In the *Ashiwake obune* (1756), a youthful essay on poetic theory, Motoori wrote that "monks do not have characteristics different from laymen. Since both are ordinary people (*bonpu*), they should not have divided feelings" (*MNz* [new] 2:28–29). Hirata Atsutane echoed this opinion later, when he declared that people were basically the same, differing only in the duties they perform. For Motoori, the meaning of such an observation pointed to the primacy of feeling and emotionality as human conditions. Humans shared feelings and emotion with others, and this was what assured a sense of commonality. Later, in *Isonokami sazamegoto* (1763), he proposed that humans were superior to all living things because they had "intentions that clarify and are profoundly touched and stimulated by things" (ibid. 2:99). Poetry and song constituted the avenues of emotional expressibility; they were realized in ordinary words that belonged to voice. Although birds and insects possessed voice, Motoori denied that they produced poetry, because voice required skill to create poetry or song. "Poetry is recited only by those who have feeling; it is not composed by those who do not have feeling . . . to say all living things have song is false." Living things had feeling (*jō*) and brought out voice naturally, it was a voice that skills had fashioned from emotion into song. Things without feeling did not emit voice by themselves; their voice had to be stimulated from the outside (ibid. 2:88).

Emotionality—the sense of feeling—also enabled the rulers to understand the ruled. Because rulers usually lived apart from ordinary folk, they "have not understood in detail the conditions of people in general" (ibid. 2:49 [*Ashiwake obune*], 167 [*Isonokami sazamegoto*]).[7] Distance, enforced by social convention and artifice, put the ruled beyond the reaches of the leadership, as if they were objects to be acted upon. Because leader and led shared a common humanity, those who occupied the lower orders of society deserved the understanding and respect of those above. The earliest songs taught such humanity and commonality and transferred the imperial will to the intention of commoners because of their shared primacy of emotion and feeling. Understanding the conditions of the people required looking no further than the songs they composed.

Ashiwake obune established the mode of Motoori's original argumentation. Poetry provided the key to learning about the ordinary folk;

it served as an instrument to remind the leadership that no substantive differences intervened between high and low (Motoori later repeated this argument in his meditations on death and the destination of the spirit). Poetry was voice, skillfully expressing emotions, and all humans participated in its production. This equation implied that there was no hierarchy in speech. Poetry recognized neither large nor small, good nor bad, Motoori asserted to counter a proper Confucian conceit; it existed only to mirror the "involvement of genuine thought, emotion, and feeling." Just as humans did not differ substantively from one another, so men and *kami* were associated in a continuous series denoting kinship. The relationship between human being and deity disclosed the nativist strategy to see things in part-whole relationships—the seen calling attention to the unseen—and revealed the idea that humans possess the spark of divinity. The argument was elaborated later by Hirata, who, by linking human productivity to divine intention, bound human activity to the initial creation of the cosmos. The major difference between the two formulations is that, where Motoori deified humans, Hirata humanized the gods. The presence of deities confirmed Motoori's reliance on wonder and mystery, on acceptance rather than rational speculation (*kotowari*) and human artifice. The inexplicable and mysterious summoned the divine and the miraculous; it inspired Motoori's poetics and his conception of feeling deeply for things. To feel, to be moved emotionally, to cry aloud, to utter the correct sounds in words from the recesses of the heart, was to understand, and understanding was a divine gift endowed only in humans.

Motoori's discussions of the function of poetry represented an effort to show how, in a world populated by apparently different objects, all things were fundamentally the same. He concluded that, even though things appeared to be different, they shared an essential sameness. The kinship of things derived from their common origin with the creation deities. All things, down to the lowest insect, he proposed, shared a single origin. Because they were all commonly created, they were endowed with the capacity to express what was most natural to them. They reflected divine intention, which disposed them to act naturally. Among humans these blessings involved a capacity to experience the world emotionally, to become one with it as sentient beings. To do otherwise constituted a violation of divine intention, indeed, a repudiation of the blessings conferred by the gods. Behind this sentiment was the belief that all humans possessed the same nature because of the will of the gods.

By the time Motoori wrote the *Uiyamabumi* (1799), poetry had been transformed into a methodological principle for the construction of a discipline of study. But it was also a discipline of life. To realize the possibilities of such a discipline and to construct a human science, it was necessary to reject the Neo-Confucian conception of nature, and its unnatural principles of organization and behavioral norms, for one capable of ensuring the natural, sensuous, and sentient. Accomplishing this goal, according to the *Uiyamabumi*, required liberating the study of humans from an artificial conception of nature, so as to express what was humanly natural. Scholarship in Motoori's day erred, because scholars had examined the section in the *Nihonshoki* related to the "divine age" and called it the "Way of the gods." Although this approach had been called Shinto (Hirata later called it vulgar Shintoism), it remained remote from the genuine Way of the gods. The object of this study had been to examine the bureaucratic offices, rites, and laws of antiquity. Others had focused on ancient customs, clothing and furniture, the ancient court, and military practices. But none had directed attention to humans, their emotional lives, and what was most natural to them (ibid. 1:7–8). Scholars pledged to study and clarify the Way adhered to Chinese-style argumentation and logic; they were fools who rarely exceeded in "fingering" the recitation of poetry. And because they failed completely to grasp the sensibility of archaic man, they never understood the ancient Way. The content of this kind of learning, Motoori asserted, was "Shinto in name only." Based on foreign understanding and interpretations, it led to an attitude that obstructed "clarifying the Way." Even among those who "recite poetry, construct sentences, and love antiquity, their concern rises only to the level of elegance, as they have forgotten the 'Way'" (ibid. 1:28–30). This denunciation meant to show how the "love for antiquity" had been elevated into an emblem of elegance and how this misrecognition had inspired antiquarian concerns for "ancient clothing" and "furniture and utensils" as "playthings" satisfying the will for style.

Motoori advised care in examining the ancient histories and songs to learn about the Way of archaic man. His interest in ancient man, as he put it, must be distinguished from the exegetical impulse of earlier writings on the ancient Way, which derived their "authority" from an interpretation of texts. In the *Uiyamabumi*, Motoori eschewed interpretation as inappropriate to reaching the Way, even though he seems to have changed his mind regarding the value of etymological studies, since in this text he valorized the function of words over time.

Despite his own exegetical excesses, stemming from a reverence for the "histories" as sources for archaic life, Motoori was convinced that even these histories were compromised by their reliance on Chinese ideographs. For this reason he ranked the *Kojiki* below the *Man'yōshū*, while he considered the *Nihonshoki* hopelessly distorted by Chinese "ornamentation." In this manner he was able to propose the superiority of poetry and song over history. Any effort to grasp the deeds of antiquity and its spirit and words must be approached through the poetry that transmitted the "words that were spoken." "It is for this reason that things done have been transmitted by the histories. But even these histories, because they have been written in words, are not outside words. Thus, it is better to know the conditions of [the ancient] spirit from songs." Motoori's reason for privileging song over history was, as we have seen, prefigured by his preference for voice over writing. As long as words and "things done" and the motivating intention coincided, later ages would have no trouble in grasping the meanings ancient man had produced and the deeds he had accomplished: "The traces by which to know correctly the circumstances of that time are in the words and songs" (ibid. 1:18). Poetry came closest to the content of the Way, which could not be taught as if it was "this or that." For poetry was an activity that must be pursued personally in the actual exercise of composition and recitation. Those who pursued learning would inevitably fail if they did not recite poetry first (ibid. 1:6). Without reciting song and poetry, Motoori continued, it would be most difficult to understand the miraculous and wondrous temperament of the ancients. Although poetry and song had different forms—one for the ancients and one for later ages—students of ancient studies were obliged, first, to recite the archaic form. Only in ancient song and poetry was there a genuine fit between content, which meant the Way or archaic times, and form, which inevitably referred to songs.

It was Motoori's conviction that one had to personally explore ancient poetry in order for its power to reveal the archaic experience, because its form called attention to the content, which was life (ibid. 1:18–19). He saw the ancients not as childish primitives but as people living close to nature who possessed wisdom—poetic elegance—and who cast their responses to the environment in metaphor. No one before Motoori had quite grasped the archaic as a meaningful response to human understanding, nor seen in the form and content of its poetry the expression of a mode of cognition that, like the rational logic of Buddhists and Confucians, sought to make sense of the world of im-

mediate experience. Motoori's pursuit of the archaic was a way of talking about his present. He believed that the problem dogging the present
originated in Neo-Confucianism and its promise to explain all things
rationally. Writing to a colleague in Kyoto (Kiyomizu Yoshitarō), he
put it the following way:

> You do not like my songs and poems, and I do not like your Confucians.
> The way of the sages is to rule the realm, order it, and pacify the people.
> It is not a thing that makes possible private ownership and individual
> enjoyment. Today it [Confucianism] can neither govern the realm nor
> tranquilize the people. . . . It is trivial in the way it regulates the indi-
> vidual. . . . Since childhood I enjoyed studying and did so excessively
> for long periods of time. I got hold of the six classics and read them. But
> I never became attached to them. The Way tranquilizes the realm in
> large things, and in small things it should rule the country. But what
> about my companions and the ordinary folk? Even though it has been
> said that the Way is supposed to do all these things, how can it be
> accomplished?[8]

Confucianism confined itself to ruling and administering the realm.
Even in this respect, it failed to take into account the ordinary folk and
their needs. The world remained filled with uncertainties and phenomena that simply defied rational explanation. Failure to explain the
inexplicable increasingly created unhappiness among the ordinary
people. Yet such failure resulted from a method devoted to understanding things in terms of principle, logic (*rikutsu*), and words abstracted
from their intended meaning (*kokoro*). Inevitably, people were induced
to act contrary to their personal nature. This was surely what Motoori
meant in the *Uiyamabumi* when he complained that it would be difficult to see the Way through the eyes of Confucianism and Buddhism
(ibid. 1:29). Violating one's natural endowment, being other than what
the gods intended, risked unhappiness; happiness involved naturalness,
or elegance—and its acquisition depended on a readiness to shed false
rationality. "If one wishes to penetrate still further into the spirit of the
true Way," he wrote in the *Naobi no mitama*, "then one must be purified from the filthy spirit of Chinese writings and proceed to the study
of the ancient texts [of Japan] with the pure spirit of the sacred land."
Then one would come gradually to know that he was not obliged to
accept the way of China. But to know this was to receive the Way of
the gods into one's own body (ibid. 9:59, 62). Granted, the accounts of

the creation and the foundation of the realm recorded in the ancient histories and songs could not always be taken literally. These texts offered a method to understand the essence of human nature as it was first manifest in the archaic age, and he was confident that his own reading of these songs and poems demonstrated to his students the poetic vocation of ancient man. But for Motoori, song and poetry had become voice and speaking in Japanese. Motoori had learned from Kamo no Mabuchi's studies of the *Man'yōshū* that the first Japanese expressed their encounter with the world of things in voice and song. Moreover, he recognized that the first records and fables of archaic times were invariably grounded in a concrete experience of the common world of things, and disclosed the naturalness and elegance of expression in song and poetry that, in turn, sought representation in a satisfactory and humanizing shape. Such a shape—or form—originated in the "true intention" (*magokoro*) or "correct heart" (*naobu kokoro*) and became the form of the world that the heart-mind perceived as natural, given, and true. Under these circumstances, representation gave way to the represented since the ancients sang the world into existence.

Motoori's examination of archaic man and the elegance of expression (*fuga, miyabi*) authorized a distinction between the natural and the artificial: the natural signalled the true, the appropriate, and the real, while the artificial constituted human contrivance (*sakashira*). Although this formulation was expressed explicitly in the *Uiyamabumi*, it can be traced back to the *Ashiwake obune*, where he first showed that the conventional order in his day between word, deed, and meaning or intent had really been quite different in archaic times. In his present, word came first, then deed, and finally intention, rather than the reverse, as he often noted to illustrate how elegance itself had become stylized and dependent on the "ornamentation" of words, without adequately accounting for the thing seeking nominal representation. Among the ancients, on the other hand, personal meaning or intention shaped both the "condition of the word and the circumstances of the deed." Ancient man perceived the world with a "true heart," as the songs constantly attested, and the "deeds done" were consistently shaped to correspond to this intention. At that time, because intention had not yet been clouded over by unreasoning reason and logic, it was natural to give the correct word to the deed or things requiring denotation. Word secured significance only when intention denoted a thing or deed for what it really was. As poetry showed, when this order was reversed, falsehood replaced truth and showy stylization governed elegance. Motoori's conception of the way words indicated the world of things implied that despite the debt of humans to the creation deities, they created themselves and their surroundings. His recognition of the natural and the artificial already had been figured by his distinction between Japan and China, culture and civilization, human and inhuman. Just as the ancients spontaneously sang songs, their representations consisted of the world of deeds and the things they made. Their songs and poems revealed a society that had found its purpose within the true shape of things. Moreover, he was convinced that the present still contained a trace of the remote world of antiquity and elegance.[9] Although he refrained from expanding this insight, his willingness to see poetic wisdom as distinctive, and as the most enduring of all human faculties, offered others a natural way to make sense of the world.

Because poetry, the form favored by the ancients, preserved the ideal identification between word, deed, and intention, the poetic mode was the first and most authoritative way for humans to grasp their world. The ancients reordered their feelings concerning the world they inhabited, and later ages came to understand their experience through its disclosure of genuine sentimentality. The *Ashiwake obune* announced early that poetry never rightly served political interests or disciplined the body. "It is nothing more than that which touches the heart" (*MNz* [new] 2:3). But the purpose of poetry was not simply to draw out real emotions, even though Motoori acknowledged the importance of such a function. Rather, poetry must be read to understand elegance (*fuga*), which marked the meaning of the poem and its intention. The poetic Way, therefore, pursued the path of elegance. By elegance Motoori did not mean flowery language or florid styles—all, he complained, hallmarks of contemporary poetic practice. Elegance represented the form of "true emotions," the heart as it was, the "real state of affairs." He warned against any attempt to separate elegance from true feelings, the style from the words used to construct sentences. As he came to understand it, elegance united with a search for the ordinary, the common, and the mundane, precisely the context of *archaic* life. It signified freshness, naïveté, honesty of expression, simplicity, and the use of ordinary words near at hand. Motoori's quest for elegance in song and poetry merged smoothly with his search for archaic man, whose example could only inspire an "imitation of antiquity" in the present. In his considerations, antiquity functioned as a transcendental signified.

Eventually, Motoori recommended using the example of the ancients and their understanding in song as a guide to the present. In earlier texts, such as the *Ashiwake obune*, his discussion rested on a contrast between ancient and contemporary poetry. The mirror he held up to his contemporaries reflected the freshness illuminated by ancient song and its consistent use of ordinary words. "Reciting song" (*uta yomi*) allowed one to enter the emotions inspiring it. In the *Uiyama-bumi* he returned to this sentiment when he wrote that the "depth between considering one's affairs and considering the things of the other is different" (ibid. 1:18). It was far more profound to compose and recite a poem than to have it recited; production involved accounting for feelings in a way that no other person could genuinely duplicate. Motoori wished by this formulation to remove the mediation of "another's things" in the grasping of a poem. The act of entering a song from a personal perspective, the place of the subject, required becoming like "ancient man" (*kojin narite*) and "acknowledging that it is possible to enter into the world of ancient elegance."

Motoori was convinced that he had supplied authoritative argumentation for the conviction that the present could become like the past, if contemporaries made an effort to conform to the example of the ancients. He also reaffirmed the power of metaphorical resemblance in the present and prefigured his conception of *mono no aware* (to be discussed shortly), which promised to close the distance between the observer (subject) and the object being observed, the knowing subject and the known. His rethinking of language back to its bodily and material dimensions provided an entry into the world of the ancients and knowledge of it. Yet it was only through the ancients that one would be able to reach a proper understanding of the present. Pitting archaic elegance against prevailing conceptions in the present, he gloomily concluded that contemporary poets were "vulgar," "foolish," and "despicable," because they used the "clumsy words of the times" and composed in a "filthy state of affairs." Invoking the idea of elegance authorized a denunciation of Chinese-style poetry and "its principal purpose to instruct people in the norms of good and evil, rewards and punishments" (ibid. 2:3).[10]

An essential element of this early formulation of elegance as a poetic function was Motoori's recognition of what he called "the real state of affairs" (*jitsujō*), "fundamental sentiments" (*honjō*), and "reciting/composing things as they are felt" (*omoi no ari no mama ni yomu*; ibid. 2:4–8, 31, 32, 37, 42). Specifically, he was referring to the moment when the poet, recognizing the real situation and perceiving things as they were, demonstrated a feel for the correct—elegant—words that would illuminate the situation. This intuitive

sense for the situation and the right words to fit it had characterized
poetry since antiquity, but in recent ages it had changed for the worse
(*kitanaku nari yuki*), and human sentiment itself had become trivialized (*ninjō mo onozukara heihaku ni naritaru*). Seeking to express such
feelings in the contemporary idiom resulted only in an abomination
(*itomi nikui*). In his day, Motoori declared, there was nothing but the
"basest poetry." Therefore, it was natural for poets of later ages to suppress the real circumstances of their own vulgar times in order to get
closer to the "real state of ancient affairs"[11] and to "imitate antiquity in
both intention and word" (ibid. 2:32, 33 [*Ashiwake obune*]).[12] A juxtaposition of contemporary practice to the ancients would clarify its "error" and "vulgarity," in contrast to their "elegance of antiquity." Beneath the notation of "difference" appeared an unformulated criticism
of the quotidian life and a solution to its "vulgarity" in the promise to
reapprehend the content of daily affairs (*jitsujō*) by invoking "true intention" (*makoto no kokoro*).

In concentrating on the status of human feelings, Motoori elevated the sensation and emotionalism of immediate, fleeting, "feminine" experiences, such as kindness, affection, tenderness, and love.
Despite recent opinion associating these values with women, he wrote,
such expressive emotionality belonged to the original spirit of all humans (ibid. 2:35–36).[13] "When we grope about for the true conditions
of our contemporaries," he remarked in the *Ashiwake obune*, "[we can
see that] it has changed since antiquity and is pitifully fleeting." Clever
masculinity—that is, invention and artifice identified with manli-
ness—fell short of expressing the real state of affairs. In the later *Isonokami sazamegoto*, Motoori located this immediate emotionality in
the origins of poetry itself (ibid. 2:88–).[14] Disclosed first by the ancients, it had existed among all the people, including the samurai,
down to his own time. Although it was concealed in the present, it was
possible to reach it by "imitating the ancients." Consequently, contemporary poets had no other choice but to "study, read, and learn about
the true conditions of antiquity." Later, in the *Uiyamabumi*, Motoori
specified his own dissatisfaction with contemporary poets by announcing, "In the poetry of later ages, only one poet in a hundred was able
to recite the true conditions. All was mere invention. But invention,
the condition of making poems, changes from time to time. If one
fabricates the conditions of the heart that touch men in all times, regardless of what one makes, it represents a decline and is not the true
state of affairs. Nor is it the elegance of antiquity" (ibid. 1:22).[15] In the

present, poets did not grasp emotions as they were but, rather, as they were fabricated. Here, Motoori suggested a rejection of Confucian rationality (articulated in his ramblings, the *Tamakatsuma*), with its inordinately heavy demand on normative behavior and its propensity for fabrication and invention as a substitute for the natural and the real.

Expression in song was the emblem of the human capacity to give representation to itself, and poetry meant figuring the natural world. The term Motoori used for "figuring," *aya*, connotes design, composing, and even form. Figuring the objects inhabiting a natural world in a poetic composition conveyed the sense that "poetry is body, recitation is function or working [*hataraki, yō*]. Still more, reciting poetry is joined to the body [because] . . . the ideograph for song [*uta*] can be read as song, recitation, making song, since all are the same" (ibid. 2:19).[16] In the *Isonokami sazamegoto* he returned to the meaning of song and recitation and argued that the ancients rarely distinguished between "body" and "function" because certain words, such as *uta*— a word that was body but also "worked"—conveyed both (ibid. 2:114– 15). In other words, *uta* could serve as both noun and verb. By making this move, Motoori was able to emphasize an emotional bond between the natural world and the process that figured objects into poetry and to demonstrate how song and its production constituted a kind of natural semiosis. He called the power motivating this figuration of the natural world *mono no aware*—the sense of being profoundly affected by certain things in everyday experience. In time, *mono no aware* also came to denote a "pathos" between subject and object so intimate that no real difference could exist between the two. Above all else, Motoori imagined *mono no aware* as a mode of representation immanent in cognition, which made it possible to control the meaning of such terms as "things as they are," the "real situation," and the "basic circumstances" in poetic theory. *Aware* represented an "expression of the profound feeling found in the heart"; it was synonymous with the production of song and poetry, which began with the creation of heaven and earth (ibid. 2:90–).[17] "Poetry springs from *mono no aware*," he wrote in the *Isonokami sazamegoto*, and "to know *mono no aware* is to have feeling for all living things; for if one feels, then he is touched by things." Basic to this theory of knowledge was the presumption of an identity of subject and object, knower and known. The equivalence of "intention" and "thing" came from the feeling released in the response to an object. The ancient texts showed the concordance between meaning and things (*mono*) and revealed "the meaning of all things

living in the world" (ibid. 2:99). In the world, because there were so
many things, speaking began when those things, reaching the eye and
ear, touched the heart. Every living thing had meaning and was, therefore, capable of eliciting feeling (here, Motoori used the ideograph for
jō to convey both meaning [*kokoro*] and feeling [*jō*]) and being touched
by other things. "All that lives is poetry" (ibid.). Among living things,
he added, humans were superior to all other things. Since humans
were supplied with sensibility and, therefore, possessed intentions that
clarified, they were in a position to be profoundly stimulated by things
that touched them, and to be moved by them more frequently. "It is a
principle that one cannot do without song" (ibid.).

It was *mono no aware* that distinguished humans from things and
birds and beasts, even though Motoori acknowledged that all humans
could not be moved by this empathic sense and that there was a difference in temperament between those who gave expression to their innermost feelings when moved by an encounter with the world of things
and those whose talents were simply "thin." Occasionally he identified
mono no aware with the skill to figure (*aya*) and give form to natural
objects in vocalized sound, which other voices, such as those of insects,
failed to produce. Perhaps it was also a rhetorical device to emphasize
a distinction between the extraordinary, who could know *mono no
aware*, and the merely ordinary, who failed to grasp the true essence of
things. If that was the case, then he inverted the criteria validating the
received system of social classes, in order to demonstrate that the possession of sensibility and elegance had nothing to do with social standing. "The man who knows *mono no aware*," he wrote in *Shibun yōryō*
(1763), "is he who has heart [feeling]; he who does not know the pathos
of things is the man without heart" (ibid. 4:59).[18] The heart or feeling
Motoori envisaged was open to the things in life and had the capacity
to penetrate their essence to discover kinship and similitude among all
living things. It was a feeling that encountered the meaning of all
things, discovered it, drew it into itself and, thus, understood true elegance. But, he warned in the *Uiyamabumi*, "all men cannot know the
purpose of elegance. Those who do not know it cannot feel deeply for
certain things. They are men without hearts" (ibid. 1:29).[19] In an earlier text, he distinguished between profound (*fukaki*) and superficial
(*asaki*) capacities to know the meaning of the heart and things and
events. Although men were superior to all things and other living crea-
tures because they could discriminate and understand things (*koto no
kokoro o yoku wakimaete mono no aware o shiru nari*), the degrees of

comprehension varied dramatically from person to person: "Among men there is thinness and thickness. There is a vast difference between a man who empathizes deeply and one who does not. Ordinarily, there are many people who now know *mono no aware*. . . . In truth, it has not been known that there is this distinction between depth and super-ficiality." (ibid. 2:100). The concept of *mono no aware* functioned to show that a demonstration of spontaneous and natural feeling, rather than studied rationality, distinguished the high from the low. It made possible the articulation of a different theory of knowledge, based on the exercise of feeling for concrete things rather than the acquisition of abstract learning. When contrasted to the prevailing division between ruler and ruled, based on the privileging of mental over manual labor, Motoori's theory of cognition constituted a serious critique of the estab-lished arrangement of authority, inasmuch as it empowered a new sub-ject who was in a position to know.

But the immediate effect of this conception of knowing was to show that poetry, a human construction inspired by the natural world of things, revealed the spark of divinity. Motoori put this convention in the form of a question he never answered: "It has been believed that the deities and men who recite the songs possess a sense of profound feeling for things. However, man must give prominence to the good-ness of poetry; the gods must receive the profoundly sincere intention informing poetry. But should it not be understood that to merely hear beautiful poetry is to have *aware*?" (ibid. 2:174). Good poetry depen-ded on appropriate figuring (*aya*) and the proper employment of words. Style alone did not make a good poem; it constituted an empty gesture if it was not "naturally" connected to the figuring of the deed itself. Hearing a beautiful poem meant that one received first the skill of the poet and then the sense of empathy inspired by the thing or deed that the composer was communicating. To occupy the subject position of the poet, the listener must bring to a reading of the poem the profound sensibility that prompted its figuration. By contrast, he continued, the Chinese attributed all things to an unseen principle (*kotowari*). "Even though they see things, they believe that there is nothing that escapes this principle." But principle went against feeling and ultimately emp-tied life of wonder and mystery. Motoori located "miraculous deeds" in the age of the gods; because men had succumbed to Chinese books, later generations doubted these deeds. Yet in the Way of the gods, there were many wondrous things that inclined toward greatness. Since the myriad gods were different from the Buddhas and sages of the countries of men, they need not rely on principle to "touch" (know) the ordinary world. As for the intention of the gods, it was difficult to doubt its existence—whether good or bad—in the hearts of humans. The deeds within heaven and earth had all been made by the acts of the gods from their august intention. For this reason, between "the feeling of humans and the principle of Chinese books, there are many things that are different." All things had been entrusted to the intention of the deities who govern everything (*yorozu o matsurigochi tamai*), and even the ordinary folk must bend their intentions to the heart of the deities. "This is called the Way of the gods," he concluded, which is another expression for the "Way of the song." The poetic Way abandoned principle and Chinese books for things that must be felt for their informing intention (ibid. 2:175).

This assertion contained a conviction that poetry represented a form of apprehension never imagined by Confucian rationalism. As early as the *Ashiwake obune* (1757), Motoori had rejected the didactic uses of poetry by trying to show the limitations of the Confucian explanatory mode. Poetry accounted for wonder, the inexplicable, the mysterious, which principle merely consigned to superstition and trivialization. Reason—*kotowari*—"fenced in" sensibility and feelings. By imposing limitations on knowing the world, it betrayed its true vocation. It was regrettable, Motoori wrote in the *Naobi no mitama*, that the ordinary folk in antiquity and the present had strayed into such "fenced areas" and become perplexed (ibid. 9:58). "Confucians believe that they have grasped the meaning of the universe through the creation of the *Yijing* and very profound words. But all that is only a deception to win people over and be masters over them" (ibid. 9:51–52).

While Motoori and his later followers were seeking to affirm the connections between poetic sensibility and the ancient Way (*kodō*), they were also conducting an assault on metaphysics, which aimed at showing the limitations it imposed upon consciousness and behavior and how it had altogether displaced the human. Yet an attack on the mediation of metaphysics was really a critique of prevailing ideological formulations. Neo-Confucian metaphysical assumptions had become institutionalized, Motoori recognized, and woven into the fabric of Tokugawa society, and a recondite philosophy had been transmuted into ideological common sense to dominate everyday life and practice. The condemnation of Chinese metaphysics constituted no innocent and unpolitical reflex by a literary aesthete; it signalled the terms in which a critique of ideology in the eighteenth century was possible. Moreover, the valorization of the Way of the gods, the poetic Way, underscored the inadequacy of both metaphysics and the prevailing ideology. The Way of the gods, he proposed in the *Uiyamabumi*, the archaic Way of Japan, had never been concerned, as both Confucianism and Buddhism had, with "noisy debates over good and evil, right and wrong." Rather, "it has been all-encompassing, unbound, and gracious; it has had the same goal as poetry" (ibid. 1:18).[20] Poetry, like the ancient Way itself, taught men how they should act toward one another, that they should express understanding and sympathy for the feelings of others as the only human measure binding people together in community.

This acknowledgement of the limitations of metaphysics is most apparent in his effort to demonstrate how song and poetry inspired deep feeling and empathy in the hearts of deities and humans. The approach Motoori employed was sensitive to the problem of knowledge, especially the prevailing division between subject and object, knower and known, authorized by Neo-Confucianism. There was more to understanding, he wrote, than what simply met the eye. "It is central to all Chinese books to believe that things not seen by the eye lack principle and are unworthy objects. Indeed, men of China believe that, in order to consider the principle of things, they must be seen and be close at hand." Because everything one saw could presumably be comprehended by an appeal to principle, anything violating this theory would appear doubtful and unworthy. But people in Japan who studied the ancient classics and poetry would gradually believe otherwise; they would discover exquisite things that could not be so easily classified. The acquisition of such learning through proper study would ultimately change the intentions of all men who embarked on this quest, and they, in turn, would transmit their learning to "ignorant men who have not yet acquired such knowledge." Even the most ordinary persons, he declared, would know that they could not exhaust all there is to know and that such a truth has remained unshaken since the beginnings of heaven and earth. The so-called sages of antiquity, who had failed to plumb the "depths of knowing," had "exhausted their own intentions and withered" in its praises: "Such things as the miracles of the age of the gods have been placed in doubt as unworthy things from the perspective of men of later ages, who have puzzled and exhausted themselves in [the study of] Chinese books. But Chinese learning is fixed to various principles with which one sorts out and classifies in order to understand. . . . It lacks [a capacity for] wonder and, thus, avoids the great" (ibid. 2:175).

People in his times had become noticeably uncertain and unhappy because they had been misled into believing that what was lamentable was really unlamentable. At this point, he came closest to articulating how ideology, through metaphysical categories, sought to present a vision of existence as if it were natural and correct. Yet this recognition of the contradictory claims of ideology was merely another manifestation of the metaphysical authority for classifying and sorting things out as if the reason for all things could be known. Human intelligence was limited, imperfect, and often deceiving, and the perception of wonder and mystery raised the possibility of doubt and uncertainty. "There are doubtful things," he wrote in the *Kuzubana*. "We consider things from the perspective of the human body, the eyes see, the ears hear things, the mouth speaks things, we walk with legs, we make all things with the hands, but all this is uncertain, as are the insects that take flight in space and flowers that bloom in the fields" (ibid. 8:128–29). Motoori centered perception in the body, which unified all sense and activities; yet he attributed the functioning of the body to some mysterious and miraculous presence that could not be seen, identified, classified, or even explained. In the universe humans could not possibly explain everything in any given time and place, and the categories authenticated by reason merely distorted the human capacity to understand. Therefore, the exercise of *mono no aware* in the composition of poetry and song promised to expand the boundaries of humanly possible knowledge, rather than to "fence" it in, by acknowledging first the natural limitations imposed by the appeal to reason. Through poetry, the human and the divine were brought together. Ancient man was temporally closer to the gods and hence, in a position to understand fully divine meaning and intention. The poets of archaic times, Motoori's transformation of the ancient sages of China, those master builders who created the first civilization, transmitted the "truth of the heart" received from the deities. Although anyone was capable of transmitting this knowledge in writing, "it is a mighty thing to learn. Therefore, it is not a thing that could be considered simply from the perspective of the rather shallow intelligence of humans." What exceeded the grasp of mere human intelligence was the creation itself and the capacity of poetry to understand it. But Motoori failed to recognize that because poetry resorted to metaphor, to the powers of figuration, in order to grasp the inexplicable, it ran the risk of confusing representation with the represented.

Enlarging the scope of knowing implied two operations: one involved concentrating on the innermost nature of things—the *mono no kokoro* and *koto no kokoro*—in order to identify the similitude of things, despite their surface diversity; the other entailed an outward expansion, since the world, like creation, was unbound. Creation and its reproduction took place in the world, and its proliferation into innumerable things required human understanding. Such knowledge meant tapping the "true heart" of the deities themselves. "Is it not the original purpose of poetry," he asked rhetorically, "to present facts that are too great for men [to grasp]?" Surely, the present departed from this truth when it delegated meaning to fancy design and induced people to read poets for titillation. The separation of poetry from its true vocation—the fostering of metaphorical understanding of things and deeds too great for ordinary comprehension—represented, for Motoori, the source of contemporary discontent and unhappiness. Knowledge of what lay beyond received forms of knowing signified that the restoration of origins was also a discourse on desire because it offered to reunite contemporaries with their original purpose and thereby remove those activities that had led them astray. Emulating the ancients was less an invitation to literally restore the past than to install its example of resemblance and identity in the present. The archaic exemplar also provided support for the conviction, found scattered through several of his texts, that past and present really corresponded to each other. To be moved by a concrete object or event and show proper feeling for it was to become one with it. The proper exercise of empathy promised a lease on identity in a world of seemingly infinite differences.

Poetry, then, recorded how the heart moved in the encounter with things and deeds. Understanding consisted of feeling and movement. "We call poetry what is composed well. Even though there has been no effort to contrive such a deed when a profound event [*koto no fukaki*] occurs, because the deep feeling is expressed according to the figuration of the poem, gods and humans who hear it will be moved [*aware*]. If they are touched by things they have heard and have experienced deep feeling, they will submit to the times and be increasingly united with the intention that designed the poem" (ibid. 2:174). Regardless of changes over time and the proliferation of things that required explanation, people would understand the meaning of things and conform to their times through the exercise of *mono no aware*. "Living in this world, a person sees, hears, and encounters all kinds of things. If they are taken into the heart and touch the heart of the things within it, then it can be said that the person knows the heart of things, the core of an event [*koto no kokoro*], knows *mono no aware*" (ibid.

2:99–100). In another text, Motoori reasserted the relationship between contemporary and true understanding. The first principle of
mono no aware, he wrote, was to realize that a deep knowledge of
things stemmed from knowing the heart of things; the second was to
recognize that knowing the heart of things meant knowing the conditions of the times. It should be noted, according to Koyasu Nobukuni,
that when Motoori referred to "things that moved the heart" (*fururu
koto*), he really meant "understanding."[21] In any case, this knowledge
entered the emotions of humans. (*MNz* [new] 4:18 [*Shibun yōryō*]).
Yet such events acquired meaning only after they were apprehended in
a poetic form that came naturally and not through the forced contrivance found in contemporary verse.

Contemporary poetic practice had induced people to falsify sentiment by writing about things that failed to strike at the heart of things
(ibid. 2:54 [*Ashiwake obune*], 172, 174 [*Isonokami sazamegoto*]).
Poems of this variety were useless and deceiving; they frequently represented a true index into changes in time, because poetry always "relates the circumstances moving the heart." An inventory of contemporary poetry showed only songs concerned with "lower-class women
and children." Despite their poor technical quality, had they been inspired by a "true heart," they could not have failed to move humans
and deities to profound feeling (*aware*). If contemporaries had retraced
their steps to reach the "elegance of antiquity," they would have been
prepared for composition in the present (ibid. 2:42, 54, 55 [*Ashiwake
obune*], 174, 175 [*Isonokami sazamegoto*]). Because *aware* did not
change from past to present, people would know it in their own age, if
they thought deeply about certain things in the past (ibid. 2:170 [*Isonokami sazamegoto*]; also 4:18 [*Shibun yōryō*]). The study of ancient exemplars in poetry and the expressions of *mono no aware* in the *Genji
monogatari* would illuminate the poetry of things and the texture of
feeling they inspired in the everyday encounter with the world.

Nativist strategy disposed writers to search out the real to recover
the tangible, authentic, and corporeal meaning that contemporary language had lost. Motoori, who shared an interest in this question with
others like Kagawa Kageki (1768–1843), framed this quest best in his
discussions of *mono no aware*. *Aware*, the sense of deep feeling, he
wrote, was found in things seen and heard; it came naturally from the
movement of the heart. In the vocalizations of the ancients, the proper
response when one was moved by a flower was to say "aah," or "hare"
when one was moved by the moon. *Aware* combined these expressions

to formulate a coherent response (ibid. 4:201). The great defect of contemporary poetry had been to lose sight of the tangibility of language
and the correspondence between things and words. Any distinction between past and present, he wrote, separated elegance (*miyabi*) from the
common. What contemporaries called poetry amounted only to the
ditties that lower-class women recited; it utilized words that had nothing to do with things capable of stimulating a deep response. Just as
tangibility in contemporary poetic practice had been replaced by orna-
mental and insufferable contrivances, so the idea of archaic elegance
and the simple but concrete expression of honest feelings had also disappeared from sight (ibid. 2:42). If the present sought to return to unadorned and unalloyed sentiment, this vanished ideal might still be
restored. The task before contemporaries, therefore, was to relocate
true feelings—touching things and being touched by them as they
were—in order to rediscover the true vocation of poetry and its capacity
to apprehend the direct encounter with the world of things.

The production of poetry must also correspond to correct intention and the appropriate selection of words. Motoori proposed that correct intention naturally determined the right selection of words, since
they would automatically spring to mind (ibid. 2:178–79). In the arrangement of the poem and in any effort to realize "elegant commonality in intention and word," it was always important to select from
what was common. "It is easy to know words that are used in daily life,
but the commonness of intentionality is difficult to grasp" (ibid. 2:178).
Although Motoori consistently advised using language that was near to
the daily life, revealing once more the identity of song and voice that
was found in common speech, he warned from the early *Ashiwake
obune* through his more mature texts, like *Isonokami sazamegoto*, that
words alone did not necessarily guarantee a true intention. The poem
must present a perfect combination of both. If the poet failed to perceive the "common element [informing the poem], he will succeed
only in repeating words." But "if the actions and deeds of humans are
read first in great depth, it will be possible to grasp the 'common thing'
in detail." Because the ancients' conception of elegance was steeped in
a penetrating understanding of the mundane, the world of common
things linking people together in a shared community of feeling and
emotion, he urged people to study their works. "In reaching elegance
in intention and meaning, one should aim first at knowing the distinction [between mere words and the transmission of intention]" (ibid.
2:179). The "common thing" referred to those aspects of daily life that
could not be understood or those that had been taken for granted as

fragments of shared experience, "those things one sees and hears that touch the heart" (*kokoro ni omoukoto o, miru mono kiku mono ni tsukete*; ibid. 2:99).

Motoori argued that poetry was born from *mono no aware* (ibid.), a conception of "knowing" that represented an enlargement of the field of knowledge and thereby increased the number of people who might participate in it. This expansion had occurred when the criterion for knowing had changed from grasping principle to recognizing "experience" and sensation, a faculty possessed by all humans. Accordingly, the things people could know were common; they "touched the heart." In this scheme, nothing should intervene to separate an expression of profound feeling for a certain thing from the act of understanding the thing that inspired it. Cognition became a moment of recognition, when a person experienced the sensation of having been "touched" or "moved" upon encountering a "thing." Since the exercise of understanding corresponded closely to experiencing a sensation, intuition became the agent of knowing. Yet such a theory inevitably dramatized the essentially nonnormative character of knowledge—its "unrational" properties—and privileged a knowing subject who possessed not refined intellect but human emotionality. Motoori insisted on defining the objects of knowing no further than the feeling and emotionality resulting from the "things one sees and hears." He evoked the lesson of the ancients, who encountered their world and gave expression to their experience from it honestly, naturally, and spontaneously, in order to constitute the experience of the encounter as the content of knowledge. By so redefining the field of knowledge and its population of knowers, he avoided precisely the kind of closure demanded by Neo-Confucianism, which had authorized the acquisition of morality as the condition for dividing knowers from nonknowers, leaders from followers, mental labor from manual. In fact, it was against the inhibiting strictures of received forms of knowing that Motoori had installed a conception of knowledge based on feeling and experience. The ancients, he wrote in the *Shibun yōryō*, possessed gentle and yielding (*sunao*) hearts that permitted them to give expression to conditions as they were, whereas contemporaries imprisoned intention in ornamentation and hypocrisy. Contemporaries faltered when they composed or recited poetry, since they had no way to grasp how the ancients had been moved. Although he recognized that the natural was still missing from daily life, he knew that recitation of ancient poetry opened the way to learning about it.

Inventing the Daily Life

When Motoori affirmed naturalness and flexibility as opposed to limiting and constraining conventions, he struck at the heart of contemporary behavioral codes. His appeals to the authority of the deities—
"all things are the work of the *kami*" (*nanigoto mo mina kami no
shiwaza ni sōrō*) and "the present must obey the laws of the present"
(*ima no yo wa ima no minori kashikomite*)—attested less to an effusive
declaration of satisfaction with the present than to an argument for the
kind of naturalness and flexibility of expression articulated in his poetic
theory. All ages, regardless of place, appeared as the work of the gods.
But to say so was not to offer unqualified approval of the present. It was
to suggest that the present changes and that this changeability, a manifestation of the unlimited divine (obviously a transformation of Ogyū
Sorai's conception of the Way), revealed the endowment of human
nature by the deities. This belief in the continuing role played by the
gods prompted Motoori to leave the object of knowing (*mono, koto*)
indefinite and unspecified, even though it was linked to the world of
common experience. In the *Genji monogatari tama no ogushi*, he
briefly described *mono* as a word possessing wide and different meanings; in its original sense, it denoted the sentient and animate (ibid.
4:202–3). But the properties of *mono* that he hoped to convey related
to circumstances (*suji*) not yet corrupted by artifice, but steadfastly free,
pure, and unaffected by foreign elements. It was impossible to react
honestly to a dishonest situation. If the real was not seen, how could it
be known? This concern led Motoori to advise his contemporaries to
"seek out the facts and deeds that are within the realm of ancient elegance," those circumstances where deep feeling inhered in certain
things (ibid. 2:40). The intention that followed things and the understanding that truly corresponded to antiquity was the "same as antiquity" (ibid. 2:156). The conditions of *mono* that offered the occasion
for a profound response were not limited, as commonly believed, to
"good events" (*yokigoto*). Rather, the circumstances provoking *aware*
were diverse; although the term itself had changed through usage, "its
meaning has remained the same" (*sono imi wa mina onaji koto nite*;
ibid. 2:105). Unspecified and indeterminate, it was the form of feeling
as well as its content, an emotional response when "touched by deeds
that have been done" (*nasu waza ni furite*). As a result, its scope was
vast, ranging from grief to happiness, joy, the strange (*okashidomo*),
and love to sadness, pity, and anger. For Motoori, the ideograph used

to convey "feel," "respond to," and "be conscious of" was *kanzuru;* it was annotated in lexicons as "to move" (*ugokinari*), referring to such things as "sentimentality" (*kanshō*), "deep emotion" (*kangai*), and any-thing else that touched, stimulated, and moved the heart (ibid. 2:100). *Aware* itself simply signalled a vocalization of emotion during moments of intense experience and expressed best the profound movement of the heart (ibid. 2:100–108).[22] Poetry served as the vocally expressive ve-hicle that shaped those "unendurable moments of showing empathy toward a thing" and seeking to transmit it to others.

Moments occasioning a profoundly emotional response were not limited merely to the poet; people resorted to poetry when they wished to express their deepest feelings. Motoori's major studies of the *Genji monogatari* aimed to show that the universe of *mono no aware* con-tained multiple, even infinite, situations that could inspire and move the occupants of this narrative fiction. Yet he was convinced that the *monogatari* could not exist outside the poetic Way; nor could the poetic Way fail to encompass various modes of writing. "Scholars should un-derstand well," he announced, "that deep feeling is the point of the *monogatari*" (ibid. 4:109–10). Only the misguided would fail to note that the subject matter of *aware* encompassed all things, however mun-dane, and combined form and content to satisfy the essential intention of the poetic Way. Anything became uncommon when it struck one's capacity to feel (ibid. 4:202–3). To suggest this was to propose, much in the manner of contemporary writers of verbal fiction (*gesakusha*), that even the common could become uncommon if viewed from a fresh and different perspective, that familiar objects could be appre-hended as the source of intensely personal, emotional experiences. Motoori was arguing for a new look at the things people took for granted and for a way out of familiar, stock responses to the things inhabiting the common world. He was trying to sensitize his contem-poraries to familiar objects from an unfamiliar point of view—the sub-ject, who was in a position to know feeling and emotionality. The result would be to see such objects in a fresh and even unfamiliar light, by an imaginative exercise that entered events and things so that they passed into the emotions of humans. To "fail to grasp the essence of things is to be without sympathy [*nasake*]; it represents a failure [of things] to enter the heart of men of the time" (ibid. 4:198). The narra-tive (*monogatari*), Motoori reasoned, did not instruct people in good or evil, as Buddhist and Confucian writings did, but in both. More important, it illuminated a variety of common experiences in great detail, such as viewing flowers, observing the moon or the passage of the seasons, listening to the cuckoo, and confronting the "suffering" pain resulting from the touch of love (ibid. 4:198–99).[23] Details of daily life, in this instance the lives of Heian aristocrats, disclosed a full knowledge of *mono no aware* in the encounter with the world of things. Yet, it was also a view of daily life removed from the mediations of metaphysics, which corralled people into unnatural, normative grooves of existence and told them what they should see and how they should behave. The lives of men and women in the great narrative vividly illustrated a lesson for the townspeople audiences: the necessity to accept and even valorize the common world of things encountered in daily life and to grasp it from the heart, to see it anew, as something different from what it seemed to be. Motoori was convinced that his own present was one of vulgarity and corruption, mirrored in the persistence of "bad poetry." Poetry became bad when it used the wrong words and conveyed false emotions and feelings. A penetration of the real essence of things permitted a viewing of the familiar with unfamiliar sensibilities; it also assured the production of the correct words for poetic expression, since the feelings conveyed were now natural, honest, and true. Motoori's conception of *mono no aware* elevated the commonality of things and objects so that people would see them in a new and unfamiliar light, in order to induce people to grasp their world for what it was rather than numbly recognizing it. In this respect, his vision converged with the contemporary practice of verbal fiction by the denizens of Edo's play world.

Although Motoori was clearly concerned with apprehending the Heian life of elegance at one level, the example did not need to be limited to an aristocracy lost to history. Contemporary writers of verbal fiction constantly employed the idea of aristocrats in history to exemplify the importance of things and deeds governing people's lives in the present. Motoori was no exception. To be sure, his use of Heian courtiers who had aestheticized their daily lives into works of art imposed restrictions on the applicability of the conception of *mono no aware*. But the constraints were not necessarily restricted to certain social classes. If, as he plainly acknowledged, the conditions of life changed from past to present, it was still true that the quality of "knowing the heart of things" and the expression of honest and natural emotion remained constant throughout the ages. The persistence of this quality always linked present to past in commonality and permitted contemporaries to "enter the realm of elegance." When speaking about passion, he advised, there was "past and present," "distance and nearness," which constituted change, but men everywhere also knew that the "feelings changed ever so slightly." Even the memory of the simplicity that distinguished ancients from contemporaries seemed to have disappeared in later times. The ancients were simple and never untrue, while later ages were known for "flowery writing" and much "deception" (*MNz* [new] 2:32 [*Ashiwake obune*], 4:97, 103 [*Shibun yōryō*]).[24] A quick survey of contemporary poems, he observed, showed that seven or eight poems in ten were devoid of feeling. Contemporaries merely borrowed elegant words from antiquity, in order to sing about the emotions of the present and simulate feelings inaccessible to them. The example of Heian courtiers derived from history and related to a whole society, not just a few talented individuals. More importantly, the *Genji monogatari* illustrated how a society of men and women was held together by a common world of things that stimulated them to make honest and sensitive responses in their lives, as if they were living in song and poetry. Antiquity also showed that all people recited song to express their encounter with all kinds of things (ibid. 2:27, 4:101–2 [*Shibun yōryō*]).[25] The observation led Motoori to conclude that contemporaries were rarely touched or moved by things, that they approached the world anaesthetized to its texture and sentience; when they insisted on producing what they called poetry and song, it was both "laughable" and "regrettable." Once more, he noted, representation was substituted for a represented, and the manipulation of archaic poetic form was made to appear prior to authentic experience.

Far from limiting sensibility and feeling to a class of courtiers, Motoori argued, long before he trained his sights on writing *Genji* criticism, that the "mastery" of poetic recitation could not be confined to skilled specialists serving up entertainment. Poetry served larger social interests by "calming the heart and ending distracting ideas" (ibid. 2:34). The effort to "straighten the self" meant learning the customs of society and required "associations with men" (*hito no tsukiai*) and "interaction in society" (*yo no majiwari*), which prepared people to govern their intentions. This sense of commonality, displayed by court society in the *Genji monogatari*, was the condition for learning ancient simplicity and elegance and for acquiring knowledge about the "gentle" (*sunao*) heart of archaic times. "Since there was no falseness and ornamentation then, the poetry was not produced in great quantity; people at that time recited/composed things as they were, things felt deeply from the standpoint of the body [personal perspective]. Therefore, songs were reality" (ibid. 2:43, 4:109).[26] All, regardless of social status, possessed the capacity to give expression to the world of things as they encountered it. Hence, there were songs for the emperor, the nobility, and the peasantry, which rose from different perspectives but were, nevertheless, informed by a "single intention."

For Motoori, Heian life was not really remote from his own times; nor was his assessment of it far from Hirata Atsutane's later effort to associate *mono* and *koto* with the daily lives of quite ordinary people. Motoori was concerned with showing the meaning of the most ordinary—and often seemingly trivial—responses of humans in their everyday situations. In his essays on the *Genji monogatari*, he demonstrated tirelessly how even the most mundane objects, such as clothes, could move a character in the narrative to express deep feeling (ibid. 4:38–110). What people did in their everyday life, Motoori seemed to propose, was far more important as an example of honest emotion than any instruction on proper or improper conduct. "The [Confucians and Buddhists] considered the passions of humans as bad conduct. Yet, there are many instances in which the passions are good" (ibid. 4:37). Nothing human could be outside the penumbra of *mono no aware*, and nothing should be beyond the natural human propensity to know, feel, and understand. "The man who follows human passion knows deep feeling for things" (ibid. 4:41).

Despite the possible range of deep feeling, the most important instances were those moments when humans sought to perform something good or beneficial for the sake of others. This sentiment attested once more to his conception of commonality and sociality, to his image of a world of things holding people together in society. In the *Genji monogatari*, he wrote, there was usually an identification between "good deeds" and the person possessing heart (ibid. 4:92, 93). The goodness or badness of an intention really depended on the quality of the deed itself. "Viewing a deed as good," he noted, "one is moved by it and, thus, comes to know a deep feeling for things" (ibid. 4:92). The term *nasake*, which referred to reaching others and performing good deeds for them, was very much related to "knowing the heart of things and the heart of events." Feeling stimulated by things or events could be applied along a wide front. The exercise of *nasake* implied a quality existing between people; the transaction between a thing or event and its power to move a respondent, as in the case of a beautiful scape or even a sorrowful moment, could easily be transformed into a relationship between people. "When one looks at an elegant cherry blossom in full bloom and knows its essence, then one understands why it is called a beautiful flower. Therefore, one feels that it is beautiful and this is what is called empathy. But, if one looks at a beautiful flower and does not believe it to be so, then [one] does not know the heart of the object" (ibid. 4:57).[27] Motoori had expressed this sentiment earlier, when he distinguished between those, like many of his contemporaries, who did not feel and who, therefore, failed to produce genuine song and poetry. "Such people," he argued in the *Shibun yōryō*, "feel no beauty and lack the capacity for empathy. . . . Moreover, when encountering the heavy grief of a man and observing his great sorrow, we must understand this sadness. It is for this reason that one knows that the event must be sorrowful. The person knows the heart of the event" (ibid. 4:57). To know the heart of such a sorrowful event, he continued, was to become naturally sorrowful; the person affected by another's grief incorporated it into his own heart and was moved by it. "When a person knows that something must be grieved for, even though he does not wish to be moved, he possesses a heart that will be drawn into it naturally. It is in this manner that there must be common feeling [*kyōkan*] and human passion" (ibid.). But, Motoori warned, the person who failed to demonstrate understanding risked losing all human contact and diminished the possibility of a sense of community. "Because a person cannot understand the heart of the event that must be grieved for, how can he see or listen to the grief of others?" Such people were not to be trusted even slightly to enter another's intentions, because they themselves had no heart capable of feeling or being moved (ibid.).

At this juncture, Motoori enlarged an earlier argument about the status of contemporary poets and the lack of honesty and feeling in their songs. He used the example of Heian society to draw attention to what constituted society—"association" rather than its absence. The archetype for his conception of an "empathic community" remained language and the way the ancients had employed it. Just as the ancients required only a small vocabulary to communicate things and deeds, in Motoori's revised conception of community, the possession of feeling—empathy—distinguished those who knew how to get to the heart of things from those who could not. The same principle of simplicity and deep feeling that informed the model of archaic society governed later examples of community. Its disappearance, which he noted in the present, meant the vanishing of community itself.

Motoori considered trust—mutual participation—as the guaranteeing condition for binding people together in common purpose and for banishing conflict (*arasoi*). Despite changes in time, it was still the heart that was capable of receiving feeling and being moved by others that qualified to be trusted to others. The reverse of this formula was also true. Confucianism and Buddhism believed that people could not be moved by evil, but the *Genji monogatari* discounted their view by its reliance on something he called "natural movement" (ibid. 4:57–58). In spite of the existence of good and evil, a person who possessed a feeling heart could not help but be swayed by events and deeds, regardless of their character, because he would know them in their essential aspect. It is worth repeating that Motoori's sense of reaching out to express deep feelings for things and events, to move or be moved by others, meant an involvement in the details of contemporary daily life, whether it was in Heian times or in eighteenth-century Edo. Involvement, *nasake*, meant corresponding to the times and understanding them as they were. A lack of involvement risked misunderstanding and forfeited the real and the appropriate for whimsy and untruths.

Motoori directed nativist discourse to the problem of knowing; he developed both a new subject and a new object of knowledge. The details of daily experience at any given historical moment now defined the content of knowledge, whose essence could be reached by the exercise of the cognitive mode called *mono no aware*. He enjoined his contemporaries to retrieve the archaic example, which grounded the object of knowledge in the details of everyday life that were presented immediately to consciousness. The people Motoori spoke about in his analysis of the *Genji monogatari* were an aristocratic elite. Yet behind them were "all the people of antiquity who recited songs about different things." The importance of these examples, apart from their homologous relationship to the urban rich constituting his audience (aristocratic in style, ordinary socially), lies in his conviction that the possession of "ancient elegance" and "knowing *mono no aware*" never depended on the prior acquisition of social power. In Motoori's scheme, different sets of criteria empowered different people, even though he kept unspecified the object of knowledge—the content of immediate experience. Knowers emerged as rather passive receivers of messages who, as exemplified in the *Genji monogatari*, were moved more often to tearful explosions or expressions of joy than to action. This view might well have accorded with Motoori's audience and explained to them, a politically impotent urban bourgeoisie (who could easily identify stylistically with an equally impotent aristocracy), that real power, the power to know things in their essence, belonged to them. But to say this is to suggest that he placed far more emphasis on the object of knowledge, the *mono* and *koto*, than on the knowing subject. His knowers, the tenants of the *Genji monogatari*, frequently appeared as passive subjects waiting to be moved by the next sensation rather than as acting agents capable of stimulating or doing and moving on their own. Conceivably, Motoori was trying to relieve action of unnatural constraints. Even so, he was still able to recognize the possibility of change over time and the inevitable encounter with different circumstances. This recognition, coupled with his constant denunciation of stylization—best brought out in his condemnation of those who "imitate ancient words"—suggests the possibility of seeing varying responses at different times in history. All he hoped to communicate in his examination of Genji's world was an example of elegance in conduct. He announced early in his critical texts that the narrative's major point was knowledge about the condition of society and an understanding of human circumstances. Throughout, the narrative showed a complete mastery of *mono no aware*, "knowing the heart of things." Yet knowing the heart of things meant "knowing the conditions of society," which derived from "knowing well the emotions of humans" (ibid. 4:18, 184). When he contrasted the narrative's perspective to a contemporary one, he was able to show how the text provided a corrective knowledge of human conditions and examples of deep emotionality. A "reading" of the narrative secured "the deeds of antiquity for us in the present," and comparison led to "sympathizing with the deep feeling for things among the ancients" (ibid. 4:186). Motoori acknowledged the importance of replicating elegance in deeds (*waza*) and, hence, affirmed the primacy of real-life conditions. But he did not go so far as to believe that the specific example of the Heian courtier was applicable to the world of his own times. There is no evidence to suggest that he was driven by an uncontrollably romantic impulse to cloak himself and his contemporaries in the garments of a vanished historical past. Unlike the characters of the narrative, people who lived in his day could not be expected to spend time draping themselves in beautiful and glossy vestments that spread out elegantly, riding in ox carts, and indulging in extravagant love affairs too complex to keep straight. Contemporaries could know through effort, however, the "profound feeling for things known by the ancients."

Motoori's defense of the daily life, whether in Heian times or in the present, identified the experience of commoners with elegance; the

emotional life of the inhabitants of the world of Genji offered a sanctuary to Tokugawa townspeople. In *Ashiwake obune* he argued that "the
Way makes elegance [*fuga*] its fundamental principle. It always stems
from the heart, and all deportment [*furumai*] must be prompted by
gracefulness. Despising the vulgar, the busy, and the restless, men
should always direct behavior to reflect the content of true song. Regardless of the person, all must make harmony their goal, easiness and
gentility their good. Those who are exhausted by poetry and who have
an air for principle and argumentation generate conflict [*arasoi*]" (ibid.
2:13). To have any meaning, contemporary life must correspond
to antiquity. Yet it is worth emphasizing that Motoori's conception
stopped short of a literal-minded definition of following "the elegance"
of the ancients; it proffered a flexible, metaphorical formulation that
was more realistic than romantic. Constantly emphasizing the immediate, the sentient, and the tangible, he was easily able to relate his
examples to the social life-world of his time and place. In *Isonokami
sazamegoto* he advised people to read the ancient anthologies and the
various narratives day and night to secure a sense of the texts' intent,
because he was confident that they could learn to recite things as they
were by immersing their own intentions in the "conditions of antiquity." If, moreover, they succeeded in changing the "polluted and despicable intentions of the present," transforming them into the intention of ancient elegance, then the study of antiquity would truly yield
results, even though in the beginning contemporaries had "imitated
deceitful things."

It would be wrong to conclude that Motoori was simply exacting
passive submissiveness from contemporary townspeople by turning
their attention toward aesthetics and sensibility rather than political
power. This might well be an interpretation of his explorations into the
world of Genji.[28] But, as I suggested above, his interest was prompted
as much by the search for concrete examples of people's responses to
the world of things on a day-to-day basis as it was inspired by the aim
of depoliticizing contemporaries. As Motoori shifted the discussion to
things and the response to them by valorizing deep feeling as the connecting link between people and things, he also saw the exercise of
mono no aware in serving political interests. Throughout the *Ashiwake
obune* he underscored the question of politics and its relationship to
song and poetry. Although he, like Kamo no Mabuchi before him,
eschewed the idea of poetry as an aid to ruling the ruled, he did acknowledge that song and poetry could be separated in such a way as to

differentiate between its "essence" (*hontai*) and the uses it might serve. Even though the substance of poetry was never political, since its purpose is to relate things that have been touched, it was possible to use songs that have already been composed to assist the "political way" (MNz [new] 2:49). In this formulation, he proposed that "men who are at the top" could use poems and songs in order to understand how people had been touched and moved by things, "to clearly know the feelings of the lower orders." Moreover, if leaders were serious, they were obliged to examine the attitudes of the people and understand them in detail; then they would look for songs and poems as records of things and deeds that were instrumental in daily life. They would use song to make something, as one might use a piece of wood (ibid. 2:50). This argument was later expanded to show how ruling derived from the "august intentions of the deities" (ibid. 2:166). Humans and deities, Motoori believed, were united by their mutual capacity to feel deeply for things (*aware*) and to be moved by them. "Its [feeling's] virtues are broad and manifold." But, he continued, everything one encountered within heaven and earth, whether good or bad, derived from the work of the *kami*. Whenever misfortunes strike high and low alike, if people from each estate offer supplication to the rough deity (*araburu kami*), they would naturally be delivered from their difficulties because virtue requires the *kami* to feel deeply and be moved. Since songs also move people to feeling, they would find consolation anew in the intention of the deities. When speaking about the virtues that moved humans to deep feeling, "men who tranquilize the people and govern the realm [*tami o osame kuni o matsurigochi*] must first clarify in detail the essentials of human intentions in society" (ibid. 2:166–67). If the leadership did not know deep feeling for things, then it would fail altogether to understand in any detail the heart of things informing the conditions of the lower classes. In this way, the exercise of *mono no aware* obliged those charged with ruling to make an effort to learn the conditions of society. Motoori was not simply talking about gathering useful information, as Ogyū Sorai had, but, rather, about transforming rulership into acts of feeling and empathy. If men who had energy did not understand the things on which "the body floats"—that is, social conditions—their capacity to express compassion in all things would be meager, indeed; they would be prevented from feeling deeply and "calculating" the many things that ordinarily touched the "despised" and the "poor." In short, the real function of *mono no aware* was to know and grasp the things that affected people in one way or another. Still, he added, the exercise of such understanding should not be restricted to the leadership, because it involved "the ordinary associations of society." Its absence threatened to throw society into irreversible disarray, where the wealthy would not understand the intentions of the poor, the young would fail to know the old, men would misunderstand women, and even children would never learn about their obligations to their parents. Motoori envisaged a political community held together by a mutual expression—among rulers and ruled and, indeed, throughout the whole division of labor—of the capacity to understand, sympathize, and be moved. Even though such a society was equally remote from both his present and the past, it nonetheless constituted a powerful ideal when juxtaposed to contemporary political arrangements. Although Motoori may very well have been concerned to provide the Tokugawa system with supplemental assistance in the interests of preserving order, his conception of order differed vastly from the one he apparently wished to support because it imagined an entirely new kind of community. For to recall the ancient exemplars of elegance meant not affectation or slavish imitation—or even "pseudo-classicism"—but the power to see and feel, to connect with others. Despite living in the "present," he offered his contemporaries the prospect of living "anciently."

Motoori's theory of *mono no aware* made possible a new kind of knowledge of things and produced a new conception of power among those who came to "know and feel deeply for" the power of daily life. It contrasted strongly with the prevailing emphasis on norms and constraints, which prescribed forms of conduct; seeing the world of things anew and grasping the familiar in an unfamiliar light provided a genuine release from the limiting and restricting codes of Confucian morality. It also seemed to suggest that official morality was somehow incomplete and insufficient to guide people in their everyday affairs and that it required a crucial supplement to preserve its authority. Yet the very impulse to add something to make up for what many acknowledged was missing conceded that serious contradictions between ideology and life had escaped containment. When he proposed that people should conform to the times, he was not so much offering a program enlisting recruits to lead quietly unpolitical lives far from considerations of power, as recognizing that unnatural constraints had forced humans to behave unnaturally. The celebration of ancient elegance meant reinstalling in contemporary life a human basis for community and association, which required neither norms nor institutions.

By addressing his message to an audience of townspeople, homologized with Heian courtiers, he provided epistemological justification for the constitution of a new kind of political subject and an adequate form of representation of its world and interests. The acknowledgement that townspeople possessed knowledge was an elaboration of the earlier seventeenth-century effort of *bushi* to explain the inevitability of their ascendancy as a ruling class because of their monopoly of virtuous knowledge. Motoori's designation of Edo townspeople as knowers of things and as masters of the quotidian experience summoned the echoes of earlier samurai, who sanctioned their right to rule by recasting themselves into sage-bureaucrats who *knew* morality.

Motoori believed he had resolved the division between language and experience by identifying things and their meaning with words, by positioning content over form, and by sublating the disparity between correct perception (*mono no aware*) and practice. It was not the form of poetic convention that determined content, but the content of genuine experience—things—that ultimately produced form. Such an arrangement was secured by identifying the sign (word) for a thing with its meaning (hermeneutics). Motoori linked the way of seeing a thing—"knowing" (*shiruwakimae*)—with the thing itself (*mono*); form was perception, but it embodied what could be seen. Thus, he brought form and content into a perfect harmony. Yet the operation implied, especially in contrast to contemporary poetry, not—as many scholars have accepted—the prospect of a stable and secure culture but one that had rigidified and lost touch with experience. Hence, Motoori's affirmation of poetic form as the adequate representation of genuine sentiment transformed frames that had supported a culture that was hierarchical and philosophically closed to those that supported its opposite, 'secular,' horizontal, open.

3 Archaism II: The Discourse on Origins

A number of interpreters have argued that Hirata Atsutane (1776–1843) turned away from the aestheticism of Motoori and his successors for a concentration on the ancient Way, from a concern for the sentient texture of things for the active intervention of the gods in quotidian life, from art and literature to natural religion. To accept this argument requires misrecognizing the immense interest Motoori showed for the question of the archaic—his effort to identify ancient exemplars with elegance and his valorization of the common world of things. Motoori and his followers continued to be concerned with illuminating the "ancient Way" and its timely message for contemporaries in the late-Tokugawa period. They differed from Hirata in their insistence that archaism meant elegance and supremacy in song and poetry, which expressed the world of things and the appropriate response to it. Hirata simply changed the content of archaism to conform to new narrative requirements and proposed an identity between things and the details of daily life. Contrasted with Motoori, Hirata privileged form over content or, at least, decided to employ cosmological narrative as a form that would permit a different discussion of objects and the introduction of new ones for discourse. The choice of narrative over poetry did not necessarily mean that Hirata was less interested in things than in deities or that Motoori neglected the importance of the deities for a valorization of things. Narrative figured a different way of relating things to one another, and the possibility of organizing content in order to talk about what could not be said in poetry. Narrative, for Hirata, was constructed on the archetypal act of the creation of the cosmos by the deities, with its claim to the connectedness and kinship of all things because of their common creation and the subsequent act to reproduce the conditions of the productive moment in worship and work, a ceaseless and ongoing practice. By this move, Hirata changed the content of archaism from the experience of elegance to subjects reproducing the conditions of existence as bestowed by the creation deities. But his privileging of form over content uncoupled the uneasy superimposition of semiosis on hermeneutics found in Motoori's intervention. For Hirata, meaning, as exemplified in the implementation of a great cosmic narrative, was more important than the signs—words—used to denote things. The promise of narrative endowed the jumble of words and things with both the proper order, as seen in his rearranging of ancient histories, and the appropriate meaning. This choice and Hirata's very considerable polemical and rhetorical skills made it appear that members of the Suzunoya had abandoned the ancient Way for the private pleasures of poetry and art, instead of apprehending the true tradition of antiquity as the Way of the gods. But Motoori and many of his followers were no less implicated in promoting the "Way of the gods."

Hirata early agreed with Motoori that poetry taught humans how to empathize with the intention behind things, as they encountered the world. His own text *Kadō taii* (1811) faithfully rehearsed the familiar arguments Motoori had already expressed in the *Ashiwake obune*, *Isonokami sazamegoto*, and the *Uiyamabumi*. Even here, however, Hirata displayed a fundamental distrust of poetry and privileged the *Kojiki* over the *Man'yōshū* as the principal source for antique intent and meaning. For all his apparent reverence for Motoori, we can note an uneasiness in his thinking concerning the status of things and content, a restless exploration of new relationships between things and even new objects for discourse as he tried to remain safely within disciplinary boundaries. The apparent shift noted by so many writers was made by enforcing a critical distance between himself and the successors to the Motoori line, Haruniwa and Ōhira, who gave substance to the shift by calling attention to Hirata's unorthodox scholarship. But Hirata also helped stoke the embers of controversy. Apart from his generally contentious and argumentative style, by the 1820s he had leveled critical charges against a number of Motoori's direct disciples.[1] The most evident target was Hattori Nakatsune (1756–1828), whose cosmological speculations (*Sandaikō*) provided the occasion for Hirata to compose what became his most celebrated text, the *Tama no miha-shira*. The "break" marked by this text (which was no break at all, but simply a manifestation of internal contestation) consisted of a shift in the choice of form. Whereas Motoori had privileged an examination of the tangible meaning of words in order to understand things as they were, Hirata employed a similar tactic to show that the meaning of things had already been specified by the deities. Motoori had not been indifferent to the religious intervention and the "ancient Way"; the link he established ran from the deities and the creation of things to their apprehension in poetic language. Hirata departed from this model by abandoning not the world of deities and things but, rather, poetic language as a mediation for understanding "true meaning." In place of poetic form, he proposed the installation of a vast cosmological narrative to tell the story of divine intervention and human intentionality.

Hirata's choice of figuration was of immense consequence. Motoori's poetics resulted in deifying humans by endowing them with the power of a divine language; Hirata's narrative ended in humanizing the divine by making the archetypal event of creation the necessity of human reproduction, practice, worship, and work. Unlike Motoori, who rewrote the *Kojiki* without tampering with its form, Hirata's narrative imagined a new form of historical consciousness that was neither "rationalistic" nor "evolutionary." Such a "history" promised to explain, represent, and even ideologize disparate and chaotic histories into an unbroken web of kinships. Implicit in this "history"—which Hirata called *koshi*, "ancient history," or *koden*, "ancient transmissions"—was the dissolution of past and present into a continuing process of production and reproduction representing the human repayment of the blessings of the deities. Its function was to satisfy the impulse to determine the mysterious spirit or essence informing national existence; at the same time it sought to apprehend things in their individuality and their formal coherence, in order to define as specifically historical the description of particular things. In Hirata's cosmic narrative—the "prose of the world"[2]—this impulse led not only to a spiritualized history but also to a historicized spirituality in its concern for local custom, the content of unique and particular experience, and the special texture of life as it restored in continuous acts of reproduction the archetypal production of the "national soil" (*kunitsuchi*). It was in the body, the folk, and the race that Hirata and his followers were able to bring these two functions of "history" together.

It is difficult to know why Hirata made the decision to abandon poetics—and its promise to illuminate proper perception—for narrative. He recognized that such a move required privileging form over content and forced him to argue against Motoori's efforts to elide the distinction between experience and expression. On the one hand, his construction of a cosmic narrative announcing the kinship of all things represented an expansion of Motoori's earlier efforts to harmonize poetry and experience and to dramatize his hope for a stable and secure culture as a solution to the coded fragmentation of life. On the other hand, it meant discounting the master's own preference for poetry over history and speaking over writing. These crossed purposes disclose a contradiction at the heart of Hirata's thinking which raises questions regarding the relationship between "context" and "text." The contemporary "history" denoted by his call to wholeness and coherence, the "referent" of his texts, signified a discursive field—intertext—that attested to the existence of fragmentation and the absence of cultural unity. "History" should not be seen as external to Hirata's discussions, functioning as the "real" that explained their condition; it must be viewed as an effect of the system of textual production. In it, the apparent signifieds associated with nativist texts were generated not by an external history—the real—but by the specific processes governing the practice of signification in the eighteenth century. Because textual production was based on a set of intertextual relations rather than an extra-textual real, the practice of reading, as nativists showed, aimed at demonstrating that "the necessity of absence"—the "relation between the 'seen' and the 'unseen'"—set the limits of their problematic. We must assume that these nativist texts remained necessarily silent on what they could not say, a studied silence or "an *otherness* through which they sought to maintain a relationship with what they were not," what, according to Pierre Macherey, occurs on the margins. By the time Hirata offered his "histories" in the 1820s, the power of narrative to transform fragmentation into a secure and stable culture was even greater than poetry, which had become a sign of the "history" that textual practice was now trying to overcome.

Although Hirata's intervention sought to supplement the received social arrangements and thereby called attention to a necessary absence, it paid a price for this "solution" by opening the way for radical transformation. His and subsequent efforts to reaffirm a prevailing ideology and resolve or, at the very least, close its contradictions became an ideological critique for groups seeking representation, order, and definition to problems often unperceived by the regime.

Hirata's decision to leave poetry for different modes has been explained as a manifestation of an intramural political controversy with

the successors to the Motoori school, notably Motoori Ōhira (1755–
1833), who had been designated as the standard-bearer of poetic studies
and with whom Hirata briefly had studied. In book 9 of the *Tamadasuki*,
where Hirata sought to construct a genealogy for *kokugaku* in order to
place himself within the correct tradition, he generously acknowledged
his great debt to Motoori and his adopted son Ōhira, the head of the
Suzunoya (*HAz* [rev] 6:513–29, 540). Hirata stated that he had tried
to continue the great work of Motoori and his successors. But it is
important to balance his effusive expression of self-service with the fact
that Hirata had fallen out with many of his contemporaries in Edo.
The specific occasion for his difficulties with members of the Suzunoya
was his criticism of their emphasis on poetic studies and ancient elegance to the exclusion of what he believed to be more urgent priorities. These priorities consisted of reviving the "ancient Way" in such
a way as to suggest that the followers of Motoori had, in fact, abandoned it. Unintentionally, his exaggerated claims prompted Ōhira to
write the *Kogakuyō* (Essentials of ancient studies, 1809) to counter
Hirata's charges and provide a coherent defense of the Suzunoya.
Hirata's critique, which joined a swelling chorus of criticism against
the Motoori school, concentrated on showing how the poetic mode
itself had become rigid, removed from the naturalness and honesty that
the master had taught and separated from the circumstances of contemporary experience. Others, like Ōkuma Kotomichi (1798–1868), denounced the Suzunoya's commitment to theories of restorationism as
unreal and its effort to assimilate the past to the present as inappropriate, because it appeared "imitative," "like looking at the Kabuki."[3]
Still, most of Motoori's contemporary critics, such as Murata Harumi
(1764–1811), Kagawa Kageki, and Ōkuma, did not contest the primacy of poetry per se but rather its putative power to transform the
present into antiquity in order to know things the way they were in the
present. Such an approach inspired a neglect for the way things really
were, Ōkuma wrote, and for "forgetting . . . our own bodies."[4] Only
Hirata, among Edo contemporaries, went so far as to recommend
abandoning poetic studies altogether, in order to return to the "forgotten body."

    By the time Hirata established his own school in Edo, the Ibu-
kiya, the central concern among nativists and "fellow travelers" was
how best to examine poetry and learn proper poetic composition. Some
writers have ascribed this narrow focusing of discourse to the presence
of large numbers of city dwellers who appropriated *kokugaku* and trans-

formed it into a "nativism of idlers [*yūmin*], hermits, and literateurs."[5]
Many of these poetically minded *kokugakusha* were indistinguishable
from *bunjin*: literateurs who, upholding an amateur ideal and growing
increasingly uneasy because of Edo's burgeoning class of idlers, turned
to poetry and fled the city for the countryside, where they pursued their
dreams of antiquity in wine and song.[6] Contemporary opinion against
the Suzunoya drew attention to how its adherents had, in fact, contributed to the degeneration of the founder's teachings and learning. Mikuni Izumi (?–1805), a loyal follower of Norinaga, complained that,
although it had been his intention to "make his life's work the study of
antiquity and the learning of the Suzunoya as it had expanded eastward
[to Edo]," he had experienced disappointment from the beginning because he encountered only members possessing "thin learning," who
were "incompetent" or in "frail health." Nothing more than an embar-
rassing intention to study antiquity prevailed.[7] Some, like Hattori Nakatsune, who were direct students of Motoori, observed that among the
approximately five hundred students of Motoori, most were inordinately disposed to a fondness for elegance. Students had been recruited
from several provinces, but not one had followed the meaning of the
teacher and his principal vocation, the study of antiquity. They had
given up trying to extract the meaning of the "august histories of the
godly age" and had usually gone no further than examining Motoori's
commentary of the *Kojiki*, rather than the text itself.[8] Some were even
convinced that Motoori's great gift to his times was simply the inaugu-
ration of the study of ancient texts regarding poetic learning to secure
a knowledge of their circumstances. Worse still, although many privately held to the teacher's views, they criticized them publicly. Generally, people like Mikuni acknowledged that the followers of the Suzunoya had not been able to meet the high standards of learning that
Motoori had reached during his lifetime. Most scholars seemed to play
it very cautiously and let things stand as they were. "They have looked
broadly at the texts," Mikuni remarked, "read the poetry well, and take
pride in their capacity to write skillfully. They are the great men of the
times. But in recent days, we can see many who have no knowledge
concerning the circumstances of learning the Way. There have been
few who have broken real ground. We have to remember to revere men
who placed intention in the service of truth."[9]

Even persons in literary groups associated with poetic activity in
Edo were critical of Motoori's valorization of song as a key to ancient
elegance and the hardened position of the school after the founder's

death. Murata Harumi, a former student of Kamo no Mabuchi who was also counted as one of the eighteen "players" (*tsūjin*) in the city, debated this point with Mikuni, as recorded in *Meidōsho*. Harumi discounted Motoori's formulations on the Way as uninformed and unknowledgeable.[10] Specifically, the issue derived from Motoori's claim that the Way, as conceived by the Chinese, did not exist in Japan (*Kus*, 150). According to Harumi, this Way was not the creation of men (an apparent attack on the Sorai school) or the imagined entity nativists referred to as the Way of the gods. "The Way," he announced, "is in nature, heaven and earth" (ibid.). Nativists had mistakenly interpreted Shinto for the Way of the gods, rather than seeing it as a mere sign of respect for certain sacred rituals and observances (ibid., 154). Indeed, it could never have been said that the *kami* Way governed the times (*yo no matsurigochi*) and tranquilized human conduct. The observance of sacred rituals corresponded to the way of the sages, and failure to take this into account had resulted in explanations that distorted facts and twisted meaning. When Harumi and others discredited the Suzunoya's conception of the Way, they discounted its privileging of certain texts and especially the function it had so confidently assigned to the "recitation of song." Even though Hirata had serious differences with Harumi, he shared this estimate, which rejected the identification of poetry and song with learning about the Way.

Responding to Harumi's critique, Mikuni offered a defense of Motoori's meditations on the Way by recalling the example of Kamo no Mabuchi and his celebration of poetic study, especially of the *Man'yōshū*. Even though Kamo had recognized that the ancients did not specifically discuss the Way of the imperial deities as their Way, he was convinced that, "to know this Way of the imperial deities, than which none is greater, depends first on learning the songs and poems in the ancient style. If introduced [in this manner], reciting songs and explaining the ancient words, then one will gain entry naturally into what is called the Way of antiquity" (ibid., 217). In these circumstances, there was no need for explicit reference to the Way. Motoori, he continued, saw the ancient Way of Japan (*sumera ōmikuni*) as the Way of the imperial deities and as "real and fundamental." Hence, to recite song and explain the ancient words was the only means available to reach this Way. Mikuni sought to show that Motoori only considered the "recitation of song" and "explanation of poems" as a method (*matsu*)—the parts and principles that would reveal the whole meaning (ibid.).[11] By following this method, he was able to elaborate a doctrine free from all impurities.

Hirata's response to this controversy is instructive since he was willing to risk losing his friendships with Murata and Mikuni by discounting their respective positions equally. His observations disclosed (as he tried so often to dramatize for his students at the Ibukiya) that his conception of the Way and his knowledge of it differed vastly from the established discussions among nativists concerning the function of song and poetic composition. In book 9 of the *Tamadasuki*, he described many of Motoori's Edo pupils as immature because, even though they had received the "august intention" of the great teacher, none had been able to apply it. Among those with a taste for discussing the superiority of composing songs and poetry to the exclusion of all other considerations, Murata Harumi stood out as the most important; he was particularly blameworthy because he had received instruction in poetics since childhood. A few years before, Hirata noted, Murata had become embroiled in a controversy with Mikuni Izumi. According to Hirata, the debate merely echoed the early nativist preoccupation with poetics. The great master Kamo no Mabuchi had established song and poetry as a primary method for studying antiquity, and the tradition was continued by Motoori and his successors. Yet both had erred, Hirata declared, because they had emphasized poetics when discussing the ancient Way, instead of the godly age. The later debate between Murata and Mikuni had no substance to it and simply recuperated this error. Hirata particularly condemned Murata for having advanced a "foolish" argument, presumably because he was further away from the Motoori school than Mikuni, who had become its standard-bearer. He denounced Mikuni's "ungentle behavior" for having provoked the debate in the first place. But the real point to recording this episode was to show his own students the irrelevance of poetry to an understanding of the ancients. In his effort to constitute a subject position for discourse, Hirata sought tirelessly—as we shall see later—to demonstrate that knowing the ancient Way differed from scholarly concentration on the niceties of poetry and poetic composition.

It was Ōhira, the nominal head of the Motoori school, who offered the surest defense against charges that the founder's teaching had degenerated into subjectivism practiced by idlers and that it had become less concerned with the ends than the means to reach it. In the *Kogakuyō* Ōhira tried to explain that, since the late eighteenth century, nativists had been locked in a discussion aimed at discounting the "ancient studies" promoted by Confucianists and Buddhists and that, until then, no one had really called attention to their claims. By his day, "ancient studies" had become commonly associated with the appeal to reason (*dōri*). For this reason, it was necessary to expose the "evils" of Confucianism and Buddhism in order to illuminate the true Way, which, he believed, had never really been known by people in all levels of society. The real point of his reference to Buddhism and Confucianism was to show his critics why an emphasis on song and poetry was the most appropriate method for grasping the true Way. Writing, which he identified with administrative ordinances, had become the vocation (*shokugyō koto*) of Confucianists, who associated it with learning itself. By contrast, the ancient ordinances had originally been prayers bestowed by the deities; they needed to be heard, not written. Discussions of learning invariably recalled Chinese things and scholarship, not learning the Way of antiquity and the ancient words (*MNz* [old] 6:535).[12] An interesting gloss, provided by Ōhira's successor, Motoori Uchitowa (1792–1855), advanced the idea that, during the time of Japan's most distant antiquity, there was simply no learning that corresponded to scholarship and the discipline contemporaries called ancient studies did not exist as a practice. In this manner Uchitowa sought to contest the Confucian conceit that had identified learning with Confucianism, "spuriously" making it appear as a tradition that originated in the age of the gods. But according to the preface to the *Kojiki*, intelligence concerning antiquity was "basic doctrine" that could be understood by pursuing "ancient studies and the ancient intention" (ibid.). Ōhira continued: "Although there were not ancient studies until antiquity [*nakamukashi*], the recitation of song is the Way that has been transmitted since the age of the gods. In the Way of poetry, there are the traces of our antiquity. To be skilled in reciting the poetry from antiquity is to know how to study its circumstances. We should rejoice in the good fortune of having a poetics . . . which has conveyed the study of antiquity and the meaning of words as well." (ibid.). Since this practice had existed for ages, it explained the reason why there must be rejoicing and esteem for the Way of studying song and poetry.

If learning—*gakumon*—was Confucian writing on administrative affairs or Buddhist metaphysics, then it was true that Japan possessed no learning in antiquity. Ancient studies sought only to recuperate the "basic doctrine" found in songs and ancient words, which were transcribed back into the discourse of contemporary life. Like Norinaga, Ōhira proposed that the essence of learning had nothing to do with ruling or not ruling (ibid. 6:540). Rather, learning spanned past and present, China and Japan; like the healing arts, it must be of value to humans. At the same time that Ōhira sought to save what he considered the true tradition transmitted by Norinaga and to vouchsafe the "poetic Way," he also tried to meet his critics by rescuing a distinction between elegance in composing poems or reading texts and the practical necessities of quotidian life. The true Way of the ancients could be discovered only in three texts—*Man'yōshū, Kojiki,* and *Nihonshoki;* he rarely, if ever, mentioned the importance of the "narratives" like *Genji* or *Ise monogatari.* His silence, supported by his preference for equating antiquity with the production of songs, contrasted sharply with Norinaga's recommendations "to the followers of the ancient Way" to look at narratives, even though he rejected the possibility of replicating their form in the present. Ōhira dismissed the narratives for an examination of the *Man'yōshū* largely because he believed they were unconnected to any understanding of the "true meaning" of antiquity. He selected a hundred poems from the *Man'yōshū* (*Man'yō yamato hyakushu*), edited them, and declared that they explained the "great Way of the Sun Goddess; the majesty of the emperor; the honest, moral, and brave intention that assists the retainers and continues to throw light on such things as the role of parents within society, beautiful wives and children, reasonable ancient facts and elegant words. One will also learn from the poems everything about antiquity and understand the essence of the Japanese spirit." [13]

In another collection (*Yamatogokoro sanbyakushu*), Ōhira insisted on the practical importance of poetry as a guide to the present. The preface of this work announced that, although many contemporaries were knowledgeable in the recitation and composition of poems and many studied books, few were interested in offering guidance in the Way to others beginning their studies (ibid. 6:285). [14] The poems included in this collection, in emulation of Norinaga's *Tamaboko hyakushu,* touched "conditions that are close at hand": they spoke to the conditions of day-to-day life, such as service to the lord, connecting bonds between children and parent, and things and articles of the ordinary folk (*aohitogusa*). Ōhira even proposed that imagining society would be impossible without the bestowal of tools and instruments of utility, including learning itself. The poems selected for this collection, Uchitowa promised, revealed the "true heart" of antiquity as it was and all "things and deeds that are elegant and rustic" (ibid. 6:285–86). They showed how people lived in the past, and they would help contemporaries reach an understanding of the true meaning of the antique intention. The poems covered all aspects of daily life and demonstrated the practicality of the poetic Way (ibid. 6:286–93). Ōhira reminded his

readers that poetry did not simply concern ornamentation, "oil lan-
terns," "cotton clothes," "inns," "bamboo umbrellas in soft rain,"
"puppet theater," and "samisen"; it also involved the emotional responses of people from all levels of society, living in the present, not
the past.[15] The poems gathered in the *Yamatogokoro sanbyakushu*, far
from rejecting the present for a restored past, celebrated its diversity
and tactility.

In *Kogakuyō* Ōhira returned to the question of how poetry and
song authorized an examination of antiquity and the relevance of antique knowledge for the present. He cited a poem by Norinaga (used
quite differently by Hirata in his *Ibuki oroshi*) that equated the recitation of poetry and elegance with the neglect of household duties.
Each social class was born into "household duties that have come down
from the time of the ancestors" (ibid. 6:542). These occupations (*waza*)
meant "household productivity" (*kasan*), while elegance (*miyabi*)
meant learning (*gakumon*). But, he added, it is important to always
differentiate what is genuinely elegant from the coarse and countrified
(*satobi, hinabi*). A preoccupation with recitation and reading—with
style and words—would lead beginners astray to "only enter the heart
of scholarship, neglect household productivity, impoverish the body,
and bring grief to wife and children and parents." Because it was "dis-
graceful" to live in society without ordinary work, it was necessary to
teach beginning students to study and endeavor mightily in household
work, which corresponded to the Way (ibid.). Ōhira urged the "diligent
men in society" to bring the whole enterprise of learning (*gakumon*)
into greater alignment with work and productivity. When the vocation
of a learning devoted to making household work prosperous became
the principle of society, it would contribute to the successful operation
of society, reflect the role of personal endeavor, and reveal the goal of
human intention (ibid. 6:543). Whether a person was skilled in learning or in the business of household work, he must always aim for
achievement and be adequate to the task; whatever the task, performing
it well would advance society.

Moreover, Ōhira proclaimed, the commitment to work, diligence, and practicality induced people to perform deeds and activities
naturally. Hence, the study of antiquity showed how the work of learning solidified the Japanese spirit (*Yamato damashii*) and established elegant meaning, thus, avoiding "imitating the Chinese intention." Specifically, it required people to "esteem the great Way of antiquity and
turn toward the gracious, august deeds of the *kami*" (ibid.). People

should never forget the beginnings of these distant ancestors, Ōhira asserted, and they should seek to replicate in their own conduct the deeds and work of the primal deities. Hirata, as we shall see, would specify further the meaning of this conception of work, but it is important that Ōhira, a leader of the Motoori school, sought to find a place for it in his general defense of the ancient Way and the poetic mode, even though he still clung to the association between elegance and the labor of learning. He clearly saw work as useful to society and somehow related to the archetypal intention of the founding deities, and his theory of archaism relied on the proposition that work related to elegance and learning. He advised that endeavoring mightily in the contemporary "work of the body" contributed to the successful operation of society, followed the drift of the times, and disclosed one's real strength. Such efforts made it possible to establish "meritorious deeds that will last for countless generations, faithfully and enduringly." The basic meaning of ancient studies was revealed in "august laws fixed by those at the top, in accordance with society and time"; in the final analysis, it referred to people working and performing tasks they were best suited to do. In short, Ōhira coupled the maintenance of order with the division of labor, authority with the performance of work, and the study of antiquity with contemporary relevance. Somewhere in this new mix, ancient elegance receded into considerations of contemporary custom and the materiality of daily life.

Ōhira by no means abandoned song and poetry. He affirmed the "Way of song" as the legitimate tradition and the true vocation of ancient studies and moved beyond to emphasize the importance of people performing in a contemporary setting. Hence, to recover the emotionality of antiquity, as disclosed in song and poetry, was to protect the Way itself. Protecting the Way called attention to its timelessness and the informing conviction of an antiquity unconstrained by mere history. The need for protection was made more urgent by Ōhira as he sought, perhaps to counter Hirata's claims, to instruct the folk in the true tradition and explain how, in recent times, the realm had been invaded by "Western principle," the last in a long line of alien intrusions beginning with Buddhism and Confucianism. Despite the claims of Western learning to "separate fire from water" and to dissect the body, Ōhira shrank from the abhorrent stain (*kegare*) it imprinted on Japan. Such "reason," sanctioned by Confucianists, violated sacred doctrine. Because the Western principle concentrated on trade, its penchant for profit would infect national institutions and customs. It re-

NB
=

duced all things to commerce and impoverished the ideas of truth, principle, loyalty, and filiality by changing them according to a reversal of the human spirit (*jinshin*). The special task of the Suzunoya was to confront this new threat to the human spirit by recruiting only students not fully committed to household tasks as their primary duty. The purpose of the school, Ōhira wrote, should be to nourish in students the basic meaning of the Way as their fundamental work. "Today," he continued, "since we are committed to broadening the Way of truth and teaching it to men, if we can abandon ourselves to those who are at the top, we will straighten the direction of society and be reunited to the basic meaning [of the Way]" (ibid. 6:540). To erect such a Way in the present, each person must look back at himself.

The charges of poetic excess and privatized withdrawal were, notwithstanding Ōhira's defense, an inescapable problem for members of the Motoori school. They could not simply announce that the school was pledged to training and disciplining young men to stand up to the critical problems of the day. Such an announcement would have provided recognition of, and self-definition to, the problem Ōhira hoped to dispel. The very absence of specific concern—the displacement of previous specific concerns in Ōhira's text—and the defense of a method aimed at preventing "reversals in the human spirit," permits a reading that reveals the presence of precisely the aporia that Ōhira sought to suppress. Ōhira's explanation of the "essentials of *kogaku*" was an attempt to meet his critics and show that poetry played a primary role in uncovering the traces of anxiety in the present. Yet the problem may very well have been created by Norinaga himself, when he separated poetic studies from the study of the ancient Way; his view of *mono no aware* privileged poetry as trace, while his examination of the *Kojiki* freed invariant truths concerning the ancient Way from sedimented distortions. Norinaga believed that his linguistic method made possible the penetration of true meaning, but because his cognitive strategy derived from an elevation of poetry, nativist linguistic theory concentrated on the poetic function of language and relied almost exclusively on poetic exemplars to speak about utterance. The successors of Norinaga followed this line faithfully over other considerations, such as philology, as Ōhira and Mikuni Izumi attested, and argued powerfully for poetry's claim as a guide for reaching the ancient Way that was superior to both exegeses and "learning." But by the early nineteenth century the ancient Way had come to mean elegance and refinement, even though its critics continued to call attention to how far the ancient Way and the study of poetry had been removed from quotidian life. In the *Uiyamabumi* Norinaga described his own aim as clarifying the ancient Way and instructing men in it. He also added that instruction in the ancient Way had always been used by the leadership to serve the changing necessities of the times. There were, in short, both practical and political dimensions to the study of antiquity, which Norinaga hoped to unite but which his successors increasingly suppressed in favor of the promise of privatization, refinement, and elegance. This trend, which Ōhira sought to stem, echoed in his *Kogakuyō* as a kind of great absent presence, occurring on the margins of his discourse yet dominating his meditations by its unacknowledged importance.

By contrast to this effort to reconnect the study of ancient poetry to the practicality of daily affairs and demonstrate its common sense and permanence, Hirata Atsutane called for the abandonment of poetry altogether as a guide to understanding the ancient Way. He argued in the *Shitsunoiwaya* (1811) that, although antiquity was encumbered by few things and words and constituted a model of simplicity and purity, the present remained mired in several kinds of activities. Differentiation and complexity inevitably led to confusion and misunderstanding. Precisely for this reason, contemporaries should actively "search out antiquity, learn about the great temperament of ancient man, and grasp the miraculous principle in the Way of the *kami*. The necessity for understanding the great intention of all the deities, the things found in the world, the deeds one performs, those who are poor and rich in body, is beyond dispute. Its meaning strengthens the desire to stay within the limits and to calculate . . . only the limits that should be. We are beings pleased to live quietly in society" (*HAz* [old] 1:79–80).[16] Hirata made clear in *Kodō taii* and other texts such as the *Tama no mihashira* that by "the limits that should be" and "living quietly in society" he meant the natural disposition or nature endowed in humans from birth by the creation deities. He explained that this "true feeling" (*makoto no nasake*) was a blessing conferred on humans by the deities from the very beginning of heaven and earth; and it was called *sei*, which meant nature, disposition or endowment. But when the term was pronounced *saga* (same ideograph), it also meant custom. The ancient Chinese (in the Zhongyong) identified heaven's command with *sei*; the Way corresponded to this nature and its practice and doctrine. Humans, Hirata proposed, were born with a specific disposition and were obliged to live according to its requirements (ibid. 1:65 [*Kodō taii*]). According to a reading of the ideograph for *sei* as *umaretsuki*, "one's nature adhering to birth," the truth of humanity moved forcefully or falsely according to how closely people conformed to the conditions of their birth, derived from the "splendid sympathy" and "compassion of heavenly deities." He assured his audience—usually students attending his lectures—that if people put into practice the Way endowed in them from birth, so as to avoid wickedness (*yokoshima*), then they would realize in themselves correctness, or the "Japanese spirit" and the "meaning of Yamato." Hirata differed considerably from Motoori in his insistence on a natural endowment that disposed humans to "compassion" and "sympathy" rather than an emotionality that led them into self-indulgence and privatization, the results of defining character as the capacity to empathize with the things of the world one encountered. This privileging of character (and hence, custom) and the individual's divinely endowed nature over the exercise of cognitive skills attesting only to personal talents possessed vast appeal, as we shall see, because it included all people rather than the few capable of expressing genuine poetic sentiment. When Motoori and Hirata referred to the "ordinary person" (*bonjin, yo no tadabito*), Motoori invariably meant the extraordinarily sensitive, while Hirata included all humans, regardless of their emotional fine-tooling. The ancient Way for Hirata was accessible to all Japanese, since its content closely resembled the lives of the ordinary folk. He not only shifted the content of archaism but also required a form to give it representation. The two writers sought adequate forms to express the production of quite different kinds of knowledge—Motoori in poetry and Hirata in narrative.

It should be recalled that Motoori's cognitive program sought to efface the distance between knower and known (the world of objects), to dissolve the difference stemming from the disjunction between subject and object, and to repair the separation between language and experience. His solution was to show how "empathy" might be achieved by the act of entering things and deeds, while the poetry produced by the ancients best manifested the actualization of this cognitive theory. By the exercise of "knowing *mono no aware*" and its empathic powers, the subject would recover kinships and similarities buried below the sedimentation of differences and recuperate a true discourse for contemporaries from a time when words reflected things in perfect transparency. Motoori privileged the poet as the only one capable of listening to the voice of this buried discourse, and poetry as its path of entry. Even his great commentary on the meaning of the *Kojiki* teased out the authentic meaning of words and names concealed by linguistic opacity, in order to relocate an original, true discourse, to actualize what nativists called, "adhering to the base." Because commentary presupposed a "sovereign text" existing beneath the language being decoded, it would illuminate what presumably had always been there.[17] This "reverence" explains why Motoori's work on the *Kojiki* was confined to the formal constraints of the text itself, why he refused either to tamper with the *Kojiki*'s "narrative" form or to employ it in some way to structure the content of nativism. Commentary and poetry "sublated" the difference between words (signs) and their meaning (hermeneutics). Poetry represented infinite possibilities to relay momentary experiences as they occurred and to reflect them transparently, just as commentary in the *Kojikiden* moved endlessly from ideograph to ideograph, name to name, seeking to establish resemblance between the word and what it can never adequately express. Motoori recruited erudition and learning in order to clarify the original text and to extract its basic emotionality—to provide a space for the constitution of the subject—not to produce knowledge. Yet, as we have already seen, the act resulted in a radical rewriting of the text itself.

Hirata, on his part, drew attention to his departure from poetry and poetic studies in texts that stressed narrative. In a letter to one of the members of Motoori's school (Natsume Fusumarō, dated on the ninth month of 1831), written in the wake of his controversy with Ōhira, he confessed that he never really understood poetry very well (*Sate tanin ni wa mōsarenu koto, shibun no koto wa moto yori shiranu otoko nareba, ijimerarete mochi isaku natte iru, michi no koto no agetsura ni kite wa, ima wa kage no yō ni natte iru*). In *Tamadasuki* he acknowledged his disbelief in the procedure that promised "entry into the domain of the ancient Way to know the profundity of things" by the exercise of reading poetry well. "Even though contemporary poets compose poetry well," he remarked, "they darken the great principles of lord and vassal and speak lightly of the penetration of things. How are we to know the real profundity of the Way?" (*HAz* [rev] 6:38–39).[18] Sharing his distrust for reading and composing poetry with his Edo audiences, he cited the following poem in the *Ibuki oroshi* lectures given at his school and then offered his interpretation as instruction: "'The elegant man who neglects his household duties can also compose poetry and read books" (*Ie no narina okotari sone miyabi o no, uta wa yomu to mo fumi yomu to mo; HAz* [old] 1:3). The verse illustrated the baneful effects of an excessive emphasis on elegance and poetics.

Family duties—work—called attention to a variety of activities people performed: "The elegant gentleman is one who studies the ancient Way, reads books and recites poetry in such an effort, but he is mired only in the recitation of poems and the reading of books. He neglects his household duties and this, to the contrary, is different from the Way" (ibid.). For Hirata, the performance of household duties defined the content of the ancient Way, which he sharply juxtaposed to the effects of poetic elegance; doing and relating to concrete things assumed a greater importance than mere feeling or being moved by a couplet. In his day, he remarked, "household work" had become the primary activity among people, and diligent performance a central value. Specifically, this required "protecting the discipline of the parents." Because the human way conformed to the fulfillment of filial obligations, he urged people not to neglect their household duties.

As conceived by Motoori, the cognitive concepts of *mono no aware* promised to bring forth expressions of human feeling and draw attention to the subsequent sensation of being moved. The reality of the outer world, events (*koto*), and things (*mono*), which interacted with human sensibility to produce the proper response, seemed to exist only for the sake of *aware*, the experience of profundity. *Aware* itself represented the primacy of the senses to know and to acquire knowledge over the constrained contrivances (*sakashira*) of rational speculation. In contrast, Hirata's sense of the real—that is, his conception of things—related to the tangible objects encountered in daily life and revealed a sensuous reverence for the texture and materiality of human passion in the world of customary reality.

The *Tamadasuki* (1829) early introduced its intention to facilitate "understanding the meaning of the Way of the *kami* for ordinary people of the times" (*HA*, 184). Hirata acknowledged that the contents of his lectures differed vastly from the "explanations" of Motoori and his adherents, since he was discussing the "untrue deeds of poetic sages" in order to demonstrate how "ordinary poets have learned this style [of dishonesty]" (*HA*, 185, 187).[19] His immediate concern was to expose fake elegance, "comic words" (*zaregoto*), and the general tendency he observed among his Edo contemporaries to confuse the way of Confucianism and Buddhism with "our ancient Way." In this struggle, he combatted the styles of the "culture of play" (*gesaku*)—with its inordinate emphasis on the witty, the comic, the parodic, and the pun—and the general reduction of poetry to the burlesque. He believed he was offering a serious program—"true learning"—to displace the lighthearted, popular ditties that passed for learning in his day. He confessed he could not understand the appeal exerted by the "laughing ridicule of men [Edo poets and writers of verbal fictions] who transform elegance and refinement into jokes" and who titillated audiences by diverting their attention away from the true Way of antiquity (ibid., 187). Embedded in this critique of contemporary writing, we can detect a denunciation of culture itself, which, Hirata believed, had debased genuine value into the carnivalesque.

Hirata did not fail to dissociate his denunciation of Edo popular culture from an attack on aristocratic style. He was sensitive to what his audiences could be expected to relate to and what might appear remote from their own experiences. These common folk could easily be led to emulate the culture of play and revel in the aping and burlesquing of genuine elegance, but there was no way they could really identify with the exquisitely refined aesthetic associated with *mono no aware*. They could be moved by ribaldry and they showed great appetite for the playful, but it was doubtful they could be animated by anything so subtle as empathy with the heart of things. To make his point he resorted to history:

> Because the civil officials [during the Fujiwara period] enacted a system that stressed [the attitude of] despising the military, they occupied the [administrative] ranks without possessing merit and made light of those below. The men in military positions occupied the lower ranks although they possessed merit and resented those above them. . . . Because the upper classes were addicted to song and poetry, wind and string instruments, refinement and luxury, there occurred frequent incidents of rebellion. (Ibid., 204)

Apparently, he was not too remote from his own times when he juxtaposed upper-class refinements (now ironically practiced by the military estates and their merchant clients) to the resentments of the lower orders. Nor was he indifferent to the contemporary possibility that such resentment and upper-class neglect could lead to disharmony among the various classes of Edo society. He enlisted the aid of examples from the various prose narratives of an earlier time (*monogatari*) and included even the "*monogatari* of the shining prince Genji," which referred to numerous rebellions occurring in and around the ancient capital. In stark contrast to Motoori, who saw the *Genji monogatari* as the finest and one of the most enduring examples of the exercise of *mono no aware*, Hirata insisted that the text had been largely misread and that it functioned to provide a different kind of instruction. He recalled that many scholars who studied antiquity and languished in leisure had proposed that the text was useful to understanding antiquity, because it was impossible "to know *mono no aware*" without it. But they were mistaken. "Among men who like to read this story, many do so because it emphasizes people looking good, looking polished." This reading seemed far from its true nature. The times in which the *Genji* was composed were degenerate, "an age of lewdness" (*inpon no yo*); "high and low were thrown together and seen as unworthy, and people believed in Buddhism. Since there were many instances that slighted and even polluted the *kami*, protecting the deities was [seen as] a superficial act" (ibid.). The resulting catalogue of abuse, woes, and disaster was so long, that it was hard to read it as an exercise in elegance and emotionality rather than as a lesson in transgression.

Hirata's dismissal of the poetic mode and its putative relationship to knowing the pathos of things was validated by examples of poets who feigned empathy with things they could not possibly have experienced. His favorite targets were medieval courtly poets like Fujiwara Teika and Ietaka, who had received favor from the retired emperor Go Toba and who had been "described as poetic sages even down to the present." The emperor had been banished to an island in 1219 after an unsuccessful effort to regain authority from the Hōjō. "The emperor suffered great humiliation," Hirata reported, "and it was the season for his retainers to die. . . . These poets, laying hold of the facts of this time, failed in their service to even look back a little on the grief that troubled the emperor. Indolently and leisurely, they composed only poetry [throughout this time]. This is a most suspicious fact." From their safe haven in Kyoto, they wrote and read poetry as if the great events of the day were not taking place. "Anyone living in the realm during those times should have expressed sadness and grief." But these poets ignored the times and, thus, "ridiculed what is called *mono no aware*." The transcribers of the *Tamadasuki* pronounced that "deeds that do not pass through the times are contrary to the heart." Specifically, the example showed how easily real feeling diluted into facile simulations by poets writing about remote events. Such activity failed altogether to relay the thing it sought to represent; its posed grief was simply "a seduction." "When one truly knows *mono no aware*," Hirata explained, "it issues forth at times when one is obliged to receive humiliation." He expressed his harshest objection to poetry's claim to apprehend things and discounted the old cliché that "those who recite poetry have empathy for their times," while those who do not "know only the words about distant things concerning the conditions of the times." He disputed the claims associated with the received formulations, in which knowing pathos—"reciting poetry well"—equaled "entering the heart of the ancient Way," and he charged that "even those court noblemen whom we have heard described as poetic sages have darkened the great principle of the Way of loyalty [*kunshin no michi*]. They have succeeded in producing only poetry distant from the empathy of things. . . . How will we know the true profundity of the Way [*ani michi no makoto no aware o shirinamu ya*]?" (ibid., 207).

Hirata's solution was to make a distinction between poetry and conduct (ibid., 208). A knowledge of origins and its attending conditions defined the real meaning of ancient studies. "Men who study antiquity," he asserted,

> learn first and quickly the great principle of the Way that informed [the past] and then make this learning part of their mind [*kokoro*]. Knowing the names of the birds, beasts, grasses, and woods comes from knowing the pathos of things that pass through the conditions left by the so-called departed spirits. Things do not happen from wickedness but spring from the true heart as it is. . . . It is, thus, honest poetry that feels these spirits, is moved by them, and weeps for men of principle [*gijin*]. (Ibid., 208)

This conception of knowledge as what can be known was rooted in the particularity of events made by people implicated in the immediate context of situations. Although human perception came supplied with a priori principles and although the categories of apprehension had been imparted by the spirits, the occurrence of events relied on the "way things are."

In book 7 of the *Tamadasuki* Hirata returned to the problem of knowing things empathically. He proposed that "the man knowing clearly knows the state of affairs of the deities of heaven and earth and is called a man who knows things [*mono shiribito*]" (HAz [rev] 6:390). His explanation had dropped *aware* as an important element in the definition of the process of knowing and sought to concretize things by identifying them with the conditions of the deities, creation, and the continuation of life. Citing a poem from a Shinto text, Hirata remarked that all things, ranging from what humans made and produced down to the leaves of grass, stemmed from the heart of the *kami*; to know these details of life qualified one to be called a knower of things. "For us," he wrote, "the term *mono* is broad in meaning and calls forth all things. . . . The man who knows things must understand the reason things are designated as they are and discriminate those things that are unclear and concealed in the deeds of heavenly and earthly deities" (ibid. 6:301, 392). When Chinese used the word that denoted "knowing," it was restricted to "knowing only small things seen by the eye in the present." But the man who truly knew things referred to an entirely different and much less constrained horizon, because he appreciated the relationship between concealed and visible things. For Hirata, men who studied the true ancient Way had learned the deeds and achievements of the deities. This was "learning about the *kami*," which many *kokugakusha* transformed into learning about ordinary people (ibid. 6:418, 421, 458).

In the *Ibuki oroshi* Hirata argued that, for ordinary contemporaries (*yo no tsunebito*), real understanding consisted of knowing the various conditions of the times well (*yoku kokora no jijō o wakae*). Such knowledge comes closest to actually knowing oneself (*HAz* [old] 1:43, 53). The meaning behind this proposition was a compelling concern for contemporaneity and a driving conviction that neither poetry nor Confucianism nor Buddhism had managed to relate to the lives of city folk (ibid. 1:55). The famous phrase from Sunzi ("Know your enemy, know yourself; in one hundred battles there will be one hundred victories") represented an effort to demonstrate that knowledge of self corresponded to knowledge of others at any given time (ibid. 1:43). His complaint against Confucianism focused especially on its incapacity to "know the times" and "endeavor suitably for the times" (ibid. 1:55). When Hirata made explicit what kind of knowledge best conformed to the age, he invariably settled on the most mundane activities—the common world of things. A knowledge of contemporary things had to relate to the lives of ordinary people or, as he clarified it in the *Tamadasuki*, the "great, august treasure [*ōmitakara*] of the emperor." "But the great, august treasure is not only the peasantry. . . . It includes people who serve the august calendar of the emperor, such as the samurai, the peasantry, artisans, and merchants." Even so, he singled out the peasants as the real subject of his discourse, however, since they "endeavor to produce important grains in order to nourish the upper classes." Like all other groups, they "must endeavor without neglecting their various house duties (*ie no nari, kagyō*). Thus, the samurai prefers the work of a samurai, the peasant farming, and the artisan and merchant are involved in their activities. . . . When people are seen performing these activities, they are things they themselves know" (*HAz* [rev] 6:437). Because knowledge connected intimately with its object, it ultimately meant people knowing themselves and performing mundane and quotidian activities, without which creation could not continue.

Hirata always emphasized immediate and practical reality over what he denounced as the empty theories of Buddhism and the excessively remote learning of Confucianists. He ceaselessly condemned both Buddhism and Confucianism because they had failed to "know the current of the times" and, therefore, encouraged people to divert their attentions from the "real state of affairs." Both had become essentially useless, since "they have not entered into the lives of the *yūmin* [here he meant common folk]. They mouth elevated but empty theories that do not possess any value whatsoever" (*HAz* [old] 1:55 [*Ibuki oroshi*]).

In his lectures at the Ibukiya, Hirata claimed that he wished to explain Japan to the ordinary folk who constituted his audience, because of its august stature (*mikuni*) and its divinely created inhabitants. Since the way to understand *mikuni* was to understand the ordinary folk, the content of learning should consist of the details of life, particularity, and custom. Hirata frequently drew attention to "knowing things" (*mono o shiru*), but he clearly steeped his conception of knowledge in the reality of things found throughout daily life. To know meant "knowing things of the times" (*yo no mono*) and "knowing the conditions of the times" (*jimu o shiru*; ibid. 1:5, 15). Denouncing the "companions of contemporary Confucianism," he explained that their

> scholarly style goes against the goal of Confucius himself. In truth, it has come to be deplorable, for they do not study Japan, which must be the basis of their studies, but, rather, read only Chinese books and do not understand what learning is for. . . . The principal purpose of learning is to secure good things that will be of use to the realm. Thus, we should learn first that *mikuni* is fundamental and then, once we are on the correct path, we can reach the learning of foreign countries. (Ibid. 1:4)

Elsewhere he admitted that he approved of foreign learning if it could be made to serve Japan.

Hirata's emphasis on the useful, the things of a world inhabited by people, contrasted with Motoori's celebration of feeling and a knowledge of emotionality and sensibility as illustrated in song and poetry. This is not to say that Hirata was insensitive to the emotional life but only to suggest that he defined emotionality differently. "First, there are the pleasures of this world," he confessed in the *Ibuki oroshi*, "rather than those of paradise. Men who pursue a suitable livelihood require sufficient rice for meals, some Nara-tea gruel [*chazuke*]. Then, they begin to eat bonita [*katsuo*] and drink chestnut wine [*kenryō*]. While eating gelatinous sweets [*neriyōkan*], they drink yellow-rose tea and smoke tobacco" (ibid. 1:47). It was less important to talk about deferred pleasures and joys than to be pleased and happy in the present. This active sense of being pleased by the involvement in things (creature comforts of daily existence) was a far cry from the "elegant" world of aesthetic sensibility that, for Motoori commenting on the *Genji monogatari*, moved humans to emotion and feeling. In Hirata's reconsideration, emotionality had come to require an involvement in the mediation of things—doing, with its promise of gratification—rather than a passive reception of the power of things.

Hirata's conception was informed by a rather strong sense of desire and passion (*ninjō*), which differed significantly from Motoori's thinking about the relationship between the two. Some of Hirata's early formulations concerning *aware* had been determined by his relationship to his first wife, a woman who apparently bore his hardships with him, assisted him in innumerable ways, and taught him, as he confessed in the *Tamadasuki*, the Way itself. Her death may very well have prompted him to discuss the problem of consolation and the rewards to be secured by involvement in one's work. Regardless of the source, Hirata was moved to propose an identification between passion, desire, and the performance of daily tasks. Passion expressed respect for the spirits (*kishin*), which he associated with the ancestors and gods. In time, this sense of passion, desire, and respect required an involvement in household duties, a process of repaying the blessings of the gods that was completed only in the last instance. Desire, for Hirata, moved people to act by fixing a relationship between themselves and the things of quotidian life that established the condition of their humanity and formed the distinguishing characteristic of "ordinary people." Despite Motoori's intention to equip humans with essential emotionality, such affective senses were often reserved for people who, like the sensitive souls flitting in and out of the *Genji monogatari*, were separated from the rest of humanity by virtue of their capacity to express elegance (*mi-yabi*). Far from rejecting this kind of emotionality as a formative factor in the human makeup, Hirata changed its object, so as to make it accessible to all.

Many of these distinctions were worked out in the different ways the two writers conceived of death. For Hirata, consolation made humans into agents responsible for their earthly actions and accountable to the world of spirits and ancestors for their behavior in the visible world. He offered solace to those who, previously, had been led to believe in *yomi* as the only prospect awaiting people after death, by inventing an invisible realm that stretched out horizontally from the visible world of work and worship; he also made such solace contingent on acting in a productive manner during one's life, which meant returning the "blessings" of the *kami*. By contrast, Motoori's meditations on death resigned people to the grim prospect of migrating to the place of pollution regardless of how well they had conducted their lives, or indeed, the social status they had occupied while among the living.

The two men held different conceptions of antiquity and its function. Motoori saw the past as a source of emulation, imitation not in any literal sense but as an enduring reminder of pure and authentic sentiment—elegance—expressed in the form of poetry. Antiquity represented the limitless expanses of the pure and true heart (*magokoro*) before it was distorted by foreign teachings and the rational mode of speculation. Although he insisted on differences between past and present, he also asserted that "antiquity and the present are not so distant from each other." By regenerating affective values, he hoped to offer contemporaries the possibility of retrieving this sense of the pure, unadorned emotion in their own lives. Imagining a past rooted in "ancient elegance" and its poetry, his notion of restoration was linked to the exercise of imitative empathy. Ultimately, Motoori was interested in the quality of contemporary life and how to rescue it from constraints, conventions, triviality, and artificiality. Satisfied that the gods would authenticate any political form, he was convinced that if his contemporaries made an effort to realize their original human nature, politics would take care of itself. But the passive dimensions of this formula prevailed over its invitation to active performance.

Hirata's difference from Motoori appeared first in his rejection of poetic sentiment and sentient emotionality as modes of knowledge and in his preference for more tactile feelings experienced in the encounter with things. We have seen how this alteration of a subject resulted in time in a more active conception of humans as agents. When speaking of antiquity, he envisaged not simply a repository of pure feeling but, rather, a spatial structure possessing communal possibilities. Using studies of antiquity, he wove together a "true account" (*makoto tsutae*) of ancient history (*koshi*) from a variety of sources. Past and present differed dramatically, Hirata remarked; contemporaries had the responsibility to note such changes by ridding their times of "erroneous custom" in order to return to the true past, the proper ground for understanding the present. To resolve the problem of "understanding" the present, he "selected" a narrative of the remote past.

Narrative form promised to repair the disjunction—the absence of linkage—between past and present so as to make them indistinguishable. In perceiving this lack, Hirata believed that poetry had failed to yoke past and present into a continuous presence, even though poetic theory had strained to secure this effect in declarations calling for the correspondence between intent, word, and thing. His distrust of this kind of metaphor explains his preference for narrative and the bonding powers of metonymy, for a syntagmatic rather than a paradigmatic hermeneutic. We must read his effort to install narrative as an attempt to supply what was lacking in poetry. He was convinced that poetry had failed to express tangibility and concreteness, even though it had privileged the "thing"—*mono*—and Motoori had valorized quotidian life as found in the *Genji monogatari*. Hirata emphasized the need for greater tangibility by contrasting the importance of connectedness with the solitary thing of poetic association and by specifying the object of knowing as the contemporary life of society (*yo no mono shiruwakimae*) rather than an empathic penetration of things serving the interest of aesthetic sensibility. The distinction between a knowledge derived from narrative and one inspired by poetic sensation signified a difference between active intervention and passive experience, as he explained in the *Tamadasuki* when he condemned medieval poets for removing themselves from the turbulence of society.

A supplement, according to Jacques Derrida, occupies a space by filling a void that, hitherto, has been uncharted by received conventions of knowledge and discourse; it replaces and intervenes "in place of" that void. In the Derridean formulation, the supplement—narrative—is a substitution for another signifier, not a representation of an "absent signified"; it fosters a relationship to the sense of presence that is deficient in poetry. For Hirata, narrative offered the recovery of an "absent origin" that poetry had inadvertently delayed in its concentration on things unconnected to the times and the realm (*kunitsuchi*).

The Prose of the World

Although poetry failed to convey the true Way and ended by communicating merely an effect (elegance), a definition of the nature of the
ancient Way was still a condition for representing the Way. Whereas
Motoori, and especially his successors, sought to establish poetic elegance as the ancient Way, Hirata altered the focus from mere representation to a central event that he submitted to representation. The event
that illuminated the ancient Way was the divine creation and blessing
of the cosmos, to make a land for human habitation. In good metonymical fashion, this event was made to stand for the whole. Hence,
the creation, a productive moment, substituted for the subsequent reproduction of a habitable space by the folk (*aohitogusa*); to refer to the
time of creation was to speak of all history. Hirata's explanation of the
event, therefore, inhered in its description, which, as we shall see, was
based on a self-conscious selectivity. Understanding history stemmed
from a simple enlargement of the central event of creation; narrative,
which contained this content, rearticulated its parts into archetypal
categories of cause and effect, agent and act. Under such circumstances
Fredric Jameson has observed of certain forms of historiography that
the events' logic authorized "an interpretation," which is articulated
into the "logical succession" of a totality. But in Hirata's case, the
"raw material" on which he worked, the latent content constituting his
"narrative," was already formed and shaped; it was meaningful insofar
as it derived from the components of a concrete social life—words,
objects, practices, experience, and people.[20] Hirata's reworking of received components into a "story line" that was an expansion of the basic
event, his decision to select and arrange certain texts to illuminate the
whole, and his inclusion of certain terms, words, concepts, objects,
and practices already filled with meaning, all combined to project the
logic of the content. The operation resulted in a new system of narrative. Unlike prevailing Confucian codes, it sought to forge an identity
of the present and antiquity (*koshi*) and to show how this past had
erected a world whose parts fitted into a seamless totality still available
to the present, where one thing functioned for another and the products of history resembled their producers. Its effect was to show contemporaries that their present resembled "archaic history."

Opening up a space for different combinations—interpretive
strategies—enabled Hirata to depart from poetry to construct a narrative. His narrative, which sought to explain the relationship between
all things in the cosmos, constituted a "prose of the world"; it resembled

the earlier explanations by linguists to account for the most basic units in the construction of language. Hirata's strategy in selecting a "narrative" was authorized by the impulse to order language into a constructed series whose combinatory system could be examined. To view words as representative modes capable of analysis into constituent parts and relationships and then to construct general grammatical tables called attention to the question of origins. Ordering demanded a reduction of elements to their simplest components. It demanded that their relationships be traced back to the moment of genesis, which began with divine intervention.

Unlike Motoori, who commented on the language of the *Kojiki* to illuminate its hidden truths but refused to alter its formal structure, Hirata constructed a new narrative from its several accounts, in order to organize their content into a single story line. Here, he came close to the original method used to compile the *Kojiki*. But the similarity soon ends, because Hirata was openly opposed to the uncertainty of the chronicle's plural accounts, which detracted from the authority of the unified plot called the ancient Way. He wrote even the heavily exegetical *Koshiden*, devoted to explaining names and difficult phrases, within the framework of the narrative he had selected. Displacing the primacy of commentary by a symbolic approach, he welded together a number of strategic syncopes from a variety of texts, including the *Kojiki*, to figure a story that disclosed the central drama of all history. In contrast to Confucian "histories" of the Tokugawa period, Hirata revealed the process of producing his text—the signs of work— as a reminder of genuine historical thinking, to recall for his readers a preclass social structure and a time before organization had separated the conditions of production from its product. His narrative program fulfilled the goal of nativist poetics to create a space for the subject of the enounced—the "I" who speaks—insofar as the content of "archaic history" was the story of production and reproduction and the partnership of gods and humans in carrying out this enterprise. Poetics had invited readers to "recite" ancient poetry in order to show that there should be no real difference between past and present; so too, Hirata's narrative aimed at demonstrating that the godly creation of the realm and the human reproduction of the conditions of social existence recognized no boundary between antiquity and the present. When he reminded the people in his audience that they were the subject of the "ancient Way," he was saying that a continuation of the creation was impossible without their constant involvement in making the land hab-

itable. Hirata's method itself prefigured the crucial element of his narrative by "returning" to a time before the contemporary division of
labor that correlated the social structure with a separation between
mental and manual work.

Hirata acknowledged that the variety of accounts presented a staggering obstacle to knowing the true story, and he recalled that Motoori
had often accepted conflicting assertions because they were recorded in
the *Kojiki*. His collage of syncopes constituted a constructed or combined representation that "selected" the true transmission from several
texts. He did not say that *he* selected the accounts that aggregated into
a true line but only that they had been selected by virtue of their truthfulness. But it is obvious that he was the instrument of truthful selection. In his operation, the *Kojiki*, which Motoori had elevated into the
text of texts, functioned simply as one account among others. The process of selecting the correct accounts relied upon what Hirata called
seibun—"making a written text"—which, he believed, syntagmatically
authorized a form of relating gods, humans, and the land in fixed relationships so as to eliminate the distinction between past and present
and to secure the part for the whole effect. The purpose of this bonding,
which represented the fundamental relationships enabling life and its
continuation, was to show that the Way consisted of both the divine
creation of the land for human habitation and the human necessity of
reproducing the conditions of existence. A true account of antiquity
was one that would naturally illuminate the reproduction of the creation in custom as the single story line. In the *Koshichō* Hirata sought
to justify his enabling strategy to construct a narrative that would represent the "true transmission"; he explained that *seibun* "binds together
the writings of antiquity. Although many works [from that time] exist,
because some are slight when compared to the *Kojiki* and the *Nihonshoki*, the two greats are joined and the lesser ones are incorporated in
them. . . . Even though there are names for these books, when they
are put together to make a written text, it has the sign [*shirushi*] of
ancient history" (*HAz* [rev] 5:234).[21] The program to bind several texts
together constituted a *sign* that was adequate to the Way itself, a single
story line he wished to have recounted as a represented rather than a
representation.

Hirata struck on a method for making a narrative that required
selecting "widely from among the ancient histories." He was apparently
indifferent to the possibility of conflicting reports between the selected
texts. The "smaller texts" were as useful as the "greats" in constituting

the narrative, because they offered basic components that could be combined to produce a composition, just as basic linguistic units such as particles and verb endings were joined to make an utterance. In addition to the two major chronicles, he used Shinto prayers (*norito*), ancient chronicles and records like *Kogo shūi, Kabane ujiroku*, and *Izumo fudoki*, and even writings from much later periods, such as *Shintō gokisho*, regional gazetteers, and *Motomotoshū*. He first excerpted different opinions, similar sentiments, and detailed descriptions from the several texts, then collated them for an assessment of an underlying unity that reflected an invariant reality. "Even though there are differing opinions concerning the facts [*furukoto*] of the entire period of the gods, they [the facts] are still scarce; many transmitted . . . have been included, while others . . . have been omitted. When looking at the differing explanations and considering them in detail, they appear to be linked together in a single [story] line [*hitosuji*]" (ibid. 5:230). In the surplus of accounts, a "straight line," a single story line, disclosed an authentic ancient history—concealed but still present under the array of fact and opinion—which his composition (*seibun*) now promised to illuminate. Hirata explained that he made his discovery only seven years after he had begun his course of study of the ancient texts. Starting from the *Amatsu norito, Kojiki, Nihonshoki, Kabane ujiroku*, and *Kogo shūi*, he proceeded to examine Motoori's *Kojikiden*; then he collated the ancient texts with the "master's" commentary, reassessed the various accounts, and was struck by the disparity between Motoori's explanations and those found in the ancient sources (*kokoro ni kakarite*). He confessed that it was difficult to understand the "existence of differences like this, when the true transmission must surely be a single [story] line."

He argued that the diverse texts were, in reality, unified by an underlying principle. For this reason, he contested Motoori's reverence for the *Kojiki* and advanced the rather unconventional view, at least for a nativist, that the "historical facts of the 'prayers' (*norito*) are superior and more correct than the accounts of the *Kojiki* and its record of the godly age." The prayers revealed the principle or unifying reason (*kotowari*) of all things and, thus, disclosed the purpose of true facts, because they referred to the "Way that corresponds to the gods" (ibid. 5:28–29). Privileging ancient Shinto prayers seemed justified, he believed, because their content contained the unchanging "purpose of real things," sanctioned by the identification of the true Way and the principle underlying all things. Ancient history proliferated and expanded on the contents of the Way; that it could be known proved there had been such a Way. "In seeking to know how to inquire into the facts of the entire age of the gods," Hirata wrote,

> how heaven and earth came about, still more to learn of the august virtue of the gods, it is necessary to look well at the conditions of heaven and earth and the times [in which they were created]. Reverently, [we] have to read the sacred classics from the standpoint of completing the volume on the age of the gods. But later, the eye must fasten on the three supporting deities who made the creation and originally bestowed life. It is a deed that must be considered; since [they] despised the body, their spirit departed from the earth after a while and flew to the empty sky. It was their intention to view the earth from this [elevated] perspective. (*HAz* [old] 7:54 [*Koshiden*, book 1])

In the *Tama no mihashira* Hirata sought to furnish the first fable with cosmic import in order to demonstrate the essential relationship between the creation of the cosmos and the human purpose and to prove the existence of this single story line, which the surplus of accounts and transmissions seemed to have postponed.

At one level, Hirata's narrative, a working-over of earlier forms, resembled texts like the *Jinnō shōtōki*, which had provided a unified story to support claims of imperial legitimacy in the fourteenth century, or—according to Koyasu Nobukuni—Arai Hakuseki's *Koshitsū* (1716), which sought to balance "real facts" with "principle."[22] Nearer to Hirata's own time is the example of Rai Sanyō's *Nihon gaishi* (1829), which, as it followed the canonical Confucian convention to stress praise and blame, tried to show the disjunction between those who had name and those who had reality. The similarity ends here, however, since the elements and components Hirata pressed into a story line presented a vastly different content. Earlier, we argued that content has its own logic: by centering an event or certain events, it projects through enlargement a description inherent in the event itself. The logic of content in Hirata's narrative and the explanatory categories it authorized consisted of recounting an experience that recalled a pre-class, folk past and a sense of time founded on a collective, work-oriented agricultural order.[23] Yet this story remained suppressed beneath Hirata's articulation of the event of creation and his explanation of the relatedness of all things in the cosmos. It will be our task to reveal it and restore the original message his cosmic narrative often concealed, to lay bare a latent content that a manifest content disguised by forms of censorship in the act of working upon it. But to explain why this latent story was so distorted requires us to understand its relationship to the operation of concealment itself.[24]

In the preface of the *Tama no mihashira*, Hirata complained that Hattori Nakatsune's *Sandaikō* (*HA*, 225–69; the work was a cosmological text composed in the late eighteenth century by a student of Motoori Norinaga) had not really understood that, even in the "ancient traditions, there are mixed and diverse explanations." Since Hattori's thinking had failed to account for this fact, it appeared necessary to select (*erabu*) national history anew, in order to correct the errors compounded by the *Sandaikō*. Although Hirata used the occasion provided by Hattori to criticize the successors of the Motoori tradition, it is important to note that he accepted both the form of cosmological speculation and the relationship between an explanation of the cosmos and subsequent national history found in the *Sandaikō*. While Motoori had not constituted the field in this explanatory mode, he offered Hattori his imprimatur in an appendix of Volume 17 of the *Kojikiden*: "Even men of the Western countries, who have considered such things well and deeply, have not yet thought about the considerations of heaven, earth, and hell [*yomi*] as excellently as Hattori Nakatsune. It is clear from this [explanation] that there is nothing doubtful about either *Takamagahara* or the night country. The ancient legends that explain these are very precious, and so are his reasons why the imperial land [is what it is]" (ibid., 270). The *Sandaikō* subsumed, under the authority of "ancient tradition," the process of creation of the various deities and how it corresponded to the formation of the world. In a series of ten diagrams that recalled both earlier mandalas and contemporary verbal fictions (*kibiyōshi*), Hattori sought to give graphic representation to this process of creation. It was his innovation to figure the creation into a systematic theory and to order coherently the inhering relationships under the sanction of founding myths—the relationships between the cosmos and the creation work of the *kami*.

Cosmological thinking, as a cognitive mode figuring a discursive field, usually dogmatizes religious or philosophical views and attempts to link the morphology of forms to a larger world view. The parts in the linkage obviously produce a totality greater than its constituent units. We know that this impulse, which informed the *Sandaikō*, was shared by Hirata, whose *Tama no mihashira* is even more comprehensive. The importance of Hattori's effort was to figure the parts of the creation of the cosmos, as suggested by innumerable accounts, into a systematic story.

Hirata's conception of selectivity derived directly from this strategy. His notion of "selecting" (evocative of contemporary Confucian justification for "choosing") presupposed a differentiation between primal myths and the various successor legends. Early in the *Tama no mihashira*, Hirata remarked that the three deities who appeared even before the formation of heaven, earth, and hell—Ame no mina-kanushi no kami, Takami musubi no kami, and Kami musubi no kami—existed not on *Takamagahara*, the "high island plain," as supposed by Motoori and Hattori, but in an "empty space" (*amatsumi sora*). His interpretation suggested the presence of archetypal *kami*, even before the "beginning of heaven and earth." Hirata did not deduce this condition from an examination of the ancient legends but, rather, the reverse; his theory of the cosmos as a totality was a determining factor in what he chose to select from the ancient legends. He gradually changed these accounts by interpreting (selecting) them in light of the cosmic structure—by directing the stories toward the goal of a cosmological narrative and a system of Shintoistic religious beliefs.[25] As he endeavored to order the process by which the cosmos was created and to find a place for the various deities who seemed to be coeval with it, he raised the question of what we might call pregeneric *kami*—the primal sources of creativity. This was undoubtedly what he meant when he referred to the principle underlying all things. In the *Tama no mihashira* he stressed the importance of only two of these deities, the two *kami* of creative productivity (Takami musubi no kami and Kami musubi no kami). Hirata was most concerned with emphasizing the creative capacity of *kami*, who possessed powers enabling them to produce and to manage the creation and growth of all things, humans, and successive *kami*. He identified the two creation deities with Kamuroki and Kamuromi, which *norito* had held to be the ancestral deities of the emperor, and classified one as female and the other as male. Reconstituting the field in terms of creation deities who made all things determined the degree to which Hirata's cosmological strategy "selected" a single story line; his emphasis on creation and creativity, productivity and reproductivity, disclosed the search for a means to connect the various parts constituting the world into a unified system.

Hirata's response to the problem of good and evil as raised by Motoori, the status of the afterworld and the visible world, and his subsequent choice to resolve this question over others, shows clearly the relationship between the structure of his cosmological vision and the external world to which it was supposed to relate. Like Motoori, he apprehended the world in what we have called a metaphorical mode, but he realized that the particularity of things identified by metaphor required an explanation of their interconnection. This "grasping together" of the parts of a whole greater than the sum of the constituent components (Hirata's "single story line"), this ascription of wholeness and organic unity to elements of a system, is a modality often expressed in the trope of metonymy. Thus, in the *Tama no mihashira* Hirata promised, while concentrating on structuring a cosmology and a cosmogony, to explain how heaven, earth, and hell related to one another and, ultimately, to the world of living things. The formation of the world, he explained, grew out of differentiation of the formless floating mass into heaven (*ame*), earth (*tsuchi*), and hell (*yomi*) and their subsequent hardening or solidification (*katamaru*). Such an explanation appeared necessary in order to understand where people went after life and to comprehend the vast difference between two kinds of knowledge, Chinese (*karagokoro*) and Japanese (*yamatogokoro*). Hirata believed that a necessary condition for understanding the "Japanese mind" required a knowledge of where one's spirit settled after physical death, which Chinese knowledge had failed to provide. "It is the obligation of the Yamato spirit of the people who study antiquity [to determine] the supports [*hashira*] on which the [cosmos] is constructed" (*HA*, 12).[26] It was in connection with the desire to console people and to allay their fears concerning the destination of the spirit after death that Hirata employed a rather elaborate cosmology to relate the journey of the "spirit" and its final resting place to the three realms of heaven, earth, and hell as a manifestation of the creation deities and the centrality of Japan. "By not learning the whereabouts of the spirits [*tama*] [we] are forced to depend upon explanations which come . . . from countries that lie in the direction of the filthy base [*kitanaki soko*], indeed, the underworld itself [*yomi*]" (ibid.). By linking his conception of good and evil to a concern for the destination of the spirit after death, he significantly improved on Motoori's moral ambivalence and the view (represented in Hattori's cosmology) that the spirits of all people returned to the foul and polluted world of *yomi*. Hirata argued that, before it was possible to know where the spirits of humans went after death, it was necessary to understand how the divisions into heaven, earth, and hell came about. This explanation was important if he was to show that the origins of the underworld were of such a nature that human spirits could not migrate there. Like Motoori before him, the question of death and uncertainty in the afterlife seemed urgent, and only a knowledge of its condition could promise relief and consolation to the fearful spirit (*anshin*). Hirata's location of the spirits' destination and his conceptualization of a hidden world (*mukai*) inhabited by the spirits of the dead led him to rethink the creation and establish a morphology of heaven, earth, and hell. For this reason alone, he wrote early in the *Tama no mihashira*, "*Sumera ōmikuni* is the august country and the supporting foundation for all other countries, and it excels all countries in all things as to inspire awe and obedience. Because our country has known the true principle, it sits as the Great Lord [*ōkimi*] of the ten thousand countries. For this reason, we should understand the whereabouts of the spirits." (*HA*, 13).

Hirata accepted Hattori's version of heaven and hell as representing the sun and moon, respectively, and incorporated it into his own system, but he disputed the relationship between *yomi* and the hidden world, which he called *yūmeikai*, where the spirits resided as its tenants. The separation, which was his great innovation, was only possible after he had successfully demonstrated the origins and morphology of this realm. The ancient legends had stated that the underworld was the place of permanent pollution, to which the deity Izanami no mikoto descended after death. Although he agreed with others that such a place was unspeakably foul, he rejected the conclusion that *yomi* was the afterlife world for departed spirits. *Yomi*, he reasoned, was formed in the lower areas (*shitatsukata*). Because it was physically separated from earth, it could not receive the light of heaven (which Hirata etymologically identified with the sun); as a result, it had been doomed to darkness since the time of its formation. For this reason, it was called the "night-seeing country." But earlier writers had confused *yomi* (opaqueness) with *yomi* (night-seeing). Hirata argued that once *yomi* congealed into form, it was forever separated from heaven and earth, and this "lower depth" or "root country" (*soko no kuni, ne no kuni*) became *yomi kuni*—the "night-seeing land." Owing to the separation, departed spirits could never migrate to this place of pollution (*HA*, 25–26).

Yet this argument presupposed that spirits could not possibly partake of the essence of *yomi*, because they possess a different substance from it. "The reason human spirits (*hito no tama*) do not migrate to *yomi*," Hirata wrote,

> is known from the real facts of the age of the gods and from understanding why people are born and what happens to them after death. To begin with, even though people are born as bestowals of their parents, the basic

cause of their creation is the mysterious and marvelous creation powers of the deities, who have produced the four materials [*yokusa*] in humans of wind and fire, water and earth, blessing people with a spirit [*tamashii*], which they give to them at birth. At the time of death, water and earth become a corpse [*nakigara*] since we see its remains before us; we can see that the spirit [*tama*], together with wind and fire, are set free. . . . The reason for this is that wind and fire correspond to heaven, while earth and water belong to the soil. (Ibid., 104–5)

Even though he believed that the spirits belonged to heaven—"because they have surely been given by the creation deities . . . it is for this reason they must go to heaven"—he worked out a conception of a hidden realm both omnipresent and coterminous with earth as the final sanctuary for the departed spirits. Just as the various *kami* had existed in this place for a long time, so the spirits of humans found their final destination there. And "even though . . . this governance coexists with the visible realm (*utsushi kuni*), it is concealed from contemporary men who are not able to see what is hidden." The boundaries of the two realms differed, although they were often located "in the neighborhood of gravesites," and humans who lived in the visible world were prevented from seeing the "hidden" and "dark" world of spirits (ibid., 109). He reassured his audience that such a world resembled the one they already occupied in all details, since the spirits shared their essence with heaven.

At this juncture, Hirata presented his central distinction between "visible things" and "invisible and mysterious things." Originally, "visible things" (*arawanigoto*) referred to "ruling" in this world; "invisible and mysterious things" (*kamigoto*) meant simply the affairs of the *kami*, especially religious ceremony. This crucial division, authorized by the *Nihonshoki*, had been accepted by Motoori, who added a new dimension to the word *kamigoto* by making it denote the deeds the gods performed. This gloss meant that *kami* ruled supreme over all things in the world, including human conduct. Even contemporaries must differentiate their conduct from that of the gods. Each sphere had its principle of sovereignty: the emperor ruled in the visible by virtue of divine descent from the Sun Goddess, while Ōkuninushi no kami, a descendent of Susanowo, the wind god and brother of Amaterasu, supposedly assisted governance in the invisible. In the *Tamakushige* Motoori framed this relationship in the metaphor of puppeteer and puppet.[27] Hirata went further to make the "hidden realm," rather than

yomi—as Motoori had imagined—the final resting place of all spirits.
In the *Tama no mihashira* he wrote: "To the extent that ordinary men
and things exist in the present, these are visible affairs. They are the
august people of *Sumera ōmikuni*. But death and spirits and things that
are like spirits and ghosts belong to concealment and darkness
[*yūmei*]. . . . They are subject to the invisible government of the Great
Deity—Ōkuninushi" (*HA*, 77). Elsewhere, he added that governing
the people of the realm became an "august political affair of the imperial court—deeds conducted visibly before contemporary man." But
after death the conduct of the spirits fell under the jurisdiction of the
hidden realm.

For Hirata, *kamigoto* represented an unseen reality. An invisible
domain where the gods carried out their affairs, it concerned the creation of heaven and earth as well as the sacred affairs of the world of
darkness and concealment. Elevation of this realm to equivalence with
the world of the living provided authority to his argument concerning
consolation. "It is difficult to accept the old explanations that dead
spirits migrate to the land of *yomi*. But where do the spirits of people
who have died in this country go?" If this question was not clarified,
there would be no chance for achieving genuine happiness. The question was rhetorical, since Hirata had already established the coexistence
of a realm that remained unseen and hidden to all but the departed
spirits and a visible world inhabited by the living. Even ancient man
and the revered Motoori, he charged, had not known of the location
of the spirits. Although Hirata acknowledged a twinge of uncertainty
when he admitted that "generally, I have not seen the facts or old legends to [confirm] this," his method, nevertheless, gave confidence:
"When talking about the destination of these spirits, it is known clearly
from the *intention* [my italics] of the ancient legends and the real facts
of contemporary times, that it [hidden world] has existed in this country
eternally. It is also seen in the *Man'yōshū*" (ibid., 108).

Thus, while people were alive, they were ruled by the emperor;
after death, they submitted to the authority of the ruler of the hidden
realm, Ōkuninushi no kami. This conception of afterlife did not correspond to *yomi*, the dreaded world imagined by Motoori and Hattori.
Rather, Hirata's afterworld resembled the living world in all aspects.
"When the old die," he explained in *Koshiden*, "their bodies return to
the earth, but since their spiritual character does not diminish, it mi-
grates to the world of mystery and concealment to follow the august
role of Ōkuninushi no kami. . . . Because this, too, was established by

the creation deities . . . it can be said that *kamigoto* is the Way of the *kami*" (*HAz* [old] 9:44). In this concealed realm, the departed resided as they had in the visible world; it was dark only to those who could not see it—the living bodies—and in it such things as clothing, food, and shelter were supplied. Once people died, Hirata wrote consolingly, they migrated to "*yūmei* and they become spirits [*tama*], that is, *kami* . . . since they do not reside in *yomi*; where they do live, which is in the vicinity of graves, they construct shrines and smaller places of worship [*hokora*] to celebrate" (*HA*, 112). It is important to note here that Hirata envisaged the hidden realm standing in a spatially homologous relationship to the visible world of the living. The site of the hidden world was contiguous to the village in which the living were born, lived and died.

The spirits that migrated to this place are obliged to receive the judgment of Ōkuninushi no kami with respect to their conduct while they were among the living. According to Hirata, in the spirit world high and low, good and evil, strong and weak did not necessarily correspond to these distinctions in the visible world. Like the emperor of the visible world, Ōkuninushi no kami, when informed of human deeds, "bestows retributions [*mukui*] on the living; investigates and judges the good and evil of the *kami* [spirits] who have entered the hidden world; determines as guilty [*tsumiokashi*] those who have gone against the will [*magokoro*] which the great *kami* of creation have bestowed; and rewards as good those who have endeavored consistently to conform to their nature" (*HAz* [old] 9:45 [*Koshiden*, book 23]). This arrangement of rewards and punishment in the afterlife, which many Japanese scholars have attributed to Hirata's reading of the Bible and his familiarity with Christianity, permitted him to raise the question of good and evil and to explain to his contemporaries both the origin of deeds and the consequences of their effects.[28] He dismissed Motoori's earlier assertion that the "occurrence of evil deeds" came from the "spirit of the bent or evil deity" (Magatsubi no kami) for an optimistic view that the "roughness" of this deity was essentially a good quality and clearly not the cause of the misdeeds humans commit. The spirit of Magatsubi no kami simply imparted to humans the capacity to discriminate between good and evil. In discriminating between the two realms, Hirata was, in fact, locating the source of responsibility for deeds in the world of humans themselves. This analysis was a far cry from Motoori's pronouncement that humans resembled puppets directed by godly puppeteers whose own "reason" always remained concealed, even when they acted as the causal agents of manifest events, such as fortune and misfortune. In his lectures to Edo townsmen (*Ibuki oroshi*), Hirata meditated on a poem of Motoori's that declared, "When there are good deeds, evil appears; when evil prevails, good appears—this is the way of the times" (*yukikoto ni magakoto itsugi magakoto ni yukikoto itsugi yo no naka no michi*). He explained that, because Motoori perceived "misdeeds (*ashi*) originating directly from the good, and vice versa, humans cannot know anything more than the way things are. In Motoori's explanation, humans are similar to puppets. The *kami* manipulate puppets who are humans" (*HAz* [old] 1:18). Because all things stemmed from the creation deities, Hirata argued, humans were not in a position to actually know how the deities calculated their own intentions concerning the "bestowal of effects." But this approval of Motoori's view meant only accepting the less problematic idea that the *kami* were responsible for the "making of humans"—what the ancient texts called "*kami* affairs" (*kamigoto*). Beyond this, their "august intention" could not be fathomed by humans. Although he clearly affirmed the importance of the *kami*, he also recognized the centrality of human agency. If Motoori had withdrawn from interfering with the *Kojiki's* formal properties because he saw the text as a divine production, not susceptible to human intervention, he was also unwilling to see human behavior apart from divine agency. Hirata, by contrast, emboldened to stitch together a "true account" of *koshi*, easily located responsibility for conduct in human willfulness. To be sure, prayer helped to gain divine intercession, but humans, in the end, had to make an inexhaustible effort to express their natural—that is, god-given—endowment (ibid.). In the *Tama no mihashira* Hirata advanced the idea that the gods gave the land to humans as a trust, which subsequently obliged the folk, in successive generations, to act in accordance with their endowment. Surely, this was the meaning of his ambiguous remark in the *Ibuki oroshi* that humans were not independent (ibid.). But, it also meant that humans, owing to the character conferred by the deities, were duty-bound to act and work in repayment for divine blessings. How they did so was their responsibility.

Departed "ether-spirits" (*reiki*), who migrate to the concealed world, were judged by Ōkuninushi for acts committed in the visible world. The principal purpose of Ōkuninushi no kami was to judge whether these "souls" had acted in accordance with or contrary to their nature as derived from the creation deities. All humans were endowed with a heart (*shinkon*) and the four elements (wind, fire, water, and earth), the most important of which was wind. Since wind produced breath and enabled humans to speak, it conferred both life and meaning (Izanagi exhaled and created the *kami* of wind). Life and breathing were rendered as *iki*, and their termination signaled "death" in the visible world. But "life" continued in the concealed world. "When people breathe, it is the wind, and we must never forget that the wind deity was thought to have been born from the august breath [*miibuki*] of Izanagi no mikoto. Moreover, does not the warmth of the human body partake of fire? Does not the moisture of the body belong to water? Or, when a corpse is interred, is not its essence converted into spirit?" (HA, 103–4).

This sense of the interconnection between the creation and humans figured Hirata's cosmological narrative. The same deities who created the cosmos gave life to humans. Despite the Chinese theory of yin and yang and the five elements, he explained, one hundred sages had not yet been able to account for the "wonders of sexual union and birth. How will such understanding be secured?" Even though the sexual union of parents produced children, it was originally "bestowed by the august spirit of the creation and supporting *kami*, Takami musubi no kami and Kami musubi no kami" (HAz [old] 1:27 [*Ibuki oroshi*]). These two creation deities existed before the formation of heaven and earth and formed the terrestrial spheres before all else. After this, they busied themselves (*asobashi*) creating humans and all other things (ibid. 1:28). Here, Hirata brought together two interrelated ideas: (1) "because they are esteemed deities, they have been called the gods of creation," and (2) their principal creative accomplishment was humans themselves. The coupling rested on the continuity of a series of linguistic associations:

> The meaning of the word *musubi*—in *musubi no kami*—takes the ideograph conveying "to live"; when the ideograph is read as *sansuru*, it is creation and productivity. The suffix *bi* [in *musubi*] evokes something strange and wondrous. These *kami* did not rely on anything in [the making of] words in the divine age. Because the divine virtue that carried the august creation existed in strange and wondrous *kami*, the creation deities were elevated. The meaning of the word *musu* today has the same connotation as the *musu* when a woman gives birth to [produces] a child. (Ibid.)

The analysis acquired further authority from old songs, which emphasized the centrality of humans as the product of the creation deities. "The songs [*uta*]," he exclaimed, "are proof that humans were produced by the august virtue of these *kami* of creation." He invoked an ancient poem as a reminder: "When one looks on the lords, the *kami* are indeed angry—who would create heartless men?" According to Hirata, the poem contained the following meaning: although the lord might, in fact, be heartless in his treatment of people below and, thus, inspire the anger of the deities, even the *kami* were capable of creating heartless humans (ibid.).

Hirata's cosmic narrative established a distinction between the genuinely natural and the unnatural, a real history of the visible world over the claims of a history of contrivance, first nature against second nature. Essentially, the move entailed a critical rejection of Confucianism, which represented, for him, artifice remote from the Japanese experience. When, on several occasions, he attacked the Tokugawa Confucian thinker Dazai Shundai (1680–1747) as a fool for thinking that the "convention of nature in the august realm has to imitate China . . . according . . . to the classics," he revealed the importance of this distinction for understanding the natural and the appropriate in contrast to mere deception (ibid. 1:56). A defense of the natural—the interchangeability of the creation, the land, and the folk—relied less on philosophic speculation than on the establishment of a new common sense. He drew on familiar proverbs and stories but defamiliarized the stock responses they evoked by inserting them into his new narrative. The following two examples of proverbs (*kotowazu*) "well known to the ordinary people" demonstrate both the operation of this conception of defamiliarization and the effort to explain the significance of the natural. The first story deals with the attempt to use an ordinary bird, instead of a cormorant, to catch fish.

> Above a clear and rapid river there were two or three large monkeys. The first was perched on a rock and fell sound asleep; the second was nearby, concealed sometimes and unconcealed at other times. A crow flew to the rock and landed alongside the monkey who was sleeping. All seemed well. He pecked his bill at the monkey's foot and the monkey failed to move even slightly. Since the monkey appeared to be dead, the bird flew to the top of his head. When the bird began to pick at the eye, the monkey took hold of the bird's foot. The second monkey, which had been nearby, suddenly appeared and tied a long rope around the bird's

> foot. Even though the bird tried to fly, it could not. Well, they all went down to the river, in order to throw the bird into the water. The first monkey held the rope, while the second tried to spot a fish at the surface. When they saw a fish, they threw the bird into the river, but it died immediately. The monkeys abandoned it and went back up the mountain. (Ibid. 1:56–57)

What did it mean to use a bird for a cormorant? Hirata asked his audience. The bird, a crow, looked like a cormorant, but even though it was black, it was not able to snare a fish. "Even though the ways of foreign countries imitate the true Way, using them to rule the imperial land is like using a common bird for a cormorant" (ibid. 1:57). Confucianism, Hirata concluded, was really "monkey wisdom" (*saru chie*); importing it to Japan was like inducing the black bird to come to the river.

In another example of how artifice masked as culture forfeited naturalness, Hirata cited the case of Kibi no kimi who, in an effort to expand the skills and technology of ancient Japan, journeyed to China. "There he purchased knowledge and skills with money. The Chinese appeared miserly and mysterious, and all that money has ever bought is a stench." Hirata worried that Kibi had established a recognized method for securing new information by paying for it, a practice that was alien to Japan before his trip. His intention was to demonstrate the naturalness of things, which originated not from any shabby financial arrangement with the Chinese but as "divinely mysterious gifts that bestow good value." Since antiquity, the Chinese had measured all value in terms of gold; everything there was either bought or sold for money. But valuing gold was useless and meaningless, because real value corresponded to use. Only utility satisfied an appropriate definition of the natural. Associating use-value with the common world of things, he concluded that life was impossible without either. "In truth, we esteem only those things we cannot do without on a daily basis: chiefly, grains and cereals, beginning with rice; next, limited things, such as salt, silkworms, cotton, reeds for roof-thatching. If one possesses these items, there will be no scarcity of food, clothing and shelter" (ibid. 1:58–59). Money was not simply the root of evil; it was the source of invention, artificiality, and representation, and exemplified best the human propensity for the unnatural. On this occasion, Hirata also worried that money installed differences among people. A better Way had existed in Japan before the massive importation of money and civilization: "In Japan the principal treasures are cereals, salt, iron, cotton, wood, reed, etc. Our master [Motoori] wrote the following poem: 'The people who make things are the august treasure.' The ancient word for peasant [*hyakushō*] was *ōmitakara*—august treasure. People who create the aforementioned treasures [namely, the peasantry, artisans, and craftsmen] have always enjoyed the love of the deities and the emperor" (ibid. 1:60). The treasures of life related to the natural and barest necessities of existence as well as to their creators and consumers. Elsewhere in the *Ibuki oroshi* Hirata advised his students that esteem belonged only to those things that made life possible and to the essentiality of agricultural work. Hirata saw both product and producer as the source of all human life, and their relationship (peasant and land) a symbolic representation of the interaction between creation and custom, production and reproduction.

> Even barbarian countries that fail to know anything about their origins must still pass through [the activity of] agriculture. When thinking about agriculture, it is something that must be esteemed. Still more, Japanese, belonging to a realm founded on rice seedlings, must search out the basis of their country. In this connection, I usually recall a poem from Motoori: "Whenever one eats, day and night, men of the times think about the blessings of the gods and the abundance we have received." (Ibid.)

Confucians had forgotten this truth; to know it enforced awe and respect for the deities who gave it. Thereupon, Hirata urged, these "blessings" should be the principal reason for men to study the ancient Way. Although such study involved great difficulties, the effort must be made. Otherwise, people, although born as humans, risked descending to the inferior "level of the birds and beasts." Nature meant not a beckoning to a simple and raw state but, rather, a recovery of the basic necessities of life, which he and other nativists considered essential to human nature itself. Animals could not learn the Way of humans as humans, he reminded his audience, and humans should not fail to respond to what they must know. "Men whose spirit is poisoned in such a manner [that they cannot know the human Way] are inferior to dogs, cats and rats" (ibid. 1:61).

Hirata's conception of the natural was rooted in the links between peasant producer and agricultural production, made possible by the "blessings of the gods," especially the *musubi no kami*. But the natural came to mean producing within a divinely appointed space designated by the *kami* for just such a purpose; it was a definition *by* culture. In the *Tamadasuki* Hirata stressed the importance of these creation deities in such a way as to make their function clear to his audience. After they had created all things and especially other gods, he said, Izanami and Izanagi—more immediate procreators who, unlike the *musubi no kami*, had acquired some of the features of the human personality—appeared and "first give birth to the land (*kuni*) and then later to its people—*aohitogusa*" (*HA*, 191).[29] "Once they had completed this, they decided to give birth to a variety of things with which the *aohitogusa* could increase, expand, and prosper." Yet, Hirata added, the discussions of the beginnings of wind, fire, metal, earth, and the several deities did not adequately explain how these things were created for the "sake of the ordinary folk" (*Makoto ni wa hitokusa no tame ni nashimaseri to mōsamu ni shingoto ni arazu*; ibid.). In the *Koshiden* he commented that the *aohitogusa* originated from the time of Izanami and Izanagi and were praised as gods (*Sono wa Izanagi, Izanami kami no miyo yori hyaku aohitogusa umawarite sono yo ni kami to tonaishi, wa naka ni omodachitaru kami o mōseru koto ni kokoro tsukarezarishi wake nari*; *HAz* [old] 7:8 [*Koshiden*, book 2], 41 [book 3]). Although no real canonical explanation connected the creation to the people, he believed that it was the intention of the creation deities. His assertion was perfectly consistent with a strategy that had already decided to select a true account of antiquity from the several extant records. Hirata not only established a systematic classification of things related to each other and reducible to a common origin, he also interpreted the creation itself to serve the purpose of the people, not the gods. In the *Tama no mihashira*, toward the end of the second book, he considered this relationship between the gods, the creation, and people. Responding to a passage about creation, Hirata noted: "In the world more people are born than die daily. This is the reason for the august passage [from the classic histories] 'a thousand necks are strangled daily [*hitoichi chikashira kubiri korosamu*] and fifteen hundred parturition huts [*ubuya*] are erected'" (*HA*, 101). The great prayer for purification [*Ōharai*], he explained, contained the following passage: "Many people of heaven were born in the realm" (*kuni naka ni nari idemu, ame no masuhitora*). The passage referred to "people," *aohitogusa*—diffuse, luxuriant, and dense with the growth of grass. Undoubtedly, Hirata chose the word deliberately in order to evoke the association of creation and growth, which permitted him to position the people in a natural and original series consisting of land, plant and vegetable life, wind, fire, metal, and water. "Death of all people is the action of the *kami* of *yomi*, while birth and productivity are the blessings of Izanagi no ōkami" (ibid.). Thus, the creation, from its beginning, had sustained and maintained the ordinary people.[30] Just as a creation without people challenged belief in divine trust, so production without reproduction defied the very intention of the gods.

Hirata's maneuver to suture the apparent split between creation and folk, production and reproduction, and divine intention and human will, encouraged the idea that the human community came into existence simultaneously with the formation of the land. The folk had always nourished the land and been nourished by it, in an act that ceaselessly continued the creation. The formulation also invited the conclusion that the land and folk had existed even prior to the emperor. The relationship between creation and folk acquired greater force and specificity in the *Tamadasuki* (as we shall see later) and became a major principle when nativists turned to the construction of a viable theory of politics to accommodate the swift succession of events in the last years of the Tokugawa period. By coupling naturally the creation and community, Hirata's successors were able to expand the formulation and apply it to contemporary events. The most important effect of this politicization was to show, by a strategy of reduction to a common origin, that restoration best exemplified this mode of relating things and that its content clearly signified the priority of both land and folk over other claims. Although Hirata never actually proposed this explanation, he came close when considering the meaning of *mono no aware* in the *Koshiden* (book 13). As for knowers, he wrote, they "are men who know how to discriminate the origins of reason behind all things. . . . Today we can say that men only understand the small things that they can see before them [*utsutsu*]. This was not the case in antiquity, which knew the sources of the Way of the gods" (*HAz* [old] 8:19).

Hirata's discussion of the reductive strategy leading to an understanding of the reason underlying all things brought him back to the present. Because his use of the metonymic mode permitted him to reduce things to origins (in order to retrieve essence and tangible meaning), it also allowed him to show how the self-evident had always existed as a timeless presence. A return to essences seemed to offer liberation from the specific structural forms of political enterprises in order to recover the basic sources of authority itself; it authorized a restoration of the actual content of power from its historical displacements. By reducing the parts to the whole, nativists, like the thinkers of the Mito school and the founders of new religions, were in a position to designate the part as a substitute for the whole. Underlying this program and authenticating it was Hirata's belief in the primary importance of humans and their capacity to perform and his identification of truly human activity with some larger purpose. In this scheme, language, work, and worship bespoke not nature—although such activities were seen as a "natural" series—but other people in terms of a shared purpose and kinship, subjects constituted through practice in order to reproduce the conditions of community. Hirata clearly meant to establish this relationship of reciprocity when he bonded the creation to the folk's capacity to "produce" and "expand" potentialities that conformed to the original intention of the gods. The idea of the ordinary people and the knowledge they are able to acquire was to occupy a central position in late-Tokugawa nativist thought. Ōkuni Takamasa, for example, seized upon the "natural" relationship between the creation deities and the *aohitogusa* and employed it to establish a discipline stressing "learning about the people" as a necessary presupposition for "learning about the deities."

In the heavily cosmological text *Tama no mihashira*, Hirata applied a logic that fixed the equivalence of the creation, deities, and folk. It subverted prevailing conceptions of political space, based on a system of closed differences, by showing how they canceled each other because they invariably expressed something identical underlying them all. The "something" guaranteeing identity (similitude) was the creation, to be sure; more important, it was a common reference to an external referent. Hirata's text aimed to demonstrate why the souls of the dead could not possibly migrate to *yomi* and why they went instead to the invisible world. He designed this explanation to show how all folk shared an equivalence because they occupied the same space in the "national land" and belonged to it even after death (HA, 108–9). This was why the souls of the dead were always to be found in the vicinity of where they, as humans, had been born and lived. The ordinary people, like the land itself as it moved from growth to harvest, did not really die but underwent a transformation in shape. Their spirits returned to the invisible realm where they had originated, to be judged by Ōkuninushi no kami. Hirata's suggestion that spirits returned to their origins in order to be judged for their performance in the visible world promoted the priority of the ruler of the hidden realm over governance in the visible realm (*arahitogami*).

In the *Tamadasuki*, Hirata proposed that all things had been made for the folk since the time of creation. "In the august words of

Izanami and Izanagi, it is decreed that, as evil exists for the *aohitogusa*, so also does good. The words also decree to all living *aohitogusa* beauty and blessings" (ibid., 191). In a gloss, he explained that the prefixes that such divine ordinances employed to indicate the *aohitogusa* carried the same meaning as *utsu*—living, the real. His interpretation fixed the centrality of the ordinary people in the creation of things by privileging the relationship between the *aohitogusa and the "living."* He completed the organic metaphor when he wrote that in the "ancient explanations, when one talks about the *aohitogusa*, the proliferation and expansion of people [*hito no fuehirogoru*] compares with the density and luxuriance of grass" (ibid.).

The association between the creation and the people shaped Hirata's political program. Izanagi gave birth to Amaterasu in order to rule and nourish the "august realm of the heavenly sun." After she had esconced herself in a palace in heaven called Hi no ukamiya, she decreed that the deity Ninigi no mikoto should "ascend to the position of emperor, so as to rule the people who have become dense and luxuriant under heaven because of the august intention of Amaterasu ōmikami and the creation gods." Hirata argued that the way to serve the "intention" of the creation deities was "to govern their beautiful people [*aohitogusa*] who have become dense and luxuriant" (ibid., 192). The emperor (*ōkimi*), who was also correct and reverential, must be mindful of how disorder spread and undermined tranquility. He must "lower himself" in order to bestow blessings, pacify, and rule the people. Cosmology supported the central duty of imperial rule to govern not from a distance but close at hand. For this reason, emperors since the time of Ninigi were obliged to descend from heaven.

> When the emperor descended to earth, Amaterasu decreed to Ninigi all the land within the abundant reed plain as a realm that must be governed. Consider well the sacred words that have established governing the *aohitogusa* as a principal duty. If one seeks to rule without the *aohitogusa*, one should discriminate deeply and well about how useless it would be to govern the realm (Ibid.)

Hirata also tried to establish a primary relationship between Ninigi and the creation deities (the later Izanagi and Izanami, as against the primal Takami musubi no kami and Kami musubi no kami) in order to explain how the land existed for the people and why ruling meant caring for both. In the *Ibuki oroshi* he criticized the Chinese for making "ruling" the subject, rather than the realm itself, as was the

Japanese practice. He called attention to the necessity to "learn about the deities" and advised that *kami* people should know about first were the creation gods. Accordingly, the *Tamadasuki* asserted that, since it was believed that the deities were the ancestral *kami* of heaven, earth, men, and all things, they were deserving of special affection and love. Because it was according to the "divine intention of the deities that emperors descend to separate themselves from their heavenly roost, they had no other function but to rule the people tranquilly." Thus, the great intention (*ōmikokoro*) of the Sun Goddess and the imperial creation deities was the "august intention" of the emperors themselves. Hirata reasoned that when Amaterasu decreed to her descendants, beginning with Ninigi, that loving the *aohitogusa* meant preparing for them a variety of grains and foodstuffs, this bounty referred to things people use in their daily life that were necessary to their continued existence. Clearly, the "sprouting forth of *aohitogusa*" in the world manifested the creation of Izanagi and Izanami and, beyond it, the spirits of the creation deities. "Since Ninigi no mikoto and his descendants were to rule the realm conforming to these ordinances, both land and people are the august objects of Amaterasu ōmikami. The sign of imperial command is the duty to govern the realm" (ibid.).

The discussion focused on the project of governance that the deities had "intended." When Ninigi descended to earth, he was charged with a detailed plan of polity (*go matsurigoto*) as he was entrusted to rule the land of the ancestral *kami*. The term *matsurigoto* has great importance, because it indicates a governance more religious than political. Although Motoori had earlier (in the *Kojikiden*) explained that the meaning of the ideograph *matsuri* in the compound *matsurigoto* (ideograph for the contemporary word meaning politics) meant service (*sumeragi no ōmikoto o uketamawarite, onoono sono waza o tsukaematsuru, kore tenka no matsurigoto narebanari*),[31] Hirata transformed the meaning into "religious ceremony" (*HAz* [rev] 6:554–55). The *Koshiden* prescribed that men who know divination and magic were called knowers of things. When acquiring such knowledge, it was important to read the ancient prayers (*norito*) relating to the ceremonies of the wind god as the surest way to reach the "sources (*moto*) of the *go matsurigoto*, which have been discarded and forgotten a long time ago" (*HAz* [old] 8:11, 12). Considerations of governance should inspire people to think more about the practice of worshiping the deities (*kamimatsuri*), which had been transmitted to the present since the creation. Because governance of this kind existed, it relied on the spirit

(*kokoro*) of all the heavenly and earthly deities. Therefore, the purpose
of human governance was, from the beginning, to celebrate the deities
who created the realm and the people. Its duty was first to worship and
pacify the "crooked god" (*araburukami*) so as not to bring calamity and
then to offer respect in various ways to the several deities in order to
increase their blessings. "There is no other deed for the *aohitogusa*
under heaven but to express their thanks in worship and celebration"
(*HA*, 193). Elsewhere, in the *Daidō wakumon*, a political history
chronicling legitimacy, he affirmed that

> the rule of the realm is called "illustrious *matsurigoto*"! In the august
> customs of the divine land, the realm is ruled according to divine inten-
> tion. Since the celebration of the deities is primary, the ideograph for
> political affairs is read as *mimatsurigoto*. From the beginning worship
> and governance were one and the same thing, and this is the reason for
> the name "the divine land" [*shinkoku*]. If commoners today understand
> that there is a distinction between *kami* worship and governing the
> realm in the ideograph for *matsurigoto*, they have committed a great
> error. (*HAz* [old] 2:2)

This conception implied neither the trickery nor the contrivance usually associated with the political practices of foreign countries (that is,
China). Again, the contrast with Motoori is instructive. As pointed out
earlier, Motoori's understanding of the term *matsurigoto* referred to
performance for the emperor and seemed, therefore, to accommodate
a system of hierarchical offices in a fixed administrative order. Although he acknowledged religious ceremony as an important function,
"among things involved in governing the realm of the lord . . . its root
is not religious but service, when one thinks about it." In Hirata's rethinking, *matsurigoto* clearly meant a unification of polity and religion, which required the folk to live their lives as if in a continual
ceremony to the gods. Specifically, this meant not an administrative
hierarchy pledged to maintain order in the name of the emperor but,
rather, a repayment of constant work and worship to the deities for their
blessings. Conceivably, Hirata's reformulation of service into work and
worship could strengthen support for the emperor and the current administrative system. Yet his reevaluation of the histories and his subsequent decision to appeal to an external referent by restructuring the
role of Ōkuninushi no kami constituted a move to a different political
logic. Hirata's specific tactic was to substitute a "logic of equivalence"

for a "logic of difference" and to reduce the number of offices (differences) by expanding the elements that could be substituted for one another (similitude). By unifying governance and worship, he reduced separate claims to identity. In ideological terms, he dissolved history into nature and closed the perceived gap between different realms of activity (daily life and governance) and sacred and secular time. In time, Hirata's reformulation of *matsurigoto* made available a theory of wholeness, which others would appropriate to displace the fragmentation they were beginning to notice in the countryside.

As a result, the ordinary folk and the land were bonded in common ancestry and purpose to make possible a conception of community vastly different from the prevailing world of political hierarchies. By seeking to supplant a logic of difference with a logic of equivalence, Hirata simplified politics instead of fortifying existing arrangements; he established the terms for even greater antagonism when, in fact, he was trying to eliminate conflict. In other words, his intervention divided political space into opposing camps instead of removing the possible sources of conflict, and it served the very contingency his theory of "necessity" was trying to overcome. In any case, he suggested one meaning of the phrase "to learn about the deities is to learn about the folk [*aohitogusa*]" (ibid. 7:42, 43 [*Koshiden*, book 3], 11 [book 4]), because the word for learn, *narau*, also meant practice and imitation and possessed associations of religious celebration and worship. Late-Tokugawa nativists like Ōkuni Takamasa reversed the formulary to emphasize the primacy of people and community. Yet even this move was prefigured by Hirata's striking insistence on a linkage between people and gods, community and its divine origins. "Because the production of land and people have been entrusted [to the folk] by the heavenly deities as the great principle [*omoki kotowari*], great stress must be placed upon it and the importance of loving the people" (ibid. 7:12 [book 4]). Throughout the *Koshiden*, Hirata returned to the question of the folk who, along with the realm, represented blessings from the creation deities, and he reiterated the conviction that the "divine intention" "loved" the ordinary people and provided everything for their nourishment (ibid., 24 [book 5]).[32] This suggested the priority of community and land over the emperor and the assertion that authority resided in the divine intention to create the land for people to occupy and actualize its potential. This gift represented a trust, an obligation extended to the folk to "increase" and "expand" the natural bounty of the national soil. When Hirata asked earlier what the point would be to a realm without the *aohitogusa*, he was calling forth this conception of authority and community.

Whether intentional or not, the effect of a strategy determined to trace the relationship of all things back to their common origins (manifested in Hirata's decision to "select" a true history) was to elevate what might be called the Izumo version of the creation myths. According to it, the emperor ruled simply as a mediator between a living community and the creation deities. Power inhered in the community because of the partnership between *kami* and folk, as illustrated in the formulary enjoining people to learn about the gods or imitate them. But the reverse was equally true: if people made an effort to learn about the ordinary folk, they would reach the gods. Hirata acknowledged that gods and people differed, even though he recognized a primal relationship between the human and the divine. Common emotionality bound both gods and people in kinship (ibid., 11 [book 4]). The principal deity of the Izumo version of the myths was closer to the founding creation deities than the claimants of the Ise version, such as the Sun Goddess and her progeny, whose antiquity appeared further away from the "nature" Hirata was trying to install and nearer to the "history" he was seeking to displace. Hirata's declaration to "select" a narrative decentered the emperor from the plot of creation and displaced political power altogether to the divine production (creation) and human reproduction of the conditions of social existence (custom) as the central story line of "history."

The prevailing Ise mythology (whose claims Meiji Restorers later reified) had long validated imperial authority; it considered the emperor prior to community. Hirata's political language and logic reduced the emperor to the role of mediator in the visible world, whose governance was restricted to the "living and visible *aohitogusa*." We already know that his cosmological classification actually established the two realms of visible and invisible and acknowledged an equivalence between their activities. Since people inevitably returned to the invisible realm after death and submitted to the governance of Ōkuninushi no kami, the authority of this world seemed to claim priority over the visible. It signalled the authority of horizontal community. The nativist chronotope,[33] with its emphasis on the invisible realm—the place in which all received impartial judgment for past behavior—and its valorization of the essentially human character bestowed by the gods, obliged people to work together in order to reproduce the social conditions of existence, the plan of creation itself. It not only spoke for people who had not possessed a voice by which to represent themselves, it also prompted a shift to the claims of community over hierarchic political structures. The nativists' search for origins, their concern for relating things to one another in a constructed series with a common genesis, and Hirata's selection of a true history embedded in nature and the natural, combined to figure communitarian and horizontalist claims and authorize them as a true tradition. We will see later that Hirata devoted special attention to the question of tutelary shrines (*ubusuna no kami*) and local village deities in the *Tamadasuki*. There, he tried to show how local religious practices served as contemporary reminders to the community of the autonomy and authority conferred by the creation deities. Such institutions and practices represented contemporary instances of an authority existing prior to publicly constituted hierarchical governance; they also functioned, in Hirata's considerations, as sources of social control and reminders to the community that ultimate judgment rested with Ōkuninushi no kami and his invisible governance. "It is the august office [*omushiku*] of the emperor", he wrote, "to receive the great and august intentions of the creation deities as its own purpose in order to rule the realm, by making *kami* affairs principal in the *matsurigoto* and by bestowing love on the ordinary people" (*HA*, 194). And we know that Hirata and his successors identified godly affairs ("learning about the *kami*") and human affairs ("learning about the ordinary people").

The Chronotope of Collective Time

It would be a mistake to assume that Hirata's cosmic narrative was only prompted by impulses to return to the golden age of a simpler time in the history of the folk, just as it is incomplete to propose, as many Japanese interpreters have, that his thought intended to support a flagging feudal order by reminding people of their ethical duties. We must remember that his elaborate construction, recalling a different time and order of things, was inserted in the world of late-eighteenth- and early-nineteenth-century Japanese society, as remote from the conditions the narrative recounted as our world is from Hirata's. We must also account for the often-neglected juxtaposition of the content of the nativist narrative to received official versions of "history." By propinquity, the nativist narrative revealed a profound contrast between differing versions of "history" and the subject of the enounced, not to mention the producer of the respective discourses. This disjunction

signified a recognition that prevailing formalizations required supplementation if their claims were to remain uncontested. The supplement, which the nativist narrative undoubtedly represented, intervened
in contemporary history precisely because its content was organized
around a story line in which large numbers of people—the folk—who
had remained marginal to Confucian "histories" were invited to constitute themselves and their lives as the subject of the discourse. The
terms employed in the narrative worked over the materials of ancient
histories, largely taken on and in their own terms. But these terms can
be reread as a diversion, if not a displacement, for a message quite
different from the one described in the manifest content. Just as it
would be wrong to conclude that death and the destination of spirits
was the problem dogging nativist discourse and that it was more compelling at this moment in Japan's history than at any other time, so it
is insufficient to see Hirata's narrative as an instance of innocent cosmological speculation. The solution to the question of death permitted
nativism to conceptualize life, through the form of a cosmological narrative, as a crucible of things produced by the creation deities (*musubi
no kami*) for the ordinary folk; this crucible was produced to show the
necessary wholeness of existence and the web of relationships in kinship that held life together in a continuum of interchanges between
gods and humans, life and death, production and reproduction, birth
and growth, creation and custom, and past and present.

But it was also the task of the narrative to provide a "natural justification" for the historical intention producing it.[34] It transformed the
"reality of the world," as it was received in the late eighteenth century,
into an "image of the world" in which contingency appeared eternal
and culture was reapprehended as nature. The passage from culture to
nature abolished the "complexity of human acts" and provided them
with the "simplicity of essences"; it organized a world free of all contradictions, because the image of a totality held all things together in
kinship. The artifice of culture, "emptied of the history" that produced
it, was filled with nature; the "world displayed a harmony of essences."
Although it was a world made by the gods for human habitation, the
significance of human action was lessened because of the intervention
of the deities. To reproduce in custom the act of creation, to "imitate"
the *kami*, was an intention endowed by the gods; therefore, it constituted a natural, not a cultural or historical, activity. Although this view
could easily be used to induce large numbers of people to fall into line
and work hard and, hence, suggest by an absence that they are failing

to perform work, it could just as easily prompt people to see themselves as authors of their own action once they were inserted in a world vastly different from the one in which they lived. The nativist narrative ultimately signified a collective world of preclass, folk essences, existing prior to the various contemporary divisions of labor and life; the focus on this world explains the rural appropriation of nativism in the 1830s and 1840s.

Owing to the creation of the land by the gods for the people and the human partnership directed to "reproduce" this primal act, time (by contrast to Hirata's own time) was collective: it was measured in events and moments essential to the agricultural collectivity; work (the central agency of reproduction) and the consumption of things were also collective, especially when contrasted to late-Edo life, which Hirata and others regularly denounced for its profligacy, private consumption, and self-interest. The time envisaged in his narrative was linked to work (and worship, as we shall see) and remained inseparable from everyday life as long as it did not interfere with the continuation of the productive process. It was, as M. M. Bakhtin would have said, the time of labor; everything was measured by the collective work process, and there was no possibility yet of the individualization of interior time.[35] By shaping time, collective work called attention to growth and productive increase, and time confirmed merely the process, not its proliferation. When Hirata explained that the *aohitogusa* represented luxuriant growth, resembling thick grass, he drew attention to the question of growth and increase and showed how no real division could exist between humans and plant life. The perishability of things, even death, appeared simply as moments in the broader matrix. The death of the body did not mean an end to life: the corpse was returned to the soil to replenish and nourish it, and the spirit was removed to another place to continue life under altered conditions. Because the time of the narrative was still collective, individuals were not yet isolated or differentiated as, of course, they were in Hirata's time. Growth, old age, and death were subordinated to the cycle of agricultural production.

Hirata privileged reproduction ("returning the blessings of the gods") as the purpose of narrative time, which moved ceaselessly toward a future that never came (desire of the Other); humans worked indefinitely to reproduce the conditions of social existence for succeeding generations, in order to assure the continuity of the species. Custom signified the continuing creation that was never completed. Work aimed for growth and reproduction for the future both in agriculture and in human life. In this version, Hirata singled out consumption as a sign of contemporary unhappiness in Edo, and sought to reunite it with physical labor, the activity of the body. By this move, he intended to diminish commodification and the self-contained, isolated pleasures that interfered with the matrix of collective work. But the centering of reproduction dissolved any real distinction between time zones, past, present and future. The time Hirata restored in his narrative was spatial and concrete, rooted in the land that humans must work to make habitable in order to sustain the order prescribed by the gods. Nativists, it is worth recalling, rejected China principally because it juxtaposed culture—contrivance—to nature. Hirata's narrative restored human activity to nature, just as linguists relocated language in the world of things, where human life and the life of nature were measured by the same events on a single scale, bonding the reproductive act to consciousness itself. Collective life and collective time combined to constitute the wisdom of the national soil (*kunitsuchi*).

The sense of time in Hirata's narrative sought to restore unity in the face of contemporary individualization, which had installed differing scales to measure personal events and historical time. Aizawa Seishisai's (1782–1863) elevation of the *daijōsai* (Great Thanksgiving Rite) in the Mito discourse sought to produce the same effect by rejoining personal time to the collective rhythm. For Hirata, whose sensitivity to the privatization of life is well recorded, it was vital to summon a time before the existence of the private sphere, before the invention of private life. His narrative pictured life as a unity that held the various parts—birth, growth, reproduction, and death—as manifestations of collective existence, not as instances of personal affairs, because of their links to the labor of the body. By collective work, humans encountered these cosmic moments and saw themselves in a relationship to the deities, who were everywhere. They, the cosmos, and all the deities participated in a series of mutual transactions constituting the human plot; all things and objects were drawn into the orbit of life as totality to become living, animate participants in its events. Their participation in the plot was placed in the foreground, rather than serving as "background" or as a remote landscape separated from the locus of human activity.[36]

Even before the agrarian appropriation of Hirata's nativism, it is evident that his narrative bespoke what M. M. Bakhtin has called a chronotope in defining the matrix of preclass, folk time in contrast to the matrices of objects and phenomena of contemporary literary practice (*gesaku*) and discursive writings (*keiseisaimin*). Hirata's restoration of this chronotope and its implicit juxtaposition to contemporary matrices implied the existence of two opposing conceptions of life. The reverse of the folk, preclass chronotope figured in his narrative was a contemporary social order that had isolated life sequences into firmly established discrete events, where time itself was separated between personal life and "history," between private rhythms and public, disunified, fragmented, and different duties. In its place, Hirata offered the unity of time in a single event—the creation and its endless replication—so as to demonstrate by contiguity that all phenomena and objects represented only the parts of the whole. His narrative fused humans and nature in a common undertaking. In the series of occurrences recorded in his narrative, events had no individual or existential status; rather, they were categories. All events were seen simply as equivalents of all others—eating, reproduction, creature comforts, work, worship, death, all constituted the matrix under the sign of custom. And custom was the single event of creation. Edo life, *sekan*, was already highly stratified and differentiated into discrete divisions, and forms of activity were separated from physical work. Consumption was privatized and compartmentalized; it had been removed from collective life and had become an end in itself, as attested by contemporary verbal fictions and "custom." The members of the collectivity had experienced a vast transformation from producers into consumers. Food, drink, sexual activity, pleasure, and death were increasingly severed from the matrix that, in an earlier time, had given them unified meaning. Everyday life was becoming atomized.

Hirata's narrative sublated the differentiation between productivity (work), religion (worship—that is, repayment to the gods), and everyday life (custom) by unifying these activities in the body. Here, he owed much to the contemporary privileging of the body in popular literature, art, and entertainment, but he differed from occupants of the world of play in his insistence on using the body for disciplined work rather than specialized activities. He spoke of folk time to arrest what he believed was the personalization of everyday life, where the elements of the unified matrix—eating, drinking, sexuality, pleasure, and death—were transmuted into privatized, everyday affairs. Popular verbal fiction (*gesaku*), for example, valorized sexual love over fertility and reproduction, and it designated drinking and eating as objects of pleasure rather than necessities to maintain collective work. In the late eighteenth century, death, which in the preclass matrix had belonged

to life, was separated from the totality and made to look fearsome, causing unhappiness and diverting people from an authentic existence to
search for surrogates that would "console" their anxiety. Hirata tried to
allay popular fear and anxiety by showing that death simply meant a
transformation that restored the collective identity. His narrative differed decisively from Motoori's rewriting of a sacred text not simply in
his decision to emplot a "single story line," even though this marked
an important departure, but in his attempt to provide a mediation between an absolute past and an uncertain present. For Motoori, the
Kojiki described an epic time, a time of the founders—deities, even
heroes—remote and separated from his time. Even though his cognitive mode—*mono no aware*—functioned to close this distance, it was
purchased at the price of rooting the operation of knowing in poetic
perception and the power of metaphor. Metaphor may have led to tangibility but not to practice. By contrast, Hirata sought to reconstitute
the collective matrix by restoring the centrality of work as the agent of
the reproductive process that each human was capable of performing
in the present. Work called attention to the powers of practical achievement to integrate a totality whose components lay dispersed throughout
contemporary society as fragments obeying their own movement.[37]

Although Hirata aimed to shore up the failing moorings of the
bakuhan system, he also drew attention to a profound distinction between alienated and unalienated work. By relating work to its preclass,
folk chronotope, he was able to offer his contemporaries an explanation
of the meaningfulness of work and its necessity for maintaining the
social whole. He proposed that alienated work represented a separation
from the time matrix in which all activities were interrelated, a time
before the separation of manual and mental labor, when all forms of
conduct corresponded to sensuous practice. But to propose this argument was also to imply its opposite. The contemporary matrix had
caused both meaninglessness ("unhappiness") and alienation—forms
of individuation and privatization. This perception resembled an earlier argument that considered the present to be the place where language and experience had become uncoupled although, in fact, they
amounted to the same thing. Here was the full promise of a syntagmatic hermeneutic. Nativist linguistics called attention to the separation between language and experience and sought to overcome it by
returning to an unalienated language in a different time and place. By
the same token, Hirata's valorization of a preclass, folk matrix reminded his present of a time when working had been intimately impli-

cated in the web of life, and vice versa. In his day, there was good reason to suppose that work had been separated from life and language from experience. The solution to each involved a metonymic operation that enabled nativists to retrace the relationships to a time before they had become "alienated." Making this move inevitably involved an act of criticism of contemporary society and its rulership with far-reaching consequences.

To juxtapose this vision—an "imaginary" resolution—to prevailing formalizations is to reveal that the formalizations were no longer capable of concealing fundamental contradictions; it also allows us to reread Hirata's narrative as a different kind of supplement to what was apparently lacking in official ideological claims to represent the social order. Especially because of the kind of resolution he offered, this supplement constituted a political intervention that contested official Tokugawa ideology where it was weakest by providing a completely different conception of order to make up for what apparently was missing; it was subsequently amplified by rural nativists to legitimize their secession from the control system. Whereas, in Motoori the poet was delegated to resolve the "contradictions" found in the social order (all deriving from the disjunction between language and experience) by the exercise of imaginative empathy, in Hirata the collectivity itself was to act in concert with the cosmos by the operation of practical and sensuous activity (work and worship) to overcome fragmentation, in which the personalized poetic perception of the poet stood as a symptom. In rural *kokugaku* the poet was displaced by the peasant sage, and a discourse on origins became a discourse on practice and politics.

Finally, Hirata's discourse, at the ideological level, was concerned with the question of social indeterminacy. What his narrative seemed bent on accomplishing was a strategic displacement, or even occultation, of the social divisions and historical creativity which had brought contemporary society to its present state of circumstances. In fact, Hirata's narrative worked to prevent an opposition between the "imaginary" and the "real," since it was this recognition that led him to call attention to the question of social indeterminacy in the first place. The real, as he articulated it, had already been *determined* at the time of the creation. Hence, his narrative called for a knowledge whose basis, origins, could not be secured by simply appealing to the process of knowledge, that is, by interpreting the visible.[38] As a discourse, it succeeded momentarily, like other contemporary discourses, in controlling the possibility of articulating the social itself, by defining the roles people occupied as natural endowments devised by the deities in the invisible world, as effects of the invisible realm, the cause of which—divine intention—was never perceptible to humans. In this sense, it is possible to argue that Hirata's aim was to dissimulate existing social divisions in the presentation of another world, the world of creation and origins, and the "materialized invisibility" of the founding moment in the continual cycle of reproduction.[39] Through the power, or, perhaps I should say the seduction, of narrative, Hirata was able to persuade his audiences (who went on to reemplot the overdetermined rural scene with this story line, in order to fulfill the promise of the figure) that the discourse enunciated about the order of the cosmos and the order of the social originated from elsewhere, outside of history, at the moment of origins and creation, which was still self-present in the practice of worship and work.

4 Routinizing the Ancient Way

Religion and the Problem of Routinization

In the early 1830s, nativism left the cities for the countryside. Its transport to rural Japan, especially to the eastern regions and the vicinity of the Japan Sea, produced a transformation of its message that conformed to the needs of its new placement. *Kokugaku* had been, from the time of its inception, an urban phenomenon. All the great schools and academies were located either in the Osaka and Kyoto region (Kamigata) or in Edo. Even Hirata and Motoori's successors in the Suzunoya anchored their activities in Edo and recruited their students principally from the vast population of commoners (*yūmin*) and samurai quartered in the city's environs. Differing interpretations of *kokugaku* did not necessarily specify any one social group in the general effort to constitute a subject for discourse, since the adherents of both the Suzunoya and the Hirata persuasion sought to reach the "ordinary person of the times" and the "people born in the august land," wherever they were located and whatever station they occupied in the social formation. Yet once nativism was appropriated by rural notables to resolve the question of order and to arrest the diminishing productivity plaguing the countryside, the alliance signified a historical conjuncture of different domains of the social order.

Although I will offer a detailed explanation of this historical conjuncture and the subsequent ruralization of nativism in the following chapter, it is important to suggest here that there was nothing in nativism that necessitated its rural appropriation. Nativism and agricultural life were relatively independent of each other in the late eighteenth and early nineteenth centuries; there was no inner necessity compelling them to draw together into a natural partnership, even though much of the imagery of nativism was derived from texts and stories steeped in creation, productivity, and growth. Although Hirata attracted large numbers of students to his school, the Ibukiya, they were by no means recruited principally from the countryside. His lectures' turn to agricultural life was prompted less by a heightened consciousness of the primacy of rural Japan as a central place than by the constraint that the basic categories and concepts he wished to support were rooted in a preurban environment. For their part, agriculture and village life had no need of an elaborate projection.

Even before the nativist message reached the countryside, it was necessary to make the conception of the ancient Way meaningful and accessible to large numbers of ordinary people and to transform the narrative of creation and custom in order to make contact with contemporary reality. The crucial link was provided by Hirata's efforts to constitute a subject for discourse through the routinization of his teachings at the Ibukiya, which established a "natural" relationship between his conception of the Way and the content of everyday life lived by his subject, the ordinary folk. Matsumoto Sannosuke, in his pioneering and now-classic study of late-Tokugawa *kokugaku*, has referred to this routinization as a process of the "positivization" (*sekkyokuka*) or "religionization" (*shūkyōka*) of nativism after Hirata's intervention.[1] Acknowledging that it was less the purpose of his study to explain this strong turn toward practicality than to demonstrate the process of politicization during the late-Tokugawa period, Matsumoto suggested that the concretizing of nativism stemmed from Hirata's rejection of poetic studies and his differences with the Motoori school. By implication, he added, the contextual force of late-Tokugawa history figured Hirata's decision to concentrate on the positive nature of faith and the centrality of daily life. His explanation relied, however, on the larger interpretive code that emplotted nativism in the role of an ideological support for the failing managerial order in its need to secure "voluntary" assent to its coalition of authority.

A different explanation is available if we take into account the metonymic strategy that permitted nativists to reduce the field of cognition to a syntagmatic chain in order to trace things back to their concrete beginnings. This move was not inspired by a romantic impulse to recover a golden age of antiquity, which would make nativism appear as an instance of feudal atavism. Rather, its purpose was to show

the fundamental identity of past and present by disposing its practitioners to apprehend phenomena in part-whole relationships. In other
words, metonymy was used to reach a series of metaphorical identifi-
cations and thereby recover a tangibility lost to the present. Metaphorical identification offered the means to refer to contemporary life without actually doing so, by describing a shared structure in ancient
mythohistory and poetry that had been suppressed. Behind this conviction lay the larger belief, accepted by both Motoori and Hirata, that
the content of life they were defining related to the life of the ordinary
person, who had remained outside the Neo-Confucian field of knowledge. To this end, Motoori's strategy led to the apprehension of the
primacy of things in their particularity (*mono*), since all things expressed the powers of the *kami*—who had originally established the
correspondence of individual and type—and their relationship to the
larger cosmic totality (*Hito wa mina, musubi no kami mitama ni yorite,
umaretsuru mani mani, karada ni arubeki kagiri no waza wa, onozukara
shirite yoku nasuru mono ni shi areba*; MNz 9:59 [*Naobi no mitama*]).
When Motoori referred to Shinto—the Way of the gods—as "things as
they are," which "follow the customs of the times," he intended only
to emphasize the importance of thingness and particularity and, therefore, the necessity of restoring the primal tangibility of the godly age in
the present. Motoori apprehended the field of knowledge as a metaphorical identification of individual things, objects and humans, immediate and knowable, in the direction of integrating all the parts in a
spiritual and timeless whole. This, too, was the purpose informing Hirata's decision to map a cosmological narrative that would account for
the relations of things, in order to demonstrate the tangible identity of
the sacred and the secular, the divine and the mundane, and the extraordinary and the ordinary. This strategy inspired a shared concern
for the texture of daily life and its primacy as a subject of knowledge.
Hirata merely enlarged Motoori's vision of Shinto as contemporary custom into a vast totality, including both the ancient Way and the daily
affairs of the present.

By the 1820s, Hirata could juxtapose the integrative powers of cosmology (now demonstrating the irreducible relationship of all things in
contiguity) to the surrounding structures of social, economic, and political life, which, to many at the time, were showing signs of fragmentation, disruption, disorganization, and division. The cosmological text
became a social text, and the transmutation supplied both the occasion
and the means to install structure in place of random eventfulness. His

elaborate narrative also functioned to encode the world as he saw it and to account for the appearance and incidence of differences, unrelated things, that were threatening received modes of epistemological organization. His hope was to integrate the world of experience with the world of things.

We know that cosmological explanation driven by a logic of likeness seeks to satisfy the need for integration by differentiating and classifying relationships among things into a greater totality, which is capable of securing similitude. A flurry of such speculation had already broken out in the late eighteenth century, and *kokugakusha* found in it the promise of a systematic production of their conception of reality. Claude Lévi-Strauss's later observation concerning cosmologies seems appropriate here: "Although experience contradicts theory, social life validates cosmology. Hence, cosmology is true."[2] In the late-Edo period, activity everywhere attested to and signified how theory was contradicted at every turn by experience, so that it could no longer be discounted as mere anomaly. Moreover, writers who constructed cosmologies were beginning to include objects from contemporary experience in their efforts to integrate and totalize. Neo-Confucianism, in whatever form, sought to resolve the contradiction between representation and experience by heaping theory upon theory to bridge the widening separation between principle or reason (*ri*) and social life. Nativism, with other disciplines, refashioned the textual materials of mythohistory into an explanation of contemporary life itself and offered meaning to the experiences and practices of social groups when, before, there had been none. *Kokugakusha* were able to show a structural homology between their conception of cosmology and its propensity for dividing things between the seen and the unseen, between creation and the quotidian life of the most ordinary person. Reconstituting the "real" purpose of Shinto in this way, nativists were able to draw attention to the linkages between past and present, creation and custom, deity and human, divine plan and daily practice (worship and work), as if no real differences intruded, and to show, above all else, how relationships between things could never have been other than connected and successive from the time of creation.

Metaphorical identification resulted in another achievement. In producing a contemporary reality with the perspective of antiquity and the social structure of the present and in insisting on concreteness and particularity as parts related to the whole, nativism was able to show the similarity of series between religion and daily life, between the affairs of the *kami* and human life and labor. To refer to the Way of the gods summoned life itself, the minute details filling the ordinary person's days and the reproductive powers of work. Talking about the ordinary life and work in this sense suggested a religious celebration, since work had come to express both a constant reverence for the gods and the ancestors for their blessings and a continuing epiphany of thanks. In the world of late-Tokugawa discourse, Hirata's reworking of the two realms (hidden and visible) possessed untapped possibilities that his cosmology and classification of things had already disclosed. Although his cosmology functioned later as the form to defamiliarize objects near at hand—to jar stock responses in order to renew perception and reenliven lived experience in a fresh and authoritative way—many among his contemporaries rejected this impulse. Motoori Ōhira regarded "discussions that investigate all things and events and calculate the condition of the universe [*tenchi*]" as "useless." Even though it was proper to "forget about the Chinese mind and despise Buddhism," he acknowledged, the cosmological explanations of Hirata, Hattori, and Gotō Ishin equally failed to grasp the ancient Way of the imperial land. Others denounced thinkers like Hirata for having "imitated the learning of Dutch scholars, whether there is consent or not" (*MNz* [old] 6:45).[3]

Hirata exploded on numerous occasions in response to contemporary criticism. He expressed dissatisfaction with established modes of learning and dramatically showed a distrust of scholars in general, who seemed to have neither grasped the essential problems of the day nor accepted his production of reality. His perception of a specific problem finally convinced him of the necessity of finding an instrument to convey his message to a broader constituency. Many, as we shall see, shared Hirata's conviction that perception itself had failed and that it was now necessary to "reach what one can see" (*kami mireba oyobanu koto no okaredo kasanugite mimu oyobu kagiri o*)."[4] In Suzuki Shigetane's assertion, "In these times there are two kinds of fools, those who do not pray to the *kami* and those who do not carry on their affairs" (*Yo ni chisha futatsu ari. Sono hitotsu wa, kami o inorazaru hito nari. Sono hitotsu, koto o okonowazaru hito nari*),"[5] we have a partial explanation of Hirata's self-appointed activity to teach the realm and his decision to routinize the learning of the ancient Way by unifying worship and work. But, as will become apparent, Hirata's conception of knowledge bypassed contemporary standards of learning and scholarship altogether, in order to make contact with Edo townspeople.

Sender and Receiver: Constituting a Subject for Discourse

Hirata saw the connection between discourse and audience early. In the lectures presented in the *Tamadasuki* and the *Ibuki oroshi* (both compiled by students about 1827), he declared that his objective was to clarify the content of the "ancient Way" to a larger audience of townsmen. In these lectures we are able to see that what he tried to talk about related "naturally" to the lives of ordinary folk. Not only did his message concentrate on knowing the ancient Way (in contrast to Motoori's decision to know *mono no aware*) and how it corresponded with the content of everyday life, but he endowed his lectures with contemporary idioms, often recalling *rakugo* in his use of familiar devices such as anecdotes, stories, and folk proverbs in order to reach the people he was addressing and be understood by them. The employment of the idioms of common speech in the *Tamadasuki* and the *Ibuki oroshi* show best the nativist disposition to emphasize the spoken word over writing.

Although the teacher-student relationship structured the setting in which Hirata conveyed his message to the audience, it does not explain how the propositional content of his lectures was received and understood. The relationship between him and those who wrote, spoke, and even acted in the idiom of the narrative code of archaism was not a simple one between master and disciple; nor was it easily reducible to the influence of an overwhelming vision and the brilliance of the lonely genius, even though Hirata was not reluctant to picture himself in such heroic terms. Before contact could be made, a number of conditions establishing the possibility for intersubjective communication were necessary to convince his interlocutors that they, not simply Hirata, were the subjects of discourse. The construction of a world view meant identifying an audience that already existed in part or in some potential form, or creating one where there was none, inscribed in the very code—the prose of the world—to which the discourse referred. The activation of this audience required casting it in a role it could not have played in a systematic manner.

The utterances of a discourse, which assume the presence of an audience, must give expression to those who are in a position to receive; they may also, perhaps, satisfy vague expectations that have not yet been disclosed in coherent articulation. The discourse opens up a space for tenants to occupy, but as they fill it they may change its requirements. Although the discursive disclosure of the world appropriates an audience, it is appropriated itself by those who listen/read as they actualize its meaning. The achievement of appropriation is an event. What has been appropriated—made one's own by the listener/reader—is neither the intention of another subject or something mental nor even some design hidden behind the text of utterances; it is rather, in Paul Ricoeur's words, "the projection of the world, the proposal of a mode of being-in-the-world, which the text discloses in front of itself by means of its non-ostensive references."[6] In the act of appropriation, the subject is constituted by the matter of the discourse.

Understanding the discourse requires a recipient (the addressee in Roman Jakobson's model) to cast himself in a role before the discourse (either as a listener or, more important, as a reader of its texts), so as to follow the message that is being communicated in a specific style, language, and mode of figuration; tracing the "arrow" of meaning and making the effort to think in accordance with it establishes the condition for self-understanding.[7] To follow the message and plot the traces of the arrow of meaning is to identify with its production, becoming the subject of the enounced, as if the recipient is the author rather than the reading audience of the utterances being expressed. When Hirata and rural nativists, who spent a good deal of time writing and lecturing to village constituencies, suggested that the drama of creation authorized a narrative devoted to the necessity of reproduction and that its subject was the ordinary folk and the centrality of daily affairs, this message as a formalized articulation enjoined receivers/readers to see themselves as the authors and characters of the story line appointed by the gods to reproduce the creation in their day-to-day activities. Custom called attention to the quotidian life of the ordinary folk and signified the continuous act of reproducing the creation. Producing the discourse, therefore, was assimilated to the act of reproducing the social conditions of existence of a certain kind, removed from the actuality of contemporary conditions in the early nineteenth century: the referential code summoning the identity of belief and mundane activity, divine intervention and human intention, recognizable by all was joined to a message that expanded on the necessity of quotidian life. Intersubjectivity, in this connection, meant securing the conditions for communication between what was being said and those who were listening/reading, between the text of utterances and the social text of common existence; it resulted in lowering differences between sender and receiver. In part, this effect was initially accomplished in the Ibukiya by assigning the authorship of the central texts of the discourse to those who, presumably, had been student/auditors. Texts such as the *Ibuki oroshi* and the *Tamadasuki* had originally been lectures given by Hirata, but because they were identifiably transcribed by "listeners," the teacher's voice meshed with several other voices as the texts were prepared for reading. The signature "Hirata," signifying authorship, appeared but the person of Hirata was absent, and the voice of the individual receded into the collective utterance of the ordinary person.

In the message of the lectures, reproduction referred not simply or only to the necessity of sustaining the conditions of social existence—following the "arrow" of creation as authorized by the "prose of the world"—but also to the ideological reproduction of the productive relationships, especially the role of subject/agent, whose activity satisfied the continuing requirements of the creation. Following Althusser, we can say that ideological reproduction meant interpolating the ordinary folk as subjects, subjecting them to an Other (Subject)—the "deities" (and whatever else they represented in social politics)—and compelling a mutual recognition of this relationship. By this operation, the subject would be put in a position to recognize (better yet, to *mis*recognize) himself. But in order to be effective, ideological reproduction must ensure that recognition will lead to a reproduction of the social conditions of collective existence.[8] Here, then, is the decisive juncture between narrative and discourse: narrative, as a function of language, reports the object of action and ceaselessly drives discourse toward action in behalf of the object; the language of poetry glorifies itself at the expense of the referential function of discourse.[9]

Audiences and texts share language, and language bonds senders and receivers in a common mode of praxis expressing and reflecting their experiences of the world. This field of praxis is an instance of a linguistic code that brings writer, readers, and texts together as elements in a larger referential code to convey a message with a recognizable cognitive content. We shall see that Hirata and his school employed the common idiom—the language from the streets—and a fund of rhetorical devices to establish a language code to convey a message that their audiences could grasp since its content derived from the daily experience of the folk. This technique forged the identity of a specific language and its object and demonstrated the natural relationship existing between a recognizable linguistic idiom and the cognitive elements, the ordinary life of work and worship, that it constituted as a message from which to draw meaning. In this way, nativists were able to shift the terms from a discourse that emphasized the practice of representing culture to one that authorized a genuine cultural praxis steeped in common sense. Reproduction, in late-Tokugawa nativism, did not mean a simple duplication of the conditions of existence but, rather, the retrieval of a preclass, folk matrix that it juxtaposed to prevailing forms of life and labor. The call for a practice of reproduction became a praxis, since it promised to *produce* a completely different kind of social and political life. When Hirata rejected the prevailing practice of representing culture because it was removed from the actual conditions of daily life, he drew attention to the division between mental and manual labor; his insistence on a praxis promising to reinstate a preclass, folk matrix testified to his effort to overcome the very divisions of labor that had produced the historical configuration. He was convinced, as Marx was later to write, that culture—mental labor— "might flatter itself as being independent of the social process" even though its forms of consciousness continued to belong to a complex division of labor that was free from neither history nor life. Hirata defined culture as mental labor in the narrowest sense—as the problem itself that contemporaries had to overcome—and rejected its pretensions because of its removal from the social/life processes.

Hirata took his lead from contemporaries who had already tried to provide a way to fulfill the aspiration, which many believed was universal, of securing "composure of the heart." Even Motoori had shown a keen interest in the sources of unhappiness; he had explained, in the end, that people were obliged to shoulder their burdens because nothing else could be done about it. In Hirata's time, religionists offered consolation to allay the general fear of death. Hirata questioned their solutions and the *Ibuki oroshi* recorded his objections. Contemporary Shintoists, he said, had returned to the question concerning the composure of the heart. In seeking to expand the Way of the gods, they had decided to combine the explanations of yin and yang, the five elements, and Buddhism (*HAz* [old] 1:14–16 [*Ibuki oroshi*], 101, 106–11 [*Zoku shintō taii*]). Hirata discounted any view that employed imported and alien religious explanations to offer consolation, seeing in them a continuing deception and cause for unhappiness. Such accounts, he stated, were never able to truly "compose the hearts" of those who believed in the "Way of the gods." If people were born in Japan and lived their lives there, they were obliged to reflect on such blessings and never weaken in their resolve not to be seduced by facile foreign theories. "The followers of Shinto who study antiquity will be awakened to the consoling heart." Vulgar Shintoists were inferior to persons, like himself, who pursued the ancient Way. Prevailing forms of Shinto, such as Yoshida, Ryōbu, or Yuitsu, invariably corrupted true belief because of their accommodation to Chinese thought and Buddhism.

In drawing attention to the ideological seduction of the ordinary folk as the cause of contemporary unhappiness, Hirata managed to turn the focus of concern away from the problem of death and toward a consideration of the question of the ordinary people, who, when correctly informed of the teachings of the ancient Way, would "awaken to the consoling heart." In *Godō benkōhon* he wrote, recalling an argument proposed earlier by Kamo no Mabuchi, that he could observe no real difference between living things. Responding to a question concerning the Buddhist notion of enlightenment, he reasoned:

> Because, in the beginning, man is born and lives in the manner of insects, it is not unusual to say that there are no differences between emperor, aristocracy, and peasantry. Emperor and aristocrats only ornament their personal apparel with outward finery. In the *Tsurezuregusa* of Kenkō it is asked, "Are not all species, down to the leaves that grow on bamboo trees, the same as humans?" Even though it is believed that ordinary people are different from emperor and aristocracy, it is not so. (Ibid. 1:20, also 15, 27)

The *Ibuki oroshi* and the *Tamadasuki* were filled with references to "ordinary men of the times" (*yo no tsunebito*), "meek commoners" (*tadabito no sunaobito*), "ordinary people" (*bonjin*), and "commoners" (*tadabito*). The *Ibuki oroshi* frequently referred to special foods, drink, and other creature comforts that must have been familiar and vital to the lives of Edo commoners, while the *Tamadasuki* was structured around well-known deities and shrines and the regular devotional practices punctuating the household calendar. They were both steeped in the texture of the most immediate experiences from daily life—such as table manners, kinship relationships, and household duties—in order to illustrate the points they wished to make. Both of these texts represent important instances of how Hirata used the subject of "the ancient Way" to talk about the ordinary folk. In the last book of the *Tamadasuki*, Hirata assessed the significance of *kokugaku* and the contributions of his predecessors. He acknowledged that both Kamo and Motoori had established the foundations for further study of the ancient Way by differentiating it from the mere examination of antiquity (*ko-*

gaku) and saw his own contribution as enlarging the concerns of *ko-kugaku* and giving it a new orientation. Unlike earlier writers, who had identified poetic studies with the ancient Way, he proposed to examine in detail the beliefs and customs of the ordinary people, their lives, daily practices, hopes, fears, and aspirations. The purpose of "true" nativism, he argued, was knowing about the aspects of life that affected people most.[10]

Hirata chose the form of lectures and discussions to present the content of his message; the tactic of using the spoken word to show his audience that they formed the subject of the discourse on archaism achieved both centering and self-presence. He also decided that these texts (*Ibuki oroshi* and *Tamadasuki*) should be called "instructional readers" (*kōhon*) in order to draw the attention of his listeners and readers to the central purpose of the lectures and discussions. The written versions of the lectures appeared as a combination of Chinese ideographs and the phonetic syllabary. Yet the Chinese ideographs often possessed only phonetic value, as if to replicate the convention found in the earliest texts. Such a practice could have been a positive obstacle to real understanding, but we know that in presenting the texts first as lectures, Hirata employed the language of daily speech. Far from obstructing communication, this technique allowed Hirata to use language to constitute a subject position for discourse of all folk born and raised in the "divine land graced with the spirit of language [*koto-dama*]." Although the written form obeyed the ancient practice of representing Japanese with Chinese ideographs, the sound values signified the language of everyday speech. The real spirit of language, the authentic spirit of the language of the gods and the people, endured in the spoken word, the language of everyday life, which lay beneath the surface of artificial written signs.

Hirata linked the possession of speech to the "spirit of Japan" and the folk who lived in the divine land. To be Japanese entailed speaking a language that had been conferred by the deities. "Without this spirit," he told his audiences, "we would lack an unbending will, much in the manner of the Chinese and Indians" (*HAz* [old] 1:45 [*Ibuki oroshi*]). The possession of language equipped humans (Japanese) to know the true intention of the *kami* Way. In his day, Hirata complained, Confucianists "no longer use the beautiful language of the imperial land, but rather a barbaric tongue [Chinese] . . . which, in reality, resembles the sounds of birds and beasts" (ibid. 1:8). The problem of language was fundamental to understanding, as evidenced in the example of foreign languages that misconstrued reality. "Owing to their sounds, the use of foreign languages misunderstands the means and ends [of things]. They are contrary to expressing things [*mono ii*]" (ibid. 1:9). Reading the Great Learning provided only the rules with which to govern and tranquilize all under heaven. Such a formulary could not be expressed in Japanese, where it would be read in reverse order.

> In China it is said, "rule the realm, tranquilize all under heaven." Because, in Chinese word order, "to rule" modifies and precedes "the realm," the realm is the object and ruling is the subject. The meaning of this arrangement makes the realm seem less important than the act of governing. Yet governing itself is simply the operation any visitor or guest can perform. According to Japanese, there has been a clear-cut distinction between subject and object [*mune to karada*], effect and body, as one refers first to the realm [body] and then later to the act of ruling—*kuni o osamaru*. This is reality. (Ibid.)

Hirata worried about the effects of languages that "mix sounds and ideographs," because they risked mistaking means for ends. During his time, he feared, when many did not even know the difference between Chinese and authentic Japanese, the dominant influence of the former contributed to the corruption of the latter. This corruption (*mikuni no kotoba ga ōkii ni waruku natte*) prevented people from realizing a true understanding of what the "intention of the deities has established." Chinese locutions acted as a screen that prevented the grasping of reality and invariably threw things into confusion. But Hirata, who was concerned with the ordinary people who constituted both his audience and the subject for discourse, acknowledged that a simple invocation of ancient words would also lead to misunderstanding. "In order to expand the ancient Way," he advised, "it is necessary to discriminate the errors in common custom. . . . If things are expressed in ancient words, it will trouble [*togame*] the speech of ordinary folk" (ibid. 1:40). Only by entering the spirit of the times and showing how the present differed from the past was it possible to restore the true meaning of antiquity. In a discussion of the distinction in speech of different classes of people, he noted that differing usages did not necessarily mean that those at the bottom of the social hierarchy understood less well than the masters (*danna*; ibid. 1:42). It was easy to find equivalents in "daily speech" for "remote ancient words that would not be understood," in order to guarantee harmony and "avoid differences among ordinary people" (ibid. 1:42–43). Hirata wanted to discount the fetishism of elegance (*miyabi*). He condemned foreign languages because of their distance from daily usage—which he called "work" and linguists had associated with practice (ibid. 1:9). A clear knowledge of the ancient Way, especially its intention and its solidification of the Japanese spirit (*Yamato damashii o tsukikatame*), required the acquisition of self-knowledge (a view dismissed by his contemporary, Shiba Kōkan, ?1747–1818).

Hirata used ordinary language as a model for both the authentically useful and the spirit of antiquity. His discussions revealed a sharp sensitivity to the political functions of language, and the logic employed in his rejection of the Great Learning could comfortably be applied to the whole realm of human expression. "There are men," he stated, "who regard [Chinese] as if it were something elegant. But it could be said of them that they have forgotten, that they resemble the saying, 'When losing the senses, elegance is also forgotten" (ibid.). Seeing how Chinese sounds had delayed understanding among the folk, Hirata was convinced of the power of language over consciousness and conduct and the importance of close congruities among language, daily life, and custom. His conception of the ordinary person resembled his estimation of daily speech; both became meaningful only in the course of practice. It was still necessary, however, to show how artifice, especially the use of Chinese, diverted people from grasping the truly natural, ordinary, and functional. By revealing the true nature of reality as it was represented in the unadorned language of the ancients, it would be possible to establish in the present an expressive means to transparently reflect what people thought and did. The true Way, he asserted, could never be studied with Chinese words, which referred to a different and remote reality and reflected experience distant from the Japanese consciousness. "If Confucius had been born in Japan," he said, echoing an earlier sentiment of Yamazaki Ansai's (1618–1682), "he would have known that the goals of the Spring and Autumn period have nothing to do with Japan."

Hirata's own writing, taken from speech, stressed short, crisp, and economical sentences. He self-consciously strove to work out an easily intelligible style, and his sentences often read like spare pronouncements. The following example from the *Ibuki oroshi* is illustrative: *Sessha ga mikuni ni to mōshita naraba, kono mikuni no koto ja. To kokoroesae sureba yoroshii no de gozaru* ["Since I live in the august land, it is well if I am informed of its deeds"]. In formal Japanese, this would be written: *Mazu watakushi ga mikuni to itta baai ni wa kono mikuni no koto o sashite iru no da to iu fū ni kokoroete itadaku no ga mottomo yoroshii de gozaru* (ibid. 1:4; see 10).[11] In Hirata's version *mikuni*, "imperial land," was written in *kana*; in the "translation" it would normally be written in ideographs. This example shows the economy involved in constructing meaning for his audiences. On other occasions, Hirata often employed simple locutions to express long and complex ideas that had been worked out in his more formal and exegetical writings. The following example, which distilled the principal argument of the first book of *Kodō taii*, informed his audience that learning, until quite recently, had been dominated by the followers of Confucius and Confucians:

> Learning of this kind consists principally of studying Chinese books; nothing about Japan can be grasped by relying on such sources. What should the purpose of learning be? Although in the past, learning has concentrated on foreign countries, its principal goal should be to learn good things useful to Japan. Thus, the order of learning begins first with a study of facts relating to Japan and then moves to an examination of foreign realms [*Tsuide ja ni yotte mōsu ga. Ima no yo no juseihai no gakufū. Ōkata wa kōshi no kokoro ni somuku koto nomi de. Makoto ni tansoku no itari de gozaru. Sono wa moto to shi manabubeki mikuni no manabi o sezu. Kanseki nomi o gaku de iru ga. Gakumon wa nan no tame ni suru koto to kokoroetaru ka. Subete gakumon no michi wa. Tatoe gaikoku no koto o manabu ni mo ittase. Sono manabu chūi wa. Sono yokigoto o totte. Kono mikuni no goyō ni sen tote. Manabu koto ja ni yotte. Mazu mikuni no koto o moto to shi manande. Sate tōtsukuni no manabi ni oyobu ga jundō de gozaru*]. (Ibid.)

Hirata's lectures were also studded with anecdotes and proverbs, which familiarized unfamiliar arguments for his listeners or rendered strange what they had taken for granted.

Hirata purposely lectured in a manner that would make his message accessible to commoners; in order to constitute the subject for discourse, he also differentiated his pronouncements from mere scholarship and pedantry. "It is customary," he announced in the *Ibuki oroshi*,

> to read the august texts of the imperial land in order to learn the facts of our country. Indeed, it is not curious that children become accustomed to our style of writing. The male writing of Chinese ideographs and the

> stories of China jar the ears of . . . children and often surprise them.
> When one inquires into the true and honest Way, based upon popular
> taste, one finds that it occurs unintentionally. The followers of Confu-
> cianism despise this popular custom and when they read books of the
> august country, they invariably misunderstand meaning, because they
> rely, from beginning to end, on Chinese ideographs. (Ibid. 1:4–5)

In this passage, Hirata employed the term *zoku* to connote the popular
and customary, but it had the pejorative association of "vulgar" as well.
Despite his own scholarly achievements, of which he never tired of
reminding his readers, he squarely sided with the discredited learning
associated with women and children—popular, customary, often spontaneous and vulgar, derived from daily experience.[12] Elsewhere in the
same text he turned to excoriating people who believed that it was necessary to read Japanese books with the assistance of Chinese ideographs,
as an example of shameful behavior that even Confucius would have
censured. It was essential to know and understand the words of one's
own country to secure a real understanding of the people's lives. The
rhythm of his lectures was often broken by bombasts of contempt
hurled at both scholars and scholarship—"this humble person hates
scholars" (*sessha wa tokaku gakusha kirai de*), "scholarly tales" (*ga-
kumonbanashi*), and "vulgar scholars" (*zokushi*)—to dramatize the
point that the learning he was promoting did not have to rely on em-
bellishments and concealments, on culture, to validate the truth. Only
the most humble and ordinary persons, precisely those who had not
been corrupted by false learning, possessed the capacity for grasping
these truths naturally and honestly. The truths were disclosed in the
language of daily speech used by commoners, because they originated
in the quotidian experience of the folk. Foreign languages such as Chinese failed to "correspond to the wondrous and miraculous effect
[*myōyō*] of the spirit of language [*kotodama*]," which was preserved
only in customary forms of reading and speech found among the most
ordinary people. Just as the spirit of language derived from the specific
experience of those "born in the divine land," so the language of the
commoners was the most suitable form for talking about the details
of their lives. He advised scholars to strive for "elegant forgetfulness"—purposeful lapses of memory—if they were to break out of the
lockstep of Chinese for the more natural, active, and truthful language
of the gods that was found among the ordinary folk.

By focusing on listeners who were closer to grasping the essential
truths of antiquity because they lived them and because their language

reflected the common experience, Hirata was able to make the ordinary folk the subject of discourse. In a single stroke, he made the vulgar and popular into the elegant, the mundane and ordinary into the extraordinary, the speechless and silent into the speaking voice, the marginal and peripheral into the center. Yet the same operation demoted the elegant and the extraordinary into the vulgar and common. In the preface to his *Godō benkōhon,* his students, who compiled these lectures, explained that Hirata gave these talks "in response to the needs of the people." Because the students of the lectures had just begun their course of studies, the lectures were, by necessity, "strongly mixed with colloquial language and slang [*sensei no kōsetsu no tsuyokuwata zokugo rigen nado mo majirite*]" (ibid. 1:1). Since the most humble possessed a shallow intention and believed anything they heard, it was necessary to show "what kind of things have obstructed the Way of the imperial land." Hirata labeled as "enemies" people who had "entered into a variety of foreign ways" to corrupt the Japanese Way. He continued, "if one is to rebuke such arguments, it must be done strongly. It is not done by declaring them [his enemies] evil men who are simply deficient in principle. Whatever they do and however it is done should not be even slightly considered." A strong argument used the language at hand. "To mingle popular language and slang so that people, who are without leisure to read books, one will come to know the principles of the imperial Way easily. In truth, it is for this reason that the true feelings that touch the Way are important" (ibid.). The truest feelings were held by folk who remained free from foreign defilement, the ordinary people of the streets who had no time for books and lengthy scholarly discussions of doctrine. This theme reappeared in the preface to the *Tamadasuki,* where we are told by the compilers that Hirata condemned florid prose for the simplicity of common usage. In Book 10 of this text, he was even more explicit in his rejection of the wiles and deceits of scholarship and in his admiration for the unadorned learning common to the ordinary folk. He interpreted a poem by Motoori—*kimomukō kokoro sakujiri nakanaka ni Kara no oshie zo hito ashikusuru*—to mean that, even though Chinese learning sought to teach people to do good, it resulted only in making them shallow and clever. Under the regime of Chinese learning, people were compelled to consider things too minutely; they showed right and wrong too closely and ended up confusing real learning with private knowledge. The distinction between private knowledge and public learning dramatized the distance between the Other (China) and what was near at hand (the custom of the people). Chinese learning forced people to value knowledge too highly, as the criterion for their superiority. Once more, Hirata drew attention to the simplicity of children as an example of ordinary people who need never worry about becoming "mature scholars of Chinese." Only those who possessed a determined heart—and children—could become genuine scholars. "If one asks why it is so," he wrote, "it is because even those who read only Chinese texts are naïve, when seen from this perspective. I have not yet seen a person whom we might call a true scholar." True understanding was reached not by reading books but by exercising a natural endowment. The way of man came naturally from within himself, according to the powers of the creation deities; it was not learned from Chinese books. The things that should be known from the beginning came from birth (*HAz* [rev] 6:570–72). This intelligence, although natural, must be imparted to children by their parents. Where parents were unable to offer such learning, then it was the vocation of the scholar to do so. Precisely for this reason, it was unnecessary for people to read too many books (recalling Kamo's earlier resentment toward learning too many Chinese ideographs). People invariably read too little but always enough to harm them: "If I [*sessha*] have read one book and then explain to another the truths I have learned, and if the other person hears and grasps it, then it is good. I do not think that people need to become scholars. They need only to hear and understand the intention of the ancient Way as I have explained it. If they have tried to understand the present, it is good" (ibid. 6:572–73).

Hirata aimed to discount all prevailing forms of knowledge and the "culture" they authorized and to completely contest the accepted common sense about the role of learning, its objects, and intellectual entitlements. He regarded the form of culture that contemporary scholarship authenticated as dangerous, especially for the ordinary folk who, by and large, had been excluded from it, since it produced unhappiness everywhere and privileged certain things, objects, and groups. As a result, he saw a division between people designated to know and those barred from knowing, that caused the formation of a mass of "pretentious babblers" who inflicted real damage on the social order. He condemned contemporary scholars because they saw themselves as qualitatively different from the ordinary folk, and their activity as vastly superior to the skills of daily life. Common language (*zokugen*) and slang (*rigen*)—the code employed in "lecturing/listening" (*tokikika*)—manifested the appropriate form to discuss the "realm of the gods" and the "godly people who live there" (ibid. 15:109–11). There should be no "hesitation" whatsoever, the preface to the *Ibuki oroshi* announced, to "mix" discussions of the Way with commoner language and slang, because "it is easier for people who have no leisure to read books" (ibid. 15:111). Consequently, Hirata underscored a learning directly rooted in the practicalities of everyday life, rather than ornamentation, arcane subjects, or elegance. "Even though the scholars of today have books that they understand," he wrote in the *Nyūgaku mondō*, "they still have not gained the Way." It was mistaken to assume that the mere acquisition of texts led to an understanding of the Way. If a person possessed practicality, he had no need for instruction; if he lacked the practicality of the Way, then learning was necessary.[13] Hirata sought to dramatize the kind of practical learning that would best serve the needs of the realm (*mikuni no yo*; HAz [old] 1:4 [*Ibuki oroshi*]). Everything else was mere frame and ornamentation.

In the course of elevating a learning useful to the realm, Hirata denounced scholars of all stripes, but especially Confucians, Buddhists, *bunjin* (whom he identified with writers of verbal fiction), and vulgar Shintoists. To reinforce his stance and, perhaps, his solidarity with the ordinary folk, he openly disavowed his status as a scholar. "This humble person," he announced, "hates scholars. The scholars of Edo do not devote themselves to bringing people together. Still, the ordinary people are not nauseating. Since it is good to assemble people together, I am fond of this kind of association. If you ask a commoner, he will speak, but, ordinarily, he does not like to listen to a [scholarly] tale." Hirata boasted that many could be found among the ordinary folk who—like himself—rarely considered themselves scholars in the conventional sense but possessed broad learning capable of serving the needs of the realm. This conception of broad learning characterized Hirata's approach to useful knowledge. A practical learning, as he envisaged it, knew no limits and boundaries, because it avoided constraints imposed by self-interest (as seen in the practice of contemporaries) in pursuit of the useful. Most "scholars are noisy fellows," he complained, "who explain the Way. Such people as Confucians, Buddhists, Taoists, Shintoists, Intuitionists (followers of *Ōyōmeigaku*) lengthen a bad list indefinitely." These scholars often feared obeying the "sincerity of august national custom" and ignored "emphasizing the court" in their studies. They poisoned the people's best intentions and neglected the emperor. "Even though there is an abundance of men in society who study, what fools they all are!" This blindness existed in contemporary scholarship because there were simply too many men "who despise the eye and respect the ear"—Hirata was referring to the willingness of people to listen to hearsay and to follow scholarly fads without actually assessing their usefulness. It was far better to study the "words and sayings of men who are nearby, men of our realm, rather than the sayings of foreigners or only the deeds expressed by the ancients." His criticism aimed at showing that arcane knowledge, usually of distant things and monopolized by scholars, had no relevance for large numbers of people, that the immediate was more useful than the mediate or the distant, the remote or the foreign. Scholarship controlled knowledge and, thus, excluded the ordinary person from participating in it. We must, however, note the irony informing his disclaimers of learning and scholarship and his effort to reach the commoners and bring them together by talking about the familiar and near at hand.

We have already argued that Hirata's purpose was to allay popular fears and superstitions concerning the destination of the spirits after death. Yet he was less concerned with the spirit world than with the quality of daily life, as it should be lived by ordinary folk. Far from merely stoking superstitious beliefs, Hirata wanted to show that as long as people prepared adequately for death, which meant living useful and productive lives, they had no reason to worry about the judgments administered in the invisible realm. "By tightening the intention and investigating the body," he wrote, "one will escape calamity after death." Moreover, "if people know the end, they will be skilled in the beginning; if they know death, they will be skilled in living; and, if they know the limits of household resources, they will be moderate in expenses." When people believed that life was not long, they would "spend empty days," "be ruled by lust," become implicated in commodities, meritorious achievements, and wealth; and intention, he promised, would harden into arrogance (*HAz* [rev] 7:23 [*Honkyō gaihen*]).[14] Living a productive and useful life would forestall disorder and harsh judgment in the afterlife; knowing about death required skill in the task of living. Hence, it was living, rather than death, that commanded Hirata's intention as he tried to reach the ordinary folk, who had been excluded from the concerns of conventional knowledge.

Knowing how the folk lived greatly benefited the realm and prepared the proper path for the departure of the spirit after death. It was important to rely on knowing the requirements of everyday life, not superstitious beliefs or magic, to achieve real consolation toward the prospect of death. "When a temple is constructed these days," he wrote in the *Tamadasuki*, "it is an excessive expense that must surely inflict harm on the realm. It is not a convenience to . . . people and afterward it distresses them. What should we say about tranquilizing people today? Govern society and nourish subordinates and the household [*kenzoku*]." Hirata found it easy to imagine that prosperity could be enjoyed without prayer, since goodness and evil, on which fortune and misfortune depended, meant understanding or "misunderstanding our household duties." He asked rhetorically, How will we know the depth of divine intention, rather than the method of the sages, which is so inferior to our Way? (ibid. 6:50–51). It was not necessary to rely on the outward trappings of faith, if the household duties were understood properly. Household duties merely reminded people of the divine intention of the deities, just as worship at Inari shrines directed prayers to the fox who functioned as a "messenger" of the "chief deities"; despite the popular beliefs of Edo folk, the fox merely called attention to the august virtue of all of the deities. Diligence in work repayed the obligations people owed for accepting divine virtue.

Hirata discussed the people he wished to reach in the *Ibuki oroshi*. "Men of high rank have leisure to read a great many books and, thus, the means to guide the people; men of medium rank [*chūtō*] do not have time to look at books and do not possess the means to guide people. . . . Those who have time and can read are few in numbers." But others required assistance. If they were not offered the opportunity to hear about the Way, they would surely abandon it. "Although men without learning in our times find it difficult to know the Way, they do not have sufficient time to read books." Yet even more than those who were able to consult books, those who were not should be encouraged to seek out the true Way of antiquity. For "those who hear the Way have realized a greater achievement than those who have gained it through study." Hirata's elevation of those who listened and acquired a genuine understanding of the Way suggests that, by constituting a subject out of the ordinary people, he was promising to eliminate the profound division prevailing between those who ruled and those who followed, between mental discipline and physical labor. It explains Hirata's decision to differentiate the showy scholarship associated with Confucians and Chinese books from the true bearing of the ancient Way. The former obscured the latter, authorized improper relationships, and caused confusion and unhappiness. If "scholarship" were eliminated, the Way would dissolve the separation between head (scholarship) and hand (household duties) and reinstate the correct arrangement of things. In the new arrangement, knowledge would become intransitive, since the distance between knower and known would no longer exist. Hirata made ordinary persons, "those who do not have time to read books," knowers of what might be called a "finalist" knowledge. They controlled a knowledge of themselves and the activities considered most necessary and natural to their daily lives, which required only "seeing correctly and hearing correctly" (ibid. 6:509). Hirata's own work, the construction of a message, turned increasingly toward explaining quotidian life, which he associated in both the *Ibuki oroshi* and the *Tamadasuki* with "household duties" (*kagyō*). The content of this knowledge corresponded to "learning about the *kami*." Yet knowing and understanding the *kami* (the folk) demanded real "diligence to avoid neglecting one's household duties," which comprised the "true Way of antiquity." Household duties rested on the twin axes of worship and work in their interaction to create custom. In this way, message merged with practice and sender with receiver to articulate a discourse on practice.

Message: The Work of Worship

In the *Tamadasuki* and the starchy enjoinment to worship, *Maichō shinbai shiki*, Hirata outlined in some detail the way worship interacted with the most mundane forms of daily life and the way the lives and activities of ordinary people represented a religious moment. The "hailing" of daily forms of worship and the description in detail of various worshipful observances was a strategy nativists increasingly employed to make archaism meaningful to a wider audience, but the terms of a program pledged to "hailing" or "interpellating" a subject invariably altered the nature of the message itself. The *Tamadasuki*, like the *Ibuki oroshi*, announced its purpose to inform the "unread" in the ways of the ancient Way. But its emphasis on the relationships between forms of worship, agricultural work, and productivity highlighted the centrality of daily life. Hirata imagined these mundane activities as living examples of the archaic precedent and authoritative proof that no real disjunction separated the present from the preclass, folk past his narrative recounted. But in the exposition, the ancient Way forfeited its privileged status to the ordinary life of the folk in the present. For peasant leaders, many of whom had passed through Hirata's school, the emphasis on the unity of work and worship, life and labor, offered a solution to unrelieved divisiveness, fragmentation, and the threat of decreasing productivity and conferred a form of representation on their leadership. Because *kokugaku* had res-

cued the ordinary folk from the margins of official discourse, it could
enforce a community of interests among the upper and lower peasantry
and overcome the ambiguity of the relationship between village leaders
and their followers. The status of the ancestors and the centrality of the
village deities bound the various parts of the village into a whole. Together, they constituted a world of relationships more "real" and fundamental than those found in the visible realm of public power. The
flow of ties, transactions, and traffic between the hidden world of ancestors and tutelary deities and the visible world of work and social
relations disclosed a commonality of interest and purpose that transcended ascribed status and mundane duty. In this arrangement, village
leadership and the peasantry were encouraged to recognize no differentiations, since relationships flowed horizontally from the deities and
ancestors in the hidden world to the visible world of worship and work,
in order to establish an unbroken chain between the ancestors, gods,
life, and practice. Nativism in this manifestation was more rural than
urban, given to the sanctity of the household, the village, and agricultural work rather than to the uncertainties of play in Edo and Kyoto.
Yet it also aimed at dissolving the more basic division between rural
and urban that underlay the perceived fragmentation of life, as well as
the more immediate separation between manual and mental.

Hirata's lectures in the *Tamadasuki* endeavored to make the content of the ancient Way clear and accessible to the ordinary folk. They
systematized a cycle of prayers that represented an "august transmission
of the gods." To offer respect would "incline the intention of the ordinary people to learn the august Way of the gods," and study would
illuminate "understanding for contemporaries who live in society." "In-
clining the intention of ordinary people" to understand the deities obviously referred to a spiritual attitude informing people as they performed their daily duties; "understanding for contemporaries living in
society" required grasping things and deeds close at hand by people
living in the present. These admonishments did not simply enjoin worship or its understanding in prayer. Instead, the lectures were directed
toward teaching people the fundamentals of an authentic life by systematically showing them how the basic desiderata of daily life conformed to specific prayers that had to be repeated at certain times. The
operation reveals how nativism sought to routinize its message. Just as
people performed various kinds of household work every day, they observed forms of worship "day and night," as if there was a seamless fit
between worship and other life-supporting activities. Although much

of the *Tamadasuki* concentrated on the relationship between prayer and forms of daily performance, the connection was expressed best in book 3: "The two deities Shinatsuhiko and Shinatsuhime are wind gods. After Izanagi gave birth to the land, he was pleased to announce that it was only full of scented, misty fog. There existed a breath that blew this away. This breath began in the wind, which resided in these two *kami*. . . . Since these wind gods possessed the capacity to blow away anything, it is clear that they are able to blow away the evil that afflicts." Hirata explained that *iki*—breath—really meant life and work (*iki hataraku*). Because the breathing of things that live and work was ordained by these two deities, people were invited to pray for long life (literally, long breath). In addition, these two deities had the name *shina*, "long breath." Wind, the breath of the deities, went everywhere, but because it sustained and passed between heaven and earth, the breath of humans was really wind. It made voice and words. Owing to the fact that all things relied on this "august breath" (*miiki*) and the spirit of these deities, "we are obliged to offer our thanks to these heavenly and earthly gods" (ibid. 6:130–39).

The incorporation of religious respect into the texture of daily life, the spirit of the deities into the body ("the living are the body of these ancestors"), the regularization of worship and work into a single series became the condition by which the routinization of the Way led to a form of rationalization. It has been observed by a number of writers, notably Matsumoto Sannosuke, that the process of "religionization" refined the system of native beliefs by internalizing a normative structure among the ruled:

> The obstacles to evangelizing nativist beliefs were removed by Atsutane. The means of evangelizing and instrumentalizing Shinto deeply permeated the interior emotional life of the people. The practice of moralistic norms was not permitted to terminate, as in the case of Confucianism, in the formal and external realm. The proof of practice was not an external symbol, because it had to be pursued internally in one's feelings. . . . A *kokugaku* that rejected external norms for the interior feelings of humans would easily and thoroughly rule them, because it revered the emotionality of the ruled.[15]

Far from signalling "excessive irrationalism," this internalization of belief rationalized the process of faith by removing reliance on external objects and norms and relocating expressions of belief in the interior

emotional life. Behind this process, which enjoined the folk to give
thanks regularly to specific deities within the matrix of their daily lives,
was the cosmic plan and Hirata's demonstration of the connectedness
of things, people, and gods. It was this cosmic connection that was
internalized; ultimately it authorized the recognition (or, perhaps, the
misrecognition) that a person's received vocation was equivalent to an
act of religious observance of cosmic import. This connection also explains, as we shall show later, why Hirata's routinization concentrated
on the household as the most basic unit in the visible world and how
the various activities associated with it—worship and work—summoned the hidden world of ancestors, deities, and creation gods. While
Matsumoto and, beyond him, Maruyama Masao are surely correct in
seeing the internalization produced by the nativist discourse and its
privileging of emotionality as a significant intellectual move in late-
Tokugawa Japan, it is by no means clear that its sole function was to
strengthen an adherence to crumbling moral and political external
norms. Although Hirata railed against Confucianism and especially its
myopic view of the "spiritual life" (*kishinron*), he was just as concerned
with removing corrupting and superstitious beliefs from native religious
practices. In this respect, nativism occupied a common ground with
many of the new religions of the late-Tokugawa period, which sought
to purge worship of its excessive reliance upon external rituals, imagery,
and magic. Over and over again, in texts like the *Shutsujō shogo*, Hirata excoriated Buddhism, especially for leading people astray by relying on external practices such as magical incantations, superstition,
and the material paraphernalia of ritual. In the *Ibuki oroshi* he condemned vulgar Shintoists for mixing native beliefs with Buddhism and
the cosmology of yin and yang, which authorized its own set of super-
stitiously religious practices.

Routinization and rationalization sought to overcome an excessive reliance on the external norms manifested in objects, imagery,
magic, and ritual. Although a case might be made that the process of
dis-enchantment ultimately encouraged the ruled to submit voluntarily
to the rulership, the terms of internalization also figured a conception
of order—the relationship between the visible realm and the hidden
governance—that was far from the one that *kokugaku* supposedly was
made to serve politically. In fact, its real effect, as will be seen later,
was to displace politics altogether by centering the household and the
village and to provide a clearly dangerous alternative to the prevailing
arrangement of authority. The *Tamadasuki* specified this rejection

when it explained that the origins of slighting ancestor worship derived from the "raw artificiality" of "stinking Confucianists" and "Buddhist priests who sell mountains of medicinal nostrums" (*HAz* [rev] 6:576). It also roundly denounced the ornamentation of Buddhist altars (*but-sudan*) as false and empty practices designed to deceive foolish people (ibid.). Elsewhere in this text Hirata dismissed the Bon Festival (the fourteenth and fifteenth days of the seventh month, commemorating the departed spirits) as "foolish observances" and even recommended its abolition, principally because its dependence on Buddhist rites of "false and empty decoration" were disrespectful to the departed spirits of the ancestors (ibid. 6:585–86). "In my family," he declared, "I have put a stop to it." In another instance, the text recorded a conversation that one of Hirata's followers, Ishi Atsuta, had concerning the practice among many of the ordinary folk since time immemorial of installing images of Amida and Kannon and Buddhist saints on the household shrine shelf. After hearing about the ancient Way, people experienced an immediate desire to remove the imagery from the household since it was no longer necessary. Yet they were also afraid because they believed that removal would provoke divine recrimination. Ishi counseled his interlocutor that, since the choice of including Buddhist imagery on the shrine shelf had always been a personal affair, no harm would come from removing the images of Shinran and Nichiren. Indeed, because Japan was the land of the heavenly and earthly deities who must be respected, it was important not to place such Buddhist icons either on the top of the shelf or in front of the household (ibid. 6:589–91).

The most obvious contact between discourse and audience was provided by the creation deities and the deities of heaven and earth concerned with agricultural production and its centrality in the cosmological scheme. Although their implications for an ethic of work were substantial, it most likely would have remained unrealized had it not been associated with an emphasis on the household (*ie*), the veneration of the ancestors, and a continuing reference to the tutelary and guardian deities. In book 10 of the *Tamadasuki* (compiled by one of Hirata's sons some years after the original lectures) Hirata discussed the importance of the ancestors, and in book 5 the primary function of tutelary worship. It is hard to imagine a more systematic account of ancestor veneration in Tokugawa Japan than Hirata's meditations, which represent one of the truly conscious efforts to integrate such long-standing practices into a coherent religious framework that was more nativistic than Buddhistic. The associations we ordinarily make concerning ancestor veneration have been invariably identified with Buddhism rather than Shinto. Shinto had easily accommodated itself to the practice of venerating ancestors, but Hirata made it—along with tutelary and guardian deities and the other significant deities in the Shinto pantheon—part of a regular, daily series of worship and celebration. His purpose stemmed from the larger cosmological agenda, as well as an earlier prompting from Motoori, who sought to dissociate both ancestor veneration and filial piety from their strong Chinese associations. The impulse shared a general desire of the Tokugawa period to purge certain religious practices of foreign impurities. Beyond this general purpose lay Hirata's belief that the ancestral spirits and village deities represented a vital link between the two realms articulated by his cosmological system of classification.

Ancestor veneration offered Hirata the most basic relationship capable of explaining to his audience the vital link between the visible and invisible worlds. By arguing that the spirits inhabited the same place as the living, he was able to propose a union of the dead and the living and to demonstrate the essential similitude of the hidden and visible realms that was so essential to his theory of consolation. When Hirata showed that ancestor veneration—filiality in its most extreme form—manifested pure Japanese sentiment, he was able to use the practice to exemplify the most "natural" and fundamental structural relationship between the living and the dead, between the world of the deities (*kamigoto*) and the visible world (*arawanigoto*), and thereby collapse what hitherto had been seen as differences into a series of resemblances. Everybody had ancestors and would, in time, become one.

In an afterword to his catalogue of daily prayers, *Maichō shinbai shiki* (depending upon the version, there are either twenty-five or twenty-eight prayers, which he subsequently explicated in *Tamadasuki*), Hirata noted that it was just as important to make observances to one's ancestors as it was to other deities. "Whether an antique custom or a contemporary one," he wrote, "these prayers must be entrusted to men." Men who wished to fulfill their household duties were also obliged to pray to the deities of the *ie* (no. 14) and to the shelf reserved for the ancestors (no. 25). The former, he explained, "focuses the heart on worshiping the *kami* who are in the two shrines at Ise (Inner and Outer—the latter sheltering Toyouke [the founding agricultural god])"; the latter would "direct the heart to concentrate on the spirits that are celebrated in the household, such as those of the distant august ancestors and the ancestors of the generations. Apart from having noted that, one must worship, without fail, the various and sundry clan deities [*ujigami*] and the deities of occupations [*nariwai*]" (ibid. 6:18–19). In his brief endnote, Hirata not only singled out, from a very large inventory of religious obligations, the necessity to offer prayer to the household deities and ancestors; he also yoked these prayers to the various clan and tutelary deities, the gods of work, whether one was "working hard at his household occupation or immersed in leisure" (no. 18).

Worship at the *kamidana* (spirit shelf) could confer great blessings and good fortune and instruct the people in the "achievements in the Way to learn about the *kami* [*kami narau*]"; it also provides a central key to our discussion of worship, work and the ruralization of *kokugaku*. Hirata described the observance in detail. "Facing the spirit shelf of the ancestral generations, [this] prayer is offered in the manner of prayer to ordinary deities":

> To the distant spirits of the ancestors and the generations [past]. To all the honorable spirits of relatives and to all spirits celebrated at the ceremonial shrine. [I] offer prudent respect before the august spirits and pray that there will be no harm and injury to household or body. Protect [me] day and night. Increasingly bestow prosperity upon the descendants of [our] great-grandchildren and lengthen their lives so as to serve excellently the august ceremonies. Tranquilly and peacefully hear [our] requests and grant [us] good fortune. This prayer is offered in fear and awe. (Ibid. 6:17)

Then Hirata instructed the worshipers to lift up their heads and clap their hands twice. He advised that such practices must be followed in order to accomplish the "work of purification" (*misogiwaza*) of polluted things, and people "must never neglect to worship the ancestors." This prayer prefaces the last book of the *Tamadasuki*, in which Hirata proposed to explicate the importance of the ancestors to the living. The ceremonial shrine (*matsuriya*), what the vulgar and uninformed called the *butsudan*, was where the household worshiped the spirits of the departed. The distant, honorable ancestors were simply the primal ancestors of the household; the "generations of ancestors" were those who succeeded, from one generation to another, the primal ancestor. He digressed to argue that the word for parent—*oya*—did not originally refer to parents only but embraced the whole series of kin relatives who were first called "distant parents" (*tōtsu oya*). In the prayer, the relatives were brothers who issued from the distant ancestor down through the generations; they included the near relatives on the mother's side (*mata hakata no chikaki shinruitachi*). "All of the spirits worshiped at this shrine are related, apart from those above who are not mourned within the lineage of the distant relatives but who, for some special purpose, are the august spirits of people or retainers who have performed meritoriously for the household" (*HAz* 6:551).

Thus, Hirata established a set of contiguous linkages that extended back to the beginning of the race and the formation of the household and laterally to contain within the province of worship those who were not related by blood either on the brothers' or the mother's side. Each linkage called attention to a metonymical relationship between the part and the whole; whatever the specific relationship, worship referred to the whole household. He used the same strategy to elevate the tutelary and guardian deities, and a century later, the ethnologist Yanagita Kunio (1875–1962) would return to it in his effort to regain the wholeness of life he feared was disappearing from modern Japan. But in his explication of the prayer, Hirata was trying to establish the connection between the household and the primal ancestral descendants. Everything went back to the creation deities. He explained that the request for protection from harm and the realization of good fortune actually tied the ancestors, however remote, to the living. It asked the ancestors to "increasingly bestow prosperity upon the descendants of [our] grandchildren. Grandchildren means children of children. The vulgar call these *mago*, but, in reality, it is correct to use *hiko*. Since *yahiko* are the children of grandchildren, they are commonly [vulgarly] called the children of *himago*. The words of today extend to children and grandchildren, but also to great-grandchildren and great-great-grandchildren [*yashiago*] for all times to follow" (ibid. 6:552). The importance of this practice, according to Hirata, was best understood when contrasted with Chinese custom, where the specificity of terms actually prevented the inclusion of more distant relations within the circle of veneration; in Japan, the generality of terms established the principle of inclusion going back to the beginning. The promise of inclusion was the purpose of enjoining the god-spirits to continually provide long life, which in turn encouraged regular worship for advancing the prosperity of the household in the visible world.

Hirata's cosmologically sanctioned boundaries between seen and unseen also prompted him to hold the living responsible for the veneration of all the departed. The status of the spirits allowed them to live in another realm, never disappearing but taking on different shapes in places such as cemeteries and spirit shrines where they were worshiped. This view also meant that the spirits dwelt within the household itself. "Because there are boundaries between the visible and invisible, we cannot see their [departed relatives'] shapes from our perspective. Even though they cannot speak to us from their side, from time to time they show their form and send instructions. Understand well that, although their shapes cannot be seen, they have not been extinguished" (ibid. 6:553). The point to this discussion was to demonstrate that just as the household was the basic grouping, the ancestors were the most fundamental focus of worship and belief. The act of worshiping ancestors invoked the whole pantheon and, indeed, creation itself. "It is important to especially understand the spirits attached to the household, although one might go so far as to speak about the ancestors; even though one may neglect the worship of other deities, one must exhaustively worship the ancestors morning and night without fail" (ibid.). The creation itself provided the reason for emphasizing ancestors, who should never be forgotten. In the beginning, the creation deities of heaven and earth decreed that Ninigi no mikoto shall descend to earth to rule, in order to transmit this form of the worship of god-spirits to the imperial descendants for all time to come. This was the original meaning of governance, and "through the august rites of the heavenly realm, the honorable generations were governed exceedingly well, according to the performance of this honorable ceremonial [*mimatsuri*], and there were no eventful happenings [*nanigoto mo nakarashi*]." This arrangement lasted through the reign of Jinmu tennō, who, when confronted by special matters, prayed to and requested supplication from the heavenly ancestors (*koto ni gokigan araseraretaru mikoto to miete*). In time, when peace came to reign over the realm, the imperial ancestors were worshiped in the Tomi mountains as a return of thanks for the fortunes conferred.

Hirata argued that, even though the ancient Way could be called political, it was still a practice similar to the reverence for the ancestors. "Nothing was done by august considerations of the august person [of the emperor] alone"; rather, "it was well to perform honorable deeds only on receiving the opinion of the imperial ancestral deities." There are a number of implications of this passage that have gone unnoticed in the conventional literature concerning *kokugaku*: (1) Hirata clearly saw events occurring only when certain archetypal rites were not being observed; history represented "eventful happenings" and, thus, a departure from some conception of normative order; (2) the emperor, far from being the autonomous agent beyond good and evil imagined by later Meiji theorists of monarchical absolutism, was accountable for his actions to the ancestors, the deities, and society itself; and (3) proper political conduct now appeared as nothing more than ancestor veneration, society worshiping itself. Therefore, Hirata could say that "calling the august deed of governing the realm *matsurigoto* came from performing the ceremonies to the deities of heaven and earth" (ibid. 6:554–55). This kind of ceremonial worship guaranteed peace and tranquility and protection from plague, pestilence, and famine. What other functions was government supposed to perform? Moreover, he advised, it was precisely ancestral respect in remote antiquity that made people peaceful and secured the unification of ceremony and governance for generations (*nochi yo saisei itchi itasu nado*).

Confucianism and Buddhism distracted emperors, beguiled and bewitched them into confusion, and ultimately dissuaded them from performing such ceremonies to the ancestors. Everywhere, officials showed contempt for and neglect toward the spirits and filiality. To offset the baneful consequences of this change—what Hirata described as an "eventful happening"—he reformulated the "Regulations of the palace from the Emperor Juntoku [1210–21; *Juntoku in no tennō no kinpi goshō*]." The importance of this reformulation lies in Hirata's decision to substitute the household for the palace, changing the whole purport of the regulations to satisfy his argument:

> In the laws made in the household, the first order of attention is to the ancestors, and then to other matters. At sunrise and sunset, the heart should never neglect reverence to the ancestors. Plainly, never turn away from the direction of the spirit shelf of the ancestors and their burial grounds. As they make possible ten thousand things, one must first offer ceremony to them. Remembering this extends to daily spiritual offerings only and not to anything else. From time to time, furnish special things [for offerings], as well as the first fruits of things prepared daily. When good or evil is attached to the household, good things should be explained to the ancestral spirits; if bad things [occur], they have to be conveyed to the spirits, and prayer has to be offered to them so as to secure goodness directly. In the words of the prayer, "To request that the person succeed and that the household flourish, and that neither harm nor injury will come to body and household, we pray for protection day and night." In the Man'yō there is the following poem transmitted from the divine age of Ōnamochi and Sukunabikona: "When

one sees mother and father, respect them; when one sees wife and child, have compassion for them" (ibid. 6:555–56).[16]

Hirata's argument here turned on the centrality of performing the necessary duties toward the ancestors in order to enforce the inseparability of the spirits and deities from the household. Politically, this sentiment had been formalized in his discussion of "august ordinances." Here, he proposed that the living body merely represented a priest of the ancestors. Although contemporary practice related the priestly office to the performance of shrine duties, the ancients saw priests (*kannushi*) as worshipers of the *kami*. Therefore, the person who celebrated the spirits of his ancestors was the priest of the ancestors (ibid. 6:557). In turn, the "living body" became the substance of spirituality (ibid., 567). Quoting Motoori—"Mother and father are the deities of our household; the children of men exhaust their hearts for our gods"—Hirata was able to reconceptualize this relationship and to point to one of the possible meanings for the term "visible deity" (*arahitogami*; ibid.). He hoped to show that children offered respect and celebration to their parents, who were the living deities of the household and who would most surely join the spiritual ancestors in the unseen world (ibid.). He authenticated the fusion of household and worship by referring—once again—to poetic examples transmitted to the time of the Man'yō from the age of his favorite deities, Ōnamochi (Ōkuninushi no kami) and Sukunabikona (ibid.).

Hirata tried to personalize this sense of reverence by enumerating the kind of offerings that would best satisfy parents in their unseen abode after they died. They should be presented only things they liked most when alive. Hirata instructed his own children—in one of the few moments of levity in a sea of unrelieved seriousness—to make offerings of fish and vegetables after his death. Moreover, it was the obligation of the descendants to "personally purify the spirit shelf daily. [The duty] to furnish the branch of the *sakaki* tree and water is transmitted from [the customs of] antiquity" (ibid. 6:577–78). Although it was true that the spirits lived in the household, it was still necessary to make regular visits to the cemetery on the anniversary of their deaths. Since spirits resided in several places like "divided flames," the cemetery and the households of their children stood as the natural places for worship. Ultimately, this argument showed that, since Japan itself housed the deities and, thus, represented a macrocosm of the household, it was necessary to offer respect to the gods of heaven and earth. Household worship called attention to the whole—the worship of the national deities and the land. It also helped to explain why he advised that Buddhist images, which he detested, should not be placed upon the spirit shelves or, indeed, in front of each house (ibid. 6:590–91).

Substitution (part-for-whole relationships in contiguity) of household for realm, descendants for ancestral spirits, and living deities for unseen gods acquired greater force in Hirata's explanations of the worship of tutelary and guardian *kami*. Again, he sought to demonstrate that things nearest at hand—daily customs, practices, and observances—always related to larger, seemingly remote referents and represented transformations of them. Just as the household now became the focus of worship, the village, which constituted a collectivity of households, served as the center of collective worship. Custom mediated belief and made it meaningful in larger terms. The household represented the most basic grouping in Hirata's conception of the invisible world; the village defined its outer boundaries. The village, household, spirits (ancestors), and distant deities combined to form a series of concentric rings that held together because each naturally connected the next in contiguity.

Like Hirata's prayer to the ancestors, which called for protection and good fortune for the *ie*, his invocation to the guardian and tutelary deities sought to secure protection and prosperity for the village community. "Grant all protection to this village [*sato*]," the prayer intoned. "Before the great tutelary deities [we] offer prudent respect. Protect [the village] day and night, and grant [it] prosperity. In fear and awe this prayer is earnestly offered" (ibid. 6:291). Once more following his impulse to explain the "true" meaning of terms, Hirata advanced the interpretation that the correct word for "tutelary" (*ubusuna*) could be found first in the *Owari fudoki*, where *ubusuna* was the name for the shrine that young princesses entered for childbirth—that is, an imperial parturition hut. These young women were imperial princesses of the Emperor Keikō (A.D. 71–130). Prayers were offered for tranquil births. "Today," Hirata continued, "the *ubusuna no kami* are called guardians of places where everyone was born." In time, these tutelary deities fused with the clan deities (*ujigami*).

Despite their later merging, differences existed between the two in the beginning. The tutelary deities appeared in areas that they presumably governed, and, in time, they became tutelary or guardian gods. The clan gods, however, were said to be the ancestral deities of

particular clansmen. But the reason why these tutelary gods were not
the ancestral deities of the clans lay in the ancient practice of designating as *ujigami* only deities associated with both a single household and
a lineage system. *Uji* was, in fact, the same word as *uchi*—within—
and, thus, the meaning associated with deities referred to prayer and
intimate service within either the village (*kyō*) or the larger lineage
(ibid. 6:292–93). Thus, *uchigami*—*kami* within—meant or was similar to *ujigami*. Moreover, the term denoting those who were within the
clan (*ujiko*) resembled *uchiko* (children—family—within), which no
doubt referred to the group or lineage system. Ultimately, *ujiko* carried
the meaning of "children who are within these *kami*" (ibid. 6:293).
Hirata's discussion aimed at showing that linguistic similarities and resemblances in antiquity invited later folk to blur the distinctions between tutelary gods and clan deities. Yet, significant differences existed
between the functions of clan deities and tutelary gods. "On the side of
the tutelary deities are the men born in the areas as leaders of the clan
[*ujiko*]; on the side of the clan deities, it is our intention to call the
several men who serve there as clansmen" (ibid. 6:295). That is to say,
the tutelary gods served as deities to those members of the clan who
originated in the area of the clan itself; the guardian deities of the clan
functioned to unify the members of the clan who worked for the group
in some capacity.

Hirata believed that the distant ancestors of households were
probably clan deities. Among the villages of the contemporary countryside, the deities of landlords (*jinushi*) were called clan deities, and
shrines had been erected to them. But these gods were the ancestral
deities of particular households. Eventually, worship of the deities of
landlords and of the ancestral deities of the village households became unified. Such worshipers, then, must be called the *ujiko*—members of the clan or parishioners of the shrine of these deities. Later,
Hirata added, it became common practice to refer to all the deities of
the landlords as *ujigami*—clan or guardian gods. The association took
precedence because, since antiquity, "one respects the ancestral deities
of the *ie* and the gods of the masters" (ibid. 6:296). Moreover, the
"august virtue" (*miitsu*) of the spirits of specific areas differed widely.
Humans and animals derived divine powers from the fact that they had
been created by gods. Yet their characteristics differed from region to
region. Thus, "although the *ubusuna no kami* are the spirits of the
earth, they are also the spirit deities in each region throughout the
islands. In one region they are called regional spirits [*kuni tamashii*],

in another tutelary gods. Such distinctions correspond to differences in the topography of the land and the places in which they reside." Regardless of these regional differences, Hirata believed that the variations were largely superficial, because the spirit deities all submitted to the invisible governance of Ōkuninushi no kami. "Moreover," he wrote, "there are the *kuni tamashii* in some regions, and the *ubusuna no kami* in others, who have been directed to share the administration of the realm among themselves and who assist Ōkuninushi no kami, whose basis of rule is the concealed governance" (ibid. 6:298). "They [these various regional guardian gods] administer the great foundation of *matsurigoto* [from the hidden realm] that tranquilizes the realm" (ibid.). In each locale, the men who presided had been entrusted to specially attend to the detail of administration, which, in itself, represented an imitation of divine authority (*So o wakachi osamuru hitobito o yosashite, osameshimetamō arisama ni, ito yoku nite zo omouwarumeru*). People who managed to carry out this authoritative responsibility usually "forget about themselves and are called *daimyōjin*" (ibid. 6:299).

Authority was not merely rooted in the hidden governance; it was also manifest in the tutelary shrines of the various regions. For Hirata, the shrines administered the will and intention of Ōkuninushi no kami (ibid. 6:300–301). Such governance ensured good fortune in that places possessed both belief and a program of appropriate observances to the various tutelary and patron deities. The expression of faith made possible an intimate link between *kami* and humans. This relationship, bound by prayer, kept the village community integral. Intercession by the gods, and the subsequent division of labor they established, which expressed a "bestowal of virtue," assured humans of continuing divine reciprocity and assistance. In his discussion of the function of the local patron deities, Hirata formulated a conception of mutual assistance (good fortune from the gods, repayment of thanks from humans) that could serve as a model for both village and household. Conversely, the assistance that characterized the household or the village could just as easily be projected onto the deities and their deeds. Whichever the case, the major role of the deities involved protection, which came to mean continuing good fortune, whereupon the thankful community returned the blessing with prayer and hard work. Clearly, Hirata was suggesting that the gods helped those who helped themselves. Prayer and work denoted the difference between continued wholeness (order) and fragmentation and decreased productivity (disorder). "If there are deeds that inflict injury and harm on men who are bewitched," he advised, "these tutelary deities are solely directed to administering, protecting, and driving off [such spirits]. Men who serve and believe only ordinarily in these deities will themselves tend toward the mildest protection [*onozukara mimamori mo atsukaranu sama nari*]. One must believe fervently in this heart [of the deities] . . . and men who are closely protected by the tutelary deities are not able to inflict harm and injury" (ibid. 6:311). Ordinary folk (*tadabito*) often vacillated in their resolve concerning these patron gods. Generally, the reason was that people of his time had left the area of their origins (*ubusuna*) and taken up residence elsewhere. Yet it was a human activity for people to carry out observances and express a sense of loyalty to a place and its deity. He cautioned against a conflict of loyalties between the "guardian deities of the place to which a person has moved and the gods of his place of origin" and warned that such divided loyalties go against the "plan of the gods." Therefore, "men who leave the place of their birth and live elsewhere must first worship the gods of their home place. They must [then] make observances to the deities of the place in which they currently reside." In this way, the sense of connectedness with one's native place would be preserved, as well as one's recognition of respect for his new surroundings. Hirata was convinced that local equilibrium would be conserved, despite continuing mobility and emigration from villages. It is possible that he was seeking a means to arrest the constant dissolution of ties and collective purpose—if not the erosion of productivity itself—by anchoring people to a place by primary religious obligations. He believed that movement away from one's native place to another part of the country was part of a divine plan and that, since people were obliged to return to their home place to make their required offerings, they should be furnished with "protecting cards" (*mamorifuda*) during the time of their travels (ibid. 6:313). It seems likely, however, that owing to his conviction of the centrality of the tutelary belief system and the function such deities played in the lives of ordinary folk, he actually believed it was better for people to stay in their place of birth than to risk the slackening of faith that removal would surely encourage.

Faith and the social importance of place demanded concrete assurances that people were settling their debt of thanks to the deities and ancestral spirits. Here, it was not difficult to move from simple, formal religious observances—worship—to more enduring forms of thankful expression such as work. Within the framework of his discussions of worship, Hirata raised the problem of work as a way of returning the blessings of the *kami*. Although other nativists refined this relationship later in the Tokugawa period, it is clear that Hirata figured work as an active element in belief. His conception of work lay in his concern for repaying the blessings of the *kami*. In book 3 of the *Tamadasuki*, he stated that, because all things had been granted to ordinary people for their use, it was important to return this trust (*yosashi*) to the various deities who had bestowed them. The discussion singled out—purposely, it seems—the agricultural god, Toyouke no kami, for "the source of clothing, shelter, and food today depend upon [his] august spirit" (ibid. 6:130–31). According to Hirata, this deity regulated rainfall, growth, and harvest; along with others associated with him, he directed the sea lanes, the forested lands, and the mountains. Hirata saw this accomplishment as the condition for a program of daily worship. Failure to express such thanks, he added, would invariably result in shame, and "personal shame inflicts shame on the deities" (ibid. 6:142). When praising this deity for its "manifest august achievements (*miisaoshi*), people could expect such things from its august body (*mikabane*) as the several grains, horses, cattle, and mulberry worms. These things have been ordained so that the ordinary people might be able to exist" (ibid. 6:170). "We must know well," Hirata asserted, "and be attached to the profound intention that has ordained all things for the beautiful ordinary people." Moreover, this agricultural deity was responsible for the making of houses; houses for people were built from wood and roofs were thatched with rush, the original materials that were provided by Toyouke no kami during the age of the gods. In antiquity, the completion of a house was marked by a ceremony of moving, and all worshiped this deity. But these observances are not limited only to the moment of moving; they were carried on at all times. They were used to commemorate the place, which itself was called a deity. The central deity of this ceremony was called *Yabune no mikoto* (*yabune* was a place where people lived; it referred to a "roofed boat" but actually meant any utensil). The Commentary on the Imperial Ordinances proclaimed that it was Toyouke no kami whom the masses worshiped as the deity of the houses they inhabited (ibid. 6:180–81).

The special focus of Hirata's concern for worship and the repayment of blessings was rice cultivation. Since, in Japan, rice had been granted as a gift from the heavenly deities, the people partook of it almost as if its consumption represented the ingestion of the divine.

Despite the claims of the Chinese that they had been the first to cultivate rice, Japanese rice was both first and superior. The Chinese reports
were unfounded—their rice could not be considered "beautiful, like
the rice of the august realm. Because [Chinese] rice is inferior and was
begun by the mandate of men, those who eat it are weak and enervated
[*myūjaku*]" (ibid. 6:172). Hirata was convinced that such rice consumption accounted for the failure of various political experiments in
China and their inevitable consequences (ibid. 6:172–73). Japanese
rice was superior to the rice of all countries, and those who consumed
it took in a divine food that guaranteed their uniqueness and superiority
over all others. Hirata based his conviction of this superiority on what
he believed was the naturally endowed strength of the Japanese over
other peoples.

To prove this assertion, he compared the methods of cultivation
of the Japanese and other peoples. He declared that it "can be seen that
the essence of cultivation [in Japan] has not changed since its inception" as it had in China and in other countries (ibid. 6:173–74). "If
people pray intensely to Toyouke, to the great intention that has blessed
the ordinary people, it is because we have been graced with the august
spirit of this deity" (ibid. 6:173). Because people recognized that rice
was the major agricultural product resulting from this deity's manifold
blessings, everywhere in the realm they must express their respect in
some form of daily worship. Yet worship, for Hirata, did not simply
mean performing a series of ritualistic gestures. Rather, it referred to a
total attitude that was disclosed in all activities from eating through
work itself; it was manifest in the most basic level of worship in the
household, where all assembled at mealtimes, and in the fields, where
they labored daily (ibid. 6:177). To make this point, he enlisted the
support of Motoori and quoted from the ever-quotable *Tamaboko hyakushu:* "When eating things morning and night, men of the times always think of the blessings of Toyouke no kami" (ibid.). The passage
conveyed to Hirata the necessity for people to fix their attitudes on life-
supporting activities; worship could easily be reconstituted as work or,
indeed, as eating itself, if one realized the correct mental set. Each
reinforced the other; eating made possible work, which satisfied the
divine blessings.

Hirata stressed the identity of worship and work as components of
a single series and endowed both with the meaning of activity. In this
sense, he envisaged the act of consumption as a form of religious devotion. People should never forget the blessings of the grains that had

been ordained so that "beloved ordinary folk" might be able to live, to eat, and to plant. "One thinks of this when approaching the chopsticks and the rice bowl; and, one thinks of the labor of the peasant who cultivates the rice (*mata kore o tsukureru hyakushō no waza o mo omoi*)." Nor was it permissible to lose sight of the intention informing the word "to eat" (*taburu*). Eating and working were religious acts. After contemporaries finished eating, they must dedicate themselves by lifting their chopsticks and their tray to their heads. This mindfulness of obligations, which recognized the great intention, had slackened among Hirata's contemporaries.

> In our times, people quarrel at mealtime, between parents, wives, and brothers, and end by doing such things as throwing their bowls and trays [at each other]. . . . This bad conduct is, indeed, like dogs who quarrel when eating. The correct etiquette in eating, by people of the imperial land, is unparalleled among the nations of the world. However lowly a person, each has a tray separate from his parents, his own chopsticks and vegetables. . . . When barbarians see this, they admire us. (Ibid.)

Good table manners, which both Chinese and foreigners—who "ate from a common dish"—had failed to develop, illustrated both proper conduct and devotion. It is hardly surprising that Hirata concentrated on household dynamics at mealtime and raised the image of rancor and riot characterizing a family meal. He was, it should be recalled, ever sensitive to the incidence of conflict in his society and the possible causes of violence. Whether it occurred in a family or in an agrarian community, the intrusion of violence represented a failure of the mechanisms of social solidarity. The solution, he believed, was devotion, achieved by relating work to activity, worship, and consumption. The acts themselves would be sufficient reminders of respect for the deities.

Indeed, Hirata remarked, the gods frowned upon such bad habits, which were absent in antiquity (ibid. 6:178). "The reason why there are so many people in our times who have learned ideas so remote from the ancients is that, when they eat in the morning and at night, they do not understand the basic bond that has been bestowed by the *kami*." An abundance of food dulled people to their obligations; they became ungrateful (literally, their feelings toward the important are thinned) and, thus, they "cease to inquire about the meaning of the word 'to eat.'" Earlier in the *Tamadasuki*, Hirata had explained that the word "to eat" also meant "to grant," "to receive," "to bestow" (ibid. 6:174). Therefore, "because the imperial land has been granted the blessing of the gods, [people] are accustomed to these great, august gifts of sufficient rice and grains, even though they do not think to be thankful" (ibid. 6:178).

Hirata demonstrated the same kind of relationship between clothing and shelter and the gods. The agricultural deity (Toyouke) had made these necessities available as a blessing given in great abundance. Hirata underscored the exchange relationship between gods and humans in his discussions of both the heaven-sent grains cultivated only in Japan and the materials used to construct houses and make clothing. In the *Tamadasuki*, he used silk to show that, although the deities made such blessings accessible to humans, it was human mediation that converted them into food, housing, and clothing. Hirata wanted to establish a conception of work as a naturalized and dehistoricized activity as a condition for his discourse. The appeal to naturalness necessitated the argument that human practice—working—should not separate people from nature but restore them to it. It also established the terms by which the creation itself—the means of existence—might be reproduced: the "spirit of the body of Toyouke . . . in our times" was manifested in the products that living contemporaries had made. Hirata's logic led him to propose that abundance materially transmitted spiritual blessings. It also explained why humans in generation after generation were expected to pledge themselves to both work and worship. According to Suzuki Shigetane, spirit was synonymous with the "concealed body"; according to Hirata, it meant a body always performing, whether in the visible world or in the hidden realm of Ōkuninushi. Thankfulness had to be expressed actively; eating and prayer both constituted acts of worship to the "spirit of Toyouke." No real distinction existed between "spirit" and "body," "life" and "death."

In this way, worship came to mean an exchange for products and things and thereby signified the "blessings" and "abundances" that this deity had made available to the ordinary people to carry on the job of living. Yet it was work that put people back into "nature" and established the modes of a natural social reproduction to transform the "gift" into actuality. Work made custom and a "historyless history" (Hirata's "uneventful history") possible; this new sense of "history" came to symbolize the return of blessings to the gods who made it all possible. In his discussion of the Great Yearly Deity (Ōtoshi no kami), the August Yearly Deity (Mitoshi no kami), and the Youthful Yearly

Deity (Wakatoshi no kami), Hirata made this linkage explicit. These "yearly" deities, he explained, were related to the rice field (ibid. 6:432). The word for year became *tayoshi*, meaning "relying on the fields" or "entrustment of the fields." *Tayo* was condensed to *to*. "Therefore, it was said that *toshi* refers to cereals and grains. These are the spirits of these yearly deities and are formed in the fields. The grains are collected once a year" (ibid.). Here, Hirata was less interested in the occasion of the blessing than in the yearly activity by which the grains matured and were harvested. Yet behind the yearly cycle, summoned by invoking the yearly deities, stood the more important activity of work itself, which always transformed seed into fruit and back again into seed.

Hirata's discussions of the Way concretized the content of the narrative to conform to basic and timeless features of ordinary life that all could recognize as their own. In joining a cosmic story line to a discourse on quotidian life, he and others were able to amplify a different, preclass mode of production—an archaic economy—and the necessity to reproduce it in the present. This archaic system of production (and reproduction) did not refer simply to a time that had long passed but rather to a place (in other people's terms—rural Japan) that still preserved its operations in the life of the ordinary folk. But the active reproduction of these conditions of place meant the virtual nonreproduction of the existing requirements of contemporary social life. Code was used to displace context in order to restore paradigm to the place of syntagmatic events.

The ideological implications of this maneuver were consequential. The essence of this archaic economy, as articulated within the matrix of the narrative, lay in the concealment of the ends that the economic was supposed to serve; it was an acknowledged refusal to conceptualize the economic as a separate activity.[17] When this version of life was juxtaposed to contemporary life, Hirata and his rural followers were able to show real disapproval of current economic practices serving explicit ends, such as the maximization of interest and profit. In the narrative, there was an "idolatry of nature" that made it impossible to think of nature as mere raw material, as it surely must have been in the late eighteenth and early nineteenth centuries, or to see human activity—"household duties"—as labor separated from nature and life itself. Surely, this fusion of meaning is what nativists meant when they denoted "work" by "household duties." Given their logic of equivalence, work as apprehended in the narrative could not be seen as an activity independent of the household or, indeed, of the collective existence. Nativists were seeking to solve the problem of autonomized labor serving noncollective ends. Their move to an archaic site occluded the view of the economy as a separate form of activity derived from a struggle; it prevented them from grasping the economy as a system—as Pierre Bourdieu has described—"governed by the laws of interested calculation, competition, or exploitation."[18] Rural nativists, as we shall see, were acutely sensitive to economic activities such as competition and calculation, which seemed to undermine the solidarity of the collectivity and to throw it into disarray, conflict, and fragmentation.

Discourse appeared in Hirata's thinking as an act almost deliberately directed toward concealing the relationship between work and its product and dissolving the various forms of work into worship and the repayment of the gods. Here is one possible function of his discussion of the Great Yearly Deity, which related the word for "year" to the trust associated with rice fields and the spirits who produced grains harvested once annually. The reality of production, consisting of countless acts of work throughout the year, became subsumed by simple reproduction and made to appear as a repetitive process culminating in a regular harvest representing the gift of the gods. In this scheme, work simply "assisted" nature, rather than standing in an adversarial relationship to it. But Hirata and his rural supporters may have been acknowledging, by an act of distancing and repression, the natural world's dis-enchantment, which would function as a condition for the discovery and development of labor. Late-Tokugawa Japan offered abundant testimony to the fact that economic activity was directed principally toward economic ends—money—and away from archaic undifferentiation. And it seems likely that nativists recognized in rural disorder and the installation of new social relationships the effects of this dis-enchantment. To counter the consequences of social labor, they increasingly insisted on integrating work into the larger matrix of life and death, production and reproduction. The promise of the archaic narrative lay precisely in its capacity to disguise more material interests and to prevent the economy from being seen as a separate practice with its own goals. They consistently repressed work socially or made it a part of a larger system governed by the rhythm of nature, where life and death formed a partnership with nature; to this end, they made the repetition of the undifferentiated conditions of existence (where no part was conceivable without the others) to stand in a distanced relationship with the contemporary social world. Distance revealed the failure of contemporary official ideology not only to stem a drift toward the fragmentation and autonomization of practice but also, just as important, to account for and repair the rupture between the representation of a world and the world itself.

5 Ruralization I: Figure and Fulfillment

Historical Conjuncture

Hirata's routinization of the ancient Way in quotidian life and his emphasis on the ceaseless interaction between worship and work provided the points of contact by which rural Japan could appropriate nativism. His systematization of ancestor worship into a large framework of belief linking the ancestors to the creation deities; his explanations of the central importance of the various clan and tutelary deities, which recharged fundamental religious practices and sensibilities in the countryside; his renewed emphasis on the *musubi no kami*, which increasingly functioned as a theoretical basis for self-strengthening rehabilitation in order to increase production and wealth; and his projection of consolation, which promised immortality of the spirits by binding human performance in the visible world to its dispensation in the hidden—all of these modifications of nativist thought struck responsive chords in the villages of late-Tokugawa Japan and provided the means to resolve the problems of the countryside and to reconstitute life anew. Hirata's routinized message seemed to single out the village as the focal unit for such activity and to make it the intersection between the visible and hidden worlds, conferring upon it a kind of sacral autonomy and a justification for secession and self-strengthening resuscitation.

Many people saw the breakup of village life and the erosion of received productive relationships in the changing conditions in the countryside, announced by large-scale out-migration from villages; the growth of an agricultural day-labor force; and, in the Tenpō period (1830–44), the regularization of peasant disturbances, conflict, and rebellion.[1] The perceived threat of new productive arrangements to rural order and continued agricultural output occasioned the application of *kokugaku* to transform agricultural life into a coherent world vision. This process made use of Hirata's concentration on the household unit and his insistence on the solidarity of the village with the world of the ancestors and deities. By rearranging the most basic components of the human community and showing the cosmic necessity of a chain of linkages guaranteeing harmony and unity, he offered a possible defense against the forces that promised to disrupt life in the countryside. Hirata's formulations drew attention to ordering the microcosm; it could safely be assumed that disorder in the macrocosm would take care of itself if "natural" relationships were reinstated. Yet it was the presence of new productive relationships, not the cognitive content of *kokugaku* per se, that offered the "raw material" for subsequent speculation and the establishment of formal representation. Until the late-Tokugawa period, these new productive relations, described by many Japanese historians as the "conditions of world renewal" (*yonaoshi no jōkyō*), were seen by contemporaries either as signs of moral failure or as unformed expressions implying no worldview.[2] We know from the language of peasant rebellions, however, that they were hardly formless and spontaneous outbursts of peasant energy, and in the actual *yonaoshi* disturbances of the last years of the Tokugawa period, we have impressive testimony to both purposeful action and a coherent world vision.[3]

Although new rural arrangements induced peasant notables to find forms of representation adequate to their altered conditions of existence, vast transformations in material life alone could not account for the subsequent changes in consciousness implied by the rural adoption of *kokugaku*. The installation of the nativist discourse in rural Japan achieved a conjuncture comparable to the one noted by Max Weber, in which capitalism was mediated by new forms of Protestant spirituality, each representing independent kinds of activity from different sectors of the social formation.[4] Agricultural life, as it was conceived in the 1820s and 1830s, made possible the speculation leading to the construction of a coherent worldview, even though it was quite independent of the form and content of nativism, which supplied its representation. A new view of nature, steeped in an earlier productive process, was made to accommodate the "raw material" of agricultural life in the Tenpō years for a generalized conception of reality. Because this operation was inspired by the content of contemporary rural life, it derived principally from the side of social relationships. But these "raw" materials were neither innocent nor raw; they possessed their own sedimentation of meaning, capable of transforming and even altering the nativist message. Still, the impulse that prompted the creation of a coherent view must have found in the nativist message familiar points of contact, in order for rural appropriators to make the alliance appear natural.

To suggest a partnership between a specific message and a receiver is to propose that cultural form was used to comprehend the content of contemporary history and mobilize structure, in order to determine the course of events. The principal function of the nativist discourse, once it left the cities, was to account for the overdeterminations in the historical field—which had become alienating and unfamiliar—by refamiliarizing events and thus changing their meaning and significance for the whole set of events that constituted the life of the times.[5] *Kokugaku* was applied increasingly as a method to resolve rural disorder, to "detraumatize" events in the contemporary historical field that were acting in an overdetermined way as causal forces, by removing them from the "plot structure in which they had acquired a dominant place" and either inserting them in a subordinate place or simply neutralizing them into ordinary elements in another conception of the social world.[6] In this manner, *kokugaku* was utilized to decenter events in the real historical field to allow the operation of another principle of organization. We have already seen how nativism sought to dehistoricize the world and to establish an unmediated relationship between humans and nature. This plot structure, explained in great detail in Hirata's cosmic narrative, was now effectively employed in rural Japan to distance the historical field, which threatened to dissolve the ties of agricultural life into dispersed fragments. Although a "real" set of historical determinations may well have inspired the alliance between *kokugaku* and its rural audience, the principal condition for appropriation—that is, the fit—was the removal of history altogether as an object of discourse. Nativism provided rural notables an explanation that offered a detour around history, the circumstances producing the contemporary crisis, by promising to restore natural relationships from a time and matrix that history had suppressed. Because it was itself a discourse trying to overcome the historical field, nativism offered relief from events so charged with meaning that they had been alienated from the specific social world of a group.

This function was inherent in Hirata's cosmic narrative, which summoned a preclass, folk matrix. It was explicit in the *Tamadasuki*, which, in concentrating on the structure of linkages between human practice and the ancestors and deities, demonstrated what was meant by an "eventless history." Yet the call for an "eventless history" constituted a radical decentering. Throughout the first two books of this text, Hirata provided an account of political history down to the Tokugawa period. The purpose of this "history," an eventful history contrasted to the eventlessness of "real" history, was to show how neglect of the ancient Way had led to the decline of the imperial court. The principal agent in this antihistory was Buddhism, which despised human ethics and opposed the naturalness of human passion; its overall effect was to pollute what had been pure and clear. Hirata showed how Buddhism had undermined filiality, compassion for women and wives, the increase of children, harmony within the family, trust among friends, mercy toward servants (*dohi*), and the prosperity of the household. The continuing decline of the imperial dignity and the demise of the ancient Way weakened the "august protection of the deities." Within the court there was only audacity and insolence, and in the military there was rampancy and domination. Since the time of the Hōgen period (1156–58), the realm had fallen into grievous conflict, and, as a result, a series of rebellions had occurred, beginning with the Great Treason of the Jōkyū (1221) era, the struggle between the Southern and Northern Courts and the civil disturbances of the degenerate age of the Ashikaga. Under these trying circumstances, the imperial authority became enfeebled. Such conflict, Hirata proposed, induced its participants to forget the *kokutai* of the imperial land by persuading them to form excessive attachments to the luxurious customs of the Chinese and of Buddhist law. It made *kami* affairs appear as an unscrupulous activity, because there were many events that defiled and polluted the deities of heaven and earth. Eventful history signified, for Hirata, the "staining" of these deities by "bewitching gods" who angered them and brought calamity everywhere by perpetrating evil deeds. A great transformation came about with the adoption of political power by the military families, who went on to erect a system based on the ancient intention and Way, which differed from one derived from Tang dynasty customs that "privileged the civil and despised the military." New groups made the military essential; they turned toward the ancient Way and sought to realize the divine plan (*kamihakari*) of the imperial deities, which had been contracted in the hidden realm of the gods and ancestors. Since they were dealing with two courts claiming imperial status, it was difficult to avoid an "august struggle" within the imperial genealogy. The military estates moved to return to the "exhausted and burned-out unity of the Southern Court" because they believed that the Hōjō, "rough-ened" by the evil *kami*, had inaugurated the rebellion. The divine plan was ultimately realized by the intercession of the Sun Goddess and the spirit of the deity of correctness. But the prosperity of imperial authority and the ebb and flow of national destiny depended upon the correct conduct of *kami* affairs. After Oda Nobunaga and Toyotomi Hideyoshi appeared, countrywide disorder was suppressed and the ancient rites (*kogi*) were once again restored by revering the imperial court. Toku-gawa Ieyasu pacified the realm and promoted the order of the ancient Way based on the classics of the court. It was Hirata's belief that the court, under the patronage of the Tokugawa, had turned the reinstate-ment of *kami* affairs into its principal consideration, and it was this move which inspired the Mito school to produce the *Dai Nihonshi* and *kokugakusha* like Kada no Azumamaro, Motoori Norinaga, and Kamo no Mabuchi to make ancient studies flourish (*HAz* [rev] 6:1–127).

    This view identified eventfulness with the decline of *kami* affairs and the suppression of the ancient Way; genuine historical reality was supposed to be uneventful because it was based on "godly intention," the "deliberation of the gods," the "planning of the *kami*," the "pact contracted in the hidden realm," and the "deliberations made in the concealed governance" of Ōkuninushi no kami.[7] This conception of "history" juxtaposed the authority of the hidden realm to the phe-nomena of the visible and proposed that history could be produced only by rejoining the former to the latter. The locus of real "history" re-mained in the invisible world, while the events of the visible realm exemplified the influence of the alien, strange, and unnatural—the Other. This view established a congruence of the prosperity of the im-perial court—and the realm as a whole—with the rise and fall of the Way of the gods. The great appeal of Hirata's cosmological narrative was its capacity to displace the event-ridden field of contemporary his-tory, to render occurrences strange and alienating for a plot structure that was contracted in the age of the gods and was still available in the hidden realm inhabited by the *kami* and the ancestors. Overdetermi-nation quite simply meant overinterpretation.

    For rural Japan, the truly radical *effect* of changing the plot struc-ture was to make quotidian life identical with a mode of cognition, to take the logic of daily affairs—what Pierre Bourdieu has called a *habi-tus*—and make it into a system of thought.[8] The *habitus* refers to the space that generates practices reproducing the "regularities immanent in the objective conditions . . . while adjusting to the demands in-

scribed as objective potential ties," as defined by the cognitive structures motivating the *habitus*. Hence, the *habitus* represents a socially
constituted system of cognitive and motivating structures and signifies
a form of internalizing the external among those who inhabit its space
by defining for them what constitutes the reasonable, unarbitrary, and
natural. This space can refer to a village, a region, or the wider entity
of an ethnocultural realm, what *kokugakusha* called *kunitsuchi*. In
fact, as we shall see, the village, as envisaged by rural nativists, was a
substitute for the broader realm and interchangeable with it.

The dispositions characterizing the *habitus* are engendered by
objective conditions that prompt "aspirations" and "practices" com-
patible with external requirements. Bourdieu argues that the most "im-
probable practices are excluded as unthinkable."⁹ As a result, economic and social necessity, constraining the relatively autonomous
universe of family relationships (sexual division of labor, domestic morality, cares, strife, tastes, etc.), produce the structures of the *habitus*,
which become, in turn, the basis for perceiving and appreciating all
subsequent experiences.¹⁰ Encouraged by Hirata's conception of a cosmic narrative, later nativists increasingly defined the *habitus* as the
world of the corporate village. Hirata's narrative showed, in minute
detail, the structural relationship between the hidden and visible
realms, the linkage between cosmology and creation on the one hand
and the daily life-experience of ordinary folk, prayer, and practical activity on the other; it demonstrated a causal principle of determination
in the divine planning of the deities from the beginning of time. Moreover, this identification of *habitus* with a mode of cognition reflected
an acknowledgment by Hirata and his rural followers that the environ-
ments that they encountered were remote from the practices they were
supposed to fit. In rural Japan during the late-Tokugawa period, conflict, following the lines of the *habitus*, took place between differing
conceptions of space; contestation would appear in the projection of
differing conceptions of the *habitus*. What I have elsewhere called "secession" signified different ways to constitute social space.¹¹ Henceforth, the production of conditions of existence that imposed differing
definitions of the impossible, the possible, and the probable would
prompt one group to experience as natural or reasonable what another
would find unthinkable.

The *habitus* produces practices that tend to reproduce the regu-
larities immanent in objective social conditions; it also seeks to ad-
just to these demands as recognizable potentialities in the situation.

Bourdieu writes that such practices, whatever they consist of, cannot be deduced either from objective conditions or from the conditions that produced their principle of production. They can only be accounted for by relating the objective structure, which defines the conditions underlying the production of the *habitus*, to the conditions in which the particular *habitus* operates. In the construction of the *habitus* as an effect of the renarrativization of the contemporary historical field, nativists showed the relationship between the creation, with its mode of divine production, and the consequent necessity to perform agricultural work as a reproductive act. They centered this activity in a village that, they assumed, was self-sufficient and autonomous by virtue of its kinship with the primal community. Hirata transformed history into nature by linking the *habitus*—*kunitsuchi*—to the creation of the divine land and to the reproduction of practice in prayer and work. History, as he conceived it, unfolded as an unending transaction between genesis and its reproduction and operated as an unconscious exchange; what it reproduced became incorporated into the second nature of the *habitus* itself. By making history into nature, he could summon the mysteries of preestablished harmony and account for an appearance in the present as having objective and timeless meaning. For him, humans functioned as agents who unwittingly produced and reproduced "objective" meaning by reenacting practices, such as worship and work, because their nature permitted no other choice. Bourdieu has proposed that, because "subjects do not know . . . what they are doing . . . what they do has more meaning than they know."[12] Hirata's nativism showed that the *kunitsuchi*—*habitus*—represented a universalizing mediation that without either explicit reason or some form of signifying intent, ultimately demanded practice to be "sensible" and "reasonable." The *habitus*, itself a product of the humus of history, produced individual and collective practices in accordance with schemes engendered by history. When the fit between history and nature appeared imperiled, as Hirata noted, there was an attempt to resituate the system of dispositions, a surviving past, as a synchronic fact. Once Hirata began to call for a "true account of antiquity," he was, in effect, recognizing the importance of reincorporating history into nature and providing a program to rural nativists.

Kokugaku reconstituted this *habitus* into a natural entity, understood as a system of lasting, transposable dispositions integrating past experiences, that could function once more as a matrix of perceptions, appreciations, and action. Rural nativists sought to establish the essen-

tial character of *habitus*—a correspondence between the objective order (social structure) in the form of a communal village and the subjective principles of organization (mental and cognitive structures)—so as
to make the fit between the natural and social worlds appear self-
evident. In Bourdieu's terminology, the way this fit is articulated is
called a *doxa*. In the nativist project, the effort found expression in
concerns for "vulgar" doctrines and an obsession with orthodoxy. *Kokugakusha* felt that the social world had lost its character as a natural
phenomenon and regarded the situation as an occasion to raise questions concerning the natural or conventional status of social facts. A
crisis was necessary to prompt this consideration for "correct" teachings
over vulgar views, but it need not have been sufficient to produce a
critical discourse.

In short, rural nativists moved to reinstate what they believed to
have been self-evident in village life, thereby exposing as arbitrary what
had hitherto been taken for granted, precisely at the moment when the
ruled were beginning to use collective action as a means to call attention to a dissatisfaction with the circumstances of their lives. In order
to defend the rural elite against the threat of disorder posed by collective
action in the countryside, nativists turned their attention to supporting
the authority of the *doxa*. But any attempt to reestablish the self-evident
would invariably result in displacement and reformulation. As subsequent experience showed, the form of this orthodoxy ultimately uncovered the arbitrary principle of the prevailing system of classifications
used by the Tokugawa and served as the substantive and symbolic
means to reject the definition of the real that had been imposed upon
society. *Kokugaku* had always aimed to reinstate orthodoxy, to remind
contemporaries of "straight" and "correct" opinions. Yet its appearance
on the horizon of official discourse revealed the vast division between
what could be stated and thought in Tokugawa Japan and what was to
be taken for granted. It also drew a dividing line between the most
radical form of misrecognition and the awakening of a new political
consciousness. Rural nativists, who saw how a crisis in the everyday
order affected language and experience, tried to create an "extraordinary discourse" that might give coherence to the range of experiences
contemporary life now made possible. Hitherto private experience—
official discourse's suppressed alterity, which *kokugaku* assigned to the
hidden world—gained public recognition in thought and practice.
This program prescribed attention to the true and divine language in
order to support its claim as a language authorized by the group of

which it spoke and which it represented, whether the members belonged to an upper peasantry pitted against an official managerial class or to the Japanese confronting the Other. The things it sought to designate not only gained discursive entry, which they had been denied before, but also legitimacy. Because *kokugaku*, like many other disciplines in the late-Tokugawa period, derived its power from the capacity to objectify unformulated experiences and to make what had been private into a public statement, it signalled a return of the repressed.

Roman Jakobson has argued that it is never possible to begin with a specific historical context; one can only end with it. If this is the case, *kokugaku* was distanced from the history that generated it in the first place. As a discourse, it was linked not to real history but to the way contemporaries encoded and emplotted history. In any event, this history had to be considered part of the message it wished to convey, if the discourse was to gain recognition. We have already argued that it was the purpose of nativism *not* to take history as its most immediate object. But its apparent lack of real history represented an overdetermined relationship between discourse and historical reality. Nativist texts regularly contrasted "evil events" and "good times," correct doctrine and evil and vulgar views, but they referred more to the immediate historical field than to any struggle over authoritative doctrine. When Hirata embarked upon a campaign to discredit all forms of contemporary thought, he acknowledged the kinship between the incidence of overdetermination and the appearance of surplus interpretations and showed how the appeal to doctrinal differences functioned as a trope for real historicity.

This contextual component—history as referent—assumed vital importance. Whatever the range of experimentation with different forms and multiple messages, such activity could be comprehended and contacts could be made only if the sociocultural context—history—was recognized by an audience whose own experience conformed to the modes of message and conveyance adopted by the writers in accordance with the rules of a specific discourse. When I argued earlier that nativist discourse sought to reconstitute the root metaphors of a discredited Neo-Confucianism, I was providing an instance of "innovation" corresponding to a larger code. The nativist effort to envisage the world in categories of similitude and resemblance and in the form of cosmology sanctioning a series of contiguous relationships testified to a negotiation with an ideological experience of real history. History may have entered nativist texts in the form of a struggle between correct

and incorrect doctrine, as many *kokugakusha* have insisted. It nonetheless provided the means to talk about real history, because it trig-
gered a series of associations that signified disorder and disease in society. Nativists believed that adopting incorrect doctrine incited riot and
rebellion by devaluing productivity; in their discussion, they made
work equivalent to religious doctrine. The *kokugaku* discursive strategy
had two obvious consequences: it designated all Japanese similar to one
another—related as kin and each resembling the other—as well as to
other things by virtue of their singularly divine origins, when, in fact,
the experience of contemporary history ran counter to this representation; and it identified a certain kind of social world with religious duty
because of the unitary source of the creation of all things. Its decisive
shift to work as religious duty merely conformed to the ideological experience of "real" history in rural Japan. Privileging the role assigned
to work—projecting it as the primary purpose in the doctrinal world of
kokugaku and forming the whole and self-sufficient communitarian
village that it bespoke—was by necessity an operation cut loose from
"real" history and presented to allow for the range, permutation, and
flexibility denied to mere reproduction. It defamiliarized lived experience to distance it from history and to solve the encoded problem of
doctrinal heterodoxy and its baneful effects on the human order. This
view suggests that nativist discourse functioned as a "necessity of ideology" rather than a product of it.[13] When *kokugakusha* began to talk
about the creation, divine productivity, and the necessity of work in the
cosmic plan, the resulting representation of a nonexistent Tokugawa
Japan disclosed one of the ways late-Tokugawa society might signify
itself. By bringing the contemporary countryside into the net of nativism, writers were able to organize experience into the new categories
and classifications suggested by Hirata and some of his followers. Yet
the act of bringing nativism into the countryside to resolve current
problems permitted the conceptualization of new spaces for performance and productive work and the valorization of communal interests
over private interests as a means of overcoming the perceived threat of
division, difference, and inequality. Nativists, along with other rural
activists of differing persuasions, such as Ninomiya Sontoku (1787–
1856) and Ōhara Yūgaku (1797–1858), all agreed that the spirit of
work must be informed by a strict prohibition against the pursuit of
private property. Most rural writers believed that real private interests
could only be secured by first elevating the collective interest of
the village. Writers like Miyahiro Sadao (1797–1858) and Miyauchi

Yoshinaga (1798–1843), as well as Ōhara, proposed that recovering the household was possible only by recovering the village. Such activity, carried out in the world of the countryside, testified to the political failure that must have caused the contemporary crisis. Specifically, the conceptualization of a new space withdrawn from the control system— a space in which the village relied on its own resources and efforts to reproduce the basic modes of social life and achieved, along the way, a sense of a whole-in-the-part—logically dramatized the question of polity and political leadership. The perception of contemporary failure encouraged nativism to enjoin ordinary people—the peasants—to resolve the question of sufficient food and the equal distribution of resources by their own energies. The meaning of *ken'yaku*—economizing—changed as the word was reappropriated and reapplied to rural problems in the late-Tokugawa period along a whole front of intellectual persuasions. It now counted less as a moral admonition, as it had originally, than as an invitation to accumulate wealth by production for the sake of the village community under the informed guidance of agricultural sages, usually village officials, elders, or wealthy notables. Again, this solution was prefigured in Hirata's writings that defined the boundaries for practice. Behind it lay the authority of the creation deities and their archetypal achievement—creation for the ordinary people, who would work and worship continually to return these blessings.

When peasant leaders in the villages, the main beneficiaries of *kokugaku* in rural Japan, sanctioned a form of secession and autonomy by turning the agricultural community back on itself—to the peasant— when before it had served the interests of the lord, they raised the question of the politicality that such an act entailed. By presenting this program, the village leaders—officials, local notables, and headmen (*nanushi*)—found it necessary to reconceive their own role to satisfy both new spatial requirements and their previous long-standing relationship to the *bakuhan* authority system. The overdetermination of contradictions manifest in the late-Tokugawa period appeared in the dilemma these people increasingly experienced. The ambivalence of their position has been noted by a number of writers;[14] it ultimately led to a genuine failure of nerve that prompted the village leaders to join the resolution of their problems to the solution of the crisis encountered by the general peasantry. But, owing to the dual nature of their position, the groups constituting village leadership could have chosen either of two directions. Because they represented the closed world of

the village community, they functioned in two contradictory ways that
the late-Tokugawa failure merely exacerbated. (1) Many village leaders
were peasants who spent time cultivating and managing their own
fields. Because productivity represented a primary principle in their
lives, their involvement in work lent authority to their performance as
village administrators who regulated activities essential to the preservation of daily life in the community. (2) Often, these men were also
charged with carrying out a variety of duties for the lord, such as tax
collecting, adjudicating law disputes, and policing. Here, they served
as the grass roots representatives of the domainal or shogunal bureau-
cracies at their farthest edge. As transmitters of higher authority (from
outside the village), they conducted themselves as members of the official managerial class and received feudal privileges in compensation
for their work. The apparent irreconcilability of these two roles came
into sharp focus at the moment when the authority system began to
extract more revenue in order to meet rising prices and growing in-
debtedness. Often these village leaders have been seen simply as em-
bodiments of feudal class-power and its inexhaustible propensity to extract revenue. And not without justification. By collecting revenue and
performing other services, they found themselves contributing willingly
to the ruin and destruction of the very communities over which they
presided; in their efforts to find greater quantities of revenue or simply
to meet quotas for their feudal masters in bad years, they undoubtedly
hastened the breakup of the small, enclosed world of the village that
had conferred status and power on them. Opposition to their efforts
exploded periodically in expressions of violence, rebellion, and intervillage disputes (*ikki, murakata sōdō*) that, more often than not, struck
out directly against this rural leadership.

The rural leadership found itself in the unenviable position of
being attacked as the lowest—and therefore the closest—representative
of the authority system while obliged by feudal necessity to extract more
revenue from the people below. Undoubtedly, these circumstances imperiled the leaders' lives, not to mention their social positions and fortunes, as they were caught between angry peasants and a relentless
administration. Yet they easily could have thrown in their lot with feudal authority to resolve their personal dilemma and salvage their in-
vestments. Instead, they linked their interests to the general peasantry
and called for the construction of a self-sufficient unit, cut off from
feudal authority and the world of shrinking benevolence (*jinseiron*),
that they believed would guarantee the expansion of productivity and

the enhancement of their role as leaders in the countryside. Historians have argued that these slight recognitions of a general problem failed to disclose even the rumor of critical consciousness against the Tokugawa order.[15] But if the call for secession and the announcement of programs of self-sufficiency—the move to the periphery—did not represent a calculated attack on the authority system at its center, it represented nothing. The various forms of secession in the late-Tokugawa period (*yōgaku*, *Mitogaku*, *kokugaku*, new religions) rejected received political and social conventions by reconstituting a part that might substitute for the whole. Their advocacy of withdrawal from the control system—on the grounds that it no longer was able to supply relief, assistance, and security as it had been delegated to do by tradition— struck at the heart of the Tokugawa arrangement of power and challenged the very principles it had employed to authenticate its conception of polity and society.

Kokugaku provided the necessary arguments and defined the group constituting village leadership so that it could conceptualize the resolution of its dilemma in a program designed to rehabilitate the general peasantry. Nativism encoded the problem so as to persuade the leadership not to pursue its own interests but to devise a plan capable of resolving the general peasant problem of poverty, chronic distress, and the breakup of the village unit. Its emphasis on productivity as the means of continuing and expanding the creation surely inspired a necessary identification of village elite and general peasantry. It also offered a concrete method for realizing such a possibility, in a program encouraging the self-sufficient reproduction of the modes of communal life and a new kind of political role for the village leadership.

Something resembling a sense of "class" solidarity was forged within this group in late-Tokugawa times.[16] Village leadership moved to form a network of contacts between officials and notables of other villages in the widening crisis, rather than merely associating with the lower peasantry within their own towns. By a variety of devices ensuring the establishment of intervillage bonds—such as marriage, the common education of youth, and service in youth groups (*wakamonogumi*) fostering life-long friendships—it became increasingly possible to construct the framework for a form of group solidarity and consciousness. This sense of solidarity was reinforced by sharing the style of life conferred by the possession of wealth. Wealth, above all else, offered leisure for study and intellectual speculation and thereby transformed the rural rich into a local intelligentsia. This social style enforced a distance between the rural rich and the general peasantry as associations grew among the upper peasantry of various villages; at the same time, it brought the village leaders closer to home because their local positions enabled them to assume responsibility for the preservation of village custom. Local village leaders found themselves increasingly implicated in maintaining the integrity of their own village communities. In this way, political leadership became fused with intellectual and cultural custodianship. Such ties were usually expressed by a genuine emotional affection for one's "native place" and one's ancestors, who, although departed, still resided (according to *kokugakusha*) in the vicinity of the village. They were also manifest in a growing sense of responsibility for solving problems related to the village as a whole, which stemmed from a recognition that those who occupied a different status in the ranking system and resided outside the village—usually samurai and high-ranking officials in castle towns—could not be expected to either care for the continuing sanctity of the village or take concerted action in its behalf, even though obliged by an ancient moral injunction of benevolence. Each individual, the village elite believed, had to perform the good that was most humanly possible within his or her appointed station. The village rich were required to acknowledge themselves as "men who know things"—as knowing subjects who, facing the peril of the contemporary crisis, could recognize the necessity to relieve poverty among the general peasantry as a condition for their own survival. They therefore assumed a responsibility commensurate with their station in life that was easily related to nativist sanctions of entrustment and enabling (*miyosashi*).

It was not the structural relationship between *kokugaku* and its audience of village notables alone that explained the intellectual choice. To be sure, fundamental attitudes found in village belief-systems corresponded to the nativist emphasis on such things as the worship of clan deities and tutelary gods, which contained rich and familiar associations of local folk elements; the systematization of ancestor reverence, which linked the departed spirits to the creation deities; the establishment of a theory of consolation concerning the afterlife and the migration of the spirits to the hidden world; and the centrality of the creation deities themselves, which, in giving life to all things, provided a theoretical basis for the self-strengthening rehabilitation of the villages according to increased work and productivity. Nativism often gave such beliefs coherent expression where none had previously existed. Yet village notables also chose *kokugaku* because it offered a systematic theory sanctioning their presumption of responsibility and local leadership. Once a decision was made to use their position to resolve the village problem and to find a way to reassure rural recovery and order, it was necessary to authenticate such action. They enlisted the authority of a hierarchical arrangement of political responsibilities, ranging from the creation deities through the Sun Goddess down to the emperor and retainers, in which each level represented a link in a cosmic chain of power. *Kokugaku* had always been mindful of the flow of authority, in both temporal and spatial dimensions. It believed that power derived from the divine act of creation—from the beginning—and was transmitted from deities to humans; spatially, this transmission descended from the emperor down to rural officials. In this scheme, each rank represented a part that could function as a substitute for the whole. The arrangement was referred to as *taisei inin*, the entrustment of imperial administration or the delegation of imperial authority. The idea was implicit in some of Motoori's formulations, and it was discussed by Hirata in several texts. But it gained new importance, if not expression itself, in the environment of late-Tokugawa rural concerns, where it was increasingly employed to validate the position of village leaders. Beyond its obvious uses by the rural elite, the theory of *taisei inin*—entrustment and enabling—had larger consequences. When village notables assigned authority to themselves by manipulating the implied arrangement in the idea of imperial trust, their positions easily called attention to the whole syntagm of delegated authority; so too, they could substitute the village as they conceived it for the larger realm. In this part-to-whole scheme, the village became an autonomous community, while the shape of the larger realm, for which it served as a substitute, remained vague. Underlying this new political possibility, we find an interesting correspondence with nativist strategy, with its assertion of part/whole relationships. The theory of delegating authority—trusting others to carry on the divine administration and enabling them to act in an authoritative manner—was rooted in the archetypal event of the creation deities, who conferred a trust upon their descendants and, hence, established the means to continue and expand the work of creation. The result for people like Miyahiro Sadao, Suzuki Shigetane, Katsura Takashige, and Ōkuni Takamasa was a plan to recover the village community as an autonomous and reconstituted whole—which introduced the dangerous possibility of a form of secession from the Tokugawa control system.

To transform *habitus* into the self-sufficient village, it was necessary to envisage the village as the living embodiment of creation, production, and reproduction; this process required a reemplotting of the content of everyday life in terms of the cosmic narrative. To show that the most mundane events of daily life were significations of the cosmic narrative, rural nativists resorted to the device of defamiliarizing everyday life by joining its content to divine intention and divine planning—making ordinary custom appear as the custom of the gods, and vice versa. They began to shake off old associations and responses concerning the routine of life and re-present them in a new and meaningful light, as something fresh and even strange. Agricultural work, which in everyday life was taken for granted, was reapprehended as the source of wealth itself, validated by the organization of the land; the familiar village was now seen as the *kunitsuchi*, an autonomous and self-sufficient space, a sacred place located at the intersection of the hidden and visible worlds; and the local notables were transformed into natural leaders who derived their authority from the gods. The emplotment of daily life in the modality of the cosmological narrative meant that rural life and organization were represented in the fiction of a self-enclosed communal corporation marked by horizontal ties of "kinship" rather than the vertical bonds of ascribed status and power; it substituted friendship, affection, and reciprocity for the fragmentation and conflict reflecting the impersonal relationships of the authority system.

Classifying the Cosmos

At the most fundamental level, cosmological speculation mandated a system of classifications, but the step to systematic defamiliarization also required the comprehensive ordering and description of living things into a "naturalized" history. I have already proposed that nativism sought to reconstitute history and culture into natural categories, to transmute what people ordinarily accepted as second nature into a first nature. This move sought to remove intervening mediations between humans and nature and to show that no real difference existed between animate and inanimate. Hirata's critique of eventful history and his reconstruction of narrative went a long way to prepare the ground for classifying the cosmos. The specific intent of the nativist defamiliarization strategy was to show that the aspects and activities of daily life that the common folk had taken for granted were not culturally constituted or historically determined habits but part of a natural order older than both culture and history. It also demonstrated that the close-at-hand was full of unrecognized meaning. The activities of daily life formed an unbroken chain back to the moment of creation; they manifested, in every present, the intentions of the gods who created the cosmos and of the people who continued life by their productive labor. Owing to the *musubi no kami*, all things were "naturally" related and formed a continuous series from the divine age of the *kami*, which was less a time than a place of concealment, the unseen world, that authorized the creation of the visible world of humans, where the "plan" was constantly actualized. Life was possible only because of the structural relationship between the unseen and the seen, between production and reproduction. By problematizing this relationship and defining its terms in detail, nativists believed they had found a way to classify the totality of existence.

One of the consequences of reducing life to a binary system of visible and invisible realms was the dissolution of historical time into a timeless spatial order of enduring relationships and activities. The impulse to dehistoricize the human order into a natural structure may have originated in the nativist linguistic project, which had tried to close the gap between expression and experience by returning language back to things. The possibility of restoring concrete meaning to words and reinstating a genuinely translucent correspondence between word, thing, and intention implied that words could concretely denote things and their relationships in an expanded series representing the totality of life—the seen and the unseen. The subsequent effort to demonstrate the relationship of invisible and visible and to classify—nominate—the things belonging to each realm could only have resulted from the prior recognition that a distance separated language from things. Classifying the relationship between invisible and visible, although distinct from language itself, promised to make language more natural and authentic. The taxonomy of the invisible and visible constituted a secondary language that, because it was grounded in the language of everyday life, reworked that language in an attempt to perfect it. It moved beyond everyday language to discover what lay behind it and what constituted it. Classification remained within language, since it functioned as an act of nomination and description. Here, language reflected nativist theory, which held that the continuity and presence of nature preceded nomination and therefore served as the condition for it; nomination also derived, however, from the act of reproducing the creation, which could be found in the sources of work and wealth.

Once classifying the cosmos was completed and the proper relationships between visible and invisible were straightened out, the representation that emerged vastly expanded the realm of visible affairs to illustrate that the activities—work—that people performed to produce wealth were central, not habitually marginal, to the entirety of existence itself. The organization of visible existence and its relationship to an invisible realm generated, as we shall see later, an "empirical" domain for a system of describable and orderable knowledge. The passage from *arawarinigoto* and *kamigoto* to classification meant primarily that the world of the visible no longer stood, as originally supposed, as the place of imperial governance and genealogy; now it appeared as something more—as the space where people carried out the life-sustaining activities authorized by creation. Although Hirata's meditations prefigured this move, it was only when nativism was exported to the countryside that this broadening of the visible world and reordering of priorities (recentering alterities) was accomplished.

Mutobe Yoshika (1806–65), one of Hirata's students and the son of a Shinto priest of the Muko shrine in Yamashiro, published in the 1840s (the date is unauthenticated) a compendium titled "Discussions of the order of the visible and the invisible" (*Ken'yūjun kōron*). This work sought to provide a comprehensive ordering of the things believed to correspond to the major taxonomic categories Hirata had earlier established. (The text was ultimately brought to the attention of Emperor Kōmei, before whom Mutobe was asked to lecture.) Mutobe's tract is a detailed classification table that tried not simply to catalogue things and objects in terms of their proper order or series but also to show how the *musubi no kami* guaranteed linkage and unity.

Mutobe's purpose was to detail the findings of his teacher and to classify the various explanations concerning the ancient Way from the perspective of "the two paths of the visible and the invisible" (*Kjk* 3:8). Although Hirata's researches had called into doubt many of the received explanations relating to the origins of the cosmos and the beginning of the earth, Mutobe acknowledged that followers of Hirata's learning had found it difficult to understand (ibid. 3:7). As a result, many students sought foreign explanations, which invariably omitted much and led them astray. Hence, the *Ken'yūjun kōron* proposed to provide in-depth instruction concerning "the astronomical phenomenon" (*tenshō*), "the earthly body" (*jitai*), and especially the contents of the visible and invisible. Mutobe reworked Hirata's cosmological speculations and reduced their main focus to an examination of these two realms as they constituted the "basic meaning" of ancient studies. His reason lay in the conviction that all people, whether "elevated" or "despised," and all things, regardless of their status in the cosmos, entered the visible world through birth, which, therefore, constituted the "basic factor" (*moto iware*) of human limitation. This limitation referred to humans knowing the conditions of their existence and recognizing that they possessed a spiritual form within them that enforced a basic intention that must be expressed in all things. "If the distinction between the visible and invisible is well understood first," Mutobe announced, "then it will be possible to grasp the basic intentions" (ibid. 3:8). The visible world, which he identified with the "ordinances of the public," corresponded to the body in the visible present; although it incorporated things that could be seen and heard, its requirements were easy to understand but difficult to carry out. By contrast, the invisible realm could neither be seen by the human eye nor heard by the ear; it was difficult to grasp but easy to doubt. The *Ken'yūjun kōron* sought to lessen both difficulties by enunciating the fundamental relationship between the two realms and removing the aporias that had led contemporaries away from the basic intention. Mutobe was convinced that enunciation of the ancient Way would eliminate the "bent" and reinstall the "straight." When the ancient traditions were ordered (*yorikamugaete*) and the customs of the gods maintained according to the divine dictates, even the words of a humble person like himself would not be ignored by listeners/readers (ibid. 3:10). Apparently applying a practice (devised by linguists) that privileged the enunciated over the act of enunciation, he actually closed the distance separating the two moments. Mutobe showed the authority of this sense of immediacy in the act of maintaining divine custom, by presenting an imaginary unity between the subject of enunciation and the subject of the enounced, meaning and simultaneity. Any such move, however fictive, suppresses how something is said for what is being said; it is likely to command assent more readily, since it works to draw the listener/reader away from the production of the enunciation to the presence of a speaking voice. The subject of the enounced invites the receiver of the message to constitute himself or herself as the producer of the speaking voice who is "always already there," complete and self-present.

The first book of *Ken'yūjun kōron* explained the creation of the cosmos, heaven, and earth and the establishment of a code of ethical conduct based upon the principle of master-retainer discrimination (ibid.). Early in his text, Mutobe acknowledged the association between the foundation of the cosmos and the implementation of a moral code in the conduct of public affairs. Moral behavior originating in the five relationships belonged to the world of visible affairs. From the be-

ginning, human conduct in the visible world (*kenkai*) reflected the disposition humans received in the invisible realm, so that behavior conforming to moral principles in the former became evidence (or even
a sign) that people were satisfying the character conferred on them
by the *kami*. Visible affairs were public and concerned "deeds" relating to contemporary governance, the "august administration of the
realm—that is, bright and visible—which constitutes a public bestowal
that is clearly benevolent according to the unchanging and eternal ordinances (*eitaifueki no chokujō yoreru koto nite, ima mo kenmei no
goseiji wa, ōyake yori akiraka ni jinsei o shikihodokoshi tamō ni*)" (*Kus*,
224; *Kjk* 2:36).

As Mutobe sought to show the relationships between the hidden
and visible worlds, he concentrated on three large areas: the origins of
procreation, the protection of the visible world, and the destiny of spirits after death. The innovation of his method of explanation, which
centered on how such concerns might be made meaningful for contemporaries, was to combine the creation deities with the tutelary deities, which he called *ubusuna no kami* (*Kus*, 226). "Even though the
realm is wide and expansive, there has not been a place in which these
ubusuna no kami have not resided since the age of antiquity; there have
not been men who have not been subjected to the august principle of
yin [*mikage*]" (ibid., 224). Mutobe remarked further to support this
vital connection:

> The basic origin of all things that created the world, whether human or
> inanimate, relies on the dependent energies [*onrai*] of the creation dei-
> ties. As for the origins of these basic dependencies, the creation of the
> national soil [*kokudo*] and its hardening was entrusted to the two sup-
> porting *kami*, Izanagi and Izanami. This great achievement is recorded
> in the incident of the dripping spear. These two supporting deities
> founded the realm and also bestowed the birth of the various *kami* of
> wind, fire, metal, water, soil, as well as the ten thousand things. Because
> the hidden realm of the creation deities is administered by such *kami*, it
> belongs to the realm of divine achievements; it is reported to the heavens
> that the two supporting deities, the five supporting *ōmikami*, and the
> five deities of creation administer the hidden government of the invisible
> realm. Later, they decided to entrust this creation to [the governance] of
> Ōkuninushi no ōkami. Since then, the ten thousand things of the hid-
> den government [*yūmei*] connected to this earth are under the gover-
> nance of Ōkuninushi no ōkami. The procreation of humans is chiefly
> managed by the great deities of creation. . . . These . . . deities reside

in their respective regions, provinces, and villages, their home place
[*furasato*], and it has been decreed that they are to be managed by the
tutelary gods [*ubusuna no kami*]. Moreover, they [the creation deities]
have divided the various duties between the time of procreation and later
administration. (Ibid.; *Kjk* 3:2–3)

Elsewhere Mutobe noted that the allocation of boundary divisions and
duties to the various areas meant only that each place had its own
tutelary deity down to the present (*Kus*, 224; *Kjk* 2:20). The importance of Mutobe's "observation" concerning the centrality of tutelary
deities lies in his willingness to accept Hirata's interpretation of the
origins of heaven and earth and his showing, at the same time, how
this message constantly found a "living" embodiment in the figure of
the tutelary deities, who reminded contemporaries of their divine origins. "In our own times," he wrote in *Ken'yūjun kōron*, "humans daily
grasp, in their lives, the spirit of roughness and calm from the things
that are chiefly conducted in the various shrines; they also grasp the
secret governance of procreation and its administration, by virtue of the
deities who have been divided among the tutelary gods of the various
areas" (*Kjk* 3:3).

In contrast to Hirata, Mutobe privileged the process of creation,
especially "becoming" (*naru*) and making; he thereby succeeded in fixing the centrality of the tutelary gods, who symbolized the activity of
creation as an ongoing process. "The tutelary gods," Mutobe wrote in
his programmatic tract *Ubusunasha kodenshō*, "refer to the basic deities who give birth to all things in creation" (*Kus*, 225; *Kjk* 3:3–7). He
asserted that scholars who had previously written about these deities
had been greatly mistaken. Even though many gods had managed the
various villages throughout the ages, they were all manifestations of the
same two creation gods. Mutobe explained that the people who mis-
apprehended the real nature of the tutelary deities misunderstood the
symbolic presence of multiple representations. In the end, each shrine,
whatever its specific representation, unmistakenly manifested the same
idea. Tutelary worship not only reminded the living of the unity of
creation but reconsecrated the moral example of the gods in each
generation.

Even though mortals were prevented from seeing the invisible
realm, Mutobe stated, its whereabouts were fixed by shrines devoted to
a tutelary deity (*Kus*, 224; *Kjk* 3:3). Recalling Hirata's earlier location
of *yūmei* in the precincts of cemeteries, Mutobe transferred the site of

Ōkuninushi's realm to the local tutelary shrines. This association was significant. The bond between the visible and invisible realms drew its adhesive powers from the presence of tutelary shrines in each area of the country; the shrine reminded the living of the creation deities and, beyond, of the shadowy realm of invisible affairs. The lands of these deities, which they subsequently administered, gave birth (*umare*) to humans; and they provided the five grains, trees and grass, birds and insects, fish, wood, and metal to maintain their creation. "All birth relies on the female principle (*mikage*) of these tutelary deities" (*Kus*, 225). Hence, the familiar deities of local shrines, whom rural folk had habitually worshiped, appeared now as the gods who made possible birth and becoming and who protected the land. In Tokugawa times, it should be noted, people believed in clan gods (*ujigami*) who watched over a region or a smaller precinct. With the passage of time, many clan gods became the *kami* of villages. The presence of these deities in all the villages of the realm and their settled figuration as *ubusuna no kami* inclined Mutobe to imagine a unity among the various deities of creation and to perceive a natural association between the village and the act of creation itself.

Although Mutobe's classifying practice, stipulating a fundamental separation between visible and invisible affairs, accepted the familiar division mandating the emperors, the unbroken line of descendants from the Sun Goddess, to administer the visible realm, he also believed that governing the hidden realm was the responsibility of the descendants of Ōkuninushi no kami and the various *kami*, as well as the tutelary gods residing in every sector of the land. The emperors always administered affairs publicly and visibly (I believe that nativists identified public—*ōyake*—with what they understood as visible affairs); they were pledged to realize the ideal of a "benevolent polity" (*jinsei*) immersed in virtue and dedicated to the tranquility of high and low, rulers and ruled. The rulers of the invisible realm, inaugurated by Ōkuninushi's progeny, represented the creation of things and, of course, the spirits of the dead. Mutobe's effort to resituate the invisible realm and to enhance the role of Ōkuninushi and his descendants, celebrated at the Grand Shrine of Izumo, owed much to Hirata's formulations, but his move to yoke commoners to peasants and explicitly recenter an alterity in the form of a competing source of political authority marks a special contribution to the discursive field. Although much of what he said might easily be interpreted conservatively as a means of maintaining established structures, his decision to underscore the relationship between the invisible world, Ōkuninushi, and the creation of things (humans and agricultural products and the ancestors) endowed rural Japan with special importance and went a long way toward establishing its autonomy by appealing to a different (and dangerous) source of authority and power. Mutobe managed to alter Hirata's conception of the "hidden world" by connecting the tutelary deities that characterized most agricultural communities to the descendants of Ōkuninushi; he thereby convincingly demonstrated that life-giving forces occupied a supremely important position in the invisible world of things. "Nurturing all things is a fact related to the invisible governance" (ibid.; cf. *Kjk* 3:48). The implication of this shift was an alternative conception of political authority (which I will deal with elsewhere) or, at least, an equivalence between two kinds of governance, public and private, that Hirata had only barely suggested. By raising the claims of the invisible realm to parity with the visible, Mutobe had opened the way for the eventual displacement of the latter by the former.

Declaring that the "tutelary gods have taken charge of the foundations of creation, the protection of our times (*kenze*), and the destiny of our spirits after death" (*Kus*, 226), what else needed to be accounted for? Mutobe explained that the tutelary deities selected the forms of man and woman to express the shape of the human body and supplied these forms with the passions of love and pity (*airen*). Passion lay at the base of the true heart that informed the values of benevolence, sympathy, loyalty, and truthfulness, which were all bestowals of the creation deities. Love and sympathy spilled over into sexual desire. Nothing seemed more basic and illustrated better the prior principle of all creation than the actualization of love and sympathy in the sexual bonding of man and woman. Man and woman in sexual union signified a skill that derived from the region of the invisible governance (*mukaisei*), even though it was "carried" out in the visible world. Although Mutobe revealed some familiarity with an internal physiological process, for him the real explanation for the "miracle" of sexual congress and procreation resided in the hidden realm and remained beyond human understanding. "When the semen of the male is activated (*seiki kappatsushite*) and the woman's ovary (*ransō*) receives the injection, the ovum that makes life embarks upon its course" (*Kjk* 3:3–5).[17] Yet the mysteries of birth and becoming, the divine gift of life itself belonged ultimately to the administration of hidden government. The responsibility for nurturing life resided with the tutelary deities, who administered this operation in the visible world, even though their source of authority lay elsewhere. Owing to the importance of these deities, Mutobe insisted on regular expressions of respect and thanks to them. "The shrines of tutelary deities," he wrote, "are very important. Since they are, we must first offer prayer daily to these deities; next, we should make regular visits to the shrines of the *ubusuna*. The prayers and ceremonies that are offered should never be neglected" (*Kus*, 229). For, he promised, regular and punctual offerings to the various tutelary deities throughout the realm guaranteed prosperity and abundance. His overriding conviction of the epiphanic power of the tutelary gods led Mutobe to call for the establishment of a countrywide movement pledged to respect them (ibid., 222; *Kjk* 4:1–15), a sentiment that was rearticulated by Yanagita Kunio immediately after Japan's defeat in the Pacific War.

It was in this respect that his celebration of "practicality" acquired meaning and related to his belief that work, the performance of duties, concretized a sacred trust. "Within our times," he wrote,

> the remains and the family inheritances and professions are things that have been transmitted to us from our ancestors. Those people who belong to the civilian and military estates endeavor in work because of their elevated status. [Mutobe was especially referring to samurai, who served in domainal bureaucracies.] The masses [*shomin*] work in occupations related to our tutelary gods, even though they now live in towns [*machi*] and village hamlets, as they are all attached to domainal lords and land managers [*jito*] of the various estates. Among the small number living in idleness and amusement, there are those who conduct their affairs in quiet leisure. We must not aim at withdrawing [from society] and securing an easy and comfortable life. (*Kjk* 2:9, also p. 7; *Kus*, 228)

Mutobe was warning contemporaries of the steady migration of folk from the countryside into the cities and urging the retention of tutelary belief as a necessary deterrent to fragmentation and the decline of agricultural work. It is significant that he recognized the erosion of order by newer divisions between city and countryside and the corresponding consequences for the division of labor. Elsewhere in *Ken'yūjun kōron*, he coupled the necessity of work with the religious celebration of the tutelary shrines and the deities of creation, echoing the occupational theory articulated by Suzuki Shigetane in *Yotsugigusa* (1849). Mutobe was convinced that those who worked in commerce, industry, and agriculture produced wealth only if they continued to be sincerely loyal, which meant sticking with their occupations (*Kjk* 2:7–8; *Kus*, 225). Acknowledging the unwelcome existence of differentiations within the workplace, he tried to explain them away by proposing that they all originated in the affairs of the invisible world. Without such an ordering authorized by the gods, there would be no hope for the accumulation of wealth (*Kjk* 2:7). Nothing was more important, he added, than agricultural productivity generating wealth and national well-being (ibid. 2:8). He equated his central conception of "production" and "becoming" (*naru*), with their rich associations of birth, making, and doing, with the act of working; as a consequence, they appeared equivalent to household duties (*kagyō*), which peasants especially were expected to execute diligently in order to bring things to their fruition. If the leadership utilized the accumulated wealth for the good of society, he wrote, "it will illuminate our lives," for the task of working for family productivity, from infancy to old age, expressed accurately the "basic meaning of our ancient Way" (ibid. 2:9). Arguably the most important point in Mutobe's considerations of productivity was his reincorporation of the proliferated divisions of labor into the basic classifications of visible and invisible. His identification of the masses and work with the tutelary deities minimized the incidence of the division of labor and its consequences for contemporary society by showing how they were subordinate to the larger cosmological categories of visible and invisible that authorized them. By showing how proper moral conduct was *necessarily* a sacred obligation signifying a recognition of the order established by the relationship of the visible and the invisible, Mutobe had opened the way for political possibilities implying rural autonomy and secession. Owing to the powers of the "hidden world" over the spirits of the dead and, therefore, the living, he advised, not even the "elevated" could win immunity from the judgment and powers of the tutelary gods (*Kus*, 230).

The Rhetoric of Place: Shrine and Village

When Mutobe classified the cosmos as an orderly series based on the natural relationship between this world and the other (visible and invisible), he designated the countryside as the locus of this universe. In his theory of the creation deities, whose presence was embodied in the tutelary shrine, and in his conception of production, he was able to provide the terms to translate nativist cosmology into a self-contained rural world, even though he refrained from actually taking this step. This operation, transmuting cosmology into rural space and place, was essentially the work of others; it resembled a palimpsest where the new markings were inscribed on the "text" or "map" of an older set of co-ordinates denoting agricultural life. Cosmology, especially when re-duced to the basic structural relationship between the visible and invis-ible realms, was superimposed upon village life as it existed in the 1830s and 1840s, with the effect of removing it (the village) from his-tory (the corrosive division of labor) in order to resituate it in the time-less zone of structure. Mutobe managed to find equivalents in contem-porary rural life corresponding to the components (ideologemes) of the nativist cosmological vision. Since it was believed that the cosmos was now held together in a series of relationships between parts and whole, village life was used to show a natural connectedness among its diverse elements, signifying a unified structure, complete, immediate, and self-sufficient. But because cosmology was superimposed like a palimp-sest, the real "text" of village life was never wholly erased under the new form. Despite the effort to represent the village as a self-contained microcosm analogous to the macrocosm, the superimposition often functioned as a transparency, reflecting precisely those conditions of the rural world it sought to conceal or displace. This juxtaposition of space to time resulted in a ceaseless contradiction between the two poles and brought together an impossible synthesis between older social relationships (preclass) and newer socioeconomic forces, between the claims of an unchanging communal order and the authority of histori-cal motion. The *kokugaku* effort to make the fit must be seen as an instance of "maximum ideological production," as Gayatri Spivak has called such operations. What started as an attempt to arrest rural dis-order and its threat to productivity ended in the secession of the village from the control system—history—as a means of making the palimp-sest into a thick representation, removing the tension between what representation now claimed and what could still be seen beneath it.

The transmission and adaptation of the nativist message to the countryside was undoubtedly related to the nature of village society in the late eighteenth and early nineteenth centuries. I have proposed that the peculiar nature of the Tokugawa village and its apparent fragmen-tation by the penetration of new economic forces prepared the way for a reconstruction of the village by local leaders (who had the most to lose from rural disorder) along communitarian lines. This view is based on the conviction that the village, as it was constituted in Tokugawa

Japan, represented a holistic unit. Yet the resulting picture of a corporate body, continuous since the beginning of human habitation, was a
calculated fiction inspired rather late in the Tokugawa period by rural
notables allied with *kokugaku* to project an image of a naturally corporate and integral unit, self-contained and self-sufficient. The reason
for this move was undoubtedly the fear of rural disorder and decreasing
agricultural productivity. The terms of the crisis in the countryside
offered both the occasion and the opportunity to rural leaders to constitute themselves as the natural leaders of self-sufficient political units,
accountable neither to feudal authorities nor to their peasant constituencies. Resolving the rural question led to a restructuring of the village
into a unified and economically self-sufficient cosmos and to the installation of conceptions of political trust legitimizing the claims of
local notables to natural leadership. The only way to offset the palimp-
sest effect was to withdraw the village from the control system and to
induce the peasants to fend for themselves. Withdrawal had the unin-
tended effect of making nativism into a contesting ideology bound to
clash with the authority system.

Increasingly, it was believed that the Tokugawa village possessed
a structure of ties based on relationships in place and blood. These
relationships combined to create a natural communal unit. The strategic purpose of such a claim was to show that such structures were
reinforced by a variety of communal, cooperative activities, which
made possible the reproduction of the peasantry's means of social existence. People lived, worked, worshiped, and died in the same place,
with others to whom they were bound by natural relationships of kinship, friendship, and, above all else, divine necessity.

This is not to say that Tokugawa villages lacked classes or hierarchical status relationships. But regardless of social distinctions, the village was able to enforce communal responsibility and, thus, reproduce
the character of the cooperative, communal unit, despite the prevailing
impulse toward "private activity." Even though villagers might pursue
their private interests, the weight of the communal consciousness,
which stressed kinship and necessary reciprocity as natural endowments, still guaranteed the performance of crucially important activities ensuring reproduction. The place of the village became the
"natural environment" for carrying out reproduction. The village and
reproduction were complementary; one was unimaginable without the
other.

Much of this operation was possible because the Tokugawa village remained relatively isolated. Secluded, often closed, even insular,

the village was able to hold its inhabitants in the grip of a strong communal consciousness. The system was cemented by the nativist conception of common worship of the *ujigami*, guardian deities, and tutelary gods, and reverence for the ancestors who, it was believed, resided in the vicinity of the village as spirits whose "bodies are concealed." This deeply rooted religious consciousness, stemming from common practice, greatly strengthened the communal awareness of the peasantry. The intimate and often integral relationships between common practice and forms of worship and customary belief not only established the boundaries between village and nonvillage but provided a *raison d'existence* that was neither exclusively economic nor exclusively religious. Yanagita Kunio, who reified this conception for the twentieth century throughout many of his texts but especially *Senzō no hanashi*, argued that the household (*ie*), the basic grouping in the village, represented the fundamental unit to which the ancestors belonged. The household in the village rarely exceeded the structural boundaries of the *ie*, because it constituted an inheritance transmitted by the ancestors. Even the larger *dōzoku* groupings, according to Yanagita, functioned as a household union that was, at bottom, composed of the *ie* and its ancestral associations. This social form of organization, out of which the village was constructed, necessitated continual expressions of worship and respect by the living descendants of the ancestors to whom they were related by place and blood. Thus, the continued existence of the *ie* guaranteed that the past would live in the present; ancestor veneration and the worship of the pantheon of local guardians and tutelary deities confirmed in the present the presence of the past as the surety of the future. But, it is well to recall, nativists proposed that none of this was possible without maintaining the boundaries of the village intact—that is, place itself—which meant keeping people within its confines to work and to worship, to live and to die.

The beliefs of the village related specifically to clan gods and the tutelary deities, and, as Yanagita later observed, they were primarily situational, a view articulated by nativists like Miyauchi Yoshinaga and Suzuki Shigetane (1812–63). Such beliefs often found expression within the framework of land ties that transcended the narrower ancestral world. Worshipers prayed for the safety of the village and the places of residence and work and made requests for abundant harvests by offering ceremonies to propitiate the appropriate *kami*. Often, such *kami* were idealized as the community god. The collective worship of a specific place reinforced the relationships between individual members of the village, because such observances reaffirmed the "seating order" of

positions occupied by members of the community. That is to say, such
ceremonies reconfirmed and even secured the received arrangement of
order in the village. Tutelary beliefs, the *ujigami*, and ancestor respect
constantly worked to sustain the consciousness of a corporate unity
among the inhabitants of the village.

Among the many rural nativists who gave force to this reformulation of place and the corporate unit, Miyauchi Yoshinaga was perhaps the most systematic. Yet this particular move can be noted in
virtually all of the participants of the discourse. Miyauchi, another
student of Hirata's, shared with Mutobe the belief in the centrality
of tutelary shrine worship and its powers in the visible realm. Like
Mutobe, he was a priest. As commercial capital spread in the countryside, notably in his region of Shimōsa, he elevated the tutelary deities
to secure harmony within the village and meet the threat of fragmentation announced by the advent of new economic forces. A good portion of his major text, *Tooyamabiko* (1834), concentrated on the incidence of contemporary misfortune, its sources, and how it might be
overcome. The text contained frequent references to "ill luck," "evil
times," and "unhappiness," which, no doubt, referred to contemporary
rural conditions such as famines, riots, and collective violence. Encoded as instances of misfortune and evil, these events now functioned
as signs of new economic forces and productive relations that were
eroding received arrangements in the countryside. This form of coding
suggests that the purpose of Miyauchi's text was to displace such
changes, as Hirata had already indicated, from the received plot line
and to transpose terms in order to eliminate the commercialization of
the countryside—the apparent cause of recent eventfulness—as an event
of central importance. Here, the shrine, embodying a sense of timeless
structure and place, replaced events in order to lower the historical
temperature.

"I have heard that bad times, rebellion, and the illness of men,"
he declared, "are due to the ordinances of the two supporting deities."
Fortune and good government, which prevented rebellion, stemmed
from the intention of the heavenly and earthly deities and represented
a "wonderful truth." But, he added, bad times, rebellion, and disease
"come from committing great transgressions and must be seen as
changing times. People do not possess evil hearts. Those at the top
[lords] behave as lords, while those below behave as subordinates. If
conditions are protected and there is no change [*kawari koto nakaba*],
none of these things would ever occur." Miyauchi, like many contem-

porary founders of new religions, saw disease, misfortune, and peasant
disturbances as omens portending the failure of leadership. Bad administration existed when the leaders exploited and mistreated the peasantry and, thus, failed to take notice of the importance of their labors.
The peasants were consequently encouraged to "rob before the eyes of
the lord, neglect paying their taxes, thicken personal selfishness [*onore
ga watakushi o atsukushi*], despoil the boundaries of the fields, pilfer
water from the fields of others; artisans become increasingly sparing in
their endeavors, omit things before the eye; merchants buy cheap and
sell dear, indulge in profit making in commercial transactions, miscal-
culate and mismark, and steal" (ibid., 322–33).

Miyauchi believed that rebellion, disorder, and disease were
everybody's business. When the lord committed violations against the
people, the people would surely retaliate. Committing transgressions
meant going against sacred doctrine and divine word; belief in both
promised to banish evil and redeem the good (ibid., 313–14). The reality of the divine age taught that, if good was to be realized and evil
eliminated, it was necessary to "fear the meaning of the godly age and
honor the doctrines of the imperial Way." When the deeds of the divine age were known—that is, when humans realized that they were not
able to do anything alone—the foundation of imperial doctrine would
be established. Here, Miyauchi drew attention to the waste that "bad
times" and "disorder" inevitably caused (ibid., 325). Only disaster
awaited those who "follow disorder," since many ordinary people died
needlessly. But by pursuing the august reign (which meant merging
real deeds with imperial doctrine—*mioshie*), the ordinary folk would proliferate. Misfortunes came from neglecting imperial doctrine, which
had been a trust from the creation deities; such neglect necessitated an
inquiry into the "foundations" in order to cast off the roots of these evil
events (ibid., 326). Elsewhere in the text, Miyauchi identified imperial
doctrine with the "great, correct Way of the imperial deities (*ōmasa
michi*)" and remarked that when men "relate the august reason of the
great source of the truth of words, they are admonishing the doctrine
of the deities" (ibid., 339). Truth always intended proper deeds, which
were "preceded by words which come from the mouth. That is to say,
it is august doctrine to make word and deed the same and to make truth
the mutual union of word and conduct. Once words leave the mouth,
they are joined by deeds" (ibid.).

For Miyauchi, disorder and disease belonged to the same series,
because they invariably diminished productivity. Although they were

difficult to avoid, they could be overcome through acts of "supplication." If the source (*moto*) of an illness was known, its occurrence could be arrested; by knowing the basic cause of rebellion, people would be in a position to avoid it before it happened (*Kore wa makoto ni sono toki ni ate wa, sono maga ni awanu yo ni negitatematsuredomo, nogaregataki kotowari no areba, yamu wa sono okuru moto no iware o shirite, sono moto o fusegi, midare mo okuru moto no iware o shirite, okurazaru mae ni, sono moto o fuseginaba, ika de byōran no okurubeki koto ya aramu*; ibid., 326). Odd and unpredictable occurrences rarely happened, if people understood their basic causes. Nothing equaled injury and illness inflicted on the body and the body's inability to deal with the "hot and cold" diseases inspired by the seven passions.

Miyauchi's meditations referred to the confusions of contemporary life, which he described as a time of heterodox opinion. Heterodoxy led to excessive self-interest. Praying to the *kami* was bonded to things and deeds, and this realignment would dictate the proper order of activity. But to mistake the order of priorities was to open the way for evil. Miyauchi envisaged an order related to the deities who came first in the creation, beginning with the two supporting gods and descending to lesser *kami*. To violate this sacred arrangement of reverence was to throw the "ordinary [*tsune*] principle"–divine truths–into disarray. When this happened, the Way itself dissembled and its "disappearance" imperiled the times (ibid., 329). Order was synonymous with a continuous series. Miyauchi cited the example of successive numbers, from one to ten, to demonstrate the necessity of an unbroken chain. "If the number one is hidden, there cannot be the number ten. If the number one is mistaken for the order of things, it is difficult to speak about normalcy." When the order of things became jumbled, its backside appeared in the form of disorder. Because order denoted occupational status and the maintenance of various duties signifying work (*waza*), he advised protecting "the rules of the times" and knowing that the hidden governance guaranteed the maintenance of ordinances in the visible world (ibid., 330). The contemporary laws, as familiar as people's occupations, took on an unfamiliar appearance when they were associated with the "wondrous, august deeds" performed by the deities of heaven and earth. This entrustment, which first meant creating the world for human habitation, eventually validated imperial administration. Miyauchi explained that the foundation of imperial governance was a continual ceremonializing of the deities. "Today," he wrote, "this governance has been transmitted to the Tokugawa shogun and his family." But the same kind of governance existed in the hidden world, where its purpose was to assist the visible. The logic for this mapping, already worked out by Mutobe, lay in the conviction that since the body could be seen in the visible realm it submitted to imperial governance; the heart, which could not be seen by the human eye, resided in concealed deeds directed by the administration of Ōkuni-nushi no kami.

After rehearsing this familiar supposition of nativist cosmology, Miyauchi asked: Could evil deeds befall the times if the rules were protected by the invisible governance? Answering this question correctly depended on understanding the words used to describe work. Among ordinary folk, he argued, there prevailed a variety of occupations—literally, a "variety of boundaries of the body." For "boundary," he employed the ideographs for social status (*bungen*), which in contemporary usage brought forth associations relating to work. Although these "boundaries" usually called attention to work (*waza*), he complained, they fell short of covering the range of possibilities. If one accepted the variety of samurai, peasants, and merchants found among the people, the distinctions equaled "the divisions of the body." But must they all be called work? The term *waza*, he reasoned, associated work with bringing the five cereals to completion and signified becoming or producing, which Mutobe had designated *naru*. Miyauchi prescribed that work always implied the activity of agricultural cultivation and, therefore, the task of making a livelihood (*nariwai*; ibid., 332). He cited the example of the division of measurements utilized in the performance of household duties. These forms of measuring represented the skill of calculation bestowed by the deities, which men had been appointed to receive and apply in making a livelihood. The various measurements referred to specific functions, differentiations that constituted boundaries (*hodo*) extended to men and to things in heaven, earth, and hell. Humans were differentiated from all other things, and they were obliged to develop "natural" divisions as part of their unique endowment. In this discussion, Miyauchi offered the example of the body's organization into hands, feet, mouth, and other parts as a model for the division of labor. But, he warned, there should be no mixing of series, no crossing over the lines differentiating one group of functions from another. Positioning samurai, peasants, artisans, and merchants as boundaries defining different forms of work corresponded to employing units of measurement, such as *bun*, *sun*, *shaku*, and *jō*, to measure different kinds of things. Both cases fixed limits and boundaries.

Differentiations amounted to order, he wrote, and order necessitated its own principle of preservation. The other world always protected the ordinances of this world, for "if the limitations of the body are not calculated and if one exceeds such divisions, the august ordinances will be transgressed and the foundations for disaster shall be laid." Each occupational grouping had its own functional divisions. Such divisions obliged people to observe and forever remember the boundaries and limits of "sufficiency." "How not to forget or lose interest?" he asked rhetorically. The answer lay not in the contemporary impulse leading to selfishness and acquisitiveness (*horisogokoro*). The selfish person never found anything adequate or recognized limitations to sufficiency. Miyauchi was convinced that examples of unbridled greed among contemporaries represented the urge to violate "boundaries" and invite not good fortune but only disaster. "If people extend the boundaries received from the earthly and heavenly deities, they will neglect their productive duties (*nariwai*) and be impudent toward them. Ordinarily, this kind of activity leads to poverty and insufficiency." Men who exceeded such divisions and abandoned their bodies and families went beyond working for the household. Poverty and insufficiency were predictably caused by people immersed in pleasure and play. Miyauchi noted the familiarly encoded cycle of decline, in which the son born into a wealthy household grew weary of his duties and squandered inherited resources in the pursuit of aesthetic and sexual excitement, ultimately forfeiting the good fortune of the household. The decline of good fortune meant going against a trust derived from the parents and the imperial ordinances of the deities.

The preservation of the established boundaries by observing the household duties required both performance and prayer to the ancestral deities. Continual observance in work and worship ensured that the household would be free of misfortune and promised "brightness" and happiness. To dramatize the centrality of work, Miyauchi distinguished between the origins of real wealth, already being amplified by Satō Shin'en (1769–1850), as we shall see, and the contemporary understanding of it. In his time, treasure commonly meant the acquisition of money and forms of hoarding; people who requested good fortune ordinarily desired more money from the gods (ibid., 335). A lack of money among the upper orders was considered an annoyance and eventually inflicted hardship among members of the lower classes, who could not make ends meet. Because people had become so attached to the uses of money, they had forgotten about the real sources of wealth.

"Treasure" meant people working in the fields and carried with it the additional meaning of rice field. "Among merchants, artisans, and samurai," he wrote, "certain services are performed for money. But those things that derive from agricultural production [*takara* was written for rice field] are called treasures. Thus, the source of wealth is the rice field." In recent times, this source had dried up, wealth was being needlessly squandered, and the gods were moved to anger. Divine anger manifested itself in periodic famines. To avert such misfortune, the folk would have to retrace their steps and return to the source of wealth, so that, once more, they could concentrate on agriculture and bring to fruition (*naru*) the blessings of the gods. Offenders and violators of the divine blessings committed transgressions (*tsumi*) and resembled the "annoying pests" who "gather together and destroy households. Isn't this weakening [the will to] work?" In this passage, Miyauchi used the term *mure tsudoi* to convey "pests banding together," but it actually referred to contemporary jacqueries (ibid., 336).

In his discussions concerning work and its relationship to worship, Miyauchi introduced the metaphor of fire to designate imperial majesty, which he compared to the "force of fire." This imagery depicted imperial majesty as a substance similar to fire because of its potentialities when related to other things. Unless fire mixed with some other element, he wrote, such as wood or oil, it remained useless. The same relationship described imperial majesty. But fire, like imperial dignity, played a role larger than mere metaphor. All things relied on the force of fire and emanated from the deity of fire, since the time of creation (ibid., 341–42). Traditionally, the word for "fire" identified phonetically with "day"—both were sounded as *hi*—and this homonymic relationship proved the equivalence of divine purpose and quotidian life (ibid., 346–47). Miyauchi's concentration on the function of fire turned his attention to the status of the tutelary shrines. Shrines were like an adhesive; they anchored life, work, and worship. Their presence reinforced the unilinear link between creation and continuing custom. Here, the shrine assumed the shape of a fortress defending *place* against the invasion of historical change. It came to symbolize the place of the village; worship in tutelary shrines came to mean the worship of place. Miyauchi saw in the shrines a connection with the ancestors and the primal deities and a guarantee of continued production and good fortune. In his thoughts concerning tutelary worship, he aimed at securing the certainty of a place of social solidarity and the effect of substituting the part for the whole. Shrines reminded people of their formal religious duties to both place and past and enforced their obligations to continue the collective work of productivity in the present. They also were responsible for the "birth of children," he added: "Although humans are born and live in the present and return to the hidden realm after death, we know that they are protected by the tutelary deities in these places" (ibid., 350). Birth and life in the present came as endowments from the time of Izanagi and Izanami; although the parents granted them, they derived from the creative powers of these two creation deities. People were born to place in each present and submitted to the governance of imperial genealogy. They were obliged to follow the august system of the creation deities, keep watch over their intentions, serve those who were above and love those things that were below, and perform occupations conforming to their endowment (*onoono nanigashi ni tsukitaru shokubun o itonami*). Moreover, people were enjoined to pursue the divine morality of the gods and to differentiate correctly the visible things from the invisible (ibid.).

The shrines signified the birth and becoming of the body. Body derived its existence, its heat, from the deity of fire. In humans, this was called spirit. Spirit supplied warmth to the body, which turned cold upon death because the spirit left it. These departed spirits returned to the tutelary shrines, where they took up a new kind of existence (*shinibito o ieru koto to kikue, sono tama o todomuru tokoro o hokora to iu mo*; ibid., 351). Miyauchi proposed that even ancient prayers referred to the places where the spirits resided. They showed the relationship between the spirit and creation, and fire and blood, calling it *hichi*— "fire blood"—and defining it as the basic composition of the human body. This meant that life—the body—was transmitted directly by the parents to their children and from children to grandchildren. Yet behind the Way of "true blood," as he put it, there prevailed the idea of lineage and ancestor veneration. The "great basis" (*ōmoto*), which was related to the proliferation of things caused by the spirit of creation deities, bequeathed to humans the "several allocations and administrations." "Therefore, people born in such-and-such village, according to the principle of the *kami* Way, are divided among the places of the tutelary gods of these villages." This division took place at birth, when children were "divided into individual spirits" (ibid., 353). Before individual differentiation occurred, only an undivided spirit existed, a "basic spirit" whose unfolding was like a light radiating first from a basic source and then gradually refracting outward from place to place. The differentiated spirits were, similarly, refractions of the creation; knowledge of such sacred affairs of creation resided in the tutelary deities (ibid.). Although tutelary meant only the place of birth, the gods also protected villages because of the relationship of birth to place; the places they guarded were the prior locus (*osaki*) of the great deities of the two supporting *kami*. Thus, the clans of the villages joined with the great intention of these *kami* to constitute the only possible promise of renewal and "rebirth" (ibid.). Because bodies were given birth and differentiated into spirits in each village, they were called clan members (*ujiko*), but for Miyauchi, they were members of the tutelary shrine. The reason for the birth of the individual body resided in a mysterious and wondrous act bestowed by the deities, but it remained too difficult to explain in words. Giving life took the name for body (*mi*) and honored (*mi*), and connoted respect. Body (*mi*) and honored (*mi*) were the same word. In our times, Miyauchi explained, the word denoting respect for things was called *on*, a corruption of the word *ōmichu*. The root of this word had changed from a respect for body to a reverence for things. Yet it was not entirely mistaken, since it still carried the essential meaning of reverence for body (as an object; ibid., 354). The crucial link was provided by becoming and existence, *naru* and *aru*. Becoming changed into being: "As things are born, they exist, they are bodies that become and exist. Making shape gives way to [settled] shape, form to body." Words conveying thanks such as *arigatashi* and *katajikenashi* simply referred back to expressions of gratitude for the blessings of the gods, who made human bodies in the present and gave life. Thanks for the body immediately implied knowing how to esteem it, which, in turn, led to thankful respect to the deities and the parents. To neglect this truth risked reversing the whole chain of associations, the proper order symbolized in the tutelary shrine; it left the body open to the blandishments of private temptation and lust. Under these circumstances, the body as a vehicle of respect would be forgotten, and with it the parents, wife, and children, household, and, ultimately, place itself, which remained prior to all.

Cosmologizing Agriculture: The Origins of Wealth

Hirata Atsutane's cosmological narrative constituted a form that called attention to a certain message and a point of contact with a specific rural audience. Mutobe proposed that the form of the cosmic narrative defined the relationship between the invisible and visible realms and fixed the boundaries of place as the settled division between the appropriate and transgression. It also served to structure a content—a signi-fied—which Satō Shin'en located in the production of wealth. This content qualified as an "inner form," a subtext to the cosmic text of naming and fixing boundaries. Yet considerations of wealth and the necessity of work were only possible—as we shall see in Suzuki Masa-yuki—after determining the place of production, which itself depended on producing a space that could be named and subdivided. Classifying the cosmos according to a binary opposition between invisible and vis-ible expanded the field of human activity immeasurably, especially when compared to the conception of public space found in Confucian narratives. Whereas nativist theory imagined a space that would in-clude both the performance of work and the application of proper moral conduct, Confucian discourse, until the development of politi-cal economism, could only accommodate the latter. Nativism, with its expanded conception of space and place, was able to privilege both the sources of wealth and the necessity of work in a way no other dis-course had managed to conceptualize. Since explaining the cosmos was indistinguishable from illuminating the principle of creation in which things came to exist as a result of the concourse and union of deities (Hirata in the *Tama no mihashira* had associated the invisible with female organs and visibility with male parts), the archetypal act of producing things—habitation and folk—now necessitated wealth and work. Here, too, the supplement of narrative performed the task of incorporating the past into the present in order to secure both presence and plenitude.

Satō Shin'en was probably the earliest to make this connection between origins and continuous productivity, and he showed clearly how cosmology might be used to talk about things closer to daily life in rural Japan. Yet we can note the same impulse in other writers, such as Mutobe Yoshika, Suzuki Shigetane, and Suzuki Masayuki. Even though Satō's cosmological efforts were largely inspired by Hirata, he went further to emphasize the importance of the origins of wealth and productivity, which in Hirata's text remained a secondary considera-tion. Satō's major cosmological texts, the *Yōzōka ikuron* and the *Ten-chūki*, were written about 1825; their contents are similar. In the pref-ace of the *Tenchūki*, he confessed that, after reading such books as Motoori's *Kojikiden*, Hattori Nakatsune's *Sandaikō*, and Hirata's *Tama no mihashira*, he came to "excel in the real facts of antiquity and to understand [*satori*], gradually, the genesis [*gen'un*] of the creation deities in terms of such principles as life, heaven, and earth" (*Tck*

12:128). Undoubtedly, his familiarity with Hirata's powerful cosmological program provided the occasion for his own work. Satō was, like Hirata, from Akita in northern Japan, and records from the Ibukiya list him as having enrolled sometime in 1815. Not much is known about his relationship with Hirata, except that he was forty-seven years old at the time he enrolled and, thus, seven years older than his teacher.

Satō proposed to link his own conception of political economy, with its concentration on the sources of wealth, to the format of cosmology. Rather than study the classic texts, he drew most of his outline from Hirata's *Koshiden* and the cosmology of Yoshio Shunzō (or Junzō), *Ensai kanshō zusetsu* (1823), "Map of Far Western meteorological observations." Hirata had argued that the creation deities, embodied in the tutelary shrines of contemporary villages, were the originators of the cosmos and all things. Although this view coincided with folk beliefs, it was being undermined by new texts translated from the Dutch. Satō's *Yōzōka ikuron* often noted the destructive influence of these texts and argued that not even Western science successfully explained the motive forces behind such things as the movement of the heavenly bodies and the rotation of the earth. Yet, like so many contemporaries, he realized that the new knowledge disclosed a view of the cosmos constructed on principles of observation, deduction, and measurement. It seems to have been his intention to bring together the newer explanations (method) with the findings of nativist learning (substance).

Satō accepted the basic elements of Hirata's combinatory strategy, his story line concerning the creation, including the major dramatis personae among the deities, and the archetypal fables accounting for the beginnings of all things. He differed from the established discourse in his effort to explain growth and productivity. Whereas Hattori and Hirata had been satisfied to attribute the origin of things and subsequent production to the miraculous powers of the creation deities, Satō, accepting the centrality of the deity Ame no minakanushi no kami and the commands to the creation deities to make the world, explained growth and productivity as a result of warmth and light emanating from the sun's rays. He agreed that the creation of the cosmos represented a divine act defying rational explanation, one in which Izanagi and Izanami were directed to form the heavens and earth, and asserted that—despite accounts insisting on reason and principle—the rotation of the globe and the centrality of the sun constituted the "private destiny of creation" (*musubi no shiun*). "Even though Copernicus could skillfully chart the principles of movement by which the ten

thousand stars revolved openly, it is not yet known what gives occurrence to this phenomenon of movement. It is known that the divine
principles on which the rotation is based are a private destiny [of the
creation deities]" (Yi, 237, 220).[18] People born in the imperial land had
been able to avoid being constrained by the contrivances of others,
since they possessed a superior wisdom in the ancient classics. Satō's
argument rested on accepting the tales found in the earlier chronicles;
his return to the authority of the first fables disclosed the familiar nativist distrust for rational explanation. Yet when comparing his account to
that of Hattori or Hirata, it is evident that he relied heavily on data
derived from observation, measurement, and deduction (Yi, 246–47;
Nmc, 294).[19]

The sun, not heaven, was the source of life. The central deity
Ame no minakanushi no kami created heaven and earth and "imparted
the blessing of love to people; this deity augmented the nurture of the
people and brought to completion morality and the cultivation of the
Way among the ordinary folk. This kami decreed to the two deities of
creation to begin the work of bestowing birth on all things" (Yi, 196–
97; Nmc, 267; Tck, 138–39). The origin of things (animals, earth,
rock, plants, and trees) consisted in a mixture of water, soil, salt, and
oils, and revealed the divine intentionality (ten no kokoro; Yi, 248;
Nmc, 300). The purpose of the divine will was "to nourish" and bestow
the blessings of creation upon people. "When one seeks to assist the
work of nature by giving nourishment to all things in heaven and earth,
one will surely turn to agricultural activities as the best way to realize
enrichment. Even though it is necessary to investigate the reason [dōri]
of all things minutely, if agricultural affairs are not emphasized, this
activity will result in the discrimination of useless things" (Yi, 239–
40; Nmc, 296). Divine intention was chained to human endowment
to work in agricultural activity; humans, it seemed, had no choice but
to produce things and enrich agriculture out of divine compulsion.

Nourishment, enrichment, and productivity invoked sexuality
and the archetypal union between the two supporting deities. "The
feelings inspired by yin and yang are rich and elaborate; the joy uniting
male and female is profound." Satō, in this connection, drew from the
fable Hirata had articulated in the Tama no mihashira concerning how
the various spheres had formed from the "drippings of the spear of
heaven" and how residues "hardened into the eight islands." Human
procreation and the growing of things stood as a transformation of this
primal act. The "spear of heaven" (ama no nuboku) resembled the

shape of the penis (which Hirata called male support, *mihashira*), and
all things acquired life as a result of the concourse between male and
female deities. Satō acknowledged the importance of this fable, in
which the jeweled spear was thrust into the primal ooze, and concluded that its associations were self-evident for understanding the basis
of heaven and earth (*Yi*, 238; *Nmc*, 295). If the reason of heaven and
earth did not furnish male and female, he wrote, there could be no
propagation of the species. Therefore, "to give birth and life to things
of the world, there must be male and female." Male and female possessed the vigor (*kekki*) to feel mutually and to "rejoice in sexual intercourse." Continuing life through reproduction carried forth the wondrous work of the creation gods. But sexual union as a productive act
belonged to the series that included agricultural work and productivity
as manifestations of the divine will. Satō showed, before many rural
nativists, that the production of foodstuffs and agricultural work in no
way differed from the creation of the cosmos, and he linked creation
and agriculture by noting that children were created as potential members of a rural work force (*Yi*, 239–40; *Nmc*, 296).

Men and women were given their respective shapes to propagate
the species. "The vitality of men and women is the sexual spirit heaven
imparts. The young woman's ovum is the flesh that nourishes on earth.
What one gains from the father is the demon (*oni*) of animality, from
the mother, spirit." At the time of death, Satō claimed, recalling Hirata's earlier meditations on the subject, the sexual spirit ascended
while the flesh descended. "Things that have been bestowed by heaven
return to heaven, and things that have come from the earth are restored
to the earth." The father, acting as a surrogate for heaven, made the
birth of the individual possible, while the mother, acting for earth,
nourished the individual into maturity. Heaven and earth appeared
now as father and mother writ large. "The blessing [*on*] of heaven and
earth and the meritorious services of father and mother are not fundamentally different."

By appealing to a logic of similitude, Satō sought to clarify what
he believed were indistinguishable linkages between the human and
spirit worlds, betwen "visible" and "invisible" realms. He proposed that
people passed from the invisible to the visible realm accompanied by
messengers, and *kami* guardians continued to follow humans during
their stay on earth. "From the time of birth to the moment of death,
the [sexual] spirit is connected to the deities" (*Yi*, 241; *Nmc*, 297). This
was so because humans inhabited the earth, which served primarily as

the place for them to practice and carry out the Way and give expression to virtue. The presence of the *kami* guaranteed that sexual union would satisfy the divine purpose. Satō resorted to this rather elaborate explanation so as to underline the importance of agriculture and rural labor. Westerners, he observed, had developed marvelous techniques, "which bring fire from water and water from fire," but when closely compared to the agricultural technology of Japan, these techniques were found to be decidedly inferior. He associated the centrality of the agricultural program with the divine cosmological project. "The Way of the cosmos was brought together by mixing metal, stone, salt, and mud"; the union of male and female generated the species that would work in order to continue the creation. Agricultural labor equaled life and creation.

Satō detected in the first fables the microcosm of the natural history of the race. "The Sun Goddess decreed that the imperial founders should show people how to make life abundant and prosperous" (*Yi*, 250; *Nmc*, 300). Ama no kumahito (probably a messenger), hearing of the sacred virtue of Toyouke no kami, was moved to tears by such achievements. Even when Toyouke died, the deity's body gained a new lease on life by the production of its parts: the head yielded horses and cattle; the forehead, millet; the eyebrows, cocoons (*mayu*); one eye, Deccan grass (*hie*); the other, rice seedlings (*ina*); and the sex organs, soybeans (*daizu*), red beans (*azuki*), and barley (*mugi*). The heavenly messenger came to collect these things and give them to Amaterasu who, receiving them, was overjoyed and said, "These are the things that people who live on earth must use to make a living and use as food." The millet, Deccan grass, and beans were made into seeds for vegetable plots; the rice was made into seed for wet fields. The Sun Goddess enjoined the Ama no murakimi, who were leaders of the peasantry, to have the seeds of rice sown for the first time in the narrow, long fields of heaven. By autumn, ears of rice, bent under their own weight and eight span long, were everywhere a splendid sight to behold. Still more, she took the silkworm cocoons in her mouth and began to spin thread from them. This act inaugurated sericulture. Satō concluded the story as follows:

> Toyouke no kami today is the great deity of the outer shrine of Ise. But, in antiquity, the shrine devoted to the worship of this deity was located in a central village in the region of Tango; later, during the reign of the Emperor Yūryaku, it was moved, owing to a decree from the Sun God-

dess, to the area of Watarai in Ise. . . . . Among the various *kami* to whom Izanami gave birth was Hitama no kami, who, in union with Haniyasuhime no kami, gave birth to Waku musubi no kami. Now, Waku musubi no kami gave birth to Toyouke no kami, a deity who possesses a broad and deep virtue. All things used and consumed in the world of humans, such as food, lodging, tools and utensils, and domestic animals, have issued forth from this deity. Ever since the beginnings of the realm, emperors have revered greatly the virtue of this *kami*; worship and celebration at the outer shrine prospered, because emperors felt it their duty to worship this deity first; and since that time, this ritual has been decreed by all subsequent emperors.

Recounting this fable supported Satō's principal argument concerning the centrality of agriculture as the source of wealth and the necessity of work. The *kami* intended to provide the folk with the conditions of wealth. But the gift carried the obligation of acknowledging the importance of agriculture and sharing the conviction of the gods, who worked to make the ordinary life of the people prosperous. Among the affairs of the earth, nothing was more urgent than agriculture. Early emperors recognized its primacy, bequeathing the divine intention to their descendants to divide the seedlings between wet and dry fields and taking the initiative among the populace to endeavor in cultivation. "The simplicity of antiquity," Satō noted, "was never to despise work, but rather to fear that not enough energy and vitality were being expended" (*Yi*, 251; *Nmc*, 301). Humans could expect continuing assistance from the gods. Susanowo no kami, for example, planted a variety of trees for human use; Ōtoshi no kami implemented a system of agricultural administration that was passed down to the emperors; and Ōnamochi no kami managed the *habitus* (*kunitsuchi*), opened up fields and paddies, sowed several kinds of cereal seeds, and decreed the fructification of all things. Others followed in this divine work, representing an archetypal and divine division of labor, even though earth was designated a place for humans to make their way, not an abode for the gods. Once the land was completed and things reached their full growth, humans appeared to make their living on earth. Although this fable served in the *Yōzōka ikuron* to authenticate the rural project, Satō also used it to amplify the role played by Ōnamochi no kami, who, in several versions of the myth, was Ōkuninushi no kami, ruler of the invisible governance. He expanded Hirata's exegetical explanation of the role played by this deity and supplied further validation to the nativist valorization of the Izumo tradition and its claims to recognition.

We have already seen that in Hirata's classification scheme, Ōkuninushi acquired new importance largely as a result of the division between things seen and unseen, realms visible and invisible. Satō's reformulation resituated the deity within the much larger context of creating the land, bringing it to completion, and readying it for human habitation. This move was hardly accidental or innocent, and Satō could not have been insensitive to its consequences for political theory. Although he had no trouble finding authority for this version, it would be wrong to suggest that his argument for the primacy of the land and the priority of Ōkuninushi and the folk over the imperial genealogy reflected *only* the operation of the nativist metonymic strategy to trace things back to their origins. Meiji leaders, recognizing the possible consequences of this version of the myths, moved quickly to eliminate its political influence by reducing the shrine at Izumo to the status of a state sect. Others in the twentieth century returned to this tradition in their efforts to promote the claims of community over the state and bureaucratic necessity.

In any event, once the work of Ōkuninushi was completed, according to Satō, Ōnamochi no kami (as Satō called him in the text) turned over the administration of the realm to the imperial descendants. Satō's discussion falls short of a full-scale assessment of the meaning of this figuration for the ancient historical field and the possibility of historical conflict among clans competing for power. The transfer of authority was apparently made during the age of the gods, he wrote, since it was never the *kami*'s intention to "live forever on earth," but always to revert to concealment.

Satō was unrestrained in his admiration for the achievements of Ōkuninushi no kami. "Among the descendants of Susanowo no kami," he wrote, "none is more splendid." It was this deity who provided the imperial descendants with the "divine intention; . . . he made the reeds and bulrushes grow luxuriantly, gave shape to the soil, cultivated the rice paddies, opened up new fields for cultivation, and endeavored in the administration of agricultural affairs. He directed the wind that blows, the rain that falls, and [caused] the national events [*kokuji*]. . . . In time, the realm was enriched, things were abundant, and the people lived prosperously" (*Yi*, 253; *Nmc*, 302). He identified Ōkuninushi no kami's accomplishments as the central experience of the creation and the condition for subsequent imperial rule. Satō was convinced that

the fable authorized the act of coupling agriculture to the actual management of the land, which made the visible governance dependent on
the invisible authority of Ōkuninushi no kami. It also sanctioned all
subsequent efforts to unite tutelary deities and village religious observances in the present to the creation and the governance of the invisible
realm. The completion of the earth signified this deity's great enterprise
and profound virtue. Before withdrawal into the unseen realm, Ōkuninushi no kami turned to the task of ridding the earth of pollution,
evil *kami*, and the spirits who inflicted pain and injury upon humans.
In doing so, this deity, who was synonymous with creativity, acquired
the additional association of a great military hero who, destroying evil
and tranquilizing the realm, enabled the people to pursue their agricultural program.

Despite Ōkuninushi's withdrawal, the imperial descendants continued to oversee rural affairs as the central concern of political management among the living. The folk were obliged to practice agricultural work on the authority of *yūmeikai*; the unseen world reminded
men to work for the achievement of abundance, to practice morality,
and to follow the ancient Way. "If one does not follow the character of
the heavenly endowment, and does not practice the way of human
ethics, if one leads a life of idleness . . . for private desire, then it would
be necessary to receive the punishment of the invisible government"
(*Yi*, 257, also 262–63; *Nmc*, 307, also 310–11). Punishment in the
concealed realm amounted to hardship, distress, and poverty in the
visible and resulted from the kind of willful conduct that characterized
those who went against their endowment to work and to produce (*Yi*,
266–68; *Nmc*, 316–18). Yet, Satō remarked, the necessity to perform
reflected the responsibility of the lord as much as the duty of the ordinary peasant. Earlier in the *Yōzōka ikuron*, he noted that emperors
rarely acted out of private concern but, rather, from sincerity (*shissei*),
since they "earnestly love the people" (*Yi*, 254; *Nmc*, 304). The rulers
were obliged to exhaust their own efforts to promote agricultural affairs
in fulfillment of the inheritance from Ōnamochi no kami, who, at the
time of the creation, linked political authority (management) to agricultural productivity. Although this theory, as we shall see, was appropriated by rural nativists to legitimize the authority of local leadership,
Satō saw it as the basis of a policy of enlightened agriculture and wise
political management, and, alternately, of state intervention in the accumulation of wealth. Fear of heaven alone was not enough to induce
political managers to administer wisely; lords must study the "reason"

of heaven, observe the movement of the stars, measure the ebb tide of the seas, determine latitudes and longitudes, investigate in detail the conditions of the weather, prepare for the advance of heavy rainfalls and regular dry spells, clarify the nature of soils, open up new paddies and fields, arrange for irrigation projects, manage dikes and barriers efficiently, and learn more about fertilizers to endeavor in agriculture with a full heart. Such actions, Satō promised, would continue the intention of the gods from the time of creation (*Yi*, 273; *Nmc*, 323).

The Worship of Work

In routinizing the ancient Way, Hirata, as we have seen, expanded his definition of the visible realm to include not simply the political management of the folk but their contemporary conduct as well. Although he was initially referring to ethical behavior, his lectures specified the content by equating it with the details of daily life. Behind this valorization of the life activities of the folk lay the principle of creation itself and the authority of the creation deities. The principle of creating all things, we have seen, was reduced by both Hirata and Satō Shin'en to the union of male and female and the natural production and reproduction of species. Satō further refined this formulation by envisaging the visible realm as the place for producing wealth, once the deities had made the land habitable for human cultivation. But human cultivation was seen merely as a continuation of the principle of creation. In this supplement, the principle of creation came to mean the birth and increase of all things; it was intimately related to the production of agricultural goods as the completion of the primal creative act. Even though Satō emphasized the role of human activity (work) in this continuing process, it was still only marginal to the central role of the deities, who prepared the conditions for subsequent cultivation. Yet it was precisely this principle of creation that nativist scholars like Suzuki Masayuki (1837–71) elevated into a principal metaphor for the Way itself. By transmuting the ancient Way of Hirata—the creation of the cosmos—into the Way of "generating life" (*seisei*) as a continuous activity, these scholars brought to completion the *kokugaku* conception of work as a religious observance.[20]

Suzuki Masayuki came from the Shimōsa region and was undoubtedly exposed to the nativism that had for some time distinguished the intellectual life of the area. Many of the loose threads concerning productivity and procreation and the centrality of the tutelary shrines as reminders of the ever-present relationship between practical activity and divine intention acquired systematic exposition in his major text, the *Tsukisakaki*, composed sometime in 1867. It was at this point that a discourse begun as a consideration of death and the destination of the spirits became a meditation on the forces of life. Like Satō Shin'en, Suzuki Masayuki was not officially affiliated with any one school; he has often been portrayed as an independent scholar and an autodidact. Yet his writings reveal conceptions, relationships, and concerns that place him securely within the nativist discourse. By his own acknowledgment, his "learning was without benefit of a teacher and spanned a period of six or seven years" of intensive study in preparation for the composition of the *Tsukisakaki*. He made it a point to describe his method: he had studied with no specific "master" but read the books of many and thought about what they meant, so that he could disclose best the power of a discourse to speak through an individual's voice, diminish the dimension of personal authorship, and represent something larger than the sum of its parts or its participants.

In the *Tsukisakaki* Suzuki demonstrated simultaneously the fundamental role work played in the activity of the living force (*seisei*) and the way performance itself represented the fulfillment of the cosmic plan. The cosmic plan affirmed what he called the "way of life formation," the "true principles" informing all things. Life formation referred to the Way of heavenly and earthly deities in their divine abode, Takamagahara. Specifically, it pointed to the work (*hataraki*) of the august spirits and the intention of the heavenly and earthly deities who gave birth to all things and provided for abundance (*umahara*) and prosperity. For humans, divine endowment ranged from the five relationships to the union of male and female and the availability of food and drink. But the Way also included the possibility of production and, therefore, development, change, and even success. Hence, Suzuki identified the "true principle" of the life force with productivity in general and proposed that it reflected the "logic" or "reason" of the heavenly and earthly deities. Before accepting the multitude of words that permanently systematized and organized the human image, it was necessary to grasp how people expressed their distinctive and original productive character. Rather than accept beliefs founded on words alone, it was necessary to determine how they reflected practice or conformed to the logic of productivity. If good seed or land was lacking, there was no chance of purchasing decent results. Even though the gods provided everything, people still constituted an active agency in the "generation of life"; humans must enter into a partnership with the gods. This partnership stemmed from a similarity between things (*mono*) and principle (*kotowari*). "Since all principles adhere to things, if there are things, so there is principle," he wrote in book 4 of the *Tsukisakaki*. Yet the conduct of principle derived from the divine. Hence, the foundation of principle remained in things, while its source lay with the earthly and heavenly deities. To consider deeply the will informing the creation of things by the deities of heaven and earth was to know the principle of things. Life, according to the true definition, existed only where humans followed principle. Viewing things and events in their productivity and grasping the true principle as it was concretized in production was the only way to secure a genuine understanding of life. Since the source of life could not be envisaged without considering things, humans who practiced the Way must abandon private knowledge and reaffirm their own intention, "if they wish to lead lives that place the body within the occurrences and existence of the times and the changing events and things." A firm belief in putting one's body at the disposal of the world of things meant not passive acceptance but active encouragement of human endeavor and effort (*SMk*, 246–48).

Suzuki tightened the causal relationship between the hidden realm and the visible world: "The success or failure of all things in the universe are produced in the invisible world and are settled in the visible." Without the hidden, nothing would ever be produced in the visible; without the visible, there would be no becoming. "Occurrence" and "becoming" were mediated by the concealed and the visible; visible and invisible were intimately bound to spirit and intention. Despite the earlier associations of the invisible with *kami* affairs and the visible with the human order, Suzuki argued that the gods could not do without the world of the seen, and humans would not be able to function without the world of the unseen.[21] Unlike Mutobe Yoshika, who sought to taxonomize what belonged to the two realms in order to diminish the real division of labor, Suzuki's discussions aimed only at showing that the visible, the site of becoming (*naru*), could be seen, while the invisible, the sanctuary of principle, could not. The invisible world of principle made possible the manifestation of things in the visible. Even though the spirits inhabiting the hidden realm ultimately determined the world of the living, potential forms were actualized only in the space reserved for the act of becoming and production in society.[22] These spirits gave birth to children, who reproduced themselves ceaselessly down to the present. Their life-giving powers were inexhaustible

and unchanging. Suzuki proposed, "The generation of all things results from the heavenly and earthly deities at the time of origins, but
they do not make each thing." The deities managed the spirits and
imparted blessings to them, but the actual "generation of things is
caused by the spirits." In this division of divine labor, he was careful to
separate the primal deities who created heaven and earth from the spirits—*tama*—who apparently came a little later as humanity proliferated
(*Nmc*, 380). "The spirits," he wrote, "are the *kami* who inhabit the
human body; the spirits of parents have all been divided and transmitted by the heavenly deities" (ibid., 338).[23] "The spirits borrow
strength from the heavenly and earthly deities and then perform their
work [*hataraki*], and it is for this reason that the heavenly deities believe
that all things will prosper. Beginning with Izanagi and Izanami, who
divided the spirits and gave birth to the myriad deities and peoples, all
must similarly endeavor for the enterprise [*jigyō*] of the generation of
life" (*Nmc*, 387).

The relationship between the two worlds appeared more complex
than before. The deeds that *kami* performed were visible, while their
august intention was concealed. Their intention was seen, while their
spirit was not. But the enterprises of humans invariably occurred in the
present, the visible world, whereas the working of their intention belonged to the hidden realm (ibid., 401). Suzuki hoped to distinguish
these two realms to show that the things humans did, made, and even
destroyed revealed intentions devised in the hidden world. The ultimate relationship between these two worlds was mutually reinforcing;
the combination projected a model of reciprocity for will and action
among humans. Suzuki differed from Motoori and Hirata in his refusal
to accept the explanation that the hidden world functioned in the form
of an invisible governance; his purpose was to demonstrate that the two
realms existed in both humans and deities.

Suzuki's contention concerning the necessity to "endeavor"
rested on the authority of the *Nihonshoki* (like Suzuki Shigetane, he
contested the primacy of the *Kojiki* and Hirata's dim estimate of the
Nihonshoki as an expression of Chinese intentionality), particularly the
passages announcing the goal of the creation to provide the basis for
the generation of all living things. These passages, he stated, showed
that the beginning of things and the separation of heaven, earth, and
yomi had been created by the deities of heaven and earth and were
"encouraged by the enterprise of giving life." Now, this principle of
generation found expression best in the establishment of the funda-

household

mental relationships between husband and wife, parent and child, older brother and younger brother, friend and friend; the guarantee that people performed in this spirit of mutual assistance came from the emotionality of man and woman and the availability of sufficient food and drink. All these signified the "enterprise of generation." Moreover, the descent of the imperial line from heaven, the privileging of a power figure in four of the five relationships, and the construction of governance in the visible world constituted the work of generating life, because they were able to "ward" off mutual conflict. This sensitivity to conflict, without necessarily specifying its content, drew attention to the "absent" contemporary history at the heart of Suzuki's texts and nativist discourse in general and became the unstated problem they sought to resolve. Suzuki believed that the basic endowments and arrangements were generated in order to prevent conflict before it occurred (ibid., 387–88).[24] In his last major text, *Jiansaku*, he turned directly to the question of human conflict, in order to show how its conditions might be removed. Everywhere, he observed, there was human conflict. If the heart incorporated conflict, it risked struggle, which inevitably led to rebellion. The basis of all conflict was the discontented heart. When the human heart became dissatisfied, chances for avoiding conflict diminished because of the wedge driven between "we" and "they".[25] Although a number of reasons had been advanced to explain the causes of rebellions throughout the realm in past and present, all of these occurrences could be reduced to the action of unruly passion, which became conflictual precisely at the point when humans were swayed from their original duty and position (*honbun*)— when interests collided. Here, Suzuki relocated the purpose of "correct governance" in the management of human passion to eliminate "private intention" from the "august heart of the heavenly and earthly deities" and to equalize the realm (*tenka o kinpeishi*; *Kcks* 5:151).

Underlying his theory that life was generated to overcome conflict was a conviction that human intention had to reflect in performance the life-giving activities. Suzuki wanted to show that because work— agricultural labor—required people to maintain the proper ethical conduct, it forestalled conflict, which undermined the generation of life activity. The reverse side of human conflict was mutual assistance and aid. "Humans," he asserted, "are all born according to the Way of generating life by the deities of heaven and earth, and it is, thus, their way to endeavor and conduct this Way of generating life" (*Nmc*, 355; *Kcks* 5:126 [*Jiansaku*]; *Shigaku zasshi* 67, no. 6:68 [*Minsei yoron*]). In order to accomplish this great task, they must first revise the content of the five relationships.

Such a revision should begin with the duties of the lords; it was their obligation to explain the Way of generating life as the central aim of humanity because they "receive the great trust . . . from the deities of heaven and earth." Owing to this "divine" responsibility, they must ceaselessly encourage goodness and dispense punishments among the folk. Although their task was not easy, they must coordinate the intentions of the deities with their own and avoid the temptation to harbor even the slightest private consideration. They must "pursue good men and rid the realm of distorted things [*nejiketa mono*]." Specifically, they must punish the wicked and "exhaust the heart in the governance of generating life, extending compassion to the ordinary folk and vouchsafing the prosperity of the times." Politics existed only for humans to promote life-giving activity. In another context, Suzuki remarked that a diminution of productivity and work invariably resulted from incompetent and irresponsible political management. As for the retainers—now interpreted broadly to include the ordinary folk—he advised them to make their intentions conform to the goal of generating life, to abandon selfishness, and to assist the lord in working for the establishment of public rectitude. Parents were duty-bound to make "household work" an expression of intention directed toward the accomplishment of life-generating activity. In practice, this meant instructing the young and diverting them from mistaken paths. If they failed in this undertaking, he warned, the prosperity and longevity of the household would be imperiled, since it depended on proper observances and performances. "One should never cause the decline of the household duties of the ancestors, which comes from a failure to encourage work and instruct the young and from forgetting that one is a parent." Children, for their part, were bound to fulfill the life-giving duties already enacted by their parents and to defend their teachings. Moreover, "by promoting work, they will shed light on the household." To neglect work; to avoid defending the Way "inclined" by the parents; to become addicted to wine, women, and tobacco; and to forfeit productivity—any of these transgressions would lead inevitably to shame on the parents and ancestors. The role of husbands demanded constant attention to work and productivity, prudence and sound judgment, in order to implement correct doctrine and avoid the confusion caused by sensual pleasures, indulgences inspired by an excessive "listening to the sweet words of women." Wives were to uphold the teachings of their husbands, pursue \

harmony and union, rear their children properly, and assist in the prosecution of household duties. Among brothers, the oldest must love the younger and follow the path of goodness; the younger must respect the older and adhere to his instructions. By promoting the general interest of the household well, by working at all levels, they—the brothers—would assist the father and mother in securing the goal of life generation. Discord at any point in the five relationships led to conflict over finances, especially among brothers, and should be avoided at all possible costs. Finally, the relationship between friend and friend was rooted in a sense of mutual assistance, specified in material terms. True friendship, the bond of affection linking members of a community into an organized whole, meant lending aid to others in troubled times, since the offer of assistance continued the work of generation. Suzuki's remodeling of the five relationships demonstrated that working together to generate life united people and diverted conflict. But, he added, serving this goal required the effort of bringing virtue to completion, which meant "realizing the virtue of having been born" (*Nmc*, 331, 333). "Exhausting energies for the Way" secured the "real learning, by which persons complete the virtue they have received at birth." When the folk recognized the primacy of the Way, they recalled the creation of things and the subsequent imperative for all living things to fulfill its demand of generating life by work and productive activity.

The equation between "completing the virtue one receives at birth" and working came close to the formulation advanced earlier by Suzuki Shigetane, who envisaged labor as the necessity of life (ibid., 336, also 339). "Labor" here meant not social labor but the exercise of reciprocity to secure life-supporting necessities. The original cooperation among the deities of creation exemplified the pattern for human organization to follow. "To work alone," Suzuki Masayuki cautioned, "will, in general, fail to accomplish anything" (ibid., 336). The human body still provided the authority for this conviction, because its parts functioned in concert to carry out work and speech. The body, in late-Tokugawa times, played an enormously important role; it usually denoted in discourse the terms by which a subject position was constituted for articulation. In Suzuki's texts, which resembled many of the "new" religions of the late-Tokugawa period, the body appeared as the "form" of the spirit and, therefore, the agent of intentional action initiated in the hidden realm, the analogue to the enunciated voice of the act of enunciation. The relationship of the parts of the body constituted an exemplar for human reciprocity. The eyes saw, the ears heard, the mouth spoke, the hands held, and the feet moved; each part relied on a mutuality in order for the whole to function properly. The principle of mutual reciprocity in work—people working together to accomplish a great undertaking—remained fixed and unchanging; things mutually assembled for work represented the "profound consideration of the heavenly and earthly deities and the miraculous creation" (ibid., 336–37; *Kcks* 5:128–29 [*Jiansaku*]).

Suzuki's articulation of the centrality of work and the cosmic necessity of mutual reciprocity, manifested in the activities of the myriad deities and the operation of the human body, constituted an ideological intervention that, as we have already seen, instantiated contemporary history. The *Tsukisakaki* shows a keen awareness of the ironclad relationship between work and the achievement of an orderly community. "When people go against the Way of generating life, the realm will become disordered, and it will be difficult to accomplish the important enterprises related to the generation of life." Destruction of the necessary work ethic would drive the realm into riot and rebellion, and it would be a long time before order was reestablished; retainers (people) would turn on their lords and Japan would follow the customs of China (*Nmc*, 337). Although Suzuki acknowledged that order and disorder, the success and failure of things, relied on interaction between the hidden and visible realms, he also believed that rebellion resulting from the neglect of work would be the fault of the lords (*Nmc*, 340, 345). Riot and rebellion occurred because the leadership obstructed the Way and, thus, prevented the people from carrying out activities necessary to the Way.

This judgment conveys a clear evaluative standard of good and evil. A disruption in the reciprocal relationship between ruler and ruled, leading to altered conditions in the countryside, meant that the leadership had, in some way, failed to implement correct intention. Evil appeared when change occurred, and change invariably testified to the diminution of the productive process (ibid., 376, 345; also *Shigaku zasshi*, 129 [*Jiansaku*]). In this way, *kokugakusha* like Suzuki used their discourse to resituate the ruled—the producers—as the subject, whose performance depended on the conduct of the rulership. Failure to produce drew attention to the responsibility of the leaders and their willful interference with the activities that made the continuation of life possible and meaningful. Just as parents gave life, the lord must provide all of the conditions necessary for accomplishing the generation of life. Yet the land alone served as the basis of this activity (*Nmc*,

346). Although, for Suzuki, this relationship represented the good, it also explained the periodic occurrence of evil. "Evil," he wrote, "is born from within good things. Because the Way of generating life is a good thing, evil abuses come from it and mingle with it" (ibid., 347). Work and production could be misused by the lords for private and selfish purposes. Private desire itself showed its affinity with "evil doctrines," a misrecognition fostered by the study of Confucian books. Only private desire disturbed the heart and plunged the realm into disorder—which Suzuki compared to a "deep valley." He was convinced that false doctrine and private desire inhibited the Way, causing a shift in the modes of life-giving activity inscribed in the earth itself. "Even though birds fly in the sky," he warned, "they are still not able to live apart from the earth," as if to suggest that humans, too, had no alternative. The earth stood as the place where the life-generating activity was carried to completion (ibid., 351). Hence, people were bound to the soil, because there could be no real separation from the land and the deities who made it. But, on closer inspection, the deities were really the ancestors of contemporaries, those who had already served their time to ensure that life continued into succeeding generations (ibid., 345, 378). "The lords, parents, and the land have all been conferred by the deities as the foundation on which to carry out the business of life in the visible realm." Although existence was unimaginable without these three blessings, it was grievous that, with the flourishing of private desire, people began to forget this "foundation and fail to take notice of their moral obligations. . . . During times of immorality, the realm will become entirely disordered and one's body no longer safe" (ibid., 352–53). Suzuki yoked private impulse, unmanaged passions, and what he called "desiring pleasure" to "neglecting one's occupation and livelihood." He discovered the locus of desire in behavior caused by the confusion brought on by "evil doctrines" imported from abroad (China). His solution to the confusion was to "jettison the evil and mistaken teachings of foreign countries for a return to the intention informing foundations . . . casting off contemporary abuses for the study of the ancient [Japanese] spirit." If false doctrines led to "private knowledge," he reasoned, then supplication to the gods would avert misfortune, secure happiness, and bring tranquility and a quiet heart.

Suzuki Masayuki took the nativist conception of work farther than most of his contemporaries in discourse; he grounded being in an inaugural productive activity, whereas it had previously resided in the spoken language. But this operation actually amounted to the same

thing. Earlier nativists had seen the cosmic plan manifest its purpose
in the speaking of a divine language; Suzuki transformed the divine
intention into the working body. Yet work required the activity of the
body. Although he readily acknowledged the divine intention informing creation and saw the "creation of life as an obligation that all must
repay," he was less sure about making the act of work a moment of
worship. His discussions of the necessity of "completing the virtue one
has been born with" relied less on recognizing specific religious practices, such as observances and ceremonies related to tutelary shrines,
than on performing useful work. This is not to say that he saw work
and worship as separable. Just as divine necessity instigated work and
productive activity, the subsequent realization of the sacred trust to
work by the body represented an elision of religiosity and motivated
labor, precisely the kind of internalization Hirata had established as a
condition for proper ethical conduct. Suzuki removed work from a
reliance on external forms of religious observance. He also established
the conditions for a later separation of work from religious ceremony
without undermining the motivating power to perform, thereby preparing the way for a conception of work unmediated by any other consideration than its own necessity. None of this would have been possible
without the nativist insistence that the relationship between worship
and work was mediated by the body's capacity to redirect desire. We
have already seen that Suzuki rejected the status of Ōkuninushi no
kami as the ruler of the invisible governance, while accepting the functional relationship between the two realms. This refusal subsequently
authorized the separation of explicitly religious observances from the
performance of productive activity. In Suzuki's "rationalized" version
of nativist discourse, spirits and *kami* reappeared as the ancestors of
humans in the present, necessitating a recognition of the mutual interaction of godly and human activity. In a certain sense, he was arguing
for the human origins of community (ibid., 378). Mutuality between
deities and humans was sanctioned by the more fundamental relationship between the invisible and visible realms and functioned, therefore,
as the archetype for the mutual assistance governing human society.
He was equally convinced that, if contemporaries would adequately
consider the age of the gods and the time of humans, it would be easy
to find and clarify many areas of mutuality. Yet, this very interaction
of divine and human beings made it possible for him to weight the
emphasis toward humans as subjects (as their bodies were the form of
spirits) and toward work (*seisei*) as their ontic grounding.

It should be recalled that Suzuki saw evil occurring from the good, not from the intervention of a divine agency such as the "bent" god Magatsubi no kami. The incidence of evil necessarily depended on the extent to which the good—working—was being accomplished. Since evil had no autonomous existence, it had no positive permanence. Only a change in circumstances could transform good into evil (ibid., 364). Such a change occurred when humans wanted more life-generating activity. Humans desired sweet drinks and elegant goods, fine clothes and households; men desired beautiful women and wished to satisfy emotions induced by life-generating activity. But such demands became evil when they turned into surplus desire. The responsibility for punishments and rewards, then, rested not with an invisible governance, as imagined by Hirata and Mutobe, but in the visible world with the lords, who were obliged to exercise proper judgment. Convinced that goodness would always prevail if people selected the correct path, Suzuki also recognized that good fortune or punishment depended entirely on the path chosen (ibid., 360). Yet the proper path had been illuminated since the beginning of time: people knew that they were bound to "complete virtue" in the interest of continuing life and to abstain from private behavior, which led to excess and the disruption of the very processes by which life was continually generated.

6 Ruralization II: Act and Authority

Authority for Action

As nativism developed, its expansion under the direction of local notables, who saw in it a solution to rural problems, came to mean declaring the right to representation—a political act that would run counter to official discourse. Nativists, especially those in the countryside, interpreted events in a way that provided specificity to discourse as a suitable method for solving the contemporary dilemma of disorder and fragmentation. We have seen that nativism envisaged a new structure of relationships based on kinship, affection, friendship, and personalized associations, testifying to a communal consciousness centered in the village and symbolized by the shrine. These new associations were based upon human, not political, and "natural," not "historical," considerations. Under such authority, nativists sought to arrest historical time and return the ordinary folk to the status of people without history. The kind of institutions they hoped to reinstate and the relationships they wished to establish aimed at overcoming the differentiations and the succession of history that had been introduced in the form of political experiments. But to annul political history in this way was a political act, even though nativist discourse insisted on maintaining an explicitly apolitical posture.[1] By leaping over history, nativists believed it would be possible to direct the folk back to the proper route, which led to a "cold society," a collective time when the historical temperature was lower. Getting outside history, it was believed, was the necessary preparation for channeling relationships so that they would correspond to "natural" and "self-evident" principles binding the human commu-

273

nity, in the general effort to reproduce the social conditions of existence. This meant removing all factors that interfered with the continuity of the collectivity and the equilibrium of the *habitus*. As Claude
Lévi-Strauss has proposed, "The object of cold societies is to make it
the case that the order of temporal succession should have as little
influence as possible on their content."[2] At this juncture, nativism became a method for authorizing forms of action and a discourse for a
theory of politics.

But nativism, it is well to recall, had already conceived of politics
as a *matsurigoto* serving gods and people, not merely the ruling emperor and his imperial retainers; it had made possible the formulation
of a new political space founded on the "national soil" (*habitus*) for its
divinely created inhabitants. When nativists began to propose that the
creation deities produced the land for the sake of the ordinary people,
they fixed the coordinates for a new kind of map. Such a community
would realize true human nature as disclosed in the ancient Way and
thereby become the place where humans, endowed with the divine
disposition to work, would naturally reproduce the conditions of social
existence and repay the blessings of the gods. Community spoke of
people interacting with and assisting one another in a common purpose. Even the drudgery of daily life and the particularity of a common
world of things, in its most solitary moment, called attention to others.
Hirata himself had proposed to the ordinary folk that the example of
the creation of the cosmos served as a model of "mutual assistance of
divine deeds on earth" and described this natural reciprocity as a
"knowledge of origins" that the *aohitogusa* must constantly realize in
their daily affairs (*HAz* [old] 7:24 [*Koshiden*, book 5]).

Embedded in this projection of community and in the reason for
its appeal in the environment of the Tenpō years were old fears of division, private activity, and selfishness (*watakushigoto*), which had
dogged thoughtful men in the sixteenth century. This parallel between
the present and the past was not lost on nativists. Confucian writers of
the earlier period, living amid the civil anarchy that the Tokugawa
ultimately arrested, interpreted events as an expression of selfishness
and unbridled private interest. They sought to halt privatism by extin-
guishing passion, emotion, and feeling as determinants of human behavior and by elevating the pursuit of the public good (*kōgi*). Just as the
early-Tokugawa Confucianists presented their fears of difference and
division as a kind of unyielding nemesis, so nativists, writing two hundred years later under vastly altered historical conditions, confronted

the prospect of increasing and continuing peasant disturbances and encoded such conduct as signs of the persistence of private interest
and selfishness. The recurrence of rebellion—Miyauchi's "swarms of
pests"—offered an analogue to the difference and division earlier writers had noted as the cause of civil conflict. Rural notables perceived
the growing turbulence dominating rural life in the late-Tokugawa period as a threat to agricultural productivity. For this reason, many nativists concentrated on explaining the sources of wealth and the necessity of work. They pictured the manifestation of private behavior as an
offense against the gods and an unnatural state of affairs brought on by
unnatural desires. By "unnatural" they really meant unsocial, the spectacle of people acting for themselves rather than for others. This portrayal of privatism recalls sixteenth-century descriptions of difference
and division in contemporary life and shows why nativists linked publicly motivated conduct with sameness. The nativists' solution consisted in a decision to achieve "sameness" by advancing a program demanding communal action sanctioned by a conception of commonly
shared purpose. Mutual assistance and cooperation, they announced,
was the natural constitution of human beings and represented the only
basis for a social organization that could resolve the problems of an
unsettled society. Some form of mutual assistance, whether in work or
another kind of activity, satisfied the archetypal achievement of the
creation gods and foreclosed the risk of losing the blessings the deities
had conferred upon humans.

Peasant disturbances were becoming familiar and even common
in the countryside in the 1830s and 1840s, and their frequency reminded thoughtful men of the consequences for the social order. The
rising tide of turbulence prompted many *kokugakusha* to reassert the
claims of communitarian purpose. Other participants in the discourse,
who were involved in practical agricultural activities and aligned with
the upper reaches of peasant society, found it in their interest to induce
peasants to go back to work. But it would be wrong to attribute simple
self-interest to their activities. At the same time that they devised elaborate explanations to center work, they were also mindful that, if such
an effort were not made, the very conditions of social life as they knew
it and indeed the human order itself—including them as well as the
general peasantry—might disappear in a cataclysm of destruction. Nativism offered not simply a theory of representation—a new emplotment of the story line—but also an evaluation and critique of the contemporary arrangement of affairs. This evaluative and critical project

was always implied in its projection of wealth and work and in its valorization of the shrine and the village. It supported the conviction that
the well-being and order of things in Tokugawa society could no longer
rely on the direction of a managerial class and the apparatus of a feudal
institutional authority. Its new representations authenticated practice
and necessitated a different kind of structure, which enabled ordinary
people to return to performing their "natural" duties without interference. The new representations became the basis of a system of knowledge constituted of interest based on the necessity of reproducing the
creation; the new structure led to a theory of action, a redefinition of
authority along communitarian (village) lines, and a new conception
of leadership. Community became a system of mutual assistance leading to production and reproduction and a crucible in which relationships among humans might be transformed. In time, it became the
domain of cultural intentionality.

The question for nativists in the Tenpō years was how to conceptualize a space for action that would escape the debilitating divisiveness
of politics. Their answer was a communitarian society, pledged to reproducing its own conditions of existence without relying on outside
structures; the social unit they envisaged was more religious than political, relying on a "natural" sense of order derived from the necessity
of human reciprocity rather than an obedience determined by institutions. They believed they had discovered a principle capable of inducing people to act purposefully in the collective interest, and, in fact,
action came to mean performing productively for the collectivity. Yet
this vision of productive collective activity was the counterpoint to what
they saw as the collective but unproductive behavior enacted by large-
scale peasant movements in the countryside. It shared with collective
disturbances the belief that the peasantry must rely on its own resources
and not on the mediating structures of a failing authority system. Ironically, both the nativist communitarian vision and the practice of peasant rebellions in the late-Tokugawa period concluded that society's
business was not other people's business. Action could be measured
only in terms of its value to the goals of the community and the necessity of self-reproduction. Although Hirata had established a system of
evaluating performance in his formulations concerning the hidden
world and the judgmental role of Ōkuninushi no kami, others elevated
meaningful action serving the communal interest to a level of primary
importance. Nowhere was this inflection expressed in more extreme
terms than by Ikuta Yorozu (1810–38), whose texts came to constitute
a form of meaningful action and whose decision to rebel came to rep-

resent an action-text endowed with meaning. Even though Ikuta abandoned the production of texts to take up arms against the feudal system, his decision did not signify a break, since the propositional content of both text-as-event and event-as-text was provided by nativism.[3]

Ikuta Yorozu has always appeared to historians as an anomaly, an accident, or a paradox; sometimes, he has been represented as a combination of all three.[4] His rebellion in Echigo (1838) has often been compared to the Ōshio uprising in Osaka (1837), which apparently served as its model. Ikuta quite self-consciously summoned the example of Ōshio Heihachirō, appropriating Ōshio's slogans for his own banners and identifying with him deeply because both were members of the samurai class and both had been schooled in 'intuitionism' (ōyōmeigaku).[5] But, Ikuta's actions were neither anomalous nor paradoxical; that he was a high-ranking samurai striking against the feudal authority explains neither his decision nor his commitment to an action philosophy. For Ikuta, the decision to act was not separable from the act of writing texts on contemporary issues; his texts provided coherent meaning to and a disclosure of the action he embarked on in 1837–38, which claimed his life.

Ikuta came to nativism rather late in his short life. He was twenty-four years old when he entered Hirata's Ibukiya. Before this time, he had received a fairly diverse but conventional education for his status. According to the Ibukiya's registration record, Ikuta was "introduced" to the school by a friend who was a member of the upper peasantry (gōnō). This fact is important, because it suggests that in the early nineteenth century status lines had been replaced by other criteria, such as education, for the establishment of peer relationships. That a fairly high-ranking samurai would count a rich peasant as one of his closest friends suggests not willful eccentricity but the presence of new possibilities for alliances and coalitions in Tokugawa society. Hirata's school recruited all kinds of people; we know, too, from other evidence, that young samurai associated with a wide range of people in their educational travels around the country. Schools were usually the focus of such new ties and the forum for new horizontal relationships. Ikuta had already established such relationships before entering Hirata's school; his experience in the school merely reaffirmed this social style. The question Ikuta's experience poses is, Why did he choose *kokugaku?*

Ikuta's interest in nativism stemmed from its reconstruction of social theory and its penetrating assessment of contemporary life. Hirata, following Motoori, had directed his energies toward explaining the sources of contemporary discontent, asking why large numbers of people appeared to be unhappy and resorted to rebellion and what they must do to realize security, peace, and tranquility. Ikuta was attracted to these proffered solutions to contemporary unhappiness and to the new discipline that announced its determination to "learn about the *kami*." Once he became an adherent, he even devoted a text to its systematization and further dissemination: the *Daigaku kaitei gaihen* (1825) was written in conscious emulation of Hirata's *Tamadasuki* and proposed to explain to contemporaries the meaning of the ancient Way by ranging over a number of subjects from cosmogony to the importance of the tutelary shrines. One of its sections dealt with the question of "learning about the *kami*"; although it has been lost, reports of its contents suggest that Ikuta, like many nativists in the late-Tokugawa, sought to construct a basic discipline to represent the convergence of divine custom and human understanding.[6] "In truth," Ikuta wrote, "there is nothing that has explained the things of practical studies with the conscientiousness of the great man of our Ibukiya [Hirata]. It is an important discipline that has become unfashionable to acquire." His praise for nativism itself was even stronger. In response to criticism from fellow retainers of Tatebayashi *han*, he wrote what was to become his celebrated *Ryōyaki kuchinigashi* (1826), which he prefaced with the following poem: "Painful medicine, indeed, to awaken men who are drunk and sleeping from Chinese books." The title of the text had been suggested by Hirata in one of his lectures, when he informed his audience that "good medicine is like something painful to the mouth." He concluded that people had become ill from too much exposure to foreign ideas and too little knowledge of the "true Way." As a result, the time was ripe for "imparting the good medicine of the true Way" (*HAz* [old] 1:3 [*Ibuki oroshi*]). In Ikuta's text, he followed Hirata's advice to seize the moment and transmuted an attack on nativism into an offensive drive against the various forms of Confucianism by emphasizing the primacy of action—"strong and painful medicine"—in order to finally discount all competing claims.

In the *Ryōyaki kuchinigashi*, Ikuta proposed that, in the effort to shake up those caught in the drunken stupor caused by Chinese learning, not even the strongest medicine worked (*Ito nigaki, kusuri wa nomedo karabumi no yoi no neburi wa nao samezu ya mo; IYz*, 365). He had before him the example of Motoori, who had launched a critical campaign against Confucians and noted that they had become "drunk on the poisonous wine" that was the Chinese "heart." According to Ikuta, this statement proved that scholars had not yet awakened to the purity of the "imperial idea." Motoori had offered his *Kuzubana* (Arrowroot) as an antidote, which served metaphorically and literally as a medicine to cure men of the torpor brought on by "poisonous wine."[7] Inspired by this precedent, Ikuta envisaged his own purpose to jar his adversaries from "false consciousness" as preparation for establishing the "true discipline" and securing happiness and tranquility. In the *Ryōyaki kuchinigashi*, he explained that because he now was serving the Way of the imperial country, he had become an "imperial force." But "you [his critics] are men of the imperial country who serve the way of a barbarian nation and follow the management of traitors called sages [*seijin*]. [Their activity] is like drawing out a bow against the imperial forces" (*IYz*, 407). By insisting that he be called an "imperial force" (*kangun*), Ikuta implied that he was interested in dramatizing the problematic relationship between words and performance; indeed, the metaphor of administering strong and painful medicine itself revealed a performative dimension that writing could hardly satisfy. Thus, for Ikuta, the primacy of *kokugaku* as a true discipline was revealed in its capacity to enjoin people to perform in the interest of practicality. In an encomium to Hirata—"in our time, equal to Confucius"—he explained how his learning had brought "peace and tranquility" and, ultimately, "relief" to those who believed in it (ibid., 374).

This association between words and performance was further demonstrated in Ikuta's assault on Confucians, who were currently making the grandiose claim that their teachings guaranteed tranquility and order. Ikuta responded first by pointing to "rebellion and disorder during the period of the warring states," caused by "men of great evil" attempting to establish imperial dynasties. "Confucianists like you should know this well by now, and Chinese books are filled with such examples of ostentation." Because they were drunk on poisonous wine, he added, they charged that "we [Japanese] do not hear about the correct governance of the period of the Three Dynasties. But, the Three Dynasties, when compared to the natural [*mui*] polity of our great unity [*daidō*], cannot be described too strongly as a time of complete disorder" (ibid., 378–79).

Ikuta's argument rested on the belief that Confucian teachings deflected perception from its true object. Because Confucianists must shoulder the responsibility for ostentation and a "partiality for China," they were unwittingly forced to "enter into their ears such words" and, thus, "drunkenly confuse order for disorder" (ibid., 379). Yet, he continued, "since we are men of the imperial country, let us favor this place; should we not follow the true heart . . . ? There is a saying, 'If there is reality, then there is no need for metaphor [*hiyū*],' but when one does not talk about this reality, which can be investigated in [the Japanese] classics, there is pollution" (ibid.). The failure to know reality brought on drunkenness caused by imbibing the "wine of Chinese learning" and led to pollution. In this way, Ikuta believed he had found a sanction for shaking men awake from their stupor and producing texts identified with the necessity of acting.

Ikuta's intense interest in "awakening" people to the truth was no doubt prompted by a more basic concern for feeling and the self, which he shared with other nativists. In an early text written in Chinese, called "Theory of poems and songs (*Shikaron*)," he posed the following question: "How can we prevent abuses in poetry, if its content is unimportant and the words are bent?" His answer recommended returning to the genuine expression of subjective feeling and emotionality. "If a person inclines to this argument and is involved in literature and . . . does not affirm emotion [*shujō*], then, even though he might talk about poetry and songs, he has not grasped it nor gained the Way. The Way is only emotion" (ibid., 33). Later, in the *Daigaku kaitei gaihen* (marking his formal acceptance of *kokugaku*), Ikuta saw this subjectivity as the possession of all by virtue of their common birth from the creation deities (ibid., 147–48), for which poems and songs served as a constant reminder (ibid., 164–65). Feeling, subjective emotion, became the motive force for the "respect" and "reverence" expressed in activity. Ikuta diminished principle (*kotowari*) in comparison to the "blessings of the *kami*," transforming "blessings" into emotion and feeling. When activated, the pledge of such blessings was performance which guaranteed that "the people would experience long periods of peace and tranquility [*aohitogusa mo nakadono ni yo o heru koto yo*]" (ibid., 270). These blessings were constantly illustrated by the power of prayer to bring rainfall and radiance, "to destroy harmful insects and to raise grains that will not be ruined by excessive water. . . . Are not such blessings wondrous and majestic?" (ibid.).

In an exegetical text explaining the meaning of the Great Purification Rite (*miki ichiren*), Ikuta was convinced that "interpreting the words of the Great Purification Rite is, in truth, like carrying the name of the realm; like the breath of the wind deity, which emanates from the farthest mountainous reaches and sweeps away the clouds, as a

waterfall cascades down a slope, so these words illuminate the true
heart of the *kami* age correctly and translucently [*kiyoaki*]" (ibid., 440).
According to ancient custom, it was necessary, as it was in the present,
to make offerings to the good fortune of the creation deities (ibid., 286).
Specific tasks drew attention to the deity to whom the appeal should be
made. But all roads led back to the deity of agriculture, Toyouke no
kami, whose place of worship had always been located in the outer
shrine at Ise. This deity possessed many names, depending on locale
and region (ibid., 288). "This particular deity and all the regional *kami*
representing his transformations are important because the households
we live in and the food and clothing we need come from the august
spirit of this deity" (ibid., 289). Collectively, these agricultural deities
were responsible for long periods of tranquility and prosperity; to express thanks, prayers must be offered daily in the households. After all,
Ikuta advised, people could not construct houses without using grass
and wood; since grass and wood were gifts of good fortune from the
agricultural god, it was appropriate for prayers to be offered. The process was continuous: after "praying well to the deities of the household,
offerings next must be made to such *kami* as protector deities, creation
deities, clan deities [tutelary, *ujigami*] in the various villages and
towns. . . . Once this is accomplished, one must then serve and work
for these *kami* [*Yoku kono kami nado ni tsukaematsurite nochi ni wa,
sono hitobito no shinmi tatematsuramu kokorogokoro no mani mani,
ikanaru kami ni mo tsukōbekiwari*]" (ibid., 296). Celebrations of the
kami and offerings of continual thanks for their blessings (*sawai*) must
not be prompted by expectations of material wealth (*kono wa zai o
tsuyasu koto ni arazu*). And if offerings required a show of money, "it
would not be difficult for the rich man to carry it out," while the poor
would be forced to make sacrifices (ibid., 296–97). To offer prayer to
the *kami* was a wondrous thing. In Buddhism, by comparison, even
though a person was admonished to "abandon the body and exhaust
his wealth," there were many who did not do so freely. The returns
were measured in terms of how much one was actually willing to give
up. Despite the small number of people who offered even a little prayer
to the *kami*, the effort would constitute a moving example; "since such
people have been born in the august land of the gods, are they not the
saplings of the *kami*?" (ibid., 297).

Ikuta sought to make this relationship between deities and people
the principal prop of his political theory. But it was his preoccupation
with origins that cemented the relationship between deity, people, and

land that existed before the emperor. "Even today," he wrote in book 4 of the *Daigaku kaitei gaihen*, "although the august body of Ukemochi no kami [another name for the agricultural deity] has died, we are still subject to the august blessings and favor of this deity. Are not foodstuffs, clothing, and shelter revealed in the august spirit of this deity? Even though we are attached to the august blessings and favor of this spirit, do not men know this? How can the ordinary people of our times want more than food, clothing, and housing?" (ibid., 313). Here, especially, he summoned the Izumo version and its record of the "majestic," "glorious" deeds of Susanowo. Even though such deeds were "old facts [*furukoto*], it is important to pray to and beckon this deity and the creation gods to come out of concealment at this time. For if they are not summoned today as in the past, the times will be as an endless night [*kono yo ima mo tokoyo yukamashi*]" (ibid., 314). Ikuta wanted to show that the evil usually associated with Susanowo represented a misunderstanding, that even this deity could bestow peace and harmony (*nagomi*). Contemporary men did not know the reasons for respecting this *kami*. Although the present was filled with both good and evil things, the final decision required a return to the good by appealing to the intervention of Susanowo. In this way, Ikuta believed that even the most degenerate of times could recover goodness by returning to antiquity (*otoroeshi yo mo inishie ni, tachiekaerubeki yo koso matarure*; ibid.). The actual method for accomplishing this return was provided by the Great Purification Rite; its reenactment represented reverence for the august and wise age of the ancient emperors (*hijiri*). This purification (*misogi*) dissolved "evil deeds" and guaranteed the possibility of returning to "ancient deeds" (the good). Susanowo had been entrusted to accomplish much (giving birth to offspring, bringing metal and money from Korea, etc.) before he finally entered the land of *yomi*. Out of respect, his several offspring "hardened and gave shape to the land." They banished evil to the base country (*ne no kuni*) and, following the words of Susanowo, became the deities of the trunk land (*ki no kuni*) and returned to it.

> Under the august name of Yachioko no kami, assumed by Ōkuninushi no kami, this deity became the great master [*ushi*] of the land [*kunitsuchi*]. The wonder of Ōnamuji sukunami kami [Ōnamochi, Ōkuninushi] gave birth to the reeds and sedge and gave shape to the land; he was responsible for the *kami* who cultivated the fields and invented the tools and utensils for furrowing and plowing. How moving! The way of medi-

cine and the direction of charms and enchantments, the deeds of deities who heal animals and humans suffering from illnesses should, in reality, stand as signs [*shirushi*] for our times. (Ibid.)

The relationship between godly blessings down through the ages and the human necessity to repay them demanded performance in the present. The archetypal achievements (*miisao*) of antiquity required replication in human activity. An inquiry showed, Ikuta asserted, that the times were short on good deeds (*yogoto*, here Ikuta used the ideograph for "old" to indicate "good") but long on evil deeds. He asked his generation, "How can we, lacking governmental rank, hope to realize comparable achievements in our times?" (ibid., 316). Archaic achievements pointed to the necessity of reinstalling the good and returning to a more fundamental form of life, one representing the appropriate repayment of divine blessings. But, he continued, How can contemporary man continue the great achievements found in the ancient histories? A wise selection from the works of the native tradition (*ware kuniburi no fumi*—next to *fumi*, *fudoki* [gazetteers] was written in *furigana*) clearly showed the ordinary men of later ages how to secure these blessings. But, he advised, people should endeavor mightily, not simply think about performing such tasks in their hearts (ibid.). In each age, there were many hindrances to the accomplishment of the good, but if people expected to realize it, they must be prepared to die (ibid., 317). "Our spirits will leap to the imperial court. . . . By still inquiring about such teachings [*kokugaku*], our spirit will offer, in our times, good to men who are good and punish sternly men who are evil" (ibid.). Earlier in the *Daigaku kaitei gaihen*, in a discussion relating to the origins of the cosmos, Ikuta had argued that the land had been formed for men to become deities in the realm, "enshrining quakingly and movingly" the intention of the spirit that performed loyal and sincere deeds for the gods, the emperor and the country (*tenka ni kami naru hito ni narite kami ni sumera ni kuni ni chūsei naru isao o nasamu to tama no mihashira*; ibid., 174). His conception of support (*mihashira*) employed ideographs that conveyed the meaning of "spiritual intention," which transformed men into gods by motivating them and equipping them with the proper intentionality—the will—to perform outstanding achievements.

Ikuta believed that this spirit or will informed all humans. It resided in the heart. Although Hirata had argued that such a spirit corresponded to wind and fire, and the body to earth and water, Ikuta apprehended the substance of spirit slightly differently, to mean something more than spiritual life after bodily death. It was something that flowed, he explained, between the heart (*kokoro*) and the top of the head (*itadaki*). "In the body of men, it corresponds to the hidden governance. Even though the human body relates to the visible world . . . there is an invisible governance within it; just as things and events cannot be separated, so there can be no parting of the visible and invisible realms" (ibid., 321). Even though this allusion to visible and invisible worlds struck familiar chords, Ikuta's adaptation of it suggested that the motivating impulse—will or intention—sprang from an invisible governance within the body. Spirit was, therefore, responsible for the capacity to memorize and to conceptualize; thinking was transmitted through the activity of hands and feet, and the activation of things (*hatarakubutsu*) merely manifested the spirit's government (*tsukasa-doru*) of movement (*hataraki*, written for *undō* to denote movement, although it also means work) and mental reflection (ibid., 323). There was another spirit that left the body to soar (*tobikakaru*); because it ultimately inhabited the invisible world (*mukai*), it differed from the spirit that moved. They mirrored the relationship between the two worlds: the process by which the spirit acted to allow men to conceptualize and to perform was structurally similar to the idea of an invisible governance directing men's activities in the visible world (ibid., 324–25). This relationship, which Ikuta detailed, merely affirmed the belief that things and deeds could not be separated because of the constant interaction between the invisible and visible realms.

Contemporaries had failed to grasp this truth, even though the ancient texts offered proof of the interaction between the two realms for the present. Ordinarily, people could not see the hidden realm, because they were imprisoned in bodies that consisted of materiality (water and soil). Yet in the words of the creation deities, men would know that the visible world was entrusted to the emperor, and the world of hidden affairs to the governance of Ōkuninushi no kami (ibid., 326). Ikuta brought to mind his promise to awaken men from their drunken stupor by noting that contemporaries were prevented from seeing the truth because their reliance on Chinese explanations had blinded them to the two realms (literally, because the eyes of contemporary man have been obstructed—*utsushi yobito no me ni saegiredomo*). The conception of the will and purpose characterizing ordinary people not only provided a sanction for action that Hirata had never made explicit; it also became an important part of the subsequent disciplinization of *kokugaku.* We know that one of the missing sections of Ikuta's *Daigaku kaitei gaihen* dealt with "learning about the *kami,*" and it is conceivable that he went on to show how such concerns implied "learning about the ordinary people" (to use Ōkuni Takamasa's phrase). The elements of such a systematization of knowledge were already present in Hirata's transformation of Motoori's conception of human nature and in Ikuta's interpretation of divine and human achievement and the agency of spirit.

For Ikuta Yorozu, the complex set of relationships between divine and human agencies and the reconceptualization of spirit as motive force and intentionality sanctioned action and performance. This conception undoubtedly inspired his decision to rebel in 1838, against odds that could only lead to defeat and suicide. Despite Ikuta's obvious and self-conscious identification with Ōshio Heihachirō, it would be difficult to argue that the wellsprings for his rebellion resided in Ōyōmei intuitionism. Owing to Ikuta's deep immersion in nativism, it seems more appropriate to propose that, for him, action was located in the delicate relationship between will and the necessity for achievement, as a counterpart to his conception of *miisao.* When people acted in such a manner, they would transform themselves into *kami* of the realm.

Before Ikuta decided on rebellion, he wrote a text about the conditions of peasant disturbances and the immediate circumstances leading to such desperate acts. In the *Iwa ni musu koke* (1828), he devised a plan for domainal reform that contained a reasoned account of why peasants rebelled. Although this text has often been cited as an example of Ikuta's activist nativism, it falls considerably short of explaining his motivation for sedition, since it deals only with the possible conditions attending it. For our discussion, it serves two functions. First, the purpose of this text for Ikuta was unquestionably defined in his earlier, more self-consciously nativist writings. Hence, we must apply his principal nativist ideas as a semantic device to decode the meaning of the *Iwa ni musu koke.* Seen in light of his conceptions of will, act, and achievement, the text discloses that, under special conditions, peasants—ordinary people—were justified in rebelling, in order to accomplish deeds essential to a world created by the blessings of the *kami.* To act in this way promised a return to these blessings and the recovery of a world that consisted of divine favor and the reciprocating achievements of humans. Under such circumstances, even a peasant rebellion could be seen as an effort to "restore" the goodness of antiquity. Second, Ikuta specified the context in which peasants were driven to act; the text represented a means to move outward toward another ring of mediations and the world of contemporary history as he understood it. Previously, interpreters have assumed that, because this text engaged the question of rebellion, it was reducible to the conditions Ikuta recorded and, thus, explainable by them. But the economic "facts" that formed Ikuta's context did not explain the action he sought to describe; they only provided the opportunity to offer an "interpretation."

The title of the text, *Iwa ni musu koke*, was drawn from a poem anthologized in the *Kokinshū* (tenth century); it refers to the moss that grows in the crevices of rocks. As a metaphor, it announced Ikuta's intended argument, since the moss relies on the rock and grows in its frugal and unkind environment. "The moss on the rock is thin," he explained, "and appears to have only one layer, with nothing below to support it; this book might also be thrown away as a mat of moss" (*Kus*, 10). Ikuta suggested that his book, like the moss, was really thicker than it seemed and that it stood in the same relationship to contemporary history as the moss did to the rock. But the imagery of the moss possessed another meaning: the layers of peasant discontent that appeared only as surface phenomena but were deeply rooted in long-standing grievances.

The model for this text, according to Ikuta, was Motoori's *Hihon tamakushige*, which recorded in detail late-eighteenth-century rural conditions in Kii Domain. According to Ikuta's reading of Motoori's text, the influx of wealth and the imbalances it caused in society resulted in ruinous relations between the high and the low and in the loss of fundamental purpose. Motoori observed from his own reading of earlier war tales that rulers in antiquity lived off nature without taxation. So spare and austere were they in their personal lives that they "washed their hair in rain water, combed it in the wind, made armor and helmets out of clothes, and lived on their saddle and stirrup [*ame ni kamiarai, kaze ni kushikezuri, katsuchū o ifuku to shi, kura abumi o kyosho*]." (*Kus*, 30–31). Ikuta was impressed that Motoori had engaged the problem of economic change and its social consequences; he approved of such aims, even as he questioned the appropriateness of the master's measures.

Ikuta was convinced that Hirata's teachings offered the best guide to resolving the contemporary malaise. Because Hirata had understood the truth that ancient principles inaugurated good government (*go matsurigoto*), he provided the only realistic assessment of contemporary life and its solution. "In truth," Ikuta wrote, "I have followed the study of antiquity and learned how to discriminate the true Way." Serious study affirmed his belief that men had somewhere abandoned both the utility and practicality so fundamental to a tranquil social order (ibid., 45). Confucian concepts such as the "extension of knowledge," the "investigation of things," and "mental discipline" (exhausting the mind) amounted to little more than "empty words and explanations" if unaccompanied by practice (ibid., 44). The proof for such harsh judgment was already piling up in the successive failures of the Tokugawa system to realize its obligation to maintain order and tranquility. As a result, a "reversal" in the order of things had occurred (*un'en naru koto*) and society now faced the prospect of disorder.

Ikuta saw the problem manifested in the incidence of poverty that was exacerbated by superfluous domainal offices drawing on meager resources and levying excessive taxes (ibid., 15–16). He called for a search for standards that had not yet been eroded by time (*bansei fukiyu no o sadame*). His solution to the proliferation of bureaucratic offices and the resulting unrelieved drain on resources was to return the bureaucrat-retainers to the land as cultivators, in order to increase agricultural productivity. Their return resembled, in the words of a Neo-Confucian parable, "rain falling on hardened soil, a rebellion terminating to give birth to order" (ibid., 16). The argument against superfluity rested upon Ikuta's sense of utility: just as his call for a return to the soil resonated with nativist associations concerning land, increased productivity, and the essentials of life conferred by the deities, so the decrease in officeholders satisfied an antistructural theory of politics. Removing unnecessary offices and their occupants and generally reducing the size of the domain's administrative apparatus would replenish choked resources. The plan, he believed, would satisfy two important conditions: it would lessen the number of nonfunctioning officeholders on the dole and put more people into the field for cultivation. "Essentially, we have all kinds of distress and suffering; because we have forgotten about the utility of things and flowed on the crest of elegant but useless items, hardships have accumulated" (ibid., 17). Although it took little talent to adorn life with elegant things, "we must all make our lives accord with the manner of peasants [*ōkata hyakushō dōyō no kurushikata ni ainari mōsubeki sōrō*]" (ibid.).

Ikuta worried that people were encountering inconveniences that affected their capacity to make a living. "They leave families that they have been used to and go to work that they are not accustomed to and eat food that is strange to them" (ibid., 18). Failing to practice strict economies, people became interested only in the elegant and lived so "carelessly" and dangerously that they invited poverty. All of this behavior reflected a political administration that combined laxity (*kan*) with valor (*mō*); although valor must be retained, the abuses of laxity must be eliminated, and sending samurai back to the land as cultivators seemed to offer the best solution.

Ikuta's program, which was to be applied to Tatebayashi *han*, called for a reduction of expenditures, the elimination of surplus offices and occupants, and the establishment of economies (ibid., 18–23). Economic reform by returning samurai to agricultural cultivation was its principal premise; its overall effect was to "thin out the upper ranks" and "thicken the lower." In addition to reducing officeholders, Ikuta recommended standardizing the stipendiary system among upper-echelon retainers at a considerably lower rate. He itemized the benefits his program would bring. (1) The savings would be converted into cash so as to benefit reserves in the domainal treasury; (2) the several offices would be rationalized and its occupants "now fewer in number, would spend more time in administrative and other kinds of work and, therefore, eliminate excessive expenditures"; (3) retainers would thereafter share the way of life of the peasants. Here, Ikuta sounded a familiar nativist call for a return to a more natural style of life, thus, avoiding the spectacle of difference and division among people (*onozukara junboku shitsuso no fuzoku to nari*; ibid., 19). (4) Litigation in village disputes would thereafter be simplified—this provision referred not only to a reorganization of the system of village conciliation once the samurai took up residence among the peasantry but also to the establishment of a clearer sense of justice in settling current disputes, which often exploded into larger disturbances. (5) Greater attention must be paid to military preparedness among the samurai settled in the countryside. Ikuta was confident that "when a law [returning samurai to the land] is carried through today, all in the domain will, unfailingly, receive the blessings of the lord. . . . After ten or fifteen years . . . all rebellions will have been crushed, and the domain rid of the pollution of its enemies" (ibid., 20–21). (6) In place of the mansions of the castle town and the domain's buildings in Edo, there would be planted useful trees, such as paulownia, chestnut, and persimmon. Moreover, the domain would be able to calculate the revenues of the land tax from new agricultural developments. (7) The desolation of agricultural villages would be arrested. Ikuta referred to the growing attraction of ele-

gance and luxury among the peasantry and the resulting migration of
poorer tenants from the land to towns and cities for a better life. His
analysis undoubtedly relied on Motoori's evaluation of rural conditions
in Kii, but it also dramatized explicitly how bad the present appeared
when compared to the past (ibid., 22). By emphasizing tighter economies and increased agricultural productivity, Ikuta was convinced that
the "poverty of the present will become an ancient tale." In times of
bad harvest or crop failure or when work was seriously disrupted, the
yearly tax obligations should be decreased. In proper "Confucian"
form, he was convinced that "good government always provides compassion and benevolence; it also offers relief and assistance in dire
times."

At the same time that Ikuta demonstrated the benefits of his
policy, he hoped to amplify certain conclusions consistent with his nativist strategy. In the context of the fifth point, for example, he expressed what can only be described as a theory of peasant rebellion.
During times of continuous crop failure and resultant famine, the peasantry would naturally form rebellious coalitions (*shizen to ikki totō
itashi*); "The lower classes display a somewhat contemptuous attitude
toward their superiors, because the domain has been too accustomed
to long periods of benevolent administration" (ibid., 20). It seems likely
that these observations stemmed from his prior conviction that the domainal administration had been too long removed from the countryside to recognize the needs of small cultivators. At the same time, Ikuta
recognized the difficulty involved in persuading people to return to the
"good." A policy aimed at returning to agricultural production would
not only satisfy the basic conditions for continuing the creation (reproducing the means of social life); it would also remove the distinctions
that divided people and hindered production. The domainal lord himself, Ikuta advised, was experiencing the kind of distress provoking the
peasantry and was no longer in a position to depend upon the privilege
of status or precedent. Circumstances now necessitated social relationships that had less to do with received power (*kunshindō*) than with
horizontality, authorized by common birth and relatedness as the principles holding people together. It is not surprising, therefore, that he
called attention to the "extreme estrangement between the lord and the
vassal. The conditions of the lower orders are never communicated to
the top, and talent and ability are never expressed" (ibid., 34). He
warned against the "importance of status" and recommended the
speedy implementation of principles of social solidarity by which

people might more "naturally" relate to one another. Waste was attributed to extravagance, and loss of domainal revenues to samurai who
qualified merely by virtue of ascribed status and whose only talent was
misconduct. "The warriors who are warriors [today] fall short of their
original character. In truth, they are like dependent female children,
and it is for this reason that men at the top see status as important,
while those below dread it" (ibid., 35, 37). Toward the end of the *Iwa
ni musu koke*, Ikuta introduced the question of meaning and how one
should understand the conditions he described and the reforms he proposed. In commenting on the personal importance of nativism, he asserted once again that, in "clarifying the true principles of the ancient
Way (*kokugaku*), there are no lords at the top nor people at the bottom"
(ibid., 38). Like many of his rural colleagues, he had used his different
social perspective to construct the conditions for an autonomous and
self-sufficient community, free from the fragmenting divisions of class
and status and capable of providing for itself.

Ikuta's text, like his later decision to rebel, attested to the circumstances of the 1820s and the 1830s and provided a glimpse of the
conditions of "world renewal." He now regarded political status and its
resulting economic failure as the principal causes of contemporary discontent and disorder. Like so many of his nativist contemporaries, he
urged the resolution of fragmentation and division in the form of a
secession justifying the reconstituted part—the reconstructed domainal
community—that would serve as an adequate substitute for the whole.
In his thought, the program of "returning samurai to the land as man-
agers/cultivators" [*dōchaku*], long a staple in the Confucian reform
diet, acquired nativist associations and disclosed a policy promising to
ruralize all classes. Ikuta turned increasingly toward the examples of
contemporaries like Miyahiro Sadao (1794–1858) (concurrently calling for an autonomous and self-sufficient village) and Ōkura Nagatsune
(1768–?) for their praiseworthy achievements in agricultural intelligence (ibid., 42).[8] In a system of valuation favoring agricultural production and the leveling of all classes, nothing mattered more than
practice and knowledge (*sono tochi nite tsukurikitaritaru mono no hoka
wa, tsukurikokoromi sōrōwazu; Kus*, 42).

If nativism appeared in the *Iwa ni musu koke* as a method to be
applied to rural problems, it was because Ikuta believed *kokugaku* offered the means to analyze society in terms of an essentialist conception
of origins, capable of providing a solution to contemporary social problems. Although his perception of contemporary history was undoubt-

edly shared by a wide range of people during the Tenpō years, his analysis led not simply to the stale and familiar call for moral economy but to the searching conclusion that social fragmentation inevitably accompanied the "excessive importance of status." Status differentiations, he believed, generated differences leading to the devastating fragmentation of society as a unit. Only nativism could have inspired such a conclusion, since, as a discourse, it was already pledged to explain and overcome the problem of proliferating differences. Ikuta consistently viewed contemporary history from this perspective; the sanctions resulting from his recognitions inspired a course of action promising to dissolve the inequalities caused by the status system. Sometime in 1837, Ikuta, moved by the example of Ōshio to relieve peasants in Osaka, decided on the course of rebellion. Riots over famine and the rising price of rice had already penetrated Kashiwazaki in Echigo, where he had opened a school devoted to disseminating *kokugaku*. At the time of Ōshio's uprising, Ikuta wrote a letter to a friend in Oda (dated the fourteenth day of the fourth month in the seventh year of the Tenpō era) in which he confessed his admiration for Ōshio, gave his personal thanks for the circulation of detailed notices concerning the uprising, and expressed the general belief that the incident represented a "creative moment." He gathered intelligence on the uprising, concluded that the rich merchants and peasants of Kashiwazaki had neglected poor relief, and decided to follow the route to action paved by Ōshio. A few months later, he and a small group of companions hoisted their banners bearing slogans such as "Serve the Heavenly Mandate, Punish the Traitors of the Realm" and "Gather Loyal Retainers, Relieve and Assist the People," recruited from Ōshio's own arsenal of sayings, and attacked the garrison at Kashiwazaki. The rebellion was quickly put down, and Ikuta committed suicide. Yet the uprising continued to agitate thoughtful men throughout the late-Tokugawa period. Hirata, on hearing of the sedition of one of his students, quickly dissociated himself from Ikuta and discounted his scholarly accomplishments, although other accounts report that he was deeply moved. Other nativists, who "rejoiced" in tranquil times during the Tenpō years, regarded Ikuta's political radicalism as a dramatic and unique reminder of how prolonged peace had lulled them into believing problems no longer existed. Despite his description of himself as a "great heretic" (*dai itan*), Ikuta's achievement continued to live within the nativist camp. His sense of a great deed, illustrated by his own example, and his proposal for a self-reliant program that could function as a measure of such a deed, announced *kokugaku*'s encounter with late-Tokugawa history.

Entrustment and Enabling

The importance of Ikuta's radical heresy, notwithstanding Hirata's own ambivalence, is that it brought the contemporary world more directly within the apprehension of nativist discourse. It also brought nativism increasingly into the world of contemporary social life. Seeing nativism as a method for specifying the nature of a problem and its resolution, Ikuta used it to call for action, in order to accomplish a great deed comparable to the "august achievement" (*miisao*). Under the familiar format of *dōchaku*, his writings aimed to authorize the transformation of the domain into an autonomous, self-sufficient, and self-producing unit. Echoes of Ikuta's solution could be detected in the contemporary efforts of Mito writers and activists. By returning people to a fundamental agricultural life and making them all peasants ("treasures of the land"), Ikuta believed he had found a way out of the progressive economic failure he and others had come to recognize. He imagined contemporary history to be a manifestation of the divisions and differences created by artificial status distinctions and their endless proliferation. Such distinctions not only produced vast inequalities, they also undermined productivity. Hence, the importance of a "solution" authenticating action and the promise of a "return to the good" that was antiquity. Despite Ikuta's failure as a rebel, his achievement was considerable: he defined the contemporary problematic by showing the manifest forms of difference and division, and he devised a solution that sanctioned secession from the Tokugawa control system in order to establish a self-contained and self-sufficient community, harmonious and whole, as a defense against the corrosions of contemporary history. And, along the way, he successfully demonstrated the close relationship between text and social text, intellectual production and performance.

The problems of village deterioration and chronic poverty among the peasantry were real enough, and they inspired efforts to find authoritative solutions. Ikuta Yorozu stated this theme best in the *Iwa ni musu no koke*: "Since antiquity, the peasantry have labored excessively with mind and body. Although they have suffered great hardships from yearly taxes, they have not been permitted to forget their obligations from morning to night. Compassion might be a token of gratitude [to them]. We must be prepared to decrease the yearly taxes and to relieve their hardship even a little. The daimyo and lower officials should be aware that this should be their primary intention" (ibid., 41). Claiming that the yearly land tax the peasantry shouldered was disproportionate to what it received in return, Ikuta concluded that the real cause of the decline of the living standard among the peasantry was the severity of the official collection of revenues: "Although the peasants, from begin-ning to end, are the august treasure of the imperial court [here he used the ideographs for peasants, *hyakushō*, but wrote *ōmitakara* in *furi-gana*] and entrusted to the daimyo of the realm, they are, in truth, an important trust" (ibid.). Ikuta seemed bent on suggesting that the peas-antry in his day embodied a sacred trust too important to leave to the daimyo and their subordinates. He outlined a strategy—a "good method," as he described it—to specify this conception of trust and the way to meet its "divine" requirements. He called for a plan that would carefully manage domainal resources to divert peasant anger and pre-vent periodic revolts and advocated the establishment of a system of storehouses that would make food available for relief to the peasantry during times of crop failure and pestilence: "There will be small por-tions of rice yearly for people in the high, middle, and low orders. In later years, if the amount of rice yield increases, then it can be used for military purposes." The abundance of rice depended on careful plan-ning and informed management, which meant gathering the necessary intelligence developed by rural "sages" for increasing agricultural pro-duction (ibid., 42).

Ikuta's program emphasized the principles authorizing secession rather than concrete measures leading to its realization. Nativists had little trouble finding the scriptural authority for their conception of trust, even though the ancients had not envisaged it as a political idea that would lead to the formation of specific policies. In no time at all, nativists converted the archaic ideal into a powerful instrument, by reinterpreting a variety of textual references to the divine act of handing over the land to the imperial descendants. Ancient texts usually em-ployed terms such as *koto yosashi* or *miyosashi* to denote "trust." For nativist scholars, these words were reducible to two meanings: a literal reference to an actual event in which the gods gave something to other gods or to the imperial descendants; and a figurative act designating the land as the object of the bestowal. In either case, divine trust involved associations of enablement. In the *Kojiki*, *koto yosashi* was used to de-scribe the divine act of conferring the heavenly spear on those ordained

to "form" and "solidify" the realm out of the briny ooze, and to designate the ordinance that entrusted Amaterasu to rule the "high island
plain," after giving the "rich reedy plain and wet rice land" to her
descendants.

According to Motoori, owing to the ministration of Amaterasu
ōmikami and the transfer of her authority to the imperial court, the
realm of Japan was relegated to the administrative policy of the descendants of Tokugawa Ieyasu, who, in turn, transmitted it through the
daimyo to the masses (*shomin*). As a result of this chain of descending
authority, the masses, Motoori wrote, must always consider the ordinances and commandments of the shogun important, because they
represented the divinely ordained decrees of the Sun Goddess. Ultimately, Motoori molded this argument to secure political submission
from the general populace and obedience to contemporary feudal
lords.

By contrast, the really significant theoretical reformulation of the
idea of trust was made by Hirata Atsutane in a number of texts. In *Zoku
shintō taii*, he sought to inform his audience of the meaning of "true
Shinto" by presenting its main features (*taii*) and exposing its vulgar
variants. He offered the following explanation of the all-encompassing
importance of trust and its implications for political enabling:

> True Shinto is like the outline of the ancient Way; it deigns [to explain]
> the creation of the heavens and earth; beginning with the heavenly dei-
> ties Takami musubi no kami and Kami musubi no kami, they were suc-
> ceeded by Izanagi and Izanami, who began the basis of all things that
> exist today. Moreover, these *kami* have given birth to the deities that
> have ruled over the various divisions of things. This virtuous achieve-
> ment was transmitted to the Sun Goddess. When the Emperor Ninigi
> no mikoto was commanded to descend from heaven [to earth], the dei-
> ties of the heavenly ancestral creators ordained Amaterasu ōmikami's
> august imperial descendants to govern all that is under heaven, and to
> transmit this in the form of a *mimatsurigoto*. Under this bestowed trust
> [*miyosashi*], the reigns of the emperors [*miyo miyo no sumeragi*] have
> not acceded to any personal impertinence [*onore mikoto no misakashira
> o mikuwaeasobasazu*]. (*HAz* [rev] 8:113–14)

Here, then, was the "way to govern the times together with the realm"
and the real meaning of Shinto. Proof of this contention, Hirata commented, could be found in the *Nihonshoki* account of the fourth
month in the third year of the reign of Emperor Kōtoku (r. 645–54).

During this time there was an ordinance for the great chieftains (*Omi Muraji*) and the peasantry under heaven to rectify their lineages. It proclaimed: "To follow the Way of the gods, our descendants [literally, my children] have been entrusted to govern the land. It was imparted from the beginning of the realm that it [Japan] is a country ruled by emperors." In one of the notes to this text, Hirata observed that the word *kannagara*, "following the Way of the gods," was ultimately expressed as Shinto. Specifically, the entry in the *Nihonshoki* referred to the reform of titles used during the Taika period. In the past, there had been charges of numerous cases in which *muraji* had arrogated imperial titles and deprived emperors of their office. Because emperors had been entrusted (*koto yosashi*) to rule the land in accordance with the plan of the deities, there could be no other arrangement: "It is something requiring thanks" (ibid. 8:114; also *Kus*, 598). This arrangement disclosed to him the true intention of the ancient Way and the locus of Shinto itself. The two phrases, "following the Way of the gods" and "possessing Shinto in oneself", meant that one obeyed "the august laws that have been designated as ordinances, like the entrustment of the august ancestral *kami* to the emperor" (ibid.).

Hirata turned to this conception again in the *Koshiden*, when explicating a passage from the *Kojiki* (*HAz* [old] 7:18). The particular entry described the act of the "heavenly deities in giving to Izanagi and Izanami the jeweled spear with the trust to stir up the briny primal ooze, in order to make, harden, and shape the realm" (ibid. 7:12). This identification of giving the spear with the charge to make the land constituted the most important example of trust summoned in late-Tokugawa nativist discourse. In the writings of Ōkuni Takamasa, Suzuki Shigetane, and his pupil Katsura Takashige, it not only became the basis for a theory of political trust, obliging a leadership to meet its responsibilities for assisting the people; it also was used to elevate the importance of work among the populace. Hirata himself, in the *Koshiden*, shifted the object of trust to Susanowo and his descendant Ōkuninushi no kami. "Returning the entrustment of Susanowo to the visible realm, these august achievements were transmitted," Hirata declared, and "sternly Ōkuninushi continued the august deeds of the ancestral deities, according to the august trust of the imperial ancestral *kami*" (ibid. 9:24). Creating the realm called attention to the intervention of Ōkuninushi no kami, whose accomplishments necessitated expanding the idea of trust to include the continuation of the creation. In the end, the two sides of meaning—literal and figurative—became complementarities in the construction of a broader political theory.

In another consideration, Hirata defined the use of *koto yosashi* in the context of political trust and enabling. The term could be written either as "word" (*koto*) or as "event" (*koto*); the word *yosasu* was homonymous with combinations associated with "imparting assistance to the times." The sense of imparting assistance, he reasoned, could also be written with the ideograph for "trust" (*makasu*) and meant that "something is entrusted to a person [*koto o sono hito ni yosemakasete*]" (ibid. 7:18). Moreover, the association carried with it a sense of performance (*torikonō*). In an example from the early-Heian period, Hirata showed how entrustment and its enactment related to the administration of the realm (*sono kuni no matsurigoto o sono hito ni yosamakasu kokoro nari*).

The sense of caring for and providing assistance to people (*buiku*) and the appropriate administration for meeting such needs (*minsei*) marked the transformation of the theory of entrustment into a sanction for enabling in rural Japan. This is what the conception of trust came to mean for rural nativists searching for a validation of their programs of secession, autonomy, and self-sufficiency, especially for thoughtful and high-ranking peasants like Miyahiro Sadao and Hirayama Chūemon and for rural Shintoists like Miyauchi Yoshinaga and Mutobe Yoshika. This transformation made *kokugaku* appear as an authoritative method for solving local problems. The method became indistinguishable from the theory of caring and assistance, which village leaders saw as an expression of the trust embodied in an administration willing to carry out its sacred duty to the people. People like Miyahiro and Miyauchi began to plan ways to bring permanent relief to the rural poor and unemployed. Although the major focus of their thinking tried to give work a new dignity, a natural result of their efforts was a political justification for the establishment of a relief program and its administration. The purpose of such a program was to anchor administrative responsibility in a leadership that would accept the "divine" charge to rehabilitate the village-as-a-whole through the exercise of autonomous action. Miyahiro Sadao in his *Kokueki honron* proposed that the wealth of any region would depend on instructing people in the Way; he thereby shared a belief with rural thinkers like Ninomiya Sontoku and Ōhara Yūgaku that people had to be initiated into a spirit of work by showing them how it related to a world larger than mere day-to-day subsistence and the paying of taxes. For Miyahiro, this belief meant teaching people about the necessity of producing children in greater numbers, so as to increase the labor force and ease the financial burden on the present population. "Because there are so few people," he asserted, "it is difficult to generate wealth and open up new lands for cultivation. Since the august intention of the bright deities of heaven and earth has been to produce all things, it should be our aim to confer as many children as possible among the masses under heaven" (*Kus*, 293).[9] Generating wealth by a systematic increase in the working population appeared as the sure answer to the economic problems facing rural life.

As a village official, Miyahiro Sadao stood in a precarious position between rulership and ruled. He was painfully aware of the increasing conflict provoked among the lower peasantry by demands for the payment of yearly taxes. Yet, he noted, "even though squeezing the lower classes by the upper is rare, the poor take to deceiving the wealthy. They stand up to public ordinances and aim at moving at another pace. Their chief purpose has been to rob from others [the lords]" (*Kus*, 292).

Miyahiro's central concern was to find ways to cement the relationship between service and work. Like others, he accepted explanations attesting to the importance of the creation deities in agricultural life, yet, more than most, his interests aimed at promoting a practical agricultural discipline and finding the conditions appropriate for carrying it out. Like Suzuki Masayuki, who also came from the region of Shimōsa, Miyahiro clearly represented an instance of how a tradition of agricultural thinking and practice combined in the 1830s and 1840s with the ideologemes of nativism to transform the discourse into a rural message. This merging of discourses, noted in Satō Shin'en as well, permitted Miyahiro to refigure work in the modality of divine service and to invest the village notables with sacred trust in order to bring about regional wealth (*kokueki*). Miyahiro stressed the primacy of the tutelary deities from a perspective different from that of either Mutobe or Miyauchi, perhaps because he was not a priest. Describing himself as a "potato-digging village official" (*imohori nanushi*), which dramatized both his attachment to practical agricultural work and his official status, he was no less insistent on the intimate relationship between certain deities and the world of daily life. But the texture of this relationship was more immediately material, more accessible to rural life. In the *Minke yōjutsu*, he identified the male deity in the figure of a phallus carved from natural stone as a Shinto tablet (*mitamashiro*) cor-

responding to the *musubi no kami* themselves (*Kcks* 5:278). He tried
to show that its existence gave specificity and self-presence to the deities
in the familiar world near at hand. The *mitamashiro* constantly reminded the folk that the creation deities caused birth and growth,
much as the Buddhist mortuary tablets (*ihai*) summoned obligations of
respect to the dead ancestors among the living (*ko no umareru koto wa
makoto ni musubi no ōkami migokoro ni shite sunawachi kamiakitsu
no miukemono nareba*; ibid. 5:271). In his own region, he added, there
was an old family whose *ujigami* happened to be a stone deity shaped
naturally like a male organ. When women without children worshiped
at the shrine of this deity, legend reported, they would give birth to
children. "Since this [shrine] became the august tablet of the creation
deities, childless women were obliged to make offerings to it." There
were examples of families in other places whose patron deities had assumed the form of a phallus-shaped stone, and other representations
served as tablets of the creation deities which symbolized their productive powers and were said to give the gift of descendants (*kodane*; ibid.
5:278). The creation of all things from the initial activity of the two
deities functioned as the Japanese equivalent of the yin-yang principle
(a powerful conception in Tokugawa rural belief-systems), the male/
female opposition, now in material form, constantly interacting to
make possible life itself and the growth of all things. Miyahiro specified
this principle of procreation in his discussions of the importance of
pollination and crossbreeding and cited as an example the operation of
grafting male-to-female bamboo shoots (ibid. 5:294).[10] Sexual intercourse, like the primal act it signified, did not exist to serve anything
so mundane as pleasure, leisure, or entertainment; it represented the
natural activity that unified all life. "From the beginnings of the two
support *ōmikami*, Izanagi no mikoto and Izanami no mikoto, down to
the birds and beasts who receive no instruction, the intercourse of male
and female is a way, like nature, that has been transmitted to us. Since
the procreation of descendants is a great enterprise, it must be revered"
(*Kcks* 5:267). Time and again, Miyahiro, like so many nativists, returned to the archetypal account in the narratives of the origins and
creation of the islands and the resulting imagery of the drippings of life-
giving salt water, and its vivid evocations of semen from the jeweled
sphere (phallus), which "hardened" into the islands in an act of
procreation.

The act of creation and its consequence for all life was catalyzed
by the regularity of agricultural work and the rhythm of the seasons,

the cycle of growth and harvest, procreation and birth. "In our country," he wrote, "since it has been governed peacefully and tranquilly first by the *matsurigoto* of the deities of heaven and earth, we are pleased to say that *kami* affairs take precedence, after which come all other things. Therefore, the first regulation is the obligation to attend the shrines, and this is seen as a chiefly religious ceremony [*saishi*]. A religious ceremony of the *kami* is carried on in the households assigned to the various status rankings [*shokubun*] among high and low" (ibid. 5:263). Miyahiro proposed that, just as *bushi* worshiped the war *kami* (*gunkami*) and whores their respective patron spirits (*rei*), peasants made offerings to the great "Yearly Deities," who guaranteed life. Regardless of one's social standing, the act of worship represented the respect owed to the gods. Yet, writing as an agriculturalist, he saw work as another form of religious respect, just as he saw procreation as the principle underlying the fundamental unity of life. Sexual intercourse must now be read as a religious activity reenacting the archetypal event, and agricultural work must be seen as a comparable sacred moment, recalling the creation of the land itself. As all things constituted links in the cosmic chain, so the ties between the living and their ancestors, who made the living possible, formed a bridge to the *musubi no kami*. "To worship the spirits of ancestors and the generation of departed spirits and ancestors of the households, we must never neglect praying for the happiness of these spirits in the next world" (ibid. 5:265). When the spirits of the ancestors were forced to live in "distress," they would not be able to protect their descendants living in the visible world (*kenkai*). Visible and invisible were intimately related: "Humans receive the blessings of the *kami* of the invisible world, and thus, good fortune; the spirits [*kishin*] of the invisible world receive the ceremonies [*matsuri*] of humans in the visible world, and since it is their aim to gain good fortune in the next life, those who pray for the glory of the household must never neglect to worship the deities and ancestors" (ibid. 5:266).

Reverence for life and labor, then, signaled a religious act. Miyahiro was as offended by the practice of infanticide (*mabiki*) as he was opposed to the neglect of agricultural duties. Both constituted fundamental violations of the sacred principles of creation granted by the *musubi no kami*. Miyahiro was convinced that infanticide bordered on "disloyalty to the realm" and "unfiliality toward the deities" (ibid. 5:271), since "the prosperity and decline of the realm depends on whether *mabiki* is or is not conducted. The enlightened lords [*meikun*] governing the great realm must make the first principle of political affairs the prohibition of infanticide" (ibid. 5:272). As for the neglect of agricultural duties, he argued constantly and forcefully that, since the beginning of creation, agricultural work had functioned as the foundation of the realm. But this function did not depend solely on people's efforts. Agricultural work assumed primary, religious significance because of the role of seed selection and cultivation (ibid. 5:290). Seed selection called forth all kinds of associations of creativity and creation, and the sexual imagery of its life-giving and unifying principles embodied in microscosm the entirety of the cosmic moment (*Kus*, 295).

Just as Miyahiro opposed infanticide as a violation of the sacred gift of creation, he rejected the practice of sending young boys to the Buddhist priesthood (ibid.). He saw the penis (*dankon*) as an endowment from the deities and believed that males carried a sacred responsibility to use what was god-given. "Males are supplied with a penis" through which feeling (*nasake*) passed between men and women. As a result of the concourse of man and woman, he continued, "descendants are born and the species is created in every generation. This is the sign by which they honor and serve the ordinances of the *kami*" (ibid.). In this instance, Miyahiro changed the meaning of *nasake* from its earlier association with empathy and a compassion for others and for things in nature. He added that it was important to know that the penis was a utensil (*dōgu*) given to males to be used for procreation. He asked rhetorically: "Could the *musubi no kami* have made a useless organ [*fuyō no ibutsu*] in the body of man? . . . It was put there to be used . . . and, in truth, it is a tool by which to honor the generation [*seisei*] of descendants" (ibid.). Thus, to either assassinate (this is the word Miyahiro used to describe infanticide) or abort a fetus, or, indeed, to even prevent the implementation of the *kami*'s utensil, risked violating the expectations of the deities (ibid.).

In this regard, Miyahiro bolstered his interest in the concourse of yin and yang by appealing to near contemporaries and earlier Edo agriculturalists such as Miyazaki Antei. Many during his age, he remarked, portrayed the sexual genders of rice seedlings and concluded that, since "one yin and one yang compose the Way of heaven and earth and are called creation deities . . . they are the wondrous *kami* said to make all things" (*Kcks* 5:290). Miyazaki had confirmed, in the great text *Nōgyō zensho*, the essential truth of the theory of male-female coupling in seeds (*shunyūsetsu*) and the importance of wise and skillful selection. But all agricultural writings affirmed the principle that "selecting grain seeds for rice fields resembles the act of intercourse between men and women, when [it is put to the service of] procreating life. If one does not respect male-female intercourse as a principle, one will give birth to a bad offspring; and if one does not respect [the method of] sowing grains, the harvest will inevitably be poor" (ibid. 5:298–99). The way one received the blessings of the *kami* to realize a beautiful harvest and an abundant life ultimately relied on "sowing" the soil and praying to the deities of heaven and earth from the heart (ibid.).

The faith implications of Miyahiro's denunciations of the priesthood were clear; they suggest the powerful pull of Shinto as it was reformulated into a popular and agriculturally oriented religion in the late-Tokugawa period. Here, as in the texts of many Neo-Shinto contemporaries, life and labor (not to mention language itself) were sanctified as acts of worship and religious celebration. He shared with his *kokugaku* contemporaries a profound concern for the factors influencing increased productivity and wealth (*kokueki*). His late-Tenpō essay, *Kokueki honron*, showed how labor, if a sufficient work force existed, continually expressed the blessings of the *kami* and secured the prospect of expanded productivity (it is very important to recall that political economists of the times were equally concerned with the problem of increasing the capacity of "national wealth" but resorted to different tactics). The basis of regional wealth, he wrote, "is found in the way of human ethics. When people of the realm erect such a way, they will respond to the spirits [and to the *kami* who influence the present], and good fortune will be lowered toward them. . . . When the people [*aohitogusa*] know humility before the spirits, they will be generated daily; and when the race is generated [*fueru*], finances too will be created, and with the creation of finances, there will be regional wealth" (*Kus*, 292). Although the first necessity of "regional wealth" was to teach the Way (which he called *moppara zenkō zenshin seichoku*—"good intentions are straight and correct"), it was equally important to "increase the race" (*hitodane o fuyasu koto;* ibid., 293). With a small population, the question would always be how to increase productivity and accumulate wealth, which, he acknowledged, was as difficult as "opening up new lands for cultivation" when there were few workers available (ibid.).[11] Hence, his decision to concentrate on the strategic role played by the creation *kami* in augmenting the production of the race and the growth of grains. Between the sowing of species and the sowing of rice, Miyahiro recognized no barriers. "Because the deities of heaven and earth raise the ten thousand things from their august heart, it is their intention to grant much to the (Japanese) race among all the peoples under heaven" (ibid., 293).

Beyond expressing concern for wealth and increased productivity (in people and things—how could they be separated?), Miyahiro was deeply disturbed by the recently perceived moral failure. He was convinced that it was important to emphasize the requirements of established codes. Even though right behavior meant that people worked diligently in their own occupations, Miyahiro believed that when ethical requirements were not met, "misfortune will be lowered upon the people." He recast bad behavior—the requirements established by Confucian codes of loyalty and filiality for securing proper conduct—in the language of religious transgression and restricted it to violations of the division of labor, which meant acting against the endowment of one's basic character.

Losses (*sonmō*) to the realm derived directly from "human hearts" that behaved incorrectly; "bent" conduct polluted the heart and body and defiled the household and realm. Defilement came to mean irretrievable loss. Because such acts of unethical conduct violated the intention of the spirits, they risked eradicating their blessings. Hence, the frequent occurrence of bad years, bad harvests, fire, famine, and epidemics. Worse still, "the population will decrease and wealth dissipate. The losses that have occurred in the realm are due to the august reprimands of all these spirits and deities" (ibid., 292). Recognizing the unsettled times, he despairingly concluded that the folk had lost moral resolve: "When we investigate attentively the activities of men in recent times [*tsura tsura chikaki yo no hito shogyō o utagai miru ni*], [we discover that] even though cases of the rich robbing the poor are rare, the low cheat and deceive [*itsuwari*] the high; they have violated the august public laws [*kami to shite shimo o kasumuru wa mare naredomo, shimo to shite wa kami o itsuwari, ōyake no miokite ni tagai*], and they have aimed at taking what belongs to others" (ibid.).

Miyahiro's immediate purpose was not simply to excoriate the masses for their lack of character but to uncover the factors affecting what he called "losses to the realm and the household." Work itself and all of its associations, sexual and otherwise, formed a contiguous series—a chain of relationships made possible by divine appointment—and any slackening in the line constituted "deeds that do not correspond to the august heart of all these deities" (ibid., 293). He was, of course, particularly hard on those among the lower orders who "cheat and deceive their superiors," since they sought to take another's wealth by force. Miyahiro saw the disruptions caused by peasant riots and rebellions as examples of cheating, robbing, and deceiving, and he read them as grim inscriptions of the way divine displeasure wreaked misfortune and undermined wealth and productivity. As a sign, rebellion differed little from infanticide, abortion, packing off young boys to monasteries, or idleness and neglect, and, as a village official, he was acutely sensitive to activities that disturbed the regularity of the productive process and those factors that might cause a diminution in output. His inventory included any activity that imperiled divine favor by turning against the natural duty to work and increase productivity. Yet he knew—perhaps out of a self-serving impulse to sanction the position of his own class in a time of rural troubles—that the appearance of incidents in which "many among the low deceive the high" escalated jurisdictional quarrels and tenant disputes, which he and his colleagues were forced to resolve. Success or failure in arresting disorder depended on the availability of expert leadership, which he and his class were supposed to embody in rural Japan (a sentiment shared by Ninomiya Sontoku). "The fineness or coarseness of agricultural work," he wrote, probably speaking of himself, "rests on the availability of skill or incompetence, which accounts for the wealth or poverty of the realm. . . . It is a custom of our times that, while the presence of able men [*kuwashikimono*] who are skilled is a rare phenomenon, there are many negligent men [*sorō naru mono*] who are unskilled. There are virtually no agricultural masters" (ibid., 296).

To offset this deficiency, Miyahiro called for an official edict, enlisting "polished men" versed in agricultural knowledge and technology (*shūgei*) to teach and guide, as a religious duty, the unskilled in the fundamentals of "regional wealth." Miyahiro bolstered the idea of entrustment and relief by appealing to the importance of self-sufficiency, because he felt that the relationship between village officials and peasants constituted a fundamental compact. Although he advised the peasantry to understand and preserve the "commands (*gechi*) of the village leader (*myōshu*), which are like the public laws," he also insisted that such a trust be invested in local leaders (*Kcks* 5:316; see also *Kus*, 308). Accepting an argument that placed leadership in a line of entrustment descending from the emperor to shogun and daimyo (*ryōshu*), he was confident that each presided over his own jurisdictional space without fear of conflict (*Kcks* 5:316).

In this scheme, the village chief naturally assumed responsibility for the space within the larger area of the domain, "an office that must make its chief duty the administration and charge of the peasantry under its jurisdiction." Miyahiro recognized the uncertainty of contemporary domainal leadership, which was remote from and often uninformed in local rural conditions, especially in years of bad harvests or crop failures. For this reason, the responsibility for local administration was even greater than the authorities in the castle town imagined. Understandably, local notables extended relief to peasants when it was difficult for them to meet their feudal dues and when the regional authorities remained ignorant of the real conditions. Because local leaders occupied positions that permitted them to know rural conditions, their trust and responsibility ran deep. Village leaders must attend to all the families, to natural disasters and the general well-being of the village, since "uneconomical policies result in the shame of the village, and the shame of the village becomes the shame of the lord" (ibid. 5:317). Demonstrable incompetence among local leaders represented not only a form of disloyalty to the feudal authorities but also an act of disbelief and impiety toward the deities, resulting in pollution against the gods and the village by overstepping the established "boundaries" of appropriate conduct. What Miyahiro feared most was the ever-present threat of conflict and division within the village. When village leaders truly understood their responsibility, they would be informed of all the "public events" that transpired between their offices and the general peasantry (ibid. 5:319). If conflict broke out among the villagers, village leaders must approach it "without a private heart," in order to adjudicate it fairly. The single most important obligation of the village official must always be to promote the general interest of harmony within the village and to try to avoid "improprieties" and "wicked ways" toward other villagers and villages as well. Village shame caused disharmony and conflict. The trust of leadership was to avoid disorder, to "guide ignorant peasants, reconcile affairs within the village so as to avoid public litigation [kōji soshō] caused by making public office into a private desire, and exhaust all personal energy in governing the village" (ibid.). Such actions characterized "a true village chief," even though many still ignored their trust and plunged shamelessly into the pursuit of luxury and "private desires" to the general neglect of their duties.

Miyahiro's considerations of trust made it appear as if the village was already set apart from other administrative structures and in need of reorganization. He explained the necessity of self-sufficiency and economic determination in this "new" context. If local leaders successfully administered their villages during times of crop failure or bad harvest, he was confident that there would be no need to rely on authorities outside the immediate area of jurisdiction and agricultural activity. Well aware of the putative moral obligation of the lord to extend relief to hard-pressed peasants during bad years, he was equally convinced that, by his time, "benevolent polity" (*jinsei*) had become a remote and inaccessible ideal (ibid. 5:317). If there was "a foolish ruler (*ankun*) who has misgoverned (*fusei*) . . . he surely will not attend to providing relief to the peasantry." In such circumstances, the responsibility for care and assistance passed from the territorial lord to the village leader, for "the village chief who has replaced domainal officials (*jitō*) in giving relief to the poor is the glorious achievement (*ōtegara*) of local leadership" (ibid.). Miyahiro advised that, because of the poor performance of domainal administration, accepting responsibility for trust involved an even greater commitment from village leaders, who "replace *daikan*." "During times of bad harvest," he wrote, a person

> cannot rely on the august assistance of the regional lords and officials. He helps himself with his own savings and effort. He must understand that he should not bother or depend upon the leadership in such times [*tokaku agaru no yakkai ni narazaru kokoroetarubeshi*]. However, if one bestows august relief on the lower orders through the agency of a benevolent administration from the domainal leadership, they should accept it thankfully. Refusal to accept is an expression of disloyalty toward the lord. This [assistance] is based upon *jinsei*. (Ibid. 5:304)

Since there was little reason to expect any "benevolence," he concentrated on explaining the necessity of village self-reliance. Contemporary experience had already discredited the claims of a "benevolent polity." Villagers were expected to help themselves by mutual effort, economy, and thrift (*ken'yaku*). Moreover, encouraging village thrift and trying to make the prospect of self-help appear attractive enhanced the political role played by people like Miyahiro in the syntagm of trust and authority. Yet even before turning to the singularity of the village unit, Miyahiro had already drawn attention to the relationship between "enriching the region" (*kuni o tomashi*) and "promoting the household" (*ie o okusu*) in *Nōgyō yōshū*, which he wrote in 1826.

Ken'yaku, as already suggested, no longer meant just a regimen

of belt tightening. Ninomiya Sontoku had previously argued that it
exceeded mere thrift, because its content concerned specific forms of
utility. Although "revering *ken'yaku* . . . means despising large mansions and detesting [elegant] clothing, it also demands using capital to
bolster the supply of foodstuffs and realizing wealth within the realm
for people's relief." Miyahiro, like Sontoku earlier, defined the aim of
ken'yaku as the collective effort to accumulate capital for providing
assistance to cultivators in needy times (ibid. 5:305–6).[12] His notion of
relief referred to the rehabilitation of the village and entailed inducing
peasants to accumulate wealth for themselves rather than saving to
stave off waste. In Sontoku's earlier estimate, a view shared by Miyahiro
(he devoted a whole chapter of *Minke yōjutsu* to *ken'yaku*), the major
task that confronted a local leadership was to find ways to accumulate
capital for the village. Miyahiro agreed with both Ninomiya and Ōhara
that *ken'yaku* inspired men to return their lives to the barest essentials,
the "treasures of the *kami*," as it was frequently expressed. It also encouraged "abolishing all planning for luxury and [excessive] consumption; *ken'yaku* permits [people] to calculate [*hakaru*] how to increase
the treasury of the region" (*Kcks* 5:305).[13] Village leaders stood as me-
diators of the trust to amass wealth; their authority derived from divine
entrustment (*miyosashi*) and the subsequent ordinances issued by the
emperor through the shogun and regional lords, reaching down to the
village level. Despite his own affiliation with the upper peasantry, Miyahiro insisted on the responsibility of the rural rich to maintain the
"sanctity" of the communal order. He tried to enlist people for work in
a larger purpose, defining for himself the meaning of "public," and he
advised the rich against separating their interests from the collective
goals of the peasantry. He suggested that hegemonic claims required a
measure of sacrifice from the ruler, if the consent of the ruled was to
be secured without using force and coercion. In order not to exacerbate
existing class relations or contribute to the conflict inherent in hard
times, the "share of the wealthy families is to hoard much grain to assist
people in years of famine. It is their first obligation to bestow assistance
on those who have been inconvenienced" (ibid. 5:306). Miyahiro saw
the wealthy as the recipients of fortunate heredity, and their "true
wealth as the accumulation of ancestors that has been transmitted over
several generations to their descendants." He was satisfied that such
wealth existed, because it meant that men had not forgotten the blessings bestowed on their families and households. "If one accumulates
and, thus, leaves behind secret charity [*intoku*], it should not, over the

generations, be limited to the glory and honor of one household" (ibid. 5:307). On the contrary, it must become an endowment put back into the service of the community-as-a-whole.

Embodying Habitus

Miyahiro's conception of trust, authorizing notables to lead the village toward "self-strengthening" by mutual assistance, represented a nativist rereading of the text of contemporary rural affairs. Inasmuch as he specified a certain group and a strong agrarian consciousness steeped in the day-to-day concern for cultivation, his nativism constituted a tactical superimposition on a received ordering of the rural world. It offered local notables, like himself, the occasion to assert their leadership by inserting their position in the familiar chain of divine trust, so as to assume primary responsibility for the well-being of the village. As we have already seen, this conceptualization of well-being depended upon a self-sufficient village, free from outside dependencies, accountabilities, and interference. If Miyahiro's response was limited because of its complicity in immediate agricultural affairs, it nevertheless showed contemporary ruralists how divine trust could be appropriated from the prevailing authority system and made to legitimize the claims of local leadership, privileging the place of the village as the new locus of political responsibility. The chain of command employed by feudal nobles was simply extended to the notables in the countryside (including them now, when before they had been excluded), resolving the ambiguity of their position between officialdom and peasantry by demonstrating their placement in the syntagm of authority. Just as the figure of the peasant sage-leader (substituting for Motoori's poet and knower of *mono no aware*) displaced the received structure of authority in the countryside, so the village was made to stand for *habitus*, the part for the whole.

Writers like Miyahiro, Mutobe, and Miyauchi provided the ideologemes, the most basic units, with which to construct a unified ideological representation adequate to rural interests. Resembling the basic linguistic elements and playing a similar role, these units consisted of recurring themes and utterances and included the following: the role of the creation deities, the importance of the tutelary shrines, the cosmic significance of union and differentiation, the model of the village, and the countless considerations relating to trust. In time, they were combined into a comprehensive and coherent view, establishing the identity of a particular place and a broader political space, village and *habitus*, part and whole. This new combinatory process was supposed to facilitate the transaction between part and whole in such a way as to make it appear a naturally negotiable relationship, adequate to eliminating any trace of contradiction or conflict. But just as any effort to extend the notion of enabling to sanction village trust was bound to be interpreted as a political act bordering on sedition, so any larger attempt to envisage a new dimension of political space, inspired by the example of the imaginary village, would be seen as a challenge to the received arrangement of institutional power. The resulting projection of *habitus* as the means to realize a fit between "objective" conditions and subjective principles merged place and collective practices with the cognitive principles that turned history back into natural structure. This move consciously created a tradition that, nativists proposed, "goes without saying, because it comes without having been said." Yet we know that any act to return to *doxa* and orthodoxy is prompted by a disenchantment with the world as it is officially encoded. Hence, nativists directed their efforts toward transforming *doxa* into heterodoxy, confirming Ikuta Yorozu's ironic self-estimate that he was a "great heretic," and previous heterodoxy—unofficial opinions connected with the ruled—into "correct doctrine," a new *doxa*.

In the 1840s and 1850s, Suzuki Shigetane's intervention launched nativism on this course to suture the split between "self-evident" experience and the cognitive principles that now interpreted the world as a place for "creating," "managing," "solidifying," and "doing." Suzuki considered himself a student of Hirata Atsutane, but he studied with the great nativist system-builder Ōkuni Takamasa as well. Much of his textual work concentrated on exegeses of ancient Shinto prayers and the *Nihonshoki*. His investigation of the ancient chronicles of Japan (*Nihonshokiden*) was often critical of Hirata's "historical" studies and ultimately, in the early 1850s, plunged him into a troublesome quarrel with Kanetane, Atsutane's successor. He also became embroiled in late-Tokugawa loyalist politics and ended his life as an early casualty of the drive toward restoration in the 1860s. His major contribution to nativist discourse was to ideologize *habitus*, now incarnated in the self-sufficient village, as the timeless intersection of past and present, absence and presence, and gods and humans.

Suzuki first disclosed the operation of suturing in the exegetical *Nihonshokiden*, where he sought to demonstrate the impossibility of separating the creation deities from the presence of tutelary gods in his day. Each called attention to the other in an endless interchange of absence and presence. Authority for this observation came from an account of the reign of Emperor Bunretsu (498–506) that described the occurrence of an earthquake as *nai* (earth shaking) and an account from the seventh year of Suiko's reign (598) that reported a ceremony to the gods of the heaven and earth, after the "earth moved" and "houses were entirely destroyed" (*Nsd* 1:111).[14] The *na*, he explained, really meant earth, and *i* referred to moving and shaking. In the *Nihonshoki* the word used to denote tutelary was *ubusuna*, and carried the meaning of the place where production or birth was accomplished (ibid.). Even today, the term employed to mean tutelary still conveyed the meaning of "becoming" (*naru*). The *na*, employed originally to represent soil or place, served as a phonetic sign with different ideographs to designate "great lords" (*oona daimyo*), who maintained large portions of land, and lesser lords (*kona shomyo*), who possessed smaller estates. Village heads were called *nanushi*, and *nariwai* (he used ideographs that sound out the word for household duties) was the name for producing things in the earth, originating from rural cultivation. The *tami*—the people divided into the four estates of samurai, peasants, artisans, and merchants—were originally called "bodies in the field" (*ta*—field, *mi*—body). Household duties originated from agricultural cultivation but were extended to include most activities outside it.

Because of the identity of the earth with the process of becoming and producing implied in agricultural cultivation, there could be no real difference between things (*mono*) and deeds (*koto*). Although there appeared to be a differentiation, Suzuki noted, "deeds become the function of things, and things the substance [body] of deeds" (*Nsd* 1:112). Just as there could be no separation between things and deeds, there could be no temporal distance between the "names of the gods" and reality. "Nothing is apart from the names of deities . . . that bring power [to things]." The names of the gods summoned the "definite form of deeds and conduct and are invoked by anybody who does likewise." When for example, a mirror was made, the mirror-making deity was there, and when a jewel was carved, there was the ordinance of the jewel ancestor. Because these acts were transmitted by the deities who created the cosmos in the distant age of the gods, a similarity existed between the "transmitted reality" of the godly age and the things of today (ibid. 1:114, also 110). The shape of the cosmos's beginning existed in the present. Suzuki portrayed this identity of divine names and contemporary reality in a metaphor that made the relationship appear seamless: "The realm is like a cart, the gods are like men who pull it" (ibid. 1:155).

The reference to evoking the "names of the gods" when something was made or created closed the perceived distance between things and the causal principles of the creation. It also gave substantiality— body—to things by proposing that each object immediately invoked the name of the appropriate deity. "The deities, whose bodies are concealed," Suzuki explained, "give body [jintai] to the cosmos and the cosmos, the august body of the kami, is like the skeleton of men who can be seen." Because the cosmos was composed of godly bodies hidden from view, the kami Way corresponded to their intention and to the conditions of the cosmos—which came to mean the same thing. If humans desired to accept this intention and see it through, they must do so adequately; if they stopped short of this intention, they must do so according to its requirements (ibid. 1:93). The importance of names and naming derived from the observation that the phoneme [na] generated a whole series of terms, synonyms and antonyms, drawn from the paradigmatic pool of associations, which were evoked when na— name—was used in the syntagmatic chain. In the syntagmatic chain, when one term was chosen all other possibilities in the associated pool were excluded; here, Suzuki replenished the chain by demonstrating that all the possibilities were present in the single word for name—na. By listing the associations participating in the phoneme [na], he could simultaneously call attention to the range of paradigmatic substitutions available to the term for name and provide a device that might offset the inclusion of one term and the necessary exclusion of others in the now-occupied space. The point was to bring different meanings along the syntagmatic chain and show similarity in difference; substitutions in the chain would avoid keeping other possible meanings outside, excluded from the chain in order for the signifier to align with a signified to produce a specific sense. The desired effect was to secure the simultaneity of sameness and difference, presence and absence. Yet all of the absences that were barred in order for meaning to take place constituted the Other.

Suzuki insisted that the meaning of all the possible associations generated by the term na or the term mi [body] revealed the Other as the very condition for producing syntagmatic sense. He used this tactic throughout the Nihonshokiden, as well as in his texts on language, to recover the presence of all those absent associations—differences and

connections simultaneously—and to forestall the split between conscious and unconscious intent. Confident that he had found a way of
removing the implicit desire of the Other—the absent associations in
any utterance—he worked to reduce difference to similitude by showing its kinship with the other, the self-same of what is being said. All
things had names according to having been made, Suzuki noted, and
the phonetic suggestion of *nasu* (to make) in the word *ubusuna*, tutelary, referred to "making names." To do was to name. Moreover, the
name of Okuninushi no kami became the *na*—name—of Ōnamochi
no mikoto and thereby brought forth the act of "making" (*tsukuri
nari*). Becoming—*naru*—meant having names. In the *kunitsuchi*, the
mountains and rivers had names; the becoming of mountains and rivers
was expressed in the union of things and names. The middle—*naka*—
of Ame no minakanushi no mikoto, primal central deity of heaven,
was the place that later became the cosmos, where all things were
placed (*na*—become, *ka* [*tokoro*]—place); *nushi* was "giving name"—
nasu—and must be joined to "creating the universe" (*nashitsuku*).
Industry was *nari*, similar to *naryū*, which denoted giving birth—
to things. Things [*mono*] were *morosa*—"several names"—but were
called *mono* because they did not yet have names. Moreover, things that
did not yet exist must not assume names, Suzuki quoted approvingly
from the Laozi, because naming, not morality, was the "mother of
everything." If the cosmos did not exist, there were no-things, there
was no naming. "For the reason that there is no-thing made if it is not
a thing, naming is at the beginning of the universe; and, if there is a
cosmos, there are deities who have created all things" (ibid. 1:84–85).
The meaning of names was, therefore, adequate to all living things on
earth. In addition, the making of substantial things through the "daily
and nightly" effort of the deities was called body. Among humans as
well as plants, trees, and grass, trunk (*miki*) was called "body stem"
(*mikuki*), and ripeness and maturity also referred to the body. The *mi*
that evoked the associations of the fullness of things was similar to
"beauty" (*mi*), which called forth an "esteem for things"; *mi* also resembled "refinement" and "polish," not to mention spirit itself, and
substance. All of these associations led back to the centrality of the
body, which now incorporated all action and meaning. In the chain
of associations Suzuki inventoried, the term for body claimed kinship with "learning," "working," "substitution," "genealogy," "parents,"
"binding," "birth," and "living" (ibid. 1:308).

    This endless series of identities recruited from the paradigmatic

axis closed the apparent split between presence and absence and eliminated the desire (differences) of the Other by scaling it down to other,
a "desire" invariably attending the operation of language by virtue of
the formation of the subject of the discourse (as a result of the split from
the excluded or absent Other) and, thus, constituting the unattainable.
The human body, as conceived by Suzuki, acted in the capacity of the
practical geometer (Bourdieu's term)[15] that drew attention to making
and doing for the *habitus* (Nsd 1:256–57).[16] The body performed and
made in relationship to other bodies and reduced all subsequent operations to its requirements. Underlying the body's "doing" and "making"
was the ceaseless process of union and differentiation—the constant
emanation of things from the concourse of fundamental oppositions,
which was first manifested in the joining of the two creation deities to
make the cosmos and subsequently continued by the sexual congress
of man and woman. *Habitus*, or *kunitsuchi*, encompassed the practice
of the body in a permanent interchange with other doing bodies to
make the realm livable and sufficient: "The endpoint of cosmic experience is said to be a livable and sufficient realm. But this is not only
limited to the age of the gods and antiquity. The extension of the *kunitsuchi* is like the growth of the human body" (Nsd 1:351). Suzuki was
satisfied that this union of opposites and its producing force proved the
presence of the cosmic body by obliterating the presumed separation
between the age of the gods and every present.

Suzuki wrote the *Yotsugigusa* (The Book of Succession) in 1849,
as the title suggests, the text concerns the problem of continuing descendants. The immediate impulse informing it seems to have been
the growing incidence of infanticide (*mabiki*) in the Kantō and Tōhoku
regions. Whereas Miyahiro saw infanticide as a serious deterrent to
agricultural productivity, Suzuki believed that the practice affected the
continuity of the species itself. The procreation of the species and the
preservation of the descendants implied equivalence with the creation
of the cosmos and the deeds of the *musubi no kami*. "The Great Way
of the imperial realm," he announced, "gives birth to descendants and
nourishes them according to the feeling uniting man and woman into
husband and wife" (Kus, 232). What could be a more fundamental
definition of doing and making than the creation of the body? It may
very well be that his privileging of human sexuality, as the basis for the
reproductive act that "makes the body," was the nativist answer to
the *gesaku* transformation of sexuality into pleasure and eroticism.
Each form certainly called forth a different conception of the social

order. Yet his valorization of the union of female and male also contrasted sharply with the model for social structure found in the more conventional and impersonal relationships between lord and retainer; it attributed greater significance to the role of husband and wife and the creation of descendants in society than to any other category of activity. Suzuki proposed that this divine gift—the making of bodies—could not be distinguished from the special place designated by the creation deities, the middle, where the act of making the space sufficient and habitable actualized something out of nothingness by the meritorious deeds of creating, managing, solidifying, and doing (ibid.).

In combination, these deeds—*tsukuri, osame, katame, nasu*—brought about the transformation of a land that had existed only in a fluid and chaotic state (*tada yoeru kuni*). The two supporting kami, Izanagi and Izanami, united conjugally and worked together to transform the realm and make all things. People succeeded to this task; even though they were divided into several regions and classes, they completed the assignment of giving form to the shapeless realm. (Suzuki, it should be noted, was more generous than Satō Shin'en in the role he was willing to allot to humans.) The achievement served as a celebration of the deities and most resembled persons working in their own occupation (*jinmin kōgyō no tatsu tokoro kore nari*). The central values involved in bringing about the transformation of the potential into the actual all related to work and performance. "The human species, according to the blessings of the two supporting gods . . . even though differentiated, create, manage, solidify, and make with their own occupations in mutual assistance and mutual protection."

Suzuki acknowledged a natural division of labor authenticated by the conjugal union of opposites and the differentiation of the household. Despite such differences, all combined into a single purpose in order to realize the great transformation (ibid., 241; *Nsd* 1:357). The act of transforming specified the content of Shinto and gave it new meaning (*Kus*, 240; *Nsd* 1:357). Along with the division of labor came a functional differentiation of values corresponding to a variety of activities. *Tsukuri*, for example, referred to the various divisions in society, the familiar estates of samurai, peasants, artisans, and merchants, and the importance of these occupations in making clothing, food, and shelter available for the *habitus* (*Kus*, 242; *Nsd* 1:260–61). He envisaged the concept of *osame* as "regulating the realm, the household, and one's own body and mediating the five relationships." *Katame* corresponded to samurai conduct and specifically required constant practice (*seiren*) in the martial arts, preparedness for the defense of the realm, and a rejection of profit and desire. It differed considerably from the practices of peasants and merchants who, in imitating the warriors' way of life, put themselves in moral jeopardy by violating their own inherited occupational status. *Katame* stood as the principle that protected the various occupations from becoming something else. The idea of *nasu* was expressed best in "exhausting the body in the service of meritorious deeds. Being born into the world of humans, all have been given useful things by the deities, such as clothing, food, and shelter" (*Kus*, 242–43; *Nsd* 1:362). Actualizing these values in performance established a kinship between a person's occupation and the creation. Once more, Suzuki turned to repairing the putative split between absence and presence. "When one performs the deed of making a potential realm into a sufficient one, it is like inheriting the divine deeds of these *kami*. . . . Deity and self [*onore*] share the same body." Performing according to the divine blessing incorporated the spirit of the creation deities. For this reason, the people (not simply the peasantry) were the "treasures of the realm."

Behind this conception of transforming the realm through the activity of the body looms the larger conception of enabling trust and divine assistance. "The emperor," he wrote in his densely explicated commentary on Shinto prayers, *Engishiki norito kōgi* (1848), "exists to offer prayer to the imperial deities of the heavenly and earthly shrines, in accordance with the grant received from such deities, and to bestow assistance [*butamai*] and blessings upon the august treasure [people] of the land. The existence of [imperial] retainers is no different from the deeds performed by the emperor. They serve with a pure and bright intention [*kokoro*] to help mutually and assist the great august polity" (*Nk* 1:13–14). Suzuki described the functions of the great treasure (*ōmitakara*), which he wrote in phonetic script alongside the ideographs denoting the "public people." He called attention to people's duty to "preserve the household enterprises given by the gods, making substance for food, clothing, and shelter . . . and mutually aiding in the establishment of achievement for men of the times" (ibid. 1:14). Because of their clear and direct linkages, each sector of society assumed the responsibility for fulfilling the promises of *ōmimatsurigoto* (the ideographs denote politics, governance). Community became the place for performing duties for the mutual benefit of other people, "making things for others and meeting the necessities of the times"; it therefore concretized the idea of *matsurigoto*. Recalling both Miyahiro and Ōkuni, Suzuki made this arrangement depend on the performance of virtuous acts for others. Under a regime of reciprocity, nothing seemed less important than structure.

By writing the word *koto* in phonetic script to accompany the ideographs for "achievement" and "virtue," Suzuki avoided linking deeds and events to the initiative of the received structure of institutional authority. Like many nativists, he rejected bureaucratic instrumentality as an adequate surrogate for the true polity, the *mimatsurigoto*. This antistructural theme in nativism recurred regularly in the work of a number of writers and in different guises. Transformed, it reappeared later in the twentieth-century criticisms of folklorists, self-conscious romantics, and contemporary social historians (*minshūshi*) to forestall the bureaucratic standardization of life. Among late-Tokugawa *kokugakusha* like Suzuki Shigetane, the revised concept of trust necessitated a commitment to a full-scale rejection of the received institutional order. Suzuki referred to the special offerings made during the second month—originally made at the beginning of the year—to commemorate the trust (*koto yosashi*) granted by the imperial deities to the emperor; he also cited the duty to perform "deeds of tilling the fields by the great treasure [peasantry], which explains why the emperor begins the cultivation [every year]" (ibid. 1:23, 24). Although the trust to cultivate the fields had originally established the conditions that led to naming the peasantry (*hyakushō*) as the "treasure of the lands," it carried contemporary relevance because it possessed the authority of an imperial ordinance. A reinstatement of this trust would be the necessary condition for "changing men and things in his day" (ibid. 1:23). Suzuki believed that men should submit to such a trust. Although he recognized differences from one area to another among the leaders as custodians of the people, he was convinced that the practice of trust—*koto yosashi*—and not simply the political structure prevented separateness and fragmentation (*ai hanarenu nari*). For this reason, he asserted that love bound the emperor and the ordinary people (*aohitogusa*) and was most evident when each performed for the other (ibid. 1:75).

For Suzuki, trust and performance were forged in the divine commandments, which "created, formed, and solidified the realm." He was especially interested in recounting the story line that revealed how Susanowo, Ōkuninushi, and Sukunabikona were entrusted to make the land habitable (ibid. 1:99). The realm of contemporary life derived from this prior act of the gods to make the land cultivable and habitable (ibid. 1:90; Nsd 1:351; *Kus*, 232). To forget about this trust and the "management of creation" imperiled the land itself. Suzuki contended that if the court slackened in its resolve to administer the fundamental political teachings, it would drive the realm into "rebellion" and "riot" and "impoverish the land." When the peasantry forgot about its trust, households and families were thrown into disharmony and the ordinances disappeared in discord. Abdicating the trust of the imperial ancestors and the heavenly deities most surely invited their anger and rage (*Nk* 1:92, 95). The political administration could never exist apart from the effort to make the realm livable and adequate to human needs; therefore, the activities of "making, forming, and solidifying" were equivalent to the "administration of the land; by knowing this well, the peasantry will prosper and the realm will be tranquil." If the relationship between human necessity and governance fell apart, doom and destruction awaited the land (ibid. 1:95). Trust demanded recognizing that the land was where people resided and the ten thousand things existed for their use (ibid. 1:155). Here, Suzuki distinguished between a "universal realm" (*tenka*), perhaps the cosmos itself, and the national land (*kunitsuchi*). The broader realm, the universe, represented the place inhabited by the imperial descendants, but the national land housed the ordinary people (*sōsei*). Although he warned against concluding from this relationship that the imperial deities were only remotely involved in directing human destiny, he did acknowledge that the folk occupied a principal position in the national land, comparable to the one filled by the emperor in the universal realm. They (the people) stood in a basic relationship to the emperor that required them to offer "what the land yields as the season's first products. Upon receiving this offering, the imperial descendants then give it to the imperial deities" (ibid.). The text forcefully insisted on the equivalence of the diverse functions of emperor, folk, and gods. Their relationship remained as natural as the Great Way and permitted no real distinction between high and low or revered and despised, since each had been assigned their own duties and a place for fulfilling them. When high and low carried out their services in their respective places, the land's administration ran smoothly and tranquilly. Any other institutional arrangement would be superfluous.

Suzuki's theory of trust necessitated an adequate explanation for the meaning of creation. "The body," he wrote, "comes from the heavenly ancestral gods and its spirit belongs to them. At the same time that people possess their body and spirit, they must recognize that the gods also possess them. . . . Because the deities have accepted the great deed [*kamuwaza*] that has made, shaped, and solidified this floating land, for this reason [they have ordained] loving the ordinary folk" (*Kus*, 235). Divine love acknowledged that the folk had transformed the watery realm into a habitable place. That deed established a permanent partnership between the heavenly deities—called the "imperial ancestral gods"—and humanity. In this association founded on ancestry, "the progenitor of father and mother is called ancestor; the founder of these ancestors is named grand ancestor [*sōso*], and his creator is designated the original ancestor [*kōso*; literally, high ancestor]. If one gradually works his way upstream, he will reach the ancestors of the realm's human species, who are the imperial ancestral deities." When people recognized this chain of relationships, they would understand why service to the parents was such a great event. But, he added, there were too many people who held superstitious and irreverent attitudes toward the deities. These views induced people to ignore their parents and to trivialize and neglect the duties that, as children, they were obliged to fulfill. The hidden governance of Ōkuninushi discouraged the folk from straying off the path of filial obligations, by reminding them that everyone must ultimately submit to judgment for his behavior in the visible world, and the "way whereby people serve parents who are close at hand is none other than the great Way of heaven and earth that reaches back to the most distant deities." Suzuki noted that, although some people knew they must "look up to and serve the imperial court [*chōtei o aoigimatsurubeki koto o hoboshite*]", others, who had been enjoined to follow and obey since the time of the ancestors, still held scorn in their hearts for their rulers. It is difficult to ascertain to whom he was referring in this condemnation, but the observation apparently persuaded him to redraw the map of political trust in order to unite the sacred imperative with the "new" idea of direct rule, which would create a "hundred military and civilian offices for managing the administration of the country. Because men pledge service to the folk, they are designated as leaders whom all must follow." Since the imperial seal (*gomiyōdai*) signified these offices, "where [these leaders] command, there one will find the trust [*mikoto yosashi*] of the court, and wherever these men serve, there one will find service to the court" (ibid., 236). More than a decade before the Meiji Restoration, Suzuki Shigetane had already shifted the discussion of politics from the content to the substance of authority, and he had envisaged an arrangement whereby the principle of direct rule preceded the form of ruling and administration.

Part for Whole

The logic underlying Suzuki's conception of trust was applied by his student Katsura Takashige (1816–71) to show how this utopia of the body could contribute to a critique of prevailing society from the perspective of the ruled. Katsura came from a long line of wealthy peasants who had served as village officials (*daishōya*) in Niitsu of Echigo, in northwestern Japan. He spent some time assisting Suzuki, who had recruited a large following from the rural rich of the area, and helped compile his lectures on the *Engishiki norito*. After Katsura completed his "apprenticeship," he turned to interpreting Suzuki's *Yotsugigusa* in the dialect of the region, in an effort to make it more accessible to audiences in Niitsu. Called the *Yotsugigusa tsumiwake*, this text also sought to explain the terse and often cryptic pronouncements of Suzuki's original. [17]

    In this text (written in 1849?), Katsura engaged the question of trust and responsibility. As a rural leader, he no doubt shared with people like Miyahiro, Mutobe and Miyauchi the anxieties of their position in the circumstances of the times. Katsura refrained from mounting a frontal assault on the authority system and its causal relationship to the deteriorating conditions in the countryside. "To criticize the politics of the leaders from the perspective of the ruled, who represent the human power of the times," he advised in the *Yotsugigusa tsumiwake*, "entails discussing the propriety [right and wrong] of officials [*yūshi*]." Lower-ranking officials, empowered by the territorial lords, acted contemptuously toward the people and often appeared as men "who abandon their parents or as students who slight their teachers." "Small men," he observed, "ridicule the elders as old-fashioned; they borrow elegant foods and clothing [they never repay]. . . . Poor cultivators [*kosaka mizunomi*] are portrayed as trash by the landlords and wealthy farmers, while they, in turn, boast about their exploits in avoiding payments of debt. Incidents like these show that the signs point to a violent and disobedient overturn and that there is dissatisfaction and unhappiness everywhere" (Yt, 71b–72a). [18] Katsura's inventory of disorder neglected no segment of society. Even wives and children, he reported, were driven from their homes to other villages. As early as the 1840s, this picture of rural society suggested a rampant disregard

for duties and obligations, the breakup of conventional social relationships, and the drift toward "violent overturn." Katsura was closer to
social conditions than most Tokugawa commentators, by virtue of
class, location, and contemporary history. His perception, nearer to the
texture of social life than Miyahiro's assessment, disclosed a world in
which lower officials pursued self-interest, wealthy peasants (*shōya*)
willfully ignored the needs of their less fortunate contemporaries, and
small-scale cultivators and tenants avoided their financial obligations
at every opportunity. To restore "order" to the countryside, Katsura
later produced the *Saisei yōryaku* (1863), which mapped a terrain of
responsibility that headmen and local officials should follow. Here, he
argued that village officials should comprehend their obligations toward the peasants even if they scorned such people (*Kus*, 253–54).

Time changed things and relationships; older customs gave way
to newer practices. Looking back on earlier Tokugawa times as a possible model for his present, Katsura recalled that the troubles and dis-
orders of the sixteenth century were succeeded by a great peace. "At
that time," he wrote in the *Yotsugigusa tsumiwake*, "the popular spirit
was simple, and, although today we speak ill of those days, the realm
had suffered for nearly three hundred years before them. . . . Laws and
the entire system were reformed, and gradually became precedent [liter-
ally, exhortations]. These precedents and ordinances were understood
by officials, who frequently had to exhort the peasantry [*ōmitakara*] in
order to diminish their impertinence toward human intention" (*Yt*,
70b–71a). Juxtaposing human intention (*jinshin*) to moral intention
(*dōshin*), much in the manner of his contemporary Ōhara Yūgaku,
Katsura tried to show how human intention must always be mediated
by prior concerns for the larger, collective interest (*dōshin*) so that it
would not result in selfishness. His anxiety about the present was directly allied to his fears that such precedents of the past had been lost
to the pursuit of private interests.

Katsura's analysis concentrated on the importance of the conception of trust. Like his teacher, Suzuki Shigetane, he was convinced
that a clarification of how the idea had been employed in archaic practice would disclose to contemporaries its timeless relevance. He seized
on a passage from Suzuki's *Yotsugigusa* that had identified people by
reinterpreting the importance of the two principal transformations of
the godly age. Suzuki had explained that the first transformation involved transmuting the "floating existence" into a solidified national
land by the active achievement (*sachi*, the ideograph also connoted

virtue) of the principal values of "making," "hardening," and "shaping." In the second transformation, the land was worked to yield the great necessities of human life, such as clothing, food, and shelter. By this act, the land was "transformed into society" (*seken o yūzūshi*) that, to this day, carried the mark of its origins in the "collective deeds and duties of the principal values interacting with one another." The second transformation led to the organization of social life and culture; its important element was the trust granted to the people by the ancestral heavenly deities (*amatsu mioyagami no mikoto yosashi*; ibid., 28a). Since the time of origins, people had been engaged in different but, ultimately, common endeavors to transform the realm into a habitable place; for that reason, they were called the great treasure. At this juncture, Katsura commented that people were born to do certain things and perform a variety of useful tasks as a trust from the ancestral deities. Those who endeavored in the service of the court and performed necessary needs stood first among the treasures of the land, but no difference separated a trust enjoining a person to work in his respective occupation and one that offered service to the emperor (ibid., 28b).

The idea of public service ran through much of the nativist discourse, but its articulation had to do less with providing ideological support for the rulership—although it could be appropriated for this purpose—than with *kokugaku* conceptions of being, work, and community. Concerned with the immediate problems confronting rural society, Katsura employed the idea of trust to spur people on to perform their duties and thereby solve the problem of decreasing productivity. "Since today's emergency," he observed, "involves the food supply, the peasantry, among the three classes [peasants, artisans, and merchants], must be understood as the most important." But each group was important to the operation of the whole order, and the current ranking system could show how trust cut across the various divisions to secure a whole greater than its individual parts. The existence of the parts working in harmony called attention to the whole. This reference to the ranking system permitted him to demonstrate how divine trust fell to village officials like himself in the discharge of their duties. Because village officials encountered the folk daily, they were qualified to administer to the people's needs. Katsura's argument, which implied that the realm's administrative system depended on village officials because they interacted daily with the masses, led to a theory that privileged the lowest level in the hierarchic chain as the strongest link.

In the *Saisei yōryaku*, Katsura explained that because local officials (*kyōrui*) and village headmen resided in the areas of their jurisdiction, they were entrusted by the gods and the emperor to assist the peasantry (*moto moto nōmin o oazukari mōshite; Kus*, 270). Specifically, their entrustment consisted of "planning for increased agricultural productivity and collecting the yearly taxes, lecturing on agricultural governance and clarifying its way." By putting themselves on the line "with their bodies," Katsura declared, "and by refraining from words, they will enter the vital spirit of the peasantry." That is, actions, not words, would enable village officials to understand the peasantry. In effective village management, the proliferation of words was the problem and not the solution, since it distanced the officials from the ruled. "There are many village heads today," he confessed, "who do not even know the names of the variety of rice seedlings!" (ibid.). If village officials remained apart from the work and activity of their villagers, the area under cultivation would decline in productivity and invite disorder. "If they [village heads] do not lose the simplicity of the agricultural household, calm will prevail . . . within the community. The ruled will learn from rulers and imitate the idleness they observe among village officials. When ordinary folk become too accustomed to [the example of] luxury and extravagance, then one person will decide to imitate the powerful farmer, then two, and three, until the whole village is affected" (ibid.). Like falling dominoes, the process of decline in the countryside would be set into irreversible motion and would encompass the whole realm. "Fields inherited from the distant ancestors will collapse [from disuse], and the peasant cultivators will lose their land." Since this scenario sprang from official mismanagement at the village level, "we must be on our guard, fearful and ever watchful." Katsura's portrayal of rural decline presented the image of a corporate body, the realm, composed of villages that either guaranteed or imperiled the integrity of the whole. If the parts failed—if villages declined, then the whole of society faced the prospect of dissolution. By the same token, society as a whole would survive if the villages were ably and efficiently administered.

Katsura believed he had found a model of order in the early-Tokugawa period. Because the Keichō and Genna eras (early seventeenth century) had successfully installed the "simplicity of the human spirit," the present could draw lessons from their experience in its own effort to restore human intention to its original status (*Yt*, 70b, 71a).[19] He found it most interesting that the earlier period had relied simply on trust between ruler and ruled and that it had no need for conventional political devices such as laws, ordinances, punishments, and rewards. Trust, he explained, was conveyed to people through "preaching" and "exhortations" from elders and superiors, who instructed underlings and servants (*dōhi*). To recuperate this example, it was important

> first of all, to depend upon the august heart that deepens and widens the *kami* learning of the people within the imperial court; then, this learning is transmitted from court officials [priests] who have made their intention identical with the great august heart to the regional lords, country officials, village chiefs, and headmen, and then it is taught to the peasantry. The peasantry also receive and transmit their intention to instruct the women, children, and servants in each household in the learning of the deities. In this manner, the great intention of the emperor is transmitted downward. (*Yt*, 71b)

The original transmission of the great august heart invested the human intention (*jinshin*) with "rectitude," "straightness," and "simplicity." In time such human values fell into disrepute, owing to the "bent teachings" of Buddhism and Confucianism and even more to the neglect of the leadership and its abdication of trust (ibid., 72a). Katsura's indictment of the leadership was double-edged: at the upper levels, officials had ignored the trust they were supposed to uphold; at the lower levels, in the villages, the time was right for local officials to exercise real rulership. Both the *Yotsugigusa tsumiwake* and the *Saisei yōryaku*, written some fifteen years later, attested to his abiding belief in the powers of local leadership to stem disorder and disbelief in the interests of the reconstituted community.

This reiteration of the character of local leadership in the rural reaches prompted a redefinition of hierarchy. Yet Katsura's formulations differed vastly from more conventional conceptions of ranking. Like most *kokugakusha*, he believed in hierarchy, since nativist cosmological strategy had already fixed its importance in the univeral organization. From Motoori through Hirata and Satō, nativists were consistently convinced that life organized itself in terms of natural structures, preferences, and priorities. This inclination for differentiation underlay Hirata's elaborate diagrammatic exploration, which sought to explain the reasons for the ordering system. After all, the deities and creation were sorted out in classifications of priorities and categories of significance; life merely reflected the cosmic plan. For rural writers like Katsura, *kokugaku* signalled a full return to the problem of hierarchy, but at a different level of cognition. A return to hierarchy meant focusing on the position of leadership in the village, the space of the reconstituted community now serving the whole that nativists had designated as the form of the social life-world. This transposition to a new level resulted in a definition of the relationship between ruler and ruled that was radically different from the one conceived by the Neo-Confucians. In a very real sense, writers like Katsura and Suzuki Masayuki, his contemporary working in Shimōsa, pushed the *kokugaku* argument to its logical conclusions. Once nativism became a method for resolving problems in the countryside—the questions of proliferating peasant disorder; the withdrawal of assistance, relief, and even security; and the erosion of productivity because of market arrangements—it was natural to assume that the autonomous village, the metonymical part, would constitute the appropriate jurisdictional unit. Because the objective of restoration was now the self-sufficient space represented by the village, nothing counted more than the affirmation of the village elite in its "new" position of responsibility by invoking the whole machinery of trust and enablement. Even the discussions of relief and mutual assistance informing most nativist texts converged on the availability of an effective administration (*minsei*) in the village, and nowhere else. In the short run, this solution also satisfied the requirements of local necessity—the scene of politics—and encouraged secession and withdrawal to the periphery. Yet what fulfilled local expectations—substituting the part for an unenvisioned whole—invariably failed in the long run, when the character of events changed and thoughtful men were forced to imagine what the whole might look like.

The great systematizer of nativism, Ōkuni Takamasa, when confronted by the problem of making a local solution serve a wider interest, broadened the idea of trust to satisfy a larger context, so as to validate the authority recently appropriated by local leaders. Ōkuni took the term *yosachi* to refer to the realm itself. Three entrustments had been granted in the age of the gods, he wrote in the *Hongaku kyoyō* (1851), and two in the age of men. It was, of course, the earlier three grants (*sando no kuni yosachi*) that held for him archetypal importance. The first came from the several heavenly deities to Izanagi and Izanami and entrusted the "heaven and stars"; the second was from Izanagi and Izanami to Amaterasu and consisted of the entrustment of the sun and the moon; and the third was Amaterasu's entrustment of the realm to the imperial ancestor Ninigi no mikoto.[20] Ōkuni described these trusts as eternal and inimitable divine ordinances. In the human world, the two great grants were the trusts to Sukunabikona and, later, to Ōkuninushi to solidify the realm and make it livable. Their "example" signified the basis for both a program to achieve productive life by mutual assistance between the local leadership and the peasantry and a larger license for the imperial restoration of a cultural order. The linkage was forged first at the mythic level, in the example of the grant (*yosashi*) to Ōkuninushi to render and subsequently restore the national land to human cultivation and habitation. Transferred to the human order, it authenticated demands on behalf of the local leadership and the peasantry to realize this "trust" in a harmonious and productive life.

Much of this theory was worked out in his discussions of the *aohitogusa* and the necessity of the leadership to learn about their "customs." In the *Yamatogokoro* (1848), where he first developed his ideas about ordinary people, Ōkuni observed that a principal manifestation of the lord as the source of leadership was his willingness to care for the people (*bumin*). Leaders were obliged to make the act of caring a fundamental principle of their ruling duties. Such a responsibility should be exercised at all times, especially in normal times, and not be implemented only during moments of necessity. "When the people are oppressed, their spirit is separated from the regime. . . . The lord must not neglect his skills of caring for the people" (*OTz* 3:183–84). The rulers, therefore, were required first to provide standards and exemplars for the people; their lives and demeanor should reflect simplicity. Ōkuni stressed the importance for leaders to preserve and protect "ancient methods" in the present. Therefore, they must administer to peasants and merchants without grumbling over personal difficulties in collecting regular yearly taxes and payments to the government; for their part, the commoners should not default on the payment of debts.

> The peasantry's first intention should be not to default on the payment of yearly taxes. As for village officials, they should fix their intention on trying not to trouble the peasantry, on avoiding selfishness and egotism, and on trying to avoid, where possible, disputes over the distribution and allotments in the fields, laziness, luxury, and gambling. Peasants are persons who ought to work with all their might, and it is a bad thing for them to pursue pleasure. If there are people troubled by long illnesses in the villages, it is well for officials to be attentive. The reluctance to assume responsibility in public affairs is the shame of village officials. (Ibid. 2:323)

Although Ōkuni came down hard on the village leaders, he was no less demanding than others, like Miyahiro and Katsura, who believed that only local leaders were qualified to rule in the changed countryside. Nevertheless, it is noteworthy that he concentrated upon this class as the recipient of trust, enabling it to lead the peasants by providing needed assistance. To this end, the *hongaku* movement, led by one of Ōkuni's students, Oka Kumaomi in Tsuwano *han*, declared that its principal aim was care and relief, founded upon a "great loyalty" for all, "down to peasants, merchants, and artisans."[21]

7 Knowledge, Interest, and the Cultural Order

Hermeneutics and History

For nativists, the autonomous village became a manifestation of the unchanging *habitus*, or *mimatsurigoto*, which itself validated a return to origins; the village stood as the part now substituting for the whole. When *kokugakusha* spoke of mutual assistance and the importance of self-sufficiency, they steeped their claims in the authority of a primal moment of creation. They expressed political authority in the language of entrustment and enabling, which they believed described the most fundamental relationship between the creation deities and the ordinary folk. We have seen how nativists extended the syntagm of trust from the deities down through the emperor, shogun, daimyo, and village officials, and why, at each stage, they enjoined people to repay the blessings of the *kami*. In the village, this repayment meant carrying out practices that would achieve mutual assistance and self-sufficiency. To act in this manner, it was believed, would fulfill in the present the potentialities of the ancient community. This conviction functioned as a strategy to offset rural disorder, but it could also be applied to the realm as a whole.

Entrustment could work in two ways: at the level of the village head and at the level of the emperor. Emphasis on one or the other depended largely on the nature of contemporary events and how they were perceived—how people privileged events and whether they saw them as a peril to the survival of a region or to the realm as a whole. In part, this explains the nativist decision to save the village first and only later to turn to the support of a higher authority system aimed at

326

arresting rural disorder and foreign colonization. The decision to save the village by removing it from "history" and the decision to join the imperial cause to arrest peasant unrest amounted to the same thing.

Nativists like Miyahiro Sadao and Katsura Takashige, who sought to formulate the principles by which to reconstitute village life, were determined to take responsibility out of the hands of feudal officials in order to restore it to the community. They also hoped to reduce the regularity of peasant disturbances, by removing what they believed were the conditions prompting such outbursts of collective violence. When, in 1867 and 1868, they joined the ranks of imperial loyalists bent on overturning the *bakufu*, they saw the restoration of the emperor as a way to return authority back to the community. Underlying this interpretation was the nativist preference for a communitarian order rather than a hierarchical administrative polity as the most natural form of social interaction. Restoring authority to the emperor really returned power to the body; community, the most fundamental form of human organization, simply consisted of bodies interacting with one another to make the realm livable and sufficient. Between emperor and people no intervening institutions were necessary to fulfill the divine intention, because both shared the same body. Hierarchical organization, as implemented by the Tokugawa arrangement, was steeped in the legitimizing principles of nature, which authorized both a model of society that reflected its tiered structure and a moral system that bound people together in vertical relationships. Nativism, along with the new religions, envisaged a society based on other principles of organization, which projected bodies interacting with one another to create a formation of horizontal relationships. The failure of the Tokugawa clan to secure control over the forces that affected productivity and its incapacity to offer assistance and maintain order resulted in a loss of the legitimizing principles that had for so long authorized its rule and conception of society. This loss of legitimacy called attention to the failure of a hierarchical organization to maintain tranquillity and prosperity. In the face of this failure, nativists, along with others, projected their own claims to interest and designated a form of withdrawal from the control system. Disbelief in politics led to its displacement, but this skepticism was also grounded in newly-defined interests.

Nativists had good reason for abandoning politics, as they understood it, and looking elsewhere. In part, they were prompted by the construction of a different conception of social order. But "the will to formulate discourse" came to be supplemented by the perception that

the administrative hierarchy simply was not working. Both the countryside and the cities were rocked by disorder, while the authorities increasingly suffered from a numbing incapacity to act decisively. To look
elsewhere—that is, to displace politics altogether—meant constructing
a new kind of social order, founded on different principles. The nativist
choice of social community was at the heart of many schemes of the
time that called for a return to antiquity. The sense of a community
authorized by the nativist idea of an order held together by natural and
tangible necessities—not artificially constructed status groupings and
power relationships—derived from a spurious conception of nature. It
contained an implicit criticism of the prevailing political system, which,
many believed, diverted people from serving themselves and realizing
their own interests and made them serve the goals of an impersonal and
distant managerial class. In this arrangement, society existed to maintain political power relationships, rather than the reverse. The new
schemes resituated power in the body, which would establish the necessary relationships to make the realm sufficient and habitable. All of the
attempts in the late-Tokugawa period to establish self-sufficient communities by collective effort recognized that, if people did not help
themselves, nobody else would. Nativists believed that nativism, along
with other discourses, had a natural right to express their interests, as if
such articulation was vital to the general interest of society. Matters
pertaining to the general interest were no longer other people's business, but the business of the social body. The articulation of claims
related to interest relied less on traditional dogma than principles of
knowledge that were often critical and even rational. The will to discourse mandated organized movements often appealing to different
classes of people—*kokugaku*, groups devoted to western studies (*yōgaku*), *Mitogaku*, and new religious constituencies—to work for secession and voluntary association.[1]

    The idea of voluntary association—people banding together to
discuss and protect their interests—represented a new sense of politics
in the late-Tokugawa period. Openly discussing and actively pursuing
what many people now believed to be in the interest of society-as-a-
whole (later in the early-Meiji era, this goal was specified as the pursuit
of happiness) flew in the face of a traditional order founded on a definition of social constituencies according to "natural" categories and
involuntary relationships. Under prevailing circumstances, people had
their interest defined for them, instead of defining it themselves. What
appeared in late-Tokugawa times was a genuine public sphere where

none had existed before; its constant principle of expansion was the willful formation of discourses, seeking to represent certain groups on the basis of new forms and systems of knowledge constituted from interest. All of these new discourses implied the possibility of discussion free from prevailing constraints, and all were directed to interests that most affected the lives and work of the people they resolved to "represent." For many of these groups, the concept of restoration served as a code signifying both the will to discourse and the appeal to systems of knowledge founded on definable interests. This was particularly true of *kokugaku*, which, in the hothouse atmosphere of late-Tokugawa politics, projected a vision of restoring a lapsed structure in time as its contribution to resolving the uncertainty of the present—what the nativist Ōkuni Takamasa called "adhering to the base." Yet, this call for a return to foundations was, as we shall see, indistinguishable from the systematization of a knowledge field that qualified people to act authoritatively. The upshot of the restorationist urge was the displacement of the hierarchical system demanded by politics for a cultural order capable of providing self-definition to groups that hitherto had been excluded or simply marginalized from the defining function of discourse. In this will to knowledge, nativism, along with other late-Tokugawa discourses, organized the relationships between objects constituting the epistemological field, so as to center a subject and certain activities in discourse. Nativism fulfilled its function as a syntagmatic hermeneutic by designating culture as the site where meaning was to be produced, as a more than adequate substitute for politics and institutional power.

As a cultural hermeneutic, *kokugaku* promised an understanding of reality by the clarification of practical effective knowledge. "Reality," Jürgen Habermas has written, "is constituted in a framework that is the form of life-communicating groups and is organized through ordinary language. What is real can be experienced according to the interpretations of a prevailing symbolic system."[2] The nativist claim to the status of a hermeneutic lay in its rejection of abstract reason and principle (*ri*) and its devaluation of written language (Chinese) for the immediacy of speech. It derived its process of articulating "methodological rules" to form a discourse from the structure of life, which reproduced the conditions of existence in socially organized work and the interactions mediated by a common language capable of producing mutual understanding.[3] As Habermas has proposed, such "conditions of life have an interest structure." Among nativists, inquiry, as we have seen, was synonymous with a ceaseless attempt at self-formation, and meaning was identical to creating the cosmos and to custom. Like Habermas, they spoke "of a technical or practical knowledge-constitutive interest, insofar as the life structures of instrumental action and symbolic intention perform the meaning of the validity of possible statements . . . in such a manner that, to the extent that these statements are cognitions, they have a function only in these life structures: that is, to the extent that they are technically exploited or practically efficacious."[4]

When referring to knowledge constituted of interest, we do not mean a reduction to immediately and empirically identifiable motives prompting people to act. Throughout this study, we have called attention to how nativist theory aimed at reproducing the conditions of social existence by purposeful action, work, mutual understanding, and language. In this sense, interest provided *kokugaku* with both the actual content of its system of knowledge and the cognitive principles of organization.[5] At the most basic human level, work and language formed a matrix for interaction and communication; work required mutual understanding if it were to be carried out, and language needed the interaction of bodies—the dialogic relationship of people doing things together—to communicate the experience among the participants. A study of origins—*hongaku*, or *honkyō*, as it was increasingly described by late-Tokugawa nativists—called forth a knowledge of the fundamentals necessary to reproduce social life, whether in the cognition of things (Motoori) or in the creation of the cosmos and the life of the ordinary people (Hirata). Precisely because the reproduction of social life was believed to be based on a knowledge constituted on the interest of working and communicating, it was less a biological process—even though nativists tried to demonstrate the necessity of nature—than a cultural one; self-definition, which existed from the moment of creation when naming first occurred, implied conscious, methodical inquiry. In short, nativists argued that the interest structure constituting their system of knowledge lay embedded in the life-process in which it functioned; in addition, they proposed that the operation of reproducing social life could not be understood without considering the relationship between knowing and practice. In their formulations, practice, or action, established the conditions of possible knowledge, which, in turn, relied upon the cognitive principles derived from the putative structure of life. With this coupling of knowledge and action, which bordered on tautology, the conceptualizing powers of language to capture the life-world and the performance of practical affairs constituted nativism as a form of self-reflection that—if it did not bring "emancipation" by its critique of social ideology—at least promised to alter the received categories of life. Here was the meaning of restoration for the nativists who turned to it in the contest for power that dominated late-Tokugawa history. But, as we shall see later, here, too, was the reason for nativism's failure to establish its conception as the normative one in the competition among restorations.

Hence, a return to basics—to fundamental learning, to the elevation of daily affairs and their importance for reproducing the communal unit, to aid and relief, to mutual assistance and understanding, to practicality and productivity—did not necessarily "reflect" conditions in the late-Tokugawa period, as most interpreters have supposed; instead, it provided an interpretation that transformed the seriality of blank events into "facts." Praxis intersected with history in the nativist conception of cultural order, which had been generated by the disciplinization of self-knowledge. Events were apprehended in such a way as to provide specificity to the new discursive claims of interest and transpose them into principles of general concern. The will to form discourse in the late-Tokugawa period pointed toward the establishment of a dialectical relationship between knowledge and the determination of cultural order, and, more important, toward relating specific epistemologies to the creation of cultural form. This was also true of *Mitogaku*, the new religions, and Western studies, and each, in its own way, applied a strategy that stressed the substitution of the part for the whole. Usually, they appointed a space for practice that could represent the interests of a certain group as a displacement for the social whole. If there was any sense of consensus in the late-Tokugawa period, it was that the question of the whole required serious engagement. The real problem was to determine which part(s) would constitute the unenvisaged whole. As each group attempted to identify the purpose of society, it sought a different source of authority, which might center and explain activity that had hitherto been marginalized and a space that could serve as a locus for such representation. Any discussion involving politics or administration as it was officially practiced risked conflict with the authorities because it challenged the officials' claim to define objects for political discourse. To avoid conflict necessitated finding a space outside the prevailing conception of the social formation, one different enough that it did not duplicate the place traditionally occupied by shogunal officeholders yet meaningful enough that it could give significant representation to the activities of groups seeking self-identity. A reconstitution of culture along these lines permitted discourses like *koku-gaku* to conceptualize new cultural orders as substitutes for political forms. As a result, *Mito* writers emphasized the primacy of the domain sanctioned by the essentialist *kokutai;* nativists concentrated on the village authenticated by its relationship to the creation deities; the new religions announced the establishment of sacred communities along horizontalist lines (*kō* organization) and formed *yonaoshi* groups that acted to give permanence to their conception of epiphany; and the adherents of "Western studies" (samurai from smaller *fudai* domains, usually associated with the *bakufu* and merchants) pledged their determination to install a mercantilist state, more moral then political. These cultural forms became political when—each in its own way—they announced their withdrawal from the central control system after concluding that the shogunal system, hitherto identified with the whole, had become less and less able to provide the services that its arrogation of the center had obliged it to offer. Among nativists, secession from the center was validated by the promise to find a cultural order in a timeless and self-sufficient community devoted both to reproducing the conditions of its social existence and to balancing the claims of spatial atemporality, illuminated by its systematization of knowledge, with the incursions of contemporary history. Although nativist theoreticians envisioned that such an act would move thought and activity to the periphery, events transformed this simple withdrawal into a contest to determine who and which discourse would occupy the center by reconstituting it again.

Nowhere was this ensuing relationship between the disciplinization of knowledge and the authorization of cultural form articulated more systematically than in the writings of Ōkuni Takamasa (1792–1871), which attempted to shape a space consistent with the cognitive principles of nativism. Nowhere was the relationship between knowledge and action better exemplified than in the texts of Tomobayashi Mitsuhira (1813–64), which, in attempting to resuscitate the poetic mode of knowing established by Motoori and his successors, made the theory of restoration an exercise that promised to realign emotionality with praxis. In Chapter 8, which is an extension of this discussion, we will consider nativism as an interpretive moment in the process leading to the Meiji Restoration of 1868.

"Learning the Customs of the Folk"

On the occasion of Tokugawa Nariaki's commemoration of Jinmu tennō's twenty-five hundredth anniversary, Ōkuni Takamasa announced a new theory of learning. He had met Nariaki, the lord of Mito, in 1853 and dedicated *Gakuunron*, published in the same year, to him. The essay concentrated on the nature of the times, the changing whims of fortune, and the necessity for identifying new kinds of knowledge. Ōkuni observed that the rhythm of history was characterized by large-scale cycles that periodically stimulated fundamental changes. "Cycles surrender to the spirit, to fortune, to the trends. Until the present, we have been in a trend that promotes the teachings of Confucianism and Buddhism. This trend has lasted a long time. From the time of Jinmu's foundation of the realm, it was six hundred years before the first foreigners crossed over to Japan. We should calculate when this trend from west to east occurred first." Ōkuni believed his calculations had uncovered the great turning points in the cycles of history, which always represented the promotion of new modes of learning (*gakuun*). By locating the principle of change (*kiun*) in the introduction of new forms of learning, he was convinced that he had found the laws of historical motion. Until recently, he wrote, men had neither noted the regularity of these changes nor clearly recognized the relationship between such changes and new modes of learning. It had been assumed that the last ten thousand years have been unitary. But "we can halve these stretches of time seven times and show, in each segment, a relationship between imperial fortune and the decline of learning" (*OTz* 4:1–2).[6]

In his discussion of historical motion, Ōkuni showed the extent to which the discourse on knowledge had always been implicated in considerations of power. Like writers of the Mito school, he had argued that history moved according to something called the "drift of the times" (*kabusu*, literally, tilting one way or another), which explained the flow of historical change by divine deeds (*yo no ugokiutsuru mo mina kami no mishiwaza*). In *Gakuunron* he added the notion of large-scale cycles announced by the introduction of new modes of knowing. "There are 1,250 years from the reign of Empress Suiko to 1844, 2,500 years from Jinmu tennō to 1841." During that time, he reasoned, there had been two major breaks. "If one thinks along these lines, today is the time for such a change in the trend of learning, which has come down to us from antiquity. The origins of the Great Way [*daidō*] of our country have been buried" (*OTz* 4:7–8). Under the sanctions of this new principle of temporal unfolding, history had validated the present as the appointed moment to install a new kind of knowledge. Signs pointing to such a change, the first major alteration in learning in 1,250 years, had first been disclosed in the eighteenth-century formulations of Kamo no Mabuchi and Motoori Norinaga, who "drew out the ancient way of *Sumera mikuni*, which has remained buried . . . to be used by the leadership for the people." Ōkuni was prompted to continue the work of historical necessity by disciplinizing the new knowledge and offering it to his times as a learning that satisfied the "drift of the times."

In the *Hongaku kyoyō*, Ōkuni reported that the trend or "bend" of learning lasted from Jinmu (r. 660–585 B.C.) to Suiko (r. A.D. 592–628) and totaled 1,250 years. During the regency of Shōtoku taishi (under Empress Suiko), the "old customs were abolished by imitating all things according to foreign ways. For the last 1,250 years, we can observe the declining fortune of our country. . . . But the decline contained the [seed of the] prospering fortune of today" (*HA*, 415). Indeed, it was to the credit of the *kokugakusha* to have reminded the realm of its origins and "to return to the history when the *kami* Way flourished" (ibid., 418). In order to retrieve prosperous fortune, it was necessary to "adhere to the origins" (*moto ni tsuku*), a pairing as "natural" as right and left in eyes, ears, hands, and legs or the happiness that came from enacting a ceremony for the gods (*kami no matsuri*; ibid., 452). Ōkuni's appeal to the source recalls *Mito* writers and their conception of restoration; its function was comparable: it enabled nativists to redefine the original state of the social order. But adherence to origins meant calling forth the "restoration of state foundation under Jinmu tennō." Here, Ōkuni was drawing from the lessons of Western Christianity. The West, he wrote, had violated the basis of social order because it had not used it to erect sovereignty. Rather, "we must know that, in the 1,850 years since the founding of Christianity, there has been a spiritual head as the basis." The reckoning of time in the West proceeded from the founding of a new religion, whereas in Japan it was "opposed to this" (ibid., 426). "We . . . have made Jinmu tennō the basis and have erected a chronology that dates twenty-five hundred years from this founding restoration [*chūkō kigen*]." Ōkuni linked a knowledge of basics—a concern for origins and ends—to the time for a change in the politcal drift by invoking the "founding restoration of Jinmu tennō." There is no mistaking the objectives impelling this restorationist projection, now authorized by the new discipline, nor need there be any doubt that "learning about the *kami*" really meant "learning about the people."

In fashioning a discipline that might get back to basics, Ōkuni searched for a method that would allow him to apprehend the world in terms of similitudes, integrations, unities, and harmonies, despite the apparent presence of differences. The titles of some of his key essays show this interest in sameness—*Dōi hon* (Book of differences and similarities), *Shinri ikkan* (Integration of deity and principle)—not to mention the central direction of his thinking itself. In an early work, *Amatsu norito futo norito kō* (1834), he proposed that if the differences between, say, the world of deities and the world of people remained unchanged, then it would be difficult to integrate principle and the divine, the rational and the unrational (*OTz* 7:151–66). In his concern for creating harmony from similitude, especially between deities and humans, upper and lower, he paradoxically revealed the portion of his thought that sought to engage the world of contemporary history, when he began contemplating proposals for the dissolution of "differences" between the ordinary people and "those who are at the top." He approached this problem first by trying to minimize the differences produced by class affiliations. Although he enjoyed military status, he confessed, he had always endeavored to cut across class lines. As a member of the lower orders of the warrior class, he wrote, he always "attended to the intentions of his superiors." At the same time, he spent a good deal of time considering how people might come to understand the spirit of the country of Japan (ibid. 1:163). Elsewhere in the same text, he clarified this sentiment when he explained the necessity to think about the folk, instead of exclusively considering the upper classes, because they all had been born in Japan. Despite the importance of social divisions, birth and place eliminated essential differences and secured kinship. Ōkuni's disciplinization of nativism presupposed a social imaginary that was a unity held together by similitudes and resemblances. The only possible definition of the social derived from a logic of likeness that banished principles and practices separating people by virtue of social—that is, artificial—distinctions. In his theory of social holism, Ōkuni offered contemporaries an analysis of their society and a solution to the problem of difference or fragmentation dogging it. He demanded the establishment of a community founded on principles of similitude and resemblance, specified by birth and place, in order to eliminate the spectacle of difference, manifested most recently in the conflict between superiors and subordinates. Plainly, he was referring to contemporary peasant disturbances and the acceleration of disorder in the countryside.

Ōkuni's specific strategy, which called for the installation of "basic studies" and explaining "fundamental doctrine" (*honkyō, moto oshie*), was never far from the more enduring protocols of the nativist

discourse and represented almost perfectly the nativist choice of metonymy. We have already seen how nativists early disclosed their preoccupation with genesis and the most tangible forms of meaning and
the real. By its capacious reductive powers, nativism was enabled to
locate the essence of an object or a series in one or another part of
the totality. Far from concentrating on the totality, a tactic closer to
Neo-Confucianism and its privileging of the paradigmatic, nativism—
especially after Ōkuni systematized it—favored the part as a substitute
for the whole. Ōkuni envisaged "basic" studies as a discipline concerned with a proper understanding of origins, which was capable of
revealing essences rather than mere phenomenal form. This consideration, which revealed his conception of interest, had profound consequences for political theory and subsequent political practice; it permitted writers like Ōkuni to discuss politics politically, without seeming
to do so, by associating the prevailing political system with temporal
form and emphasizing the priority of an essential authority and its unchanging character. Above all else, the focus on origins redirected him
from merely contemplating the forms of political activity to actively
trying to grasp the sources of its authority. Even though we will return
to this subject later in this chapter, it is important to say here that the
upshot of this interest in the primacy of unchanging essences created
by the deities was its dismissal of the prevailing arrangements of power.
Finally, this shift to a conception of cultural order produced by the
appeal to origins and essences resituated an alterity in the place of the
center, culture over politics, the immediate over the mediate, and the
permanent and lasting over the temporal.

Acknowledging that the word for "basic studies," *hongaku*, could
not be found in the ancient writings, but undismayed by this "absence," Ōkuni believed that its "presence" was inscribed in the texts.
Owing to the existence of something called "basic teachings" (*moto
oshie*), he reasoned, it was justifiable to "call *hongaku* those skills
whereby we are able to learn the essence [*mune*] of those teachings"
(*HA*, 408). Hirata had employed a term close to "basic teachings" in
his *Tama no mihashira*, when he referred to "fundamental learning,"
moto manabi. But, according to Ōkuni, his own idea of "basic teachings" differed considerably from Hirata's earlier conception. Even in
the preface of the *Kojiki*, there were references to the concept of "fundamental teachings," although the text failed to use the word *hongaku*.
"At the time of the formation of the islands," Ōkuni continued, "the
nobleman Ō no Yasumaro no nushi [nobleman in charge of editing

Kojiki] relied on fundamental teachings . . . so that the people of the times would celebrate the deities" (ibid., 440). Consequently, fundamental doctrine (*honkyō*) referred to the study of origins and the conditions attending the genesis of the land, as well as to the truths accompanying its birth (*umu*). It differed from both Confucianism and Buddhism, because it authoritatively "explained the [original] shape of heaven and earth and taught the Way according to which men [of this country] must conduct themselves" (ibid., 405). Deriving its superiority from the fact that its formulation had preceded the importation of foreign teachings to Japan, it had, from the beginning, successfully managed to "unite high and low in harmony [*kamishimo wagō shi*]." When contrasted to the claims of foreign doctrines, it had demonstrated its vast powers to govern the times well (ibid., 404). Yet at the same time that these teachings were being applied to the governance of the realm, they were also operating as a practical ethic incorporating such Confucian-sounding values as loyalty, filiality, and constancy, long before the reception of either Confucianism or Buddhism in ancient Japan. This ethic was inscribed in the sacred language of divine and imperial ordinances, which were "as eternal as heaven and earth themselves" (ibid., 408–9).

Since the age of the gods, Ōkuni asserted, people and gods had been united in community by their sharing of a divine language. In showing how the language of ordinances immediately reflected the divine presence, Ōkuni hoped to identify the leading elements and principles of language that would bring people together in community. Convinced that only communication and common understanding could provide the necessary conditions for the constitution of a viable social order, he resituated the earlier nativist conviction concerning the inaugural act of speaking and its importance for the origins of the empathic community in an environment charged with political and social uncertainty. Among Japanese, he remarked, all things had been understood in terms of "five sacred shapes", represented by the following divine words: *to*, *(h)o*, *kami*, *emi*, and *tame*. The word *to* referred to earth, *(h)o* to the sun, *kami* to deity, *emi* to man, and *tame* to things (*HA*, 411; *OTz* 7:137.). Man smiled and laughed (*emi*), and thereby formed a shape that pointed to the intention to speak. The voices of *emi* harmonized the vowel sounds—[a i u e o]—with consonantal sounds to form combinations such as [ha hi fu he ho] (*HA*, 411). This "linguistic" argument appeared early in *Amatsu norito futo norito kō*, where Ōkuni examined the language of prayer as recorded

in the sections on worship in the *Engishiki* (volume 8), an early compendium of rituals and rites. In this text, he contended that the recitation of prayer had attended the origins of language as the primal act of
utterance of archaic Japanese. The recollection of these prayers in the
present, he added, would not only remind contemporaries of the ancient Way of the gods but would also reveal the terms and conditions
that brought people together in community in the archaic ages. Because this community was principally a gathering of worshipers, the
ancient Japanese had banded together first to protect themselves from
pollution. Using the language of the gods, the community had won
immunity from pollution and protection against transgression. "Our
Shinto", he wrote, "aims at the truth of the inner heart. Evil men are
those who embellish the surface but conceal a polluted heart within
the heart. Being born in our country, we incline toward the way of the
realm, which is purifying the heart. To do so means that one must
always react to the aims of these prayers" (*OTz* 7:124). Prayerful performance depended on the prior classification of things in the visible
or invisible realms. As a result, transgressions (*tsumi*) could be committed against either the visible or invisible realm, but both were
judged by the "spirit deities" (ibid. 7:124–25). Although transgressions
in the visible realm were important, polluting acts against the invisible
governance were more serious offenses. Ōkuni was convinced that ut-
tering the sacred phrases of prayers to the deities would purify the heart
and prevent polluting acts in the visible realm. By praying in the present to the deities in the invisible world, the visible world would be put
into even greater dependence on it (ibid. 7:126).[7] "When one knows
well and skillfully the intention of the five sacred words . . . one will
be able to avoid . . . the punishments of both the invisible and visible
realms" (ibid. 7:128). In Ōkuni's scheme, the visible world was incorporated into the invisible.

Ōkuni's explanation of sacral sounds and shapes attested to the
materiality of language and its bodily source in order to demonstrate
the reason for presuming unity and association; it also sought to show
the identity of humans and gods by relating the five sacred word/shapes
to specific deities. He considered the pairing of Takami musubi no kami
with *kami*, Kami musubi no kami with *emi*, and Ame no minakanushi no kami with *tame* as the most important. The last relationship
seemed primary, because of the role it played in Ōkuni's interpretation
of genesis and its centrality when compared to the creation deities. It is
significant that he paired the word *tame*—"for," "on account of"—

with the central deity, who gave things "because of." He enlisted the example of the gift of rice to the Japanese people to explain the coupling between the word *tame* and the deity Ame no minakanushi no kami. "People born in Japan," he wrote, "will consider the way of Japan. By this, they should know that this country's rice is superior [over that of other rice-producing countries]. Rice is what people eat and what pulls the heart of man to heaven. We Japanese eat rice regularly, and it is because of this that we should excel all other countries in the truth of loyalty, filiality, and constancy" (HA, 412). As a heavenly gift, rice symbolized an exchange between deity and human and secured the relationship between sound and shape for all time to come. Rice constantly reminded people of such harmonies in the world of the present.

The word *to* meant "place" and referred to the place on which humans stood erect (*tatsu*). But it was also the place where rice grew. *Emi* (smile, man, mouth) called forth the cracking open of the rice seedlings, as they are brought before the eye. The rice, once seen, was put into the mouth, chewed, and passed into the stomach. Ōkuni then followed the itinerary of the ingested rice, as if trailing the traces of divinity itself, to its ultimate destination. Rice nourished the body, and its wastes were returned to the land. "The grain is *for* [*tame*] man; the wastes [*kasu*] are *for* the subsequent growth of rice" (ibid., 414). *Tame* also occupied a central position in the process leading to the formation of community. At birth, men were made to discover their dependence on *tame* (and, thus, deity), and they devoted themselves to learning how to perform deeds that bound them to the world of things and other people. In the *Shinri ikansho* (book 3), Ōkuni tried to explain the integration of deity and principle (*ri*) by showing how harmony and union resulted from seeming opposites and differences. The operation required reducing things to basic equivalences that functioned interchangeably. Yet, his logic now insisted that some kind of binary opposition (which he never clarified) informed all things and made the world an endless series of complementarities. The relationship between convexity (*totsu*) and concavity (*ō*) exemplified this binary principle: "The earth is convex, the sun concave; settlement convex, fields and plains concave. . . . Within the concave, we find the convex and vice versa. . . . The peasant grows food, cuts trees, catches fish . . . in order to assist [other] men. To make things for man's utilization is convex power that assists man; to search for such exchange is concave power that means to be assisted by men" (OTz 5:188–201). Even the obvious and familiar oppositions, such as "rich people" and "poor folk," fitted as necessary complementary pairings (ibid. 5:199). Although the idea of harmony plainly commanded Ōkuni's gaze, he still relied on a more basic conception of human nature, which served as one of the principal themes in the construction of *hongaku*.

Despite the vast powers of *tame* to secure a condition of itself-for-others, nothing was ever accomplished without the mediation of personal intention. Evil people, Ōkuni announced, always made the body their only goal—that is, gratifying the body by satisfying its endless needs; therefore, they did things *for* themselves alone. But the good invariably made doing things *for* others (spouse, family, parents, lord) their principal purpose in life. "One must always consider things for human use, far and wide for the times [*Hiroku hito no (tame), yo no (tame) o omou mono nari*]."

In *Amatsu norito futo norito kō*, Ōkuni proposed that *to* also meant earth, the national soil (*kunitsuchi*); it denoted a place of entry—a threshold, door, gate, etc.—and a subsequent range of associations that signified acting for something outside of one's own body. The sacred/secular complementarity inscribed in the five sacred sounds/shapes showed that performance always served something outside the immediate needs of the performer. To speak, Ōkuni noted, called attention to others and their requirements; language usage was inconceivable without an addressee and a dialogic relationship. This model of relationship informed the behavior of humans, who must, by virtue of their humanity, assist others. Failure to make this connection resulted in both silence and selfishness. Here, he condemned Confucianism and Buddhism for confusing the self (*watakushi*) for the "we" (*ware*), consequently misrecognizing the selfishness of human desire as the purpose of *ware* (ibid. 1:339). *Ware*, defined as a concern for the collectivity, revealed its centrality (*naka*) and the meaning of assistance, doing *for*.

Ōkuni explained that *tame* meant "to do," and "its chief objective is to plan for all" (ibid. 7:163–64). It also disclosed the original intention of the creation and the decision of the deities to give things because of the existence of humans. This exchange between deity and human was mirrored in relationships among humans when they assisted one another. The word *tame*, then, provided the key to the real nature of man (*hito no michi*) because it conveyed two meanings simultaneously.

> If one uses Japanese, there are ten syllabic sounds; in Chinese, four ideographs. . . . First, in Japanese, we have *ai tasuku* [mutual assis-

tance] and *moto ni tsuku* [adhering to origins], while in Chinese it is written differently. The three values of loyalty [*chū*], filiality, [*kō*], and constancy (*tei*) specify the Way that adheres to basics, while work and propriety stand for mutual assistance. Internally, all must strive for loyalty, filiality, and constancy; externally, they must endeavor to work. One must never lose the sense of propriety, as both work and propriety are deeds of the body . . . and loyalty, filiality, and constancy, the virtues of the heart. . . . Even when they appear divided into two opposing values, they are, in truth, one and the same in the word *tame*. It [*tame*] represents a return to the middle Way. (*HA*, 414–15)

Changes in the destiny of Japan, introduced by the importation of foreign doctrine, had buried these aims, which had been first revealed to the people in the "ancient words" of prayer at the time of creation.

When Ōkuni described "mutual assistance" and "adhering to origins" as a return to the middle Way, he was proposing that fundamental teachings originating in the antique experience established a golden mean to regulate the conduct of people. The idea of the middle or centrality (*naka*) closely corresponded to his conception of a supreme deity, Ame no minakanushi no kami, the chief deity who dwelt in heaven, directed the cosmos, and produced the two creation gods. When Ōkuni turned to the claims of international law, late in the Tokugawa period, he envisaged Japan as a mediator, owing to its centrality among the countries of the globe. Yet this reformulation was merely an enlargement of a view that saw man—a creature of mutual assistance, a mediator—standing at the center of the universe and affirmed his superiority over all other forms of life because of his centrality in the world of things. In the earlier *Shinri ikansho*, man occupied a position between the world of things and the world of deities, and *naka* was what brought all things together in harmony and union: Japan and China and the West (*nishiguni*), lord and people, we and they, birds, beasts, insects, trees, and plant life (*OTz* 5:233). But at the same time that the conception of the middle appeared as a universal cement holding all things together, it also prescribed a program for performance by insisting that working *for* something or somebody outside of the self avoided differences and divisions, that is, a divided heart. Bonding harmonious conduct to the activity of the "ordinary folk"—to their "custom"—demanded defining a subject position with interests (*aohitogusa narae*) that authorized a new and important field of knowledge.

According to the belief that real knowledge pertained to people working for others—their customs, as Ōkuni put it—the evaluation of good and evil relied entirely on whether men left "their bodies open to the earth" or their intention to heaven. In another formulation, he asserted that, when humans "adhere to the fundamentals," they would be in a position to realize "mutual assistance" (*HA*, 420). Household duties and "productive" work best exemplified the way people assisted each other in an endless exchange of reciprocities. These exchanges constituted the source of meaning, which conventional interpretive strategies (Neo-Confucianism) had hitherto neglected. To extract meaning from this basic experience—this knowledge of the everyday—Ōkuni expanded his idea of the golden mean; he proposed that reciprocity depended on "adhering to fundamentals" and conveyed the sense of "men helping us" (ibid., 427). Although the idea of a mean belonged to the classic Chinese philosophy embodied in *Zhongyong*, its content had remained a lifeless abstraction since antiquity. Mutual assistance and reciprocity referred to concrete service to the community for itself. When peasants, for example, paid their yearly taxes, they were rendering assistance to the upper classes. But the upper classes could not expect the lower orders to assist them without offering reciprocal forms of help. Since the lower classes always feared theft, the rulers should work quickly to eliminate it (ibid., 427–28). Recalling the earlier admonitions of such writers as Mutobe Yoshika and Suzuki Shigetane, Ōkuni recommended eradicating anything that diverted the lower classes from their duties, such as burglary, gambling, excessive taxation (especially in bad years), official bribery, and speculation. Although he expressed concern for factors that undermined the execution of household duties (one's occupation) and diminished agricultural production, he also saw this discussion of meaning and reciprocity as the occasion to define the function of officials as people who mediate assistance between high and low (*Yakunin to iu mono no arite, kami yori o tasuke tamō waza o tasuke tatematsuri, shimo yori kami o tasuke tatematsuru waza mo tasukete*).

In reformulating the received idea of the "ordinary folk" (*aohito-gusa*), with its attendant will to interest and knowledge, Ōkuni found a way to combine convincingly his concern for the creation, and its consequence for community, with his views on class relations.[8] He specified the nature of learning: its subject—the ordinary folk, and the object of their interests—custom. We have seen how nativists restructured the received conception of human nature into a subjective, autonomous, and acting agent, who derived meaning from performing reciprocally. The earlier engagement of passion and emotionality as conditions of one's humanity opposed more formal Confucian efforts to diminish such qualities as personal selfishness, or to ignore them altogether, in any serious consideration of human purpose. Already in his notion of mutual assistance, Ōkuni had emphasized the importance of feeling for others and pursuing larger interests beyond oneself. Unquestionably, humans possessed the capacity to feel and to express emotional states. "A man who actively abandons his father, mother, wife, and children is a man without human feeling [*ninjō*]; even though he might possess the shape of a man, he is not" (*OTz* 1:315). In *Koden tsūryaku*, he asserted that people occupying the lower orders of society, "since they are the *aohitogusa*, know, from beginning to end, the profundity of feeling and passion, while those who have not yet learned about the ordinary people [do not know]" (ibid. 7:79). Although he stopped short of proposing that only the lower classes understood the passions of life, he was certain that, until his day, no one had considered that they understood them at all. To realize genuine passion required knowing reciprocity towards others and acquiring a knowledge that constituted its own interests. As a result, he reformulated "ordinariness" to convey associations of human sociality and equated its preservation with the *necessity of interest*. Once the act of "mutual assistance" was supplied with compassion (*awaremi*), status seemed less important than the capacity to express human feeling for others. Basic humanity, defined now as compassion, displaced hierarchy, an unnatural social construct, for a new system of valuation to classify people. Ōkuni's decision to concentrate on the fundamentals of being human, before class or status distinctions, directed discourse toward the ordinary folk and toward imagining new criteria for organizing the social that would inevitably challenge privileged rank.

Ideas of creation and birth, *musubi* and *musu*, play a significant role in Ōkuni's discussions of the ordinary folk. Etymologically, the term *musubu*, designating the creation deities, orginally meant "blending parts," "joining separations," and "gathering things that are separated." Additionally, "deities possessing the august name [suffix] signifying *musubi* have also been given the name of middle. . . . *Musubi*, then, gathers and unifies [things] in the middle" (ibid. 6:82–183). According to Ōkuni's reworking of these archaic words, harmony and the human necessity to act for others came to denote the activity of bringing things together and growing food for the sake of men. Joining things at the center was associated with events such as birth, growth, creativity, and productivity and consequently acquired a greater degree of specificity than it had in the thought of Motoori and Hirata. Whereas Hirata had employed *musu* and *musubi* to indicate the creative and life-giving powers identified with the two creation deities, Ōkuni acknowledged that the terms conveyed birth and production and added that they also carried the sense of people and things coming together. Coupling creation with the center, he produced the following formulary: "People are joined at the center because of the creation." In book 4 of the *Koden tsukai*, he discussed the central importance of community and showed how it consisted of men brought together at the center, a sentiment that came close to Hirata's conviction that the creation deities produced solely for the sake of the people. Writing in *Honkyō genmyo*, Hirata concluded: "The great intention of the creation deities was to give form to the national soil and, thus, bestow life and growth on the people. Indeed, the fact of creation itself and productivity was the chief aim and was, therefore, affixed to the divine virtue of creation [union; *Kunitsuchi o nashikatameyo to miyosashitamō. sono wa hitokusa o ikisodatsushi tamawan to no ōmikokoro nite, sanseisan koto o sen to musubi no shintoku o fuzokushi tamaeru ni zo arikeri*]" (*HAz* [rev] 8:103).

Even if Ōkuni's conception of the *aohitogusa* relied on Hirata's earlier formulations, it is vital to grasp the meaning he gave it and the function it played in organizing a field of native knowledge. Hirata had made scattered references to the *aohitogusa* throughout his writings, especially in passages concerned with the *musubi no kami* and the creation. But only in a few places, like the incomplete *Shintō genmyo* (1820s?), did he specify a coupling of "customs of the *kami*" or "learning about the *kami*" to the condition of "learning about the people." In this short essay, Hirata spoke of the familiar division between visible and invisible, the allotment of functions to the two realms, and the respective political responsibilities of each. He acknowledged that the "great accomplishments" bestowed by the creation deities had been to create the cosmos and, through Izanagi and Izanami, to give shape to the national land and birth to the people. Their acts, he continued, have preserved the intention of the primal *kami*. With the separation of realms after the creation, the emperor assumed dominion over the visible realm and, through the divine ordination to govern (here, Hirata used the ideograph for "to know"), established a *matsuri*—the religious polity of the descendants of the heavenly deities. Hirata proclaimed that the heavenly deities would "conduct the people in conformity to the supports [*hashira*] of the heart." In the hidden realm, there had been a constant endeavor to realize the deeds of be-

nevolence, mercy (*utsukushimi, jinai*), and charity in the Way of the
gods. Giving to this realm followed the "august steps of Ōkuninushi no
kami." According to the character with which the *kami* had endowed
each person, no one should ever go beyond what he or she was. Hirata
explained that such behavior "satisfied the aim of the ancient words
kami narae (*kami* custom). As seen first in the *Book on the Ōjin
Emperor*, 'Formerly in the past, one who knows the customs of the
gods will know about the ordinary people and the facts of the times'"
(ibid., 8:98).

Hirata used the term *aohitogusa* to preserve its organic associations and to secure an identity of people, luxuriant growth, and the
general creation. Knowledge about the gods—their "custom"—meant
the creation; it easily merged with knowing about the people, who inhabited the land and without whom the creation would be meaningless
and the "talk about ruling the realm, useless." The times, he advised,
must always be viewed from the perspective of the ordinary people
(*bonjin; HAz* [old] 4:15; [new] 6:9). Ōkuni accepted this interpretation
and extended the range of its associations by adding mutual assistance
and "relief" (*sukuu*) as conditions for knowing about the people. Very
early in his writings, he had raised the issue of the *aohitogusa* and the
necessity of making their lives the subject of knowledge. Throughout
the 1850s, perhaps the most prolific time of his life, this issue appeared
regularly in his texts, as if prompted by some sort of special urgency. In
the *Yamatogokoro*, he wrote that the human species (*hito no tane*) was
divided into two parts:

> According to ancient traditions from China, these parts are called the
> large, or great, men and the small men. But, in our ancient words, the
> two parts are divided into *kami* learning and learning about the *aohito-
> gusa*. As for *kami narau*, the ideograph for deity is such that it conveys
> the character of upper [*mata kami o atsuru kami nite*], and refers to the
> great men and lords recognized by the Chinese tradition. *Aohitogusa* are
> the small people [perhaps "mean people," here] designated by the Chi-
> nese. *Narau* is really learning. When one learns about the deities, even
> a small person will be transformed into a lord, a great man; and, when
> the lord and great man learns about the ordinary people, he will come
> to resemble the folk. This is the great doctrine of our country. (*OTz*
> 3:18, 43)

Reference to the small people was not necessarily pejorative, because
he was undoubtedly calling attention to the mass of commoners. But,

by arguing that they, the ordinary folk, now required study because of their identity of interests with the gods, he was clearly saying that the real differences between high and low originated only in imperfect knowledge and "distorted communication."

Very early in his career, then, Ōkuni engaged the problem of developing a discourse that would permit a serious consideration of the ordinary folk. Utilizing a method that considered status divisions unnatural categories produced by misunderstanding and ignorance, he attempted to show that such differentiations derived from the Chinese need to establish arbitrary distinctions between ruler and ruled in order to maintain political order. Since Japanese history had happily escaped the cycle of usurpation, with the subsequent necessity to represent it as the manifestation of moral principle, the way was now open to reinstate the natural categories of high and low that had attended the creation. In his explanation, the deities claimed the upper rank, while the rest of mankind occupied the lower order. Ōkuni recognized that, within the human species—now called the "ordinary folk"—differences would always exist as forms of social convention, but they paled before the greater truth that all were human. This is what he meant when he recommended "knowledge of the deities." If people learned about the deities, if they "imitated" their creators, they would understand that the creation and the informing divine intention were motivated to make the earth the place of human habitation. No real difference between high and low marked the divine plan of creation; since gods and folk shared a partnership from the beginning, knowledge of the former could only lead to learning about the latter, and vice versa. This arrangement explicitly eliminated the sharp differentiation between ruler and ruled; it revealed, in the context of the 1860s, how Ōkuni had maneuvered to displace the perceived differences between social classes, necessitated by politics, and their consequences for order.

As a hedge against the political conflict, Ōkuni proposed that the status of the ordinary folk was equivalent to service to the heavenly deities. In a passage from the *Man'yōshū*, quoted earlier and often by Ikuta Yorozu, he announced that wherever people went, on the sea, mountains, or plains, they should be willing to give their lives to the emperor (*Umi yukaba mitsuku kabane. Yama yukaba kusa musu kabane. Ōkimi no he ni koso shiname. Kaeri miwaseji nodo ni wa shinaji*). Its sentiment, he remarked, informed the "intent behind the learning of the ordinary people" (ibid. 3:19). But, far from authorizing a one-sided devotion from the lower orders toward the ruling class as a form of involuntary submission, as imagined by later interpreters, Ōkuni's insistence on reciprocity demanded a two-way relationship. Under the moderating influence of assistance, the conventional divisions within society give way to interest in harmony and unity. "Formerly," he stated, "signifying the *aohitogusa* happened [to belong to] the august doctrine of *kami* customs" (ibid.). Reciprocity eradicated the difference between social groups because of the principle of base and ends. The lord represented the base, and one's body conformed to the end; parents constituted the base, and one's self became the end. When observing the self—"our bodies"—he explained, we find the end in any reciprocal relationship. Recent reports had attested to a reversal in this relationship, and the ordinary folk had turned their attention away from lord and parent to their own bodies. Evidence for this reversal of base/ends appeared everywhere in the pursuit of pleasure and the corresponding neglect of household duties (work). The shift was manifested dramatically in an excessive lust for life and a genuine fear of death. Yet the original doctrine, calling attention to the ordinary folk, expected people to die willingly for their sovereign.

What Ōkuni envisioned for the contemporary context was an entirely new social imaginary, which accommodated differences in character rather than distinctions mandated by social status. Although status remained locked into maintaining permanent power relations, character attested to the changeability of people and the possibility of transforming "great men" into "mean men," and vice versa. The major division among people corresponded to the separation between those who feared and disliked death and those who remained unconcerned. Nothing was greater or more noble than the man who never thought about his own safety and death. If people chose to forget their own bodies—desire—and ceased acting out of personal self-interest, they would realize a change from one status to another. "To dislike death expresses our selfishness [*waga watakushi*]. When people willingly oppose one another, then they are unwilling to 'die' for the public [interest; *ōyake*]. But if small men are not limited by a dislike for death and by personal concerns, then they will know [the meaning of] death" (ibid. 3:20). Only character accounted for the real divisions between great and small. The small invariably forgot their duties, attaching "themselves to their families, fields and houses, and personal treasures." The problem facing the folk was how to overcome the "attachments that bind one to selfishness" in order to become "great." In another text, he condemned the ruling classes for their willingness to become addicted to "beautiful concubines" and "elegant finery," their inordinate concerns for the luxuries of life, and their failure to understand the substance of feeling rather than just its form and its design (*kazari*). At the same time, he warned the lower classes against imitating upper-class habits and advised them "to learn well the customs of the *kami*" (ibid. 7:79–80). Public activity emerged from the most basic "household duties" and "work," in order to carry out "mutual assistance" and "relief." Character meant "making the lord the base" and contrasted with traditional Chinese convention, which ostensibly "made the people [*tami*] the base" (ibid. 3:130–31). We know that Ōkuni was no longer referring to simple hierarchical distinctions. People could change their character; the lord could become mean, and the small person a lord. The realization of the powers and transformative dimensions of character illuminated the surest way to overcome conflict and avoid discord.

Nativism seemed obsessed with the problem of conflict and harmony. Perhaps it represented an exaggeration of real circumstances and, therefore, a sanction for ideological claims enjoining the lower classes to work harder. But, historical reports are nothing, if not exaggerations of some kind or other. Despite the obvious ideological function we can tease out of nativist meditations on work and productivity, it would be wrong either to dismiss the effort to overcome division and fragmentation as unimportant or to trivialize the calls for community as simply an ideological dissimulation. Although it is true that nativists possessed the epistemological means to apprehend certain events as manifestations of difference and division, it would be incorrect to conclude from this that what they described was mere illusion. Their explanations were necessary to restore to the world the harmony of similitude that they believed had been lost since the eighteenth century. Ōkuni was really no exception to this project, and his writings, especially in the 1850s, attested to his conviction that life had to be reconstituted along more humanly communitarian lines. At the time, such an observation was not particularly exceptional, since *kokugakusha* shared with the founders of several new, syncretic religions the belief that the principle for binding people together could only be found in the genuinely human impulse to help others. Men were still men, Ōkuni wrote in *Honkyō shinri setsu*, despite their different appearances; therefore, they were fundamentally similar because of the humanity they shared (ibid. 5:32–33). To know about the deities was the only way the ordinary people—humans—would know how to install a truly human community in their time.

Man stood between the world of deities and the world of things. Yet all were linked in "mutual concern," which was the great intention of the creation gods (ibid. 5:54–55). Things were good only when they submitted to the intention of gods, bad when they went against it. The optimal good occurred when *kami*, humans, and things were involved in mutual assistance; evil appeared when they injured each other (*aisokonau*). Ōkuni believed that men must always conform to the fundamentals of human community, which meant helping others in the common effort to live as humans, because these basic principles "teach all men the blessings of the ends." Assistance showed each the only possible course for life. "The deeds of the deities join the base to the ends" (ibid. 5:37). When the folk actualized the divine intention correctly, they would find the way to establish a genuinely human community. Expanding on Hirata's earlier humanization of deity, Ōkuni saw man/god the measure of all things. "Men occupy the middle ground between the gods and things," he wrote, "when they face the top, they worship the deities, and when they turn to the bottom [things], they bring out the character of things [*Hito wa kami to mono to no naka ni orite, kami wa kami o matsuri shimo wa mono no saga o togushimubeki mono ni nan*]" (ibid. 5:44–47). Humans celebrated the gods to receive their continuing blessings in the world which enabled them to bring the nature of things to their realization. To bring things to their realization meant providing food, clothing, and shelter out of the stuff and substance of the natural resources granted by the gods. The actual bringing of things to realization was the objective of work. Here, Ōkuni transformed reproduction from a private household duty to a public necessity. The "end" represented the finished product; work served as the agency or means. His conception established the conditions of community and made the continual reproduction of the social modes of existence a public and collective enterprise. In addition, Ōkuni contributed another meaning to Shinto by equating it, as a natural religion, with the common necessity of bringing things to their realization.

If social failure was manifest in difference and fragmentation, then devising a conception of humanity involved eliminating the spectacle of both. Ōkuni proposed a new form of learning that would show how the folk could be ennobled if they knew their own interest and returned to the teachings of the *kami*. He believed that by persuading them to shift their concerns from the self to the relief and assistance of others, he had found a way to transform all people into the "heart of a noble" (ibid. 5:236–38). But, he was quick to warn, men who had been ennobled merely by the status system thought only of preserving things, and "lack the heart that assists and relieves." Ordinariness had lost its real and original meaning under the bewitching influence of Confucianism and Buddhism, and people had been induced to forget that it had once been associated with the teaching of the deities. Once the "customs of the ordinary folk" were reunited with the "learning of the gods" as specified in the ancient texts, the present would have the chance to recover the true meaning of humanity. The consequences of this argument were radical, because Ōkuni was trying to dissolve social difference—the cold, impersonal status lines regulating Tokugawa Japan—and introduce "hot" relationships determined by mutuality, reciprocity, and affection toward others. In place of a society mediated by status, Ōkuni imagined a community of affection pledged to the collective reproduction of the necessary means for social existence. By making reproduction, originally tied to household duties, the principal determinant of the social and by bringing people together, Ōkuni successfully transformed the realm of private intimacy into the public sphere of interest. The very duties necessitating the household's survival now became the imperative of the social collectivity. In one broadly arched gesture, his nativism transmuted a contemporary dystopia into an arcadian utopia.

If men differed from the animal kingdom, it was because their nature disposed them to help others (ibid. 5:259). This inherent humanity proceeded from the act of creation itself. Just as the gods had given humans the necessities of life, so humans had no choice other than to extend assistance to others in times of hardship and distress; and this is what the ancients meant by the phrase "to learn the custom of the gods is to learn the custom of the ordinary folk" (ibid. 5:276). Ōkuni explained that the deities in heaven were dispatched to earth to intercede for the ordinary folk, and they immediately "discerned well the understanding between man and things and therefore preserved these distinctions." But people failed to grasp these distinctions—their true interests; now, denied the Way, they urgently required correct instruction. The purpose of doctrine was to make people similar, as they had been at the time of the creation.

> When the ordinary folk learn about what is elevated, [the gods] will, by themselves, elevate their own hearts [intention]. Even their bodies will come to stand at an elevated level. Among those who stand above learning about the ordinary people, their hearts, too, will be lowered to the

level of the folk. Even their bodies will be . . . lowered to the level of
the ordinary folk. If, then, one imitates the patterns of the deities carefully, one will become a good person; if one learns them badly, he will
become an audacious person. (Ibid. 5:278)

In another place, Ōkuni advised that, when the folk preserved the teachings of the gods well, they would—regardless of their humble status as
ordinary folk—equal the divine descendants who had been sent to earth
from heaven. And "when these doctrines are preserved, even the heavenly descendants will be lowered to the level of the ordinary people"
(ibid. 1:309). Because the formula *kami narae* appeared everywhere in
the ancient texts but had been forgotten since those remote times, "it
is a good time to consider the occurrence of divine learning." Here,
Ōkuni infused contemporary meaning into the archaic phrase, defamiliarizing it, by arguing that the word *kami* contained the homonymic association of high and upper and as a result, referred to the
ruling class. In the *Bunsei kyojitsuron*, he noted that *kami* (deity) and
kami (upper) had the same pronunciation. Since they did, learning
about the deities equaled learning about the truly elevated and manifested the truth that "upper designates the blessings of the people as the
great treasure of the land. In learning this, one will come to know that
humans relieve and assist other humans" (ibid. 1:313).

Conventional distinctions must be rearranged according to a new
catalogue because "men must learn about the high." They must not
learn to be like the upper classes in body—that is, they must not merely
emulate the status of the upper classes. "They ought to learn about
what is elevated and corrects the heart; they must never consider that
body alone is at the top. They must learn about the ordinary folk, but
they must avoid being like the ordinary people [of today]" (ibid. 5:282).
In another text, he advised that human desire must be reunited with
the desire of the gods. Indeed, the "customs" of the *kami* were identical
to the "desire of the deities" (ibid. 2:310–11). When men assisted
other men, they were expressing the deeds of the gods (ibid. 1:305).
This bonding of godly deeds to human nature, at the heart of Ōkuni's
thoughts about politics leading to a community of interests, satisfied
the logic of a strategy that imagined the project of creation as a blessing
for humans and reciprocity as a gift exchange.

In the present, only ordinary people failed to make the fundamentals their chief objective (ibid. 1:312–14). When those who made
it their business to be informed about the ordinary people discovered

how they had elevated personal willfulness, laziness, and desire in their lives, they would be moved to compassion. They would also learn that the ordinary folk had not conformed to the ancestral instructions nor "listened to the practicum of loyalty." By failing to accept the archaic precedent, the present diminished its chances for realizing peace and tranquillity (ibid. 1:314). In his times, Ōkuni noted, the prospects for a revival were promising, as there were already several lords who had begun to make an effort to "learn about the people" and who must, as a result, be considered by all as "our strength." Henceforth, it should be the intention of the upper orders (the *kami*) "to make us good," just as it was a necessity to apply the august doctrine that held, "To learn of the deities is to learn of the ordinary people" (ibid.).

The equation of divine patterns and human purpose had profound consequences for nativist political theory and the problem of historical consciousness. We might recall that Hirata had given forceful testimony to a conception of political community that posed serious questions for the problem of historical awareness. The metonymic emphasis on contiguous relationships—on sequences, not process (Ōkuni's major breaks)—and the search for genesis put the question of history squarely in the service of political community. The location of the sources of social cohesion would determine the conditions under which history (life) might be apprehended. In nativist discourse, the creation deities had replaced Ogyū Sorai's archetypal kings in order to explain the beginnings of the universe and the Way that men were supposed to follow. Yet this substitution ultimately robbed nativists of any claim to universality, despite the fact that the principles they enunciated were often the same as those promoted by theorists of political economy (*keisei saimin*). More than most, Ōkuni tried to broaden the claims founded on the basis of particularistic deities and experience; he tried, for example, to raise Ame no minakanushi no kami to the status of a universal deity. His late-Tokugawa essay on international law (*Shinshin Kōhōron*) tried to demonstrate how the centrality of the realm and its deities made Japan superior to all other nations. But his explanation of superiority rested on particularity and uniqueness, not on values that might be obtained by all people in all times. He proposed that Shinto could be understood by all nations as the basis of a truly international order. Unfortunately, he was betrayed by the powerful historicist and particularistic underpinnings of *kokugaku*: its appeal to creation was meant to serve not humanity in general but Japan and the Japanese alone. The interests specifying the cultural order were local; the inhabitants were Japanese, not the whole of the human species. Despite his effort, no doubt inspired by his encounter with Western legal and political theory, to universalize an experience intimately rooted in particularized custom (which was celebrated as true knowledge and the divine appointment of the race), Ōkuni failed to make nativism the fundamental discipline for all peoples. His effort to dissolve difference opened the way for a valorization of sameness, whose force depended on a logic of racial and cultural exceptionalism.

It was precisely this exceptionalist experience, elevating the claims of culturally specific custom, that determined the character of nativist politics and history. Although its theory of human purpose upheld values such as mutuality and reciprocity, they were bound to the particular deeds of the deities (ibid. 2:305). Because Ōkuni was concerned with essentials rather than form, his political views concentrated on explaining the sources of community and authority rather than their temporal manifestations.

Consequently, his writings emphasized the genesis of community in the creation rather than the forms of political activity. This is not to say that he minimized the forms of temporal political activity but only that he called attention to the prior importance of the authorization of politics, which in his thinking, was the social solidarity of the community. Following Hirata, Ōkuni drove home the point that the community existed before the establishment of political structure dispensing authoritative decisions. Political forms would not have been possible without the identification of the divine intention and the human purpose. Hirata, it should be recalled, had already announced that ruling would be pointless if there were no people (*aohitogusa*) to rule. Now, Ōkuni pushed this argument further to conclude that whatever happened was the result of the deeds of the *kami*. "Although the true heart of the realm was buried for twelve hundred years, since the time of the reign of Empress Suiko, it is the work of the gods that it has reappeared." The term he used to denote gods (*kami*) in phonetic script was written with the ideograph meaning creator (*zōbutsushu*; ibid. 5:84). Everything, then, resulted from the activity of the deities. History was simply the product of the "plan of the *kami*" (*kami hakari*) or the consequence of their calculations. Time was not successive nor even progressive, but merely a discontinuous series of sequences. The sequences were made possible by experience and custom, formed by human praxis and guided by new knowledge to reproduce the conditions of creation. But it was the creation deities, he wrote in *Honkyō shinri setsu*, "who have determined the enterprises of humans, which have been linked to [the world of] things" (ibid. 5:47). Politically, the movement and the changes of the ages followed the deeds of all the deities. Whether or not the contemporary system changed depended on the plan of the gods (ibid. 5:275). Although the current system, in which the emperor conferred rank on the several lords and the shogun set about dividing land, was a good one, there was no good reason to suppose that the "present-day system is one for eternity" (ibid.). The specific form of governance was matchless in its performance, he declared, but it was still only a form. Ōkuni accepted the possibility of favoring one system over another, but he revealed a preference for feudalism over the Chinese-style centralized polity (*gunken*) that had prevailed in Japan's middle ages. He based his choice on the observable failure of the *gunken* system, which "without fail has inflicted hardship upon the lower classes," while feudalism, although difficult to establish, had resulted in the way things were. He remained silent on the status of contemporary political affairs as administered by the Tokugawa order, but the context of these passages suggests only limited approval. More important, however, was his conviction that such forms owed less to the "plan of the deities" than to the customs of men. The actual character of any political order rested on the specific experiences and events of the times, and, to prove the point, he cited the example of Tokugawa Ieyasu, whose personal efforts brought forth the feudal system. The actual performance of a regime relied on human agency, and its record of political success or failure represented the interplay between good and bad custom.

This juxtaposition of divine deed and human experience, or custom, raised a paradox. To consider that politics—or, indeed, whatever happened—stemmed from the activity of the gods was, of course, to reassert the classic nativist principle formulated first by Motoori, who employed the puppeteer/puppet metaphor to describe the way things occurred. At the same time, however, Ōkuni was convinced that the political performance of any age depended on human competence. In the *Hongaku kyoyō*, when he asserted that even the rise and fall of regimes represented the "divine planning of the two ancestral deities of the emperor," he was proposing that even political failure constituted an instance of the divine plan. But throughout his texts, he stressed the existence and agency of custom—experience—and insisted on relating its meaning to the phrase *aohitogusa narau na*. This conception referred to the customs of the people, which originally followed the pattern of divine intention. Good custom really meant conforming to the archetypal model, exemplified by the yoking of divine custom to the custom of the ordinary people. What people learned from the *kami* in order to form custom was "adherence to the fundamentals" and the provision of "relief and mutual assistance." Ōkuni's appeal to the ancient formulary was not prompted simply by the necessity to demonstrate the primacy of custom, even though much of nativism since Hirata had been propelled by this consideration. He meant to show that, originally, there were gods who created the land and people who returned thanks by bringing things to their realization. Social solidarity was achieved because people worked and behaved in strict observance of the pattern of the *kami*.

Ōkuni was aware of changes over time. We have already shown how he sliced up time into momentous sequences brought on by the introduction of new learning. But time also represented the actions of humans as they intersected or, better yet, intercepted the "plan of the deities." "Human society [*ningen sekai*] is consolidated and dispersed," he wrote in the *Koden tsūryaku*, and "it is broken up and reconsolidated. This is called impersonal destiny [*kiun*]" (*OTz* 6:191).[9] This notion explained the rise and fall of political regimes and the belief that, when things rose they would inevitably fall, and once down, they would rise up again (*kabusu*). In politics, the destiny leading to consolidation (*atsumaru*)—that is, sociality—required human effort. Not even the intervention of the gods could secure unified social life, if humans failed to perform.[10] Thus, political fortune and misfortune could be attributed to human conduct and will and to the performance of the leaders. Yet, we know from the formulary on *kami* learning that such efforts had to match divine intention if they were to succeed. In the *Yamatogokoro* he asserted, "In this time, there should be an interdependence between the deeds of the deities and human effort [*Kore yo no naka wa, kami waza jinryoko to aimochi no yo no naka nari*]" (*OTz* 3:118).[11] His advice was to implement some sort of program promising a return to an antique political ideal, in which governance responded to its sacred entrustment. The leaders must view things from the perspective of the ordinary people to retrieve the obligations that had been abandoned. Changes in historical destiny represented instances when socialness was either established or abolished, and he had no trouble declaring that Emperor Jinmu's reign signaled a change (*kabusu*) in the historical destiny of the realm (*OTz* 1:226).[12] Ōkuninushi no kami's accomplishment, which made the earth habitable for humans, had marked another such change. The vision of community that informed his theory of sequential changes made it a rather crude philosophy of history. He believed the country's history began with Emperor Jinmu. But Jinmu was also important because he established feudalism as the form for political activity. "Emperor Jinmu," he wrote, "ruled by virtue of a change in destiny [*kiun ni kabusu to iu koto no aru koto no shiroshimeshi*]: he divided and distributed the land among his retainers and did not begrudge them [anything]. Moreover, he was neither arrogant nor luxurious in his style. He made frugality his chief aim because he feared the possibility of change."[13] After Shōtoku taishi, rulers began to "begrudge retainers land," and wealth was gradually concentrated in the hands of the imperial court. Such a trend led to vast and dangerous changes. "Once more dissent developed, and the changes it caused have inadvertently reached down to the present." In brief, Ōkuni celebrated Jinmu's reign because it conformed to his conception of what constituted the social life. Jinmu began the feudal system, whereas successive descendants introduced private interest and contributed to the erosion of society. Ironically, feudalism was identified with the public interest and with the impulse providing mutual assistance and relief, while the *gunken* system was seen to promote privatism and selfishness.

In this discussion, Ōkuni specified his views regarding the imperial office. Throughout nativist discourse, the emperor appeared as a figure of absolute political authority, yet it is hard to square this assumption with much of nativist thinking. Nativists were inclined to juxtapose the hidden governance of Ōkuninushi to the visible world of the emperor (Sumera no mikoto) and his descendants. They seemed to rank the former above the latter and to see the visible world as a function of invisible governance. Despite their apparent valorization of the continuity of the imperial line and the necessity to fulfill all obligations to the imperial position, such behavior was, in fact, intended to satisfy the requirements of the invisible realm. Along with many contemporaries, Ōkuni saw the imperial office as secondary in significance to the creation deities and the community, as his theory of sequences and change and his opinions concerning Jinmu demonstrated. If we remember that he believed that history and destiny were marked by people either "coming together" or "breaking apart," then the notion of people banding together manifested an idea of solidarity because of its synonymy with creating the land. Feudalism, he believed, best represented this ideal of "assemblage," while a centralized bureaucracy promised "scattering": a foreshadowing of the early-Meiji debate over the relative merits of the two and of the later ethnologic attack on Meiji bureaucratism. Change, the principle of *kabusu*, specifically meant one thing overtaken by another; it showed how the leadership might shape destiny by ruling in accordance with unselfish ideals. Yet destiny could assure the opposite consequences, if the leadership decided to act in its own interests. Ōkuni showed rather concretely how the emperor—far from acting as an absolute and autonomous political agent (as imagined by Meiji theorists to authenticate their conception of bureaucracy)—was really hemmed in by the ordinances of the creation deities and the requirements of learning about the ordinary people. Interestingly, the "people's emperor" of early-Meiji rebels like Etō Shinpei and Saigō Takamori and of later-twentieth-century would-be restorationists was closer to this image than the absolute construct of the Meiji constitution. In the *Bunsei kyojitsuron*, Ōkuni explained that the emperor had always obeyed and respected the imperial office. He meant that the emperor had not been permitted to transfer or hand over the office to retainers, "even the *kabane*, to whom he is related." But, he continued, "when there is no imperial heir to succeed to the office, then it is necessary to make an exception to the rule. The ordinances of the deities are external and the imperial office is pledged to preserve them for all times to come and is bound by them" (*OTz* 1:226).[14] Action undertaken by the emperor was always restricted by the ordinances of the imperial ancestors. The emperor was not granted the absolute authority of discretionary powers from these heavenly ancestors—the creation deities—but, rather, he followed their injunctions faithfully and had his demeanor reflected among his retainers.[15] Hence, the emperor served to remind the community, which was coeval with creation, of its divine obligations.

Ōkuni made this argument more explicit when he discussed the frequency of political failure in Japan's history. Even the emperor was susceptible to criticism. "Among the emperors throughout the ages, those who have been arrogant have not had flourishing and prosperous reigns. They have entrusted their rule to retainers. But those who have protected their position well have known brilliant reigns" (*OTz* 1:92–93). Clearly, the emperor was not the awesome, absolute figure fictionalized later; he had to account for his actions to the ordinances of the creation deities on one side and to the community on the other. When the emperor acted out of subjective will, arbitrarily and "privately," he opened the way for momentous and destructive changes—for "breaking apart"—as the history of the *gunken* system illustrated. But when a monarch refrained from "haughtiness and extravagance, entrusts governance [*matsurigoto*] to military families . . . when great and small lords do not shirk from preparedness, and when they love the peasantry and the merchant class as the great treasures of the land . . . the present will experience a glorious reign" (ibid. 1:378).[16]

Poetic Knowledge and Politics

Ōkuni Takamasa's understanding of proper political procedure depended on knowledge concerning the *aohitogusa* and the plan of the deities. On the other hand, Tomobayashi Mitsuhira's coupling of poetic learning and Shinto sanctioned action without apparent political self-interest.[17] Tomobayashi sought to establish the conditions of purity in the political circumstances of the 1860s by reinstating the poetic tradition of Kamo no Mabuchi and his teacher, Ban Tomoyuki. Part of this purity, which involved a distancing from the "polluting" world of contemporary political practice, stemmed, no doubt, from Tomobayashi's intense Buddhist affiliation, yet much of it was inspired by his commitment to nativist theories of poetics. He believed that poetic knowledge alone revealed the true meaning of Shinto and that its method would thoroughly "cleanse and purify the heart." He dramatized this conception of purity first as a teacher in several regions and then as an activist. He participated in the ill-fated uprising of the Tenchūgumi at Yamato Gojō in 1862; he was apprehended and, two years later, executed in Rokkaku Prison in Kyoto.[18] His passion for poetry merged with an interest in contemporary political possibility to produce commitment and action. The importance of Tomobayashi's program lay in his attempt to revivify the poetic tradition of Motoori as a guide to the current situation. As a result, his efforts must be read as a measure aimed at depoliticizing contemporary action and ridding *kokugaku* of its inordinate reliance on abstract theorizing and the representational power of signs rather than things.

When Ōkuni Takamasa transmuted the nativist narrative of origins and reproduction into a philosophy of history that privileged an "eventless" experience, he intended to sublate the contradiction between a "local knowledge" (particularism) and its broader applicability, between basic studies founded on the timeless necessity to recuperate the creation (interest) and the authority of a "scientific" discipline. Ōkuni's project was bound to fail; eventually it dissolved into the shallow sanctions that buttressed the proclamations of jingoists bent upon imposing Japan's "centrality." But his move to accommodate the discourse to the newly encountered international environment revealed different pressures and limits from those that had originally functioned as nativism's principle of determination. Ōkuni's perception of this new context led to an expansive intervention and a systematic effort to disciplinize new-found interests into a "rational" field of knowledge. But his solution relied too heavily on the requirement to dispel difference in order to recover similitude; it was too closely linked to the way a historically specific circumstance was encoded. Once this strategy was applied to determine Japan's place in a wider world, it could only transpose the terms of difference—and, thus, the locus of the Other—from China to the West. In this relationship, sameness summoned all that was genuinely Japanese and, hence, superior to what was now misrecognized as different and Other. This ideology of cultural exceptionalism was ultimately appropriated by imperialists and the *homo economicus*; in the middle of the nineteenth century, it established closure in the nativist discourse and prevented the dialectic between identity and difference that had characterized the *kokugaku* of Kamo and Motoori. Ōkuni, following Hirata, attempted to organize nativist intelligence into a comprehensive discipline called *hongaku*, whose authority rested on a natural relationship between the folk and the gods, between divine interest and human knowledge of it. But both interest and the knowledge constituted on it were more Japanese than human. Closure meant that only the Japanese, deriving from the national deities their duties to reproduce the conditions of life in a specific social space, were in a position to know this exceptional knowledge, to grasp it through the activities of their bodies—through the agency of the Japanese language (*kotodama*) and through work (worship) pledged to fulfill the sacred trust. Hirata's dismissal of poetry undermined and Ōkuni's disciplinization of "basic studies" eliminated the possibility of either antiphony or polyphony for nativism.

To forestall this closure or at least modify its demands, it was necessary to reinstate a space for poetics in the nativist discourse by returning epistemology back to metaphor. The effort to do so was best exemplified by Tomobayashi Mitsuhira, who tried to revitalize an earlier *kokugaku* in order to contest the established signs of a knowledge of sameness. He "rediscovered" deeper, buried kinships between things so to hear a submerged and forgotten discourse and, hence, to "recall the time when words glittered" in their resemblance to the world of things.[19] To lay claim to a discourse promising a disclosure of a still-deeper kinship of things meant to recover a poetic knowledge prior to

signs. The poet became the knower who possessed a knowledge superior to the mere relationship between signs. He saw not signs (*kotoba*)
but things (*mono*) and heard that "other language" of sameness, without either words or discourse.[20] The return to the immediacy of *mono
no aware*, derived from a time when there was still the opportunity for
the subject to appear fully present to itself in a signified without a signifier, to achieve the status of being represented without the means of
representation—that is, in just being there—meant juxtaposing the
claims of privileged poetic knowledge to history.[21] The forceful re-
appearance of the poet in a discourse and culture steeped in representation and signs constitued what Foucault has called an "archaic sil-
houette," but it also called forth a powerful effort to contest the closure
that the historical narrative and its easy substitution of signs for things
had established.

We must read Tomobayashi's text (thought and action) in relationship to Ōkuni's disciplinization of divine interest and folk knowledge
in the late-Tokugawa period. It would be wrong to see his intervention
as a lone, dissenting voice in late-Tokugawa *kokugaku*, because he represented a coherent tradition of thinking on poetics tracing back to
Ōhira, Norinaga, and Kamo. Yet the contesting power of his particular
attempt to valorize immediacy and presence and, by extension, poetics
itself, became meaningful only in contrast to the closure demanded by
history as an act of enunciation.[22] A search for a poetic space was accompanied by an attempt to show that, even though experience was represented in language, it was not dependent on any means of representation in producing the represented.[23] Denying the means of representation
for the direct encounter with things drew attention to all representational forms—historical narrative and the disciplining of knowledge—
that were indistinguishable from the language they employed to produce
the represented. With Tomobayashi, language was once more turned
back to experience, which was prior to it, so that the enounced did not
appear as the mere result of the enunciation.

According to the *Kadō taii*, Tomobayashi was convinced that
transparency characterized language and constituted the condition attending the beginning of Japanese words (*TMz*, 189). Poetry became
the highest expression of "good voice." When poetry or song was good,
it had strength, purity, and elegance; there was no need to call it poetry
(ibid., 190). It followed that poetry, because of its transparence, was
really experience itself—"things as they are"—which reflected the purity and clarity of Japanese intention. And when things were as they
were, they were not trammeled by words. Experience remained outside

and prior to poetry; it avoided relying on the force of words and, rather, endowed them with power. Poetry was a spontaneous outpouring of feelings (*uta wa kokoro ni omou koto o machi mawarazu*), neither thought-out beforehand (*enryo sezu*) nor connected to rules and methods (ibid.). The essence of things as they were appeared in speech directly translated into poetry. In the *Kadō taii*, Tomobayashi proposed that good poetry—which had no need to be labeled poetry—declared its freedom from all conventions that obviated the act of enunciation. Far from being hindered (*todomarinaki*) by words, it was a transparent overlay reflecting the way things were. To this end, the poet took great pains to execute song. It was bad to manufacture (*koshiraeru*) elegance and worse to contrive stanzas and patterns. All that was necessary for the poet was to employ the basic sounds as they existed in the beginning, in order to bring out the "flower embedded in words."

In the time of the *Kokinshū*, Tomobayashi wrote, people relied inordinately on the rules governing poetic composition, detrimentally widening the disparity between emotion and expression (literally, the things that touched the heart were not arranged correctly). Because composition was chained to the manipulation of devices, it became "weak-boned" and "stylistically feminine" (ibid., 191).[24] Tomobayashi contrasted this femininity with the masculinity found in the *Man'yō* poems (first "identified" by Kamo no Mabuchi); he explained that it referred to a whole tradition of poetics that had carelessly submitted to conventions, methods, and figuration—rhetoric without calling it by name—and, therefore, to the forms of enunciation that obscured the way things were. Poetry of this kind was never able to rise above the level of mere representation. Accordingly, feminine style inadvertently revealed its dependence on the mediation of rhetoric, which prevented the direct and spontaneous outburst of emotionality. As the poems of the *Man'yōshū* showed, masculinity consistently eluded the snare of representational devices to give spontaneous and direct expression to the "heart that has been touched." Just as poetic production never needed "interrupting conventions," so action must be liberated from forethought and calculation. In place of this deformed and "feminine" tradition, Tomobayashi recommended bringing things as they were into a "straight line"—which meant dismissing the notion of poetry as mere imitation of experience for one that specified poetry as experience itself.

To grasp poetry from the perspective of experience rather than expression, he advised applying a method that "excavates purport, [intentionality], words, and tone," the deep structure of authentic composition. "Purport" meant "getting into the heart of the self" by the act of "seeing" and "hearing." "We should know," he remarked, "that everything can be recited in song." Since humans possessed a variety of aptitudes and appetites, it was not possible to fix only the things that one person liked and disliked as the standard of excellence. Rather, poetry consisted of reciting things that "all of us like," avoiding both logic and baseness. Antiquity produced a proliferation of beautiful words that could be grasped from archaic songs; by the same token, vulgar words, contrived words, trivial things, and fraudulence must always be eliminated. Finally, tone should exemplify a perfect correspondence between voice and stanza, for when it failed to, the "man who hears will not rejoice in the intention" (ibid., 190). Tone was a quality that designated such distinctions as "greatness and smallness," "heaviness and lightness," and "distance and nearness." When the intention of a person was aroused, the tones of the words appeared agitated and excited; but when intention was at rest, the words became gentle. Tomobayashi was convinced that a poetics that observed these requirements would transform "living things" into "active things" and mere recitation into living song.

Even so, he seems to have undermined his own position, since "words" and "tone" call attention to language as a material process of enunciation. Inadvertently, he acknowledged how difficult, if not impossible, it was to remove poetry from the ranks of representation so as to make it identical with experience (a problem that nativist linguists first noted). Accordingly, Tomobayashi recognized that poetry differed from life and had to rely on the "force of words" and qualities (called *shina*, material articles) to make necessary distinctions. More important, he argued that the poet should not "imitate men" (other people), even though by actualizing intent, word, and tone, they might have achieved the purity and transparence attending the beginnings of song in Japan (ibid., 192). Because the appropriate word and tone accounted for intention, he believed it possible to recite song "strongly," "clearly," and "elegantly," making it live and active; such an accomplishment was "following the intention of the deities." But the poet always fell short of divine expression because his songs were, at best, imitations that could never escape the forms of representation for emotion and feeling. Ironically, Tomobayashi was closer to the means of representation, especially as it had been used to construct a narrative and disciplinize knowledge, than he had imagined. His effort to contest closure resulted in supplying a supplement to it.

Tomobayashi's attempt to reinstate a poetics in the environment of late-Tokugawa political events may well have been prompted by the continuing struggle between those nativists who, with Hirata, promoted the ancient Way as a guide to the social life-world and those who carried on the tradition of Motoori Norinaga, equating *kokugaku* with poetic elegance. Yet this in-house struggle among *kokugakusha* failed to diminish Tomobayashi's conviction that the poetic expressiveness and the nonmimetic status of the real tradition of antiquity was still accessible. Poetry reminded the folk of the origins of heaven and earth; it had appeared at the same time as the creation. It was coterminous with both heaven and earth, he wrote in the *Sono no ike mizu*, and supplied the means whereby the deities gave expression to their innermost thoughts (*Kus*, 474). Tomobayashi acknowledged that he was not sure why poetry came into existence so early, but he was certain that it had. "Poetic recitation began," according to one of the prefaces of the *Kokinshū* which he called "true," "when Susanowo no mikoto reached Izumokuni, [where] he began to compose a thirty-one syllable poem." According to both the *Kojiki* and the *Nihonshoki*, Susanowo had been banished because of his large inventory of misdeeds:

> After this, the myriad deities deliberated on Susanowo no mikoto's transgressions [*tsumi toga*], submitted [a penalty of] a thousand tables of restitutive gifts, cut off his beard as well as the nails of his hands and feet, and finally drove him away. From heaven, he made his way to the Hi River in the land of Izumo; there, he heard somebody crying and decided to investigate it. [He found] an old couple and a beautiful maiden crying. Susanowo asked, "Who are you and why do you cry?" They answered, "We [the old man] have descended from the *kami* of the realm [*kuni tsukami*], my name is Ashinazuchi; my wife's name is Chinazuchi. This girl is our daughter and her name is Kushinada-hime. The reason we are crying is because, previously, we had eight daughters, and every year the Eight-Tailed Serpent has eaten one. We are crying because he will come again and eat this young woman." Susanowo replied, "If I [kill the serpent], will the young maiden serve me?" The old man answered, "She will serve to follow your decrees [*mikoto*]." From that point, the Storm God proceeded to devise a plan in order to slay the serpent . . . which he executed. . . . When he cut off the tails, he found in one a sword, which was called Kusanagi.

Susanowo looked for a place to build his palace in Izumo, Tomobayashi continued; he finally came upon a location that was known, even up to the present, as Suga. The deity was reputed to have said of the place, "My heart is refreshed [*Waga kokoro sugasugashi*]"; there he constructed his palace. When Susanowo built his palace at Suga, clouds rose to inspire the first Japanese poem (*waka*): "Many clouds rising around the many-fenced palace of Izumo; To receive my spouse I have made this many-fenced palace, that many-fenced palace [*Yagumo tatsu Izumo yaegaki tsuma gome ni yaegaki tsukuru sono yaegaki wo*]" (*Kus*, 475–77; see also *TMz*, 152–53).

For Tomobayashi, this archetypal event demonstrated that both poetic wisdom and poetic expressiveness began with the gods. That so obdurate and mischievous a deity as Susanowo had been the first to shape the poetic project suggested some interesting possibilities. Much of the nativist idiom after Hirata had concentrated on the Izumo version of the myths to authenticate new claims. Despite Tomobayashi's affiliation with the Motoori wing, through Ban Tomoyuki, and his insistence upon the priority of poetics as the basis of true knowledge, his effort to locate the origins of poetry in the Izumo tradition disclosed an acceptance of the most fundamental associations raised by this version. Susanowo's exile to Izumo provided the opportunity to overcome his reputation for misdeeds. He assisted the old man and woman, "once he had observed their distress and inconvenience." In the act of slaying the serpent, according to Tomobayashi in *Yomiuta ōmune*,

> [he] had served the heavenly deities by performing a good deed that had sprung from the innermost feelings of his august heart. Thus, he began poetry. Therefore, men who seek to recite/compose poetry must first know the *aware* of things, whether [responding to the] caution of evil deeds or performing good ones. They must maintain a heart that is pure and fresh, and if they do good, personal poetry is possible. In learning the deeds of this *kami*, we make his heart and intention into ours. (*TMz*, 153)

Such assistance from the *kami* "cleanses the heart all the more, governs the household, and purifies the body." Poets who applied the method of divine recitation, he wrote in *Sono no ike mizu*, thus knew how to purify the household as well as the body; and by asking for divine assistance, "they will be able to offer true emotion for themselves and others" (*Kus*, 477).[25]

Tomobayashi next asked, "Why study the poetic Way?" He had already hinted at the answer in his discussion of divine expressibility and true emotions. Only poetry, by virtue of the archetypal example, could express what was genuinely honest and innermost. The capacity to recite poetry disclosed what was most fundamentally honest, pure, and sincere. Recognition of this quality enabled people to conduct themselves correctly in their daily life and permitted them to purify themselves, "govern" the household, and express loyalty to superiors and elders (*Kus*, 478). It allowed people "to know the *kokutai* and exhaust the cleansed heart for the emperor; the self that knows the ancestral deities will endeavor in its household duties (*ie no nari*). For men of today, there is no higher principle than serving the emperor and working for the ancestors" (ibid.). If a person hoped to know the *kokutai*—which, in Tomobayashi's understanding, referred to duties— he was advised to read the classics, especially the great poetic collection, the *Man'yōshū*. Tomobayashi was returning to a tradition of nativism illustrated best by both Keichū (who first equated the poetic project with Susanowo) and Kamo no Mabuchi, which sought to emphasize poetry as a function of governance. Kamo, who also revered the *Man'yōshū*, had seen in these early poems evidence of masculinity and martial values. Tomobayashi's reconsideration of the poetic project both acknowledged the masculine moment in primal poetry, as illustrated by Susanowo's achievement, and reinforced the linkage between service, household duties, and loyalty to the emperor.

> To know the *kokutai* is to know the ancestors and, thus, to exhaust loyal intention to the emperor and hard work in one's household duties. Those who make the eminent virtues of the divine realm [that is, the projections from the *Man'yō*] the learning of the gods will love the deities of heaven and earth. This fact, whereby the gods have bestowed assistance and good fortune, is found in the long poem of volume 5 of the *Man'yōshū*: "Yamato, the several islands that have been transmitted to us, is the country blessed with the language of the gods transmitting this land, which has been assisted by the *kotodama*; men of the present must see this before their eyes and know it."

Tomobayashi reported that, even in his times, the presence of this divine language signified godly assistance, which only Japan knew. When the folk grasped the meaning of this sign, they would be in a position to "acquire the divine learning of ancient customs" (ibid., 481). Poetry and the study of poetics spoke to the most fundamental aspects of life. "If a person stands squarely in the Way of poetry and knows the *kokutai*," he wrote, "if he also knows the ancestors and endeavors in the performance of household duties, he will transmit his name to generations to come, illuminate the name of his parents, who are in concealment, and esteem all men and love them" (ibid., 484).

In contrast to Hirata's position, Tomobayashi sought to elide any difference between poetics and Shinto, which most nativists now conceived as worship and the performance of daily duties for the deities. For this reason he condemned Hirata's poetic views as erroneous—a misunderstanding and an example of "shallow theories." Poets, he declared, were comparable to the sages. "They respect the deities as their principal aim in life, make requests of the divine spirits, learn the divine deeds and incorporate them" (ibid., 465). But, he continued, too many men today had abandoned poetry because they had failed to penetrate the meaning of its tradition. "Hirata Atusutane no nushi examined [in the *Kadō taii*] the essentials of the poetic Way in some detail . . . but he endeavored only argumentatively. In the direction of poetic composition, he shows his lack of skill because of his reliance on the learning of the ancient Way" (ibid.). To counter this baneful influence, Tomobayashi produced a text in 1854 titled *The Principles of the poetic Way (Kadō taii)*, with the object of offsetting Hirata's general dismissal of poetic knowledge. Actually, however, Tomobayashi's views differed little from the opinions of people promoting an active theory of restorationism.

It was the purpose of this essay, as well as many of his theoretical writings on poetry, to demonstrate both the superiority of poetic learning and its equivalence with everyday life. Even in his self-conscious reluctance to follow Motoori's example of emulating ancient elegance and living anciently, he seemed closer to the nativism of the Hirata wing. "The imperial land," he wote, "with its unbroken and unprecedented lineage," is the "warp," while "poetic learning" is the "woof" (ibid., 467–68). Because the poetic "woof" was the "eminent deeds of the *Man'yō*," he recommended "weaving" poetry of this kind into the fabric of life. From the very beginning, poetic learning penetrated the realm to its innermost reaches and united the hidden and visible worlds; it defined the arrangement of things within heaven and earth and, thus, constituted the Great Way, which stood with the imperial lineage and made it shine brilliantly (ibid., 472–73). Elsewhere, in the *Yomiuta ōmune* (1856), he observed that when a person composed poetry, he could not be prevented from talking about Shinto. Poetry was the Great Way of the imperial land, and it protected human lives (*ningen issei no karada no mamori naru wo, TMz*, 153). The argument in the *Kadō taii* was more explicit. In the *Nihonshoki's* account of Emperor Kōtoku (r. 645–54), Shinto meant following the Way of the deities; it was called *kannagara*. It meant avoiding personal intention but entrusting one's body to the deities in all things. The example of Susanowo performing a deed out of honest feeling, in order to assist the old couple and their daughter, and his subsequent exhilaration upon building a palace in the clouds of Izumo both attested to the relationship between action and the "principle of purity and honesty." Such principles did not cloud the heart (intention) and "if one shows an unclouded heart, [the act], then, must consist of performing a good deed" (ibid., 187). Real intention, drawing its inspiration from the deeds of the deities, always resulted in "good deeds." Once again, Tomobayashi summoned the powerful example of Susanowo, who, expelled from heaven for committing serious misdeeds and mischief, was miraculously prompted to perform a good act, which immediately inspired poetic expression.

Tomobayashi's recognition of the performance of good deeds, propelled by an unclouded heart and pure intention, suggests the degree to which Motoori's formulations about knowing the profundity of things and being moved by them had been altered in the electric environment of late-Tokugawa politics. Motoori was not explicitly interested in accounting for political action. His thoughts on empathy inclined toward the passive and meditative and entertained the possibility of a variety of deeds—joyful, exuberant, painful, or sad—that moved humans to express their innermost feelings in the poetic mode. Tomobayashi, deeply immersed in a discourse that, by his time, had acquired strong associations of practicality and daily life, jettisoned this earlier sense of poetic knowledge for one that celebrated useful deeds. When he considered the essentials of poetics, he unreservedly declared that "good deeds are nothing more than endeavoring in behalf of one's personal vocation [*shokubun*]" (ibid.). For "if one does not neglect his vocation, he must be personally pure and cleansed. When one's heart is pure and cleansed, it will be mirrored well in all events, all things, and all vistas. When one projects well and concentrates on the means [work] . . . it will result in the famous poetry of nature [*shizen no meika*]" (ibid., 188).[26] In this reconsideration, he transformed political action into "natural poetry."

Rather than a mere private indulgence, isolated from the public world of sober duty and hard work, a number of interpreters of Motoori's theories envisioned poetry as playing a vital role in the public world of action and duty. Tomobayashi's transformation of Motoori's poetic vision, which accommodated its usefulness to a specific set of contemporary circumstances, emptied poetry of its private associations and rejoined it to the public world. Although such possibilities were inherent in Motoori's views, they remained muted because of his effort to illustrate the texture of the private side of public life. Motoori undoubtedly conceived of the private as standing in some sort of metonymic relationship to the public, the whole. Having made this recognition, he needed little coaxing to expand or even alter the content of this space, if conditions demanded it. Regardless of how we look on the function Motoori assigned to poetic learning, we know that Tomobayashi plainly rejected any presumed association between poetry and privatization. "The *kannagara*", he announced in the *Sono no ike mizu*, "does not mingle at all with the private emotions of men, because it is the Way of the gods. It entrusts the body to the august deeds of the *kami* of heaven and earth; it earnestly [enjoins men to] offer prayers to these deities and service to the lord and parents" (*Kus*, 466).[27] Tomobayashi believed that Motoori had identified the *kami* with "wondrous and miraculous things" and that all things must therefore be wondrous and miraculous, if they had been moved by the deities.[28] The recognition of wonder was a nativist response to the Confucian reliance on rational speculation and the primacy of principle (*kotowari*). But Tomobayashi sought not merely to rehearse the familiar *kokugaku* complaint about Confucianism and Buddhism but to establish a specific form of knowledge as the basis of conduct and activity.

> In our times . . . all things and events in heaven and earth, whether good or bad, are from the august intention of the deities, who have existed to govern all things. How can we calculate this with *limited knowledge?* [My italics.] If there are principles that cannot calculate [such things], then we beg to pray every morning and night that the divine spirits permit us to endeavor, each in his own household duties, to be loyal to the emperor, respect the parents, and love wives and children. All things will be greatly tranquil. At every turn, one cannot manage [things] with personal, small knowledge. (*TMz*, 69)[29]

Governance referred to "*kami* worship" (*TMz*, 70–71) and the importance of understanding man's relationship to the *kami*, when "a person uses his personal, small knowledge, he will not possibly understand why our imperial land is the divine land."

The bond between Shinto and poetic knowledge was "true feeling." Separation from honest feelings prevented poetic production from encountering the Great Way of the imperial land (ibid., 108). It was inconceivable to sever poetry from the Great Way, which was the "way of man" (ibid., 106). Poetry transformed people, as any form of knowledge did. If poetry sprang from honest emotion, it would naturally change one to "honesty" and "simplicity" and lead to naive sentience, which would make possible the acceptance of the world as it was and would enjoin everyone to perform his work and duties. Poetry was able to tranform because it informed the heart and purified and cleansed it; it reflected all things in the heart. As a form of knowledge it excelled because it enabled people to act correctly rather than to merely speculate about the unanswerable. This return to the natural apprehension of the world as it was illuminated the meaning of the "famous poem of nature." Shinto and true emotion "project and emulate well those things" found in nature; emotion and true feeling, which were purified and cleansed and without planning, were rooted in the *kannagara*, which, as a form of knowledge, ᠄made its substance "true reality" and "freshness." Thus, the sense of similitude and equivalence realized by uniting poetry to Shinto would inspire "men to stand in the poetic Way," to exert their true feelings for others and perform deeds only after assessing the true conditions of the times. Poetics should serve as the model for human conduct so that everyone became his own poet. By apprehending poetry as the language of sameness, people's performance would be diverted from willful, evil deeds (*Kus*, 477).

Like Ōkuni, Tomobayashi saw *kokugaku* as a mode of knowledge that would permit the recovery of the "real" and the "essential." He wrote that the Japanese spirit, which had inspired ancient custom as illustrated by the "eminent virtues" of the *Man'yō*, itself forged in a military environment, "lay buried for more than a thousand years" (ibid., 452–58). Recalling Ōkuni's observation that the present provided the first opportunity in over a thousand years to introduce a new form of knowledge, Tomobayashi appointed it as the moment of opportunity for a recovery of the "eminent virtues." The discovery of a buried past—the poetic knowledge of things prior to signs, disclosing deeper relationships—would enable men to "read and recall well the great and august customs of the wondrous imperial country. Learning would incline toward learning about the *kami*." In the *Inagisho*, he explained that men who studied the imperial country invariably learned the poetry of high antiquity (*TMz*, 107–8). This poetry instructed them in the true emotions of ancient men, allowing them to "accumulate these feelings in their own body, to nourish the parents and serve the emperor (*kimi*)" (ibid., 108). The poetics he was seeking to reinstate was very similar to the *kami* learning that so many of his contemporaries were trying to promote. Knowledge of the *kami*, as he reasoned in the *Sono no ike mizu*, "following the ancient Way and revering it as an object" meant "praying to the deities and learning about their august deeds so as to absorb them in one's body." He promised that the "principles that should be learned from the deities in all things will cast a spell on the evil words of ordinary people from foreign countries." The source of real knowledge remained the *Man'yōshū*, which, he believed, recorded the true words and deeds of the gods (*Kus*, 465).

When contrasting ancient elegance to contemporary convention, the former appeared fresh and honest, the latter, stale and vulgar (*TMz*, 120). Any discussion of ancient and contemporary poetry revealed an ambivalence over the relationship between past and present and a concern for overcoming the gulf between them. Although some poets favored ancient elegance and others were partial to novelty and originality, the two were not necessarily incompatible. The disparity became manifest when men who made such distinctions "failed to recognize the beauty of language" (*kotoba no myōshu o shirazu*; ibid., 117). Tomobayashi's solution proposed, first, that poets should try to make "ancient words fit their own things"; then, they must seek to accommodate (*kanaemukoto*) new forms of expression to the antique intention. Appropriating the ancient language took only a moment, but it would secure permanent entry for the poet into the world of ancient elegance—or, as Tomobayashi expressed it, "it will be difficult to avoid succeeding the ancients." Using new words to correspond to the antique intention was not an invitation to abandon contemporary modes of expression. Far from it. "Referring to new words separates one from the world of vulgarity [*zokushū*]; skillful accommodations to the ancients means that one should not neglect ancient words and that one ought to search them out and read them." The example of the ancients taught the contemporary poet the meaning of innovation and newness. Purity, freshness, and newness were not bound by time; they remained available in every present. "Therefore, one must strive to make ancient forms of expression one's own by grasping their purity and newness; by paying attention to newness, we should strive to accommodate [the forms] to the ancient intention . . . Scholars should first discriminate well the distinction between the elegant and the vulgar; then they should despise words that are coarse and rustic." (ibid., 118). However, he warned, antiquity had realized a high degree of skill and elegance and beauty, but "contemporary cleverness is differentiated by its superficiality."

Tomobayashi elaborated on this tension between past and present in the *Kakiuchi shichikusa* and disclosed his real interest in contemporaneity. He asserted that the gap between "ancient elegance" and "later vulgarity" was rooted in a "slavish imitation of the past." Changes within time constantly occurred; they merely reflected the "flow of the trend of the time" (*jiun*), a ceaseless condition of nature that characterized poetry as well (ibid., 145). "The differences are in style and taste. In antiquity, the intention, words, and form [arrangement] belonged to antiquity; in the middle ages and later times . . . it was a style that was designed by each age." The present must be mindful of the special conditions of each age in order to understand the relationship between what was being said and how it was expressed. Poets were obliged to concern themselves with the special style of each age and accommodate themselves to the human passion of those times. This was no less true of the past than of the present. "Men who read and compose poetry must first seek out the old traces of the *kiki* and *Man'yō* to understand the simple and honest taste of high antiquity. When also surveying widely the poetic collections of later ages to *understand the development of those times* [my italics], they will know the new character of those times." A poet should neither abandon the ancient intention nor cling to convention but "bring to recitation the honesty of his innermost thoughts" (ibid., 146). [30] In another place, he asserted that, if people made an effort to study the histories and the early poetic collections, they would find abundant examples of pure and honest emotionality that could inspire them to fix feeling as the real objective of poetry. But, he cautioned, first they were required to recognize that the structure of style must always correspond to their own times (*TMz*, 109).

Contemporary poetic intention changed the selection of things that moved the poet. Tomobayashi favored the special whims and arbitrary turns of poetic convention that always differed from time to time, because they disclosed the innovation and freshness of the ancient intention. Antiquity taught men that poetry functioned to present only the most honest and innermost feelings, not convention and artifice. He eschewed a strict adherence to norms and precedents, which were invariably produced by time-bound necessity. Both his poetic theory and his advice to "entrust the body to the deities" invited contemporaries to actively engage their immediate environment, to be "touched" by it, and to continually express their emotions. [31] In a reference to later

poetic collections, Tomobayashi reaffirmed the conviction that a knowledge of circumstances was always the undisputed condition of understanding. It was important to understand the transformation of human
passion (*ninjō no hentai*) as well as the development of the times, and
to recite and compose according to the styles of "the age" (*TMz*, 109).
His aim, here, was to emphasize the knowability of conditions and
change; the poetic metaphor was merely his way of illustrating the usefulness of this theory of knowledge for serving the deities and the times.

> Since the seven passions of joy, anger, empathy [*aware*], pleasure, love,
> evil, and desire are touched by things that adhere to events and, thus,
> change, there are times in which the intention [*kokoro*] inclines toward
> beautiful and bright flowers, and there are also times it tends towards the
> mysteriously sublime [*yūgen*]. Therefore, one should not alter or mend
> the inclination of the heart that is with excellence, sternness, gentleness,
> or simplicity, with remarkable effect or tranquillity. One should recite
> only what is there. (Ibid., 113)

To the last, Tomobayashi sought to show that poetics represented an
exemplar of knowing that could couple with personal perceptions of
the present and with experience; *the* poetic Way of antiquity he articulated, according to one writer, became *his* poetic Way, just as his conception of Shinto demanded action in the present as a sign of "entrusting his body to the deities."[32] But experience prior to poetry also
required compromising the "way things are" with forms of representation, in order to reach contemporaries.

Politically, it is hard to imagine the kind of order he had in mind.
At one level, his notion of order resembled, most of all, the attempts
to join worship to governance and to eliminate all structures but the
imperial court. In its recommendation that "all things be entrusted to
the imperial court"—which was merely another way of referring to
Shinto—Tomobayashi's vision was closest to *Bunkyū* loyalists like
Maki Izumi, who worried less about enduring structures than about
overthrowing the Tokugawa. By calling attention to the imperial court,
Tomobayashi tried to retain a distant sensation and imagery while en-
gaging contemporary circumstances. "In all things," he wrote in the
Sansei itchi setsu, "one exists to esteem the worship of *kami* and does
not, therefore, use his personal knowledge." The reason for this dismissal of "personal knowledge" was his conviction that, if people abdi-
cated their responsibility to celebrate the *kami*, they would forever re-

main ignorant of the way polity was governed in antiquity. Tomobayashi believed that his present had been called upon to resolve the struggle over the ancient Way, "to emphasize celebration of the godly Way now and in the years to come" (*TMz*, 73). The time was ripe for people to "know the august and great customs of that time [antiquity], if we are to have an imperial polity, that is, a divine polity" (ibid., 70). Since the end of the Zhou period and the age of Confucius, he remarked, the Chinese had relied upon mere human wisdom, whereas, with the *kami*, celebration had never been constrained by any one moment or restricted to the achievements of a few men in a remote era. Rather, the example of the gods accumulated for all time (ibid.). Fearful that the times had become too limited in vision and the blessings of the deities too scarce, Tomobayashi wondered whether the moment had not yet arrived to "begin restoring the ancient customs [*inishieburi*] of the divine age" (ibid., 73).

Tomobayashi's poetic discourse recalled a tradition of thinking that insisted on a correspondence between writing and the apparatus of a sinified, bureaucratic state structure. Just as Kamo no Mabuchi had envisaged the elimination of that correspondence—or at the very least its displacement—by returning to speech and the simplicity of things ("a time that required few words"), so Tomobayashi's valorization of "singing only of things as they are" and his retrieval of a "divine polity" reintroduced to late-Tokugawa discussions the earlier equation of writing with state formation (China) and its possible eradication by restoring the poetic Way (speech) and the action of the body (Japan). But in a struggle already devoted to resolving the clash of claims between authority and structural form, nothing mattered less than a theory proposing to remove politics altogether. Because Tomobayashi's "interest" failed to dispel the aporias of signs, his claim of representation remained remote from the environment of action.

8 Accomplices of Restoration

Figures of Restoration

On January 3, 1868, domainal activists with connections at court issued an edict calling for a "restoration of ancient imperial governance" (*ōsei fukko*). The set of events culminating in the overthrow of the Tokugawa *bakufu* and the return of direct imperial rule, which has come to be known as the Meiji Restoration, inaugurated Japan's transport to the modern world of wealth and power. Yet at the time, it seemed like a local event with no more significance than—as the historian Tōyama Shigeki has described it—a coup d'état. The alliance composed of activists representing domains such as Chōshū, Satsuma, and Hizen and courtiers like Iwakura Tomomi, Nakayama Tadayasu, and Sanjō Sanetomi agreed on little else than the dissolution of shogunal authority for imperial leadership. The edict promised nothing more than a reshuffling of feudal arrangements, even though summoning imperial governance introduced the powerful principle of political authority already inscribed in the nativist preoccupation with trust and enabling. Returning to an imperial polity meant reclimbing the ladder of authority to get to the top, just as recovering the original traces of the moment of creation necessitated discourse. Both operations led to the ancestral deities and creators of the cosmos; both promised the recovery of an absent origin. Behind this theory of origins was the conviction that once the lines of power were realigned to conform to the ancient precedent, then the structures mediating the relationship between emperor and folk would also be rectified. Invoking the sign of antiquity gave the bold plotters of restoration the greatest degree of

374

flexibility and the least amount of binding associations. A restoration so conceived offered the opportunity of retrieving both presence and absence.

The edict, drafted by nativists, specified that even though the new governance would "wash away old abuses and customs," the model of restoration would be the state foundation of Emperor Jinmu. The paradox of a political change pledged to dissolve old institutions (the Tokugawa past) but steeping its claims in the example of the founder of the Japanese state made perfectly good sense to the people who made the Restoration. The reference to Jinmu, evocative of Ōkuni Takamasa's earlier views, offered to liberate the new and uncertain leadership from specific political associations for a conception of authority unmediated by either history or recent institutional experience. At the same time, the general call permitted the activists to tackle the issues that had dogged the *bakufu* in its last days—disorder among the populace, secessionary movements among the domains, and new religious communities, and the ever-present threat of foreign colonization.

Throughout the Tokugawa period the conception of restoration was associated less with specific political content than with tactics and a theory of action. This is not to say that writers and activists did not formulate ideals concerning the organization and conduct of a prior time. Since the eighteenth century thinkers had dreamed and talked about restoration. Yamagata Daini, in *Ryūshi shinron* (1764), envisaged a populist agrarian past on which he was willing to act; writers of the Mito school increasingly referred to a *chūkō* in their programs to "restore" their domain to military and financial self-sufficiency; and court factions (*oshitsuke*) in the 1850s began to see in the idea of an imperial restoration a sanction for political mobilization and action. By the late 1850s and early 1860s the concept of restoration lost whatever specificity it might have held for its proponents when it merged with new forms of imperial loyalism and cultural xenophobia to provide focus to a broad spectrum of malcontents bent on organizing activity against the Tokugawa. In no time at all there were as many plans and schemes for a restoration as there were loyalists milling around in the streets of Kyoto, plotting sedition in the city's tea houses, inns, and geisha quarters. Among nativists, the idea of restoration was always synonymous with the recovery of origins, and when the discourse was exported to the countryside in the 1830s and 1840s, it became linked to the idea of reclaiming the communitarian potentialities of a pure and unadorned Shinto, as the surest guide to life and death in the

present. Although the ancient map that glittered through the superimposed layers reflected the new agricultural orientation, nowhere was
it possible to detect a plan or blueprint instructing the present in the
details of the past. Nor was such discovery necessary. For nativists,
discussing this past was like talking about the invisible world. For
the great nativist theorists like Motoori, Hirata, and Ōkuni restoration—adhering to foundations—was necessitated by an epistemological strategy rather than a specific concept or solution reached by discourse; it made discourse possible, organizing the world in a certain
modality and talking about certain relationships. But a discourse on
origins that was so often indistinguishable from the origin of discourse
did not necessarily authorize a political restoration. The nativist belief
in a cosmological and ontological division between the visible and invisible worlds, and the classifications derived from this opposition, resulted in a displacement of the former by the latter—the manifest
polity, with its administrative and institutional trappings, displaced by
an undifferentiated communitarian order, the agricultural *habitus*,
faintly distinguished by hierarchy and division. Yet this displacement
scarcely amounted to a program, since the very substitution of realms
that lay at the heart of the *kokugaku* conception of knowledge inhibited
the mapping of a restorationist political order.

When nativism collided with contemporary history in the late-
Tokugawa period, it became implicated in the very events it had tried
to reemplot. The ensuing struggle in the 1850s and 1860s increasingly
narrowed its focus. It sought to restructure the center in order to arrest
withdrawals to the periphery—which had become the problem, not the
solution—and to resolve definitively the clash of claims between community and polity. Formerly, the nativists' displacing strategy had sanctioned withdrawal to *habitus*, an unspecified cultural order designated
as the place of practice and reproduction; in the context of this new
problematic, they were compelled to offer their conception of a restored community as a solution in order to be accepted in the competition. But the installation of a vague cultural order as a substitute for
what they *misrecognized* as random eventfulness amounted to little
more than an accommodation to and complicity in events that had
overtaken them. Paradoxically, nativists found themselves embroiled as
accomplices in an eventful history that their discourse had already discounted as unreal; withdrawal to the periphery was the condition for
removing themselves from the center where history and politics occurred. This move to the periphery, as it already has been suggested,

was sanctioned by the part/whole strategy. Once nativism became implicated in agricultural affairs and a specific place, however, invoking the part as a displacement for the whole became a substitution that worked to defer the center altogether and delay reaching it until the "last instance." The distance between the nativist evaluation of contemporary history and the empirical domain proved too great to close by transmuting the part/whole relationship into a substitution of the periphery for the center. Ultimately, the space between religion and politics proved too wide to span and, more important, too contradictory to conceal ideologically. Hence, nativism became an accomplice in a plot that privileged time and political possibility—the center—rather than the frozen moment of an atemporal communitarian sanctuary located in the place of the periphery—that is, a "no place."

Both Ōkuni and Tomobayashi saw action as the means to withdraw from the uncertanties of time and to forestall the privatism and fragmentation that, they believed, the mediation of politics caused. Yet displacement was not the same as replacement, and interpretation did not add up to "changing the world." Nativism, as we have seen, had formulated a theory of action to serve a different plot structure. The aim of the new story line was not to overthrow the Tokugawa *bakufu* for an even greater structure of political authority. Once nativists became involved in the movement to bring down the Tokugawa and to restore imperial governance, their theory of action, which aimed to secure a communitarian order outside politics, was compromised and finally jettisoned by the power brokers of the Meiji government. Disbelief in politics failed to bring about the destruction of politics. By 1868 all that was left of nativism was its hermeneutic, which tried desperately to make sense of what was happening. This impulse was expressed best in the texts of Yano Gendō (also Harumichi, 1823–87), who tried to transform the event of the Meiji Restoration into an interpretative moment and to show that the purpose of restoration was to reinstate the nativist system of knowledge—fundamental doctrine (*honkyō*)—as the epistemological basis for a unification of religion and polity (*saisei itchi*) and to secure for *kokugaku* the privileged position of a master code. Yano hoped to make all political policy and decision making dependent on nativist principles of knowledge, to redirect power to the discourse on knowledge as compensation for its forfeiture of the communitarian vision. In this way, the nativist conception of restoration, scaled down in scope to a mere hermeneutic, was defeated by a Restoration that erected a centralized political organization capable of performing the services that the Tokugawa had been found unable to deliver, and more.

This is not to suggest that the nativist complicity was foreordained, nor that its failure stemmed from an uncontrollable romanticism and nostalgia for the good old days of antiquity. Its vision of a communitarian order failed, like those informing the new religions and the *yonaoshi* determination to "dance toward the millennium," because its image of the "past" was too radical for the present and bordered upon utopia. In its call to move to the periphery, it posed a threat of unimaginable proportions to the convention of politics and the sanctity of the center; and in its valorization of place as the repository for *the* fundamental conditions of social existence, reproduced by the bodily unification of mental and manual labor to secure sufficiency and the promise of livability, it discounted the divisions of labor demanded by politics to justify claims of authority, power, and hierarchy. It challenged both the feudal order, which maintained politics safely apart from culture, and the modern bureaucratic order, which would use culture to depoliticize the masses.

Although the idea of restoration failed to specify the details of the new order that was derived from the past yet applicable to the present and future, it still functioned as a system of meaning sanctioning forms of action. In the 1850s and 1860s restoration was a code word for action; its frequent use signified the attempt to discredit and even overthrow the *bakufu*. It was the path to restoration, the recovery of traces—not the restoration itself—that recruited would-be restorationists. Moreover, this was no less true of *kokugakusha* like Tomobayashi Mitsuhira, Yano Gendō, Tsunoda Tadayuki and others who participated in restorationist politics in the early 1860s than it was of loyalists with intellectual commitments to Mito or to some retrograde form of Neo-Confucianism. A reading of Arima Shinshichi's *Miyako nikki*, Kusaka Genzui's *Kairan jōgi* and *Kaiwan shirigoto*, Hirano Kuniomi's *Kaiten sansaku* and *Jinmu hitsukatsu*, Ogō Kazutoshi's *Ōsei fukko gikyoroku* and Kiyokawa Hachirō's *Senchū shimatsu*, Ōhashi Totsuan's *Seiken kaifuku hisaku* to name the best-known texts (all written about the same time), shows that the idea of restoration was weakest in actually conceptualizing its goals and strongest in commanding purposeful commitment and loyalty in the service of a great cause. For all these men, and others too numerous to mention, the Mito discourse, with its sense of moral purpose and rectitude, not to mention its reformist experience in resuscitating the domain economically and militarily, and *koku-gaku*, with its compelling religious vision and belief in the necessity of sacred trust, offered a justification for dangerous action and self-sacrifice. These texts were written by men whose own discourse disposed them to valorize sincerity over contemplation and conceptualization, practicality over mere prudentiality; they were, like Yamagata Daini, Ōshio Heihachirō, and Ikuta Yorozu before them, interested in how to talk about the possibility of action and the appropriate tactics for it, rather than its ultimate object. Hence, it is not surprising to note declarations of intent, demonstrations of will, and effusive proclamations of sincerity in many of these restorationist texts. Another feature of these texts is their acknowledged immersion in the events of the 1850s and 1860s, as if contemporary history was their collective object. Arima Shinshichi, for example, a Satsuma activist, recorded in *Miyako nikki* his responses to the events of the *Bunkyū* years. Yet inscribed in his evaluation of the current situation was a theory of restoration that could meet the requirements of action and the awareness of the central position of the imperial court in any subsequent political program. "We must drive off the rough and indecent retainers [of the *bakufu*]," he wrote, "so as to learn again the origins of the realm for the return to the divine age" (*Ksi* 3:297). Similar sentiments scattered throughout the writings of Ōhashi, Ogō, and Kiyokawa manifested an intention to bring about a restoration, instead of providing details of the anticipated imperial order, and privileged the authority of personal experience as a surrogate for a definitive solution. It was precisely this blindness that organized the rhetoric of restoration and constituted the unstated principle of its production. Behind the maze of proclamations of self-righteous sincerity was an effort to put under erasure the necessity of devising a viable order consistent with the activity launched by the *sonnō jōi* movement. When it was ultimately recognized that personal intensity alone was not enough to mobilize large numbers of people, activists turned to the only model of a restoration accessible to them—the nativist vision of returning to an agricultural arcadia that had existed before historical time. The figure of restoration was reduced to the syntax of events leading to the Restoration. Because of the intervention of writers like Maki Izumi, especially after he reentered public life in 1860, the nativist rhetoric of place was assimilated to the "grammar" of action as if the operation was unproblematic. As a metaphorical figure, restoration had been simply another way for nativists to talk about the tangibility of life, the necessity of work to reproduce the conditions of place, and the identity of all things in the creation as timeless constants without which existence would have been unimaginable. Once this trope was reduced to the syntax of events leading to the overthrow of the Tokugawa *bakufu*, it became a political image supplementing a movement in linear historical time.

Restorationists recruited this figure to cloak sincere and willful action proceeding along a "syntactical" chain in order to supply their opposition to the Tokugawa with a purpose sufficiently general to escape charges of self-interest. Under Maki's direction the movement was figured to make the course of sedition and terror appear as the logical necessity of the promise of an agrarian arcadia, even though it is difficult to say whether the adherents of the anti-Tokugawa cause ever really intended, by their overthrow of the shogunate, to reinstate a simple agricultural community existing outside political time. But the power of this figure bonded disparate groups and interest in common agreement despite the apparent tension between rhetoric and syntax. Events were to show that a restoration envisaged by nativists was one thing, while the Restoration as the culmination of an eventful history was something entirely different. Even though the Restoration sought early to resolve this tense and very problematic relationship by reorganizing the central authority to make possible the destruction of the Tokugawa and to arrest the centrifugation it had been unable to stem, the tension became a fundamental legacy for modern Japan. The Meiji restorers promised, in the opening decree announcing the Restoration, that the aim of the new polity was to return to the "events of antiquity and Jinmu tennō's state foundations"; it also proclaimed, almost simultaneously in the Five Charter Oath (1869), that it was determined to "search for new knowledge throughout the world" and to "eliminate old customs." The former led to a belief in cultural exceptionalism and even to presumptions of superiority in Japan's relations with foreigners; it would seek, much like the nativists in the Tokugawa period, to emphasize the basic similarity of all Japanese in the face of the differentiating and alienating influence of foreign culture, and the separation between the claims of similitude (Japan) and difference (the Other). The latter inspired the creation of a modern state and the transformation of Japanese society under a regime of new forms of Western knowledge and a mandate of progressive historical time. Although the call to timeless origins and place came to authenticate all proposals proclaiming essence and spirituality, claiming to know what was irreducibly

Japanese even though society had changed visibly and materially, the search for new knowledge, the logical outcome of the linearity of events, was identified with progressive development, modernity, and the West. The terms of cultural uniqueness stressed ends and essences, while the pursuit of rational knowledge privileged means and instrumentality; in the end, tension was expressed in a struggle between culture and civilization and in a desperate quest to resolve the aporia that had been prefigured by the assimilation of restoration to Restoration.

It was Maki Izumi (1813–64) who used the nativist rhetoric of restoration to figure the action that led to the Restoration.[1] Among participants in the *sonnō jōi* movement, he, more than most, structured the idea of an *ōsei fukko* (restoration) into a coherent theory of purpose to supplement what hitherto had been action in the service of will and sincerity. Maki is especially interesting for us because of his prominent role in the restorationist putsches of the 1860s and because he was also a Shinto priest. Despite his generous acknowledgements of homage to the Mito discourse he was, in his writing about restoration, close to the nativist vision and undoubtedly owed much to rural *kokugaku* and its formulation of the self-sufficient agricultural community. Yet the particular meld testified to how—in the production of meaning—texts and their readers were spread over discourses and ideologies belonging to differing modes of cultural production. To see Maki's texts as a form of productivity is to locate it in relation to prevailing language codes and to fix its status in terms of an intertextuality. Maki's writings on restoration took utterances from other texts, principally from Mito and *kokugaku*, which intersected and neutralized one another in the service of different ends.

Maki turned to the idea of an *ōsei fukko* as a policy to destroy the *bakufu* in 1860, after he had heared of Ōhashi Totsuan's abortive restorationist plot in Edo. A year later he drafted the *Missho sōan*, proposing the implementation of a restorationist plan. Yet even before this proposal, Maki had called for an *ōsei fukko* in the *Keii gusetsu*, written sometime in the summer of 1858. This text announced that to bring about a great event it was necessary to link the warp to the woof. "We call the warp that which, with great loyalty [*taigi*], penetrates both beginning and end. The woof comes later; according to appropriate conditions, it meshes with the warp. Today the warp [moral purpose] and the woof [conditions] are separated" (*MIki*, 5). Imagining a grid crossed by horizontal and vertical strands, he contended that the universe required one supreme ruler, who, because of Japan's special origins, happened to be the imperial descendents of the gods. Geography confirmed his conviction; echoing a sentiment of Ōkuni Takamasa, he noted that Japan stood at the head of the great world land mass (*taiji*). This sense of political and geographical centrality prompted Maki to discuss origins and the necessity of "understanding foundations" (*sōgyō*) in a way that was strikingly similar to the nativist idea of "adhering to the base" and probably meant the same thing (ibid., 6). For Maki, the need to understand foundations led to the formulation of a theory of restoration. By foundations he meant returning to the times of the founder, Jinmu tennō, the legendary founder of the state (*taisō mo chūkō nari*); the "deed that spreads imperial authority is foundation" (ibid.). Emperor Tenji (r. 668–71) had also implemented a restoration founded on origins because he, too, had returned to a system of central control (*gunken*). Foundation and origin revealed the shape of restoration. A return to foundations, as expressed in the examples of Jinmu and Tenji, represented a normative principle—the warp—unmoving and fixed. Like Ōkuni, who also saw the necessity of knowing the trends of the times in order to seize the opportune moment to reinstate the timeless and fixed principles of creation, Maki observed that the times were propitious for contemporaries to weave together the threads of normative values and contemporary conditions, past to present, to produce a new textile (text-ile). He also raised the question of merit and ability as the necessary requirement for achieving a lasting restoration (ibid.). This point is important, because a theory of merit found its way into the later restoration edict, as well as the proposals of many writers, activists, and ideologues who tried to describe the content of restoration. The final defense was put best by the courtier Iwakura Tomomi when he declared that the future of the restoration would take care of itself if policy was directed by men of talent and ability. The concern for *jinzai*—talent and ability—in the recruitment of responsible leaders offered the same kind of promise as the summons to origins: both, so it was believed, represented a return to basics, pure, simple, unadorned, and unfettered by intervening associations, and to the prospect of a timeless ancient order available to the present.

Throughout the *Keii gusetsu* and other texts by Maki, we find an equation between ability and the acquisition of practical knowledge in the final accomplishment of a restoration. The utility of learning (already a part of the nativist discourse), which he observed among the ancient sages of China, constituted the "primary virtue of the realm" (*tenka daiichitō no toku arite*) and therefore the single most important criterion in the recruitment of administrators (ibid., 7). Maki ranked this principle, along with foundations and restoration, in the class of things belonging to the warp. When foundation signified restoration, restoration—the original—became nothing more than the guidance of talented and able men, who, by virtue of their natural endowments, were learned in matters of practical utility.

In describing the woof, Maki called for the "destruction of old abuses" as a condition for any new program. This meant simply carrying out a restoration of foundations in his time. Such a restoration was not just supposed to remind Japanese of the creation or even the most ancient kernel of their experience; it was also supposed to link them to a different time from their own and, paradoxically, set free in them everything that was not contemporaneous. He warned against the "haughtiness" and "pomposity" of persons who were not able to shake loose from timeworn customs and advised that the destruction of old abuses should not be left to court nobles "who would come to everything—old examples and antique precedents—as if they are important ordinances, without taking into consideration feelings and social conditions [*ninjō setai*]" (ibid., 11). Maki observed that practices that contemporaries located in antiquity went back no further than the Nara period—what he called "near antiquity." "In our time," he continued, "everything has to be destroyed in order to return to distant antiquity [*tōku inishie ni tachikaeri*]. Roughly, it is like taking hold of the example of Emperor Jinmu and the age of the gods through the time of Emperor Tenji" (ibid., 12). Elsewhere, in the *Missho sōan*, he reiterated a belief in a restoration of foundations dating back to the time of Emperor Jinmu and the age of the gods. "We should establish a capitol according to ancient Kashihara in the land of Yamato, imitate the system of six ministries and six provincial offices of the Zhou period, deploy an army, and organize rites and rituals" (ibid., 191). Or, as he put it in the *Gikyosaku betsuhen*, "We must return to the age of the gods in all things, as well as the doctrinal [religious and educational] prohibitions by which the realm has been ruled" (ibid., 937).

His sense of antiquity conformed to current nativist theory concerning the unification of ceremony and governance (*saisei itchi*). Maki saw in this idea the real meaning of Shinto. "The foundation of Jinmu was bequeathed by the heavenly ancestors," he wrote, "who established the Way of the gods [*shintō*]. They taught that governance is not a separate activity [from worship], that civilian and military arts share the same path, lord and vassal the same intention. The peasantry has

known this [truth] in its daily application . . . [but] since the coming
of Buddhism our Way has been suppressed" (ibid., 668).[2] The only real
prosperity the Japanese ever knew was in the "age of the gods." The
decrees of the Sun Goddess had brought forth the doctrine of governance
as ceremony (*saisei*). Maki invoked one of the central tenets of nativist
discourse to announce that the "great principle of loyalty was maintained in everyday affairs from the court down to the people. Whatever
happened all people were unified in the great principle of loyalty.
There could not be observed any differences between those who were
just born and those who were ready for death. . . . In later times, the
Great Way decreed by divine ordinance disappeared among people.
Each person acted as he or she pleased, and after the arrival of Buddhism the Great Way ceased to exist altogether" (*MIki*, 725–26).[3] If
this doctrine of governance-as-worship, so essential to the basic spirit
of ancient Shinto, was restored, Japanese could reconstruct a Shinto-
like society informed by faith and worship in daily affairs. His ideal was
consistent with his convictions as a priest and with prevailing nativist
notions concerning the possibility for order and community in the agricultural village: he proposed that the shrine in each village serve as
the locus of administrative authority. This proposition rested on the
more basic assumption, developed by rural nativists, that the village
must be reconstituted as a self-sufficient community.

In many ways, Maki's idea concerning a "one village, one shrine"
system resembled the *kokugaku* emphasis on the institution of tutelary
worship (*MIki*, 149).[4] *Kokugakusha* before him had already seen in a
revitalized tutelary belief system a way to identify governance and religious ceremony in the village community. In Maki's revised version
the elevation of the shrine satisfied a more fundamental belief in village
autonomy and the necessary inseparability of ceremony and administration. He advanced this idea as a major condition for domainal reform in his "Secret plan for renovation" (*Ishin hissaku*) during the
late-Tenpō period. Convinced that rural affairs could be advanced if
"carried out in the shrine," he argued that "skills steeped in the customs
of the domain" and prompted by "public spiritedness" would "rectify
the system of one village, one shrine" (*MIki*, 149). The shrines should
also function to educate the young of the village. Maki assigned administrative, ceremonial, and educational responsibility to priests, whose
own training symbolized the necessary merging of governance and religious ceremony. Even the physical construction of shrines must revert
back to their original architectural design, which was simple and func-

tional and organized to allow diverse duties to be carried out. He proposed a compound of buildings that would constitute the center of each village's religious, educational, and administrative activities. The final result was very close to the autonomous village imagined by people like Katsura Takashige and Suzuki Masayuki.

Maki aimed at unifying the various groups and inhabitants in the village and making them more responsible for their own affairs. Although this conception of community was characterized by a strong emphasis on horizontal ties, he, like many nativists, did not abandon hierarchy altogether. Entrustment necessitated leadership at the village level. Whereas people like Miyahiro and Katsura looked to village headmen like themselves to receive the divine trust to lead, Maki, who was a Shinto priest, enlisted the Shinto priesthood as the natural holder of authority in the rural community. In his explanations of village ceremony, he did not limit himself to religious duties but showed the character of leadership in the village and why no other hierarchical form was necessary to regulate the lives of the inhabitants. The ceremony of autumn, for example, he wrote, occurred after one hundred days of work. On one day it was necessary to offer vinegar to the gods. Since this was a requirement of the Imperial Food-Tasting Festival (*daijō niiname*), it must be carried out on that day each year throughout the domain of Saga. In front of the door of each house in each village (in the domain), there must be placed an offering of foods and rice amounting to about nine liters. In addition, there should be rice cakes, undistilled sake, and fish prepared with two vegetables produced in the area. The rites and rituals began about five o'clock in the morning. At a temporary shelter, people of the village nourished the elderly and paid respects to their superiors. Four or five shrine families beat the rice into *mochi*. They also performed sacred dances, playing only the *biwa*, the flute (*yokobue*), and the large drum (*taiko*) in order to bring about one's good character (*honshin*). After this rite, women and children visited the shrine to pay homage. Following this, the ritual of sacred wine and reverence for drinking was performed and the villagers would visit the shrines of relatives from other villages. Some shrines also conducted ritual games of play and wrestling (*sumō*) among the young of the village. If various rituals were performed strictly, people could avoid dissipation in both food and drink (ibid., 150–51).[5]

Maki's description of this particular festival aimed at showing that, apart from its religious significance, such rituals reminded people of the original meaning of antiquity. He had observed that the village banquet commemorating the harvest ritual had become increasingly more elaborate when, in ancient times, it had been a solemn and simple observance stressing thanks and social solidarity (*MIki*, 805). But it was his primary intention to call attention to the apparent disparity between theory and practice in enforcing village customs, which, he believed with others, had become disorderly. Rituals, he noted, had been emptied of all meaning and had degenerated into purposeless performances; the habits of contemporary village youths had become scandalous. Maki, it should be remembered, was responding to a perception shared by a number of thoughtful people in the 1840s and 1850s that village life was breaking up, older relationships were being eroded by new economic forces and managerial incompetence, and basic values were being drained of all meaning. The solution to the times, he believed, lay in a plan that would reaffirm the autonomy of the village community and signal a full return to the pure simplicity of antiquity.

Maki's concerns for the restoration of order in the villages disclosed a relationship between knowledge of a certain kind and the establishment of an autonomous and self-sufficient community. Here, he was closest to the nativist discourse and its insistence upon reconstituting the village community. Even later, when he had begun to think in terms of a larger political space, he expressed his preference for a feudal structure (*hōkensei*) over a more centralized polity (*gunkensei*) as a mere reaffirmation of the autonomous village. Only under a feudal arrangement, a "natural" polity, could the village retain the kind of order and autonomy he had envisaged as a requirement for restoration based upon "foundations" (ibid., 12). The broad structure—the *hōkensei*—was, for many in the late-Tokugawa period, a remote abstraction compared to the village structures where many people spent their lives. As a priest from a family of village priests, Maki's affiliations belonged to the countryside and the restoration of village life. Moreover, this attachment explains his somewhat inordinate valorization of the village priests, whom he called "village masters" (*sonshi*, ibid., 151).[6] Specifying the importance of the village and the necessity of maintaining order, he devised a scheme in which priests, as teachers and exemplars, would guarantee the integrity and safety of the village. Writing to a friend in the 1850s, he proclaimed that because "laws are dead things," it was necessary to find men who were able "to join rule to the flow of the times [*jisei*] so that they [the laws] will conform to human passions [*ninjō*]." Under such conditions laws would become "living things."[7]

Maki acknowledged that village officials performed concrete administrative tasks. But—reminiscent of Miyauchi and Miyahiro—he was
critical of their performance when he pointed to the observable fact
that the management of the villages had forfeited its moral authority
and its leadership qualities. Moral authority was like spiritual power,
and the loss of the former derived from the absence of the latter. These
were familiar complaints, voiced by many of his contemporaries. They
concentrated on showing that peculation, incompetence, and stupid-
ity—where *shōya* "are like dogs"—were rampant conditions throughout the countryside (*MIki*, 809 [*Mukashimono monogatari*]).[8] Leadership by village officials must be exemplary to justify their being called
"masters who minister the village" (*mura no bokushi*). These "pas-
tors"or "masters" were to be recruited from the priestly families of each
village; "villages without priestly families must select as *sonshi* talented
and able men from among the gentry." Maki identified talent and
ability with Shinto priests—persons who possessed a knowledge of the
divinity of daily affairs and who could put such learning into the service
of community order and interest (*MIki*, 151). Such priestly exemplars
should be assigned the direction of village schooling, devising the appropriate curricula for youth "over eight years old" and "over fifteen
years old."[9] Maki believed that education and its direction were abso-
lutely vital to the leadership of the village and its spiritual integrity. Yet
it should not stop with the education of the young. When, as he observed in the *Mukashimono monogatari*, officials had lost the spiritual
direction of their villages, the "village masters" should serve as the
model for the entire community.

But Maki was not so unreflective or self-serving as to not recognize that changes within the priesthood must be made first. In order
for priests to play the role of *sonshi*, they must return to the original
meaning of the *shinkan*. Priests had departed from the model of being
"good servants" (*yoki geboko*) of Shinto.[10] "Most priests today are fools,"
he charged, "men who mislead and deceive the people. . . . They purify polluted things with toad's eyes and they practice respect to the gods
with weeping and wailing sounds. There are many who are skilled only
in committing transgressions against the deities and in slandering
heaven itself" (*MIki*, 280). Others, who administered shrines, were
versed in the details of prayers and collected handsomely for their efforts to secure favors from the gods. Men believed that certain priests
alone could reach the gods to represent their requests. He demanded
the "prohibition of detestable charms and prayers" as a primary condi-

tion for his program of village exemplars, hoping to rouse priests to return to their original role, to manage ceremony and rite, which, he believed, was at the heart of politics and education. Contemporary conditions necessitated a revival of this foundation, so that "priests will be able to conform to the ancient office in the present." It was, in fact, this kind of knowledge that Yano Gendō cited five years after Maki's death, in his detailed plan for a restoration, to demonstrate the vital link between establishing a center for imperial studies (*kōgakusho*) and the management of a society based on the unification of governance and ceremony.

Maki's village program was designed to achieve order by banishing political administration and bureaucratic hierarchy. In their place he proposed a religious and spiritual leadership as the surest guarantee of order, community, and autonomy within the village. Although this particular sense of leadership and order seemed limited to the world of the village, it remained a major principle with Maki even when he became involved in political affairs at the national level and began to formulate a strategy for restorationist action. His major proposals, such as the *Goji no kensaku*, merely enumerated a plan for a restoration based upon the idea of an imperial campaign against the *bakufu*. They resembled the restorationist proposal he had advocated for Kurume *han* in the late 1840s and early 1850s. This particular tract, which writers like Tōyama Shigeki have cited as examples of loyalist "futility," illustrated a central tension between political reform leading to a form of local secession and the necessity of finding a national organization capable of resolving the foreign problem. Maki demonstrated a conflict of claims between emotional intensity and political rationality, especially in point 4, which promised to reconstitute the power of land and people by reducing yearly taxes. Although he recognized the necessity to do something about land, taxes, and peasants, he never really worked out how such a reorganization should be accomplished. Rather, he invested authority in a reinstated emperor, a revised version of the village *sonshi*, who, in some vague way, might be able to exercise control over land and people. But this proposal, which undoubtedly reflected both his domainal experience and his commitment to local reform, represented an enlargement of an earlier reformist impulse. His view of expulsion (*jōiron*), regardless of its reference to the arena of national affairs, stemmed from a conviction that politics meant tapping the *ikioi*—the current of the times—and exploiting the opportunities it offered in the present. *Jōiron* functioned as an occasion to promote

land reforms; it was not a goal in itself. Behind Maki's call for an imperial campaign to destroy the *bakufu* and expel the barbarian was his
dream of the Tenpō years that had advocated relief to the peasants and
reorganization of the villages, as well as protection and security in the
form of a program leading to self-sufficiency and autonomy. A restoration of the emperor simply called attention to the incapacity of the
Tokugawa—that is, the national organization—to deal with the for-
eigner and to resolve the more urgent problem of land and people. A
restoration of this kind was little more than the first step to the political
reform imagined by Maki in the Tenpō period. Maki believed that the
public spirit, exemplified by heroic and courageous *shishi*, inspired
both the achievement of national unification and the required political
reorganization, but his own conception of reform related more to the
question of secession and the realization of an agrarian communal order consistent with ancient example than to any "rational" organization. Summoning the emperor was the way people like Maki were able
to conceal the contradictions between their conception of local reform
and the national structure necessitated by the foreign presence.

Between Religion and Polity

The Restoration that was announced five years after Maki wrote the
Goji no kensaku sought to dissolve this tension. First, it considered the
question of national unity and the appropriate organization for the new
imperial authority, by displacing the question of political reform as it
related to land, people, and taxes. The very energy that nativists had
noted among the peasantry, which people like Maki had tried to harness in the organization of a peasant militia, became the question that
the unified national administration was consecrated to resolve. Restoration was made to represent interests that would contain the very energies that political reform—whether domainal or rural-agrarian—was
supposed to realize in new conceptions of authority and communitarian order. The presence of alternatives constituted a threat to any
unified national organization capable of succeeding the Tokugawa; the
continued existence of secessionary groups would surely undermine
any conception of authority. The threat was posed by the concept of
the center and periphery held by secessionary groups calling for order,
autonomy, community, and "world renewal." The center was increasingly symbolized by the emperor and the court. It provided the base on
which domainal activists and courtiers were able momentarily to unify

their differences and carry out a *coup d'état* against the shogunal authority system. This *coup d'état* was centered in the court and required
the manipulation of the emperor to create a sign sufficiently authoritative to replace the rulership of the Tokugawa family. Leading the
coup, which was ultimately described as an *ōsei fukko*, or restoration,
was a group of court noblemen such as Nakayama Tadayasu (1809–
88), Iwakura Tomomi (1825–83), and Ōgimachi Sanjō Sanenaru
(1818–1909), who had access to the young emperor. It should be noted
that as courtiers their interests were entirely identified with the center.
In their collective perception, periphery meant domainal interests. Any
political seizure in the name of the emperor represented for them a
resolution of the question of national organization and unified authority, not a concession to the various groups that justified their secessions
by appealing to the model of an ancient agricultural community. For
courtiers like Iwakura, certainly the most articulate of the group, it was
far more important to secure agreement on questions of authority than
to respond to claims for community. Faced with the power of the domains like Chōshū and Satsuma and the massive protest of peasants, it
was crucial first to establish the principle of authority in order to deal
with an uncertain future that could easily be diminished by domainal
power or, worse, disappear altogether in a mass cataclysm. In a very
real sense, courtiers like Iwakura had no power other than their proximity to the emperor. Although they had been able to persuade the
emperor to lend his approval to the idea of restoration, it was not
enough to sustain them against the domainal activists, who had real
power, or the peasants, whom they feared but did not understand. Restoration represented their triumph but it also signaled their demise. No
sooner had courtiers like Iwakura established the *ōsei fukko* in a decree
in 1868 than the real decisions about reshaping the national organization and renovating domestic society fell to those who possessed the
power of their domains (*goishin*). A reminder of the futility of the courtiers' intervention and their desperate appropriation of the nativist vision
was Yano Gendō's *Kenkin sengo*, an elaborately detailed plan for a
restorationist polity. Commissioned by Iwakura in the wake of the Restoration announcement, Yano's program sought to solidify court interests by constructing an organization based on the "unification of ceremony and polity" (*saisei itchi*). Unfortunately, a program of restoration
stripped of its primary communitarian impulse was left only to map out
the religious aspects of the new political order. When the leaders of the
new regime decided that religious life should not interfere with the

formation of state structure, the hopes for a *saisei itchi* dissolved. Ironically, the Restoration announced the end of the nativist restorationist dream.

Iwakura Tomomi turned to the idea of a restoration during his exile outside Kyoto in the last days of the Tokugawa period. Almost as if he had struck on a plan that might offer a way to mobilize events and thus secure real authority for his group, he began earnestly to write about the meaning of restoration and the reasons why it should be speedily implemented. His purpose was both strategic and tactical: restoration offered the basis of a broad plan, and it functioned as a device with which to discredit the *bakufu*. Lacking access to real material strength, Iwakura hoped that by making the emperor available to anti-Tokugawa domainal activists he would be able to secure an arrangement wherein the court might once more play an instrumental role in formulating national policy. Also, such an arrangement might prevent a domainal coalition from merely replacing the Tokugawa hegemony with a new version of the shogunate. Hence, he regarded the restoration of the emperor as the most persuasive means by which courtiers like himself could gain access to the world of political decision making from which they had been excluded since the middle ages. It is not surprising that Iwakura referred to the last great imperial restoration in Japan's history, the Kenmu Restoration of the fourteenth century, as an example of what needed to be done. He later, of course, changed his mind about the relevance of this example for the present, since it had ended in failure. In the *Shinshū kanzaisaku* (1858) he cited the example of Emperor Godaigo's (r. 1318–39) efforts to retrieve political authority from the Ashikaga and the loyalty of retainers like Kusunoki Masashige in fighting the enemies of the throne. This historical exercise showed how the present must "imitate" the example of "endeavor" in the coming struggle with the barbarians (*Ksi* 3:18). A few years later (1860) he proposed returning the "political center of trust" to the throne and linked it to the principle of "public discussion and consultation" (*yogi kōron*). Iwakura aimed to couple the great enterprise of a restoration with some conception of conciliar consensus in order to protect the "political heart of trust" (the Kantō region) and thus the imperial court from being dominated by any one faction or interest. By 1866 his understanding of an imperial restoration, expressed in the *Sōri meichū*, coincided with a moderate position that aligned the *bakufu* and the larger domains with the court. In this text, Iwakura disclosed his fears concerning *sonnō jōi* radicalism and its consequences for the realm.

Here, too, he first hinted at a different model for restoration, one that was not constrained by the failure of Godaigo to maintain himself in power against the military estate in the fourteenth century (*Ksi* 3:42).

Ultimately, Iwakura came around to a view already articulated by Maki Izumi and Ōkuni Takamasa. This position, expressed in the restoration decree of January 3, 1868, called for a restoration whereby "all matters shall seek their foundation in the work begun by Emperor Jinmu in ancient times." Between the time of his first recorded thoughts about the possibility of restoration and the Restoration, Iwakura had clearly abandoned his preference for the Kenmu example—a *chūkō*—for an *ōsei fukko* summoning the more remote example of state foundation itself. He had also moved from a moderate, pro-*bakufu* opinion to one demanding the *bakufu's* dissolution. Accompanying this change of mind was a condemnation of the shogunate for abandoning public interest to pursue private policies (ibid. 3:84). Only the model of a restoration that predated the *bakuhan* system could sanction the destruction of the shogunal order. Moreover, a restoration liberated from Tokugawa associations promised to reinstall the court in its proper place as the administrative arm of imperial authority. Such a restoration (Iwakura's language increasingly referred to it as a *kōshitsu chūkō*— a restoration of the court, not the emperor) would "hereafter throw off the private intention [*shishin*] of the *bakufu* for a foundation of public principle." But his logic betrayed his own interest in promoting the cause of the court behind the screen of an *ōsei fukko* (ibid. 3:98–99). "The essence of restoring political authority to the emperor," he wrote, "lies in expanding the national prestige and crushing the foreign barbarian. The basis for carrying this out exists in unifying the realm; unifying the realm lies in coming to a single political ordinance; to reach [the state of] a single political ordinance is the responsibility of the imperial court, which is at the center of carrying out a national administration." Iwakura was referring to a restorationist decree that only the court could issue. He was convinced that the court could constitute the axis of any new government, because the "great task of the court must be to make a general inquiry of conditions. And such inquiry must be debated before the emperor" (ibid. 3:104).

In an opinion of 1867 Iwakura listed what he believed an *ōsei fukko* should consist of. Heading the list was a return of the imperial family to secular life and the abolition of the law that obliged members of the family to become Buddhists. After this separation of court from Buddhism came a "revival of procedure under the direction of the Bureau of Shrine Affairs (Jingikan) and the executive council of the new government (Dajōkan)." These conditions pointed to the form the Restoration was to take. The resemblance between them and Yano Gendō's elaborate plan for a restoration were not accidental. Yano's *Kenkin sengo*, commissioned by Iwakura, was drafted in December, 1867. Just as Yano's detailed program for a replica of an ancient theocracy was based on Jinmu's act of foundation, Iwakura's completed conception of an *ōsei fukko* drew its inspiration and sanction from the founder's example. As suggested above, Maki and Ōkuni, too, had used the model of Jinmu's restoration. In the last days before the Restoration, the proposal was given forceful expression by Iwakura's secretary, Tamamatsu Misao, a student of Ōkuni's and the man who actually prepared the draft for the restoration edict. In an "inquiry" (*shimon*) from Iwakura to Tamamatsu concerning the "basis of an imperial restoration," the issue of what kind of example was introduced for discussion. Tamamatsu referred to an earlier record of discussions in which Iwakura, Nakayama Tadayasu, Ōgimachi Sanjō Sanenaru and Nakamikado Tsuneyuki "planned the great project of an *ōsei fukko*."[11] According to the record, the participants had discussed retrieving the system of the Kenmu Restoration and establishing an administrative order consistent with historical precedent. Iwakura had countered by arguing that the "system of the Kenmu Restoration was insufficient as a model to imitate," and hence he submitted an inquiry on this issue to Tamamatsu. Here, Tamamatsu made nativism into a practical political instrument applicable to the conditions of the immediate present. The example of the Kenmu Restoration was too limiting, he explained, and "it is essential that the restoration of ancient imperial polity broaden the magnanimity of the throne as much as possible and devise a plan of greater scope. To establish an administrative structure it must be rooted in the original foundation of Jinmu's empire. It must be a standard [*kijun*] that will plan to unify all in the universe so as to correspond to a renovation [*ishin*] of all things."[12] In the construction of the new government, Iwakura advised, the builders should follow Tamamatsu's words. The decree announcing the *ōsei fukko* proposed that the new government would "endeavor" in such a way so that all things would "adhere to the beginnings of Jinmu's establishment."

On the occasion of the restoration decree of 1868 and as a kind of acknowledgment that the new government was to be centered in the emperor and his court, Yano Gendō brought out his *Kenkin sengo*. Yano had been trained in the Hirata school; he was an activist in late-

Tokugawa loyalist politics and an associate of the Iwakura-Tamamatsu line. The *Kenkin sengo* was a memorial petition commemorating the renovation. Its title was inspired by the *Lushi chungiu* (Mr. Lu's spring and autumn), a pre-Han commentary on the "Spring and Autumn Annals." The term *kenkin* referred to a modest way to present something to a person; *sengo* was a humble expression for a trifling opinion. The effect was supposed to be ironic. *Kenkin*, it is interesting to note, was also used as a title in one of the drafts of Maki Izumi's *Keii gusetsu* a decade earlier.

Although Yano's petition was inspired by the example of "Jinmu's Restoration," it also distinguished sharply between the founder of a political order and the authenticating ancestral *kami*. "The successive reigns, beginning with the foundation of the ancestral founder Jinmu, are all based upon the basic doctrines [*honkyō*] of the imperial ancestors and heavenly deities." Drawing his inspiration from the "event" of Jinmu's earlier restoration, Yano proposed to give political substance to this example in the present. His petition, reflecting Ōkuni's earlier conception of change and new knowledge, contrasted markedly with Hirata's and Motoori's formulations of a restorationist program. In the earlier cases, it is difficult to find any explicit proposal calling for a restoration based on the state foundation of Emperor Jinmu. When Hirata referred to restoration, he was calling attention to the genesis of creation, not some later political event, since much of his thinking concentrated on demonstrating that political authority belonged to the world of visible affairs and was ancillary to the hidden realm. A discourse that poured so much effort into displacing politics by cosmology and epistemology to achieve communal order would most surely have had trouble in apprehending the political events of 1867 and 1868. Paradoxically, the function of Yano's *Kenkin sengo* was to make sense of these events within the terms of a discourse that had already discounted eventfulness as a condition of its production. As *kokugaku* confronted the Restoration, it was forced to either withdraw from the political field or try to make an accommodation to it. In the end nativists like Yano managed only to weave an "emotional fabric" out of the Restoration; they could not themselves come up with a polity pledged to "renovate all things." In its discussions of restoration, nativist discourse could only call for a return to a dehierarchicized agrarian community held together by worship and work. The power of the hidden realm was simply not adequate to actualize a Restoration in the visible world.

Yano's blueprint for a new administrative order failed to overcome the contradiction between the political precedent of Jinmu and the act of creation that had established an agricultural community prior to the monarch's drive for empire, between the claims of the hidden world and those of the visible. It should be recalled that *kokugaku* had made this division, authenticated by cosmology, into an ontological principle. The corresponding classification established a real distinction between the affairs of the gods, (growth and productivity) and the affairs of the visible world (political administration). Nor can we forget, as Yano apparently did, that the detail nativism tried to give to the hidden world was identified with daily work, worship, and custom, as if *mukai* was the model for agricultural and community life. By contrast, the visible world of politics and administration remained remote, as if the *kokugakusha* were not concerned with mundane problems of administration and governance. And that is precisely what they were saying until they were confronted by epic political events in the visible realm. Some writers have argued, in this connection, that Yano was a spokesman for the masses and that his proposal was pointedly devoted to realizing a "people's polity" (*minsei*). Although he was no doubt very much interested in signs of massive civil disobedience such as *ee ja nai ka* and *okage mairi*, these concerns did not make him an advocate of populist interests. Rather, we must see Yano's program as an effort to interpret the moment at hand, to endow it with significance and a meaningful structure, and to make sense of—if not gain control over—the events of 1867 and 1868. The *Kenkin sengo* was an elaborate attempt to *re-present* the events that had signaled the *ōsei fukko*.

Specifically, the problem Yano was compelled to resolve was how to square the primacy of the hidden realm, with all of its associations, with the momentous political events of the day. It should be recalled that *kokugakusha* believed that they had found in the invisible realm a more than adequate substitute for the official world of power and governance. They also believed that they could dismiss the claims of the visible world by the agency of reemplotment. Rural *kokugakusha* did not have to worry about reuniting the two realms, and their preference for the hidden was license for secession. But when political events sought to arrest this secessionary movement, it became necessary, as Yano clearly showed, to find a way to maintain the central importance of the hidden world before the new claims of the visible. Completing this task was considered urgent, since the visible world was now committed to terminating the arrangements by which *kokugakusha* had given substance to their world. In effect, Yano was confronted by a problem that nativist discourse had not anticipated. He and his colleagues could not reaffirm the primacy of the hidden world, which they had already established in their effort to detraumatize events occuring in the visible world, and they could not extol the claims of the visible world because of their commitment to the invisible realm.

Confounded by this contradiction, Yano Gendō sought two major goals: the unification of religious ceremony and government (*saisei itchi*) and the establishment of a permanent center for imperial studies (*kōgakusho*). The former attempted to merge the claims of the hidden world to the visible realm and, thus, give shape to a new order. The latter was related to the *kokugaku* belief in the importance of knowledge (and interest) as preparation for proper conduct and, presumably, policy making; it disclosed the nativist conviction that interest was prior to the establishment of order and that the maintenance of an order of a certain kind would depend on the availability of knowledge. Yano and other *kokugakusha* believed, perhaps as a way of validating their claims, that it was important to the stability of the new order to establish a center for the teaching of national studies and the study of imperial institutions. If Japanese society was to be guided by an administration devoted to unifying religious ceremony and governance, it would need access to an authoritative body of knowledge concerning such affairs and a group of experts able to dispense it. To this end Yano, even after the disappointment of seeing *saisei itchi* dismantled in the early years of the Meiji era, spent most of his time trying to give detail to a discipline of knowledge that he called "fundamental doctrine," *honkyō*.

Yano linked the Restoration to the reinstatement of the "tradition of fundamental teachings of the imperial ancestors and heavenly deities in all things and to the spread throughout the cosmos of the doctrines of governance with the Great Way of the gods [*kannagara no daidō*]" (*Kus*, 548). He saw the *ōsei fukko* as an occasion to implement these teachings and as the surest guarantee of order, tranquillity, and prosperity; it is obvious that he imagined the Restoration as an auspicious event signaling the end of politics and the beginning of the Way of the gods. Under the sway of this conviction he was enabled to interpret the incidence of urban unrest, the "congestion of the *ee ja nai ka* demonstrations in Kyoto and the *okage mairi* (pilgrimages to the Grand Shrine of Ise) as august approval of the imperial deities from heaven" for the events of 1867 (ibid.)[13] The disturbances in the cities and the countryside appeared as signs of heaven's intention to restore the imperial government to rule. In the preface of the *Kenkin sengo*, Yano explained that "such blessings originally derive from the governance of the hidden world [*Ōkuninushi no kami*]," and that recent events were announced by "divine signs" (*shinbu*) falling on the city of Kyoto during the *ee ja nai kai* demonstrations. The Restoration represented the recognition of the primacy of the invisible realm over the visible and revealed to all that the visible world was ultimately directed by the governance of Ōkuninushi.

Yano declared that it was clear that knowledge of the fundamentals was to be identified with the new order. "If the limits of the Great Way are brought out and established, the first political duty of the realm, owing to the religious ceremonies to the heavenly and earthly deities, will be to proclaim a unification of worship and governance." Elsewhere he asserted that a "chief duty must be *kami* learning (*kannarai*) within the Great Way of the imperial deities" (*Kus*, 558). He was confident, from the precedent of decrees of emperors Uda (r. 887–97) and Juntoku (r. 1210–21), that with the assistance of such "august learning" governance would be able to see clearly the "sources of prosperity, decline, order, and disorder in antiquity and the present" (ibid.). Moreover, the people must be nourished, which meant they must be taught and educated properly. As part of this "indoctrination," there must be a suitable emphasis on the forms of worship among the people of the realm (ibid.). The "unparalleled" *daijōsai* (Great Thanksgiving Ceremony), in particular, should be restored from the distant past; the time was right for its retrieval by the government. In the revival of such a remote ritual, he believed he had found the best case for a unified religious polity. The teachings of the imperial deities related to a knowledge of ceremony and worship, yet embedded in ceremony and worship lay the principle of governance itself. The restoration of the *daijōsai* was vital to the act of administration, just as the reinstatement of ceremonies connected to specific shrines was essential to maintain order among the people. At the same time, instructing the people in their religious duties would reinforce the realm's order and prosperity. The main purpose of government, Yano argued throughout the *Kenkin sengo*, was the performance of proper religious ceremonies; the model for such an arrangement lay in the ancient state of the Taika reforms (645) and Taihō code (701), whose decisive elements he now sought to elucidate in this text.

This conception of knowledge and its role in governing was at the heart of Yano's educational ideas. Before the Restoration he had, on numerous occasions, drafted petitions calling for the establishment of a school (*daigaku*) pledged to a *kokugaku* curriculum. And this aim was the informing force behind his involvement in the *kōgakusho* after he had offered his famous petition, the *Kenkin sengo.*[14] The *kōgakusho* barely existed for nine months, between December 1868 and September 1869. A concession to *kokugakusha* like Hirata Kanetane (nominal head of the Hirata school), Tamamatsu Misao, and Yano Gendō, it tried to put into practice Yano's conviction that knowledge of a certain kind preceded proper policy and action. Yano's first plan, in the pre-Restoration years, had been for a "university"; after the Restoration it was changed to an educational system called the *kōgakusho.* Its basic aim, expressed in a preamble probably written by Yano, was to enlist and train able men for government. But, unlike the Chinese example, the new school would educate people from all classes.

> To propagate the fundamental doctrines of the first imperial ancestors and heavenly deities, it is necessary to establish the doctrine that emperor and *kami* are not separate and that ceremony and governance are united. Allowing for the presence of such varying conditions as civilizations and barbarism, past and present, it is important to fix ceremonies to the deities of heaven and earth and a system of etiquette for high and low, government and people. Within this [system] there is to be no lack of wisdom and competence among the samurai and general population of the realm. . . . The way to order the realm and tranquilize the people by morality and ethics will be discussed and investigated close at hand; guidance and assistance will be offered at further remove. An image of talent and ability will evolve. Throughout the various regions of the realm, and in the large and small schools, the correct style will prevail. Like the ancient saying, "A trip of ten thousand *ri* begins with one step," . . . we will restore the imperial Way to the far corners of the earth and its majesty will glow throughout the world [*hakkō bankoku*]"[15]

The program of study stressed the propagation of fundamental teachings and the unification of ceremony and governance as the basic proposition for the new order. Within the university administration, which was to manage the new system, there was to be a shrine honoring the imperial ancestors and heavenly deities as a means of reinforcing the union of worship and education. The curriculum focused on *honkyō* and the classics that best demonstrated the linkage between ceremony and governance.

The sanction for the extended proposal outlined in the *Kenkin sengo* was provided by the recent popular disturbances. Incidents in the streets of the larger towns and, presumably, in the countryside represented not simply a divine sign but "blessings from the world of invisible governance" indicating its intention. Yano relied on the Izumo tradition to interpret these events as well as the establishment of a new government as gifts from Ōkuninushi no kami (not the Sun Goddess). This argument had been proposed earlier (1862) by a colleague of Yano's, Tsunoda Tadayuki (1834–1918) an activist and later editor of Hirata's collected writings, who wrote a tract reconstituting Hirata's conception of ancient history as the ground for action and policy (*Koshiryaku*). Tsunoda proclaimed that Susanowo and Amaterasu were coequal and that the creation deities had "entrusted the heavens to the Sun Goddess and this great earth to the storm god" (*Kus*, 534).[16]

Yano believed that it had been the "custom in Japan since the time of Jinmu tennō to bestow the fundamental teachings of the ancestral deities on all things" (*Kus*, 548). He made clear what he meant by "fundamental teachings" as a form of knowledge when he proposed the organization of a new polity: "The first political duty of the realm is to implement the religious ceremony to honor the heavenly and earthly deities." Specifically, this required a proclamation calling for the "unification of polity and religion, governance and ceremony" (*saisei itchi*). It necessitated the dissolution of an autonomous and self-interested politics, an act that Yano, like many *kokugakusha* and founders of new syncretic religions, saw as the first step toward a new kind of social order. After all, the recent past, and even earlier, provided impressive testimony that political self-interest, as represented by the Tokugawa system, had torn the social order into swirling and unconnected fragments seeking new forms of cohesion. To writers like Yano, whose own position had been imperiled by the new leadership, *saisei itchi* offered a guarantee against political division and interests inimical to nativism.

The unification of religion and polity promised to restore the relationship between the divine and the human, to put into practice the nativist deification of humanity; it also made possible the implementation of Yano's second major point, the establishment of a *jinsei*, "benevolent polity." Here, Yano revealed the linkage between his larger program and the effort of rural nativists to envisage an administration responsive to the needs of the people so as to provide relief and assistance in times of distress (*minsei*, ibid., 572, 577). His language barely concealed the nativist preoccupation with assistance and relief and its concern for arresting the incidence of peasant disturbances. Benevolence meant "making all people in the realm content by giving them adequate clothing, food, and shelter and by completing each person's moral character." Such actions, he believed, were natural, because "even the ancestral heavenly deities decreed family names to all living peoples. The august decree of Aramatsuri no miya proclaimed, "People are the honorable treasure of imperial shrines." The evidence from ancient sources overwhelmingly supported the idea that ruling meant providing assistance, much in the "manner of parents who nurture weak children" (ibid., 548–49). But to see this duty as a sacred obligation meant fashioning a government directed by religious purpose to initiate a policy of relief and assistance for the peasant masses. Yano illustrated the paradox of the nativist position that sought simultaneously to give peasants relief and local autonomy and to arrest rebellion by averting "evil spirits" and the appearance of "traitors" (ibid.).

Perhaps predictably, the *Kenkin sengo* remained silent on the real details of a *minsei*, which might very well have served peasant interests and avoided continuing unrest; it went directly to the task of reorganizing the nation along the lines of *saisei itchi*. Yano made accomodations to the new arrangement of power; by deliberately equating a *minsei* with a *jinsei*, he shifted the focus of attention from the village, which had occupied the gaze of many nativist writers, to the central government. His three major categories—*saisei itchi, jinsei, jinmu fusatsu* (military preparedness)—and thirty-one subprinciples resembled the basic proposals of Mitogaku and countless other domainal reform programs since the Tenpō period. (The archetype for many *han* reforms, Mito *han*, had advanced three interrelated proposals: reverence for ancestors, loving the people (*aimin*), and fostering the military spirit.) Yano's specific recommendations advised strict religious observances, such as regular visitations to the great shrines, and periodic imperial trips throughout the country in order to learn about the hardships of the peasantry (ibid., 584). To contain the "traitorous rebels in the *kinai*" (*kinai no hainan no zokutō ai okuri*, ibid., 580), he recommended the formation of farming militia (*nōhei*), which could also accommodate the surplus of samurai after the reorganization of social classes. A few years later, the Meiji government established agricultural military colonies in Hokkaido under the rubric of samurai rehabilitation (*shizoku jusan*). Because the government undoubtedly shared Yano's fears of peasant uprisings, it seems likely that such colonies, which were never really tested, were envisioned as both a hedge against internal unrest and a deterrent to foreign invasion.

Yano specified the institutional form of the new religious polity. His plan was inspired by the example of the Taika Reforms of the seventh century rather than the ill-fated Kenmu Restoration of the fourteenth century (ibid., 576, 579). He believed that the reforms had made possible an orderly society where the "people of the realm resemble the grass that yields to the wind, and the clouds that follow" (ibid., 570). But he also emphasized military preparedness as one of his three major proposals for the new restoration government. (Again, it seems likely that he, like others, was far more concerned with the threat of domestic violence than foreign invasion.) He argued for the establishment of a "divine military" that would protect the realm "against murder and assassination" (ibid., 549). Echoes of the 1860s were still very audible to him; although he, like others, could easily exaggerate the foreign threat, his experience attested to the profundity of internal disorder and the necessity to stem it. For, once all the details of his proposed order fell into place, "where the provinces are under the law and the institutes, where the *gun*, regions, towns, and villages are under the provinces . . ., where the top functions as a high command," then all would prosper with the emperor (ibid, 584–85). "To carry out the great fundamentals of a religious polity [*saisei*] in this manner will nurture all, enrich the regions and provinces, exalt the military majesty" (ibid., 585).

Yano was most literal in his understanding of a religious polity. For scholars who have brushed aside the religious claims of the Restoration government as a cynical expediency of its leaders or who have simply ignored it as a significant consideration, it should be emphasized that men like Yano and those who listened to him were seriously interested in this form as a possibility for the new government. To this end, Yano detailed the several ceremonies that should be observed and the various shrines that should be either reconstructed or simply built anew. (ibid., 551–556.). The object of his program to promote shrines and ceremony everywhere, which he exhaustively outlined in the *Kenkin sengo,* was to remind the people, in regular worship, of their duties to the deities. For Yano, following Hirata, participation in regular service served as a promising device to secure acquiescence and order. A survey of his detailed mapping of shrines and places of worship recalls Hirata's schedule of punctual, daily observances to the various deities and shrines (*Maichō shinbai shiki*).

The detail of Yano's restoration program was matched by its obvious shortsightedness; what it lacked in perception it surely made up in specificity. Although the new government nodded in the direction of *saisei itchi* and even appropriated some of his recommendations, only the forms of such a religious polity, not its content, were ever accepted. *Kokugaku* gained "official" representation by its association with imperial courtiers like Iwakura Tomomi, an associate of Ōkuni Takamasa and the patron of Tamamatsu Misao. In exchange, under the guidance of Yano Gendō, it quickly abandoned its linkages with rural life—the hidden world, so to speak—for the visible world of imperial court politics. The appropriations not only changed the essential purpose of nativism by shifting the object of focus from the resolution of rural problems to the determination of public political form but also stigmatized it as an ideology of courtiers in their struggle over decision making in the early-Meiji government. When Iwakura lost, so did *kokugaku*, but by that time it had been so eviscerated of its fundamental purpose that it was virtually unrecognizable.

The Community of Silence

Yano defended the wider interests of *kokugaku* to the end, but the end came sooner than he or any of his colleagues could have foreseen. His restoration plan aimed at minimizing disorder and outlined a new authority system to satisfy a number of new requirements that neither he nor his contemporaries in discourse had ever imagined. He framed his proposals on the basis of a new kind of knowledge, which, he believed, would determine the nature of political relationships necessary for the new order. But, it is well to remember, the order he conceived was not simply political or religious. It was both. This ambiguity, which undoubtedly lay at the heart of the nativist discourse, made it impossible for *kokugakusha* to give lasting political representation to the events of 1867 and 1868. Their conception of politics suffered from the same deficiencies as their conception of language. Nativists had sought to rescue a subterranean language, translucent and directly representative of things and emotions—a kind of private language whereby the self honestly expressed experience. Their proposed new order resembled the hidden world of Ōkuninushi—authoritative, authentic, private, and concealed; it ran aground when seeking public expression. Distinctions between hidden and visible, private and public, authentic and artificial were simply too great to overcome. Nativists failed because these oppositions provided them the sanction and the means to talk about a sublangue more translucent than public speech and a religiopolitical order more authoritative than the public administrative structure.

At the same time that *kokugaku* was pressing claims for its conception of knowledge, others were doing likewise. All could agree with

Yano that the new governance was an announcement for a new kind
of learning; they could not agree on the kind of learning that would
best serve it. In the ensuing contest, the nativist promotion of fundamental doctrine and its valorization of a cultural order, its effort to
establish a balance between the horizontalist relations of community
and the verticality of hierarchical authority (symbolized by the emperor) simply failed to gain serious acceptance. Too much of *kokugaku*
concentrated on displacing authority by community. Yet the real point
of the Restoration, which nativists saw as an end to politics, was, in
fact, to install a political order free from disorder. The restorers looked
for a new kind of knowledge that would mandate a new set of power
and authoritative relationships. Even before the Restoration writers and
activists had discussed the possibility of a practical knowledge (*jitsugaku*), universal in its applicability, instrumental in its problem-solving
capacity. Such a knowledge, which meant Western, technological, and
"social scientific" learning, was seen increasingly as the most appropriate means available to resolve the contemporary problem of disorder
and to establish a new kind of political society. Practical knowledge also
provided a way to dramatize the importance of "universalistic" standards in the recruitment of leaders for the new society. An instrumental
and practical knowledge was, in theory, accessible to all groups. Its
acquisition depended on ability and talent, not on social genealogy,
and it represented a demonstration of qualifications for responsibility.
Within ten years after the Restoration, the nativist ideal had all but
vanished, displaced by new forms of ideology and organization validated by a practical knowledge. Its leavings found expression only in
memory, in efforts to elevate a more authentic language (*genbun itchi*),
in nostalgia and cultural narcissim (*Nihonjinron*), and in a sense of
betrayal authorizing resistance to the state.

The problem was simply that restoration, as envisaged by *kokugakusha*, represented principles on which to construct a human community but not a modern political society. Any reader of Shimazaki
Tōson's moving lament for the vanished possibilities that nativism
seemed to promise people like his father, (in the figure of Aoyama
Hanzō in *Yoake mae* [Before the dawn]) will not doubt that its most
intense adherents recognized in it communitarian aspirations bordering
upon utopia. Yet, as Tōson concluded of Hanzō's ruined ideals, only
willed madness was equal to the massive disappointments experienced
by supporters of this vision once they were forced to recognize the real
drift of contemporary history. A similar fate awaited the believers in a

truly translucent language. What they received was a language more artificial than natural, open to a debasement (by its accommodation to foreign words and expressions) that would have driven people like Motoori mad.

Nativism failed where it seemed most secure. In their effort to dissolve politics into religious worship (which it shared with many of the new religions and the *yonaoshi*) *kokugakusha* could not project the principles on which to erect a state apparatus capable of ensuring order and security, which had prompted them and others to search for a solution in such devices as *saisei itchi* in the first place. To identify politics with religion was to link authority with legitimacy. But the social order they imagined was a poor foil to the state that domainal activists had erected to preserve the possibility of orderliness.

Perhaps nativists were too close to the problem. *Kokugaku* had never lost its links to the upper peasants, who, themselves, were caught between revolutionary peasants calling for a new history or an end to the old and the world of *bakuhan* officials basing their authority on vertical and hierarchical relationships in power. Their own position was marked by ambivalence—a fear of "proletarianization" yet a distrust for powerholders who had increasingly failed to deliver security and protection. This ambivalence explains the *kokugakusha*'s willingness to invest their support in a cultural order, first in the shape of the autonomous village promising to dissolve all differences and later in the state. Their belief in the village as a combination of community and responsive leadership was the understanding that Aoyama Hanzō, and others like him, brought into the "brave new world" of Meiji Japan. But *kokugaku*, from the beginning, had feared too much community was a greater threat than too much authority. Nativists believed they had found the proper solution in an emperor entrusted by the creation deities and responsive to the community for which they had made creation, who would therefore represent the people and resolve the question dogging Tokugawa Japan since the eighteenth century. The result would be a balance between community and authority. Even here, however, they were bound to be disappointed, because they became locked into the question of origins. Although they were undoubtedly correct to differentiate the actual source or content of authority from its mere form, their reliance on divine appointment and the priority of the religious obliged them ultimately to find a model that would best preserve this enduring principle of authority. Despite the power of the hidden world to confer religious authority for all time to come, it could not resolve the question of temporal form that nativist discourse had previously discounted as a secondary consideration.

The Meiji Restoration represented the least radical secession that contemporary history could offer to solve the problem of a failing control system and its incapacity to stem widespread social unrest. All in all, it resembled most the earlier Mito solution, with its primacy of vertical and hierarchical relationships, its promotion of temporal forms of political authority and power, its recommendations for greater moral discipline and its determination to settle rural unrest, and its advancement of practical knowledge as the surest guide for leadership. Mito offered the most acceptable solution to the question of authority and order, over the claims of community among the centrifugated constituencies of late-Tokugawa society. The Meiji state proposed the dissolution of the very divisions that had led groups like the *kokugakusha* to confront the question of order and security in the first place. Yet, as we know from Japan's subsequent history, the price paid for order and the security of interests was autonomy itself. The communitarian and human impulses that had characterized so much of the nativist discourse were forfeited for "governability." In modern Japan such impulses would have to find new modes of expression, as people once more sought their roots in the hidden world that, even Yano believed, had produced the real Japan. "Yamatokuni had been originally contracted in concealment during the age of the gods," he declared, and regardless of how time and forgetfulness obliterated this truth, men could always return to it as a source for new beginnings.

But the beginnings people attempted to implement came too late with too litle. Rural Japan, for example, offered the faded promise of nativism in *minzokugaku*—ethnology—in the formation of a "science" devoted to preserving custom and folk. Other forms of retrieving the original promise of *kokugaku* found imperfect expression in a truncated Shinto; in romanticism and nostalgia; in the rantings of the revolutionary Right; in the declarations of social historians to write a people's history; in the Japanese obsession with themselves and their sameness (*Nihonjinron*); and even, perhaps, in a people's movement (*shimin undō*) pledged to clean up political corruption, bureaucratic indifference, and the environment. The life represented by the hidden realm was to remain in the shadows throughout Japan's modern century as background to the brilliant achievements of bureaucratic necessity. Yet the loss of this genuinely utopian purpose—a world mediated by communal arrangements, ancestors, tutelary deities, work, and mutual assistance—would occasionally emerge from the shadows to haunt and animate fitful people to recreate its blurred promise in the harsh light of modern Japan. In the end, the political legacy nativism bequeathed to modern Japan was a radical community of silence. In its determined opposition to hierarchical structures and its move to the periphery, it forfeited all means to make the necessary accommodation to the mediation of politics. All that it seemed to offer was a form of acceptance born of political indifference to the claims of authority, a rejection of the visible world of power for the communitarian consolations of the invisible.

Epilogue: Native Knowledge and the Production of a Modern "Japanese Ideology"

In this study I have been concerned with showing how private experiences—the invisible—were made into forms of public practice, how conceptions of language and labor became subjects for discourse in the late-Tokugawa period. Once these essentially private moments entered the public realm, they became contesting instruments in a struggle between ruler and ruled and could be mobilized against the received order to realize a visionary, human community. In this sense *kokugaku*, despite its penchant for particularism and exceptionalism, remained a radically utopian vision of communitarian expectations. To this end, many of its tenets—its massive displacement of the political for the religious (the social); its consistent rejection of history for a pre-class, folk chronotope and a privileging of place; its disciplining of the body in the service of work, which rescued the body from the blandishments of pleasure announced by the culture of play (*gesakuron*); its noninstrumental conception of language, which insisted on communication not between men and other men but between a community and the world and the gods who made and gave it; and its intense conviction in human reciprocity and self-sufficiency—attest to a conception of community incomparably more visionary than any experiment recorded in the long duration of Japanese history and more threatening to settled forms of power and authority than even the Western presence.

Instead of telling a story about nativism and trying to reconstruct its "development" in narrative, I have tried to explain how nativists constructed a narrative to banish linear and progressive time. This story

407

line portrayed the folk ceaselessly reenacting the creation by reproducing the social conditions of existence through the agency of worship (speech) and work. In the displacement of contemporary reality by reemplotting the rural scene, nativists believed they had found a way to rid the historical field of overdetermined eventfulness for the security of an atemporal, divine structure. They installed code in the place of context and expanded the claims of the invisible realm spatially (well beyond their original locus in godly affairs) to replace the event-producing world of the visible.

This operation derived from a prior move to transmute private experiences—the concealed content of everyday life—into public discourse and practice by designating first speech and then work as subjects for discussion. Situating both in the body, nativists counteracted the bodily excesses of urban culture by showing how speech related folk to the gods and work expressed constant thanks and repayment for the blessings of creation. By the same token, they were able to overcome the opposition between mental and manual, theory and practice, because the body now brought separate practices together. Once essentially private and even intimate experience entered the public domain, the received public order could no longer remain the same or go unchallenged. What nativists offered was the claim of an even more authentic human community than any existing arrangement. Under the force of circumstances in the late-Tokugawa period, the nativist transformation of a private and hitherto unarticulated experience into public discourse—the "externalization of internality"—confirmed Sartre's observation that "words" invariably "wreak havoc when they find a name for what had up to then been lived namelessly."[1] In this process, the private experiences underwent dramatic changes "when they recognized themselves in the *public objectivity* of an already constituted discourse, the objective sign of recognition of their right to be spoken and to be spoken publicly."[2]

The centrality of the body, now indistinguishable from the "ordinary folk," and the daily activities of worship and work resulted in far-reaching consequences for the subsequent history of modern Japan. It should be recalled that nativism positioned its own claims to authenticity against the entrenched domination of Chinese culture in Japanese life. This is not to say that the encounter with the Other was its determining principle but only to suggest that Otherness often provided the occasion for nativists to specify their own claims. There is no good reason to suppose that the presence of the Other in the eighteenth century, like anxiety over the destination of the spirits after death, was any greater or more urgent than at another time in Japan's history. In fact, even though nativists denounced the Chinese mind-heart (*kara-gokoro*) regularly, like a ritual plaint, their own conception of language militated altogether against manipulating the Other. Because language was envisaged as the condition for establishing an empathetic community and was made to serve integration within the group, it remained situated in the space constrained by man's exchange with the gods and the world—worship and work—rather than functioning as an instrument of action upon the Other.[3]

But it is undeniably true that China as the Other initially played a role in the formation of the nativist discourse and that its "suppression" related very much to what *kokugaku* was trying to "reinstate" in Japanese life. Owing to a logic that established similitude and equivalence as identity, nativists sought to emphasize those aspects that made all Japanese irreducibly Japanese—the same and thereby different from the Other. In order to distance themselves from China and liberate life from the assimilative (and manipulative) powers of culture, nativists contested culture itself as a category, declared freedom from its alien constraints, and defined the terms of being Japanese. This attitude differed considerably, however, from one that promoted acting on or manipulating the Other. In a world teeming with differences, nativists believed, worship (speaking the Japanese language) and work (repaying the gods) conformed to the requirements of identity and protected the ordinary folk from becoming other than what the creation deities had intended. Such a strategy aimed to remove the Japanese from the Other and from both history and culture. When nativism was exported to the countryside and used to authorize the secession of the village from the control system, only the terms of the strategy had changed to satisfy the new scene, not the strategy itself. Just as the quest for similitude led to distancing and even withdrawal in late-Tokugawa Japan, sameness in modern Japan led not to explaining or even accounting for difference but to valorizing uniqueness in a world of interaction. In the Tokugawa period, worship and work represented elements of a practice pledged to protect the folk from being assimilated by the Other (China); in twentieth-century Japan they were employed increasingly to authorize a theory of uniqueness and to sanction cultural and even racial exceptionalism. In this process, recessive and particularistic associations surfaced in more dangerous combinations and were made, through the agency of the state, to harness the more communitarian and radically humanist impulses associated with nativism. The utopian and communitarian vision that, in the eyes of official discourse, branded nativism as a threat to the received order of things became, in the twentieth century, implicated in the hegemonic order itself by inducing Japanese to believe that supporting the state unquestioningly revealed the sign of being uniquely Japanese. In this process, community was transformed into a consensual order serving the state. The practice of work and worship was subordinated to the interests of the broader political unit—the state—when before it had been seen by nativists as justification for withdrawing from the authority system. Ultimately, the activity necessitated by praxis was transmuted into static forms of participation and performance.

How this transformation of nativism into modern Japan's ideology came about remains outside the immediate concerns of this study. Yet it would be incomplete if I did not at least suggest how an essentially utopian communitarian vision was neutralized politically and assimilated to a larger cultural ideology mandating a consensual order. At the heart of this hegemonic process and the production of ideology was the nativist conception of intransitive knowledge. It will be recalled that nativism, in its Tokugawa incarnation, rescued daily life, custom, and "household duties"—the alterity of an official discourse that privileged mental over manual labor—and converted them into the content of discursive knowledge. This move made the center equivalent with what hitherto had been alterity and removed the center to the place of the Other. Yet, we have also observed, this new form of knowledge presupposed closing all distances between subject and object; between the *mono* (thing) or *koto* (deed) inhabiting the daily world and its apperception (*aware, shiruwakemae*); between the knowing subject who made custom and the object of knowing, custom itself. No difference was supposed to intervene between what humans did and made and what they could possibly know; practice and hermeneutics became the same thing. Although nativists hoped to win the reward of identity by promoting this kind of intransitivity, and thereby call into question the authority of culture as a separate and autonomous domain, the solution nevertheless reaffirmed the status of culture as a primary category instead of offering immunity from its alienating claims. The unification of subject and object not only reaffirmed the centrality of culture as a privileged category of perceiving the world, but the process annexed politics to its authority. The ensuing arrangement made it increasingly difficult to imagine politics as a semi-autonomous space for pursuing forms of plural or diverse interests. Increasingly, discussions

of politics in the twentieth century were transferred to the plane of
cultural praxis, action was displaced to cultural and aesthetic intentionality, and political participation was sublimated to the claims of a timeless cultural order substituting for nature. Conversely, the separation of
a knowing subject from the object of knowing could have opened up
space in which to carry on political activity independent of the state
and made possible the autonomization of differing and even contesting
forms of practice, which might have ultimately worked themselves into
a genuine social-democratic polity in modern Japan.

When, therefore, the new Meiji government announced its decision to separate politics from religion, after it had offered nominal
support to *kokugaku* by establishing the Jingikan as a central apparatus
of government and recruiting nativists to staff it, it did so under the
sanction of instrumental-empirical knowledge (increasingly synonymous with *jitsugaku*, or practicality) that derived its powers from the
basic division between subject and object. Even so, this fundamental
separation of religion (culture) and politics (state) was repaired later in
the twentieth century in the unification of state and culture. Hence,
the discussions of the importance of culture and the distrust of politics
that surfaced in the 1920s and 1930s could only contribute to the power
of the state, not to its diminution. Although the Meiji government
earlier moved to dissemble and even discount the claims of the nativist
theory of knowledge as a master code (as envisaged most recently by
Yano Gendō) by insisting upon the necessary separation of religious
and political realms, the dispersed fragments of nativism escaped becoming mere archaeological curiosities in the next century. At the center of the dispersion was an effort to appropriate and recombine elements of *kokugaku* to form a new discipline called *minzokugaku*,
"Japanese ethnology," which itself was simply one inflection in a larger
discourse on culture.

This reemplotment at a later time was prefigured in nativism's
post-Restoration struggle to mediate new political arrangements or, failing in this role, to retain a respectable measure of freedom from state
interference. On both counts, however, nativism encountered the new
state and lost to the forces of law, utility, rationality, and the necessary
separation of religion from the state. In the competition to play a principal part in the new government, nativists saw their newly acquired
hold on power in the Bureau of Religious Affairs (Jingikan) progres-
sively undermined by successive waves of reorganization that ultimately led to the bureau's dissolution. As an equally ill-fated (if not ill-

timed) attempt to secure autonomy and reverse its fortunes, nativism mounted a campaign to win official recognition for its religious claims. Specifically, it tried to persuade the government, in the 1870s, to acknowledge the authority of Izumo and the prominence of Ōkuninushi no kami in the official pantheon of gods (consisting of Ame no minakanushi, the two creation deities, and, of course, Amaterasu). When nativists lost their power base in the Bureau of Religious Affairs, they tried to offset the political loss by linking institutional authenticity and legitimation to the prior and primary religious authority of their particular political theology. Adherents flooded the government with petitions demanding the elevation of Ōkuninushi's status to parity with the other deities in the state pantheon, in order to become an official object of worship at state shrines. The inclusion of Ōkuninushi would have guaranteed the recognition of the nativist struggle to realize the "spirit" of their conception of restoration and, more important, acknowledged an "interception" of the power symbolized by the Sun Goddess and the imperial genealogy.[4] In this way, Ōkuninushi *might have had* an opportunity to play the role of a "dangerous supplement" and compel the new power brokers to recognize that a lack needed to be filled. Here, Ōkuninushi *would have* acted "in the place of."

The promotion of the newly ideologized Izumo version, Ōkuninushi, and the entailing associations of the invisible realm constituted a desperate effort to equalize the claims of authority between the opposing contestants and signaled an early intervention in the struggle to arrest the expanding power of the imperial house and the government that ruled in its name. Nativists warned that any "separation between doctrine and polity invites immediate danger to the land." Although it was on this terrain that nativists fought and lost their cause to the government, the struggle was over something much larger than the mere separation of state and religion. Beyond that lay a more important clash over differing forms of knowledge—who was to know what and how. Here too was a prefiguration of a later contest between the "authority" of rational utility and measureable historical progress, embodied in the modern state, and its critique, which dismissed the veracity of both. The critique turned instead toward constituting a culture from the dispersed fragments of the past, as an alternative to modern civilization (*bunmei*) and the bureaucratic state that had evolved since the beginning of the Meiji period.

The earlier skirmish between state and discourse disclosed not simply a minor quarrel between secular and sacred—even though contemporaries focused on this issue—but the first stage in a continuing conflict over identity and difference. At stake was a modern knowledge that constantly threatened to introduce difference and eradicate all those aspects of "life" that Japanese shared as the sign of their irreducible sameness and a response that tried to reinstate suppressed alterities, as nativists had tried to earlier, in order to secure identity. Modern knowledge was committed to nonidentity and the possibility of the plurality of life, while the response to it submitted to the demands of equivalence and similitude; in the case of the former, the Other referred to the unrational, the irrational, the primitive, and the backward, which Western discourse usually specified as ethnically other—the African, the Asian, the Arab—whose elimination it promised; for the latter, the Other remained the repressed alterity of a more authentic life that had existed prior to the imperative of Western rationality, which had to be recalled before Japanese were altogether assimilated to the imperial requirements of Western epistemology.

In the ensuing struggle over equivalence, identity, and the terms of difference, the nativist narrative announcing the advent of subject positions for the folk and their "household duties" was resituated by ethnologists or folklorists (*minzokugakusha*) in their own campaign to combat a story line that increasingly upheld the march of modernization led by bureaucratic rationality serving the imperial state. The clash revealed a contest over which narrative best represented Japan in the new age. Yet the ethnological "transformation" of the nativist narrative was far more problematic than it was made to appear, and it introduced dangerous discontinuities even as its practitioners confidently insisted on the natural evolution of their "science" from *kokugaku*. With Hirata, narrative proceeded from a reconsideration of origins, an anamnesis of the archaic and the founding operation of *habitus* (*kunitsuchi*), whereas folklorists like Yanagita Kunio and Origuchi Shinobu regarded this calling to a time before time as a secondary consideration to the relentless search for traces of the founding operation remaining in their present. They recognized that a commitment to modernity was already exacting a heavy toll on received forms of daily life, especially as they existed in the countryside, and that it portended their total elimination in the near future. Whereas anamnesis of the archaic sanctioned a fresh beginning and the opening of the sacred, the effort to identify remaining traces in the present for preservation authorized the closure of profane culture. Even though twentieth-century ethnologists and cultural theorists failed to acknowledge this difference between the nativist program and their desperate invocation of its name, it remains crucial to understanding the production of a discourse and its later mobilization.

It is well to recall that Hirata and his nativist followers aimed at constructing a discourse of place—or as I shall propose, of a no-place—which became the site of practice once the process of renarrativizing the countryside occurred. Under the sanction of the cosmic narrative, people were enjoined to play their proper role as reproducers of the social conditions of existence and to act out the ceaseless story line as lived experience. But in the formulation of *minzokugaku*, discourse itself became place—that is to say, the former discourse on place was inverted into the place of discourse. Hence, daily life as the lived experience of the folk, which nativists consistently centered indistinguishably from the content of discourse, existed in ethnology only as an effect of a constructed discourse called folklore. What apparently had authorized the constitution of a discourse comprising native knowledge became in the discussions of the twentieth century a discourse that constituted the ordinary folk as its object. If earlier the figure of the archaic was fulfilled in the renarrativization of the countryside, fulfillment was later realized simply in the *description* of the figure of folk life.

For its most intense adherents nativism offered possibilities bordering on the utopian. All could easily agree with and even share Suzuki Masayuki's enthusiastic exaltation of the "new dawn" announced by the Meiji Restoration. In a long poem (*chōka*), a form recalling the *Man'yōshū's* own practice of employing *chōka* to represent auspicious events, Suzuki exclaimed: "Even the despised folk will not be without anything; the emperor [*ōgimi*], hidden in the shade like a night flower, will flourish increasingly; everyone will rejoice in the prosperity of the august age."[5] Yet before long, other voices began to condemn the Restoration as a deception and the deathblow to their most cherished ideals. According to Yano Gendō's short, elegiac lament for the vanished glories of Kashihara and the promise of returning to its golden age for a fresh start in the present, all that was left by 1880 was a "dream that will never be." Others, like Tōson's hero Aoyama Hanzō, seeing the Restoration turning into something totally unexpected, openly acknowledged that their hopes for a new age were dimming and disappearing, and their lives were becoming ruined remnants of vanished aspirations.

We have already observed in Ōkuni Takamasa's systematic disciplinization of nativist knowledge how *kokugaku* acquired the status of a master hermeneutic capable of explaining the meaning of *habitus*. This hermeneutic produced the sure knowledge that the *habitus* was to be found neither in the past nor in the present but somewhere in between; it was a place located neither in Japan nor elsewhere but rather at the center of the cosmos. Without historical and geographical coordinates, *habitus* appeared in nativism as a neutral moment of a radical difference, a space outside place per se, whose reality belonged to the narrative text. Yet its figurative representation functioned as witness to a critique of prevailing ideology. For Hirata, the anamnesis of the archaic was like a description of the "concealed and mysterious realm," which he, along with others, insisted was identical with the social life-world of the visible present yet radically different and genuinely other. The archaic, which served as the "model" for the hidden realm—or vice versa—was not an anti-world or even a "new" world but an Other world or the world of the Other, neither a moment in history nor a fixed location on a map, here but not yet there, the same but different. The nativist vision constituted the locus of a radical difference that, when juxtaposed to the prevailing representations of Tokugawa Japan, became a critique of ideology and a projection of a utopian communitarian order; its promise was reaffirmed in the new religious constituencies and the *yonaoshi* fervor of the last years of the Tokugawa period and the opening of the Meiji era. Ultimately, this movement toward "no place" was intercepted by the state.

When nativism was selected for reincarnation in Japanese ethnology, the founders sought, in part, to reinstate in the sociopolitical environment of the twentieth century this legacy of a critique authorized by the spatial play of differences. The modern origins of the disciplinary formation of *minzokugaku* under the leadership of Yanagita Kunio surely lie in the moment he dramatized the possible effects of the government's decision to reorganize shrines and their lands in 1908. Although the Shrine Merger Act appeared as one of a series of measures implemented by the bureaucracy by fiat (reaching down to the present-day struggle over locating an international airport at Narita), Yanagita and others used the occasion to draw attention to the sacrifices Japanese society was being forced to make for its modernist transformation. This is not to say that he had not imagined his ethnological project before 1908 but only to suggest that his prior interests in agricultural economics, folkloric studies, and tenant disputes in the countryside were given a decidedly critical, antibureaucratic slant after the promulgation of the Shrine Merger Act. From that time, he embarked upon a lifelong program to collect data, materials, and stories from the rural scene before the modern bureaucratic apparatus eliminated their last traces. Along the way, Yanagita began to see in these remnants traces of the founding operation that had successfully withstood the erosions of historical time. He grew convinced that rural Japan still offered the example of a life-world experience, the unchanging daily life, that was different from the artificial style and pace associated with the new urban industrial sites. By concentrating on a natural and ecological crisis, folklorists were able to find a language for talking about bureaucratic politics, free from the idiom of conventional party interest, political theory, or even the rhetoric of socialists. Yet the critique Yanagita launched was directed less toward political policy than toward conserving the true content of cultural form by defining it. For this reason, his involvement in the controversy over the shrine merger appeared less political than that of people like Minakata Kumagusa, with whom he eventually broke over the question of action. Yanagita, it seems, wanted to shift the question of the shrine merger and its effect on the environment to a consideration of cultural choice; he did not want political warfare, which, he believed, would have reduced the issue to the terms established by the persons promoting the policy. His concern for saving the fictive "natural village" (since the older Tokugawa rural community had virtually been eradicated by the first decade of the twentieth century) prompted him to agree with Nitobe Inazō and other like-minded ruralists who were convinced that the real problem of the day was the irreparable damage that had been inflicted on the countryside in the interest of urban development.

Nevertheless, Yanagita's principal interest was in Japan itself, as a place. The countryside had been privileged as the authentic Japan and made to function metonymically to call attention to the whole—that is, as "one's native place" (kyōdo). But Yanagita's countryside was an imaginary, constructed from a discourse aimed at conserving and preserving traces of a lost presence. Ethnology, which he sometimes referred to as a "science," became the space of discourse where he was able to constitute a timeless rural Japan that was "always already there." In finding Japan in this way, Yanagita was restoring an absent signified, rather than a different signifier that might have opened the way to a play of difference and helped to subvert the prevailing ideology of the state before World War II. As a signified, Japan became the content of a discourse, a specific place characterized by fixed identities, instead of the radical difference associated with the no-place located in the center that

people like Ōkuni Takamasa imagined. The discourse on Japanese ethnology departed from nativism by establishing a coherent and homoge-
nous subject, what Yanagita called the "ordinary and abiding people"
(*jōmin*), as a condition for eliminating the Other. Although I have
proposed that nativism also installed a subject position for the folk, the
operation presupposed the existence of an Other, whether China or the
national deities and ancestors. In either case, the Other functioned as
the place of difference whose existence constantly jeopardized the stability of fixed identities. Because the Other became yoked to the deities
who made the creation and bestowed the blessings of life on the folk,
the folk were enjoined to work ceaselessly with their bodies in order to
repay the gift and thereby to participate in an exchange that never ter-
minated. Yanagita reduced the importance of reproduction and diminished the relationship with the Other that nativists had seen as a condition for practice. He was thereby able to eliminate both the centrality
of the body working for the place of the Other and the desire that
compelled people to seek reunion with it. Because he failed to grasp
the heterogeneity of the Other (the site of difference), practice and activity (reproducing the creation) were no longer necessary, since nothing was left to function as the object of desire.

In the new arrangement, the state occupied the site of the Other
once inhabited by the gods; it identified the Subject with the Other in
order to repress otherness as the heterogenous place of language and
desire. As a result, the state produced an omnipotent Subject who mas-
tered both language and desire when before, during the Tokugawa period, there was no conceivable way for it to incorporate everything. In
modern Japan, as elsewhere, this mastery has led to the narrowing or
the elimination of the possibility of a "theoretical perspective for ideological struggle" against the dominant ideology, because nothing escaped or "was left over from the original production of the subject by
the Subject," that is, the state.[6] Modern Japanese society therefore became the place that housed an imaginary Japanese, a subject produced
by the state (beginning with the Meiji creation of a middle class) enjoined to work and achieve in order to secure the identity of likeness as
a guarantee for social solidarity. Where theorists like Yanagita and Origuchi differed from the nativists was in their willingness to substitute
the reproduction of imaginary social relationships for the reproduction
of the social conditions of existence.

It should be recalled that nativism projected a conception of the
body, work, and desire for the place of the Other in a field crisscrossed

by contradictions that it, along with other discourses, sought to resolve. Owing to its position in the matrix of relationships characterizing the historical field of late-Tokugawa Japan, nativism became an oppositional discourse working to subvert the official ideology. When, subsequently, the body and the object of desire were eliminated, the consequences were immense. Late-Tokugawa culture showed time and again that when the body was emphasized, it could be used for a variety of reasons and still not exhaust its productivity in representations. It also disclosed that the body functioned as a floating signifier, capable of being fixed to any number of "signifieds," and that it moved according to specific placements in economic, political, and ideological practices. Here, it seems, was a genuine potential for launching counter-ideologies, since it was by centering the body and its inexhaustible power for representation that the unconscious of discursive formations manage to disrupt the smooth functioning of the dominant ideologies.[7] When Japanese ethnology became committed to Japan as signified as a condition for effacing both the practice of the body (the signifier) and its endless trek toward the place of the Other, when it moved to completely remove the Other—the different—it could never hope to become anything more than an incurable nostalgia, which yearned to freeze what had been process into a timeless presence.

Instead of concentrating on reproduction and the activity of the body, Yanagita—confronting what he believed to be the spectacle of modernity and the devastating consequences of its division of labor—devoted his discipline to examining the nature of the social bonds that united people, in the hope of finding forms of cohesion capable of guaranteeing lasting social solidarity. Fearful that the mechanism of difference would not bring about social cohesion, he resorted to the logic of social likeness, which, he believed, still persisted in the villages of Japan. Later, immediately after the war, signs of disintegration seemed to be everywhere and the necessity for solidarity appeared to be more urgent than at any other time in Japan's modern history. Especially at that time he appealed to native religious practices such as tutelary and ancestor worship to reinforce the structure of resemblance; by linking individuals more closely, directly, and harmoniously with society, he hoped to make action and behavior spontaneous, unreflective, and collective. Here, too, is a possible explanation for the tragedy of Yanagita's immense achievements. It explains why the ethnological movement could do little to contest the state, apart from launching rather pallid campaigns to protest the effects of unbridled industrialism on the environment, and why the state could easily appropriate the folklorist conception attesting to sameness among all Japanese and subvert it into official declarations of cultural exceptionalism and racial uniqueness. In this way, a social science of Japan became a Japanese social science.

To sharpen the details of Japan that signified a fixed identification with the "place of one's birth," Yanagita turned to the voiceless and powerless subjects who, he believed, had occupied the native place before history. He converged with his nativist predecessors by amplifying a narrative lived by ordinary folk, who had remained silent and left no written traces or histories apart from their beliefs, customs, and practices. Like nativists, Yanagita felt compelled to find a way of representing the folk who did not write about themselves but who, nevertheless, "actually moved society until recent times." History itself had repressed this truth, excluded the role played by the folk, and remained adamantly silent on the details of the daily life. In fact, it was writing as a specific idiographic practice that had effaced the memory of the folk and their ceaseless reproduction of custom. Before the formal development of ethnology (*minzokugaku*), he observed, there had existed a history of place and the daily life (*kyōdo seikatsu*) "always already there," waiting to be rescued from concealment. By rejecting written traces and the narrative story line they embodied, Yanagita was able to turn away from signs for things in order to hear a language of sameness, without words or discourse, which had remained buried beneath the humus of historical writing. In order to avoid writing a "history" described by the language of the Other, whether reason or power or both, Yanagita sought to write a "history" of the folk and their interaction with custom, in which they spoke about themselves on their own authority, on the basis of their own experience and unmediated by another's language. He wanted to present this account as the living narrative that existed before the language of historical progress crushed it and made the folk into an object, to be exiled into museums. When he embarked upon this project he assumed the pose of a methodological innocent, presenting himself as a traditional traveler—not a teller of tales but a listener—both to collect data and to achieve the effect of being a witness to the immediacy of the folk experience. He committed himself to the impossible task of trying to speak for the folk outside the language of power and reason that had concealed them from view. He misrecognized his task, failing to see that the misfortune of the folk—the interminable misfortune of their silence and their failure to secure representation for themselves—lay precisely in the fact than as soon as a person attempted to convey their silence, he passed over to the side of the enemy, the side of history and reason, even if, at the same time, he put the claims of the enemy into question.[8]

Yanagita sought to develop a discipline devoted to the enduring presence of the folk found in surviving messages from the past and to thereby retrieve an absent signified. He also hoped to make science useful to his present. "The first objective of studying the native place," he wrote in 1935, "is, in a word, to know the past of commoners. . . . To know the route traveled by commoners down to the present is . . . to know ourselves" (YK, 279–80). He was convinced that the "footprint of the life of the peoples' past has never stopped" and that concrete, material practices involving foods, shelters, yearly rituals, and beliefs were enduring forms immune to historical change (ibid., 283). Even though those practices and material items originated in a distant past, they appeared as new manifestations when contemporaries embraced them in their daily lives. According to this vision, history was eventless and consisted of sediments piled on top of each other to resemble the imperceptible growth of a large icicle (YK, 279–80).[9] Yet the manifold layers function as palimpsests that revealed the shapes of earlier forms of practice glittering below them.

Yanagita's disclosure of a new "history" signified by the "study of place" aimed at discounting synthetic conceptions of the world or human species that overlooked the particularity of unrecorded custom. It was critical of any evolutionary scheme that emplotted the development of society according to criteria of scientific and technological progress. Commenting on H. G. Wells's *Outline of History,* Yanagita observed that despite the claim of a general history, "there are peoples who are not in this world history." Many peoples did not have writing systems, while others, like the African Bantu, had been represented by their conquerors (YK, 283–84). He condemned the paradox of a historical discipline that remained silent on the essential aspects of life dominating the Japanese—and other forgotten peoples—which were embedded in the repetition of practices that constituted the ordinary life.

Yanagita concentrated on the central role of the "abiding and ordinary folk" (*jōmin*), whose lives were regulated by intersubjective relationships inscribed in customs and things.[10] Although this interest no doubt stemmed from his concern for the cause of rural relief and his search for a method capable of avoiding class conflict, it was also prompted by a profound conviction that when ties binding people disappeared, the expected consequence would invariably be conflict and disharmony. The effect of his reconceptualization of classes into *jōmin* was to emphasize a neutral association over a socially specific referent, in order to establish the conditions for a fixed common identity rather than differences corresponding to class membership.

This concern for a supraclass identity and the guarantee of stable relationships between people led Yanagita to religion. The idea of folk religious practices was inherent in any consideration of one's native place. As Origuchi Shinobu explained, Yanagita had always been interested in the deities and ancestors and shared with the great nativist scholar Hirata Atsutane a life-long belief in the relationship of religious practices with social solidarity (*OSz* 20:349–50). They differed, however, over the function each delegated to the deities and ancestors. For Hirata, the call to the hidden world, the governance of Ōkuninushi and the ancestors beyond, was a way of emphasizing the role the ordinary folk were supposed to play in the great cosmic narrative—reproducing the conditions of social existence as a form of repayment to the blessings of the gods. For Yanagita, the reproduction of the means of life lost its primary importance; he argued that the native religious system was an irreducibly Japanese inflection because the spirits of the dead always returned to the "native place" to watch over their descendants from their "unseen" mountain perspective. Yanagita remarked in *Senzo no hanashi* (1946) that this idea conferred significance on the life of the living and offered the necessary bonding for community relationships. The spirits resided in the national soil forever, he wrote; the belief that they did not go to a distant place had been deeply rooted since the time of antiquity and had persisted continuously down to the present (*YK*, 273). By emphasizing the role of the ancestors and their relationship to the household and clan deities, he believed he had found a way to bring about the reconstruction of the native place in modern times. Ultimately, this religious view permitted him to conceptualize an alternative to the modern state and its social imaginary, which, he believed, caused conflict and struggle by privileging power relationships, individual interest, and difference. Instead, he envisaged the tutelary shrine as the form of a stable order that was more religious than political. Here, his study of the native place elucidated the spiritual topography of Japan's religious inheritance, with its centering of a communitarian consciousness produced by the household and forms of worship, which, he observed in 1931, distinguished the Orient from Western rural society.

After World War II, Yanagita expanded the role of common worship in his essays entitled "Discussions on the new nativism" (*Shin kokugakudan*). Although he had suggested a "new nativism" as early as 1935, when he called for a new method to study the native place, he now employed the term to explain to a defeated nation how the folk might restore the country's well-being and their own good fortune. Predictably, his assurances for recovery relied on the willingness of the people to reinstate in their lives the characteristic religious beliefs of Japan, which meant expanding the tutelary shrine system beyond its prewar level. War and defeat demonstrated the calamitous nature of the modern state, he argued, reaching a conclusion already advanced by Marxists for different reasons. But the resuscitation of tutelary worship would establish a communitarian order that might—in some way he never really explained—replace the structure of state altogether yet secure the guarantee of social solidarity, a view still held by his *epigones* the historian Irokawa Daikichi and the poet Yoshimoto Takaaki.

Recalling the discussions of Tokugawa nativists concerning agricultural beliefs, Yanagita explained that the word for tutelary—*ubusuna*— derived from remote antiquity and referred not simply to the place of one's birth but to the names of the deities associated with a specific locale. Actually, he wrote, the term meant the "place of the deities" and connoted both the gods of a locality and the locality itself. As a result of this association, place became an object of worship. Because it acquired the status of a sacred sanctuary, people were required to make appropriate acts of respect. "The place occupied by the folk is that of the tutelary gods or clan deities. It is not erroneous to use the terms interchangeably."[11] The worship of these sacred places was to be performed by the people who lived in the village or locale where the shrine had been erected. But, he warned, this regional tie never meant to exclude outsiders from religious participation at the shrine. It was for this reason, Yanagita observed, that people in Japan were eventually identified according to place rather than blood ties or even land ownership. Yet this proposition also showed that any place or region was as good as another and all or each could easily substitute for Japan, the "native place of one's birth," and vice versa. Japan as an expanded tutelary shrine where all paid their respect to the place of birth offered both commonality and the lasting relationships capable of ensuring social cohesion. "The space of the deities," he noted, "was really the place of the village," and worshiping the clan or guardian god was really making observances to place and its inhabitants, the "ordinary and abiding folk." "When referring to the *kamisama*, the gods, in the language of our commoners, and speaking of temples and shrines, these mean our villages and households. They are the same words for father and mothers."[12]

In the relationships and associations of tutelary belief, Yanagita was certain that he had found the necessary authority for a logic of likeness capable of reintegrating Japanese society in the immediate postwar years. He also believed that he had effectively clarified the question of respect for the communal deities, which had been recklessly manipulated by the prewar state, and had laid the ground work for replacing the discredited state Shinto with a veneration of the *kami* bonded to the household, village, and place. With the conception of *kami* respect revitalized and stripped of its debilitating associations with the state and public power, the regular visitation of large numbers of people to shrines of place might illuminate the intimate relationship between folk and the gods. Yanagita hoped that the present was the time for reviving a more simple and authentic form of *kami* worship, akin to ancestor veneration, and for eradicating definitively the state's cynical appropriation of Shinto for moral mobilization. "In order to preserve the space of the *kami*," he wrote, "we must once more restore a view that advocates the idea of the sacred place as it had existed in an earlier age."[13] He regarded the renewed belief system as synonymous with communal and household worship and called the act of society worshiping itself a "confidence of plenitude." Defeat seemed to offer the Japanese an opportunity to restore the basis of social solidarity, which the earlier commitment to modernity had nearly destroyed. By reinstalling the worship of the deities, they could secure the eternality of place for all time to come.

Yanagita devoted his discourse to identifying the ties of social cohesion stemming from a logic of likeness; he centered place and the worship of it to constitute the voiceless narrative of the "ordinary and abiding folk." On the other hand, Origuchi Shinobu sought to locate the origins of this narrative in a preliterate orality and the production of a "literature" that had existed prior to literature, which attested to an enduring sense of plenitude, presence, and immediacy. Despite Origuchi's effort to distance his discourse from Yanagita's by emphasizing its "scientific" rigor, Origuchi's own concerns rarely strayed from considerations of identity and social solidarity. At the heart of his theory, which identified the production of "literature" with a specific place, was the earlier nativist presumption that the ancients had achieved a perfect correspondence between word, thing, and intention that the subsequent adoption of writing had destroyed. In Origuchi's reformulation, literary consciousness had erupted in archaic times as a result of an interaction between the first Japanese and their encounter with the ordinary things of their placement. In order to recover this sense of authenticity, he turned to a "scientific" study of literature as the most authoritative inscription of an experience which, regardless of the domination of writing since earliest times, continued to express traces in folk consciousness.

A self-proclaimed follower of Yanagita Kunio, Origuchi fixed Hirata's brand of nativism as the indisputable sources of folk studies in Japan (OSz 20:348). He believed that nativism represented the beginning of Japan's entry into the modern world and thus constituted a vital stage in the development of an ethnological discipline. But nativism had concentrated on the question of origins and ethical practicality—the necessity of the daily life—and folk studies were first and foremost rigorously scientific and empirical. A social science made in and for Japan alone was no science at all; it was nothing more than sentimentality if it failed to develop a method capable of application elsewhere. To make good this claim, Origuchi expanded his research agenda by carrying on fieldwork in surrounding areas like the Ryukyu islands. But his interest in Okinawan shamanism was prompted by a desire to find in the present enduring examples of archaic Japanese practices. Because folkloric studies derived from nativism, they were unable to shake off the particularistic associations that could only compromise its claims to a science.

In an essay titled "The Tradition of Hirata nativism" (*Hirata kokugaku no dentō*), Origuchi insisted that Hirata was, above all else, a scholar of integrity, who possessed a broad learning characterized by moral intensity and a deep and abiding love for scholarship (OSz 20:331). More than any other thinker of his day, Hirata liberated learning from a reliance on Chinese knowledge. It was this critical moment, which Origuchi claimed to have detected in Hirata's later texts, that qualified *kokugaku* as a proto-science of ethnology. In its exploration first of language and later of religiosity, nativism constituted a "backbone" discipline that uncovered the authentic image of ancient history and its moral structure. "A nativism without this dimension," Origuchi wrote, "cannot exist." This model meant that the development of a new style of learning "must be passionate" and even sensuous. For, he continued, "it is not sufficient merely to acquire knowledge meditatively;

it [the acquisition of knowledge] must also be endowed with elements of activity." Nativism had consisted of learning an active and practical belief. "Today," he urged at the outbreak of World War II, "the time has arrived to act according to [this] exercise of moral passion. Although we must always aim for the accomplishment of this goal [practice], the time is ripe now for us to act" (*OSz* 20:318).

Origuchi believed that "Japan, since antiquity, has been at a standstill" that must be overcome for the folk to be united with their original purpose. He asserted that "the history of Japan is filled with examples of believing in miracles" (*OSz* 20:319); he was apparently referring to the basic belief system of Japanese antiquity, to which the present was destined to return for inspiration. Even though Origuchi appeared more patriotic than scientific during the war, he always insisted that a scientific ethnology should be consistent with its own origins and actively dissolve the framework authorized by narrative historical time, much in the manner of the ancient histories he and nativists examined. The aim of his own approach was to "give expression to a new nativism. The point is to look at the origins of ancient beliefs, which have been rationalized and modernized. . . . This new nativism derives from ancient practices, from the study of social and personal affairs, and instructs us on how and why we must make a fresh start" (*OSz*, 6). Neither philosophy nor religion were adequate to understand these remote facts. The fresh start he envisaged had already been inaugurated by Yanagita and folk studies. When an inquiry was made from a perspective opposed to conventional narrative, it would make possible an experiencing of past and present or past in present without encountering the discontinuous differentiations demanded by historiography. For Origuchi, such a move required abandoning "rationality," becoming steeped in the particularistic rationalities of the ancient Japanese rather than the logic of the Greeks. Contemporaries who studied national consciousness and the folk spirit invariably came up against the "blind alley" of "utility," "rationality," and "reason." The prayers from antiquity and the oral poetry of the epics were the "originating place of folk theory," which he called the "logic of the gods"; they would provide the surest entry to a place that existed before and beyond reason (ibid., 368).

The failure of rationality to grasp the shape of the past was sufficient reason to employ an alternative method of retrospection. Since antiquity was "transhistorical," a transcendental signified— retrospection, or as he called it, "regression"—permitted entry to this place of unreason through the exercise of "actual sensation" (*jikkan*), by which the observer could actively live the past in the present, and enter the "heart to view correctly the relationship between all kinds of things" (ibid., 369); he explicity applied "regression" as a method in *Okina no hassei* (ibid., 77, 79, 92). Actual sensation, as imagined by Origuchi, bore more than a passing resemblance to Motoori Norinaga's conception of "knowing *mono no aware*," but it was now resituated within the idiom of Dilthey's more accessible hermeneutic (since Japanese romantics were already praising its claims) based on empathic reenactment (*erlebnis, einführung*). Looking back years later (1950), Origuchi referred to this conception of "actual sensation" as the "expressive method," which, for him, had the same feel as the "method of representation." Because representation was limited to the level of form alone, however, he "used the term 'expressive method' because I aimed at the place where form and content interact" (*ibid.*, 370). Origuchi was convinced that his "expressive method" would chart a detour around conventional historical narrative and open the direct way to reaching antiquity by "grasping local life." He believed it was possible to make antiquity accessible to contemporaries as a living experience by dehistoricizing it. The operation would transform the ethnologist into a poet.

Origuchi appeared driven by two seemingly paradoxical agendas: he wanted to pursue the study of folk beliefs in the present, and he was interested in looking at the past as a condition for understanding the real present. For this reason he embarked upon a program of fieldwork in the Ryukyus, especially Okinawa, where he believed the transmitted legends were still enacted and "revealed the shape of ancient Japan. In the contemporary life of the Ryukyu islands, especially its interior life, we are able to see the life of men from the time of the *Man'yō* as it was" (ibid., 2:376). When he declared his intention to transcend conventional historical time to reach a place that had existed before time and reason—a vision he insisted appeared only "intermittently" in folk memory—he was referring to a past that had not yet been fixed or defined by the establishment of emperors, dynasties, and chronology. It came close to resembling a place of radical heterogeneity. Here, Origuchi turned against historians for their "unfortunate endeavor" of "slicing up time according to months and years." The past he wished to rescue could not be measured by time or fixed by political markers. He envisaged a perspective that deprivileged historical content to elevate timeless form. Empathic understanding offered reunion with antiquity, the Other, and the prospect of living among the ruins of antiq-

uity as if they existed in the present. Antiquity was spirit manifested in
the survival of artistic forms and skills.

Origuchi acknowledged the difficulty in distinguishing between
"history" and "legend," but he doubted the capacity of the so-called
historical method to actualize the "logic of antiquity." "Since the results of historical discourse [*shiron*] are supposed to be realized in the
concrete," he observed, "I think that the novel must be advanced anew
in order to discover the shape of the [human] drama. In this, I have
used the form of the novel as the expressive means to study tradition
and legend."[14] Literature, and especially the novel—by which he undoubtedly meant classic verbal fictions—permitted direct engagement
with the concrete Real as no historical method could. Consequently,
he came to favor ethnology (*minzokugaku*), which he described as an
"assisting discipline to the study of national literature" and a "classic of
life" (*OSz* 16:483–92). Ethnology called attention to the intimate
connection between literature and folklore, while history aimed to
translate the folk into a living text. "Literature," he wrote, "aims at ex-
cavating the theories of social life. Since human legends are solely
things that illuminate the individualistic causes of folk character, the
study of national literature begins from the same place where the study
of ethnology starts" (*ibid.* 15:24–25). Ethnology was the authentic reflection of national life and prompted people to recall the "seduction
of older forms of life." In the "customary" of unknown origins, Origuchi believed he had found the "classics of life." Elsewhere, he added to
this sentiment by proposing that *minzokugaku* consisted of the "affairs
transmitted from antiquity, whether they relate to households or religion" and consequently that it functioned as a "prior knowledge" (*sen-
dai no chishiki*). Antiquity escaped becoming a state in the passage of
historical time because ethnology was able to reenact the archaic life
in the present, resituating its elements not as relics but as living reminders of the continuity of forms. "In our life," Origuchi remarked,
"because we have proceeded on two paths, one whose meaning lies in
the past, the other oriented toward the future, the fixed traces of the
former [path] have been passed on to us in ethnology and folklore."
But, he noted, an ethnology so constituted could never be limited to
mere study and research. "Its actualization is not realized as knowledge
alone; it is reached through the contents of one's life" (ibid. 16:491).

In his seminal essay, "The Production of national literature"
(*Kokubungaku no hassei*, 1924), Origuchi turned to showing that a real
break existed between contemporary literary practice in Japan and its

"starting point" in a time before "literature" and writing. He complained that contemporary literary practice had departed from the aims attending the genesis of literary production. In fact, the presumption that forms and goals were uniform in antiquity and in the present was the product of later development and "literary conventions." Prose and its "power of representation" appeared rather late in the history of the folk. But even though prose managed to "tame" speech, it had no reason for existence outside conversation, which stemmed from the daily usage of the folk. Prose developed in order to transmit "great eventfulness," which speech, owing to its immediacy, could not accommodate or preserve. Composition—writing down sentences—suppressed the motive power behind poetry and obscured its links to daily speech, which Origuchi acknowledged was no longer accessible even though its founding source lay in "words of the gods" (*OSs*, 129). He hoped to demonstrate that modern literary consciousness had misrecognized the profound discontinuity between the two moments (past and present) and failed to see that archaic "literature" constituted a site of genuine difference. No method could reach it, but an empathic "leap" over the forms authorized by written literature could deliver one to this "distant place." "The so-called folk memory" was, he wrote as early as 1916, "revived intermittently throughout the ages" (ibid., 21). An unending process of recall revealed "an emotional and imagined recollection" pointing to the "mother country," a "yearning for the distant land." This place of otherness was the land of "wealth" and "good fortune." Folk memory, he argued, constantly returned to this place, which in archaic times was called the "land of eternal night" (*tokoyo*). In time, this permanently darkened world of dreaded gods was changed into a place of "good fortune" and "wealth," and its godly tenants were transformed into deities who would make periodic visits from the "distant place." For Origuchi, the revelation of a folk memory recalling a distant land not only offered an explanation for real difference—thereby explaining why folklore was the "classic of life"—but also showed the real origins of arts, skills, and literature. Ultimately, literature appeared as the site of the Other, and place became text.

In the context of this argument, Origuchi introduced his controversial conception of the *marebito*, the men-gods who came yearly from the distant land to incant prayers related to communal agricultural cultivation. These *marebito* were distinguished from the deities on high. "The original meaning of the *marebito*," he explained, "refers to the gods who come at appointed times, from the sky and from be-

yond the seas, to certain villages. They bring about bounty in a number
of things, wealth, and good fortune, and it was believed by villagers
that such accomplishments were godly deeds. These gods were not the
product of a religious imagination; the villagers of antiquity had heard
the *marebito*, at the time of their annual visitation, pushing against the
doors of houses" (ibid., 37, 138). They were guests, Origuchi explained, even "strangers," whose visitation coincided with the yearly
cycle of "village production" and whose prayers and recitations invoked
good harvest and fortune. For this reason, the later "traveling teller of
tales" (*kataribe*) sang songs and told stories about planting, production,
and the continued good fortune of the community. The *kataribe* recounted in prose poems the relationship between the gods, the household, and the land. In time, the form of recitation changed into more
"mature" genres and finally into historical narratives and verbal fictions. Origuchi noted that a similar evolution of political forms from
the village to the state seemed to accompany the passage of literary form
from orality and speech to writing and settled representation. Inscribed
in his formulation was the assumption of an original link between literary production and utterance—between "godly words" and "good
deeds"—as the most fundamental form of expression; the link recalls
both nativist considerations of language and prayer and the even more
important suggestion of desire for the distant land, the place of radical
difference. Folk memory had designated this place as the site of difference, the object of desire that is reached only in the last instance,
which never comes.

  When Origuchi specified that *tokoyo*, in its old usage, was closer
in meaning to "constancy" (*kōjō*), "unchanging" (*fuhen*), and "absolute" (*zettai*) than to "longevity" or "eternalness," he supplied an argument for the primacy of spatiality over temporality, permanence of
place over the changes of time (ibid., 167). For the ancients, the distant
land was a far-off place separated by the sea, out of sight to villagers
who stood on the shores and tried to visualize the destination site of
ancestral spirits. Only the dead went there. The archaic spirit had revealed this truth, but since that time "belief in the deities of earth has
receded." Still, "flashes" of this archaic spirit appeared in *minzokugaku*, which promised to release its light in the present. Origuchi recognized that ancient folk traditions had gradually perished in modern
Japan but also believed that there was still time to redeem them because
of the inheritance of an "unusually ancient spirit." Yet the critical
ground that Origuchi gained by resorting to a "science," which dis-

placed the source of creativity to the place of the Other, was lost because he specified the Other, an "absent signified," in exceptionalist terms in order to elucidate "national character" and folk consciousness. For this reason, his discourse never succeeded in rising above considerations of social solidarity, and it failed to transform a Japanese social science into a social science of custom. In the end, his project to identify folk studies with timeless life-forms simply reaffirmed a hermeneutic whose task was to uncover an eternal essence which was irreducibly Japanese.

Although ethnologists saw the folk as the object of "scientific" inquiry, writers like Takata Yasuma designated the folk as the subject of any social science. An academic sociologist who led the forging of an empirically rigorous social science in the 1920s, Takata shifted his perspective dramatically by the end of the decade, moving closer to the essentialism of Ferdinand Tönnies, not to mention contemporaries like Yanagita and Origuchi, from a view privileging society as the core unit of social science to one proposing harmony and solidarity (*ketsugō*) as the essence of society, from gesellschaft to gemeinschaft. The apparent reason for this move was the growing influence of Marxism in social inquiry, especially its explanation of social conflict and the volatile nature of social relationships, and Takata's own desire to "protect the folk." "Although I have always admired the socialization of interest in the progress of society," he wrote, "I am still a child of the village in spirit"; at the same time, he "adored the fresh vitality of village life, its communitarian society." "Even though I live in the midst of a city," he continued, "my heart has pursued gemeinschaft ceaselessly. Does this not show that the native place—Japan—is a broad community [*kyōdō*]."[15] What attracted Takata most to the communal mode was its "simple and honest human nature," attesting to a binding emotionality absent in urban life. Takata's heart also told him that a modern society, founded on the clash of interests, expressed the same point of view as Marxism, which saw in the murderous competition of claims the motor of social change. Thus, he proclaimed, "it is necessary to smash Marxism in order to protect the folk." Any consideration of class and its future in Japan necessitated a comparable consideration of the future of the folk. To this end, Takata developed in the late 1920s a critique of Marxism, which he eventually called "Class and the third view of history" (*Kaikyū oyobi daisan shikan*).

By a third view of history, Takata meant one that centered society and social relationships to explain history. It differed from both the "first conception of history" (the idealistic view, *die ideologische Geschichtsauffassung*), which saw the origins of historical development in the manifestation and movement of the spirit, and the second conception of history (Marxism), which interpreted social change in terms of shifts in the economic base.[16] The third view aimed to show that the determining cause of historical development was society itself. By using this view, Takata hoped to replace base by superstructure as a causal principle of historical development; this position probably explains why he dismissed the necessity of a critique against the first view of history ("In my work it is not important to conquer [*kokufuku*] the first conception of history"). Takata objected to Marxism on two counts: (1) even though it claimed to show the determination of culture—politics and law—in the base/superstructure opposition, these forms of activity revealed social relationships and thus the commanding role of society itself; and (2) it was difficult to sustain the argument that productive relationships—that is, society—were determined by productive forces. In the case of the first count, Takata obviously came closer to Marx than he wished to acknowledge since he privileged social relationships—the relationship between men—as the central element in his theory of society, while in the second, he doubled back to argue that the social relations of production were merely another way of referring to social relationships in general. Where he differed from Marxists was in the promotion of a conception of "social power" as the determining force. Through the mediation of this concept he was able to explain that class or any form of social differentiation originated, not in productive forces, but in fundamental differentiations between the powerful and the powerless based on talent and ability. Takata also sought to separate production—economic activity—altogether from the social and, in fact, argued that the relations between people constituted an independent variable in the formation of social phenomena.

At the heart of social relationships in the third view of history was the "aggregative composition" of society. "This refers to the quality and quantity of charter members who enter into social relationships. In a word, it is the form of social structure seen from the perspective of population density and heterogeneity in society. It becomes the base that determines the relations of mutuality among humans—relations of union and division. These social relationships determine the content and change of all other social phenomena."[17] In Takata's social scheme, then, the population density functioned as a first principle, which subsequently made possible, in descending order, social relationships, fixed organizations of society (political and legal system), the

economy, and spiritual culture (social consciousness). A closer examination of this social construct reveals a suppressed impulse resembling
Émile Durkheim's, to explain organic solidarity in terms of a division of labor necessitated by a quantum change in population. And
like Durkheim's, the purpose of Takata's explanation was a response to
Marxism and conflict models, which, in Takata's time, were being confirmed by contemporary events. Yet it is also important to note that
Takata grasped social relationships as form, not as substance or content,
which undoubtedly would have put him closer to Marxism. But envisaging forms independent of the forces of material production and, indeed, history itself drew Takata into a discursive kinship with contemporaries such as Yanagita and Origuchi, not to mention the cultural
critics of the 1930s who wrote cultural histories in which form was a
manifestation of the spirit.

Despite Marxian denunciations of "The Third view of history"
as a retrograde instance of "bourgeois science" or "formalism," and
even as a historical confirmation of middle-class political parties (Fu-
kumoto Kazuo), Takata's historical vision was probably the earliest and
most coherent effort in the third world before World War II to subvert
the category of a privileged conception of development from within and
to establish a critical distance between a local social experience (difference) and a historical consciousness that demanded identity. Under the
sanction of this claim to install difference, Takata was emboldened, in
the early 1930s, to call for the construction of a Japanized social science (quite in contrast to Origuchi, who started from the reverse premise but ended up in the same place nonetheless). Such a social science
should emphasize the special characteristics of Japaneseness (*Nihonteki
na mono*) and counter the hidden injuries inflicted by a mistaken acceptance of class and the social relations of production as viable social
categories. The problem, as he saw it, was to implement a transformation from "anthropologism" to "folkism" in order to explain the unity
of the folk and its capacity for "self-defense." The specific cause of
Takata's anxiety over the future of the folk was the rural problem in the
1930s, notably the process subordinating villages to the necessities of
urban industrialization, a fear shared by folklorists. But Takata's fears
did not terminate in a simple identification of social consequences and
a call for reconstruction. Like Yanagita, he believed that the process
leading to rural ruin was harmful to the life-forms of village existence,
which, in no time at all, "will become Americanized as fixed folk customs disappear." [18]

The strength of Japan was in the village, not the cities; it was spiritual, not material, emphasizing form, not content. Hence, "to protect the village is to protect this [spiritual] strength." Uniqueness resided in folk life and was signified by the "communal society that has constituted an exceptionally intimate solidarity."[19] The true tradition of Japan was the consciousness of the ordinary peasant who, over the long duration, had established harmonious social relationships as the indisputable condition of solidarity. The peasant represented a living reminder of the veracity of Takata's "third view of history." Yet by the same token Takata easily equated the expansion of the group ego, as he called it—a rereading of the Durkheimian collective consciousness guaranteeing assent—with imperialism. But folkism, he urged, should not be understood as imperial expansion but rather as the necessity of the group to transcend "certain limits." "The formation of Manchukuo," he wrote, "had nothing to do with capitalism but resulted from the [needs] of Japanese folkism."[20] The binding solidarity represented by the folk originated, at bottom, from the traditions of Japanese particularity, resting on the unparalleled *kokutai*. The meaning of group solidarity validated the continuity of a fixed sense of being Japanese reaching back to remote times (social relationships as form), and hence to the origins of culture itself, full and ever present, yet stretching out to the future.

Any effort to contest the claims of identity demanded by the Western discourse by appealing to a particularized Other ran the risk of becoming what Michel Foucault has called the "science of the same." The disciplinization of native knowledge, stemming from the Japanese critique of cultural imperialism, was never far from the very presumption of exceptionalism it sought to counteract. Once the program to establish a social science of place was envisaged as a corrective to an ideology masquerading as the truth of history, the terms of difference were assimilated to the claims of an essential similitude authorized by the idea of a cultural totality. But when the totality is no longer the conclusion but an enabling axiom, the possibility for theoretical and practical social criticism is foreclosed.[21] In Japanese social science the totality was represented by the folk, who possessed a natural, organic unity prior to all social differentiations, classes, and interest groups. In this way, culture was made to rejoin nature. The whole, like nature itself, constituted both the sum of the parts and the unity that functioned as a precondition for their fulfillment. Hence, it is not surprising to see, from our description of the disciplinizing of native knowledge (Origuchi's "prior knowledge"), how the primacy of the whole, made possible by eliding the distinction between culture and nature, presupposed forms of production and reproduction of life as "given" and "general." Moreover, this conception of the whole was relieved of economic and even social content (Takata's insistence that the social was an independent variable), from any real concrete mediations that would have specified it historically. Yanagita's formulation of the *jōmin*, representing a combination of all classes, was supposed to overcome struggle and conflict. Japanese social theorists like Yanagita and Takata inverted prevailing theories of utopia insofar as they proposed a classless society, but only at the price of imagining this arrangement within the framework of existing class society.

Minzokugaku sought to show how the folk constituted a "primal given," natural and prior to the artificial system of society. Culture, now posing as nature, became the great antagonist of history. Indeed, a central tenet of Japanese ethnology was the identity between the abiding and eternal folk and a timeless nature. Folk and nature shared a process that endlessly produced and reproduced the forms necessary to their survival into the indefinite future. As nature, the folk served as the substructure of history and their forms of life, the eternal constant in the continual flux of economic social relations. The similitude of nature was mirrored in the spirit of the folk. This transmutation of culture into nature resulted in what Herbert Marcuse has called the "depravation of history" and its reduction to a merely temporal occurrence external to the real principle of determination, which is the permanent totality.[22] Dehistoricization, as we have also seen, was the necessary precondition for devaluing time in favor of space and place and elevating the static over the dynamic. Just as there was no time in nature, so in folk life there was only interminable repetition. Yet dehistoricization and the production of place failed to conceal a blindness resulting from an interest to stabilize a particular condition of life that evidently could no longer be justified in the present historical circumstances.

It is important to recall that Yanagita's efforts to constitute the folk as the subject of ethnologic discourse presupposed their "voicelessness" as a condition for representing their timeless life. Silence—the absence of a written account of their activities—was what made the folk eternal and abiding. The native place was where the folk has always carried on, silently, the work of reproducing naturally the conditions of community, just as for Origuchi it was where oral literature originated in prayers for "fortune" and "good things." But a voiceless narrative, like an orality that leaves no traces, was never far from a politically silent community. Silence was a guarantee of political assent and indifference. Even though Yanagita's program to re-present the voiceless narrative of the folk was a challenge to "civilization" and "rationality," it was purchased at the price of establishing a community of silence that, because of its natural endowment, would refrain from participating in politics. When Origuchi equated orality with village simplicity and writing with the development of political forms he was, in effect, instating in the present an antique unpoliticality as the fundamental condition for life and art. *Minzokugaku* increasingly tried to prevent the instance of massive social disorder by making the folk voiceless once more, transforming their interests from class into supraclass and culture into nature. Although this operation was fully consistent with a critique aiming to discount the claims of new forms of knowledge and their resulting theories of political and social organization, it also carried with it baneful ideological effects.

The Marxist philosopher Tōsaka Jun called attention to this transformation of culture into nature (in *"Ninshikiron to wa nani ka"*) in the 1930s when he explained that "culture differed from nature because it mediated the actions and work of human subjects."[23] Nature, in the common sense of the word, had neither subjectivity nor the power of representation capable of externalizing the internal, objectifying the subjective, or actualizing the ideal. Tōsaka's colleague at the Yuibutsuron Kenkyūkai, Kozai Yoshishige, specified the implications for social science of this misrecognition of culture as nature. "Certain men have discovered in the elegant sensibility in which a person experiences *mono no aware* the characteristic Japanese spirit or Japanese thing. But are these enduring essences of the Japanese? I think not. These various explanations go no further than to abstract, in the name of the folk, the unique life sensibilities produced in a particular social class under determinate historical conditions."[24] Kozai went on to argue that since any concentration on the folk had become synonymous with considerations of Japanese culture, social science was inevitably transmuted into the baser metal of cultural sociology. This observation uncovered the central function played by the category of culture in the contemporary discourse on a science of society, and Tōsaka amplified it in his essays on the ideology of Japanism (*Nihon ideorogiron*, 1935), where he showed how culture posing as nature was itself a product of a certain kind of cultural hermeneutic.

Buried beneath the production of ethnographic and social-scientific texts was a problematic that posed the question of political and social order, to which the privileging of culture was offered as both

the answer and the form for subsequent discussion. Yet this turn toward
culture also represented a recognition among intellectuals and academ-
ics on both the Left and the Right of the futility of purposive forms of
action leading to transformation. The installation of culture as an unproblematic category signified the commanding position of the state
(which discourse tried to displace), the active discouragement of praxis,
and the primacy of invariant and timeless values in the materialization
of the spirit. Surely this recognition explains the efforts of many in the
1920s and early 1930s, including folklorists, to write cultural histories—
histories of the spirit, life histories—to detail the presence of eternal
values and to provide culture as nature with content; it also explains
the Marxist effort to formulate an alternative "scientific culture." In
this scheme, it was believed that culture was not made; it was created
by the folk spirit and materialized in form. The problem was not how
it was constituted, since it was a given, but how best, methodologically,
to capture a content that was always already there. Yanagita and Origuchi, no different from innumerable contemporaries, were concerned
only with choosing a content for a fixed form that best illuminated the
natural essence of the spirit; that is, they attempted only to interpret its
givenness, not to interrogate its process of constitution.

Because culture represented natural and internalized values
made manifest in form, it precluded the necessity to act in the external world; true action was realized only in the externalization of
such values. This meditation, which suppressed the difference between essence and existence, led only to acceptance, not to practice
or an active concern for the possibility of changing the status quo
and transforming state and society. Just as Yanagita and Origuchi
sought to grasp the enduring naturalness of timeless life-forms, so
Watsuji Tetsurō's cultural histories were not history at all but only
illuminations of the spirit in its passage to the "existence" and "life"
of the Japanese throughout the ages. According to Kobayashi Hideo,
history was pure contingency and accidental to existence (nature); the
surviving traces of enduring life-forms—frozen moments, as Yanagita
put it—collapsed past and present in an eternal unity. But, as we have
seen, presence and plenitude were invariably particularized. Because
knowledge was "existence," the task was to fix activity in lifeless artifacts
and to make sure that such activity exemplified natural creativity. A
theory that seized on creativity and its interpretation as equivalence
could easily be appropriated to confirm the received order of things,
if not the spiritual mobilization of the masses by the state. This cul-

tural hermeneutic, undoubtedly founded on the fear of individual interests, competition, and conflict, dissolved historically determinate classes into the larger category of a folk unmediated by history. In the end a dehistoricized culture replaced a historical society, folk was substituted for class, and the production of place supplanted the place of production.

Japanese will never be able to break away from nativism; as long as the national experience can be constituted as a form of knowledge, nativism can never be far from any consideration of the quality of cultural life and politics. Surely this explains why it has endured until today and why it has managed—despite the dispersions in time of those elements that nativists confidently brought together into a regulatory movement—to reappear in one shape or another. It explains why *Nihonjinron*—discussion about Japan—still inspires the Japanese imagination to heights of self-conceit and cultural narcissism as the surest defense against anything that seems to be different, the Other. Talk about oneself is a serious subject suitable for education, scholarship, and business that discloses a truly unique side of national personality. Yet since the 1950s, a mushrooming of books, articles, and mass media performances have raised the question of Japan's unique cultural endowment and rehearsed its various scenarios. This activity, which is big business today, was inaugurated in a context in which hopes for a genuine political democracy began to dim and massive economic expansion began to take off; it sought to turn people away from the disappointments of postwar democratic theory and practice to the blandishments of higher standards of living and consumption. The promise of *Nihonjinron* as it self-consciously recycled the nativist vision through folklorism, was to restore everything that had "eluded" the Japanese in a reconstituted unity, "to make sure that time, especially modern time, disperses nothing without it being returned back in some whole and integrated form."[25] Its most enduring result has been the creation of an "imaginary Japanese," offering the apparently natural unity of national subjectivity to those who identify with all the diverse articulations of the past, folk, and nationhood. This national subjectivity has functioned increasingly as an equivalent to the unity of the good citizen, the depoliticized, achievement-oriented Japanese whose reward is the prospect of even greater consumption. Although it would be wrong to suggest that *Nihonjinron* has led to a unified national subjectivity everywhere in society, there is, nonetheless, a good case to be made for a publicly instituted tendency toward homogeneity and conformity.

Needless to say, the constitution of an imaginary Japanese in discourse eliminates any explicit connection with class, gender, and regional affiliation. These are also less simple absences or mere omissions in the consideration of the question of race. Although the "imaginary Japanese" appears removed from racial identity, the constructed subject is, in fact, dependent on suppositions of ancestral continuity summoning divine origins that are not only Japanese and non-white but also actively exclusive of what constitutes the Other.

Nativism in the Tokugawa period attempted to regain a sense of similitude in order to overcome fragmentation and disorder. It failed, but its promise of sameness has remained as an unyielding nemesis. The terms of difference, however, like those of sameness, have been vastly altered in contemporary Japan from what they were in Tokugawa times. One of the functions of the nativist discourse was to offer consolation and sanctuary against the erosions, divisions, and differences experienced in contemporary history, to allow people once more to live and act naturally. Against the intrusions of changes clearly affecting rural life it offered—by elevating the quotidian life into timeless knowledge that could be known by those who lived it—a means to break the spell of history and culture and resist the encroachments of change. Yet the modern transformation of nativism to serve narrow and particularistic purposes has been remote from the practical discipline imagined by late-Tokugawa writers. Despite the nativists' effort to contain and make sense of change, they strove to confer the dignity of work and worship on those who performed daily tasks of production, not to differentiate them as simply racially unique. It was work itself, as a form of worship—repayment to the gods—that secured sameness, the sense of kinship and resemblance that nativists sought to restore. In doing so, they transmuted interests that had hitherto been marginal to Tokugawa society into a representation of knowledge. But the life nativists envisaged made work and worship a condition for being human and thus Japanese, whereas the shrill pronouncements of the current discourse have made being Japanese a condition for unique performance.

Between Tokugawa Japan and the present, a world was found and forfeited, and no amount of summoning can bring it back intact. Work, separated from its informing religious sanctions, could lead to the most lifelessly obsessive forms of achievement, as Max Weber has noted elsewhere and contemporary Japan has revealed in horrific intensity. The efforts of ethnologists and social scientists to revive this vision of culture and custom only succeeded in exhuming the husk of a long-abandoned life-form that, because it was already dead historically, could only deny time. Their excavation did not really escape time; it merely inspired a return to the ruins of memory and nostalgia and thus placed sentiment in the service of ideology. It would be difficult today to identify the nativist presence in the noisy nostrums of ideologues of the "Japanese-thing," even though they invariably claim such a heritage. Very little is left of the world it projected. Perhaps the case was put best by another ethnologist, Claude Lévi-Strauss, who also tried to secure a leasehold on a vanishing experience. Unlike his Japanese counterparts, who witnessed the disappearance of the "poetry of the past," and unlike the strident advocates of *Nihonjinron*, who worry less about the authenticity of culture than that of social control and economic advantage, Lévi-Strauss knew that he could ultimately give life only through an act of representation:

> And so I am caught within a circle from which there is no escape; the less human societies were able to communicate with each other and therefore to corrupt each other through contact, the less their respective emissaries were able to perceive the wealth and significance of their diversity. In short, I have only two possibilities: either I can be like some traveller of the olden days, who was faced with a stupendous spectacle, all, or almost all, of which eluded him, or I can be a modern traveller, chasing after the vestiges of a vanished reality. I lose on both counts, and more seriously than may first appear, for, while I complain of being able to glimpse no more than the shadow of the past, I may be insensitive to reality as it is taking shape at this very moment. . . . A few hundred years hence, in this same place, another traveller, as despairing as myself, will mourn the disappearance of what I might have seen, but failed to see.[26]

Notes

Prologue: Historians' Discourse and the Problem of Nativism

1. In Tetsuo Najita and Irwin Scheiner, *Japanese Thought in the Toku-gawa Period, 1600–1868: Methods and Metaphors* (Chicago: University of Chicago Press, 1978), 63–104.

2. The literature on *kokugaku* is immense. Ever since Hirata Atsutane wrote a genealogy of *kokugaku* (book 10 of *Tamadasuki*) to resituate his own intervention and to show how a tradition culminated in his thinking at the same time that his thinking departed from his predecessors, Japanese have ceaselessly examined nativism, which ultimately meant reflecting on themselves, as if the act guaranteed cultural authenticity and safeguarded ethnic purity. Such activity acquired the rhythm of ritual. No subject has commanded more enduring patronage and enjoyed greater bibliographic privilege. This obsessive concern stems in part from the nativist preoccupation, spectacularized by Hirata but noticeable in others, with defining a space for its own practice against the claims of prevailing forms of scholarship by making the production of their own texts the content of discourse. *Kokugaku* also announced "disciplinization" of native knowledge—knowledge about being Japanese—to reassert an alterity long suppressed or marginalized in a discourse that centered on China, centrality, and the middle way. (On this theme, see my article "The Functions of China in Tokugawa Thought," in Akira Iriye, ed., *The Chinese and the Japanese: Essays in Political and Cultural Interactions* [Princeton: Princeton University Press, 1980], 9–36.)

Juxtaposed to hegemonic sinocentrism, nativism sought to validate its own claims to "difference" and "heterogeneity" against an ideology that assimilated Japanese to the Other and enforced the *doxa* of similitude and resemblance. In time *kokugaku* itself became the site of similitude and contributed decisive elements to the construction of a "science of the same," as Michel

Foucault might have put it, promising to elevate Japan and the Japanese into a serious subject of knowledge. Because of its propensity to authorize a culturally exceptionalistic logic about being Japanese and the Japanese relationship to the Other, *kokugaku* was easily transformed into spurious sciences such as *Nihongaku* (Japanese studies), *Nihonjinron* (Japanese discussions about themselves), and *Nihon bunkaron* (discussions on Japanese culture) and ultimately underwent a profound metamorphosis in which its prior defense of *difference* was transmuted into an offensive proclamation of *uniqueness*. This "history" and the recurring preoccupation with questions of national character (*kokuminsei*) account for the large production of texts on nativism, and it is within the development of this peculiar discourse that we must situate the "literature." This observation also enables us to see a relationship between those moments when Japanese seemed to be most intensely aware of their reliance on the Other and the production of texts on and from *kokugaku*. The mountain of materials on the one side and the seminal interpretations on the other do not necessarily mesh; rather they reveal the often-observed (but never by positivists) disjunction between data and meaning. As an example, a bibliography appended to one of the last volumes of the revised edition of the collected works of Hirata Atsutane runs thirty pages and includes well over six hundred entries! For Motoori Norinaga, the volume of books, essays, and notes has yet to be tallied. Even for lesser *kokugakusha*, the amount of secondary literature is simply staggering and shows not simply mindless industry but how nativism has occupied, if not colonized outright, the space of modern Japanese intellectual history. My own reading has been limited to what we might call the "strong misreadings," which I will enumerate below, and lesser specialized pieces, which are cited throughout the body of this text. As intellectual history I have found useful Muraoka Tsunetsugu, "Nihon kokuminsei no seishin kenkyū," 5–72, "Kinsei ni okeru kokutai shisō no hatten," 310–54, and "Nihon seishin o ronzu," 357–82, in Muraoka Tsunetsugu, *Kokuminsei no kenkyū* (Tokyo: Sōbunsha, 1962); Itō Tasaburō, "Kokugaku no rekishi," 3–41, and "Kokugakushi kenkyū no dōkō," 133–47, in Itō, *Kinseishi no kenkyū* (Tokyo: Yoshikawa Kōbunkan, 1982; both were published earlier as separate articles); Haga Noboru, *Henkakuki ni okeru kokugaku* (Tokyo: Kyōiku Shuppan Sentā, 1980; also contains a very useful bibliography on how nativism was figured in intellectual debates), 3–33; and Hiranō Toyō, "Kokugaku shisōron," in Hongō Takamori and Fukaya Katsumi, eds., *Kōza Nihon kinseishi: Kinsei shisōron* (Tokyo: Yūhikaku, 1981), 9:154–204. Paradoxically, the stronger interpretations I have consulted begin in the postwar years and move back to the 1930s. They are Maruyama Masao, *Nihon seiji shisōshi kenkyū* (Tokyo: Tōkyō Daigaku Shuppan, 1952), trans. by Mikiso Hane as *Studies in the Intellectual History of Tokugawa Japan* (Princeton: Princeton University Press, 1974); and the writings of Maruyama's students, principally, Matsumoto Sannosuke, *Kokugaku seiji shisō no kenkyū* (Tokyo: Yūhikaku, 1957); idem, "Kokugaku no seiritsu," in Matsumoto, *Tennōsei kokka to seiji shisō* (Tokyo: Miraisha, 1969); and idem, "Bakumatsu kokugaku no shisōshiteki igi," in *Kus,*

633–61; Watanabe Hiroshi, "Michi to miyabi: Norinagagaku to 'kagaku ha' kokugaku no seiji shisōshi kenkyū" parts 1–4, *Kokka gakkai zasshi* 87, nos. 9 and 10 (Sept. 1974): 1–84; 87, nos. 11 and 12 (Nov. 1974): 1–75; 88, nos. 3 and 4 (Mar. 1975): 114–44; and 88, nos. 5 and 6 (May 1975): 1–72. Outside the Maruyama *ha*, I have derived much from the several studies of Haga Noboru, who has expanded Itō Tasaburō's earlier efforts concerning the role of regional nativism (*Sōmō no kokugaku* [Tokyo: Masago Shobō, 1966]) into a principal moment in the making of a people's history; I have found the following particularly useful: *Henkakuki ni okeru kokugaku; Bakumatsu kokugaku no tenkai* (Tokyo: Kaku Shobō, 1963); and *Kokugaku no hitobito* (Tokyo: Hyōronsha, 1975). Also useful was Koyasu Nobukuni's brilliant *Norinaga to Atsutane no sekai* (Toyko: Chūō Kōronsha, 1977).

Among prewar writers Itō Tasaburō (*Kokugaku no shiteki kōsai* [Tokyo: Ōokayama Shoten, 1932]) set some of the terms for the subsequent intellectual debate with Hani Gorō and Nagata Hiroshi that culminated in Maruyama's essays. This "debate" had less to do with Tokugawa *kokugaku* than the current political situation of the 1930s. See also Hani Gorō, "Kokugaku no tanjō" (published first in *Tanka kenkyū*, 1936), and "Kokugaku no genkai" (published first in *Shisō*, 1946), in Hani, *Nihon ni okeru kindai shisō no zentei* (Tokyo: Iwanami Shoten, 1949); Nagata Hiroshi, *Nihon hōkensei ideorogi* (Tokyo: Hakuyō, 1945; published first in 1938), 158–294; as well as idem, "Shisō taikei to shite kokugaku," *Rekishi kagaku*, July 1935, and "Kokugaku ni tsuite no saikōsai," *Rekishi kagaku*, Aug. 1935.

3. John Frow, *Marxism and Literary History* (Cambridge, Mass.: Harvard University Press, 1986), 58; also 57.

4. Paul DeMan, *The Resistance to Theory* (Minneapolis: University of Minnesota Press, 1986), 11.

5. W. B. Gallie, *Philosophy and the Historical Imagination* (New York: Schocken Books, 1968), 1.

6. Ibid., 2.

7. Although Gallie never made this claim explicit, it was, after all, the purpose of his book; see especially, 22–104. The case has, however, been made by Louis O. Mink, "Narrative Form as a Cognitive Instrument," in Robert H. Canary and Henry Kozicki, eds., *The Writing of History* (Madison: University of Wisconsin Press, 1978), 129–49.

8. Hayden White, *Tropics of Discourse* (Baltimore: Johns Hopkins University Press, 1978), 27–50.

9. Gallie, 23.

10. Ibid., 27.

11. Émile Benveniste, *Problems in General Linguistics*, trans. by Mary Elizabeth Meek (Coral Gables: University of Miami Press, 1971), 206.

12. Hayden White, *Metahistory: The Historical Imagination in Nineteenth-Century Europe* (Baltimore: Johns Hopkins University Press, 1973).

13. Fredric Jameson, *The Political Unconscious: Narrative as a Socially Symbolic Act* (Ithaca: Cornell University Press, 1981).

14. Catherine Belsey, *Critical Practice* (London and New York: Methuen, 1980), 3–7. For a recent critique of this "exhorbitation" of the language model, see Perry Anderson, *In the Tracks of Historical Materialism* (Chicago: University of Chicago Press, 1983), 32–55; and Terry Eagleton, *Literary Theory* (Minneapolis: University of Minnesota Press, 1983), 91–193.

15. Belsey, 6.

16. Benveniste, 208.

17. The terms derive from Belsey's incisive discussion of common sense, 72–73; see also 1–36.

18. Hayden White, "The Dialective of Narrative," MS, 28; this article has been published in revised form as "The Value of Narrativity as the Representation of Reality," in W. J. T. Mitchell, ed., *On Narrative*, (Chicago: University of Chicago Press, 1981), 1–23.

19. Ibid.

20. Pierre Macherey, *A Theory of Literary Production*, trans. by Geoffrey Wall (London: Routledge and Kegan Paul, 1978), 85–89. Also Belsey, 104, 109.

21. Maruyama; Matsumoto, *Kokugaku seiji shisō no kenkyū.*

22. Muraoka Tsunetsugu, *Motoori Norinaga* (Tokyo: Iwanami Shoten, 1942).

23. Pierre Bourdieu, *Outline of a Theory of Practice*, trans. by Richard Nice (Cambridge: Cambridge University Press, 1977); the passages quoted in this paragraph appear on pages 19–20.

24. The discussion on the "metaphysics of the text," and textual relations within the cultural field derives from Tony Bennett, *Formalism and Marxism* (London: Metheun, 1979), 57–60, 108, 146–47, 166–68, 173.

25. Theodor W. Adorno, *Prisms*, trans. by Samuel Weber and Sherry Weber (Cambridge, Mass.: MIT Press, 1981), 26. See also Alfred Sohn-Rethel, *Intellectual and Manual Labor* (Atlantic Highlands, N.J.: Humanities Press, 1978).

26. Quoted in Belsey, p. 138, from Pierre Macherey, *A Theory of Literary Production* (London: Routledge & Kegan Paul, 1978), 7.

27. Julia Kristeva, *Desire in Language*, trans. by Thomas Gora, Alice Jardine, and Leon Roudiez (New York: Columbia University Press, 1980), 64–89.

28. Frow, 227.

29. Ibid., 228.

30. Ibid.

1. Introduction: Discourse/Ideology : Language/Labor

1. Max Weber, *The Protestant Ethic and the Spirit of Capitalism* (New York: Chas. Scribner's Sons, 1958), 47.

2. Ibid., 64ff. See also Lucien Goldmann, *The Hidden God*, trans. by Philip Thody (London: Routledge and Kegan Paul, 1964), 119ff, and, of

course, Franz Borkenau, *Der Ubergang vom Feudalen zum burgerlichen Welt-bild* (Paris: Librairie Félix Alcan, 1934), 1–14.

3. Weber, 64–65.

4. See, for example, Borkenau, *Der Ubergang vom Feudalen*, which seeks to show how modern scientific thought, developing before and independent of manufacturing, provided, through historical conjuncture, the form of representation.

5. Barry Hindess and Paul Q. Hirst, *Pre-Capitalist Modes of Production* (London: Routledge and Kegan Paul, 1975), 278.

6. I have written on the culture of play and its consequences in the late Edo period in "Late Tokugawa Culture and Thought," in Marius Jansen, ed., *Cambridge History of Japan*, vol. 5 (forthcoming).

7. For an explanation of this cognitive strategy, see my "Consciousness of Archaic Form in the New Realism of *Kokugaku*," in Tetsuo Najita and Irwin Scheiner, eds., *Japanese Thought in the Tokugawa Period, 1600–1868: Methods and Metaphors* (Chicago: University of Chicago Press, 1978), 63–104.

8. On the question of tropes in general and metonymy in particular, I have followed Kenneth Burke, *A Grammar of Motives* (Berkeley and Los Angeles: University of California Press, 1969), 503–17; Hayden White, *Metahistory: The Historical Imagination in Nineteenth-Century Europe* (Baltimore: Johns Hopkins University Press, 1973), which is a monumental analysis of historiographical strategies as tropic prefigurations; and the pioneering essay by Roman Jakobson, "Metaphoric and Metonymic Poles," in Morris Halle, ed., *Fundamentals of Language* (The Hague: Mouton, 1956).

9. Pierre Bourdieu, *Outline of a Theory of Practice*, trans. by Richard Nice (Cambridge: Cambridge University Press, 1977), 170–71.

10. The preceding discussion owes much to Catherine Belsey, *The Subject of Tragedy* (London and New York: Methuen, 1985), 5–7.

11. Émile Benveniste, *Problems in General Linguistics*, trans. by Mary Elizabeth Meek (Coral Gables: University of Miami Press, 1971), 110. For this analysis and what follows, I have relied on Anthony Easthope, *Poetry As Discourse* (London and New York: Methuen, 1983), 1–47; and Catherine Belsey, *Critical Practice* (London and New York: Methuen, 1980).

12. V. V. Voloshinov, *Marxism and the Philosophy of Language*, trans. by L. Matejka and I. R. Titunik (New York and London: Seminar Press, 1973), 10–11; also, Easthope, 20, 22–23, and Bennett, 79.

13. Ibid., 22, 23.

14. Ibid., 23.

15. Muraoka Tsunetsugu, *Motoori Norinaga* (Tokyo: Iwanami Shoten, 1942); Hani Gorō, *Nihon ni okeru kindai shisō no zentei* (Tokyo: Iwanami Shoten, 1949).

16. *Kogaku*, the study of ancient (Chinese) texts, articulated as a critical dissatisfaction with Neo-Confucianism and its reliance on commentaries, proposed a return to writings produced before the time of Confucius. In Tokugawa

Japan, *kogaku* began in the late seventeenth century and reached maturation in the texts of Ogyū Sorai (1666–1728) in the early eighteenth. The best study is still Maruyama Masao, *Nihon seiji shisōshi kenkyū* (Tokyo: Tōkyō Daigaku Shuppan, 1952), trans. by Mikiso Hane as *Studies in the Intellectual History of Tokugawa Japan* (Princeton: Princeton University Press, 1974). An important corrective to Maruyama is Bitō Masahide, *Nihon hōken shisōshi kenkyū* (Tokyo: Aoki Shoten, 1961). I found useful Miyake Masahiko's first-rate summary of the debates and his own intervention, "Edojidai shisō," in Ishida Ichirō, ed., *Taikei Nihonshi sōsho: Shisōshi* (Tokyo: Yamakawa, 1976), 63–202.

17. This discussion derives principally from Benveniste, 205–15; Tzvetan Todorov, "Enunciation," in O. Ducrot and T. Todorov, eds., *Encyclopedic Dictionary of the Sciences of Languages*, trans. by Catherine Porter (Oxford: Blackwell, 1981); Belsey, 30–36, 56–83; Easthope; 30–47; and Boris Uspensky, *A Poetics of Composition*, trans. by Valentina Zavarin and Susan Wittig (Berkeley and Los Angeles: University of California Press, 1973), 17–56.

18. Easthope, 44–45.

19. Ibid., 46.

20. See also Matsumoto Sannosuke, *Tennōsei kokka to seiji shisō* (Tokyo: Miraisha, 1969), 33–36, for an important political reading of Kamo's literary consciousness, which I have followed.

21. Roland Barthes, *Writing Degree Zero and Elements of Semiology*, trans. by Annette Lavers and Colin Smith (Boston: Beacon Press, 1967), 62.

22. Easthope, 37; also Jacques Lacan, *Ecrits*, trans. by Alan Sheridan (New York: W. W. Norton, 1977), 153.

23. Roland Barthes, *Writing Degree Zero and Elements of Semiology*, 52; quoted in Gerard Genette, *Figures of Literary Discourse*, trans. by Alan Sheridan (New York: Columbia University Press, 1982), 40.

24. Easthope, 45. This observation refers to the "oscillation" speakers recognize that the words they speak are "determined" by outside relations.

25. Ozaki Satoakira, "Bunpō kenkyū no rekishi (1)," in *Iwanami kōza*, vol. 6, *Nihongo* (Tokyo: Iwanami Shoten, 1976), 263–90.

26. Tokieda Motoki, *Kokugo gakushi* (Tokyo: Iwanami Shoten 1962), 137–39.

27. *MNz* (old), vol. 6 contains a supplement, *Motoori Haruniwa zenshū*, *Motoori Ōhira zenshū*, *Motoori Uchitowa zenshū*.

28. Roy Andrew Miller, *Japanese and Other Altaic Languages* (Chicago: University of Chicago Press, 1967), 65–66.

29. Adachi Kenichi, *Yachimata* (Tokyo: Kawade Shobō Shinsha, 1974), 2:6–7.

30. Ibid., 7.

31. Ibid., 7–8; see also Tokieda, 149–60; Kitajima Masatoshi, *Kokugo gakushi gaisetsu* (Tokyo: Ōfusha, 1977), 52–57.

32. Tokieda, 191.

33. Ibid.

34. See also ibid., 189–90. In *OTz* 4:349, Ōkuni pointed out that even though the *kyūri* (investigation of principle) of the Dutch was as precise as its Chinese variant, it had not yet been able to explain the great principles of spirit (*tama*), ether (*ki*), and substance (*shitsu*). When compared to the *kyūri* of Japan, it was "thin." If contemporaries relied on the investigative principles of the Dutch and Chinese, he concluded, they would never know that a superior method already existed in Japan.

35. Voloshinov, 23.

2. Archaism I: The Origin of Discourse

1. Fukui Kūzō, ed., *Kokugogaku taikei* (Tokyo: Kōseikaku, 1938), 2:12.

2. Actually, Hirata argued that the use of Chinese style forfeited the "treasures of antiquity."

3. Michel Foucault, *The Order of Things*, trans. by Alan Sheridan (New York: Pantheon Books, 1970), 29.

4. See also Koyasu Nobukuni, *Norinaga to Atsutane no sekai* (Tokyo: Chūō Kōronsha, 1977), 8–9.

5. See also Koyasu, 71.

6. Koyasu, 61–65.

7. Motoori emphasized the point that, without *mono no aware*, those who were above because of their wealth, power, or age would fail to understand those who occupied the lower orders of society.

8. Quoted in Matsumoto Sannosuke, *Tennōsei kokka to seijishisō* (Tokyo: Miraisha, 1969), 38. See also Sagara Akira, *Motoori Norinaga* (Tokyo: Tōkyō Daigaku Shuppan, 1978), 18–19, for a detailed and penetrating analysis of this letter to Kiyomizu and Motoori's relationship to Kyoto-centered Confucianism. Motoori expanded this argument in his *Kuzubana*, in *MNz* (new) 8:127–33.

9. This argument is worked out by Sagara, 32–46; also see Watanabe Hiroshi, "Michi to miyabi: Norinagagaku to 'kagaku ha' kokugaku no seijishisōshi kenkyū," *Kokka gakkai zasshi*, part 1, 10; and *MNz* (new) 2:40 (*Ashiwake obune*).

10. Also see *MNz* [new] 9:20–21, where Motoori explained the distinction between the Chinese word for poetry, *shih*, and the Japanese usage *utau*, to recite, sing, or compose, and why it was important to keep these significations differentiated.

11. See Watanabe, part 1, p. 11, for this interpretation.

12. It should be noted that Motoori was criticizing slavish imitation because it invariably produced a disjunction between feelings (*jō*) and words (*kotoba, shi*) and their proper arrangement (*totonaru*). "The poetry of today," he wrote, "is a complete imitation of the ancients. It does not come from the true heart or sincere intention." But "by changing personal feeling," it was still possible to "live in the realm of ancient elegance and appear to possess it naturally." See also *MNz* (new) 2:42.

13. This point has been made forcefully by Watanabe, whom I have followed. See especially "Michi to miyabi," part 1, p. 13. Motoori was most explicit to proclaim that the "fundamental character of feeling (*jō no honzen*) never changes between ordinary folk (*bonjin*) and the sages" (*MNz* [new] 2:54).

14. Cf. Sagara, 29–32.

15. See also *MNz* (new) 2:42, 46, where Motoori noted the vast change between past and present-day poets.

16. Motoori made the distinction that "*uta* is body [substance], *yomu* is use." *Uta*, in this context, carried the polysemic association of song, poem, recitation, while *yomu* meant composing, reciting, reading, perhaps even singing.

17. Explanation of *aware* is found on pages 100–101. This particular discussion owes a great deal to Watanabe, part 1, 15–44. Sagara, 57–92; Tahara Tsuguo, *Motoori Norinaga* (Tokyo: Kodansha, 1968), 45–89; Haga Noboru, *Motoori Norinaga* (Tokyo: Kiyomizu Shoin, 1972), 61–70, although it should be said that Haga makes rather short shrift of Motoori's poetic theory. All of these interpretations rely ultimately on Watsuji Tetsurō's classic essay, "Mono no aware," in *Nihon seishinshi kenkyū*, (Tokyo: Iwanami Shoten, 1926), I have also had the occasion to consult Kobayashi Hideo's personal and profoundly meditative reflection on Motoori, *Motoori Norinaga* (Tokyo: Shinchōsha, 1977), which, because it resembles a verbal analogue to Richard Strauss's "Last Songs," reveals more about the author than it says about Motoori. In English, I have found helpful Shigeru Matsumoto, *Motoori Norinaga* (Cambridge, Mass.: Harvard University Press, 1970), 30–67.

18. See also Koyasu, 50; and Sagara, 73–92, for a strong reading of *Shibun yōryō*.

19. See also Koyasu, 50.

20. See also Watanabe, part 1, 522–24, where this relationship between the "goals of poetry" and what he calls an "unpolitical politicosocial image" is articulated. Watanabe wants to juxtapose the nativist "heart that knows *mono no aware*" to "argumentation and logic" to authenticate claims of pure feeling unmediated by "conscious calculation" and "considerations of obligations." This attitude, grounded in a binary opposition, defined *kokugaku's* conception of an "unpolitical polity." Yet, as I hope to show, an unpolitical polity is in fact a non sequitur that, although it supports Maruyama's interpretation of Tokugawa nativism, goes against the argumentation and evidence Watanabe brings to his study. Motoori was as political as anybody else in Tokugawa Japan, and his firm sense of oppositions signified both criticism of and contestation against the received political and social orders.

21. Koyasu, 42; Sagara, 77.

22. Here, Motoori referred to the expressive mode as *tansoku*, "giving expression in a sigh or lamentation."

23. See also *MNz* (new) 4:240–42, where Motoori compared the ancient and modern responses to common place scenes.

24. Also see Tahara, 63.

25. Motoori supposed that in modern times all that was left to this encounter was the mediation of skills. See also Watanabe, 539–46, which has been helpful to my own understanding of this ancient-modern opposition in Motoori's thought.

26. Motoori glossed the passage *Monogatari wa mazu yo ni ari to aru-koto ni tsukete* by stating that men who knew the *aware* of things in society are able to grasp the reality of the world in which they see, hear, and feel things.

27. This observation is prefaced with the qualification that the act of getting inside things or events meant reaching the core, *mono no kokoro, koto no kokoro*; see also *MNz* (new) 4:109.

28. This explanation stems from Maruyama's interpretation of *koku-gaku*, expanded by Watanabe, that is now accepted as common sense in the Japanese historiographical world.

3. Archaism II: The Discourse on Origins

1. See Uchino Gorō, *Edoha kokugaku ronkō*, (Tokyo: Sōrinsha, 1979), 157–71, for a consideration of the familial and personal conditions that, according to this author, account for Hirata's "unhappiness" and rageful personality. In the 1930s Hirata's contentiousness offended Watsuji Tetsurō, who saw in his thought a prescient expression of the violent jingoism and fanaticism that ultimately inflicted "great harm." For these very same reasons Watsuji's contemporary, the ethnographer Origuchi Shinobu, saw in Hirata's eccentric style the emblem of greatness and a model for himself to follow as an amateur scholar. Impoverished from beginning to end, Origuchi said, Hirata railed against bigotry and hypocrisy under the authority of learning that was both broad and genuinely catholic. See Koyasu, *Norinaga to Atsutane*, 204–17, for an interesting description of the images of Hirata in the twentieth century. I have also relied on Tahara Tsuguo's informative biography, *Hirata Atsutane* (Tokyo: Yoshikawa Kōbunkan, 1963); Haga Noboru, *Bakumatsu kokugaku no kenkyū*, (Tokyo: Kyōiku Shuppan Senta, 1980) 183–252; Muraoka Tsune-tsugu, *Norinaga to Atsutane* (Tokyo: Sobunsha, 1957); idem, "Hirata Atsu-tane—jinbutsu, gakusetsu oyobi shisō," in *Nihon shisōshi kenkyu* (2), (Tokyo: Sobunsha, 1955); Miki Shotarō, *Hirata Atsutane no kenkyū* (Kyoto: Sensatsu Sangyō Yūgen Kaisha, 1969); Sagara Akira, "Nihon no shisōshi ni okeru Hirata Atsutane," in Sagara, ed., *Nihon no meicho*, vol. 24, *Hirata Atsutane* (Tokyo: Chūō Kōronsha, 1972); Koyasu Nobukuni, "Hirata Atsutane no se-kai," in Sagara, *Hirata Atsutane*; and idem, *Norinaga to Atsutane no sekai* (Tokyo: Chūō Kōronsha, 1977), especially 52–60, 126–203.

2. According to Fredric Jameson, *Marxism and Form* (Princeton: Princeton University Press, 1971), 353, the term "prose of the world" appears as a transformation of the poetry of the epic world in Hegel's *Aesthetik*. It was also used as a title for one of Maurice Merleau-Ponty's books and as a chapter heading in Michel Foucault's *The Order of Things*. But in G. W. F. Hegel,

The Philosophy of History, trans. by J. Sibree (New York: Dover Publications, 1956), 288f, it describes the solidification of forms in the ancient world under the Roman state.

3. Watanabe Hiroshi, "Michi to miyabi: Norinagagaku to 'kagaku ha' kokugaku no seijisōshi kenkyū," pt. 2, 22. Ōkuma's denunciation appeared in his *Hitorigochi.* He is better known for the statement that preceded these comments, to the effect that he and his generation were not "ancients but rather men of Tenpō"—that is, moderns. See Haga Noboru, *Bakumatsu kokugaku no tenkai* (Tokyo: Kaku Shobō, 1963), 46–51, for a description of some of the "anti-restorationists" among Motoori's poetic pupils.

4. Watanabe, pt. 2, 22.

5. Uchino, 373.

6. Ibid.

7. *Meidōsho,* quoted in Haga Noboru, *Kokugaku no hitobito* (Tokyo: Masago Shobō, 1966), 73.

8. Watanabe, pt. 1, 2–3.

9. Quoted in Haga, *Kokugaku no hitobito,* 74–75.

10. *Kus,* 151. See also Watanabe, pt. 2, 4–8, for an analysis of Murata's poetic theory and his criticism of the Motoori school's valorization of the "poetic way."

11. In this context, *matsu* was linked to *hana* (flower) and juxtaposed to *jitsu* (full, real) and *moto* (base, ends), which were indistinguishable from the imperial way.

12. See also Watanabe, pt. 2, 25–40, 671–86, for a description of Ōhira's effort to reaffirm Motoori's "poetics" and its promise to imitate antiquity.

13. Watanabe, pt. 2, 30. The date of the text is 1820. The version used by Watanabe is apparently found in the *Motoori Ōhira zenshū,* which has not been available to me. This text is included in *MNz* (old) 6:237–48, but without the prefatory remarks. The preface to the *Tamaboko hyakushukai,* ibid. 6:196–97, contains the same meaning if not precisely the same wording.

14. *MNz* (old), 6:285. The preface is signed by a student of Ōhira's, Kajima Masane.

15. Watanabe, pt. 2, 37, whose text I have followed here, argues that in Ōhira there is a "double spiritual structure." Although Ōhira acknowledged Motoori's criticism of contemporary political life and accepted his call to "imitate antiquity," he also "advocated, in the name of the Way and the Japanese Spirit," the preservation of items from contemporary reality in need of rescuing. This meant rather than extol things in antiquity or situate the self in ancient times and call its name, one should celebrate the objects of the present that were closest to the everyday life. Yet Ōhira was not far from his father, who, according to Watanabe, rejected "contemporary society" (*ima no yo*), since both men valorized things in their immediacy and privileged the quotidian. See especially *MNz* (old) 6:287, 290, 292, where Ōhira singled out things in the contemporary world—"even though common, they belong to the

times." Hirata's discourse, as we shall see, centered things from the common world to the exclusion of everything else.

16. This sense of limits and constraints was worked out thoroughly by one of Hirata's students, Miyauchi Yoshinaga (see chapter 5). Before either Hirata or Miyauchi referred to "limits," however, Motoori Norinaga raised the issue of *kyōkai*—"environmental boundaries" constraining people socially, positions occupied as a result of karma—in a discussion on feeling (*nasake*). In the *Shibun yōryō*, Motoori proposed that feeling had to approximate one's social standing; its expression had to be appropriate to status; whether one was high or low, a woman or man, old or young, priest or lay, it had to signify the same kind of natural politics (*MNz* [new] 4:105–6).

17. See Michel Foucault, *The Order of Things*, trans. by Alan Sheridan (New York: Pantheon Books, 1970), 41.

18. See also Watanabe, pt. 1, 3.

19. Hirata also proclaimed that men of elegance slandered his writings and sought to inflict great harm on the followers of "beginning studies." "But," he concluded, "there are few men who study truth in society."

20. See Jameson, 344–45, 403, for a discussion of this kind of interpretative process.

21. Koyasu, *Norinaga to Atsutane*, 54–60. I am indebted to Koyasu for my own discussion of Hirata's narrative.

22. Ibid., 56–57.

23. The idea is taken from M. M. Bakhtin, *The Dialogic Imagination*, ed. by Michael Holquist, trans. by Caryl Emerson and Michael Holquist (Austin: University of Texas Press, 1981), 84–151. I will return to an analysis of this idea—what Bakhtin calls the preclass, folk "chronotope"—in the last section of this chapter. By chronotope Bakhtin meant the "intrinsic connectedness of temporal and spatial relationships that are artistically expressed in literature." Acknowledging its metaphoric value, Bakhtin argued in this brilliant essay ("Forms of Time and Chronotope in the Novel") that the term "expresses the inseparability of space and time (time as a fourth dimension of space)" as it is articulated in certain narratives. It is, he says, a formally constitutive category of certain forms of writing because they permit the analysis to focus on the relationship between time and space according to the ratio and nature of these categories in the text. The concept of chronotope has the advantage of not privileging either space or time but seeing them always as relational and functional (ibid., 85 and 426–27).

24. Jameson, 404.

25. Koyasu, "Hirata Atsutane," 45–48.

26. I have also found Tahara Tsuguo's reading of this text quite helpful (*"Tama no mihashira* igo ni okeru Hirata Atsutane no shisō ni tsuite," in *HA*, 565–94).

27. Quoted in Tahara Tsuguo, "The Kokugaku Thought," *Acta Asiatica* 25 (1973): 60. Hirata problematized this metaphor and returned to explaining it on numerous occasions in texts like *Ibuki oroshi* and *Shitsunoiwa*.

28. The question of Christian influence on Hirata's conception of the afterlife has a long history. In modern scholarship it goes back to Muraoka Tsunetsugu's "Hirata Atsutane no shingaku ni okeru Yasōkyō no eikyō," in *Nihonshisōshi kenkyū* (Tokyo: Oka Shoin, 1936), 297–314. (The article was published first in 1921.) More recent discussions can be found in Kobayashi Kenzō, *Hirata shintō no kenkyū* (Osaka: Koshinto Senpō Kyōhoncho, 1975), 197–200; Sagara, "Nihon no shisōshi ni okeru Hirata Atsutane," 13–17, and Miki, *Hirata Atsutane no kenkyū*, 201–20, which shows the resemblance between passages in certain texts like *Honkyō gaihen* and *Koshiden* and the Bible.

29. Earlier in this passage Hirata asserted that the two creation deities first made the foundation of heaven and earth and then decreed to Izanami and Izanagi to make the Eight Island Country (Japan) and solidify the land. Here, he used *kunitsuchi* to signify earth; later he used *kuni*, which included both the soil and the polity, since the gods were ordained to "give birth" to it. In both cases, he used the same ideograph.

30. For instances of the creation sustaining ordinary people, see the following: HAz (old) 7:8 (*Koshiden* book 7), 23–24 (book 5); 22 (book 4) 35 (book 3); 8:19 (book 18). (The pagination from one book to the next is not continuous but begins anew each time.) For an account of the ordinary people in Hirata's thought, see Hirano Toyō, "*Atsutane ni okeru kokka to 'aohitokusa,*'" *Hitotsubashi ronsō* 84, no. 1 (July 1980): 102–18.

31. Quoted in Matsumoto Sannosuke, "Bakumatsu kokugaku no shisōshiteki igi," in *Kus*, 648.

32. Hirata also established the model of divine mutual assistance among the various gods for humans to follow in their daily endeavors. When fire starts, he wrote, clouds gather, rain falls, and the wind dies down; "Likewise, there is the mutual assistance within the deeds of the *kami*"; HAz (old) 7:51 (*Koshiden*, book 6).

33. See n. 23.

34. My discussion in this section owes much to Roland Barthes, *Mythologies* (New York: Hill & Wang, 1983), 141–42.

35. Bakhtin, 206–7.

36. See ibid., 209.

37. This is the theme of my "Late Tokugawa Culture and Thought," in Marius Jansen, ed., *Cambridge History of Japan*, vol. 5 (forthcoming).

38. Claude LeFort, *The Political Forms of Modern Society*, ed. and introduced by John B. Thompson (Cambridge, Mass.: MIT Press, 1986), 198.

39. Ibid, 199.

4. Routinizing the Ancient Way

1. Matsumoto Sannosuke, *Kokugaku seijishisō no kenkyū* (Tokyo: Yuikaku, 1957), 68.

2. Claude Lévi-Strauss, *Structural Anthropology* (New York: Basic Books, 1963), 216.

3. Part of this passage is quoted in Matsumoto, 66. In the appendix to Ōhira's "Words in response to I-shin" *MNz* (old), 6:543, the author raised the question of Hirata's theory concerning the destination of the spirits after death only to discount the claim to consolation as "provokingly wrong." But he also spared no criticism on Hattori's conceptions.

4. Quoted in Haga Noboru, "Bakumatsu henkakuki ni okeru kokuga-kusha no undō to ronri," in *Kus*, 664.

5. Ibid.

6. Paul Ricoeur, *Hermeneutics and the Human Sciences*, ed. and trans. by John Thompson (Cambridge: Cambridge University Press, 1981), 192.

7. Ibid., 193.

8. Louis Althusser, *Lenin and Philosophy*, trans. by Ben Brewster (New York: Monthly Review, 1971), 181.

9. See Jean Pierre Fay, *Théorie de récit* (Paris: Hermann, 1972), 43.

10. This was the purpose of book 9 of the *Tamadasuki*, HAz (rev) 6:539–47.

11. The example is in Haga Noboru, *Henkakuki ni okeru kokugaku* (Tokyo: Kyōiku Shuppan Sentā, 1980), 100.

12. See Hirata's letter to Fujita Tōkō (1833) on the importance of prac-tical and popular learning, as quoted in Haga Noboru, *Ishin o mitomete* (To-kyo: Mainichi Shinbun, 1976), 86–87.

13. Haga, *Ishin o mitomete*, 86.

14. Quoted in Haga, *Ishin o mitomete*, 88–89.

15. Matsumoto, *Kokugaku seiji shisō no kenkyū*, 68–69; also see 76.

16. In *HAz* (old) 4:12, Hirata reproduced the same edict where he em-ployed "godly affairs." But later in book 10 of *Tamadasuki*, he apparently changed it to "ancestors." See also "Ancestral Worship in Japan," *Transactions of the Asiatic Society of Japan* 38, 4 (1910–12), 237–38.

17. See Pierre Bourdieu, *Outline of a Theory of Practice*, trans. by Rich-ard Nice (Cambridge: Cambridge University Press, 1977), 172.

18. Ibid.

5. Ruralization I: Figure and Fulfillment

1. There is a vast literature on late-Tokugawa economic and agricultural life, since, for Japanese historians, it provided the ground on which to contest the origins of capitalism. In English, the best guide is still T. C. Smith, *The Agrarian Origins of Modern Japan* (New York: Atheneum, 1966), even though Smith refuses to assess the political effects of the changes he records. I have also found useful Susan B. Hanley and Kozo Yamamura, *Economic and Demo-graphic Change in Preindustrial Japan, 1600–1868* (Princeton: Princeton Uni-versity Press, 1977), despite the rather glowing assessment of agricultural life

the authors wish to establish by demonstrating palpable and quantifiable economic growth and concluding from this that life improved considerably for the
peasantry as productivity increased and the standard of living escalated upward
under fairly systematic control of the population. Somebody in Tokugawa Japan had not been notified that life was really better, since textual production
seemed to match the proliferation of peasant disturbances in signifying poverty
and economic distress. Among Japanese works, I have used Yamaguchi Keiji
and Sasaki Junnosuke, *Bakuhan taisei*, vol. 4, *Taikei Nihon rekishi* (Tokyo:
Nihon Hyōronsha, 1972), especially 154–452. Needless to say, the picture
portrayed by Yamaguchi and Sasaki is far less rosy than that of either Smith or
Hanley and Yamamura, and it is perhaps more sensitive to the entailing political and cultural effects of late-Tokugawa economic history. See also *Iwanami
kōza*, vol. 13 (*Kinsei 5*), *Nihon rekishi* (Tokyo: Iwanami Shoten, 1977) especially 125–308; and Satō Shigerō and Kawachi Hachirō, *Bakuhansei kokka
no hōkai*, vol. 8, *Kōza Nihon kinseishi* (Tokyo: Yūhikaku, 1981).

2. Sasaki Junnosuke has written extensively on the conditions of "world
renewal." I have relied on his essay "Bakumatsu no shakai jōsei to yonaoshi,"
in *Iwanami kōza*, 13:248–308, and *Yonaoshi* (Tokyo: Iwanami Shinsho, 1979).

3. See Irwin Scheiner, "The Mindful Peasant," *Journal of Asian Studies* 32, no. 4 (Aug. 1973): 579–91; Stephen Vlastos, "Yonaoshi in Aizu,"
164–76, and George M. Wilson, "Pursuing the Millennium in the Meiji
Restoration," 177–94, in Tetsuo Najita and Victor Koschmann, eds., *Conflict
in Modern Japanese History* (Princeton: Princeton University Press, 1982).

4. Max Weber, *The Protestant Ethic and the Spirit of Capitalism* (New
York: Chas. Scribner's Sons, 1958); this argument is made explicitly by Franz
Borkenau, *Der Übergang vom Feudelen zum burgerlichen Weltbild* (Paris: Librairie Félix Akan, 1934). Borkenau wants to show how modern ideology,
rooted in scientific philosophy, merged with manufacturing to form a world-
transforming historical conjuncture. He demonstrates brilliantly that scientific
philosophy in the seventeenth century and the development of manufacturing,
which provided thought with the "raw" material for speculation, represented
unrelated activities from different sectors of the social formation. Moreover,
scientific philosophy undoubtedly antedated historically the rise of manufacturing by almost two centuries.

5. I have drawn this insight from Hayden White, *Tropics of Discourse*
(Baltimore: Johns Hopkins University Press, 1978), 87.

6. See Ibid.

7. According to Yamada Yoshio, "*Tamadasuki kaidai*," in HAz (rev)
6:17, these portions of the text revealed Hirata's theory of history. See also
ibid., 34 (*Tamadasuki*, book 1).

8. Pierre Bourdieu, *Outline of a Theory of Practice*, trans by Richard
Nice (Cambridge: Cambridge University Press, 1977). I have employed Bourdieu's conception of the *habitus* quite differently from the way he conceived
it. Although he sees the *habitus* as an existential and even historical phenom-

enon, I see it as an effect of the discourse and the renarrativization of the contemporary historical field.

9. Ibid., 77.

10. Ibid., 78.

11. See H. D. Harootunian, "Ideology as Conflict," in Najita and Koschmann, 25–61.

12. Bourdieu, 79.

13. Terry Eagleton, *Criticism and Ideology* (London: New Left Books, 1976), 71; also Pierre Macherey, A *Theory of Literary Production*, trans. by Geoffrey Will (London: Routledge and Kegan Paul, 1978), 92–95.

14. The idea is from Irwin Scheiner, "The Ambivalence of Responsibility: Village Headmen and the Community," unpublished paper.

15. This view, articulated continuously since Hugh Borton's study, "Peasant Uprisings in Japan of the Tokugawa Period," in *Transactions of the Asiatic Society of Japan*, Second series, vol. xvi, Tokyo, May, 1938, has recently been displaced by both Japanese and non-Japanese historians of the late-Tokugawa period, who have looked to increased productivity and high growth rates to conclude that better standards of living prevailed. It is not necessary to reject these calculations to conclude that in both text production and peasant disturbances, large numbers of people did not share the optimism of twentieth-century historians and economists. In many Tokugawa villages the rumor of recovery had simply not reached the peasants.

16. Haga Noboru, "Bakumatsu henkakuki ni okeru kokugakusha no undō to ronri," in *Kus*, 662–714; idem, *Bakumatsu kokugaku no kenkyū* (Tokyo: Kyōiku Shuppan Sentā, 1980), 183–365; Numata Satoshi, "Ichii sōmō no kokugaku," in Furukawa Tetsushi and Ishida Ichirō, eds., *Nihon shisōshi kōza* (Tokyo: Yuzankaku, 1977), 4:247–64.

17. See also 44–45, where Mutobe called the union and the creation of life a "divine skill."

18. I have also consulted the modern version found in Sagara, *Nihon no meicho, Hirata Atsutane* (Tokyo: Chūō Koronsha, 1972), 294, and collated it with Anzu's unannotated copy. See also *Tck*, 137–38, 143.

19. In the context of this first fable concerning the beginning of cultivation, Satō discussed the compass needle and the importance of calculation and measurement.

20. *SMk* is the most comprehensive study of Suzuki; it contains two sections of the *Jiansaku*, which is also found in *Kcks*, vol. 5. A separate volume (*bekki*) of this text was published by Itō Tasaburō, "Suzuki Masayuki 'Minsei yoron' to 'Jiansaku satsu no ichi bekki' ni tsuite," in *Shigaku zasshi* 67, no. 6 (June 1958), no. 7 (July 1958), no. 8 (Aug. 1958). Itō has also written about Suzuki in *Sōmō no kokugaku* (Tokyo: Masago Shobō, 1966), 26–46, where he presents an "introduction" to the *Minsei yoron* that is separate from the texts published in the *Shigaku zasshi*. See also Itō Tasaburō, *Kinseishi no kenkyū* (Tokyo: Yoshikawa Kōbunkan, 1982), 199–235. Before Itō, Muraoka

Tsunetsugu "rediscovered" Suzuki. See his *Nihon shisōshi kenkyū* (Tokyo: Oka Shoin, 1935), 350–79.

21. Itō, *Suzuki Masayuki kenkyū*, 249.

22. Ibid., 250; also Suzuki Masayuki, "Tsukisakaki," in *Nmc*, 386–87, 400. I have relied principally on this version of the text but have had the occasion to compare and check it against an earlier version found in *Shintō shisō no taikeiteki chojutsu* (Tokyo: Yamato Sōshi, 1890).

23. See *Jiansaku*, in *Kcks* 5:147.

24. See also ibid. 151.

25. Itō Shirō, *Suzuki Masayuki kenkyū*, 313.

6. Ruralization II: Act and Authority

1. Maruyama Masao, *Nihon seiji shisōshi kenkyū* (Tokyo: Tōkyō Daigaku Shuppan, 1952), trans by Mikiso Hane as *Studies in the Intellectual History of Tokugawa Japan* (Princeton: Princeton University Press, 1974), 133–85, 239–367 (pagination of English edition); Matsumoto Sannosuke, *Kokugaku seiji shisō no kenkyū* (Tokyo: Yūhikaku, 1957), 26–117.

2. Claude Lévi-Strauss, *The Savage Mind* (Chicago: University of Chicago Press, 1966), 234.

3. I have followed Paul Ricoeur here principally "The Model of the Text: Meaningful Action Considered as a Text," in Ricoeur, *Hermeneutics and the Human Sciences*, ed. and trans. by John Thompson (Cambridge: Cambridge University Press, 1981), 197–221.

4. See Itō Tasaburō, *Kokugakusha no michi* (Tokyo: Shintaiyo, 1944), which is actually an intellectual biography of Ikuta Yorozu. See also Itō Tasaburō, *Kinseishi no kenkyū* (Tokyo: Yoshikawa Kōbunkan, 1982), 83–103; Haga Noboru, *Henkakuki ni okeru kokugaku* (Tokyo: Kyōiku Shuppan Sentā, 1980), 155–76; and idem, *Kokugaku no hitobito* (Tokyo: Masago Shobō, 1966), 124–39.

5. See, by all means, Tetsuo Najita, "Ōshio Heichachirō (1793–1837)," in A. Craig and D. Shively, eds., *Personality in Japanese History* (Berkeley and Los Angeles: University of California Press, 1970), 155–79.

6. Itō, *Kokugakusha no michi*, 127.

7. Ibid., 142.

8. For a good analysis of Ōkura and late Tokugawa period agricultural thought, see T. C. Smith, "Ōkura Nagatsune and the Technologists," in Craig and Shively, 127–79.

9. I have also relied on Numata Satoshi, "Bakumatsu no kokugaku," in *Nihon shisōshi kōza* (Tokyo: Yūzan Kaku, 1976), 4:248–64.

10. A concern for seed and sexuality constituted the gist of Miyahiro's *Nōgyō yōshū*, in Takimoto Seiichi, ed., *Nihon keizai taiten* (Tokyo: Meiji Bunko, 1977), 57:130–70.

11. See also *Kus*, 296, where Miyahiro showed that fishing had also suffered from underemployment.

12. I have found helpful Kamada Michimasa, "Sonraku shidōsha no rekishiteki igi," *Nihonshi kenkyū* 102 (1969): 1–34.

13. See also Kamada, 7.

14. I have also used Tano Seigo, *Suzuki Shigetane no kenkyū* (Kyoto: Shintōshi Gakkai, 1968).

15. Pierre Bourdieu, *Outline of a Theory of Practice*, trans. by Richard Nice (Cambridge: Cambridge University Press, 1977), 119.

16. See also *HAz* (old), 7:24 (*Koshiden*, book 5), where Hirata located the origins of the principle that "blessed the realm's *aohitokusa*" precisely at the moment when the "heavenly deities and ancestors" received the ordinance (from the creation gods) entrusting them to "make" and "solidify" the realm. Throughout the early portions of this text, Hirata frequently returned to this idea of "making" and "solidifying" for the sake of the folk as the great and "weighty" intention of the two creation deities.

17. There is a fine article on Katsura by Numata Satoshi, "Henkakuki ni okeru ichi gōnō to kōdō," *Nihon rekishi* 282 (Nov. 1971): 61–89.

18. The pagination of this text, published privately by the Katsura family, is abbreviated, with one number given for two pages. I have added the letters *a* and *b* to indicate right and left sides respectively.

19. See also Numata, "Henkakuki ni okeru ichi gōnō to kōdō," 73.

20. I have used the version of *Hongaku kyoyō* in *HA* instead of the one found in his collected works. There is a translation of this text accompanied by a detailed biographical account of Ōkuni by Lydia Brüll, *Ōkuni Takamasa und seine Weltanschauung* (Wiesbaden: Otto Harrassowitz, 1966).

21. Haga Noboru, "Bakumatsu henkakuki ni okeru kokugakusha no undō to ronri," in *Kus*, 675.

7. Knowledge, Interest, and the Cultural Order

1. See my "Late Tokugawa Culture and Thought," in Marius Jansen, ed., *Cambridge History of Japan*, vol. 5 (forthcoming).

2. Jürgen Habermas, *Knowledge and Human Interests*, trans. by Jeremy J. Shapiro (Boston: Beacon Press, 1971), 191. This argument for the creation of a public realm and its relationship to the "discovery" of interest constitutes the central theme of Habermas's earlier *Strukturwandel der Öffentlichkeit* (Neuwied: Luchterhand, 1962). See also Raymond Guess, *The Idea of a Critical Theory* (Cambridge: Cambridge University Press, 1981), and David Held, Introduction to Critical Theory (Berkeley and Los Angeles: University of California Press, 1980), 296–329.

3. See Habermas, *Knowledge*, 194.

4. Ibid., 195–96.

5. See ibid., 196.

6. This identification was suggested first in Haga Noboru, "Ōkuni Takamasa no gakumon to shisō," in *HA*, 641. I have also relied on Haga, *Henkakuki ni okeru kokugaku* (Tokyo: Kyōiku Shuppan Sentā, 1980), 177–98;

idem, *Kokugaku no hitobito* (Tokyo: Masago Shobō, 1966), 195–218; Numata Satoshi, "Bakumatsu no kokugaku," in *Nihon shisōshi kōza* (Tokyo: Yūzan Kaku, 1976) 4:241–48; Tahara Tsuguo, "Bakumatsu kokugaku shisō no ichi ruikei," *Shirin* 44, no. 1 (1960): 46–72.

7. See also *Honkyō shinrisetsu*, *OTz* 5:65, where Ōkuni wrote, "Invisible governance is the base, the visible realm the end."

8. Haga, *Henkakuki ni okeru kokugaku*, 181–88; idem, *Kokugaku no hitobito*, 195–203.

9. See also Tahara, 61.

10. Ibid.

11. Ibid.

12. Ibid.

13. Ibid.

14. Also quoted in ibid., 55.

15. Ibid.

16. See also ibid., 65.

17. This is the argument put forth by Watanabe Hiroshi, "Michi to miyabi: Norinagagaku to 'kagaku ha' kokugaku no seiji shisōshi kenkyū," part 4, *Kokka gakkai zasshi* 88, nos. 5 and 6 (May 1975): 49–72. Although I disagree with Watanabe's description of Tomobayashi's thoughts about action as "unpolitical," I have learned much from this penetrating monograph, especially the concluding section. I have also used Haga, *Henkakuki ni okeru kokugaku*, 218–36, and idem, *Kokugaku no hitobito*, 245–54.

18. Yasuda Yojūrō, the leading ideologue of the Japanese romantic group (*Nihon romanha*) in the 1930s, brought out an edition of Tomobayashi's *Nanzan tōun roku* (Tokyo: Shogakkan, 1944) that contained, on page 7, a record of the Tenchūgumi incident, his involvement in it, and a signification of the "history and spirit of the august renovation [*goishin*]" written in jail.

19. Michel Foucault, *The Order of Things*, trans. by Alan Sheridan (New York: Pantheon Books, 1970), 49.

20. Ibid., 50.

21. Easthope, *Poetry as Discourse* (London and New York: Methuen, 1983), 124, from Jacques Lacan, *Ecrits*, trans. by Alan Sheridan (New York: W. W. Norton, 1977), 155.

22. Watanabe has fully documented this tradition of poetics derived from Motoori Norinaga. I should add here that conventional wisdom on Tomobayashi has situated him in a genealogy that goes back to Kamo no Mabuchi and the "independent" Ban Tomoyuki but also includes members of the Motoori school such as Natsume Fusumarō and Kanō Shinpei. Yet Tomobayashi was as critical of the Motoori wing as he was of Hirata's tone-deafness to poetry and broke sharply with the members of the Suzunoya over their inordinate reverence for the *Shinkokinshū*, a poetic anthology of late antiquity.

23. Easthope, 123–24.

24. Here especially, Tomobayashi struck hard at Motoori's interpretation of the voice in the Man'yō as "feminine," "soft," and "yielding."

25. See also Watanabe, part 4:51–52.
26. Ibid., 51.
27. Ibid., 50.
28. Ibid.
29. Ibid., 50–51.
30. Ibid., 53.
31. Ibid.
32. Ibid., 53–54.

8. Accomplices of Restoration

1. I have written about Maki in the "loyalist" context in *Toward Restoration* (Berkeley and Los Angeles: University of California Press, 1970), chap. 5. Also useful are Yamaguchi Muneyuki, *Maki Izumi* (Tokyo: Yoshikawa Kōbunkan, 1973), and Okawa Tsunendo, *Maki Izumi no kami no kenkyū* (Kyoto: Shintō Shigakkai, 1970).
2. See also Okawa, 177.
3. See ibid., 177–78.
4. See also ibid., 178–83. This idea was very close to Suzuki Masayuki's formulations on increasing the wealth of one village as the basis for expanded national prosperity, found in *Minsei yoron ryakuhen*. See Itō Shirō, *Suzuki Masayuki kenkyū* (Tokyo: Aoki Shoten, 1972), 170–72.
5. See also Okawa, 182.
6. See also ibid., 183–88, for a detailed description of Maki's views on local leadership, which I have abbreviated in my account.
7. Quoted in Okawa, 183.
8. See also Okawa, 183.
9. Quoted in Okawa, 185, from Maki's *Kokoku shinsaku*.
10. Ibid., 186.
11. *Iwakura kō jikki* (Tokyo, 1927), 2:54–55.
12. Ibid., 60.
13. See also Haga Noboru, *Henkakuki ni okeru kokugaku* (Tokyo: Kyōiku Shuppan Sentā, 1980), 240–41.
14. Ochi Michitoshi, *Yano Gendō no honkyōgaku* (Tokyo: Kinshōsha, 1971), 95–100.
15. Ibid., 97.
16. The notion had been advanced by Yano in 1863 in *Tamaboko monogatari*, in *Nihon kokusui zensho* (Tokyo: Nihon Kokusui Zensho Kankōkai, 1915), 17:12; see also *Kenkin sengo*, in *Kus*, 568.

Epilogue: Native Knowledge and the Production of a Modern "Japanese Ideology"

1. Quoted in Pierre Bourdieu, *Outline of a Theory of Practice*, trans. by Richard Nice (Cambridge: Cambridge University Press, 1977), 170.

2. Ibid.

3. Tzvetan Todorov, *The Conquest of America*, trans. by Richard Howard (New York: Harper & Row, 1984), 69–97.

4. This is the subject of Fujii Sadafumi, *Meiji kokugaku hasseishi no kenkyū* (Tokyo: Yoshikawa Kōbundan, 1977), which contains exhaustive documentation concerning the "fate" of nativism in the first decade of the Meiji era.

5. Itō Shirō, *Suzuki Masayuki no kenkyū* (Tokyo: Aoki Shoten, 1972), 287–88.

6. These formulations were suggested by Colin McCabe, *Tracking the Signifier* (Minneapolis: University of Minnesota Press, 1985), 107–9.

7. Ibid., 109.

8. This kind of criticism was leveled by Jacques Derrida against Michel Foucault's *Folie et deraison: Histoire de la folie à l'âge classique*, in *Writing and Difference*, trans. by Alan Bass (Chicago: University of Chicago Press, 1978), 30.

9. Kazuko Tsurumi, "Yanagita Kunio's Work as a Model of Endogenous Development," Institute of International Relations Research Papers, A-26 (Tokyo: Sophia University, 1975), 13–14.

10. Tsurumi, 7–13.

11. Quoted in Haga Noboru, "Yanagita Kunio to Origuchi Shinobu," in Furukawa Tetsushi and Ishida Ichirō, eds., *Nihon shisōshi kōza* (Tokyo: Yūzankaku, 1977), 8:223.

12. Ibid., 225.

13. Ibid., 224.

14. Quoted in Hasegawa Masaharu, "Origuchi Shinobu no 'gaku' no kōzō," in *Origuchi Shinobu o "yomu*," Takahashi Tetsu, ed. (Tokyo: Gendai Kikakushitsu, 1981), 90.

15. Kawamura Nozomu, *Nihon shakaigakushi kenkyū* (Tokyo: Ningen no Kagakusha, 1975), 2:33.

16. Ibid., 36–37.

17. Odō Yasujirō, *Takata shakaigaku* (Tokyo: Yūhikaku, 1953), 161.

18. Kawamura, 246.

19. Ibid.

20. Ibid., 247.

21. See Herbert Marcuse, *Negations*, trans. by J. J. Shapiro (Boston: Beacon Press, 1968), 7 and 22–25.

22. Ibid., 24.

23. *Tōsaka Jun zenshū* (Tokyo: Keisō shobō, 1975), 3:457.

24. Kawamura, 225.

25. Michel Foucault, *The Archaeology of Knowledge*, trans. by Alan Sheridan (New York: Pantheon Books, 1972), 12.

26. Claude Lévi-Strauss, *Triste-Tropiques*, trans. by John Weightman and Doreen Weightman (New York: Washington Square Press, 1977), 33–34.

Index

Deportment (*furumai*), 114. *See also* Conduct

Derrida, Jacques, 20, 22, 142

Desire, 140, 270, 272, 304, 351, 417, 429

Destiny, 355–57

Differences, 308, 312, 380, 409, 413, 417, 428, 432, 438, 442 n. 2; between ruler and ruled, 346; boundaries as, 249; of class, 335 (*see also* Class, social); divisive, 275, 288, 292; explanation of, nativist, 28–29, 179; hierarchical, 322–23; identity and, 35, 37, 413; logic of, 166; as order, 250; Otherness of Western learning, 359; proliferation of, 50–51, 55; reduced to similitude, through naming, 311; spatial play of, 415; of status, 290–92, 328, 343, 346, 347, 350; suppressed by metaphor, 43; in vocalization systems, 57. *See also* Other

Dignity (*igi*), 65

Discourse: ambiguity in, 402; apolitical, 273–74; bonded to social group, 25–26; carnivalesque, 19; closure in, 359; collapsing of work and worship in, 216; on culture, 411; defined, 3; as dialogue, 11; distinguishing between statement and referent, 29; folklore as, 414; historical (*shinron*), 427; intertextual, 121; language and labor as subjects of, 407; of Mito school (see *Mitogaku*); and narrative, 183; nativist, 226; official, 196–97, 225, 410, 412, 418; organizes objects in epistemological field, 329; on origins, 376; of

place, 414; political, 331, 336; power and, 5; rationalized, 271; reformed toward "naturalness," 33–40; and the rhetoric of place, 242–53; of ruralized nativism, 220; seduction of narrative, 175; subject of, 181–96; text as content of, 441 n. 2; versus history, 46–47; Western, 413

Discrimination, 29–33

"Discussions on the New Nativism" (Yanagita Kunio), 422

Disease, 246–48

Disorder, 218, 247, 248, 269, 273, 279, 287, 303, 304, 323; rural, 216, 243, 244, 328, 335; urban, 328, 396. *See also* Rebellion

Divine favor, 303. *See also* Blessings of the deities

Divine intention, 88, 99, 101, 155, 163, 175, 187, 195, 213, 222, 256–71 passim, 310, 338–62 passim, 457 n. 16

Divine labor, 265

Divine learning, 346, 351, 365, 369, 370, 397

Divine plan (*kamihakari*), 221, 222

Divine virtue, 195

Division, 274, 275, 288, 292, 304 (*see also* Fragmentation); of labor, 34, 116, 129, 145, 242, 243, 259, 265, 313, 378; in society, 313 (*see also* Class, social)

Dōchaku (managers, cultivators), 290, 292

Doctrine: correct, 308; of the deities, 247; fundamental (see *Honkyō*); and polity, 421 (*see also* Ceremony). *See also* Divine intention; Imperial doctrine

Habermas, Jürgen, 329
Habitus (*mimatsurigoto*), 14,
   222–25, 259, 326, 376, 413,
   425, 454–55 n. 8; village as,
   232–33, 307–18. See also
   Kunitsuchi
Hani Gorō, 44
Hana (essence), 65
Hanareya gakkun (Suzuki), 64
Harmony, 32, 282, 304, 334, 339,
   341, 348, 430
Hataraki (speaking and working),
   69
Hataraki kotoba. See Working
   words.
Hattori Nakatsune, 119, 123, 148,
   180, 255
Headmen, village, 228, 303, 309,
   321
Heart (*kokoro*), 66; gentleness of
   (*sunao*), 109; true, 92, 127,
   141
Heaven (*ame*), 150; light of, 151;
   spear of, 256–57, 293–95
Heavenly way (*tendō*), 83
Hegel, G. W. F., 49
Hegemony, linguistic, 43
Hell. See *Yomi*
Hermeneutics, 133, 142, 415; cultural, 437; Dilthey's, 426;
   nativist historical, 326–32; as
   practice, 410; syntagmatic,
   173. *See also* Meaning
Heterodoxy, 249
Hidden governance (*yūmei; mukaisei*), 209, 237, 239, 240,
   248, 249, 261, 284, 317, 356
Hidden world, 31–32, 38,
   151–54, 201, 222, 236, 238,
   239, 242, 261, 264, 265, 284,
   299, 394–96, 402, 404, 405,
   408, 412
Hierarchy, 322–23, 327, 378, 403
High peasantry, 226, 231. See also
   Meibōka

Hirano Kuniomi, 378
Hirata Atsutane, 20, 26–32, 37,
   47–49, 67–69, 71, 73, 83–
   89 passim, 110, 168–75 passim, 170, 177, 178, 218, 219,
   232–46 passim, 253–74 passim, 277–78, 283, 286, 291,
   294–96, 308, 322, 330, 336,
   344–76 passim, 394, 399,
   401, 413, 415, 421, 424,
   441 n. 2, 447 n. 2, 449 n. 16,
   451 n. 16, 452 nn. 28–29, 32,
   457 n. 16; on consumption,
   171; on poetry, 118–22, 125,
   133–42; and the "prose of the
   world," 143–68; and the subject of discourse, 181–96; on
   work and worship, 196–217
Hirata Kokugaku no dentō (Origuchi Shinobu), 424
Hirata Kanetane, 308, 398
Hirayama Chūemon, 296
Historical individual, Weber's, 24
History, 5; as act of enunciation,
   360; ancient (*koshi*), 79, 120,
   142 (see also *Kojiki; Nihonshoki*); as contingency, 436;
   Confucian, Tokugawa-era,
   144; contemporary, 290–92,
   379, 403, 408, 438; as discipline, 10, 20–22; discourse of
   (*shiron*), 427; "drift of the
   times," 333, 355, 371; effaced
   by ideology, 25, 49; emplot-
   ting of, 218–33; and events,
   203–5, 233, 376, 394; eventless, 214, 221, 358; and hermeneutics, nativist, 326–32;
   and legend, 427; nativist narrative as, 169; as plan of the
   deities, 352–55; political,
   273–74; progressive, 420;
   "real," 226–27; rejection of,
   407; secession from, 409; as
   study of place, 420–23; story

Nakamaya Tadayasu, 393
Nakamikado Tsuneyuki, 393
Nakamukashi (antiquity), 127. *See also* Ancient studies; Archaic man
Nakayama Tadayasu, 374, 390
Naming, 66, 68, 234, 309–11, 400; and Chinese writing, 55, 60; of deities, 309; of the unnamed, 33–34
Nanushi. See Headmen, village
Naobi no mitama (Motoori Norigana), 62, 82, 84, 91, 99
Naobu kokoro. See Correct heart
Nariwai (making a living; productive duties), 202, 249, 250
Narrative: cosmological, 79, 143–68, 178–79, 222, 223, 233, 253, 414; with discourse, 183; Hirata's prose of the world, 143–68; historical, 2, 6–9, 21; living, 419; *monogatari*, 107, 135; nativist, time in, 168–75; preferred to poctry, 118; of remote past, 142; subjectivity of, 46; supplement, 254; transformation of fragmentation by, 121; work as household duties within, 215–16. *See also* Story line
Narrative words (*katari kotoba*), 86
Naru. See Becoming
Nasake (feeling; outreach with good deeds; sympathy), 107, 110, 112, 131, 300
"National learning" (*kokugaku*). *See* Nativism
"National soil." *See Kunitsuchi*
Native categories, 14
Native place (*kyōdo*), 416, 421
Nativism, 1, 17, 25, 161; as authority for local solutions, 296; bibliography, 442–43 n. 2; classification system of, 29–

33; and "common folk" (*see* Ordinary people); and collective action, 273–92; cognitive program of, 78–79; as discipline, 335, 414; as expression of interests, 328; experience and discourse in, 33, 35–37; genealogy of, 122, 441 n. 2; *habitus* in (see *Habitus*; *Kunitsuchi*); ideological language of, 23–33; linguistic theory, 36–39, 41–75, 173–74; mediating between popular culture and Tokugawa ideology, 18, 39; model of the syntagm, 29; and the naming of the unnamed, 33–34; "new," 422–23, 425; opposed to textuality, 44; part/whole relationship in, 29–33, 308, 318–25, 336, 377 (*see also* Metonymy); political legacy of, 406; revived in Japanese ethnology (*minzokugaku*), 414–23; ruralization of, 18, 25, 26, 33, 176–77, 197, 202, 216, 381; self-critiquing of, 13; social agenda scrapped by Meiji government, 377; as subversive discourse, 410, 418; as urban phenomenon, 176
Natume Fusumarō, 458 n. 22
Naturalness, 30, 36–37, 88, 91, 93, 105, 157–60, 168
Natural resources, 349. *See also* Blessings of the deities
Nature, 131; "assisted" by work, 216; and culture, 67, 169, 434, 435; human activity restored to, 171, 172; poetry of, 367; and productivity, 219 (*see also* Entrustment)
Neo-Confucianism, 28–29, 34,

Practical knowledge, 192–93, 287
Practicality, 192–93, 287, 382–83, 403, 405
Practice, 78, 120, 224, 287, 331; as content, 77; cultural, 15; hermeneutics as, 410; historical (*see* History: as discipline); religious, 245. *See also* Action
Prayers, 73, 205, 281; archaic Shinto, 338 (see also *Norito*); in daily life, 197, 198, 201; efficacy of, 280; work and, 209–10
Priests, 384, 386–88
Principle (*ri*), 91, 264, 280, 329, 339; appeals to, 98, 100; Chinese words of, 82; ethical (*dōri*), 65; ideograph versus referent, 77; investigation of (*kyūri*), 446–47n. 34; penetration of (*kakubutsu kyūri*), 69; rational (*kotowari*), 81
Principles of the Poetic Way, The (Tomobayashi), 366
Private destiny (*musubi no shiun*), 255–56
Private interest, 274, 275, 356
Privatization, 171, 368
Procreation, 240, 262, 298–301, 312
Production, 3, 262, 289, 431; and accumulation of wealth, 228; cultural, 19; duties of (*nariwai*), 249, 251; in historical practice, 12–13; and ideology, 4, 40–50; of language, 70–75; modes of, 14; of poetry, 104–5; and reproduction, 161, 215, 216
"Production of National Literature, The" (Origuchi Shinobu), 427–28
Productivity, 172, 210, 263, 301, 455n. 15; agricultural, 196,

242, 261; bureaucratic drain on, 287, 288; deities of (*see* Deities: of agricultural production); and divine intention, 88; emanating from sun's rays, 255; forfeiture of, and shame, 267; increased through economic reforms, 287–89; relationships of, 218, 219; threatened by private interest, 275
Property: pursuit of, 227; words as, 71
"Prose of the world," 120, 143–68, 449–50n. 2
Protecting cards (*mamorifuda*), 210
Protection, divine, 210
Protestant Ethic and the Spirit of Capitalism, The (Weber), 24
Protestantism, 24
Proverbs, 157–59
Public (*ōyake*), 239
Public character of the *Kojiki*, 81
Public life, 328–29, 347, 348, 368
Public service, 320–23. *See also* Administration
Purport, poetic, 361–62. *See also* Intention; Meaning

Radicalism, 291
Rakugo, 181
Ranking system, 320. *See also* Class, social; Hierarchy
Rational speculation (*kotowari*), 88
Rationality, 96. *See also* Reason
Reading: and the *Kojiki*, 80; of nativism, problems in, 20–22
Real state of affairs (*jitsujō*), 94, 95
Reality: authentic, 44; changing, and language, 45; discursive relativity of, 5; as naturalness, 36–37; sense and meaning, 41–42
Realm: corporate image of, 321; cosmic, 316; imperial, losses